Special Edition
Using
NetWare®
5.0

Peter Kuo

John Pence

Sally Specker

que®

A Division of Macmillan Computer Publishing, USA
201 W. 103rd Street
Indianapolis, Indiana 46290

Special Edition Using NetWare® 5.0

International Standard Book Number: 0-7897-2056-6

Library of Congress Catalog Card Number: 99-61626

Printed in the United States of America

First Printing: July 1999

00   99   4   3   2   1

TRADEMARKS

WARNING AND DISCLAIMER

Executive Editor
Dean Miller

Acquisitions Editor
Gretchen Ganser

Development Editor
Maureen A. McDaniel

Managing Editor
Brice Gosnell

Project Editor
Gretchen Uphoff

Copy Editors
Cheri Clark
Michael Dietsch
Barbara Hacha

Indexer
Erika Millen

Proofreader
Andrew Beaster

Technical Editors
James Drews
Gary Ridley

Team Coordinator
Cindy Teeters

Interior Design
Ruth Harvey

Cover Design
Dan Armstrong
Ruth Harvey

Copy Writer
Eric Borgert

Layout Technicians
Brandon Allen
Stacey DeRome
Ayanna Lacey
Heather Hiatt Miller

CONTENTS

ABOUT THE AUTHORS

Peter Kuo, Ph.D., is president of DreamLAN Network Consulting Ltd., a Toronto-based consulting firm specializing in connectivity and network management. Peter is one of the world's first Master CNEs and Master CNIs and is the first Novell Certified Internet Professional (CIP) in the world. Furthermore, he is a Certified Network Expert (CNX, Ethernet, and Token Ring). In addition to presenting seminars at conferences, such as NetWorld+InterOp, NetWare Users International (NUI), and BrainShare, Peter has authored, co-authored, and contributed to many computer books from Macmillan Computer Publishing. When not working on books and articles, Peter is a volunteer sysop on the Novell Support Connection and Novell DeveloperNet Web forums, assisting Novell in providing support to a worldwide audience on many advanced subject areas, such as connectivity, network management, NetWare 4, NetWare 5, and Novell Directory Services. You can reach him at `peter@dreamlan.com`.

John Pence is president of MagicNet Network Consulting and the Network Engineer/Analyst at a major regional newspaper. He has over a decade of experience networking computers and has worked with numerous operating systems. Before becoming involved with networking computers, John was a cryptographics technician in the United States Coast Guard, which led him into electronics and ultimately networks. John is a CNE, an MCSE, and a former Novell Support Connection sysop. His specialty is using protocol analyzers to troubleshoot the really tough ones by looking at what is happening on the wire. John has co-authored one other book with Peter Kuo, *Sams Teach Yourself Windows Networking in 24 Hours*, also by Macmillan Computer Publishing. A former professional magician in his youth, John feels that networks are their own kind of magic! He can be reached via email at `jpence@jpence.com`.

Sally Specker is a senior consultant with Novell, Inc. She has worked with NetWare since 1991 (as both an independent consultant and an instructor) and joined Novell Consulting in 1996. She holds the Master CNI and Master CNE certifications from Novell. Although this is her first published book, she has written several articles for Novell's popular *AppNotes* publication. Sally can be reached at `sspecker@novell.com`.

DEDICATION

(Peter) To all my friends that put up with me, or lack of me, during this writing project.

(John) To my Team Pence members, George and Grace. Let's pickle!

(Sally) To Mike, for always smiling and bringing me Diet Coke while my head was buried in my computer during this project.

ACKNOWLEDGMENTS

Due to the vast amount of features included in NetWare 5, it has not been an easy task writing this *Special Edition Using NetWare 5.0* book. Trying to cover all the possible NetWare 5 topics in fewer than 1,000 pages is next to impossible. However, as a result of the sharp eyes and diligence of Maureen McDaniel, our development editor of the book, and the technical editors, Jim Drews and Gary Ridley, you'll find this book to be an excellent and comprehensive reference material suitable for getting your NetWare 5 network off the ground and running.

A special thanks goes to our acquisitions editor, Gretchen Ganser, for offering us the opportunity to work on this book. A big thank you also goes out to Gretchen Uphoff, our project editor, for "quarterbacking" us throughout the writing of the book.

Peter would like to extend his appreciations to a few special people. John, thanks for being such a sport for even considering writing another book with me, after what I put you through for our last book; I owe you a keg of beer, brother! Sally, we would have never finished this book on schedule without you. Finally, Dad and Mom, thanks ever so much for stocking the fridge with snacks and Classic Coke for my late-night writing marathons.

And, yet again, John would like to acknowledge Peter's continuing efforts to drag me to the top of the networking ladder. If you want to keep up with Peter, you had better be ready to run with the horsemen!

And finally, Sally would like to thank Peter and John for the opportunity to work with them on this book; it has truly been been a pleasure. Also, many thanks to my parents from whom I must have inherited the patience to follow through with a project like this. And, of course, to the rest of my family; without them, I never would have had enough names to use in my examples throughout this book!

TELL US WHAT YOU THINK!

As the reader of this book, *you* are our most important critic and commentator. We value your opinion and want to know what we're doing right, what we could do better, what areas you'd like to see us publish in, and any other words of wisdom you're willing to pass our way.

As a publisher for Que, I welcome your comments. You can fax, email, or write me directly to let me know what you did or didn't like about this book—as well as what we can do to make our books stronger.

Please note that I cannot help you with technical problems related to the topic of this book, and that due to the high volume of mail I receive, I might not be able to reply to every message.

When you write, please be sure to include this book's title and author as well as your name and phone or fax number. I will carefully review your comments and share them with the author and editors who worked on the book.

Fax:	317.581.4666
Email:	office_que@mcp.com
Mail:	Publisher
	Que Corporation
	201 West 103rd Street
	Indianapolis, IN 46290 USA

INTRODUCTION

WHO SHOULD USE THIS BOOK?

The late 1990s have been the fastest growth period for networking, and in particular, Internet technologies. The NetWare operating system has dominated the PC-based local area network arena for many years. With the introduction of NetWare 5, Novell has moved its flagship operating system into the Internet arena by rewriting its NetWare Core Protocol (NCP) to run over IP. Additionally, Novell has included several Internet standard protocols that can be used with NetWare 5 and IP, including the Network Time Protocol (NTP) and the Service Location Protocol (SLP). NetWare 5 also ships with a DNS/DHCP server that is integrated with NDS.

From the basics and introduction to the NetWare 5 operating system (such as setting up users), to its treatment of advanced topics (such as SLP and Migration Agent), *Special Edition Using NetWare 5* is for everyone, novices and experts alike, who is interested in knowing NetWare 5 better. You'll learn about the developmental history of the operating system and find new and exciting applications of control provided through the graphical user interfaces. Utilities, network environments, system administration, and communication concepts are revealed simply and effectively. In short, *this book has it all, and this book does it all.*

WHAT DO YOU NEED TO KNOW TO READ THIS BOOK?

To keep the chapters uncluttered with trivial information, the authors have made the following assumptions about what you know and what you don't know:

- You have knowledge of basic computer and DOS concepts, such as CPU, disk drives, files, and directories.
- You are familiar with some basic Windows skills such as maneuvering the mouse, jockeying through pull-down menus, navigating the keyboard, and so on.

- Although it's not necessary, it would be an asset that you have used a computer before, regardless of its operating system.

- The authors do *not* assume that you have used NetWare before.

Tip	It is *not* necessary, but it would be helpful, that you have access to a NetWare network to try out the commands discussed in this book, because that will better enforce the concept and material you have read. There isn't a better learning tool than hands-on experience.

WHAT WILL YOU LEARN WHILE READING THIS BOOK?

Other than the comprehensive and detailed treatment of each important topic in NetWare 5, you will find a lot of notes, tips, cautions, and other tidbits sewn throughout the book. The authors of this book are NetWare experts. The tidbits in this book are based on countless years of valuable hands-on, real-world experiences, or battle scars as some people call them, and expert advice from the authors of this book that you cannot easily obtain from elsewhere, without costing you a (sizable) down payment for someone's mansion.

The in-depth but detailed treatment of NetWare 5 features along with specific notes, tips, and cautions are what set this book, *Special Edition Using NetWare 5*, apart from other NetWare 5 books available on the market today.

HOW IS THIS BOOK ORGANIZED?

The information in this book progresses from simple to complex as you move through the chapters. The information is separated into seven parts. Each part has its own particular emphasis and is self-contained. You can, therefore, choose to read only those areas that appeal to your immediate needs. Don't, however, let your immediate needs deter you from eventually giving attention to the rest of the book. You'll find a wealth of information in every chapter!

Following is a brief look at the contents of each chapter in *Special Edition Using NetWare 5*:

Part I, "Introduction to NetWare 5," gets you bootstrapped about the fundamentals and the basics of NetWare 5:

- Chapter 1, "Features of NetWare 5," gives you insight into the background of NetWare and its history, and briefly discusses the new features, capabilities, and characteristics in this latest generation of the NetWare operating system.

- Chapter 2, "Related Products," provides an overview on various additional products that can enhance the function of your NetWare 5 network.

- Chapter 3, "Networking," shows the basic building blocks of a network, including different network topologies.

- Chapter 4, "Networking Data Flow," introduces you to the concepts on how data is transmitted across a network.

Part II, "Understanding Novell Directory Services," provides information about Novell Directory Services (NDS):

- Chapter 5, "Novell Directory Services Tree Basics," shows you the fundamental concepts about NDS.

- Chapter 6, "Designing the Novell Directory Services Tree," offers you guidelines and suggestions for setting up your NDS tree.

- Chapter 7, "Time Synchronization," offers you guidelines and suggestions on setting up time synchronization, including NTP.

Part III, "Installing NetWare 5," walks you through the steps necessary to set up your NetWare 5 server and configuring workstations:

- Chapter 8, "Installing NetWare 5 on New Servers," gives you step-by-step instructions on setting up your new NetWare 5 server.

- Chapter 9, "Pure IP, Compatibility Mode, and Service Location Protocol (SLP)," discusses how to configure your NetWare 5 server to run using pure IP. This chapter also discusses how to use SLP.

- Chapter 10, "Disk Management," covers NetWare 5's disk management and fault tolerance features.

- Chapter 11, "Upgrading an Existing Server," walks you through the necessary steps to upgrade servers running previous versions of NetWare to NetWare 5.

- Chapter 12, "Applying Patches," offers techniques and tips on keeping your NetWare 5 server up to date.

- Chapter 13, "Installing Workstation Software," discusses the installation of various workstation clients.

Part IV, "Managing Your NDS Tree," explores the procedures necessary to working and managing NDS objects and replicas:

- Chapter 14, "Logging In to and Navigating Around the Novell Directory Services Tree," shows you the basics of NDS tree navigation.

- Chapter 15, "Creating, Managing, and Using NDS Objects," shows you the steps for working with NDS objects.

- Chapter 16, "Managing NDS Rights, Partitions, and Replicas," covers NDS security, partitioning, and replication management techniques.

Part V, "Network Operations," deals with day-to-day operation of your NetWare 5 network:

- Chapter 17, "Organizing and Accessing Information on the NetWare Server," shows you how to access data on a NetWare server.

- Chapter 18, "Implementing Security," explores the various NetWare security features.

- Chapter 19, "Auditing," takes a look at how you can keep tabs on what's happening on your network.

- Chapter 20, "NetWare Accounting," walks you through the accounting features found in NetWare.

- Chapter 21, "Network Printing," covers all the bases—from issuing print commands, checking printer status, and canceling print jobs, to dealing with common printing problems.

- Chapter 22, "Configuring User Environment Using Login Scripts," discusses methods in which you can customize your users' working environment.

- Chapter 23, "Server Console Utilities," explores various commands and utilities that you can use at the server console.

- Chapter 24, "ZENworks," covers the details for using the Novell Application Launcher, software metering, and remote control features.

Part VI, "Maintenance and Troubleshooting," covers network maintenance and troubleshooting topics.

- Chapter 25, "Data Archiving and Backup," helps you to develop a backup and recovery plan, select an appropriate backup device, and choose backup tools to automate your system backup.

- Chapter 26, "Server Tuning for Performance," describes performance monitoring techniques, areas of performance tuning, and the many adjustments that you can make to a NetWare 5 server to bring better overall performance.

- Chapter 27, "Troubleshooting Common Problems," helps you deal with commonly encountered server issues.

Part VII, "Implementing Internet Services," introduces you to TCP/IP networking and provides you with information on configuring and using some of the more popular and important NetWare 5's Internet services:

- Chapter 28, "Introduction to TCP/IP," gives you an in-depth look into IP addressing and the various protocols found in the TCP/IP protocol suite.

- Chapter 29, "Domain Naming Systems (DNS)," teaches you the workings of DNS and how to set up and configure DNS in a NetWare 5 environment.

- Chapter 30, "Dynamic Host Configuration Protocol (DHCP)," shows you what DHCP is and how to set up and configure DHCP clients and servers.

- Chapter 31, "Network Address Translation (NAT)," describes what NAT is and how to set up your NetWare 5 server to provide the NAT functionality.
- Chapter 32, "The Netscape FastTrack Web Server," shows you how to configure and manage the Netscape FastTrack Server for NetWare.
- Chapter 33, "Lightweight Directory Access Protocol (LDAP)," presents you with information on how you can access NDS information via LDAP.
- Chapter 34, "Novell Internet Access Server (NIAS)," teaches you how to set up NIAS for in-bound and out-bound dial-up access.
- Chapter 35, "FTP Service and LPR/LPD," shows you how to configure your NetWare 5 server to provide FTP services.

CONVENTIONS USED IN THIS BOOK

This book uses several special conventions of which you should be aware. These conventions are listed here for your convenience.

Unlike some operating systems, such as UNIX, NetWare is *not* a case-sensitive operating system; that means when this book instructs you to type something at a command prompt, you can type the command in either upper- or lowercase. This book uses a special type-face for NetWare commands and filenames to set them off from standard text. If you are instructed to type something, what you are to type also appears in the special typeface. For example, if the book instructs you to type NWADMN32 and press Return, you must press the letters n, w, a, d, m, n, 3, and 2, and then press Return.

At times, you are instructed to press a key such as Return, Tab, or the spacebar. Keys sometimes are pressed in combination; when this is the case, the keys are represented in this way: Ctrl+h. This example implies you must press *and* hold the Ctrl key, press the letter h, and then release both keys.

Note

This book uses a convention for key names that might differ from what you are accustomed to. To avoid confusion in the case-sensitive UNIX environment, this book uses lowercase letters to refer to keys when uppercase might be the norm. For example, this book uses the form Ctrl+h instead of Ctrl+H (the latter form might make some of you wonder whether you should press Ctrl *and* Shift *and* h).

Note

Often, the need for Return following a command is implied and understood, so it might not be shown in the listing.

When discussing the syntax of a NetWare command, this book uses special formatting to distinguish the required portions and the variable portions. Consider the following example:

```
ndir filename
```

In this syntax, the *filename* portion of the command is variable; that is, it changes depending on what file you want the ndir command to work with. The ndir is required; it is the actual command name. Variable information is presented in *italics in a special font*; information that must be typed exactly as it appears is presented in nonitalic type.

In some cases, command information might be optional; that is, it is not required for the command to work. Following the convention used by most programs, square brackets ([]) surround those parts of the command syntax that are optional. In the following example, notice that the *filename* parameter is a variable *and* optional (it is in italics as well as surrounded by square brackets); however, to use the optional *filename* parameter, you must type it exactly as it appears (it is not in italics; it is a *literal* option):

```
ndir [filename] [/sub]
```

Throughout the book, you will find the following text items to draw your attention to important or interesting information:

Note

Notes contain asides that give you more information about the current topic. They provide insights that give you a better understanding of the task at hand or further clarification of a concept.

Tip #1001 from
Author Name

Tips tell you about NetWare commands or methods that are easier, faster, or more efficient than the traditional methods.

Caution

Cautions contain warnings about things that you should not do, or do with care, or else potential accidents or disasters can happen. These boxes help you avoid at least some of the pitfalls.

Sidebar

Longer discussions not integral to the flow of the chapter are set aside as sidebars.

INTRODUCTION TO NETWARE 5

## CHAPTER 1

FEATURES OF NETWARE 5

In this chapter

WHAT'S NEW IN NETWARE 5?

After more than six generations of software development, Novell has delivered NetWare 5 which combines the maturity and reliability of the traditional NetWare network with the global reach and open standards of the Internet. NetWare 5 enables you to create a network based on Internet protocols, while making the most of your existing network investments.

NetWare History
For those of you who are interested in a little NetWare history–prior to the release of NetWare 5, there have been the following generations of NetWare products: NetWare (the original disk-server operating system), NetWare 68 (for the Motorola 68000 series systems), NetWare 4.6x, Advanced NetWare 1.x, Advanced NetWare 2.x, NetWare 386 (NetWare 3.x), and NetWare 4.x.

For those of you who are familiar with previous versions of NetWare, the following is a summary of some of the new features you'll find in NetWare 5:

- **Core protocol independence**—NetWare 5 supports IP-only networks while retaining compatibility with IPX. It enables you to implement TCP/IP, the standard protocol of the Internet, in your existing network infrastructure without additional routing overhead and without jeopardizing control, security, or performance.

- **Compatibility Mode Driver**—The Compatibility Mode feature enables you to continue to use your IPX-dependent applications for as long as you need to—you decide when and if you will make the transition to an IP-only network. NetWare 5 also includes the industry-standard Netscape Web browser and Netscape FastTrack Server for NetWare, which you can use to set up your own Web server based on Novell Directory Services (NDS) for the Internet or your intranet.

- **Enhanced Novell Directory Services (NDS)**—NetWare 5 includes an enhanced version of NDS, featuring new role-based management (such as password management) and support for Lightweight Directory Access Protocol (LDAP) version 3.

- **Integrated Internet services**—NetWare 5 integrates domain name system (DNS) and Dynamic Host Configuration Protocol (DHCP) services with NDS for easy and centralized IP address management.

- **Java support**—Novell implemented Sun Microsystems' Java Runtime Environment (JRE) via a set of NetWare Loadable Modules (NLMs) so you're now able to run Java applications *on* the NetWare server.

- **Enhanced multiprocessor support**—The enhanced kernel in NetWare 5 is now multiprocessor enabled. This means the operating system tasks can take advantage of any additional CPUs you have installed in the server.

- **Virtual memory**—You can now run memory-hungry applications and lessen the likelihood that low memory conditions will cause an *abend*—an abnormal end, a term borrowed from the mainframe environment. Also, the virtual memory system ensures that the RAM is used more efficiently.

- **Improved memory protection**—The memory address space is now divided into OS space (ring 0) and protected memory space (ring 3). You can load NLMs in either memory space (if supported by the NLM).

- **New file system**—NetWare 5 also includes Novell Storage Services (NSS), a new 64-bit indexed storage service which enables the server to handle billions of files containing files up to 8 terabytes (TB) in size, and mounts and remounts volumes in seconds.

- **Enhanced printing services**—In addition to the legacy queue-based printing, also included is Novell Distributed Print Services (NDPS), which increases the performance and reliability of network printers.

- **Enhanced client desktop support and management**—ZENworks (Zero Effort Networks) allows you to centrally, through NDS, deploy applications to Windows 9x and NT workstations and manage desktop profiles and policies of these workstations.

- **New security features**—Included with NetWare 5 is public-key infrastructure (PKI), cryptography (128-bit encryption for North America, and 64-bit encryption for rest of world) and Secure Authentication Services (SAS). These new features, all integrated with NDS, simplify administration and offer new levels of access control.

- **Ready for the next century**—NetWare 5 is Year 2000 ready, out-of-the-box.

What's more, a 5-user version of Oracle8 for NetWare and a full copy of Netscape FastTrack Server for NetWare is included free of charge with every copy of NetWare 5. That means, you can instantly turn your NetWare 5 server into a powerful database server or a Web server, without purchasing additional software.

If you're new to NetWare or would like to learn more about NetWare, the remainder of this chapter describes the characteristics of NetWare 5, including its design goals, overall architecture, and behavioral aspects. Although this chapter doesn't discuss specific features of NetWare in-depth (which you'll find in other chapters in this book), it provides important conceptual information that can help you install, administer, and expand your NetWare installation. This chapter also provides a high-level overview of the new services included in NetWare 5.

NetWare—An Under-the-Hood Look

NetWare's origins are different than those of other popular operating systems, such as UNIX, OS/2, Windows NT, and so on. NetWare began life as a disk-serving operating system and quickly expanded to provide full file service over a network.

NetWare is the only operating system on the market today that began as a strictly *back-end*, network-based product. Back-end services are network-based operating system components, such as file systems. This focus on network-based, back-end services is the motivation for NetWare to provide maximum throughput and reliability, which explains some of its unique characteristics and differences when compared to other network operating systems. And because NetWare was initially *designed* to serve files, that's why it makes such an excellent file server operating system.

AN EVENT-DRIVEN SYSTEM

Because NetWare's role is to provide back-end services over a network, it is an *event-driven* system. When a network workstation (front end) requests to read a file residing on the server, for example, it sends a request packet to the server. The request packet triggers activity on the NetWare server: The server checks for concurrency conflicts and security violations, reads the file data, and sends the data back to the workstation over the network.

All this activity on the NetWare server is driven by an event: the reception of a request packet from the front-end workstation. This means that NetWare's capability to perform is dictated by its capability to receive and process packets that come to it over the network. NetWare, therefore, is designed to handle thousands of hardware interrupts and hundreds of network request packets per second. This high-throughput design requires an efficient overall operating system architecture and a particularly robust device driver interface.

TRADITIONAL DESIGN COMPONENTS

Some traditional operating system design components, such as virtual memory, memory protection, and preemptive multitasking, pose significant performance problems to device drivers. NetWare device drivers make heavy use of shared memory and Direct Memory Access (DMA). All three of these traditional design components negate or negatively impact the capability of device drivers to use shared memory and DMA. Because of this, NetWare's original designers decided to forgo virtual memory, memory protection, and preemptive multitasking. This was not an oversight or mistake, but a decision consistent with NetWare's focus on providing back-end services over a network. However, given the new CPU architecture and their high speeds available today, NetWare 5 now includes virtual memory, memory protection, and preemptive multitasking support.

> **Note**
>
> Preemptive multitasking, virtual memory, and memory protection all contribute to an operating system's capability to run multiple front-end (interactive) applications concurrently. These design features were specifically introduced into general-purpose operating systems to enable users on terminals to run front-end applications. NetWare specializes in back-end services, which in traditional operating systems typically run at the *kernel* level anyway (without memory protection) and must deal with the negative consequences of virtual memory and preemption.

NetWare uses the fact that it is generally much faster—100 times or more— to access information from RAM than it is from hard disk; it tries to keep as much information in RAM as possible. File allocation tables (FATs), most recently used directory entry tables (DETs), and most recently accessed files are all cached in RAM for fast access.

NetWare obtains excellent performance from commodity PC hardware because of the reasons mentioned previously. In order to take full advantage of NetWare's initial concept, you must install and configure NetWare in a manner consistent with its design characteristics.

Tip #1 from
Peter

> You'll find one of the most recommended performance enhancement suggestions is to add more RAM to the server, and not to add more CPUs or upgrade to a faster CPU.

A RICH SERVICE ENVIRONMENT

NetWare's event-driven design and the consequential requirements for high throughput demand a minimalist philosophy on the part of NetWare's designers. Each component of NetWare is designed with this philosophy in mind. NetWare's kernel is exceedingly simple and elegant.

NetWare, despite its simplicity, presents a rich environment to developers and systems designers. This is possible because of the fortunate rule that complex systems can be constructed by integrated simple components in a modular fashion. Each basic component of NetWare is sparsely coded and simple in design; however, because of the modular integration of the many basic components of NetWare, the NetWare environment is rich and complex.

This enables NetWare to present a complete back-end service platform to server-based applications developers and still maintain its high throughput. NetWare can service network request packets very quickly because it is *flat* (it has few Open Systems Interconnect, or OSI, layers; see Chapter 4, "Networking Data Flow," for more information about OSI). Being flat means that it is concerned only with the lowest layers of the OSI model: physical, data link, network, and transport. Another reason NetWare can handle request packets quickly is because its modular design leverages the basic kernel to its maximum potential.

Examples of services offered and supported by NetWare 5 include the following:

- Kernel-level scheduling and memory management
- Interprocess communication
- LAN communications
- Hardware device driver (including that of Intelligent I/O adapters, I_2O) support
- File system
- Print services
- Messaging and email
- Internetwork routing
- Programming interfaces and development environment
- Network management
- Built-in support for multiprotocol operation
- Support for multiple-file formats
- Support for database management systems

PLATFORM FOR SERVER-BASED APPLICATIONS

As a result of its focus, design, and characteristics, NetWare 5 is an ideal platform for server-based applications. (Server-based applications provide the "server" component of client/server computing.)

Server-based applications running on NetWare can gain increased performance over other platforms because of NetWare's high-throughput, event-driven design. Specifically, server-based applications running on NetWare automatically enjoy the following benefits:

- Multithreaded (or multiprocess) execution
- Full 32-bit protected mode
- Flat memory model with up to 4GB of addressable memory
- Full access to NetWare OS services

Note

At the time of writing, Novell is developing a 64-bit operating system, code named Modesto, designed to run on Intel's future IA-64 processor family beginning with the Merced processor.

Database vendors, such as Oracle, Sybase, and Informix, that have ported their multiplatform database management systems to run as NetWare server-based applications, have expressed that NetWare provides the highest possible performance, given the hardware on which it is running. This means that a NetWare server can run such applications just as fast or faster than platforms that cost many times more than a NetWare system. As a matter of fact, NetWare 5 includes a 5-user version of Oracle8 for NetWare.

THE ROLE OF THE NETWORK OPERATING SYSTEM

The history of network operating systems indicates that their role has expanded over time. NetWare went from disk-serving to file-serving, to internetworking and multiprotocol service. Today, network operating systems are expected to perform all these functions and more.

NetWare 3 and NetWare 4 have proven the utility of a network operating system that supports multiple network protocols and client file systems. In addition, previous versions of NetWare have proven the effectiveness of NetWare as a platform for server-based applications, based on the excellent performance and reliability of NLM-based applications, such as Oracle, Informix, Sybase, and Gupta.

NetWare 5 is designed to extend the role of the network even further, to the point that NetWare becomes the foundation of an enterprise network.

EXPANDABILITY

Many systems programmers believe that the role of a computer operating system is to provide a programming interface to the underlying computer hardware, and to provide a systematic way of obtaining hardware resources.

With this view in mind, NetWare's expandability becomes particularly important. NetWare enables you to add hardware resources to the server machine easily without having to reconfigure the NetWare operating system or even without having to restart the server in order for new changes to take effect.

DYNAMIC DISCOVERY

NetWare provides expandability through its dynamic discovery of underlying hardware resources installed on the server machine. Because NetWare discovers all server memory during the NetWare boot routines, it can make use of additional server memory automatically.

> **Note**
>
> Depending on your computer hardware, it may be necessary to run the hardware configuration utility after you've added more RAM to register the additional memory. Otherwise, NetWare will not see the added RAM. It is a rather common problem with EISA-based systems that NetWare doesn't detect the newly added RAM until the EISA configuration utility is run.

The same holds true for the number of volumes configured on the server. You don't have to tell the operating system how many volumes there are, a simple MOUNT ALL command makes all volumes available to the operating system. You can selectively mount and dismount volumes in real-time without having to restart the server for these changes to take effect.

LOADABLE DEVICE-DRIVER INTERFACE

NetWare's loadable device-driver interface (generically known as NetWare Loadable Modules, or NLMs) means that you can add storage devices, LAN cards, and other hardware devices to the server machine without reconfiguring the NetWare operating system. To activate such devices, you only need to load the device's driver from the NetWare server console prompt. (Conversely, you can deactivate hardware devices simply by unloading their drivers from the console prompt.)

> **Note**
>
> As an analogy, you can consider the NetWare operating system similar to a set of Lego bricks—you can add and remove pieces from it as you see fit (see Figure 1.1).

Figure 1.1
Device drivers can easily "snap" into the operating system.

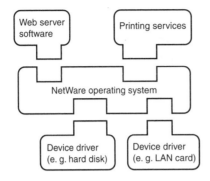

NetWare's loadable device-driver interface is especially attractive when you consider that UNIX (and other similar operating systems) require you to relink the entire operating system simply to add a driver. Windows NT requires a complete reboot in order to add or remove device drivers.

With NetWare, you can easily change certain server resources, such as LAN receive buffers, directory cache buffers, and others, simply by entering commands at the server console prompt while the server is running.

INCREASE VOLUME SIZE DYNAMICALLY

The most spectacular aspect of NetWare's expandability is the capability to increase the size of a NetWare volume while the server is running.

To do this, simply add a prepared storage partition to a volume: NetWare increases the size of that volume dynamically. (For more information about volume configuration, see Chapter 8, "Installing NetWare 5 on New Servers.")

A NEW ENGINE—A MULTIPROCESSOR KERNEL

TheNetWare 5 operating system contains a multiprocessor kernel (MPK) that fully supports symmetrical multiprocessing (SMP) hardware. Because of this, NetWare 5 does not need to load a second SMP driver as SMP NetWare 4.11 does. NetWare 5's MPK is fully multi-threaded to perform thread scheduling interrupt, exception handling, and multiprocessor synchronization, and it also adds support for preemption.

Because MPK was written to the Intel 82489DX interrupt controller specification, it can support up to 32 processors, each of which will increase your server performance; this number might increase in future releases as different controller specifications are implemented.

Note

> Server-based NLMs that have been previously developed for SMP NetWare 4.11 also work with NetWare 5's MPK without modification. Developers writing to NetWare 5's CLIB (C Library module) can use its multithreaded APIs (Application Programming Interfaces) and therefore implement MPK support to their NLMs.
>
> A Novell benchmark using Oracle 8 showed a 98% performance increase with the addition of a second processor. There was a 95% increase with the addition of a third processor, and another 89% with a fourth processor.

A number of core NetWare services are multithreaded and will therefore take advantage of MPK server systems. For example, Java can take advantage of MPK servers by allowing applications to specify which processor to bind to. NetWare 5's memory system and disk subsystem is mostly multithreaded and can take advantage of MPK systems. Other multi-threaded support includes the NetWare debugger, Media Manager, virtual memory, and abend recovery routines.

At the time of writing, the LAN and file subsystems take only partial advantage of MPK multithreading capabilities. But these include important elements—such as memory alloca-tion, Direct File System (DFS) read and write paths, and data writes through data buffers to cache buffers—that can be put on other processors. Also the packet receive buffers to cache buffers operation has also been multithreaded.

A number of NLM-based applications, such as GroupWise and Oracle, come with configu-ration parameters for SMP support; Oracle has a database setting to allow for parallelism support.

Tip #2 from
Peter

> If your software vendor isn't able to tell you whether its product is MPK-enabled, you can determine it as follows. Issue the console command SET DEVELOPER OPTION=ON and when an NLM that doesn't take advantage of MPK multithreading capabilities is loaded, it gives the following information in the color green:
>
> `<Module name>` does not have any XDC data.
>
> Don't forget to set the Developer Option to Off again when you're done testing.

NOVELL DIRECTORY SERVICES—THE FOUNDATION OF AN ENTERPRISE NETWORK

NetWare 5 is designed to provide the foundation of the enterprise network. *Enterprise net-works* tie together the disparate computing resources of the organization, enabling unlike systems to act together as a cohesive whole.

NetWare 5 binds an organization's computing resources in two ways. First, the versatile protocol and file services of NetWare enable communication among disparate computing systems. Second, NetWare Directory Services (NDS) provide a systematic and intuitive method of managing, administering, and using all the computing resources of an organization, large or small.

> **Note**
>
> Novell Directory Services organizes network resources—such as users, groups, printers, and volumes—into a hierarchical tree structure. This structure is generally referred to as the NDS tree or simply as the Directory. Throughout this book, the term *Directory*, with the capital *D*, is used to refer to the NDS structure.

Interestingly, NDS calls on all the lower-level services provided by NetWare:

- Communications protocols are necessary to query and respond to queries from other systems on the internetwork.
- File services are necessary to store the NDS Directory Information Base (DIB).
- Security services are necessary to ensure that the distributed NDS system allows only authorized information to be obtained across the internetwork.
- Transaction and concurrency control is necessary to the smooth operation of the distributed NDS DIB, such as tracking file updates on remote servers.

NetWare 5's role as the "glue" that binds an enterprise together is its most ambitious goal to date, one which draws on the heritage of NetWare's past and requires all the lower-level services that have evolved over the years to work correctly and reliably.

NDS has shaped the future of using the network. The built-in services provided by NDS, combined with the NDS programming interface, create the potential for a new generation of distributed "glue" applications—modules that bind different types of computers across geographical and organizational boundaries.

Glue applications provide a logical framework that destroys such boundaries and makes resources available universally. Although NDS is itself such a glue application, it also creates the potential for any number of higher-level modules that enable computing activities not foreseen by the designers of NDS.

SINGLE-LOGIN CAPABILITIES

In a NetWare 5 environment, a user logs into the network once using a single username and password to gain access to all authorized network resources. This means that a user logs in to the network, and NDS manages connections to NetWare servers in the same Directory tree and even connections to NetWare 3 servers if the username and password are the same.

By contrast, NetWare 3 users must log in to each network server individually with a user-name and password because of the server-centric nature of the NetWare 3 bindery; in some cases, this could mean a different username and password for each different additional server connection. Using NDS, you create each user account only once for all NetWare 5 users in your Directory tree—multiple user IDs on multiple servers are no longer needed. This single-login feature alone can save you hours of work in managing user accounts.

EASY ADMINISTRATION

Most of the NDS administrative functions are consolidated into a single, easy-to-use, graphics utility that greatly reduces the time you spend on network administration. This utility, NetWare Administrator, is a Windows-based application that enables you to make changes to the Directory with an easy point-and-click and drag-and-drop of the mouse (see Figure 1.2). Each object in the tree is represented by an icon. By clicking on the object's icon, you can retrieve information about that particular object.

Figure 1.2
The NetWare
Administrator utility is
often referred to as
NWAdmin.

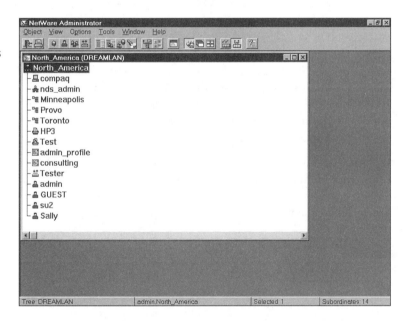

> **Note**
>
> NetWare Administrator is often referred to by one of its shorter forms. Most often, the name *NWAdmin* is used, which is named after the executable file (NWADMIN.EXE) of its initial version. With NetWare 5, the executable is called NWADMN32.EXE (a 32-bit version) so it is sometimes referred to as *NWAdmin32*. Throughout this book, you'll see these terms used interchangeably.

This object-oriented view of the Directory lets you perform many routine management functions easily: NDS objects, files, directories, and server functions can be controlled through the NWAdmin utility.

UNLIMITED SCALABILITY

Both NetWare 5 and NDS are designed to be *scalable* from a single workgroup all the way up to the enterprise level because the concept of the network is logical rather than physical. You can add to your NetWare installation one server at a time and even one user at a time. This scalability primarily is achieved through the distributed design of NDS. NDS enables you to create a multileveled global directory tree one server at a time, with no restrictions on the timing or number of servers you add to the tree.

The NDS was designed to have unlimited size, which is to say, an unlimited number of levels. This design allows a single NDS database not only to contain information about very large organizations, but also to allow the linking of multiple organizations through the merging of trees. The algorithms built in to NDS for replicating the database and checking distributed links in the tree are highly scalable—they perform very well even when the database becomes extremely large.

In 1997, Novell created a single NDS tree containing *two million* users to show the incredible extent to which the Novell Directory Services is scalable. The motivation of building this large NDS tree originated with a large Novell customer who wanted to know whether NDS would scale to 300,000 potential user accounts in a single Directory tree. Novell engineers decided to up the ante by building a fully functional million-user NDS tree, which later evolved into a two million–user tree. And although few, if any, enterprises would ever need a Directory tree of this size, Novell engineers felt that it was important to let current and potential customers know that no matter how large their Directory needs might grow to be, NDS can handle them—and do so with ease.

With the introduction of NDS 8 (the next generation of Novell Directory Services) in early 1999, Novell engineers created a single NDS tree containing *one billion users* to demonstrate that the current technology of Novell Directory Services is ready to serve enterprises of any size, including the Internet community.

> **Note**
>
> The version of NDS shipped with NetWare 5 is referred as NDS 7 as the version numbering of the DS module is 7.x. You'll read more about NDS 8 in the section "Project: Discover NDS 8" at the end of this chapter.

NDS ENHANCEMENTS IN NETWARE 5

Along with the other exciting features of NetWare 5 comes increased functionality for the Novell Directory Services. Several enhancements have been incorporated into NDS to make it more efficient and scalable, to reduce traffic across your WAN infrastructure, and to enable you to more easily manage both the NDS tree contents and your overall network system. These enhancements to NDS, organized into five main areas, are as follows:

- Improvements to the NDS replica synchronization process through the introduction of transitive synchronization

- Enhancements to reduce NDS-related network traffic via the use of WAN Traffic Manager (WanMan)
- New features for easier access to information stored in the NDS tree with the help of Catalog Services and via LDAP
- New features for easier management of objects within the NDS tree with the introduction of Inheritable Access Control Lists (ACLs)
- New features for easier management of the overall NDS system using Schema Manager and the DSDIAG (DS Diagnostic) utilities

You'll find detailed discussions about NDS in Part II, "Understanding Novell Directory Services."

CAPACITY

NetWare 5 features prodigious capacity, both in the amount of RAM the server can address and in the amount of data the server's file system can store and use.

MEMORY CAPACITY

NetWare 5 can address all physical RAM installed in the server machine, up to 4GB. Servers containing 512MB of RAM or more are not uncommon these days as hardware prices decline.

Why would you want so much memory in your server? Servers with multigigabyte file systems require more memory than you would expect. NetWare needs this additional memory to cache important volume structures (such as file allocation tables and directory entry tables). The greater the size and number of volumes on a server, the more memory is required to cache volume data structures.

Furthermore, NetWare uses all its free memory to provide a file-system cache. The file-system cache speeds up server performance by holding the data of active files in fast server RAM. This reduces the need for NetWare to read data from physical media devices, which increases performance. The greater the size of the file-system cache, the greater the increase in performance. That's why many administrators install 128MB or more of RAM in their NetWare servers.

NetWare 5 was designed to work well with large amounts of memory installed on the server machine. Its internal memory management algorithms do not slow down or become complex when they must deal with large amounts of memory. Adding RAM to your NetWare 5 server machine is one of the easiest and most cost-effective things you can do to improve server performance.

FILE SYSTEM CAPACITY

Compared with NetWare 4, the capacity of the NetWare 5 file system has been greatly enhanced. Shown in Table 1.1 is a comparison table of capabilities between the two file systems.

TABLE 1.1   FILE SYSTEM CAPACITY COMPARISON

Capability	NetWare 5	NetWare 4
Concurrent open files per server	2^{64} (or 10^{19})	100,000
Directory entries per volume	2^{64} (or 10^{19})	16 million
Volumes per server	Unlimited	64
Segments per volume	Unlimited	8
Maximum disk storage capacity	8TB	4TB
Maximum file size	8TB	4GB

> **Note**
>
> 1 terabyte (TB) is 1,024 gigabytes (GB).

> **Note**
>
> The unlimited number of volumes on a NetWare 5 server is applicable only when using the new Novell Storage Services (NSS) volume. If you're using legacy volumes, you're limited to 255 volumes.
>
> The initial NSS implementation is such that its access is through the NetWare Symantec Agent module, which has a limit of 255 volumes. Therefore, until this Agent is updated or until NetWare uses a different method to access NSS, 255 volumes is what a NetWare 5 server can currently support.

In addition to the much higher capacity of the NetWare 5 file system, NetWare 5 supports other disk management features, such as data migration and disk suballocation. These features are discussed in Chapter 10, "Disk Management."

MEMORY MANAGEMENT

For many years, trade journalists and industry analysts have criticized NetWare for its lack of memory protection. Memory protection refers to the capability of the operating system to prevent use of illegal memory references made by applications. As mentioned earlier, NetWare's designers did not include memory protection in earlier versions of NetWare for performance reasons, until now.

BETTER GARBAGE COLLECTION

In NetWare 3.*x*, memory that is freed when you unload a NLM is not necessarily all returned to the cache buffer pool; some can be placed in an allocation pool for use by other NLMs. This means that you could deplete the amount of memory used by the file cache system when you load and unload NLMs.

In NetWare 5 (and in NetWare 4), however, updated memory garbage collection routines ensure that unloaded NLMs return *all* the memory used to the file cache buffer pool. This allows the operating system to dedicate as much memory as possible to the file cache buffer pool at all times. And the more memory that is dedicated to the file cache buffer pool, the better the NetWare operating system performs.

At the same time, performance of memory allocation routines has been enhanced. This improvement is of interest primarily to software developers. Under certain conditions, such as when a NetWare server has been running nonstop for several months, users have noticed a slowdown in NetWare 3 memory allocation. The cause for this slowdown in NetWare 3 is both rare and obscure (it involves the fragmentation of freed memory in the operating system). Fragmentation of memory in NetWare 5 has virtually been eliminated by the new memory allocator and garbage collection routines.

MEMORY PROTECTION

NetWare 5 features optional memory protection. With memory protection activated, you can load NLM applications in *protected memory* (also known as *protected address space*), a memory region that has carefully controlled communication with the server operating system. The operating system creates a boundary around the protected address space. If an NLM attempts an illegal memory access (referencing areas of memory outside the boundary), the operating system disallows the memory access and unloads the offending NLM. Without memory protection, such illegal memory accesses go unchecked and have the potential to crash the NetWare server.

Note

The NetWare operating system itself cannot run in a protected address space. The operating system address space is called the *OS address space* or the *kernel address space*.

Memory protection on NetWare 5 decreases NLM performance somewhere between 3% and 10%, depending on the specific NLM and how it was designed. (This is not out of line with the performance penalty paid by other operating systems with memory protection.) Novell recommends that all NLM developers use memory protection to trap programming errors during development.

Novell suggests that server administrators run third-party NLMs in protected memory space for perhaps a month. During that time, if the NLM did not attempt any illegal memory references, the administrator can move the NLM to unprotected memory in order to gain a slight increase in NLM performance. Or, the administrator can choose to leave the NLM loaded in protected memory.

Tip #3 from
Peter

> The optional memory protection allows those who are concerned about illegal memory accesses by NLMs to protect the NetWare operating system. At the same time, however, those who run trusted applications are free to do so in unprotected memory without the slight performance penalty associated with memory protection.

VIRTUAL MEMORY

In earlier versions of NetWare, if you had a server with 64MB of RAM, that was all the memory that the server could use to load applications and NLMs, as well as offer memory for printing, user data creation and manipulation, and application access. NetWare 5 provides a virtual memory (VM) system that can move data out of memory and into a file on disk if the data is used infrequently. This means you can run more applications on the server than the amount of physical memory allows. The virtual memory system ensures that RAM is used more efficiently.

Note

> Modules that are loaded into protected address spaces use virtual memory. Both the module and the data it accesses can be swapped to disk.
>
> Modules that are not loaded into protected address spaces can still use virtual memory. However, the modules themselves cannot be swapped to disk.

Furthermore, the swapping of unused code and data out of memory to disk lessens the likelihood that low memory conditions will cause an abend.

FAULT TOLERANCE FEATURES

Fault tolerance is a design philosophy that has been part of NetWare from the beginning. Fault tolerance means that NetWare can continue operating in the face of hardware errors.

NetWare contains different levels of *system fault tolerance* (*SFT*). The need for fault tolerance became evident early in the life of NetWare because NetWare, as a server operating system, was responsible for concurrently providing resources to many workstation computers. This amounted to a single point of failure—the machine on which NetWare was running. This had the potential to bring down many other machines—the workstation machines requesting services from NetWare.

SYSTEM FAULT TOLERANCE LEVEL I (SFT I)

Level I fault tolerance is built in to the core routines of all versions of the NetWare file system. It provides for automatic, on-the-fly remapping of bad hard drive media sectors. Novell calls this feature *Hot Fix*, referring to the automatic and transparent remapping of bad media sectors. If a sector on a hard drive goes bad, NetWare automatically maps that sector to a good one from a pool of reserved sectors (see Figure 1.3).

Figure 1.3
Dynamic bad block remapping (Hot Fix).

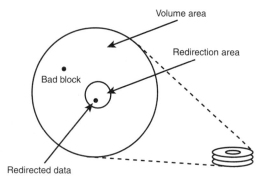

To detect bad media sectors, NetWare uses read-after-write verification. This verification involves reading data into a special buffer after NetWare has written that same data to disk. NetWare compares the data it just read to the data it just wrote and, if the two are not the same, infers that the media has suffered an error. This triggers the Hot Fix feature (see Figure 1.4).

Figure 1.4
Read-After-Write verification process.

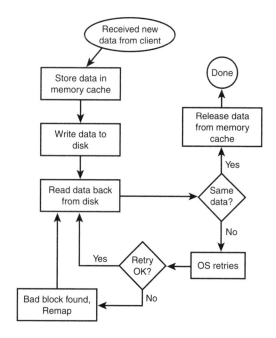

Tip #4 from
Peter

If the disk subsystem you use in the server supports Hot Fix at the hardware level, you can turn off this software feature and gain some performance.

Another aspect of SFT I is *redundant volume data structures*. Volume data structures contain essential information regarding the NetWare file system, files, directories, and free space on the media. Without these data structures, the NetWare file system cannot function. NetWare maintains redundant copies of all volume data structures and performs routine comparisons of the primary and redundant data structures. If either a primary or redundant data structure becomes corrupted, NetWare repairs it using the other copy as a reference.

Each time a volume mounts, NetWare checks each set of directory tables and FATs for internal consistency and then compares them with the other copy to ensure that both copies are valid. If a discrepancy is found, the volume will not be mounted and a warning message is displayed on the server console.

Note

If any of your volumes failed to mount, you need to run VREPAIR to correct any inconsistencies before trying to mount them again. Refer to Chapter 27, "Troubleshooting Common Problems," for more details about the VREPAIR utility.

SYSTEM FAULT TOLERANCE LEVEL II (SFT II)

Level II fault tolerance consists of all features found in SFT I plus *disk mirroring* and *duplexing*. Both mirroring and duplexing enable you to configure redundant storage devices for use with NetWare. A mirrored drive consists of two physical drives connected to the same hard drive controller (see Figure 1.5). NetWare duplicates all write operations to both drives of a mirrored set.

Figure 1.5
Disk mirroring uses two or more disk drives on the same controller.

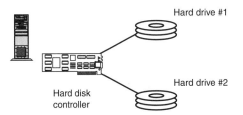

Hard drive #1

Hard disk controller

Hard drive #2

If one of the drives fails, NetWare continues to run, using the remaining drive for all read and write operations. All data on the remaining drive is up-to-date, meaning that no data loss occurred when the failed drive went down. When you replace the failed drive, NetWare automatically restores the mirror using a special background process that allows the server to remain up and running throughout the entire process.

Note

Depending on the amount of disk space that needs remirroring, the process can take up to several hours.

The difference between mirroring and duplexing is simple. Mirroring occurs when two or more drives (the mirrored set) are attached to the same drive controller. *Duplexing* occurs when each drive in the mirrored set is attached to a *different* controller (see Figure 1.6).

Figure 1.6
Disk duplexing uses
multiple disk
controllers.

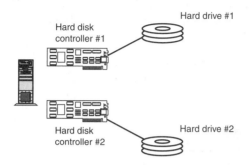

Duplexing is more robust than mirroring because it protects against drive *and* controller failure, while mirroring only protects against drive failure.

Most people don't realize that you can mirror or duplex a drive to several redundant drives—you can construct a mirrored set of many drives, rather than just two. This isn't always practical because of the cost of hard drives. You can, however, construct multidrive mirrored sets if you want.

Tip #5 from *Peter*	For large, mission-critical, servers, *redundant array of inexpensive drives* (*RAID*) technology is commonly used. See Chapter 10 for more details.

Mirroring and duplexing were built in to the NetWare operating system at a time when drive failure was more frequent than it is today (around the mid-1980s). Despite the gains in reliability of magnetic media that have occurred in the last several years, disk drives are still among the least reliable components of a computer system. Therefore, disk mirroring and duplexing are extremely important features of NetWare's fault-tolerance system.

Finally, SFT II also includes *transaction control*, or, as Novell refers to it, the *Transaction Tracking System (TTS)*.; TTS enables programs to associate groups of write operations into logical transactions. Each transaction is guaranteed to succeed (meaning that all the individual write operations are successful) or, if it doesn't succeed, NetWare restores all affected files to their prewrite state—a roll-back. NetWare then can retry the transaction, knowing that it is starting from the same point.

TTS is of interest primarily to database-management programs, which frequently makes groups of updates to database files. If one update in a group fails, the database becomes corrupted. NetWare uses TTS to ensure the integrity of the NDS database files. TTS is fully integrated with the NetWare file system. Most database-management systems that are written for use with NetWare use TTS.

SFT II is built in to all current versions of NetWare, including NetWare 5.

SYSTEM FAULT TOLERANCE LEVEL III (SFT III)

Level III fault tolerance consists of SFT II plus server mirroring, or redundant servers. Level III fault tolerance is provided in the earlier versions of the NetWare operating system as a separate product, such as NetWare 4.11 SFT III.

SFT III provides nonstop operation through the use of an entirely redundant server machine, including CPU, power supply, drives, network interface cards, and everything else. You have two completely separate server machines (see Figure 1.7).

Figure 1.7
SFT III is the duplex-ing of file server hardware.

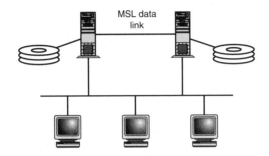

Two server machines are connected via a high-speed Mirrored Server Link (MSL). The job of the MSL is to maintain synchronization between the two machines. The entire memory image of the NetWare server is duplicated on both machines. If one machine goes down, the other machine remains running. NetWare clients experience no loss of state or interruption in service. Server-based applications, such as Oracle, run mirrored automatically.

SFT III NetWare (available since NetWare 3.11) was the first and had been the only software-based server fault tolerance solution for a long time to provide non-stop computing. Other vendors, such as Tandem and Stratus, provide non-stop operation using specially constructed redundant machines that cost hundreds of thousands of dollars. SFT III uses a patented architecture invented by Novell. Novell intentionally designed SFT III to run on high-quality, inexpensive PC hardware.

By the time NetWare 5 shipped, the SFT III technology evolved into a new product line. Novell now has a line of SFT III-like products, known as Novell High Availability Server, Novell StandbyServer, and Novell SnapShotServer (see Chapter 10 for more information). At the same time, Novell is developing a server clustering technology (Novell Cluster Services), code-named Orion.

Novell Cluster Services is a server clustering system that ensures high availability and manageability of critical network resources including data (volumes), applications, server licenses, and services. It is a multinode, NDS-enabled clustering product for NetWare 5 that supports failover, failback, and migration (load balancing) of individually managed cluster resources.

Tip #6 from
Peter

You can find out more about Novell Cluster Services from `http://www.novell.com/products/clusters/ncs.htm`.

STORAGE MANAGEMENT SERVICES

Storage Management Services (*SMS*) is Novell's data archiving technology. SMS allows for network-wide data archiving, including workstations, without regard to the native file format of the data being archived or restored. SMS also provides a modular, cross-platform programming interface for developers of archiving software and archive device drivers.

WHAT'S SMS?

The SMS architecture is built around an archive engine (called *Storage Management Engine*, or *SME*), which archives data in the platform- and media-independent SMS data format. Data is sent, via the *Storage Management Data Requester* (*SMDR*), to the archive engine by SMS *Target Service Agents* (*TSAs*) residing on remote machines. The archive engine and the TSA communicate using the high-level SMS protocol, which provides for common data storage and retrieval operations.

The SMS archive engine communicates with archive hardware using the SMS driver programming interface, known as *Storage Device Interface* (*SDI*), which in turn relies on the NetWare 5 Media Manager (a low-level media programming interface).

The basic SMS architecture is depicted in Figure 1.8.

Figure 1.8
The SMS architecture.

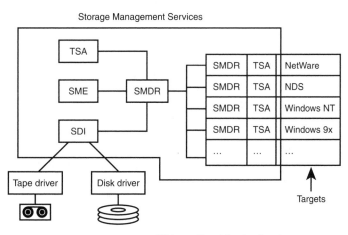

Storage Management Services

TSA = Target Service Agent
SME = Storage Management Engine
SMI = Storage Device Interface
SMDR = Storage Management Data Requester

SMS allows the archive engine to run on *any* machine on the network. It doesn't matter to SMS whether the archive server runs on a server or a workstation. For example, included with NetWare 5 is Novell's own SMS-complaint archive server, SBCON, which runs on the NetWare 5 server as an NLM. At the same time, Novell also included NWBACK32, a 32-bit Windows-based GUI application that is the workstation-equivalent to SBCON.

The format SMS uses to store data is designed to be completely media- and device-independent. This means, in theory, that you can archive data in the SMS format to an 8mm tape device using the SMS-compliant software from vendor A and restore the data using a SMS-compliant software from vendor B. However, most vendors don't implement SMS-compliance at the storage level, making this impossible.

Figure 1.8 shows the TSAs running on remote machines. These machines could be a NetWare server or any other machines on the network, including workstations of different operating systems. SMS also allows the TSA to run on the same machine as the archive server, meaning you can use SMS to back up local data.

NetWare 5 Target Service Agents

Because of enhancements made in NetWare 5, the SMS TSAs for the file system and NDS have been updated. In addition, the workstation TSAs (such as for Windows 9x and OS/2 machines) have been updated. A new TSA for Windows NT workstations has been added. The following outlines the features of the new TSAs and changes made to TSAs where enhancements have been made:

- **DOS Partition TSA**—Using this TSA you can back up and restore the DOS Partition on a NetWare server. The name of the module is TSADOSP.NLM. You need to load this TSA on each of the NetWare server whose DOS partition needs to be backed up or restored.

Tip #7 from
Peter

The DOS Partition TSA makes use of the NetWare DOS Partition APIs in order to make DOS calls. The DOS calls are implemented as Real Mode calls. In effect, when the DOS calls are made, the NetWare operating system temporarily gets suspended in order to service those calls. Hence, when many concurrent connections are made to access the DOS Partition, performance of the NetWare server might be slowed. If there are only a few connections, such a performance hit would hardly be felt and could be safely used.

In general, there's no need to access the server's DOS Partition unless you're updating boot files. Therefore, it is safe to use TSADOSP to back up your server's DOS partition.

- **Windows NT (WinNT) TSA**—The main task of the WinNT TSA is to perform backup-and-restore by reading data from and writing to the WinNT File System (NTFS) and file allocation table (FAT), and this includes backing up and restoring all the associated normal and extended attributes of the file. This WinNT TSA supports TCP/IP and SPX/IPX protocols.

- **Windows 9x TSA updated**—The updated Win9x TSA now allows users to back up and restore the target service's data over IP, as opposed to the earlier scenario where it only allows the IPX machines to backup and restore.

- **File system TSA enhanced**—To support the larger file system capacity, the TSA for NetWare server file systems (TSA500) now supports files up to 8GB in size. In addition, this TSA provides a new major resource called Server Specific Info (SSI), which appears in the list of resources displayed by SMS-based backup programs, along with the SYS volume and other volumes. The SSI data is essential in NetWare server recovery.

Tip #8 from
Peter

> In a network environment, the most likely failure scenario is the loss of a single server or its SYS volume. Because in the past this has involved a fairly complex recovery procedure, the addition of SSI resource to the SMS file system TSA simplifies server recovery in this scenario. Trustee rights assignments, ownership information, and other NetWare attributes are preserved when recovering from a server or SYS volume failure.
>
> For details on NDS disaster recovery procedures, see "Backing Up and Restoring Novell Directory Services in NetWare 4.11" in the October 1996 issue of Novell Application Notes (http://developer.novell.com/research/appnotes.htm). Although the article was written with NetWare 4.11 in mind, the same techniques apply to NetWare 5 as well.

- **NDS TSA enhanced**—The new TSANDS module backs up and restores all extensions to the NDS schema. TSANDS sends every object—those defined by both native and extended schemas—to the backup program for backup. Previous versions of TSANDS, however, do not send the definitions of the object types you have added to the NDS database. The resulting backup of NDS contains the information for objects defined in an extended schema, but not the extended schema itself that defined those objects. As a result, before restoring NDS objects, you had to first re-extend the schema so that the definitions for extended objects would exist in the tree. Otherwise, NDS would contain restored objects that it did not know how to use and would display them as Unknown objects.

  The enhanced TSANDS backs up the extensions to the NDS schema and restores those extensions by default so you no longer have to re-extend the database before NDS can recognize restored objects defined by an extended schema.

THIRD-PARTY SUPPORT

Novell designed SMS in part to allow third-party archive software vendors to support NetWare operating systems more easily. Novell encourages these vendors to release state-of-the-art archiving software that is more complete than SBCON. Most large NetWare sites choose to purchase a more complete third-party archiving package, rather than use SBCON or NWBACK32. (SBCON or NWBACK32 is perfectly acceptable for smaller organizations or in test environments.)

The primary rule you should follow when purchasing a third-party archiving system for NetWare 5 is that the package is compliant to SMS. SMS compliance is the only way vendors will be able to archive and restore the distributed and replicated NDS information base as well as file system trustee assignments.

Some of the most popular third-party archive systems for NetWare 5 today are ARCserve (Cheyenne/Computer Associates), NetWorker for NetWare (Legato Systems) and Backup Exec (Seagate).

Tip #9 from
Peter

For an update to date list of NetWare 5 certified backup solution, visit `http://developer.novell.com/npp`.

FILE SYSTEM IMPROVEMENTS

In addition to the disk space management features, such as disk suballocation, compression, and data migration, introduced in NetWare 4, NetWare 5 includes support for a new file system called Novell Storage Services (NSS).

Note

You'll read more about NetWare's disk suballocation, compression, and data migration features in Chapter 10.

In the past, some customers have been hampered by several limitations imposed by the NetWare legacy file system design and implementation. In particular, they have run into sizing limitations which in turn affect availability and suitability for larger deployments. The use of 32-bit interfaces limits users to files no greater than 2 gigabytes. The use of file allocation table (FAT)–oriented approaches to file system organization requires memory roughly linear to the number/size of files. It also takes time roughly linear to the volume size to mount a NetWare legacy volume after a clean dismount. After a crash, it might take hours before very large NetWare legacy volumes are scanned and repaired with VREPAIR, during which time they are unavailable to users.

Note

It is not uncommon to take more than 30 minutes to dismount or mount 100GB of volumes using the legacy NetWare file system.

NSS's internal and external interfaces are all 64-bits wide, allowing not only huge numbers of entities, but entities that are individually very large as well. Wide interfaces aren't enough, though. The FAT-based organization has been eliminated and replaced by high-performance, compact, and memory-efficient structures and algorithms. NSS completely decouples the amount of memory needed by a server from the amount of disk storage it maintains. You can mount NSS volumes that are terabytes in size using as little as 32MB of RAM.

The amount of time needed to mount a volume under NSS is also decoupled from its size. After a clean shutdown, a volume mounts in a fraction of a second regardless of its size. After a crash, full integrity is restored in less than a minute regardless of the volume's size, whether it contains 100MB or 100TB of data.

Note

> As a demonstration of the robustness of NSS, at Comdex '97, a 1TB NSS volume containing a billion files was deliberately crashed and recovered in 10 seconds.

On NetWare 5 servers, CD-ROM volumes are accessed through NSS. You can also mount the DOS partition on your NetWare 5 server as a NSS volume and access it using the standard file manipulation utilities and commands.

NETWARE PERIPHERAL ARCHITECTURE

Although implemented in earlier versions of NetWare, the *NetWare Peripheral Architecture* (*NWPA*) was written to provide a broader and more reliable driver support for third-party host adapters and storage devices. The NWPA architecture comes as the storage configuration for NetWare 5 and replaces existing NetWare DDFS driver specifications for developers.

NWPA takes a very modular approach to driver support by breaking them into two components types: the Host Adapter Module (HAM) and the Custom Device Module (CDM). HAM aligns itself to adapter hardware, whereas CDM associates with storage devices or autochangers attached to a host adapter bus.

Also supported in NWPA for NetWare 5 is driver hot replacement capabilities (such as hot-pluggable PCI adapters). This capability allows users to dynamically swap out a hard drive or network card without downing the server in the process. This capability can save systems administrators a lot of down time when upgrading hardware.

Note

> NetWare 5's Hot Plugging feature requires the server to have loaded the Hot Plug Monitor and Hot Plug Controller Driver modules. The Hot Plug Monitor NLM monitors the adapter's status, gives commands to unload adapter support, and turns off power to the adapter that is being replaced. The Hot Plug Controller Driver turns the power off to the slots and controls the indicator lights.
>
> The Controller driver is vendor-specific for the Hot Plug hardware. Currently there are only two supported platforms:
>
> - Compaq Proliant 6500 and 7000
> - IBM Netfinity 5500, and 7000 M10

NetWare 5 also supports the *Intelligent I/O (I₂O) Architecture Specification*, which is an open architecture for developing device drivers and can run independently of operating systems, processor platforms, or the system I/O bus. This allows hardware vendors to develop host/OS-independent I/O controllers that can offload much of the I/O processing burden from the main CPUs.

Such implementations include RAID controllers for network data storage and retrieval, ATM controllers, and network interface cards (NICs). Thus by exporting interrupt calls to another device, the server's CPU can spend its time performing other functions and services that don't involve interrupt processing, thereby increasing a server's I/O scalability.

NetWare 5 automatically detects whether the proper hardware in place, such as I₂O-aware motherboard designs and add-on network boards. With them, NetWare servers should be able to achieve faster throughput for both the I/O channels and the NetWare OS services. By splitting the workload to embedded processors on I/O controllers, user/server-requested data reads and writes can improve dramatically under heavy workloads.

SECURITY

Building on NetWare 4's security features, NetWare 5 offers richer security services that include the following:

- Public Key Infrastructure Services (PKIS)
- Novell International Cryptographic Infrastructure (NICI)
- Secure Authentication Services (SAS)
- The Audit system

These new security features are integrated NDS and simplify administration by offering single-point administration with NDS levels of access control. They also provide security for improved Internet data integrity and privacy across public networks.

PUBLIC KEY INFRASTRUCTURE SERVICES

Novell's *Public Key Infrastructure Services* (*PKIS*) enables public key cryptography and digital certificates in a NetWare environment. PKIS allows any designated NetWare 5 administrators to establish a Certificate Authority (CA) management domain within NDS. PKIS allows administrators to manage certificates and keys for Secure Sockets Layer (SSL) security for LDAP servers.

Certificate management includes services such as establishment of a CA local to your organization, certificate renewal, simplified certificate revocation with certificate suspension (without complex certificate revocation lists), creation of certificate signing requests (for use with external CAs), unlimited certificate minting services for applications, and using SSL in the NetWare environment (such as Novell LDAP Services for NDS).

Note

The use of certificates is becoming increasing popular, and is demanded by much of the public, as the push for e-commerce over the Internet continues.

NOVELL INTERNATIONAL CRYPTOGRAPHIC INFRASTRUCTURE

The *Novell International Cryptographic Infrastructure, NICI*, is an infrastructure of network cryptographic services for worldwide consumption. It supports strong cryptography and multiple cryptographic technologies in response to customer and internal Novell needs while complying with diverse national policies on the shipment and use of cryptography. Cryptography services on the NetWare platform provide fundamental security features such as confidentiality, integrity, and authentication.

The services are modular in nature, which allows new cryptographic engines, libraries, and policy managers to be dynamically added. The infrastructure is also tightly controlled, enforced through an integral OS loader which verifies modules before loading and controls access to modules only via standardized interfaces. Available cryptographic services are provided via the Novell Developer Kit (NDK).

It has been the case in the past that applications had to provide their own services if they wanted to employ cryptography. Because of the way the Novell cryptographic services are designed and provided via a standard set of APIs, application vendors can take full advantage of the services without having to incorporate cryptography in their applications. They can simply ship one version of their product worldwide, instead of having multiple versions to accommodate the many and varied national cryptography policies. Novell assures compliance with international laws and export requirements, leaving application developers free from these concerns.

SECURE AUTHENTICATION SERVICES

Authentication is a fundamental component of any security —it is how you identify yourself. A network without authentication cannot be secured. *Secure Authentication Services (SAS)* provides next-generation authentication services, as well as evolving industry authentication mechanism for the future.

SAS is built entirely on NICI. This means the following:

- The SAS service itself is based on a single executable file. Because there is no cryptography included in the SAS module, you can ship a single NLM worldwide. This provides easy administrator management and tracking. Also, any applications written to the SAS API can also be based on a single executable file.

- Applications written to the SAS application can go through a one-time and usually expedited export approval process. Novell has already received export approval for SAS and NICI. This means that application developers benefit with expedited export procedures.

- PKIS provides key management for the SSL services. In NetWare 5, SAS provides Secure Sockets Layer (SSL) support and server-based applications use the SAS API set to establish encrypted SSL connections. That means any application written to the SAS interface inherits the capability to have PKIS manage its certificates. NDS Access Control Lists (ACLs) manage access to the private key that enables SSL. Because SAS is a network service, it has its own network identity.

- Access Control Lists are set up on the SSL key object in such a way that allows only the SAS identity to read the private key. This guarantees that non-authorized entities such as users, other server applications, and even the application built on top of SAS cannot gain access to and expose or subvert the private key.

NETWARE AUDITING

Available since the early NetWare 4 era, the audit system helps you to accurately monitor and record users' access to network resources. The audit system now takes advantage of exposed NDS audit services in the following ways:

- Audit log files are represented and managed as NDS objects. That means access to the audit information and configuration is controlled by the standard NDS rights.

- Auditing is configured at the container and volume levels. The audit policy for a container or volume specifies what is audited within the volume or container and which users are audited.

Some important features that are available in NetWare 5's auditing system include the following:

- The capability to assign independent auditors that are separate and distinct from administrator privileges.

- Distributed and replicated audit information as the information is stored in NDS.

- Allows for multiple auditors.

- A high granularity of auditable events, to the user level.

- New audit events added for NetWare 5 (for example, SSL connections).

- Exportable audit data for use by reporting programs.

You'll read more about configuring and using NetWare auditing in Chapter 19, "Auditing."

PROTOCOL CHANGES

Traditionally, the NetWare clients and OS send specific requests and receive replies for services using the NetWare Core Protocols (NCPs) over internetwork packet exchange (IPX) protocol—NCP was tightly coupled to the IPX transport protocol. This is no longer the case with the NetWare 5 operating system—it is NCP protocol independent. This means that internally to the NetWare OS, NCPs can send and receive requests over IP, IPX, or a combination of these protocols.

NetWare 5 enables you to run your entire network in a pure IP environment—pure in the sense that it doesn't retain any IPX-based encapsulation. This leaves nothing but IP traffic on the wire, which reduces routing hardware and software requirements (because there's only one protocol to deal with), frees up scarce network bandwidth, eliminates the need to support other client protocols, and creates greater opportunity for remote connectivity.

Even though NetWare 5 can operate in the pure IP mode, it includes features that provide seamless compatibility with IPX-based technologies. This means you can move to an IP-only environment without having to replace valuable IPX-based applications or needlessly disrupt enterprise operations—you can move to a global IP-only LAN, WAN, and Internet/intranet solution at your own pace.

Of course, you can stick with IPX for NetWare 5 if you choose to, completely avoiding the migration to IP. Users can maintain full support for their company's investment in IPX and continue to enjoy the plug-and-play environment they are accustomed to, yet still have the option to migrate to IP. Because NetWare 5 can use either IPX or IP, you can choose to run all IP, all IPX, or anything in between.

IPX COMPATIBILITY MODE

In a pure IP NetWare 5 environment, you can continue to use IPX-based applications, resources, and services with the help of NetWare 5's Compatibility Mode. If your enterprise is running all IP applications, you don't need Compatibility Mode. However, if you are using a mix of old and new network applications, Compatibility Mode enables IPX-dependent applications to run in an IP-only environment.

In Compatibility Mode, NetWare 5 uses the Internet Engineering Task Force (IETF) *Service Location Protocol* (*SLP*) to provide service discovery functions for IPX-based applications that require them. In addition, the Migration Agent (discussed later in this chapter) translates between IP and IPX, providing a link between them during migration. These technologies enable you to move to IP without being burdened by the bandwidth aspects of IPX or having to upgrade applications and services immediately. You can gradually remove IPX-based applications from the system as they are replaced or rewritten to be transport independent.

> **Note**
>
> A difference needs to be noted between IPX-based application and NetWare-aware applications that use NCP calls. IPX-based applications are programs that specifically require the presence of IPX to function; NetWare-aware applications are programs that make NCP function calls but don't care what the underlying transport protocol is. Over 90% of the NetWare-based applications (including those of third parties) do not depend on IPX.

The Compatibility Mode also ensures backward compatibility with the NetWare 3 bindery. This service is necessary only for IP environments that still use IPX-based applications and services running on a NetWare 3 server. With the Compatibility Mode bindery NLM running on the server, dynamic objects are transformed into static objects and placed in NDS.

Thus, legacy IPX applications that depend on the bindery can still use the object information (from NDS) that is necessary for them to function properly. In this way, NetWare 5 minimizes traffic on the wire, while still providing on-demand IPX functionality.

MIGRATION AGENT—A BRIDGE BETWEEN TWO WORLDS

The Migration Agent in NetWare 5 simultaneously provides two kinds of translations: one between IPX and IP and one between the different naming and discovery services (SLP and SAP) in heterogeneous networks.

The Migration Agent is needed only when you want to link the two logical worlds of IP and IPX. It provides emulation that prevents IPX-based protocol from populating the IP world, and it replaces Service Advertising Protocol (SAP) and Routing Information Protocol (RIP) packets on behalf of IPX clients. The Migration Agent also uses IPX and IP addresses and the routing information contained in IPX packets to send them to the appropriate node.

NetWare 5 provides absolute control of both the degree and rate of change in the IPX-to-IP migration process. You can install a single NetWare 5 server with the Migration Agent NLM and Compatibility Mode loaded and attach this server to an existing IPX network. You can then build an IP segment (and, eventually, an IP network) according to your schedules. With NetWare 5 you have continuity during migration and minimal risk associated with the process.

REPLACING SAP WITH SLP

As part of the initiative to support pure IP, Novell has adopted the IETF Service Location Protocol, or SLP (RFC 2165), to provide a naming and discovery service in a TCP/IP environment. SLP replaces the service discovery function of SAP, eliminating SAP's characteristically high broadcast traffic (which happens once every 60 seconds). SLP operates by querying the network and obtaining a quick list of the available services.

The services of SLP are not required in an IP-only environment. They are required only for backward compatibility with services and applications that rely on SAP-based network discovery. SLP can be used by the IPX client to determine the IP address of the server; it is one of several options (SLP, DHCP, DNS, and local host files) available to clients for determining the IP address of an NDS server.

SLP registers information in a database and enables clients access in that database to find services. It is an extremely efficient protocol because it maintains a global database of services and only serves the local area.

JAVA SUPPORT

Java, from Sun Microsystems, introduced a new way to build applications and distribute logic in a cross-platform, processor-independent way. Applications once existed only on a central host. When LANs became populated by clients with fast CPUs, many applications moved to the client. Java provides a way to harness all that power with distributed applications that apply logic and information sharing across a network.

The acceptance of Java as a powerful object-oriented programming language has been propelled by the Internet and embedded system devices. Originally developed for software development of consumer electronic devices, Java provides the attributes of being small, fast, efficient, and portable. These attributes make Java the ideal language for distributing executable programs (logic) over the network.

Those who work with Novell products and technologies might wonder how Java fits into the Novell view of the world. Recognizing early on the value of what Java was trying to accomplish, Novell was the first server licensee of Java to create the Java Virtual Machine (JVM) for NetWare. Novell is committed to delivering access to NetWare networking services through open Java interfaces.

Novell has participated in the development of a number of APIs to create a more network-aware environment for distributed Java applications. These include the following:

- **Java Naming and Directory Interface (JNDI)**—With the help of Sun, Netscape, IBM, HP, and others, Novell has applied its expertise in directory services to develop this directory interface. It allows applications written in Java to navigate naming and directory services of all types, including NDS, DNS, and LDAP. With NDS being made available on SCO, HP, Sun, and IBM UNIX platforms, on Windows NT, and on IBM mainframe S/390, JNDI is well positioned to take advantage of the industry-wide acceptance of NDS. JNDI is being included as part of the Enterprise API set.

- **Java Network Services Interface (JNSI)**—JNSI provides Java classes to expose the native access to Novell's advanced services, such as connection management, authentication, file, NCP, print queue management, and so on.

- **Java Management API**—This combined effort from Novell, Sun, Computer Associates, Tivoli Systems, 3Com, Bay Networks, and others provides a set of extensible Java objects and methods for building applets that can manage an enterprise network over the Internet.

- **Java Telephony API**—Novell, Lucent, Intel, and Sun collaborated on this API for Java-based computer-telephony applications that work across a variety of telephony systems. It is designed to help integrate a well-known appliance, the telephone, into the intranet and Internet environments to help networks become more user-friendly.

- **Java Internationalization Services**—Along with Taligent, Novell has provided assistance and technology to Sun for the much-needed internationalization of Java. Specifically, Novell provided technology in the area of Unicode-to-Code Page conversion.

- **Java Speech Services**—Novell and Sun are collaborating to produce speech recognition and speech synthesis (text-to-speech) technology written in and accessible from Java.

- **Java Distributed Printing Services**—Novell, Sun, HP, Xerox, and others are collaborating on a new initiative to expand on the simple printing services available in Java. This interface enables richer functionality for end-user–oriented printing, such as starting and stopping print jobs and checking status. It also offers a print administration interface to manage print queues, printers, and access control.
- **JavaBeans Components**—In parallel with developing Java Class Libraries to access network services, Novell defines JavaBeans that provide high-level abstractions to network services. This provides developers an easier way to build applications that access network services.

Novell has enhanced its current products and services to take advantage of Java. Today Java is used in Novell's four major product lines:

- **NetWare 5**—Novell has incorporated the Java Virtual Machine in the NetWare 5 operating system through a set of NLMs. NetWare 5's high-performance networking services are a perfect complement to Java's comprehensive memory management and security. New Java class libraries that expose Novell's networking services make NetWare 5 an even more efficient platform for building and executing distributed applications for business intranets.
- **Novell Directory Services**—By integrating NDS with Java through JNDI, Novell enables developers to build solutions that will be easier to manage, distribute, secure, and deploy across intranets or the Internet.
- **GroupWise**—Novell is working on a Java-enabled GroupWise client. This will provide full-featured access to GroupWise via the Internet through any Java-enabled Web browser, along with an intuitive interface virtually identical to the desktop environment.
- **ManageWise**—The next generation of ManageWise (code named K2) will be Web-enabled. It is designed to let administrators quickly and easily access network information from "standard" Web browsers. Java applets for ManageWise increase administration flexibility and reduce your total cost of ownership.

INTERNET SERVICES

Included with NetWare 5 are a number of Internet-related services that permit you to use your NetWare 5 server on your intranet or as a host on the Internet.

DNS AND DHCP SERVICES

One of the difficulties of maintaining TCP/IP networks is their management. As more and more companies embrace TCP/IP as the networking protocol of choice, system administrators and IS personnel are looking for solutions to simplify the management of TCP/IP-based networks. Many who are accustomed to NetWare's relatively effortless IPX-based device naming and addressing scheme are alarmed to find that TCP/IP does not provide any automatic way to configure IP addresses and other information necessary for network devices to communicate. Even sites that have had their LANs connected to the Internet for years run up against limitations such as the increasing scarcity of available IP addresses.

Two technologies are available to help mitigate some of the inherent difficulties in maintaining TCP/IP networks. One is the domain name system (DNS), a distributed name/address database used to translate between numerical IP addresses and alphanumeric device names. The other is Dynamic Host Configuration Protocol (DHCP), a client/server protocol for assigning static and temporary IP addresses. A DHCP server can reassign IP addresses to devices instantaneously from a pool of available addresses. Although many DNS and DHCP products are available from various vendors, most traditional solutions still require significant effort on the part of network administrators to keep track of the necessary TCP/IP information, to avoid addressing conflicts, and to troubleshoot configuration errors. To simplify the configuration and management of DNS and DHCP services, Novell has developed a new product called DNS/DHCP Services.

By extending the NDS schema, NetWare 5 includes new objects that represent the DNS and DHCP data within NDS. Because the NDS database is replicated and distributed, the DNS and DHCP data is available in multiple locations across the network, creating virtual DNS and DHCP servers. This means less traffic, more fault tolerance, and greater security. Also, by eliminating the need to manage and synchronize separate DNS and DHCP servers, using NetWare 5 can significantly reduce the time requirement and cost of administering IP addresses and avoid the potential for error that exists with other methods of IP address assignment and tracking.

NetWare 5 also supports Dynamic DNS (DDNS) so the DNS servers can be updated immediately as DHCP assigns new addresses. The DHCP services in NetWare 5 also provide NDS configuration information to clients, such as their initial context, NDS server name, and tree name.

LIGHTWEIGHT DIRECTORY ACCESS PROTOCOL

Lightweight Directory Access Protocol, more commonly referred to as *LDAP*, is an industry-standard protocol that enables users to easily access X.500 directories, after which NDS is modeled. To facilitate easier access to information stored in NDS from an intranet or the Internet, NetWare 5 includes LDAP Services for NDS, which is a server-based interface between NDS and applications that comply with LDAP v3.

WEB SERVER

Turn your NetWare 5 server into a high-performance Web server using Netscape FastTrack Server for NetWare, which is included free of charge with your copy of NetWare 5. FastTrack Server is based on open Internet standards and includes Netscape Communicator client software, which enables you to create attractive and dynamic HTML pages to publish information on your intranet or across the Internet. You can create links, add graphics, and format text with simple point-and-click operations.

FastTrack Server has a rich, cross-platform environment that supports the development of custom Web-based applications. FastTrack Server provides server-side JavaScript, Perl 5, and NetBasic for building and deploying custom Web applications.

FastTrack Server delivers high performance and reliability through optimized caching, advanced use of kernel threads, HTTP 1.1 support, and sophisticated memory management. FastTrack Server supports LDAP and is integrated with NDS, which enables user and group information to be stored in a centralized directory—reducing the cost and complexity of managing your company's Web server.

For enhanced security, Netscape FastTrack Server for NetWare takes advantage of NDS authentication and SSL 3.0, the widely accepted Internet security standard that encrypts the information flow between server and client. FastTrack Server also features ACLs, which enable you to specify who has the right to access specific documents and directories. With ACLs, you can share documents across the intranet or Internet while keeping them secure from public access.

FTP SERVER AND UNIX PRINTING SERVICES

Need a fast, high-performance FTP server to compliment your Web services? Or need to transfer print jobs between NetWare and other TCP/IP-based hosts using the LPD/LPR protocol? Included free of charge with NetWare 5 is NetWare Print Services for UNIX. It comes with the following services:

- **FTP services**—This allows any FTP client to upload and download files from your NetWare server in both DOS and NFS name space. In addition this allows FTP clients to download or upload files in DOS name space from other remote NetWare servers by making a bindery connection.

- **UNIX-to-NetWare printing**—This allows any LPR client supporting Line Printer Daemon protocol (RFC 1179) to print to NetWare servers.

- **NetWare-to-UNIX printing**—This allows any NetWare client to submit print jobs to print servers supporting Line Printer Daemon protocol (RFC 1179).

- **NIS services**—This service allows NetWare servers to function as network information service (NIS) master servers or as NIS clients.

- **Telnet and XConsole services**—Telnet and XConsole services allow a remote Telnet client/XHost server user to log in to remote NetWare server console and run any of the NetWare server console commands.

SIMPLIFIED LICENSE MANAGEMENT

In NetWare 5, licensing information is stored in NDS. That means you can manage all your licenses, no matter where your servers are located, from a central location using the NetWare Administrator utility. In addition, NetWare 5 includes Novell Licensing Services (NLS), a distributed, enterprise network service that enables you to monitor and control the use of licensed applications on a network. NLS includes a license metering tool and is tightly integrated with NDS. Even third-party applications can be monitored and metered with NLS. NLS also tracks historical usage so you can produce application usage reports easily.

Tip #10 from	
Peter	You can use ZENworks in conjunction with NLS to meter all your application usage, if the applications are launched via the Novell Application Launcher.

Similar to previous versions of NetWare, NetWare 5 is still licensed on a per-server connection basis. What this means is that for every NetWare 5 server on your network, you need a server license. In addition, you need to install user connection licenses on each server corresponding to the number of users that will access that server for resources. For example, if your network consists of three NetWare 5 servers and at any given time 50 users will access each server for resource, you need three server licenses plus three 50-user licenses.

NetWare 5 user licenses come in increments of 5-, 10-, 25-, 50-, 100-, 250-, and 500-user. Novell offers special licensing agreements for sites with large numbers of users; you need about 1,000 users to qualify. Refer to http://www.novell.com/programs/ncc/ for more information about the various site licensing options.

Tip #11 from	
Peter	You can install multiple, unique, licenses of different increments on the same server. For example, you can install a 5-, 10-, and 50-user license on to the same server to get a total of 65 user connections.

CLIENT OPERATING SYSTEM SUPPORT

Since the early days, NetWare has provided support for a large variety of client operating systems. NetWare 5 provides seamless integration for Windows NT, Windows 9x, Windows 3.x, UNIX, OS/2, Mac OS, and DOS platforms and will support other popular desktop operating systems when they become available. Regardless of which type of workstation your users choose, they will have simultaneous access to the same data and network resources. By choosing the workstations and client operating systems that your users prefer, they can remain productive while you protect your investment in hardware and software.

Tip #12 from	
Peter	If you have Linux workstations, you can turn them into NetWare clients by installing Caldera NetWare for Linux, which was developed using a standard 2.0 kernel but has an updated IPX patch and a Streams protocol patch. It can be used on any conformant Linux operating system with these patches added. Caldera provides these source patches and basic instructions for installing and running the server on any Linux platform. For more information, refer to http://www.calderasystems.com/products/netware/index.html.

It should be noted that the NetWare Client for OS/2 and all OS/2 NetWare Utilities have been removed (unbundled) from NetWare 5. This means that when NetWare 5 is installed, no OS/2 Client files or OS/2 utilities are installed. During an upgrade to NetWare 5, existing OS/2 files and utilities are preserved; they are not removed from the server.

Note

> The NetWare Client for OS/2 v2.12 will function in a NetWare 5 environment, provided IPX support is enabled (IPX connectivity *only*). At the time of this writing, Novell will only offer limited technical support for customers who try to use the NetWare Client for OS/2 in a NetWare 5 environment (that is, they will offer no engineering support for bug fixes). The OS/2 client software does not support native IP connectivity to NetWare 5 servers.

Tip #13 from
Peter

> The NetWare Client for OS/2 v2.12 shipped with NetWare 4.11 and intraNetWare. So, if you have access to those versions, you have access to the client files. Alternatively, from the File Finder area on http://support.novell.com, you can download CLOS2D1.EXE, which is the disk install version, enabled for the following languages: English, German, Spanish, French, Italian, and Portuguese.
>
> Refer to http://support.novell.com/cgi-bin/search/tidfinder. cgi?2938544 for more information.

Similarly, Novell unbundled Macintosh support from NetWare 5 as Prosoft Engineering took over the development for Macintosh connectivity solutions for NetWare. Any Macintosh connectivity in the future will require a separate purchase of either the Macintosh client or the AppleShare NLMs (NetWare for Macintosh). Prosoft's NetWare offerings will be available through Novell's existing sales channel, other traditional Macintosh distribution channels, and directly from Prosoft Engineering.

Note

> Prosoft Engineering took over the development for Macintosh connectivity solutions for NetWare from Novell in late 1998. Consequently, a Mac client is not included with NetWare 5; however, you can obtain the latest Mac client from Prosoft Engineering (http://www.prosofteng.com/netware.htm). A pure IP version of the Mac client is being developed.

Note

> When NetWare 5 is installed, no Macintosh files are installed, except for Mac name space (MAC.NAM) and the APPLETLK.NLM. The Macintosh Client v5.11 (included with NetWare 4.11 and intraNetWare) functions in a NetWare 5 IPX environment.

NOVELL DISTRIBUTED PRINT SERVICES

As applications gets easier to use, users' printing needs are becoming more sophisticated. For the longest time, the user sent a print job to a network print queue, from which a print server processed the job and sent it to the printer. Because the print server is an intermediate device, it was sometimes difficult to determine printing problems. More feedback is needed for better printing functionality and management.

To address these shortcomings, Novell joined forces with Hewlett-Packard, the leader in office network printing hardware, and Xerox, the leader in enterprise printing systems, to create *Novell Distributed Print Services* (*NDPS*). Other printing manufacturers are expected to support this next-generation printing architecture as well.

NDPS is the first fully distributed print service for networks. As a client/server, application-layer print service for NetWare environments, NDPS simplifies the administration of network printing by linking print queues, printer objects, and print servers into one manageable NDS object, which communicates to the Printer Agent found on a NetWare server or in the printing device itself.

With the help of Printer Agents, NDPS makes network printing communication bidirectional, giving the user immediate feedback to common printing situations such as the type of paper in each tray, or how many print jobs are waiting for that printer. What's more, administrators and help desks can get feedback about a printer's status, such as low-on-toner or out-of-paper, and address the problem before it is reported by the users.

Details on setting up NDPS is given in Chapter 21, "Network Printing."

ZENWORKS

Novell's ZENworks is a directory-enabled service for workstation administration that significantly reduces the costs associated with managing networked PCs. The name *ZENworks* is short for *Zero Effort Networks*. The name is not intended to imply that Novell is able to eliminate the work and effort associated with deploying and maintaining a network on the administrative side (although *ZENworks* does significantly reduce the costs and complexities of maintaining networked PCs). Rather, the name *ZENworks* was chosen to suggest that network administrators can remove the obstacles and frustrations that prevent users from effortlessly accessing the resources on the network. Hence, zero effort is required from users.

ZENworks is a combination of the Novell Application Launcher (NAL), the Novell Workstation Administrator, and a remote control product. One of the many functions of NAL is that applications launched through NAL can be metered using Novell Licensing Services. Using this feature, you can determine how many copies of a given application can be used concurrently, thus conforming to your license agreements.

Note

Included on the Client software CD of your NetWare 5 package is a *ZENworks* starter pack. It is a lite version that does *not* support features such as remote control. The full version must be purchased separately.

→ For more information on ZENworks, **see** Chapter 24, "ZENworks," **page 607.**

ONLINE DOCUMENTATION

Previous versions of NetWare required that you install the documentation files and the DynxText viewer before you can access them. With NetWare 5's online documentation, you simply put the documentation CD into the CD-ROM drive of your Windows 9x or Windows NT workstation and access it directly, without having to install it or any other components. NetWare 5's online documentation is all in HTML format so you can access them using any Web browser (see Figure 1.9). A copy of Netscape Communicator 4 is included on the CD and is auto-launched if you choose to view the documentation from the CD; you don't need to have Netscape installed on your workstation to access the documentation CD.

Figure 1.9
NetWare 5's online documentation is provided in HTML format.

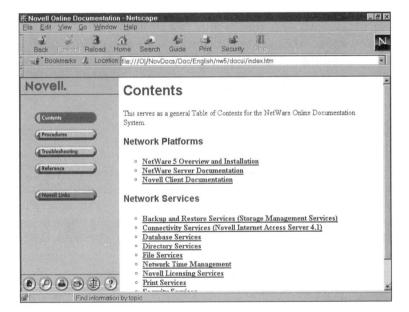

Included as part of the NetWare 5 documentation engine is a powerful Java search engine applet (see Figure 1.10). Therefore, to make the most effective use of the documentation, you need a Java-enabled Web browser, such as Netscape Navigator.

Figure 1.10
NetWare 5's online documentation can be easily searched using the included Java-based search engine.

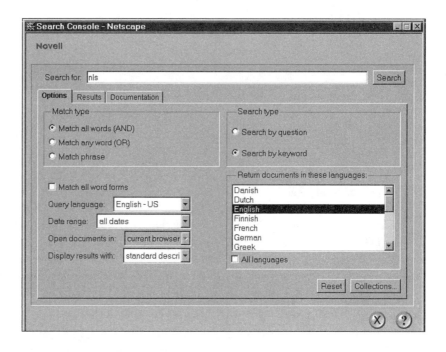

NEW AND ENHANCED UTILITIES

To reflect the enhancements made in NetWare 5, a number of existing utilities, such as NetWare Administrator and NDS Manager, have been updated and a number of new tools have been introduced.

32-BIT NETWARE ADMINISTRATOR

There were a number of different versions of the NetWare Administrator utilities in NetWare 4:

- NWADMIN (16-bit, for Windows 3.x)
- NWADMN3X (16-bit, for Windows 3.x)
- NWADMN95 (32-bit, for Windows 9x)
- NWADMNNT (32-bit, for Windows NT)
- NWADMN32 (32-bit, for Windows 9x and Windows NT)

As a result, a number of different Novell products that use different snap-in DLLs for these versions of NWAdmin; some products have a snap-in for NWADMN95 but not NWADMNNT whereas some products have snap-in DLLs for NWADMN32 only. In an effort to bring order to this snap-in chaos, a single version of NetWare Administrator, NWADMN32, is shipped with NetWare 5.

This version of NWAdmin supports multiple NDS trees and can be used to manage NDS trees that have both NetWare 4.1x and NetWare 5 servers.

Tip #14 from *Peter*	Should you choose to, you can also use this new 32-bit NWAdmin to manage a pure NetWare 4 tree. However, some options, such as inheritable ACL, will not function.

NDS MANAGER

The NDS Manager, first introduced in NetWare 4.11, is a utility that allows you to manage NDS partitioning and replication using a GUI interface (see Figure 1.11). Similar to the situation with NWAdmin, there were multiple versions of NDS Manager. In NetWare 5, a single, 32-bit, version of NDS Manager is shipped. It has been updated to include the new NDS error codes found in NetWare 5.

Figure 1.11
NDS Manager displays your NDS partitioning strategy and replica placements in a graphical manner.

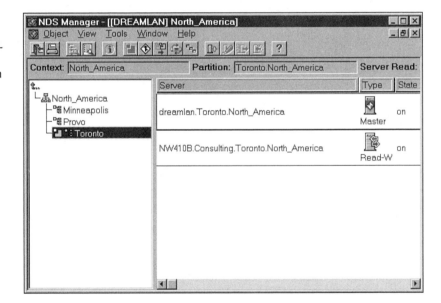

SCHEMA MANAGER

The Schema Manager utility allows you to examine and manipulate your schema definitions. It has been updated to support both NetWare 4 *and* NetWare 5 schemas. New functions have been added to the version shipped with NetWare 5. For example, you can use Schema Manager to display the schema extensions only, so you can determine how your base schema was changed (see Figure 1.12).

Figure 1.12
NDS Manager can easily generate schema change reports.

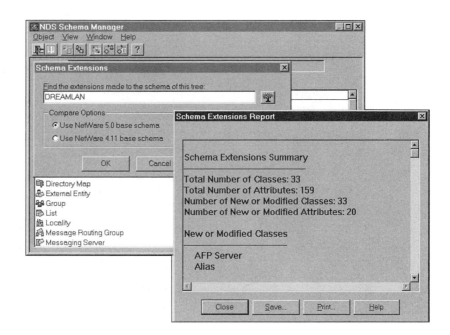

The Schema Manger is accessed through the Object pull-down menu in NDS Manager.

SBCON AND NWBACK32

Previous versions of NetWare included an SBACKUP (Server Backup) NLM that some companies used to back up their servers. However, because it was designed to be mainly an illustration of SMS technology, it was never as full-featured as one comes to expect from a "real" backup application. In NetWare 5, however, SBACKUP has been enhanced to include features such as scheduling, making it a viable backup application for small networks. SBACKUP is now called SBCON (NetWare Storage Management Console).

Other than the new SBCON utility, NetWare 5 also includes a new 32-bit workstation-based backup application called NWBACK32 (see Figure 1.13). It has the same functions as SBCON but has the added advantage of having an easy-to-use GUI.

You'll learn more about using SBCON and NWBACK32 in Chapter 25, "Data Archiving and Backup."

NLS MANAGER

New in NetWare 5 is the Novell Licensing Services (NLS) Manager. It is a graphical utility for Windows 9x and Windows NT workstations that allows you to install and create license certificates and monitor license usage so that users on the network comply with licensing requirements. You can also examine and manage NetWare license allocations (see Figure 1.14).

Figure 1.13
You can facilitate server backups using NWBACK32 from a workstation.

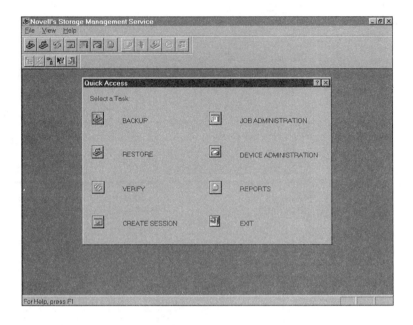

Figure 1.14
Using the Actions pull-down menu, you can create and install license certificates with NLS Manager.

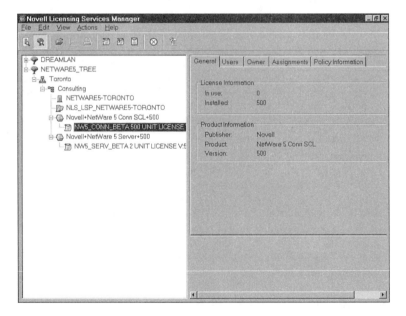

Using the Quick View (NLS Manager's default view), you can quickly get information about products and their usage and create reports to capture that information (see Figure 1.15).

Figure 1.15
The Quick View alphabetically lists product license containers installed on the network.

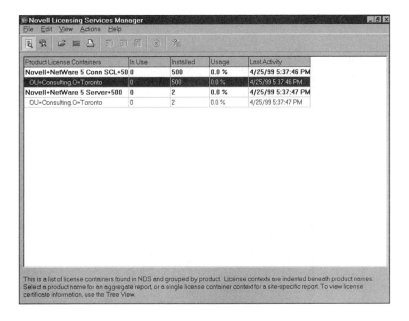

ConsoleOne

Code-named "Houston" during development, Novell ConsoleOne brings 100% Java-based GUI management to the NetWare server console. By leveraging NDS, ConsoleOne provides administrators with flexible, role-based administration. This common framework is Internet-standards–based (Java, IP, LDAP, SSL) and integrates Java applets and snap-ins allowing developers to build network management solutions with a common look and feel. It supports features such as applet launching, local volume browsing and file copying, basic management and administration, graphical server monitoring, and other GUI based management tools, as well as server-based remote console functions.

Because ConsoleOne is written in Java, it runs on both the NetWare 5 server and any Windows workstations that have JRE and the Novell Client software installed—this really illustrates the "write-once-run-anywhere" goal of Java.

ConsoleOne allows you to perform certain basic NDS object management and file system functions from the server (see Figure 1.16), something you have never been able to perform up to this time. For instance, ConsoleOne provides the capability to browse the NDS tree and to create and modify four NDS object types: user, group, organization, and organizational unit. ConsoleOne also provides full rights management within the directory structure. Some of the file system functions include creating, deleting, renaming, moving, and copying files, and viewing DOS volumes.

Figure 1.16
ConsoleOne is a
Java-based GUI man-
agement tool that
you can run on the
NetWare 5 server.

> **Note**
>
> Despite what some of the marketing literature tells you, the version of ConsoleOne that's included with NetWare 5 is really a proof-of-concept version because it doesn't have the full set of features that you'd find in NetWare Administrator.
>
> There is also presently no support for inputting Asian characters.

IMPROVED NETWARE DEVELOPMENT TOOLS

NetWare 5 caters to network developers by providing one of the world's fastest JVM for running server-based Java applications and services. And to encourage more application development for the NetWare platform, a number of new development tools have been added. Listed later in this chapter are several development environments and enhancements that are of interest to developers.

JAVA SUPPORT

By implementing Sun Microsystems' JRE on NetWare 5 servers through a set of NLMs, NetWare 5 supports Java applications running on the server. This allows a wide range of Java-developed applications to serve your network and users. Java support on NetWare 5 allows you to run Java applets on the server console, display Java applications in X Window–style formats—with full mouse and graphic support (see the discussion about ConsoleOne earlier), and run multiple Java applications on the server while the server performs other tasks.

Tip #15 from	To enable Java support on the NetWare 5 server, start the JAVA.NLM at the server console prompt. After that, you can run Java applications using the APPLET console command.
Peter	

WinSock 2 Implementation

In a big plus for developers, NetWare 5 fully supports the WinSock 2 programming interface as an industry standard. WinSock 2 is adapted from the Microsoft Windows WinSock 1.1 specification and uses sockets as its means to transport data.

NetWare 5 supports WinSock 2 on the server by supporting all the operational modes that apply to the NetWare OS. This includes traditional blocking and non-blocking modes, as well as the new asynchronous message mode (NetWare 5 does not support Windows-specific Asynchronous Windows Message Mode).

Novell's implementation includes backward compatibility for WinSock 1.1 at the source code level. Source code compatibility means that the WinSock 1.1 APIs are preserved, allowing WinSock 1.1 application source code to run on a WinSock 2 system by including the WS2NLM.H header file and relining the code to the WinSock 2 libraries.

The WinSock 2 architecture also allows simultaneous access to multiple transport protocols, which Novell fully supports. While WinSock 1.1 was implemented on TCP/IP only, WinSock 2 contains Windows Open System Architecture (WOSA)–compliant architecture, allowing applications access to protocols other than TCP/IP. WinSock 2 also provides for a name resolution mechanism when more than one transport protocol is in use.

Development Environments

In the past, developing applications for NetWare is limited to using the C and assembler programming interfaces. In an effort to help developers quickly write applications for NDS and NetWare without having to fully understand the underlying complexity, Novell Developer Support has made available several new tools. For example, you can build successful network-ready applications and utilities using your favorite Rapid Application Development (RAD) Windows programming tool, such as Visual Basic. Novell Libraries for Visual Basic gives programmers full access to all the low-level NetWare APIs that have traditionally been available only to C programmers. The Visual Basic Libraries are a set of text files that contain the NetWare API definitions which can be copied into a Visual Basic project using the Visual Basic API Viewer Add-In.

Alternatively, you can use Novell Controls for ActiveX which support full access to NDS as well as administration capabilities for NetWare servers, print queues, and volumes. All this functionality is packaged so it can be used quickly and easily in a Windows visual builder and other development tools, such as Visual Basic, Delphi, PowerBuilder, Active Server Pages for Internet Information Server, Windows Scripting Host, and Internet Explorer.

If you're a Java fan, you can use JavaBeans. Your Java applications can also access NDS through the JNDI APIs. If you're more comfortable with scripting languages, such as Visual Basic Script (or VBScript), Novell has support for them too. For example, using the Novell Script for NetWare, which is a VBScript-compatible language for script automation and Web development on the Netscape FastTrack Server for NetWare platform, you can use Novell Script's prebuilt components to access NetWare and integrate NDS, Oracle, and Btrieve databases into your Web applications. Novell scripts can quickly and easily execute Bean components and regular Java classes.

If you're a more traditional Web page designer, Perl 5 for NetWare is an effective Web programming language suitable for use with the Netscape FastTrack Server for NetWare. Perl 5 support allows you to enhance and continue your investment in Perl scripts and Perl applications.

PROJECT: DISCOVER NDS 8

Six short months after NetWare 5 started shipping, Novell introduced NDS 8, the next generation of Novell Directory Services in early 1999. NDS 8 extends its directory reach to the Internet and offers a new standard for scalable performance, reliability, and security—and eliminates the need for special purpose Internet directories.

NDS 8 has the capability to store and manage *at least* a billion objects, such as users, applications, network devices, and data—millions more than competing directories and earlier versions of NDS. And NDS 8 can perform LDAP search queries with consistent speed, even as tens of millions of objects are added to the directory. Many other directories lose significant LDAP search query performance in direct proportion to the number of users in their directories. With NDS 8's scalability, you can be confident that your infrastructure will support massive growth.

At the time of this writing, NDS 8 is available free-of-charge to NetWare 5 networks. Find out more about NDS 8 and how to obtain your copy from http://www.novell.com/products/nds/.

CHAPTER **2**

RELATED PRODUCTS

In this chapter

ENHANCING YOUR CONNECTIVITY

In many organizations today, PC-based LANs are not the only computing platforms used. There's a need in many companies to provide connectivity services and solutions between the LAN and the corporate mainframes (such as the IBM "big irons") and mid-range systems (such as IBM AS/400, HP9000, and an assortment of UNIX-based systems).

This chapter highlights several products, most of them from Novell, that can enhance the connectivity functionality of your NetWare 5 network. Although there are literally thousands of software packages that easily could have been included here, the following are indicative of various product categories. The goal of this chapter is to provide you with sufficient information on each product and category so you can make an informed decision, rather than offer a totally comprehensive review.

Note
Some categories, such as Web servers and remote dial-ins, are not covered here because they are discussed in their own chapters in Part VII of this book. For product category not covered, refer to `http://www.novell.com/catalog/solindex.html` (see Figure 2.1) and `http://www.novell.com/catalog/catindex.html` for more details.

Figure 2.1
Look up products for your specific needs from `http://www.novell.com/catalog/solindex.html`.

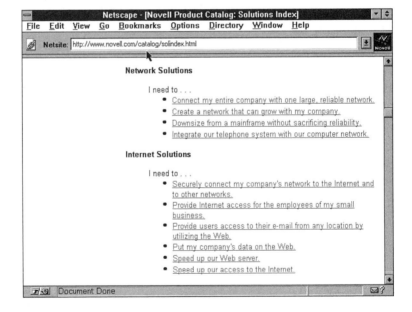

The following products are discussed in this chapter:

- NetWare for SAA
- NetWare NFS Services
- BorderManager

- ManageWise
- GroupWise
- Oracle 8 for NetWare
- NDS for NT
- NDS for Solaris
- NDS for various UNIX platforms

NETWARE FOR SAA

Many large companies generally have at least one mainframe where many mission-critical applications and huge databases reside. NetWare for SAA is a gateway product, jointly developed by Novell and IBM, that seamlessly integrates IBM's System Network Architecture (SNA) networks that mainframes and AS/400s uses, with NetWare networks.

Shown in Figure 2.1 is a typical SNA network environment. Terminals and printers are connected to *cluster controllers*, which are in turn connected to the *communication controller* (or *front-end processor*, *FEP*, as it's sometimes called). The FEP is then connected to the mainframe. Cluster controllers are often connected to FEPs over token ring links or over WAN links using synchronous modems and Synchronous Data Link Control (SDLC) protocol.

Figure 2.2
Components of an
SNA network.

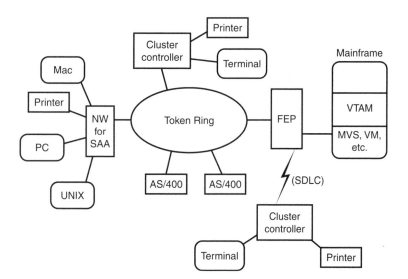

How does NetWare for SAA fit into an SNA network? You still need terminals and printers to service your SNA network. However, instead of old dumb terminals, you now use workstations running terminal emulation software thus eliminating the need of multiple terminals on your desk. You still have printers as before, but they don't need to be dedicated mainframe printers. These printers can now be LAN printers, meaning they can service print jobs from both NetWare and mainframe.

Using LAN Printers for Mainframe Printing

In order for a LAN printer to service mainframe print jobs, you can configure the workstation's terminal emulation software with a print emulation session (in addition to terminal sessions) and then use the NetWare CAPTURE command to redirect a host print job to a LAN printer. Alternatively, you can move the printing overhead off the workstations onto the NetWare for SAA server using NetWare HostPrint, which routes host print jobs directly from the mainframe to NetWare print queues, without having to go through the client workstation first.

Rather than using the rather expensive cluster controllers, a NetWare server running NetWare for SAA is used. Instead of being wired to the cluster controller, the "terminals" and "printers" are LAN-connected to the NetWare for SAA server using IPX/SPX, AppleTalk, or TCP/IP protocol. The NetWare for SAA server acts as a gateway and converts IPX/SNA, AppleTalk, or TCP/IP packets into SNA data streams before sending then on to the FEP. To the SNA network, a NetWare for SAA server functions exactly like an IBM cluster controller.

Because NetWare for SAA is implemented as a set of NLMs, you can load them on your production server or on a dedicated "application server". NetWare for SAA is tightly integrated with NDS so you have a single point of administration as well as the benefits of the security and administration features of NetWare.

Connection to the host can be made either using token ring, ethernet, FDDI, SDLC, X25/QLLC, or channel attachments. The LAN workstations can use any topology supported by the NetWare OS and supports major desktop client operating systems, including Windows NT, Windows 9x, Windows 3.1, UNIX, OS/2, Mac OS, and DOS.

The following is a highlight of the new features incorporated into NetWare for SAA version 4:

- Full access to AS/400s.
- Tight integration with NetWare OS, including NDS.
- Centralized or distributed administration and management with the following features:
  - Snap-in modules for the NetWare Administrator (NWAdmin) utility
  - SAA Server Configurator
  - SAA Services Manager (Windows-based)
  - Network-based management utilities
  - Host-based network management (NetView)
  - Network management in TCP/IP environments (via SNMP)
  - Web-based administration

- Support for multiple languages.

- Multiple Physical Unit (PU) emulation (can also act as a PU-concentrator for downstream PUs and SNA devices).

- Load balancing of dependent and independent Logical Units (LUs) across multiple PUs and multiple servers, across multiple NetWare for SAA servers, ensuring consistent response time at the workstation over IPX as well as IP.

- LU pooling across multiple PUs and multiple servers.

- Hot Standby feature for fault tolerance.

- TN3270 and TN3270E access to mainframe, and TN5250 access to AS/400.

- Support for a full range of LU types for display, printer, file transfer, and Advanced Program-to-Program Communications (APPC) sessions.

- Advanced SNA connectivity, including full Advanced Peer-to-Peer Networking (APPN) Network and End Node support.

- Support for the latest TCP/IP protocol from NetWare 5, including Service Location Protocol (SLP) for IP-client service discovery, load balancing, and rollover.

- Secure Sockets Layer (SSL) encryption. This feature allows people to use the Internet to establish secure sessions with IBM mainframe or AS/400 applications. (End users must have IBM's Host On Demand Java terminal emulator running on their PCs to use this feature, which supports TN3270 and TN5250 connections.)

PART

I

CH

2

Tip #16 from *Peter*	Included with NetWare for SAA version 3 and higher is a "Host Simulator." It is a set of NLMs that you can load on a NetWare for SAA server for testing your NetWare for SAA configurations without having access to a real mainframe.

Note that you need NetWare for SAA version 4 or higher for a NetWare 5 server.

NetWare NFS Services

If you have a requirement to share file and print services between your NetWare 5 server and UNIX machines, the most commonly recommended solution is the use of network file system (NFS) protocol. Novell's solution is the NetWare 5 NFS Services.

File-sharing service in NetWare 5 NFS Services includes NFS Gateway and the NFS Server. The NFS Gateway enables NetWare clients (such as Windows NT and Mac users) to access a UNIX file system as if it were a native NetWare volume. The NFS Server exports a NetWare volume to NFS users, enabling UNIX users (or any NFS clients) to view the traditional as well as the new NFS NetWare file system as an extension of their (UNIX) file system. UNIX clients can access NetWare volumes using the standard UNIX/NFS mount command and can share files with other NetWare client platforms, including clients running Windows NT, Windows 9x, OS/2, Mac OS, and DOS.

Tip #17 from
Peter

> Client access to NetWare 5 NFS Services does not take up licensed connections on the server. Therefore, you can have one NetWare 5 server with a 5-user license installed supporting hundred NFS clients.

Similarly, NetWare clients can access files on any UNIX system that supports the NFS protocol. NetWare NFS Services makes remote NFS file systems appear to NetWare clients as NetWare volumes. Using familiar commands native to their desktop operating systems, NetWare users can, within an NFS file system, create and use files with attributes native to the user's computing environment. For example, a Windows NT user can create files with long filenames and an OS/2 user can create and access files with extended attributes.

NetWare 5 NFS Services implements the Line Printer/Line Printer Daemon (LPR/LPD) protocol standards as its printing service. The NFS Print Sharing Services include the Print Gateway, which enables NetWare 5 clients to configure and print to UNIX (or any LPD-enabled) printers from NetWare print queues; and the LPD Print Server, which enables UNIX clients to send print jobs to NetWare print queues.

Tip #18 from
Peter

> You don't need to purchase NetWare 5 NFS Services in order to implement LPR/LPD services on your NetWare 5 network. LPR/LPD is included with the Unix Print Services that's included with your NetWare 5.

In addition, NetWare 5 NFS Services includes NFS Naming Services which offer standard Network Information Service services and support for domain name system (DNS) on NetWare 5. The NFS Naming Services provide host address translation, user and group information, and translations between NetWare and NFS user and group IDs.

Also included with NetWare NFS Services is an FTP server. It enables the transfer of files using the File Transfer Protocol (FTP) protocol.

The following are some of the product highlights:

- Supports WebNFS. The WebNFS protocol provides substantial improvements over other Internet file access protocols such as HTTP and FTP. WebNFS provides improved error recovery capabilities and greater scalability. Support for the WebNFS protocol in NetWare 5 NFS Services enables WebNFS clients to access the NetWare NFS server directly. It also enables WebNFS clients to access data on the new NetWare NSS file system, using an NFS URL (for example, `nfs://url_path`)

- Supports multiple client operating systems, such as Windows NT, Windows 9x, OS/2, Mac OS, and DOS.

- NFS Gateway volumes support multiple name spaces. This means that different NetWare clients can access titles on an NFS Gateway volume in their native environment

- Flexible access control and NetWare authentication through NDS.

- Includes an extended FTP server. The FTP Server includes a gateway that enables FTP clients to transfer files from remote NetWare servers and IBM APPC File Transfer Protocol (AFTP) hosts. The FTP Server also eliminates the need to supply the full NDS context for any given username.

- Remote management capability. Through the use of the included XCONSOLE NLM, you can remotely administer NetWare NFS Services over IP or IPX networks from any client that supports DEC VT100, VT220, or the X Window system.

NetWare 5 NFS Services is based on the industry-standard Sun Network File System protocol version 2.0.

Note

As mentioned previously, included with NetWare 5, free of charge, is UNIX Print Services (same as the NFS Print Sharing Services), which contains an FTP server as well as LPR/LPD services. You can find out more about installing and configuring them in Chapter 35, "FTP Service and LPR/LPD."

BORDERMANAGER

With the popularity of Internet today, chances are good that you'd want to (or "need" to) connect your NetWare 5 network to the Internet. However, to protect the information stored on your LAN from unauthorized access by millions of Internet users, some security measures should be taken. There are a number of ways in which you can secure your Internet connection, but the most common method is the use of a *firewall* device that sits between your LAN and the outside world.

Tip #19 from
Peter

A firewall is not limited to Internet connection. It can be used to segregate *any* IP network into two halves: a private segment and a public one. Therefore, if you're connecting your network to another one or need to keep the data of one segment private, you can install a firewall to regulate which type of IP traffic can be exchanged between the two networks.

Novell's BorderManager Enterprise Edition 3 is a comprehensive Internet security management suite with which businesses can leverage the power of NDS on NetWare, UNIX, and NT networks. This standards-based suite allows organizations of all sizes to cost-effectively deploy industry leading firewall, authentication, virtual private network (VPN), and caching services for comprehensive security protection. Taking advantage of tight integration with NDS, BorderManager Enterprise Edition 3 is the first security management solution to deliver secure single sign-on for users accessing confidential company information from the Internet, an intranet, or an extranet.

BorderManager Enterprise Edition 3 includes four integrated services:

- **BorderManager Firewall Services 3**—BorderManager Firewall Services 3 is the security foundation of the BorderManager Enterprise Edition 3 suite. With the BorderManager Firewall Services 3 NDS-based, security policy management tools you can protect the confidential data stored on your private network and control user access to intranet and Internet content. You can use the BorderManager Firewall by itself or to augment existing firewall protection.

- **BorderManager Authentication Services 3**—BorderManager Authentication Services 3 (BMAS) is the remote authentication component of the BorderManager Enterprise Edition 3 suite. With it you can allow remote access to your private network from the Internet without compromising network security. BMAS combines the security capabilities of the Remote Authentication Dial-In User Service (RADIUS) protocol with the easy and convenient management afforded by NDS.

- **BorderManager VPN Services 3**—BorderManager VPN Services 3 is a cost-effective method for allowing remote users, organizations, customers, and suppliers secure access to the confidential data on your private network. By connecting remote users through an Internet-based virtual private network, you can cut costs to as little as one-fifth the cost of using dedicated private lines and privately-owned modem pools.

- **BorderManager FastCache Services 3**—The performance foundation of the BorderManager Enterprise Edition 3 suite, BorderManager FastCache Services 3 is one of the fastest and most scalable Internet caching services. By installing BorderManager FastCache Services 3 you can significantly increase the productivity of network users.

Using the circuit-level gateways and HTTP application proxy included with BorderManager Enterprise Edition 3, you can easily control what access your users and user groups have to the Internet. You configure access rights with the NetWare Administrator (NWAdmin) utility, the same tool that you use to manage your user information. And with the logging features built-in to BorderManager Enterprise Edition 3 you can determine who requested access to what information and when. You can log information on requests accepted or rejected by the circuit-level gateways and HTTP proxy, and review the logs at your convenience.

Because BorderManager Enterprise Edition 3 services are fully integrated with NDS, both local and remote users can access these services and perform all other network tasks to which they have rights simply by logging in to the network with their NDS username and password. And all BorderManager Enterprise Edition 3 services perform authentication tasks in the background, so that established security does not inconvenience users.

Tip #20 from
Peter

The services in the BorderManager Enterprise Edition 3 product are available separately. So you can purchase and install the components you need.

> **Note**
>
> One of the most often-used features in BorderManager is Network Address Translation (NAT). It allows you to use a single legal IP address to the outside world, while on the inside of the NAT server, you can implement your own IP addressing scheme without causing conflicts. NAT also allows you to hide your IP network from view by exposing only a single registered IP address. Not originally included with NetWare 5, the NAT feature has been added, free of charge, as part of Support Pack. See Chapter 31, "Network Address Translation (NAT)" for more information about installing and configuring NAT for your NetWare 5 server.

PART

I

CH

2

MANAGEWISE

In a mid- to large-size network, it is highly desirable to be proactive, rather than reactive, to network problems; you want to fix minor issues before they lead to a major network problem causing unnecessary network downtime, thus lost productivity of your users.

Many network management packages are available on the market from many different vendors, such as IBM, HP, Computer Associates, and Novell. ManageWise is Novell's comprehensive management solution you can use to successfully manage and control your entire mixed network. It enables you to accomplish all management tasks from a single point of administration, including Novell Directory Services monitoring, NetWare and Windows NT server management, early-warning alarm notification, network traffic analysis, packet capturing and decoding, desktop management, virus protection, network inventorying, and network health reporting.

ManageWise prevents downtime by enabling proactive management and quick problem resolution. The ManageWise Console offers a bird's eye view of your network (see Figure 2.3). With the assistance of monitoring agents running on the servers, the Console can alert you of problem areas by highlighting the device that has generated an alert with alarm bell icons. If you have IP devices that supports the Simple Network Management Protocol (SNMP), you can configure them to forward traps to the Console as well. The Console also keeps historical information so you can go back and examine trends.

ManageWise supports Windows NT, Windows 95/98, Windows 3.1, DOS, OS/2, and Macintosh operating systems on desktops; NetWare and Windows NT server operating systems on file servers; common network topologies such as ethernet, Fast Ethernet, token ring, and FDDI; and standard networking protocols such as TCP/IP, IPX/SPX, or AppleTalk. Based on SNMP and RMON (Remote Monitoring) industry standards, ManageWise provides an open platform with a variety of third-party snap-ins.

Tip #21 from
Peter

> A popular ManageWise snap-in application is pager gateway. Through this interface, you can configure the ManageWise Console to send alerts to your pager, and, if you have a digital page, the error message that triggered it.

Figure 2.3
You can easily locate and determine any network alarms using the ManageWise Console.

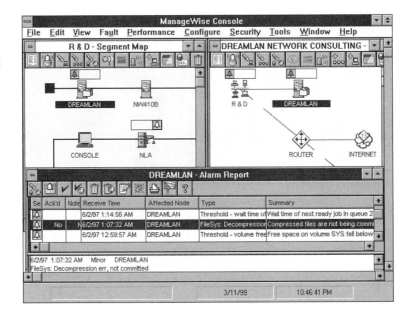

ManageWise is fully compatible with NetWare 5, and integrates completely with ZENworks to give you a comprehensive network management tool. For details on installing and configuring ZENworks, refer to Chapter 24, "ZENworks."

GROUPWISE

Electronic mail (*email*) is probably *the* most demanded network service, with Internet access running a close second. Except for the very small networks where there's only a handful of users, most, if not all, networks can use some kind of messaging system; in a mid- to large size organization, email is a must.

Many email packages are available on the market today. Depending on the feature sets and support, price varies a lot. However, there are some free and yet very good products available (Pegasus Mail is such an example). Among the popular choices, Novell's GroupWise stands out in its class.

GroupWise is a fully integrated, easy-to-use messaging system that offers a wide range of powerful communication and collaboration capabilities. Other than its standard suite of options, such as email, personal calendaring, group scheduling, imaging, automated workflow, task and document management, rules-based message management, and electronic discussions, the latest version contains features such as document management capabilities, native Internet addressing, new calendar options, and vCard support. You can also configure GroupWise to page you when a message arrives for you. Simply put, GroupWise is a groupware application.

GroupWise simplifies communications by providing the Universal Mailbox, a single access point for all types of messages, calendar information, and documents. When you're away from your workstation, you can use a laptop computer, remote client, or Web browser to access your Universal Mailbox.

GroupWise 5.5 supports LDAP, IMAP4, and POP3. It includes a Java- and HTML 3.2–enabled version of GroupWise WebAccess that provides Web browser access to your Universal Mailbox. Also included at no extra cost is GroupWise WebPublisher, a document management tool that enables users to publish documents to the Internet and to your intranet.

Like BorderManager, the GroupWise 5.5 Administrator is integrated with the NetWare Administrator (NWAdmin) utility, which means that you can easily set up, configure, and maintain your GroupWise messaging system using Novell Directory Services as your master directory. And GroupWise 5.5 provides a snap-in utility for ManageWise that enables you to monitor and manage GroupWise 5.2 agents, servers, and gateways that support SNMP.

GroupWise 5.5 supports Windows NT 4.0, Windows 9x, Windows 3.1, UNIX, and Mac OS platforms. GroupWise 5.5 for servers supports Windows NT, NetWare, and UNIX.

Available as add-on products to GroupWise are a number of gateways and utilities, allowing you to exchange GroupWise email with other popular email systems and over different message transport and communication protocols:

- Async Gateway (NLM) is an asynchronous gateway that enables GroupWise users to send and receive appointments, tasks, notes, mail, and telephone messages using a modem dial-up connection.

- Gateway for cc:Mail (NT) enables GroupWise users and Lotus cc:Mail users to exchange messages transparently. It enables users to send unlimited attachments, provide automatic exchange and synchronization of directories, and migrate from cc:Mail to GroupWise, and it offers statistical and diagnostic logging of the gateway's performance.

  You can download Gateway for cc:Mail free of charge at
  `http://www.novell.com/download`.

- Gateway for Lotus Notes (NT) enables GroupWise users and Lotus Notes users to exchange messages. It provides automatic and continuous directory synchronization.

  You can download Gateway for Lotus Notes free of charge at
  `http://www.novell.com/download`.

- Gateway for Microsoft Exchange (NT) enables GroupWise users and Microsoft Exchange users to communicate seamlessly by transporting and converting GroupWise messages into a format supported by Exchange.

  You can download Gateway for Microsoft Exchange free of charge at
  `http://www.novell.com/download`.

- Gateway for Microsoft Mail (NT) enables GroupWise users and Microsoft Mail users to exchange messages transparently. It enables users to send unlimited attachments, and GroupWise and Microsoft Mail to automatically exchange directories.

You can download Gateway for Microsoft Mail at `http://www.novell.com/download`.

■ Microsoft Mail Conversion Utility enables Microsoft Mail for Windows users to convert messages to the GroupWise system format and send them to GroupWise users.

■ Pager Gateway (NLM) enables GroupWise users to send messages to pagers as if they were sending them to other GroupWise users. Pager Gateway includes Wireless Connection Services from Neoteric, Inc.

■ X.400 Gateway (NLM) enables GroupWise users to exchange messages with users on X.400-compatible public and private email systems. It supports status messages, an unlimited number of users and attachments, and gateway aliases.

If you need to access GroupWise messaging functions from an application (that's not an email program), you can use the API Gateway NLM using a simple text-file interface. The API Gateway is included with GroupWise 4.1 Materials Pack and available with the Novell Developer Kit.

ORACLE8 FOR NETWARE

The NetWare file server is among the fastest server, in terms of I/O and fault-tolerant, available today. As such, it makes perfect sense to use NetWare servers as database servers. With the availability of high-speed CPUs and large-capacity disk drives, you can easily build a PC-based database server using NetWare 5 that rivals many RISC- or even mainframe-based database servers. There are many database vendors that have versions of their application that runs on NetWare, and among them is Oracle Corporation.

Included free with your set of NetWare 5 CDs (in North America at least, because it is labeled with a notice "This product may not be exported outside of the U.S. or Canada without prior authorization from the U.S. Department of Commerce") is an Oracle8 for NetWare CD, which contains a fully functional 5-user version of Oracle8 for NetWare, version 8.0.3.0.6. This version of Oracle8 for NetWare supports the following NetWare platforms:

■ NetWare 5

■ NetWare 5 MPK

■ NetWare 4.11/intraNetWare

■ NetWare 4.11 SMP

This CD also includes Oracle8 Client version 8.0.3.0.4 software for Intel-based operating systems, and supports the following operating systems:

■ Windows 3.1

■ Windows 95/98/NT

> **Note**
>
> The only limitation on this particular version of Oracle8 for NetWare is that the 5-user license is not additive. Therefore, you'll be unable to combine multiple 5-user licenses onto one NetWare server. Should you need more than a 5-user license, contact Oracle DMD to upgrade your license. Details on upgrading of user licenses and of support is available under Sales and License in the Oracle8 HTML pages that are included on this CD (see `StartMe.HTM`).

One major advantage that the Oracle8 Client v8 has over previous versions and other vendors' databases is that it supports NDS authentication. That means using the new client software in a NetWare 5 (or NetWare 4) environment, your users have single–sign-on access to both the network *and* database resources.

PART
I

CH
2

NDS FOR NON-NETWARE PLATFORMS

As previously mentioned, many organizations tend to have a mixture of different operating system and hardware platforms, depending on their needs and requirements. However, these operating systems generally have different management interfaces that are not compatible with each other. Wouldn't it be nice to be able to run some kind of directory service common to these operating systems so that you can manage all aspects of user information from a single utility from your desk? NDS can be that solution! Over a number of years, working with third-party vendors such as IBM, Microsoft, and Sun, Novell has ported NDS to a number of different platforms.

NDS FOR NT

In the past few years, it has been increasingly common for networks to contain both Windows NT and NetWare servers. However, in such a mixed environment, the network administrator has maintain two separate sets of user information, one for NetWare and one for Windows NT. Novell created NDS for NT to specifically address this situation.

Tip #22 from
Peter

> NDS for NT is developed using published API calls from Microsoft. Therefore, it is compatible with future versions of Windows NT servers and all Microsoft Service Packs.

By integrating the Windows NT domain database into NDS, NDS for NT is software that centralizes the administration of Windows NT and NetWare networks and reduces the complexity of managing Windows NT domains. In addition, NDS for NT does not change the domain architecture, so it is completely compatible with existing Windows NT applications. And you can still use familiar Windows NT tools to manage your NT domains.

NDS for NT eliminates the need to establish and maintain complicated trust relationships. You can add users to one or more domains, through NDS, without having to delete and re-create them. Using a NWAdmin snap-in, you can use NWAdmin to manage your entire mixed network. NWAdmin also provides flexibility: you can integrate familiar NT utilities, such as User Manager, Server Manager, and File Sharing Wizard, with NWAdmin.

In NDS for NT version 2.0, the following enhancements have been made since the 1.0 product:

- Capability to store an NDS replica on an Windows NT Server. The NDS replica can be installed on the Primary Domain Controller (PDC) or a Backup Domain Controller (BDC); no changes are needed on user workstations.
- Capability to manage NT file shares through NDS, using a NWAdmin snap-in.
- Single–sign-on for users accessing NetWare and NT servers.
- Enhanced scalability. If the only servers participating in the replica ring are NetWare 5 and NT servers running NDS for NT v2.0, the domain can scale to 65,000 objects.

Note | NDS for NT v2.0 still requires IPX, but the next version will support a pure IP environment.

NDS for NT 2.0 integrates your Windows NT Servers (3.51 and above) with your NetWare servers (4.2 and above).>

UNIXWARE 7 NETWARE SERVICES

One of the popular Intel-based implementation of the UNIX operating system is SCO's UnixWare. Initially developed as a joint venture between Novell and USL (UNIX Systems Laboratory), and later owned by Novell, UnixWare was finally sold off to SCO. At the time of the sale, Novell incorporated NDS into UnixWare 2. Now, UnixWare 7 provides standard NetWare 4.10 networking services in addition to the standard UNIX networking and application services.

NetWare Services (NWS) provides NetWare 4.10 server capabilities that integrate seamlessly into existing Novell and UNIX environments. With NWS, UnixWare 7 can also act as the primary network server for businesses that need NetWare 4.10 file, print, and directory services; LAN security; and multiple client support but who also need the reliability, stability, and application services of a UNIX system environment.

NetWare and UNIX technology have coexisted in business environments for many years. Prior to the availability of UnixWare, separate servers were required to support UNIX-based business critical applications and the day-to-day networking needs of LANs. Now, networking services developed by Novell work cooperatively with the powerful UNIX networking technologies building corporate intranets and WANs.

Unlike other solutions that use emulations or simulations, NWS allows administrators to use native, Microsoft Windows program-based NetWare tools such as NWAdmin to administer the LAN environment. Add to this the extensive LAN and WAN features of the UnixWare 7 environment and businesses get a new level of power from their networks.

The following are some of the feature highlights of UnixWare 7:

■ Full NetWare 4.10 File, Print, and Directory Services on a native UnixWare 7 environment

■ Full support for Novell Directory Services NDS APIs and Novell Cross Platform Services

■ Supports up to 150 concurrent connections and can achieve 95% of native NetWare performance (depending on hardware capacity)

■ Graphical administration tools for installing and configuring all aspects of NWS operations:

  • NDS administration and repair

  • Administration of NetWare and UNIX printers from a single tool

  • NWS volume administration

  • NWS networking configuration and tuning

■ Supports DOS, Windows, Windows 9x, UNIX, Mac NCP, and OS/2 clients

■ Works with standard SCO

■ UnixWare file systems including NFS mounted file systems

■ Transparent to clients, administrators, and network management systems (such as Novell ManageWise and so on)

Caution

Before you install UnixWare 7 into your NetWare 5 network, you should check with SCO for the latest update for the NDS code to ensure compatibility. There have been some changes to NDS in NetWare 5 that make older versions of NDS incompatible—UnixWare 7 functions like a NetWare 4.10 server.

NDS FOR SOLARIS

One of the most popular UNIX implementations is Sun's Solaris operating system. As is the case for Windows NT servers, it would be nice to be able to integrate Solaris' user information with NDS. In early 1999, shortly after the shipping of NetWare 5, Novell released NDS for Solaris.

NDS for Solaris reduces redundant administration of your Solaris environment by storing, securing, and managing information about your network in an integrated naming system—NDS—tying network platforms and applications together. Using familiar tools, such as NWAdmin, network administrators can manage users, groups, and access to multiple network applications from any location across multiple platforms.

NDS for Solaris runs on a SPARCstation II and above with Solaris 2.6.

Note

At the time of this writing, NDS for Solaris has not yet been certified for Solaris 2.7.

NOVELL NETWORK SERVICES FOR AIX

Moving to RISC-based UNIX systems, one of the common implementations is IBM's AIX UNIX on the RS/6000 system. With an agreement struck in 1987, IBM licensed NDS from Novell and has ported NDS to a number of their platforms. In the UNIX area, IBM has available *Novell Network Services 4.1 (NNS) on AIX*, which brings Novell's NetWare 4 network services to the RS/6000 system.

NNS on AIX provides a full-functioned compatible implementation of NDS, Novell distributed file and print services, network security and administration services across the RS/6000 system family. NNS enables the RS/6000 to act as server for both Internet and PC client applications using these or later versions of the following operating systems:

- DOS 5.0
- OS/2 2.1
- Windows 3.11
- Windows 9x
- Windows NT

NNS on AIX provides a single, network-based view of all network resources through NDS. The NDS database can be distributed through partitioning and replication to give seamless, reliable access to all network resources, regardless of their global location.

AIX versions 4.21 are required.

Caution

Before you install NNS on AIX into your NetWare 5 network, you should check with IBM for the latest update for the NDS code to ensure compatibility. Similar to the UnixWare 7 discussion earlier, NNS functions like a NetWare 4.10 server.

NETWARE 4.1 SERVICES FOR HP 9000

Other than IBM's AIX, another popular UNIX implementation on RISC-based systems is HP's HP/UX. Available for HP 9000 is NetWare 4.1 Services for HP 9000. It features NDS, which enables network administrators to locate information quickly and allocate resources to groups of users more efficiently, easing network administration and management. Furthermore, end users can access applications (both on NetWare and on HP/UX) without logging in more than once.

In addition to NDS support, NetWare 4.1 Services for HP 9000 (also known as NetWare/9000) also include file service that provides users with the ability to share information across the network without affecting the network's performance or reliability.

NetWare 4.1 Services for HP 9000 print services enable users to access any printer on the network without knowing where the printer is connected to the network or how the connection is established.

The one fundamental difference between NetWare/9000 and native NetWare is in the hardware interface. On native NetWare implementation, NetWare is the operating system and interfaces directly with the hardware. With NetWare/9000, it is an application running on top of the HP/UX operating system, and as such, it is a good solution for those of you who need to share file, print and management services combined with access to HP/UX applications and the use of Novell networking.

NetWare 4.1 Services for HP 9000 offers configuration integration through the standard HP/UX System Administration Manager (SAM) utility, IP tunneling (the capability to send IPX packets encapsulated in IP packets), token ring source routing and easy license administration. It also offers multiple client support, including VLM client and 32-bit client on DOS and on Windows 3.1x, and 32-bit client on Windows NT and Windows 9x.

NetWare/9000 requires HP/UX version 10 or higher.

Caution

As is the case for UnixWare 7 and Novell Network Services for AIX, prior to installing NetWare/9000 into your NetWare 5 network, you should check with HP for the latest update for the NDS code to ensure compatibility.

Novell Network Services for OS/390

In addition to its Novell Network Services for AIX, IBM released NDS for OS/390, the operating system for the S/390 mainframe, in early 1999. Novell Network Services for OS/390 is a distributed service based on Novell's multiplatform directory technology, NDS, that stores information about hardware and software resources available within a given network, whether the resources reside on corporate networks, intranets or the Internet. NNS for OS/390 can help you to reduce management costs and allows you to consolidate your PC-based directory servers on the S/390 platform (should you want to) and can help system administrators better manage their networks.

Note

With NNS for OS/390, you can place a NDS replica on the S/390 so the mainframe is part of the replica ring. In some instances, it might be desirable to make the mainframe as holders of the Master replicas because it is infrequent that a mainframe goes down.

Novell Network Services for OS/390 can be ordered separately, free of charge, as an option for OS/390 Version 2, Release 6 and higher and by customers with the OS/390 Security Server feature.

> **Note**
>
> Novell Network Services for OS/390 requires installation of the OS/390 Security Server.

PROJECT: DISCOVER NDS 8

At the time of this writing, Novell has just announced the next generation of Novell Directory Services, called NDS 8 (version 8). To learn more about NDS 8 and find out how it can help with your NetWare 5 environment, visit Novell's Internet home page at

http://www.novell.com/products/nds

## CHAPTER 3

NETWORKING

In this chapter

NETWORK INTERFACE CARDS

The *network interface card*, commonly referred to as a *NIC*, is where it all starts. The NIC is responsible for actually putting the data onto the wire. The NIC does not just start streaming 1s and 0s, but organizes the data into frames and sends it frame by frame. In the end, it all comes down to one NIC sending to another NIC on the same piece of wire.

The NIC is the interface between the operating system and the wire. The first step when putting a network card into a server is making the machine happy with the hardware setup. You must make sure that there are no interrupt or IO Port conflicts. How this is done really depends on the server hardware, for example, with a machine that has an Extended Industry Standard Architecture (EISA) bus, you would run the EISA configuration utility. PCI cards are generally automatically configured when the machine is powered up. Making sure that there are no hardware conflicts has nothing to do with the operating system, but is strictly a hardware configuration step that you need to perform.

The next step is to get NetWare talking to the card. This is done by loading a *driver*, which is the software necessary for NetWare to see the card. The driver has a .LAN extension and is supplied by the manufacturer of the card. You can almost count on being able to toss the floppy containing the driver that comes with the card. Having done that, go to the vendor's Web site and download the most current drivers. One of the first things to do when troubleshooting a NetWare server is to make sure that the server has been patched and that you are using the newest NIC and DISK drivers from the vendors.

Tip #23 from	When troubleshooting the server, the first question is, Has the server been patched? The
John	next question is, Are you using the newest NIC and disk drivers from the vendors? Things change at a rapid pace in PC space, so always check for newer drivers.

There are several considerations when choosing a NIC, the first of which is the bus within the server or workstation. If you have an EISA bus, purchasing a PCI network interface card isn't going to do you much good. So identify the type of slot within the server that you are going to use, and purchase the NIC accordingly.

The connector is equally important. For example, fiber can be run over fiber optic cable, or twisted pair wiring. Token ring can use the hermaphroditic connectors and shielded twisted pair wiring, or it can run over unshielded twisted pair and RJ45 connectors. Ethernet NICs can be cabled in using transceivers, BNC connectors, or RJ45 connectors. And as basic as it might seem, get the correct type of NIC! If you have an ethernet network, you need an ethernet NIC.

Also, it is important to know that each network interface card has a unique hardware address "burned" in to it by the manufacturer. This is known as the MAC (Media Access Control) address. As you will see in Chapter 28, "Introduction to TCP/IP," one of the user-friendly aspects of IPX is that each workstation's node address is a combination of the IPX network number and the MAC address of the workstation, so in essence, when using IPX, you do not have to do any numbering at all, which is definitely not the case when using IP! The MAC address is 6 bytes in length; the first 3 bytes indicate the vendor, and the remaining 3 bytes make up a unique number.

Tip #24 from	Not all network interface cards are created equal, so although a $30 ethernet card might be fine for a workstation, you might want to spend more on the one you put into the server. Also, don't forget support as a consideration when purchasing the server's NIC. Does the vendor have a good reputation, and does it provide updated drivers on their Web site?
John	

SERVER HARDWARE

It is amazing that people try to save money by scrimping on their server hardware or have trouble justifying the cost of a production server, when it is the most important machine on the entire network! Just because someone isn't sitting there using it for a workstation doesn't mean you should cut corners, but rather realize that everyone is using it. It isn't "just a PC"; well, it might be, but high-end servers are built differently. The components such as the fans and power supplies are much heftier than in a normal desktop. Although it might be hard to justify Suzy Secretary getting an expensive machine, if you spread the cost of the server hardware out across the number of people using it, you will find that it doesn't amount to much per user. Buy the best and most powerful machine you can afford to act as your server.

In the opinion of this author, you should go with one of the major players such as Compaq or Hewlett-Packard. Clone servers should be used only for noncritical applications or test networks. You can almost always count on something being nonstandard enough in a cheap clone that it will cause you problems. And support is a huge consideration here; can the clone vendor provide you with support and current software?

Expansion is important to keep in mind. How many slots does the motherboard have? How much memory is in the machine, and how much memory can be added? Nothing improves the performance of a server like adding memory. How much disk space does the machine come with, and how many drive bays are there for adding more? Does it have single or multiple processors? If single, can more be added?

And make sure you know what you are getting if a vendor is supplying the server as part of a complete package. In a complete package, the vendor is going to supply the server hardware and all software. Your standards might call for a minimum of 256MB RAM, mirrored disks, and dual processors. The vendor might bring in a grossly underpowered machine by your standards, arguing that it will be fine. Of course, the vendor is also saving money by this, so the server hardware you are getting has to be spec'd out at the front end of the deal, not when it shows up.

PART
I

CH
3

Again, buy the best and most powerful machine you can afford. And then realize that like workstations, it will be obsolete *very* quickly. You can often upgrade one of your most important servers, and then let that hardware trickle down to a less important one. After a few iterations of this, even your less important servers are running on hardware that is more than adequate.

The minimum server hardware requirements for installing NetWare 5 are as follows:

- Pentium or higher processor
- VGA or higher display adapter (SVGA recommended)
- 550MB of available disk space
- 64MB of RAM
- At least one network interface card
- A CD-ROM drive that reads ISO 9660–formatted CDs
- A mouse is not required, but is recommended

Keep in mind that these are *minimum* requirements. No one in his or her right mind would implement these on anything but a test server! At the extreme low end, I would recommend at least 128MB of RAM, more if you can get it. And 550MB of disk space? Enough said!

| Tip #25 from | If there is any one thing you can do to improve the performance of your server, it would be |
| John | adding memory. |

ETHERNET

Ethernet is the most prevalent technology you will encounter. It is cheap and easy to implement, and it works right out of the box; as a consequence, it is very popular.

CSMA/CD

How does ethernet work? Put simply, it works like a party line. In more technical terms, it is described as a contention-based technology, or CSMA/CD. This mouthful stands for *Carrier Sense Multiple Access/Collision Detection.*

Before I look more closely at CSMA/CD, how does one station know that another is ready to transmit? On an idle ethernet, there is no signal on the wire, so the stations need some way to sync up with each other. They do this with the preamble. The preamble is 8 bytes of alternating ones and zeros, (10101010101010101010...) that end in 11. When a station sees the preamble, it uses that to lock on, and when it sees the 11, it knows that the frame is about to begin. No part of the preamble or the 11 that ends the preamble and marks the start of the frame is saved by the adapter to be passed up to the protocol stacks, only the frame itself is.

When a station is ready to transmit, it checks to see whether the line is quiet. This is the *Carrier Sense* (*CS*) portion of CSMA/CD. If the line is quiet, it transmits and then watches to make sure its data is put on the wire correctly. If the line is busy, the station waits until the line goes quiet and then transmits. Sounds all right, but let me return to the party line analogy. If only two people are on the line, you can have a conversation with no problem. With three people, you occasionally have interruptions, and with thirty people, it will be almost impossible to conduct an intelligent conversation; you have too many interruptions, or collisions, with the other 29 people trying to talk, and all getting in each other's way.

How does this relate to ethernet? That is where the term *contention-based* comes into play. Imagine that station one has the line occupied talking to the server. Stations two and three also want to talk to the server. As soon as the line goes quiet, stations two and three both jump! Then you have a collision. The frames, or packets of data, from stations two and three are going to collide on the wire, and become worthless, requiring them to be re-sent.

The rule is that when you have a collision, you back off for some random amount of time and then try again. So stations two and three don't get to talk. They back off, and meanwhile station four jumps onto the wire. The number of machines you have fighting for time on the wire is known as the *collision domain*. If you have 1 server and 39 workstations, your collision domain is 40 machines. It doesn't matter whether any of the machines are servers or not; at the ethernet level, things are very democratic, and ethernet NICs in servers have to follow the same rules as anyone else.

The capability to detect a collision when the signals collide is the *Collision Detection* (*CD*) portion of CSMA/CD. *Multiple Access* (*MA*) means that there are no rules about sharing; if you have more than one packet to send, you can immediately attempt to send another one as soon as you get the first one off.

Are collisions normal and expected? Absolutely. Network traffic is very bursty by its very nature, and in a network of any size, you are going to have collisions as two or more stations attempt to talk at the same time. Collisions are normal; excessive collisions are an indication of a network problem that needs to be addressed.

One of the things to keep in mind when laying out an ethernet network is the size of the collision domain. With enough stations all vying for time on the wire, it is possible for the network to essentially shut down. And it is a vicious spiral; so many machines are waiting to talk that more and more collisions are almost a given. Don't misunderstand: you can have huge networks based on ethernet, but you aren't going to have all the machines on the same piece of wire.

ETHERNET FRAME FORMAT

When you bind a protocol to the NIC in your server or workstation, you need to select a frame type. In this section, you will take a look at several ethernet frame formats. Why several? In 1982, DEC, Intel, and Xerox (DIX; this is why you will sometimes see references to a DIX connector) released Version II ethernet. In 1983, Novell came out with a proprietary ethernet frame type. When the IEEE 802.3 specification was finalized, it included the 802.2

PART
I

CH
3

LLC header, making Novell's proprietary frame type incompatible. And to toss in yet another piece of the puzzle, 802.3 SNAP came along to solve some backwards compatibility issues with Version II and 802.3.

Rather than delve into the differences of the bits and bytes of the various frame types, the main thing to understand is that in order to communicate, two stations need to use a common frame type. For example, if you use Ethernet_802.2 at the server, you need to use Ethernet_802.2 at the workstations. You can have more than one frame type bound to a NIC in the server; these are called logical boards. You might have only one NIC, but have both the Ethernet_II frame type and the Ethernet_802.2 frame type bound, thus giving you two logical boards.

10BASE5 AND 10BASE2

First, what does the *Base* in 10Base5, 10Base2, and 10BaseT mean? Base stands for *baseband*, meaning that there is only one signal on the wire, taking all the available bandwidth. This is opposed to *broadband*, which is how the cable going to your television works; there are many signals on that wire.

The 10 stands for 10 megabits per second, the theoretical rate that data can flow at. The 5 and 2 stand for the distance of the maximum segment length, as shown in Table 3.1. The 5 in 10Base5 is right on at 500 meters, but the 2 in 10Base2 has been rounded up from 185 meters.

TABLE 3.1   ETHERNET NAMING CONVENTIONS

Ethernet Type	Data Rate	Maximum Segment Length in Meters	Cabling	Topology
10Base2	10Mbps	185	50 ohm coax (thin)	Bus
10Base5	10Mbps	500	50 ohm coax (thick)	Bus
10BaseT	10Mbps	100	Unshielded Twisted Pair (UTP)	Star

10Base5 and 10Base2 are older implementations of ethernet that have long since fallen from grace. The cable used for 10Base5 is either RG-8 or RG-11. This is 50-ohm cable that is semirigid, heavy, about as thick as your thumb, and very hard to work with. At various points in the line, you need to put in a transceiver, and you can then attach a workstation by using a drop cable, or transceiver cable, as shown in Figure 3.1.

Figure 3.1
To connect a workstation to a 10Base5 network, you first put a transceiver on the wire. Then, using a drop cable, you connect to the AUI connector on the NIC.

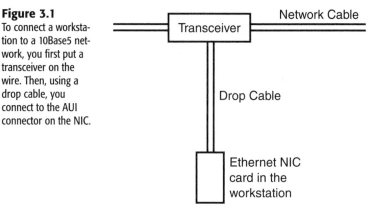

10Base2, also known as *thinnet* or *cheapernet*, was a huge improvement. As you can see from Table 3.1, 10Base2 has a much shorter segment length than 10Base5, so how can this be an improvement? The answer is the cable. RG-58 is used for thin wire ethernet, and it is much easier to work with! Thinnet cable is about as thick as a pencil, and uses BNC connectors. To attach a workstation, you put a T connector in the line, and this T connector goes directly to the BNC connector on the NIC, as shown in Figure 3.2.

Figure 3.2
Drop cables and transceivers are not used with 10Base2. Instead, you put a T connector in the line and attach this to the BNC connector on the NIC.

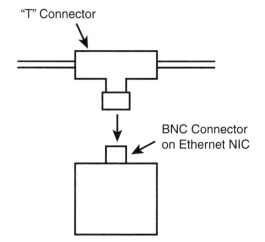

BUS TOPOLOGY

What both 10Base5 and 10Base2 have in common is the bus topology. In a bus topology, the cable goes from machine to machine in one long line, as shown in Figure 3.3.

Figure 3.3
A bus topology. You would have one long cable regardless of 10Base5 or 10Base2; the only difference would be how you tap into the cable.

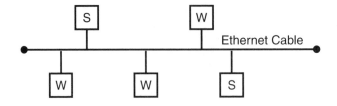

S = Server
W = Workstation

There are several problems with the bus topology:

- You might reach your maximum segment length or quickly reach the maximum number of allowed connections per segment and can no longer expand.

- Because the machines are wired in series, very much like cheap Christmas lights, a break in the cable will shut down the entire network.

- Very few buildings lend themselves to wiring by taking a long cable and snaking it from room to room.

- Troubleshooting is more difficult. At each end of the cable, there is a terminating resistor. You have to move the terminator in order to isolate a problem with the cabling.

- The cable is more expensive, and both it and the required connectors are harder to work with.

A more ideal wiring situation is one where each machine has its own piece of wire. This vastly simplifies troubleshooting, and a problem with that cable affects only one workstation instead of the entire network. This is the case with 10BaseT as you will see later in this chapter.

REPEATERS

What if you need more distance that the specifications allow? The specifications are there because the signal is good for a finite distance before attenuation and noise starts to affect the clarity of the signal. If you used only an amplifier, you could amplify the signal at some point along the line, but you would also be amplifying any noise and signal degradation.

But you can use a *repeater*. A repeater operates purely at the physical level. It does no analysis of the frame whatsoever; it merely regenerates the signal and passes it on. The new signal is an exact duplicate of the original packet. A repeater can be used to extend one of your network segments, as shown in Figure 3.4.

Figure 3.4
A repeater operates at the physical level only. The frame is regenerated and sent out the other port.

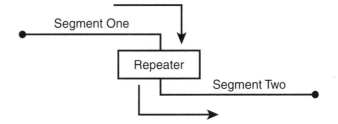

In theory, you could repeat the signal to infinity, but practically, there are rules that limit the number of repeaters.

BRIDGES

Remember the concept of a collision domain introduced earlier in this chapter? A collision domain is the number of machines vying for time on the same piece of wire. What if you have one hundred machines and two servers on the same segment, wired as shown in Figure 3.5?

Figure 3.5
A network segment with 2 file servers and 100 users.

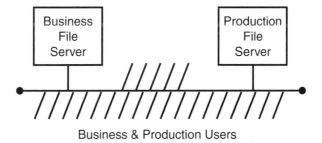

PART

I

CH

3

> **Note**
>
> A network segment is a physical division; a piece of wire. For example, you have one ethernet card in your server feeding one piece of cable. This is one segment. If you then add another network card, and pull another cable, you now have two segments. Any traffic placed on a network segment is seen by all NICs on the segment. A NIC can only send a packet to another NIC on the same piece of wire.

The load between your two hypothetical servers is pretty even, about half the staff accesses only one of them, and the remaining half uses the other server. But there are personnel who need to access both servers. You have analyzed the traffic on the wire, and have found that it is too high. How can you reduce the traffic on the wire? And with 100 machines, you believe that the collision domain is larger than you would like. How can you reduce traffic on the wire, and reduce your collision domain at the same time?

One answer (not a very good one) would be to break the network up into two discreet networks. That would reduce the traffic and collision domain, because instead of 100 users on the wire, you would have only 50, but what about the staff members who need to access both servers? They would need two computers on their desk; either that or get out of their chair and move to another station!

A better solution would be a bridge. A bridge builds up a table for each of its interfaces, and in this table it keeps up with the hardware, or MAC addresses, of the machines on each of its interfaces:

```
DLC:  ----- DLC Header -----
DLC:
DLC:  Frame 227 arrived at  09:55:14.8896; frame size is 74 (004A hex) bytes.
DLC:  Destination = Station cisco 76D1B2
DLC:  Source      = Station Prteon8432BE
DLC:  Ethertype   = 0800 (IP)
DLC:
IP: ----- IP Header -----
IP:
IP: Version = 4, header length = 20 bytes
IP: Type of service = 00
IP:       000. .... = routine
IP:       ...0 .... = normal delay
IP:       .... 0... = normal throughput
IP:       .... .0.. = normal reliability
IP: Total length   = 60 bytes
IP: Identification = 41733
IP: Flags          = 0X
IP:       .0.. .... = may fragment
IP:       ..0. .... = last fragment
IP: Fragment offset = 0 bytes
IP: Time to live    = 32 seconds/hops
IP: Protocol        = 1 (ICMP)
IP: Header checksum = AD2A (correct)
IP: Source address      = [204.78.43.220], TARZAN
IP: Destination address = [206.101.132.1]
IP: No options
IP:
```

Of the packet fragment shown previously, the bridge would look only at the destination hardware address, in this case, cisco 76D1B2. If the source, Prteon8432BE, is on the same interface as cisco 76D1B2, the bridge discards the packet. If not, it forwards it. The way this works is shown in Figure 3.6.

Figure 3.6
The bridge builds up a table of the MAC addresses on each of its interfaces. If a destination MAC address is on the same side of the bridge as the source MAC address, the bridge ignores the packet. If the destination is on the other side of the bridge, the packet gets forwarded.

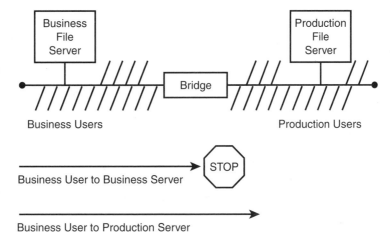

You obtain several advantages by putting in the bridge, but first think about placement of the resources. In the perfect scenario, one server and its fifty users are on one side of the bridge, and the other server and its fifty users are on the other side. In this case, you have cut the collision domain in half, because only fifty users are contending for time on the wire. Before, each user competed with 99 other users! The problem with the initial layout shown in Figure 3.5 is that if a user continually accesses only the one server, why should he or she have to compete with the fifty users who are trying to reach the other server, the one he or she cares nothing about? The bridge solves this problem for you. Not only is the collision domain reduced, but so is traffic. You don't see the traffic that the other users are generating to access their server. And your staff who need to access both servers can do it seamlessly, as they always have, without getting up.

Now, consider the worst-case scenario for locating the resources. In the worst case, the fifty users of a server are on one side of the bridge, and the server they are trying to access is located on the other side! In this case, the bridge is worthless, because it needs to forward every packet destined for the server. The bridge is a data link level device, looking only at the destination address, so to benefit from using a bridge, you have to keep in mind the placement of the servers and users. In other words, what traffic are you trying to block and who are you trying to block it from?

Tip #26 from John	Bridges are pretty much legacy hardware; rather than thinking about using bridges, think about using switches instead.

THE 5/4/3 RULE

While on the subject of repeaters, I need to mention the 5/4/3 rule. There cannot be more than five repeated segments between any two stations. There cannot be more than four repeaters between any two stations. And of the five cable segments, only three can be populated. This is often referred to as the 5/4/3 rule; 5 segments, 4 repeaters, 3 populated.

In the next section, you will see how easy it is to interconnect 10BaseT hubs. You have to be careful about daisy-chaining hubs, because these hubs are repeaters themselves. It's awfully easy to toss in another hub to service a new cubicle cluster or addition, and although it may work, you might then later add the straw that breaks the camel's back without realizing it. Remember that any path between two stations cannot cross more than five cable segments, more than four repeaters or hubs, or more than three populated cable segments.

10BASET, 100BASET, AND HUBS

You have seen some of the disadvantages of the bus topology, and one of the nice things about 10BaseT/100BaseT is that it is wired in a star topology, as shown in Figure 3.7. By *star*, I mean that from a central point, in this case the hub, the wiring can radiate out to the workstations in any direction. The 10Base5 and 10Base2 you looked at earlier requires the cable to go from point to point to point, and you wind up with one long cable snaking through the building.

Figure 3.7
10BaseT and
100BaseT require
hubs, which are
multiport repeaters.

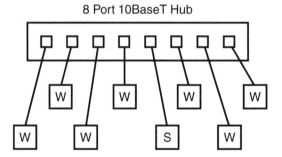

8 Port 10BaseT Hub

S = Server
W = Workstation

10BaseT/100BaseT require hubs, which are really nothing more than multiport repeaters. In Figure 3.7, you have a server and seven workstations plugged in to an eight-port hub. Even though each workstation physically has its own piece of wire, logically you can think of this as only one piece of wire. Or, referring to the earlier discussion, this is one collision domain. This concept is very important; there is no intelligence in the hub doing any checking of any type, it is simply putting the signal out to all the ports.

Seven workstations and one server isn't enough, so assume you use one hub as the "root" at the top of the tree, and then plug in other hubs, as shown in Figure 3.8. Now, how many collision domains do you have?

Figure 3.8
There are nine hubs shown here: one "master" at the top of the tree, and eight others leading to workstations, but it is still only one logical wire, or one collision domain.

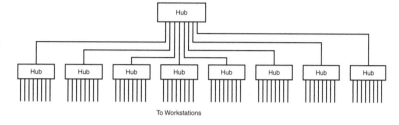

To Workstations

The answer is still one; you can think of it as one big piece of wire. In order to limit the collision domain, you would have to think in terms of bridges, switches, routers, or other physical segments by adding another NIC to the server; hubs aren't going to limit the collision domain.

Even though the wiring is physically done in a star, it's a "logical" bus topology. One of the nice things about hubs and the star topology is that each station gets its own piece of wire, which vastly simplifies troubleshooting. If the cable going to Tom's workstation gets cut or damaged, only Tom is affected; everyone else keeps working.

PART
I
CH
3

Tip #27 from
John

Make sure you document your network as you grow it. Using hubs makes additions and changes so simple and so quick, that you can easily wind up with things working, but no idea how it all plugs together. There is nothing more frustrating when troubleshooting than staring at an unlabeled cable going into a hub port; you know the cable is being used, because the link light is lit, but you have no idea which machine is using it!

Hubs come in two flavors: dumb and smart. Dumb hubs only do their job, and if you suspect a faulty port or problem with the hub, you have to physically inspect the hub or try a different port. There is no management or statistical information.

By *smart*, I mean *manageable*. Each vendor provides some sort of management console utility and, from this application, you can actually see a nice picture of the hub on your screen, lights and all. You can enable and disable ports, look at activity at the port level, get the status of the power supplies, and all other kinds of bells and whistles.

In a small environment, dumb hubs should be sufficient and will save you money. In a larger environment, such as a campus or large office installation, the extra dollars for manageable hubs would be well spent. If the hub in question is in a wiring closet halfway across campus, or in another office building, being able to check it out without making the trip is almost a necessity.

As you replace hubs, or purchase new ones, consider buying hubs with 10/100 ports; these ports operate at either 10Mbps or 100Mbps, giving you a gradual upgrade path as you move to 100BaseT from 10BaseT.

CABLING 10BASET AND 100BASET NETWORKS

If you want to memorize anything about wiring 10BaseT networks, memorize Category 5 cabling and 100 meters! The 100 meters is the key; that is how far your workstation or server can be from the hub. 100 meters is about 328 feet, or a touch longer than a football field.

Locate your hub in a central position if possible. You can think of the 100 meter specification as the radius of a circle. You can go 100 meters in any direction, which means one hub can service up to a 200 meter circle. If you plan to do your own wiring or act as the first line of defense for troubleshooting, you should invest in some sort of pair scanner or cabling test equipment. If nothing else you can use the pair scanner to get the length of any suspect runs, and most will have an "activate hub" function. This lights up the link light on the hub and the scanner buzzes to indicate network activity; instead of an activity light such as a NIC or hub has, the scanner uses noise. Using a tool like this is infinitely better and easier than saying to one of your end users, "Can you log out for a minute? I need to use that network cable for a minute".

If you are in a newer building, you probably have a premises distribution scheme already in place. In a premises distribution scheme, horizontal runs go from a wiring closet on each floor to the cubicles and offices. These horizontal runs are then terminated at punch-down blocks in the wiring closet. There are vertical runs that go from a central location to the wiring closet on each floor, as shown in Figure 3.9.

The connectivity is done with cross connects. For example, you go to the third floor, and cross-connect the horizontal run leading to John's office to one of the vertical pairs, say pair number 288. Now, down in the central location, pair 288 effectively goes all the way to John's office, and you can make it data or phone by connecting at the central point. Making a horizontal run either phone or data is as simple as making the correct cross connections.

Those of us in older buildings wind up with hubs mounted wherever space can be found, and the wiring is often enough to make the heartiest of network administrators run screaming from the electrical closet, which will be doing double duty as a wiring closet for the network.

There are many ways to get around the distance limitation of 100 meters. The simplest one is to remember that one hub can be plugged in to another hub. For example, the setup shown in Figure 3.10 would reach 400 meters.

Figure 3.9
In a premises distribution scheme, the connectivity between vertical runs and horizontal is done with cross connects.

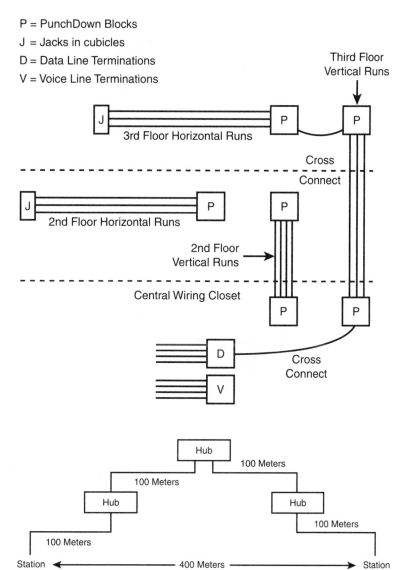

P = PunchDown Blocks
J = Jacks in cubicles
D = Data Line Terminations
V = Voice Line Terminations

Third Floor
Vertical Runs

J — 3rd Floor Horizontal Runs — P   P

Cross
Connect

J — 2nd Floor Horizontal Runs — P   P

2nd Floor
Vertical Runs

Central Wiring Closet   P   P

D

Cross
Connect

V

Figure 3.10
One of the simplest ways to get around the 100 meter limitation is to plug one hub in to another. Here, the range is 400 meters. Don't forget about the 5/4/3 rule though!

Hub

100 Meters

100 Meters

Hub   Hub

100 Meters

100 Meters

Station ◄——————— 400 Meters ———————► Station

Don't forget that the hubs are repeaters, so keep the 5/4/3 rule in mind, and keep your "hub tree" shallow. A lot also depends on the vendor's hardware. Some hubs have BNC connectors on them, and they can be attached together by running a piece of thinnet. Some have AUI connectors that would let you use an external MAU, which would even let you interconnect using fiber, thick ethernet, or some other method. Ask your vendor and read the documentation if distance is a concern.

CABLING CATEGORIES

In the early 90s, the Electronic Industries Association (EIA) and the Telecommunications Industry Association (TIA) laid out various cabling standards. Basically, different categories of cabling are suitable for different application. You can see from Table 3.2 that Category 3 cable would be sufficient for 10BaseT, which is why you often hear that it might be possible to run 10BaseT over existing phone wiring; that cable is most likely Category 3.

Category 4 cable is suitable for 10BaseT and token ring. The maximum bandwidth of Category 4 is 20MB, and a 16MB token ring falls below that.

TABLE 3.2 CATEGORIES OF UTP CABLE

Category	Description	Impedance	Maximum Bandwidth
Category 3	24 AWG solid wire	100 ohms	16MHz
Category 4	24 AWG solid wire	100 ohms	20MHz
Category 5	22 or 24 AWG solid wire	100 ohms	100MHz

Tip #28 from
John

Resistance is an electrical characteristic that is measured in ohms. Copper wire, although an excellent conductor of electricity, still has some resistance. An *ohm*, technically, is the amount of resistance in which a potential difference of one volt produces a current of one ampere. Having said that, don't confuse it with "'ohm on the range!'"

But the actual cost of the cable is negligible, especially if you looked into the difference in cost between Category 3 and Category 5. What really costs when dealing with cabling is the installation. If you are putting in new wire, make sure that it is at least Category 5, which would set you up for fast ethernet, even if you are currently only running 10BaseT. And pull more than you think you will use; it's as much trouble for the installer to pull one cable to some obscure location in the building as it is for him to pull four!

EIGHT POSITION RJ45

An RJ45 connector can terminate up to four pairs. Two of these pairs are required for 10BaseT or 100BaseT. The pin assignments and color coding are shown in Table 3.3. A quick look at Table 3.3 shows that even though you are laying down four pairs, only two pairs are actually used.

TABLE 3.3 EIA/TIA-568B AND AT&T258A CONNECTOR SPECIFICATIONS

Pin	Symbol	Function	Pair Number	Color
1	TD+	Transmit Data Plus	Pair 2	White/Orange
2	TD-	Transmit Data Minus	Pair 2	Orange
3	RD+	Receive Data Plus	Pair 3	White/Green

Pin	Symbol	Function	Pair Number	Color
4	NC	None	Pair 1	Blue
5	NC	None	Pair 1	White/Blue
6	RD-	Receive Data Minus	Pair 3	Green
7	NC	None	Pair 4	White/Brown
8	NC	None	Pair 4	Brown

The connector and pin numbers of the RJ45 plug and the RJ45 jack are shown in Figure 3.11.

Figure 3.11
The pin numbers for the RJ45 plug and the RJ45 jack.

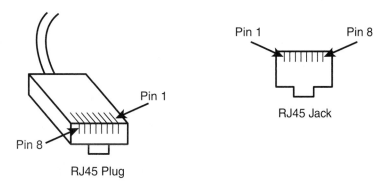

STRAIGHT-THROUGH AND CROSSOVER CABLES

Normally, when connecting a 10BaseT or 100BaseT NIC to the hub, you will use a straight-through cable. A straight-through cable is wired like it sounds, and the pinouts are shown in Table 3.4.

TABLE 3.4   STRAIGHT 10BaseT/100BaseT

Pin	Color	Color	Pin
1	White/Orange	White/Orange	1
2	Orange	Orange	2
3	White/Green	White/Green	3
4	Blue	Blue	4
5	White/Blue	White/Blue	5
6	Green	Green	6
7	White/Brown	White/Brown	7
8	Brown	Brown	8

Depending on the vendor's implementation, some hubs have an Out port. You can use normal wiring, that is, a straight-through cable and go from this Out port to connect another hub. If your hub does not have an Out port, or if you want to attach more than one hub, you need to use a crossover cable.

In a crossover cable, the transmit and receive pairs are crossed, TD+ goes to RD+, TD-goes to RD-, and so on. You implement a crossover cable as shown in Table 3.5. I am only going to show the pertinent pins: pins one and two and pins three and six. Because the other pins aren't used for 10BaseT/100BaseT, it doesn't matter how you pin them out.

TABLE 3.5   10BaseT/100BaseT Crossover Cable

Pin	Straight End	Crossed End	Pin	Function
1	White/Orange	White/Green	1	TD+ to TD-
2	Orange	Green	2	TD- to RD-
3	White/Green	White/Orange	3	RD+ to TD+
6	Green	Orange	6	RD- to RD+

Tip #29 from
John

You can use a crossover cable to implement a two-node network. This is fantastic if you have two computers at home or if you want to see whether running your new 10/100 cards at 100 will make a difference, but you don't have any 100BaseT hubs.

TOKEN RING

You can't think of token ring without thinking of IBM. The token ring standard is IEEE 802.5. Token ring isn't nearly as prevalent as ethernet, it costs more, it's more complicated, and if you use shielded twisted pair along with the IBM Data Connectors and DB9 connectors, it is harder to work with.

THE RING

Token ring is physically wired as a star, which, from the discussion of 10BaseT/100BaseT, I like. If it is wired in a star, where does the ring business come from? Each station in the ring acts as a unidirectional repeater. The cabling has two pairs of wires: one pair is used to transmit to the next station in the ring, the other pair is used to receive from the upstream station. Each station copies the data from its receive pair onto its transmit pair; it doesn't matter whether the data is meant for that station or not. So the effect created is a continuous ring from station to station.

The ring operates at one of two speeds, either 4Mbps or 16Mbps. You cannot have mixed speeds on the same ring, by which I mean that all stations are at 4Mbps, or all stations are at 16Mbps. The first station that enters the ring determines the speed that all subsequent stations use. If you try to enter the ring with a NIC configured for the wrong speed, your attempt to enter the ring will fail.

THE MAU AND THE CABLE

To get the star topology in 10BaseT/100BaseT, you used hubs. In token ring, the concept is the same but you use passive concentrators—or multiple access units (MAU)—instead of hubs.

Tip #30 from *John*	Don't confuse this MAU with the other MAU abbreviation (Medium Attachment Unit) used with Ethernet!

A traditional MAU is really nothing more than relays that are energized when a workstation enters the ring. Plugging a connector in to the MAU isn't sufficient to energize the relay; a workstation sends a voltage over its transmit pair that triggers the relay, allowing the workstation to enter the ring. Because the MAU would be in the wiring closets, the cables would always be plugged in; if this voltage was not used to energize the relay, a workstation would be in the ring even if it was off!

When a workstation is about to enter the ring, but before the relay is energized, the transmit pair of the workstation's cable is connected to its own receive pair. The NIC sends itself data frames to test itself, and the very nature of this also tests the NIC's own cable at the same time. In essence, at this point you have a ring of one, and if the adapter test passes, the NIC brings up the voltage which energizes the relay in the MAU, thus inserting itself into the ring.

I say traditional MAU because in the dark ages, when all this was starting out, you ran token ring over shielded twisted pair wiring with big hermaphroditic connectors. Compared to UTP wiring, STP is heavy and bulky! It has two pairs, and each pair has its own foil shield. These two shielded pairs are then shielded with one made of metal braid, and finally all this is put in the outer sheathing. The hermaphroditic connector was designed by IBM and is called the IBM Data Connector. These connectors are very interesting in that they are genderless. There is no male version or female version. In fact, not only will they plug in to the MAU, but they will plug in to each other; you can extend a cable or bypass a MAU in this fashion.

Now, token ring can be run over UTP and RJ45 connectors such as 10BaseT, and the concentrators or MAUs certainly don't have relays in them! If you were to walk by a computer room and see a modern MAU, feeding a token ring over unshielded twisted pair wiring, you would not be able to tell the difference between it and a 10BaseT hub. In fact, it's wired exactly like 10BaseT, the only difference being the RI and RO ports used to connect MAUs together.

A MAU has two ports on it labeled RI, for Ring In, and RO, for Ring Out. The RI and RO ports are used to connect MAUs together, and create larger networks. You take a cable from the Ring Out of one MAU into the Ring In of another MAU (see Figure 3.12).

Figure 3.12
MAUs are connected together by using the Ring In and Ring Out ports.

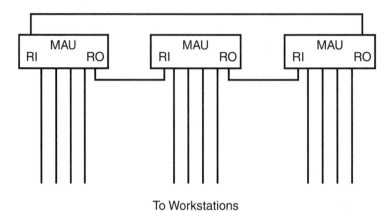

To Workstations

At the NIC end of the wire, when using the traditional shielded twisted pair cabling, you will be using a DB9 connector. The pinouts are given in Table 3.6. Pins 2–4, 7, and 8 are not used.

TABLE 3.6   DB9 CONNECTOR PINOUTS FOR STP CABLING

Pin	Function	Color
1	Receive+	Red
5	Transmit-	Black
6	Receive-	Green
9	Transmit+	Orange

In Table 3.7 , the pinouts are given for using RJ45 connectors and unshielded twisted pair cabling.

TABLE 3.7   RJ45 CONNECTOR PINOUTS FOR UTP CABLING

Pin	Function	Color
3	White/Green	Transmit-
4	Blue	Receive+
5	White/Blue	Receive-
6	Green	Transmit+

THE TOKEN AND ACCESS CONTROL

Unlike ethernet, the access mechanism to the wire isn't a free-for-all, but is rather deterministic versus contention-based. Like in the movie *Highlander*, there can be only one; only one station is allowed to talk at a time. In order to talk, you have to have permission in the form of a token.

The *token* is a special three-byte message that is always circulating around the ring when there is no other traffic. It's not really a special three-byte message, but rather the token bit is set to 0 in the access control byte. A "normal" frame also has an access control byte, only in a normal frame, there is a lot that follows the access control byte, such as frame control information, source and destination, data, and so on. The token is nothing but a start delimiter, the access control byte, and an end delimiter, there is no data or other control functions that are in data frames.

Each workstation sends the token on to the next, by copying the token off its transmit pair and onto its receive pair. When a station wants to transmit, it waits for the token. Only this time, instead of sending the token, the station sends its data instead. As I have already discussed, each workstation keeps the frames circulating; it doesn't matter whether they are the destination or not, the idea is to get the data frame back to the sender.

At some point, the data frame arrives at the intended destination; this station doesn't remove the frame from the ring, but makes a local copy and sends the frame on like all the other stations. When the frame has traveled around the ring, the sender receives it and compares it to what it originally sent to check for errors. The sender then generates a new token and passes it on down the line, and the process begins again.

THE ACTIVE MONITOR

When all goes well, the token or data continuously circles the ring. If something happens to the token and it is destroyed, perhaps by a transmission error, then what? Every ring has one station known as the *active monitor*; however, any station can take over the role of active monitor if necessary. If the active monitor leaves the ring, there is an automatic election process that occurs that forces another station to take on the role of active monitor.

It would be the job of the active monitor to notice the absence of the token and to regenerate it. In addition to keeping tabs on the token, the active monitor also is responsible for other functions, such as timing for the ring, removing frames that are constantly circulating, and more. How would the active monitor know that a frame was constantly circulating? In the token ring frame, there is an access control byte. One of the bits in the access control byte is the monitor bit. When the active monitor sees a frame and this bit is set to zero, the active monitor sets it to one. Only the active monitor sets this bit. If the frame comes back again with the monitor bit set to one, the active monitor removes the frame, because it knows that it has already seen the frame, and the frame's original transmitter has failed to remove it.

PRIORITY AND RESERVATION

As you have seen by now, the access method for token ring is far more complex than the free-for-all method that ethernet uses. In the access control byte that I have already discussed, there are reservation bits that can be set by a workstation in an attempt to reserve the next free token. There are three reservation bits and three priority bits.

The format of the access control byte is PPPTMRRR:

- PPP—Priority bits; 000 is low, and 111 is high.
- M—Monitor bit; 0 is the initial value. It will be a 1 if the active monitor has set this bit. I discussed this bit earlier when talking about the active monitor removing frames that were continually circling the ring.
- T—Token bit; 0 indicates a token, and 1 indicates a frame.
- RRR—Reservation bits; like the priority bits, 000 is low, and 111 is high.

Workstations can have a priority assigned to them, so assume that you have four workstations in a ring, as shown in Figure 3.13. Grace has a priority of 2, George has a priority of 4, and Moon and Dragon both have standard priorities of 0. Only stations with a priority equal to or better than the token's priority can capture the token and transmit data.

Figure 3.13
Token ring has the capability to attempt and reserve the next token based on priority.

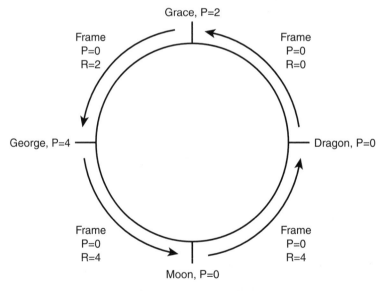

Grace, P=2

Frame P=0 R=2

Frame P=0 R=0

George, P=4

Dragon, P=0

Frame P=0 R=4

Frame P=0 R=4

Moon, P=0

P = Priority
R = Reservation

Now examine this and see exactly how it works. The ring is idle, so the token is circulating with a priority of 0. Dragon wishes to transmit, so Dragon removes the token and puts his data frame on the wire. As the frame reaches Grace, she decides that she would like to transmit, so in an attempt to reserve the next token, Grace sets the reservation bits to her priority, which is 2. So now Dragon's original frame is circulating the ring and the priority bits in the access control byte have been set to 2. As the frame passes George, he decides that he is ready to talk, so George ups the value of the reservation bits to his priority, which is 4.

Now you move to Figure 3.14. The frame has finally made it around to Dragon, at which time he absorbs his frame, and generates a new token, and sets the priority of the token to 4, as shown in Figure 3.14. Dragon sets the token priority to 4 because it is his turn to generate the token (he absorbed his frame), and the reservation bits had a value of 4 by the time his frame made it back to him.

Figure 3.14
When Dragon generates the new token, it has a priority of 4.

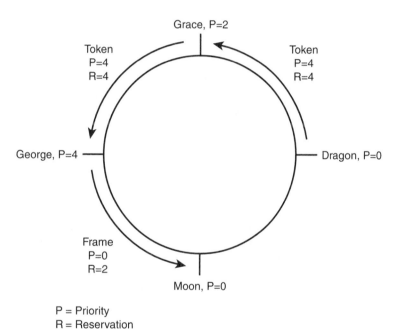

Grace, P=2

Token
P=4
R=4

Token
P=4
R=4

George, P=4

Dragon, P=0

Frame
P=0
R=2

Moon, P=0

P = Priority
R = Reservation

Because the new token has a priority of 4, Grace can't touch it. So the token circles by George and he seizes it; George is the one who originally upped the ante on the token with his higher priority. George now generates a frame. If you raise the priority of the token, you are ultimately responsible for putting it back, so George's frame has a priority of 4, but George sets the reservation bits to 2; he remembers what they were the first time the token came through his hands in Figure 3.13.

With the reservation bits set to a value of 2, it looks like Grace with a priority of 2 stands a pretty good chance to get the next token; Moon or Dragon won't be able to touch it with their priorities of 0. George's frame now circles the ring, and comes back to George, who absorbs it and generates a new token with a priority of 2, as shown in Figure 3.15.

Figure 3.15
Having achieved seizing the token, George now generates a new one with a priority of 2, the one that Grace is trying for.

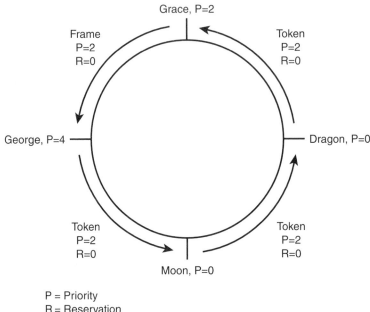

P = Priority
R = Reservation

The token that George generates with a priority of 2 circles around the ring to Grace; Moon and Dragon don't have a shot at it. Grace then seizes the token and transmits a frame with a priority of 2, and a reservation of 0. When this frame has made it around the ring and Grace absorbs it, Grace then generates a new token with the reservation and priority bits set to 0.

CONTENTION VERSUS TOKEN PASSING

Like almost any subject related to networking, a debate over contention-based access methods such as ethernet or a deterministic approach such as token ring can generate some very fervent arguments. Network administrators tend to hold rather strong opinions on almost any subject! Neither contention nor token passing is inherently better than the other; it depends on the load on the network.

On a network with only a light load, meaning one with very little traffic, contention-based access is fine. However, as a token ring advocate would be quick to point out, when you start increasing the number of machines and consequently increase the load, the network begins to slow down. This is true, but by now, you have seen numerous examples of breaking up an ethernet network into multiple collision domains. Remember, you are competing for time on the wire only with those in your collision domain. An ethernet network of 1000 machines would, as you might imagine, have very poor response times. But, an ethernet network of 1000 workstations, broken up into 50 collision domains of 20, would run fine.

On a heavily loaded network, you wouldn't want to use a contention-based access method, but would rather have the orderly "wait your turn" method of token passing. However, the end result is still going to be the same; workstations waiting for the token in order to transmit.

All things being equal, token passing would perform better under heavy loads, and contention-based access would be as good, possibly better under light loads. Contention doesn't have nearly the overhead of token passing. But not all things should be equal if you understand how to correctly implement the technology. If you understand contention based access, CSMA/CD, you aren't going to build huge collision domains when using ethernet.

FIBER DISTRIBUTED DATA INTERFACE (FDDI)

I am going to only quickly touch on Fiber Distributed Data Interface (FDDI). You seldom see fiber at the desktop; if you do, that workstation needs high bandwidth, perhaps because it moves large graphics files. If you understand token ring, you understand FDDI. FDDI, which operates at 100Mbps, is many times faster than token ring, but still uses a token passing access method. FDDI is a TIMED token ring. That is, if a station does not see a token go by every so often (the time is elected by the stations on the ring), then the station will declare a problem on the ring and the ring will reset.

You can implement FDDI over fiber optic cabling, which uses light instead of electricity for signaling, or you can implement fiber over UTP wiring. The UTP is cheaper and easier to implement, but the distance limitations are huge compared to fiber optic cabling. FDDI over UTP is know as *Copper Distributed Data Interface (CDDI)*.

FDDI, with its high-bandwidth, token-based access method, is suitable for network backbones, or stations that have enormous resource demands, such as a video or CAD application. Stations can be either dual attached or single attached to the ring. A station connecting to both rings is called a Class A station, and a station connecting to only one ring is a Class B station. FDDI is often implemented with dual counter rotating rings. One of the rings is primary, and one is secondary. Traffic normally moves only on the primary ring, but in the event of a failure of the primary ring, the secondary ring becomes operational. A Class A station can participate in the ring reconfiguration when the secondary goes active; Class B stations can't, because they are attached to only one ring.

If a dual connected station (Class A) in the ring is removed, the ring "wraps." That is, the two stations on either side of the station that was removed now connect the secondary ring to the primary ring. Data now circles over the two as one big ring. This also plays a roll in determining the size of the ring (distance-wise) because the ring could double in length when a wrap occurs. Of course if two stations are removed before the problem is fixed, you end up with two rings, a bad thing. You wind up with two rings because, when the second station is removed, the ring dutifully wraps again.

FDDI does handle the token in a different fashion from token ring, though. In token ring, there is only one token or one frame on the ring at a time. Because the speed requirements of FDDI are so high, a station generates a new token immediately after it has sent its frame. With this implementation, it is possible to have more than one frame on the wire at the same time.

SWITCHES

Bandwidth: Can you ever have too much? Most likely not; you seldom hear people complaining that their Internet connection is too fast! With today's switching technologies, you can deliver some serious bandwidth to the desktop, and possibly simplify your network configuration at the same time.

As your network has grown, assume that you have taken great pains to segment it correctly, so that traffic is contained logically; in other words, you might have a business segment and a production segment, so that the business traffic isn't seen on the production side, and vice versa. Then a new system is being implemented, which entails large graphics files being moved to and from the server. You are faced with putting in yet another segment to keep this new traffic contained.

Although this sounds great, there are a few problems. One is that there are always common machines, such as email servers, that need to be seen by everyone. The other is IP addressing, as each physical segment will require its own IP network address. You might also have only one pipe leading out to the corporate WAN or the Internet. The ideal would be a large magic box that would let you plug in a machine to any port and let it see any resource, but still contain traffic. A large enterprise switch will do this for you, but examine the idea first on a smaller scale.

The switch shown in Figure 3.16 has 10BaseT ports leading to the workstations and a 100BaseT port leading to the server. The switch is going to do only what its name implies: switch the packet to the appropriate destination, either one of the other 10BaseT ports, or out the 100BaseT port to the server. In essence, you have given each of the workstations its own private 10BaseT network. The collision domain is none!

Figure 3.16
A simple switch, with 10BaseT ports leading to the workstations and a 100BaseT port leading to the server.

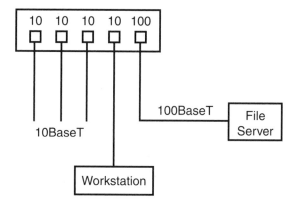

The fat pipe leading to the server is a necessity. If you take 10 country roads, and feed them all onto another country road, you obtain no benefit at all, assuming that there is traffic. In fact, you would shortly find that the traffic was backing up on the road you are feeding; it's only a country road itself, and now it has to handle the traffic from 10 others! On the other hand, if you take your 10 country roads and feed them onto an interstate, traffic could move right off the country roads and keep moving even better with no problems at all.

Another analogy is this. Take a garden hose, put 10 taps on it, and connect another garden hose to each tap. Turn on the water, and you get only a trickle at each of your 10 hoses. Now, replace the main feed with a fire hose. Tap it 10 times with garden hoses and turn on the water. You will have more than enough pressure at each of your 10 garden hoses. In this scenario, the fire hose is the fat 100BaseT pipe leading to the server, and the 10BaseT connections are the garden hoses.

Each switch port delineates one collision domain. Switched to the desktop would be the ideal; but you can also hang a hub or hubs off each switch port (see Figure 3.17).

Figure 3.17
Because each switch port defines a collision domain, you can take advantage of a small switch and still deliver benefits to your users, as opposed to switching right to the desktop.

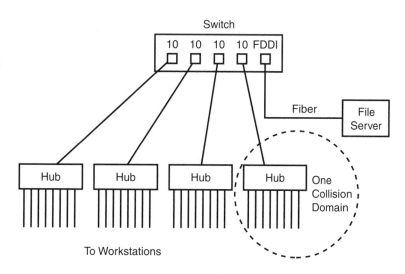

In Figure 3.17, there is an eight-port hub on each switch port. This limits the collision domain to eight workstations and lets you get a lot more workstations using each switch port, which also reduces your cost.

A small switch is fine in a small environment, but if you attempted to build a large network using them, you would be back to your original problem. The ideal would be to plug in anywhere and see what you need to see, and if you had all these small switches, you would need to tie them all together. And to benefit from the switches, you would need to use a really fast pipe to act as the backbone, as shown in Figure 3.18.

Figure 3.18
It would take a really fast pipe to tie all these switches together. Otherwise, you would start to lose the benefits you were after in the first place.

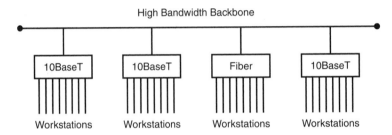

The $64,000 question is What would you use for your fast pipe? And also notice in Figure 3.18 that you have some 10BaseT switches, some 100BaseT switches, and some fiber. The backbone needs to handle all this and be capable of some huge bandwidth.

In a large enterprise class switch, you purchase what is essentially an empty chassis. Across the back of this chassis is a high speed backplane, 2Gbps or even higher. This high speed backplane is the mystery fast pipe shown in Figure 3.18. Instead of discreet standalone switches, you purchase switch modules that slide into the chassis and plug in to the backplane. The backplane provides the super-high-speed pipe that ties all the switch modules together. It's a collapsed backbone; the network is the backplane. The modules are how you access the network (backplane). The only question you need to ask is How fast do I need to access the network?

For example, you might take 10BaseT switch ports out to the desktop or to shared hubs. You could then put in a fiber module, and feed your servers off of this. Workstations that need high speed, such as those moving large graphics, you can give a 100BaseT port. But no matter what, you can plug in to any port and see anything. You have only one network segment, but its bandwidth capabilities are so huge that you don't have to worry about it.

These switch modules will be standards out the front, such as 10BaseT, 100BaseT, fiber, and so on. Across the back, they are proprietary to the vendor. The fact that they are proprietary really doesn't matter; you never see that anyway. What does matter is the huge bandwidth available to tie all the switch modules together. Another key point is that you can mix and match the modules to your heart's content. You can start out with only some 10BaseT modules, and you can slide 100BaseT modules, or fiber, token ring, and more into the slot right next to them. So a switch of this nature lets give you a flat network regardless of the topologies used.

If the entire organization is running off this one enterprise switch, you can bet that you want to have management capabilities. If you remember the smart hubs I talked about earlier, it's the same concept. The switch vendor has management software that lets you look at the details of the ports, the backplane, even the power supplies. An example of switch management software is shown in Figure 3.19.

Figure 3.19
This is Cabletron's Spectrum Element Manager looking at a Cabletron MMAC-PLUS, now known as the SmartSwitch 9000.

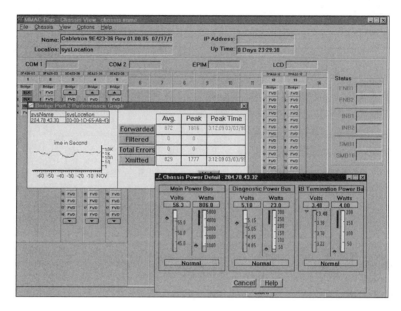

ROUTERS

So far, the hardware you have looked at has operated at a very low level. The repeater doesn't look at the packet at all; it simply sends the signal along its way. The hubs are simply repeaters, and the bridges and switches look only at the destination hardware address of the packets. The router is the first device you have seen that operates at the network layer. The router reads just enough of the IP (or IPX, Appletalk, and so on) header to make a decision as to how to forward the packet. Dealing with network level information, routers are used to connect networks together:

```
DLC:   ----- DLC Header -----
DLC:
DLC:   Frame 227 arrived at  09:55:14.8896; frame size is 74 (004A hex) bytes.
DLC:   Destination = Station cisco 76D1B2
DLC:   Source      = Station Prteon8432BE
DLC:   Ethertype   = 0800 (IP)
DLC:
IP:  ----- IP Header -----
IP:
IP: Version = 4, header length = 20 bytes
IP: Type of service = 00
IP:      000. .... = routine
```

```
IP:         ...0 .... = normal delay
IP:         .... 0... = normal throughput
IP:         .... .0.. = normal reliability
IP: Total length     = 60 bytes
IP: Identification   = 41733
IP: Flags            = 0X
IP:         .0.. .... = may fragment
IP:         ..0. .... = last fragment
IP: Fragment offset  = 0 bytes
IP: Time to live     = 32 seconds/hops
IP: Protocol         = 1 (ICMP)
IP: Header checksum  = AD2A (correct)
IP: Source address      = [204.78.43.220], TARZAN
IP: Destination address = [206.101.132.1]
IP: No options
IP:
```

Of the packet fragment shown previously, the router is concerned only with the destination address at the IP level, in this case, 206.101.132.1.

A router always has at least two interfaces, each leading to a different network, as shown in Figure 3.20.

Figure 3.20
The router always has at least two interfaces, possibly more, and is used to connect networks together.

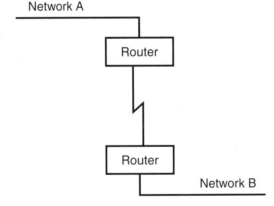

The router can be a dedicated device, doing nothing but routing, or it can be nondedicated. If you put two NICs in your server, it can act as a router between the two segments, but also still functions as a file server. An obvious consideration here is the load on the server; if it is already busy enough as a file, print, and application server, you certainly don't want to add to the load by also using it as a router.

Not only does the router connect disparate networks, but it is a solution to connecting differing topologies together. One of the router interfaces might be ethernet, whereas the other might be token ring. Workstations on either network can access resources without regard to their being on the token ring or the ethernet.

SAMPLE NETWORK IMPLEMENTATIONS USING ETHERNET

You have seen in previous figures the bus topology and the idea that hubs can be plugged in to other hubs to expand the network. But what if you have a legacy 10Base5 or 10Base2 network, and want to move to UTP wiring? Do you need to rip the entire network out and do it all at once, or is there a simpler migration path? The answer, fortunately, is the latter; there is a nice, easy way to do it one machine at time if you so desire.

Consider the network shown in Figure 3.21. Here, you have a legacy bus installation, and you want to move to UTP and hubs. Rather than rip it all out, you can simply attach the hub to your existing cable.

Figure 3.21
This hybrid network allows you to move machines off the bus and onto the new UTP network one machine at a time.

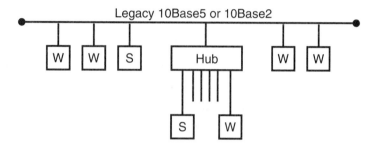

Given the setup in Figure 3.21, you can now move one machine at a time off the bus and onto the new UTP wiring. It wouldn't matter whether the machines you move are servers or workstations. Although you have two physical wiring implementations going simultaneously, this is also one logical piece of wire; and thus one collision domain.

Another approach to leaving the legacy network behind and moving to UTP wiring would be to put another NIC in the server and then begin migrating workstations, as shown in Figure 3.22.

Figure 3.22
You can put another NIC in the server that uses UTP wiring, and then begin moving workstations off the legacy network.

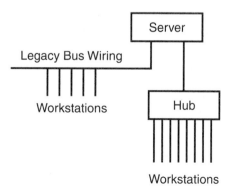

When all the workstations have been moved off the legacy cabling, you can then remove the old NIC from the server. Although this approach will certainly work, there are a few points to consider. One is that you now have two physical segments. In and of itself, this is no problem; indeed, it could be a benefit. With two physical segments, you have reduced the traffic on each side, and also you now have two collision domains, at least while the migration is going on. But if you use IP, you now need to deal with the IP addressing issues that having two segments raises. Depending on the number of IP addresses you have available, this might not be a problem. IP addressing and subnetting are covered in Chapter 28.

In the network shown in Figure 3.23, you are feeding the desktop with hubs and taking these hubs back to a switch port.

Figure 3.23
In this scenario, the desktops are on a shared hub and the hub is plugged in to a switch port. This limits the collision domain, but is still one logical network segment.

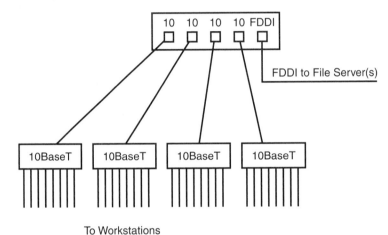

Now take a closer look at Figure 3.23. The collision domain stops at the switch port, so the size of the collision domain at the desktop is dependant on how many workstations are plugged in to the hub(s). So, you have limited the collision domains nicely. You have a fat pipe leading from the server to the switch, which is necessary in order to benefit from the switch, as I discussed earlier. How many networks are there?

The answer might surprise you, but it is one. Even though there are wires going all over the place, and even though you have multiple collision domains, you can think of this network as simply one big piece of wire. Is this really so? Assume you have bound IPX to the server with a frame type of Ethernet_802.2 net=BA5EBA11. You then add another server, and bind IPX with a frame type of Ethernet_802.2, net=BACB0. Both of those servers start squawking router configuration errors! The hubs are nothing but repeaters, and the switches are doing nothing but limiting the collision domain. Physically, it acts as one piece of wire, one logical network; there is nothing implemented here that is dividing things up into multiple networks.

PROTOCOL ANALYZERS

For any serious network analysis or baselining, you simply have to have a protocol analyzers. A protocol analyzer is essentially a phone tap for the network. Just as a phone tap lets you listen in on a phone conversation, a protocol analyzer lets you listen to the wire. You can use it for monitoring utilization for baselining, or you can actually capture and decode packets for troubleshooting purposes. When you need a protocol analyzer, nothing else will do!

The first thing a vendor of a client/server–type application does when you are having performance problems is to blame the network! With a protocol analyzer, you can actually watch and capture the entire conversation, and prove or disprove the vendor's claim. Without it, you wind up in a finger pointing contest, with the vendor claiming that "we aren't having this problem anywhere else."

The few fragments of packet traces you saw in this chapter and in the next were obtained by a protocol analyzer. Novell has two offerings in this area, ManageWise and LANalyzer. The cost of LANalyzer is trivial when you consider the information it will give you about your network, even if you don't capture and analyze packets. The main LANalyzer screen is shown in Figure 3.24.

PART
I
CH
3

Figure 3.24
Remember, when you need a protocol analyzer, nothing else will do!

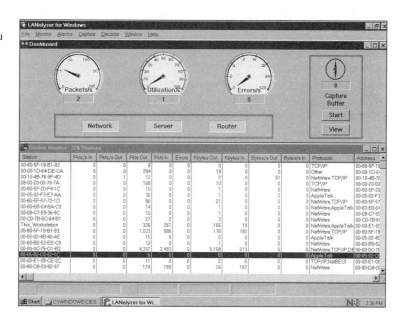

On the main screen, there are 3 gauges for Network, Server, and Router. You can also view the station addresses, packets in, packets out, errors, kilobytes in and out, which protocols are in use, and more. The gauges sound an alarm and their buttons turn red when certain thresholds are exceeded. When this happens, you can click the button in question and see the alarm list (see Figure 3.25).

Figure 3.25
The Network Alarm log shows that `Utilization of 64% exceeded threshold of 40%.`

Notice the NetWare Expert icon in Figure 3.25? Clicking it pulls up LANalyzer Help, which is context sensitive, as shown in Figure 3.26.

Figure 3.26
The context sensitive help provides an explanation, along with suggested actions.

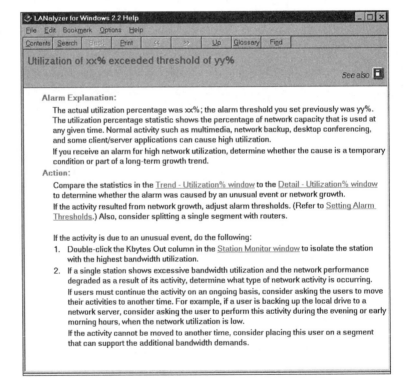

The basics already shown about LANalyzer immediately give you more information about your network than you've ever dreamed about, if you don't have something like it running already. For the more bit-and-byte oriented, you can also capture and decode packets, as shown in Figure 3.27.

Figure 3.27
LANalyzer lets you
capture and decode
packets.

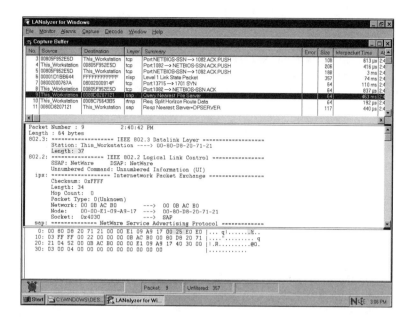

The capturing part is easy, but to make sense of what you are seeing takes an extensive knowledge of the protocols and their behavior. There are three panes shown in Figure 3.27; at the top is the Summary. Here is a high-level view of what is going on. Highlighted in the top pane, for example, is Query Nearest File Server. In the middle pane is the actual decode of the frame, and at the bottom is one that only propeller-heads can appreciate, the actual frame in Hex.

TROUBLESHOOTING

The first step in troubleshooting is to stop and do nothing. Too often, administrators rush in to make unnecessary changes that can actually obscure or compound the real issue. Get as much information as you can; for example, can anyone access the server, or is the problem limited to one workstation? If several workstations can't, but everyone else can, what do those workstations have in common? Are they all plugged in to the same hub?

And a lot depends on the level of expertise you have in-house. There are more small networks than there are large ones, so there might be little or no experience in troubleshooting; it might be that a consultant takes care of the entire shooting match.

Document the network and all changes made to critical components. Sometimes, the most innocuous change can ripple through and cause problems elsewhere on the network; these problems might not start to be noticed for days, and by that time, you might forget that you copied the C: drive from one of the inserting machines to the other.

You need equipment to baseline the network. A *baseline* is the normal average, the way things are when they run normally. For example, in the morning, when everyone is logging in and loading up applications and files, the utilization might be higher, and the response time longer. By mid-morning, the utilization might have gone down, thus improving response time. A user telling you that the network is slow probably doesn't mean much; you need to have a baseline. If the normal response time is X, and this user is getting response times slower than X, is it only the one workstation or is it the network that's really slow?

With a bus topology, you would move the terminating resistor to the halfway point on the wire, and then see whether that segment works. If not, move it halfway down the line again, as often as necessary, until you isolate the problem segment. This is known as half-stepping, and would be much quicker than starting at one end and testing machine by machine. Just the thought of it makes one grateful for 10BaseT/100BaseT, hubs, and UTP wiring!

The failure of a bridge or repeater would be obvious: the other side of the bridge or repeater would disappear! You would find that no one could access any resources that were on the other side of the dead component. The failure of a router would depend on what the router is doing. If you are using it to connect two networks together, your network would be fine; you wouldn't be able to see the other guy's, and vice versa. If the router is there only to connect you to the Internet, you would simply lose your Internet access. The failure of a switch or switch port would also be fairly obvious; you would lose contact with any resources beyond the switch port that delimits your collision domain.

An ethernet card going bad can cause wonderful problems. If the card is jabbering, or constantly talking, no one else can. Or say the NIC loses its capability to listen to the wire; as far as it's concerned, the wire is always quiet, so this workstation will cause serious collisions.

CHAPTER **4**

NETWORKING DATA FLOW

In this chapter

THE OSI MODEL

In the late '70s and early '80s, the International Standards Organization (ISO) began creating a model for Open Systems Interconnect (OSI). Before the explosion of the Web and the adoption of TCP/IP as pretty much a de facto standard (who doesn't support IP?), communicating between different systems was difficult. The idea behind the OSI model was to create a standard that everyone could and would adhere to, thus eliminating the existing complexity caused by differing vendor implementations.

The OSI protocols never really took off, but the model is very useful in discussing networking, particularly at the physical, networking, and transport levels. You will later hear me refer to IP as a network layer protocol, or TCP as a transport layer protocol, and having an understanding of the seven layers of the OSI model is necessary.

The seven layers are the physical, data link, network, transport, session, presentation, and application layers as shown in Figure 4.1.

Figure 4.1
You can remember these layers with the mnemonic "All people seem to need data processing."

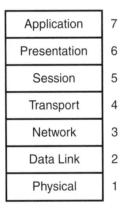

Application	7
Presentation	6
Session	5
Transport	4
Network	3
Data Link	2
Physical	1

Before you take a quick look at the function of each layer, you need to know how the model is supposed to work. It's very much like mailing someone a letter, and in this discussion, that means snail mail, not email!

You have data that you want to communicate to someone; it might be an invitation to a party or a résumé—it doesn't matter what the data is, the process is the same. The first step is to put your data (the letter) into an envelope. The standards are pretty loose where the envelope is concerned, meaning that the post office doesn't care whether you use a white envelope, a green one, a letter sized one or one that is 8 1/2×11. But what does matter is the addressing of the envelope.

You need to put the destination address on the front of the envelope, in the middle. You need to put the source address (what you would normally call the return address) in the upper-left corner of the envelope. You also need to put a stamp in the upper-right corner. Having done this, you are finished and ready to hand the envelope off to the next layer in the process. In other words, you have put a header in front of your data containing all the information necessary for its delivery, and then you hand it off to another layer, in this case, the mailbox in front of your house.

The mailman picks this up in the course of his normal route, and at the post office, it winds up in a bag with others bound for, say, Memphis, Tennessee. The bag is labeled *Memphis*; another header has essentially been placed in front of your original header, the envelope. The bag is then placed on a truck (yet another header at another layer) going through or to Memphis.

At the other end of this equation, the process is reversed. The truck is no longer necessary, so it is discarded (its header is stripped off). The bag is taken off the truck, the letters are removed (another header discarded), and finally, the letter is placed into the recipient's mailbox; when she opens it, she discards the final and original header (the envelope) and the data is in her hands.

The entire process was transparent to you. It really doesn't matter whether the post office had used a truck, train, airplane, or twenty-mule team to move the letter from city to city. Your only responsibility was to put the appropriate header in front of your data, and then to hand it off to the next layer.

The same idea is behind the OSI model. Each layer is responsible for communicating only with the layer immediately above and below itself. For the purposes of this discussion, that is done by putting the appropriate header around the data and then handing it off. Back to the mail analogy; your envelope is a header, and the letter is data. At the mailbag layer, your envelope is only one of many. The mailbag header is *Memphis*, and all the other letters—the contents of the mailbag—are just data. The truck might have many mailbags in it, but the only important thing at the truck layer is that it goes to Memphis, and the rest is all data. This concept of each layer adding a header is shown in Figure 4.2.

Figure 4.2
Each layer receives data from the level above it, adds its own header, and passes it down to the next level.

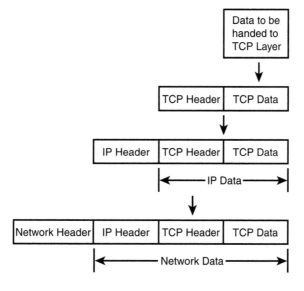

So what are the seven layers and their functions as laid out in the OSI model? Remember, this is a model, not how things necessarily work, so don't get wrapped around the axle over the upper layers. As a network administrator, you will be primarily concerned with the physical, network, and transport layers. So after a brief definition of each layer, you are going to take a more detailed look at how it all comes together by examining a workstation making a request to a server:

- **Physical (layer one)**—The physical layer is plumbing. This is how data is put on the wire. What represents a one? What represents a zero? What types of wires and connectors are used? When can I transmit? How do I know when a transmission is complete? These questions are solved by the plumbing, or physical implementation. For example, in order for two ethernet cards to send data to each other, they have to be cabled correctly, on the same network, and so on. And the rules for accessing the wire to send a packet are different for ethernet, token ring, and fiber.

Tip #31 from *John*	That last sentence is key to the idea that each layer performs its own function, or is its own level of abstraction. Imagine if you needed one version of NetWare to run on ethernet, one version for token ring, and yet another version for fiber? That would be a nightmare. Because the OS is isolated from the type of network interface card (NIC) that is in the server, you can remove your ethernet card and replace it with a token ring, and the only change you need to make is at one layer; in this case, load the token ring driver instead of the ethernet driver.

- **Data link (layer two)**—At the data link layer, a "virtual circuit" is established between the two NICs. Over this circuit, frames, or packets, are acknowledged, flow control is done, and errors are handled. This means that the upper layers do not have to worry about lost or duplicate frames, because this is handled here. You can think of the data link layer working a lot like TCP, which, as you will see later, establishes a connection, and sequences and acknowledges packets.

- **Network (layer three)**—The network layer is concerned with getting the packet to the correct network. Although an ethernet card can send a frame only to another ethernet card on the same physical network segment, the source computer and the destination computer might be on different networks. In this case, the packet would be sent to a router, which would use the information in the network header to route the packet.

- **Transport (layer four)**—The transport layer is concerned with the reliable transfer of data. Packets are sequenced and acknowledged and lost and duplicate packets are handled. There might be a large amount of data handed down to the transport layer for transmission, but the underlying network topology has its own limitations as to what size packets can be transmitted, so the transport layer also breaks the data up into suitably sized bites. It is these "chunks" of data that are tracked and acknowledged.

- **Session (layer five)**—The session layer is used to establish a session between processes. It provides session establishment, maintenance, and teardown.

- **Presentation (layer six)**—This layer formats data to be presented to the application layer.

- **Application (layer seven)**—This is the layer you know and love—or hate, as the case may be. The applications are what starts the whole process flowing. You'd be amazed at what actually occurs on the wire as a result of something as simple as clicking on an icon!

> **Note**
>
> There have been three more layers added to the OSI model, albeit facetiously. These are the political, religious, and financial layers. You can put them on top of the stack in your own order. Although not part of the ISO's model, they certainly reflect reality. Not all the decisions about the network are made by the administrator, and that's where these 3 levels come into play. People get fanatical about NT versus NetWare, IP versus IPX, and so on. The ideal solution might be too expensive, or mandates might come down from the corporate office, and suddenly, a die hard NetWare shop has NT servers cropping up!

Now that your layers are in place, how does the data flow? It flows down the stack from the application on the sending machine, across the wire, and then up the stack to the application on the receiving machine (see Figure 4.3).

PART
I
CH
4

Figure 4.3
Even though data flows up and down the stack, each layer is concerned only with communicating with its counterpart on the other side. Hence the idea of a logical, or virtual connection between the layers.

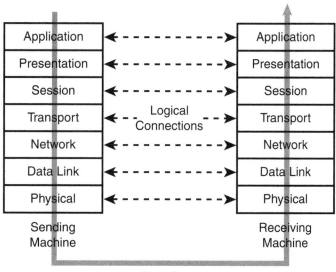

You click the map drive button, and that starts the ball rolling. The command is packaged and put on the wire, its destiny to reach the target machine. What are the virtual connections shown in Figure 4.3? Each layer is concerned only with making sure that its counterpart receives *exactly* what it got. This is the idea behind the virtual connection. Now I'll get beyond theory and take a look at some actual packets to get a clearer picture.

WHY IS THIS PACKET ON THE WIRE?

You are at a Windows 95 workstation named Tarzan. You want to map a drive to a server called Dragon. The name Dragon works fine for you, but the computer doesn't understand it at all, so the first thing that has to happen is some form of name resolution. Name resolution is a process by which user-friendly names such as *Dragon* are turned into computer friendly IP addresses.

Tarzan is configured to use Windows Internet Naming Service (WINS). A WINS server is nothing more than a NetBIOS name server, used to get the IP address of a server or workstation when all you know is the name.

Tip #32 from	Take note that WINS has nothing whatsoever to do with Novell or NetWare. WINS is
John	Microsoft's implementation of a NetBIOS name server, so don't try to find information on setting up WINS on your NetWare server, although it would make a good question to confuse your buddies with!

So before Tarzan can begin communicating with Dragon, Tarzan needs to get Dragon's IP address in order to map the drive. Tarzan does this by sending a query to the WINS server (Jane), asking for the IP address of Dragon:

```
Dest.    Source     Summary
JANE     TARZAN     DLC Ethertype=0800, size=92 bytes
                    IP   D=[204.78.43.51] S=[204.78.43.220] LEN=58 ID=48337
                    UDP D=137 S=137  LEN=58
                    WINS C ID=194 OP=QUERY NAME=DRAGON
```

→ For more information on UDP, IP, and TCP, **see** Chapter 28, "Introduction to TCP/IP," **p. 715**

You can see from the summary that the WINS query is "riding" on the User Datagram Protocol (UDP). UDP is in turn "riding" on the Internet Protocol (IP). And finally, at the physical level, you are dealing with ethernet. Here is the entire packet that contains the NetBIOS name query. Let's take a look at each layer to see whether it corresponds with the earlier discussion:

```
DLC:  ----- DLC Header -----
DLC:
DLC:  Frame 1 arrived at  06:44:17.7919; frame size is 92 (005C hex) bytes.
DLC:  Destination = Station 0008C7564D45
DLC:  Source      = Station Prteon8432BE
DLC:  Ethertype   = 0800 (IP)
DLC:
IP:  ----- IP Header -----
IP:
```

```
IP: Version = 4, header length = 20 bytes
IP: Type of service = 00
IP:      000. .... = routine
IP:      ...0 .... = normal delay
IP:      .... 0... = normal throughput
IP:      .... .0.. = normal reliability
IP: Total length    = 78 bytes
IP: Identification  = 48337
IP: Flags           = 0X
IP:      .0.. .... = may fragment
IP:      ..0. .... = last fragment
IP: Fragment offset = 0 bytes
IP: Time to live    = 128 seconds/hops
IP: Protocol        = 17 (UDP)
IP: Header checksum = 8E21 (correct)
IP: Source address      = [204.78.43.220], TARZAN
IP: Destination address = [204.78.43.51], JANE
IP: No options
IP:
UDP: ----- UDP Header -----
UDP:
UDP: Source port      = 137 (NetBIOS-ns)
UDP: Destination port = 137 (NetBIOS-ns)
UDP: Length           = 58
UDP: Checksum         = AD96 (correct)
UDP: [50 byte(s) of data]
UDP:
WINS: ----- WINS Name Service header -----
WINS:
WINS: ID = 194
WINS: Flags = 01
WINS: 0... .... = Command
WINS: .000 0... = Query
WINS: .... ..0. = Not truncated
WINS: .... ...1 = Recursion desired
WINS: Flags = 0X
WINS: ...0 .... = Non Verified data NOT acceptable
WINS: Question count = 1, Answer count = 0
WINS: Authority count = 0, Additional record count = 0
WINS:
WINS: Question section:
WINS:    Name = DRAGON
WINS:    Type = NetBIOS name service (WINS) (NetBIOS name,32)
WINS:    Class = Internet (IN,1)
WINS:
```

THE PHYSICAL LAYER

At the physical layer, there isn't a whole lot of information that needs to be conveyed. The source NIC, Prteon8432BE, is concerned only with putting the packet on the wire with a destination address of 0008C7564D45, which is the MAC address of Jane. You see that the ethertype is IP and the length is 92 bytes:

```
DLC: ----- DLC Header -----
DLC:
DLC: Frame 1 arrived at  06:44:17.7919; frame size is 92 (005C hex) bytes.
```

```
DLC:  Destination = Station 0008C7564D45
DLC:  Source      = Station Prteon8432BE
DLC:  Ethertype   = 0800 (IP)
DLC:
```

```
ADDR  HEX                                                        ASCII
0000  00 08 C7 56 4D 45 00 00  93 84 32 BE 08 00 45 00  ...VME....2...E.
0010  00 4E BC D1 00 00 80 11  8E 21 CC 4E 2B DC CC 4E  .N.......!.N+..N
0020  2B 33 00 89 00 89 00 3A  AD 96 00 C2 01 00 00 01  +3.....:........
0030  00 00 00 00 00 00 20 45  45 46 43 45 42 45 48 45  ...... EEFCEBEHE
0040  50 45 4F 43 41 43 41 43  41 43 41 43 41 43 41 43  PEOCACACACACACAC
0050  41 43 41 43 41 43 41 00  00 20 00 01              ACACACA.. ..
```

The entire packet is shown here in hex, with the ethernet header shown in bold. Starting at an address of 0x0, you can see sequentially the destination address, the source address, and the IP type. The important point here is that to the ethernet card, all the rest is nothing but data! Ethernet NICs know absolutely nothing about IP, UDP, WINS, or computer names. And notice that there is no network specific information in the ethernet header. The NIC is capable of sending a packet only to other NICs on the same piece of wire. You will see the same thing each time you move up the protocol stack: The appropriate header and anything that comes after the header are just data that has been handed down from above.

THE NETWORK LAYER

At the network layer, layer three, you see that the protocol, or language, being used is IP:

```
IP: ----- IP Header -----
IP:
IP: Version = 4, header length = 20 bytes
IP: Type of service = 00
IP:        000. .... = routine
IP:        ...0 .... = normal delay
IP:        .... 0... = normal throughput
IP:        .... .0.. = normal reliability
IP: Total length    = 78 bytes
IP: Identification   = 48337
IP: Flags           = 0X
IP:        .0.. .... = may fragment
IP:        ..0. .... = last fragment
IP: Fragment offset = 0 bytes
IP: Time to live    = 128 seconds/hops
IP: Protocol        = 17 (UDP)
IP: Header checksum = 8E21 (correct)
IP: Source address      = [204.78.43.220], TARZAN
IP: Destination address = [204.78.43.51], JANE
IP: No options
```

```
ADDR  HEX                                                        ASCII
0000  00 08 C7 56 4D 45 00 00  93 84 32 BE 08 00 45 00  ...VME....2...E.
0010  00 4E BC D1 00 00 80 11  8E 21 CC 4E 2B DC CC 4E  .N.......!.N+..N
0020  2B 33 00 89 00 89 00 3A  AD 96 00 C2 01 00 00 01  +3.....:........
0030  00 00 00 00 00 00 20 45  45 46 43 45 42 45 48 45  ...... EEFCEBEHE
0040  50 45 4F 43 41 43 41 43  41 43 41 43 41 43 41 43  PEOCACACACACACAC
0050  41 43 41 43 41 43 41 00  00 20 00 01              ACACACA.. ..
```

The IP header is shown in bold. This header is not nearly as intuitive as the ethernet header when viewed in hex, but the information is there in the decode for you. For example, the header checksum (8E21) should be easy to spot. Then what follows should be the source address of 204.78.43.220. If you convert that to hex, you would have the CC.4E.2B.DC that you can see, followed by the destination address.

The important thing here, once again, is that everything after this header is simply data to IP. As far as IP is concerned, the total length is 78 (0x4E) bytes. If you look back at the physical layer, the total length of the packet was 92 bytes—78 bytes (for IP header plus data) and 14 bytes (for ethernet header) equals a total packet length of 92 bytes.

There is nothing but network level information in the IP information. What is the network information? That this packet is destined for host 51 on IP network 204.78.43.0. Ethernet cards don't know anything about IP addressing; they only know how to send to another MAC address. If this network were token ring, the IP information shown here would be *exactly* the same! Only the physical layer information would change. You see how the network level is abstracted, or isolated, from the physical? It's the same for the rest.

THE TRANSPORT LAYER

There is no transport layer protocol used in the frame you have looked at so far. UDP, as you will see in Chapter 28, "Introduction to TCP/IP," is a connectionless protocol. From the earlier discussion of the transport layer, it should be concerned with the reliable, connection-oriented transfer of data. So you need to toss another packet into the picture, one with TCP in it; Transmission Control Protocol (TCP) is a transport layer protocol. In this frame, you have moved beyond the name resolution process, and Tarzan is now communicating directly with Dragon. Notice how the layers keep stacking? TCP on top of IP; IP on top of ethernet:

```
DLC:  ----- DLC Header -----
DLC:
DLC:  Frame 8 arrived at  09:04:49. Frame size is 138 (008A hex) bytes.
DLC:  Destination = Station 0000E109A917
DLC:  Source      = Station Prteon8432BE
DLC:  Ethertype   = 0800 (IP)
DLC:
IP:  ----- IP Header -----
IP:
IP: Version = 4, header length = 20 bytes
IP: Type of service = 58
IP:       010. .... = immediate
IP:       ...1 .... = low delay
IP:       .... 1... = high throughput
IP:       .... .0.. = normal reliability
IP: Total length    = 124 bytes
IP: Identification  = 41216
IP: Flags           = 4X
IP:       .1.. .... = don't fragment
IP:       ..0. .... = last fragment
IP: Fragment offset = 0 bytes
IP: Time to live    = 128 seconds/hops
```

```
IP: Protocol        = 6 (TCP)
IP: Header checksum = 69A6 (correct)
IP: Source address      = [204.78.43.220], TARZAN
IP: Destination address = [204.78.43.4], DRAGON
IP: No options
IP:
TCP: ----- TCP header -----
TCP:
TCP:  Source port                = 1030
TCP:  Destination port           = 139 (NetBIOS-ssn)
TCP:  Sequence number            = 117922
TCP:  Acknowledgment number      = 11615308
TCP:  Data offset                = 32 bytes
TCP:  Flags                      = 18
TCP:                    ..0. .... = (No urgent pointer)
TCP:                    ...1 .... = Acknowledgment
TCP:                    .... 1... = Push
TCP:                    .... .0.. = (No reset)
TCP:                    .... ..0. = (No SYN)
TCP:                    .... ...0 = (No FIN)
TCP:  Window                     = 8760
TCP:  Checksum                   = 1DA7 (correct)
TCP:
TCP:  Options follow
TCP:  No-op
TCP:  No-op
TCP:  Timestamp Option:
TCP:     Timestamp value      = 1048
TCP:     Timestamp echo reply = 0 (should be zero)
TCP:  [72 byte(s) of data]
TCP:
NETB: ----- NetBIOS Session protocol -----
NETB:
NETB: Type = 81 (Session request)
NETB: Flags = 00
NETB: Total session packet length = 68
NETB:  Called NetBIOS name = DRAGON
NETB: Calling NetBIOS name = TARZAN<00> <Workstation/Redirector>
NETB:
```

```
ADDR  HEX                                              ASCII
0000  00 00 E1 09 A9 17 00 00  93 84 32 BE 08 00 45 58  ..........2...EX
0010  00 7C A1 00 40 00 80 06  69 A6 CC 4E 2B DC CC 4E  .|..@...i..N+..N
0020  2B 04 04 06 00 8B 00 01  CC A2 00 B1 3C 4C 80 18  +...........<L..
0030  22 38 1D A7 00 00 01 01  08 0A 00 00 04 18 00 00  "8..............
0040  00 00 81 00 00 44 20 45  45 46 43 45 42 45 48 45  .....D EEFCEBEHE
0050  50 45 4F 43 41 43 41 43  41 43 41 43 41 43 41 43  PEOCACACACACAC
0060  41 43 41 43 41 43 41 00  20 46 45 45 42 46 43 46  ACACACA. FEEBFCF
0070  4B 45 42 45 4F 43 41 43  41 43 41 43 41 43 41 43  KEBEOCACACACAC
0080  41 43 41 43 41 43 41 41  41 00                    ACACACAAA.
```

The TCP header is shown in bold in the hex decode. You are not going to analyze each bit of this decode (more cheers from the gallery!), but something should immediately jump out at you. There is absolutely nothing here to indicate a destination. There is a destination port, which means that the receiving machine should pass this information up to port 139, but that's it. There is nothing to indicate an address of the receiving machine in any fashion. How can this be?

Well, the network layer, IP, is going to get this packet to the correct IP network. The physical layer is going to ultimately get it to the correct machine. So the transport layer is isolated from them both. Here at this level, you can see numbers for sequencing and acknowledging, which is why a transport layer protocol is considered reliable. Each side of the connection knows what to expect from the other, and each side uses this information to handle lost or duplicate packets. And true to form, everything after the TCP header shown in bold is nothing but data to TCP. In this case, the TCP data is a NetBIOS session request, but that is not important. TCP doesn't know or care.

Tip #33 from *John*	Once you really learn your protocols, you would instantly realize that server Dragon and workstation Tarzan are communicating via NetBIOS. From this, you would know that Dragon isn't a Novell server, because Novell servers don't communicate using NetBIOS. In fact, Dragon is a laptop running Windows 95 with file and print sharing turned on. But the concepts discussed in this chapter apply to any OS, not just NetWare.

THE UPPER LAYERS

You really don't need to be concerned with the upper layers. The NetBIOS session request shown in the previous section is an example, but the key point is that to the layer below it, TCP, the NetBIOS session request is nothing but data. Go back and look at the previous frame; TCP claims it is carrying 72 bytes of data. If you look at how many bytes there are after the TCP header (shown in the hex decode in bold), how many bytes will you see? You'll see 72 bytes. And again, note the stacking or layering; NetBIOS on TCP on IP on ethernet.

THE BIG PICTURE

I hope that this look at some actual packets has helped to clear up the theoretical discussion of the OSI model. Take the last packet and you see that some upper-layer data (a NetBIOS session request) was handed down to TCP (the transport layer). TCP, in turn, took this data, added its own header, and passed the whole lot down to IP (the network layer). IP in turn passed it down to the ethernet card to finally be placed on the wire.

This is shown in Figure 4.3, where I pointed out that data flows *down* the stack on the sending side, and *up* the stack on the receiving side. And the logical connections shown in Figure 4.3? The only thing that is going to relate to the TCP header is the TCP stack on the other machine. Same for IP. So you can see that there is a logical, or virtual connection between the layers.

It always comes down to one NIC sending to another NIC on the same piece of wire in the end. This is the physical layer. Getting the packet onto the right network so that the NICs can do their job is the function of the network layer. And to make sure that all the data arrives correctly is the function of the transport level. Each layer has its own function to perform and communicates only with the levels immediately above and below itself.

The protocols shown here are covered in more detail in Chapter 28. For more information on the OSI model, you should search the Web or your bookstore. And don't worry if all this alphabet soup such as IP and TCP doesn't click right away; there are volumes the size of this book and greater devoted to nothing but TCP/IP!

TROUBLESHOOTING

Of course, you cannot troubleshoot the OSI model, but it is helpful to use as a tool. Once you realize that there are layers on layers, each layer communicating with its counterpart, then you can begin breaking the network communications down into components. For example, you might be able to ping your NetWare server, by using the command `ping 204.78.43.81`, but when you try to map a drive by using the command `map n \\wizard1\sys` the attempt at mapping the drive fails.

And why is this? At a low level, the `ping` command is okay. But at a higher level, the name `wizard1` needs to be turned into an IP address that the machine can use; your workstation doesn't know anything about any `wizard1`! Using the `ping` command, you have successfully verified that the server and workstation are both alive on the wire and are capable of communicating, so you can leave the physical cabling, and IP addressing concerns alone, and move on to fixing the name resolution issue.

Breaking the communication down into components lets you focus on the real problem. In the earlier example, the user can't map a drive via the command `map n \\wizard1\sys`. As an administrator, you suspect communication problems and decide to change the network interface card in the server. This would just be a waste of time; if you understood the layers, you wouldn't focus on the server's NIC, because that has been shown to work.

UNDERSTANDING NOVELL DIRECTORY SERVICES

## CHAPTER 5

NOVELL DIRECTORY SERVICES TREE BASICS

In this chapter

WHAT IS A DIRECTORY?

Before I discuss NDS, you need to be familiar with what a Directory is. In the simplest sense, a *Directory* is a central repository for storing information. Information must be organized to be managed and used effectively. Centralizing information makes the management and utilization even easier. For example, calling Directory Assistance in the past to find a person's phone number required you to know the person's area code. This is the equivalent of having separate "Directories" for information lookup. Newer technology now allows you to call one central number (without knowing the area code) to find a person's phone number. This is the equivalent of having one centralized "Directory" for information lookup.

Note

Directory is capitalized here to distinguish the NDS database "Directory" from the NetWare file system "directory." This notation will be used throughout the book to avoid confusion.

In the networking world today, a common request from network administrators is the ability to have all their network information accessible from one location (a Directory). The benefits of this are that network administrators can use a single utility for all network administration and look-up. Additionally, users have single sign-on (SSO) capabilities, that is, they have one user account and one password versus multiple user accounts with multiple passwords.

WHAT IS NDS?

NDS is Novell's Directory Services, which enables SSO and uses centralized information management and look-up, as just discussed. NDS can contain all the information about the resources on your network, for example, users, printers, file servers, hubs/switches, and so on. Users accessing NDS use one tool (Novell's Client Software) for SSO and gaining access to these resources. Network administrators managing NDS can primarily use one tool (NetWare Administrator) to create and manage these resources.

Note

It is important to realize that *any* network service can be put into NDS, not just Novell network services. This is because NDS is extensible, meaning that it allows you to add to it anything that you want to be managed. More on the NDS schema (and extending it) later in this chapter.

NDS is a database. More specifically, NDS is a hierarchical and distributed database. It is hierarchical in the sense that it must be constructed in a certain way (discussed later in the section "Understanding the Parts of the Directory Tree"). And it is distributed in the sense that it can be broken up into smaller pieces (partitioned) and distributed to multiple locations (replicated). Partitioning and replication will be discussed in Chapter 6, "Designing the Novell Directory Services Tree."

Like other databases, NDS has Records, Fields, and Values. A good analogy is the Phone Book. All the information about one person in the phone book equals a Record. A person's First Name, Middle Initial, Last Name, Address, and Phone Number equal Fields. Finally, John J. Smith, 1234 Main Street, and 123-456-7890 equal Values of these Fields. In NDS terminology, however, the NDS database has Objects, Properties, and Values versus Records, Fields, and Values. No matter what the naming conventions are, the concepts are very similar.

The NDS database is composed of the following files, which are stored in the SYS:_NETWARE directory:

- 0.DSB—Base file, which simply holds the names of all the .DSD files.
- 0.DSD—Entry or object file, which contains the records of the NDS objects that are created to form the Tree.
- 1.DSD—Value file, which contains the property or attribute records used by the objects in the entry file.
- 2.DSD—Block file, which contains records that are used by the record in the value file.
- 3.DSD—Partition file, which contains a list of each of the partitions on the local server and in the local NDS database.
- Streams files (which are hex value names with .DSD extensions), which are used to hold variable and free-form length values, such as login scripts.

Any changes, additions, deletions, and so on made to NDS (for example, creating user objects with NetWare Administrator) are written to these files. These files together provide the NDS tree information for each server.

SYS:_NETWARE is a system-protected directory and cannot be accessed or viewed using standard utilities, like FILER or DIR. If you want to see the contents of this directory, run RCONSOLE.EXE from a workstation and follow these steps:

1. Press Alt-F1 to bring up the Available Options menu (see Figure 5.1).
2. Select Directory Scan and enter SYS:_NETWARE as the name of the directory to scan (see Figure 5.2).

PART

II

CH

5

Tip #34 from
Gally

When the DSREPAIR.NLM utlity is run to repair the NDS database, it creates temporary NDS files (except for streams files). At the end of the NDS repair, these temporary files become the permanent NDS files (unless you choose not to accept the repairs). The current .DSD files then become .DOD files (while the 0.DSB becomes 0.DOB). These .DOD and .DOB files will be overwritten by the DSREPAIR utility only after 72 hours. This feature helps Novell Technical Support troubleshoot recent NDS problems.

Figure 5.1
List of available options.

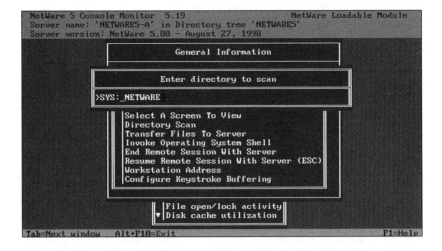

Figure 5.2
You should see a list similar to this one.

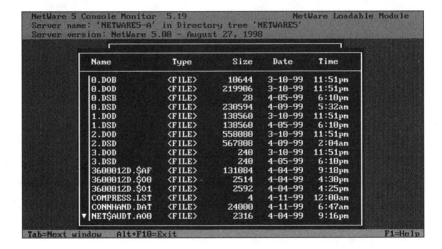

UNDERSTANDING THE PARTS OF THE DIRECTORY TREE

This section will familiarize you with the structure of NDS and the objects that comprise NDS.

NDS is modeled after the X.500 standard for Directory Services. In fact, much of the terminology used in this section is from the X.500 specification for a Directory.

NDS is structured in the form of an upside-down tree. This is why NDS is sometimes referred to as *the NDS Tree*, *the Directory Tree*, or simply *the Tree*.

There are three basic NDS object types that make up the structure of the NDS Tree and give NDS its hierarchy:

- [Root] object
- Container objects
- Leaf objects

Tip #35 from	It is important to realize that NDS does *not* contain the file system, that is, it does not contain your applications or application data files. The NetWare 5 file system is a separate system and is discussed in Chapter 17, "Organizing and Accessing Information on the NetWare Server."
Sally	

THE [ROOT] OBJECT

Every NDS Tree must have a *[Root] object*. The [Root] is created and named when you install the first NetWare 5 server. The [Root] name is also referred to as the *Tree name*. The [Root] object is the top of the inverted Tree structure. It is the container object for all other objects in the Directory hierarchy.

Note	*[Root]* and *Tree* will be used synonymously throughout this book.

Generally speaking, there is one NDS Tree per company. This is not a requirement but it is the recommended way in that one Tree allows you to achieve SSO and centralized administration which, as discussed earlier, are considered to be two very important reasons for having a Directory.

PART

II

CH

5

CONTAINER OBJECTS

Container objects are objects that can be created beneath the [Root]. Container objects organize the NDS Tree and contain other NDS objects, hence their name. There are five classes of container objects that are used to organize the NDS Tree:

- Country objects
- Organization objects
- Organizational Unit objects
- Locality objects
- State or Province objects

Tip #36 from
Sally

> It should be noted that there are other container objects in NDS, for example, NLS (Novell Licensing Services) Product container objects (used for holding License Certificate objects) and SLP Scope Unit container objects (used for holding the IP services on your network). The five container objects above are discussed here because they are the container objects that can be used to design your NDS Tree.

COUNTRY OBJECTS

Country objects are optional and are generally not used nor recommended to use except in strict X.500 environments. Country objects have an abbreviation, or an "attribute type" (in NDS terms) of *C=*. Country objects can only be created beneath the [Root].

ORGANIZATION OBJECTS

Just like every NDS Tree must have a [Root], every NDS Tree must also have one Organization object. *Organization objects* have an abbreviation, or an "attribute type" (in NDS terms), of *O=*. The required Organization object is created and named when you install the first NetWare 5 server (just as the required [Root] object was created and named at this time, too). Generally speaking, there will be one O= per company. This is not a requirement and there are exceptions to this, which are discussed in Chapter 6, "Designing the Novell Directory Services Tree.". O= objects can be created beneath the [Root], a C=, or a Locality object.

Because the Organization object is the only required container object in NDS, it would be possible to place all of your network resources (for example, users, printers, servers, and so on) in this one required container. However, much like you would not store all of your DOS files at the root of C:\, you will not (and should not in the majority of cases) store all your NDS leaf objects in this one Organization object. Instead, you will create container objects (as discussed next) to organize and hold these network resources. Additionally, these container objects will be used (when necessary) to partition and replicate NDS.

ORGANIZATIONAL UNIT OBJECTS

Organizational Unit objects are optional but, realistically, will be the most commonly used container objects in your Tree. Organizational Units have an abbreviation, or an attribute type (in NDS terms), of *OU=*. OU='s generally represent either physical locations or departments within your company, depending on which level of the Tree they are in OU='s are generally created after you install the first NetWare 5 server, using a utility called NetWare Administrator (NWAdmn32.EXE).

> **Note**
>
> NetWare Administrator (NWAdmn32.EXE) is now the primary administrator tool for creating and managing NDS. If you install a new NetWare 5 server, this is the only NetWare Administrator utility you will have. However, if you upgrade a NetWare 4 server to NetWare 5, you will retain previous versions of the NetWare Administrator utility because the upgrade does not remove these older utilities. Previous versions of NetWare Administrator include NWAdmn95 (for Windows 95), NWAdmnNT (for Windows NT), and NWAdmin (a 16-bit version for Windows). Ensure that you use the latest NWAdmn32 with NetWare 5.

Organizational Units can be compared to subdirectories in the DOS file system. Organizational units are simply containers used to organize and hold your network resources. As discussed previously, without Organizational Units all of your NDS leaf objects would be in the one required Organization object, which is generally not recommended.

OU='s can be created beneath an O=, another OU=, or a Locality object.

LOCALITY OBJECTS

Like the Country object, the Locality object is characteristic of the X.500 specification but is not commonly used within NDS. It is mentioned here because it is an available container object in NDS. Like an Organizational Unit object, it can hold your network resources but is generally not used in practice.

Locality objects can be created beneath a C=, O=, OU=, or even another Locality object.

STATE OR PROVINCE OBJECTS

Like the Country and Locality objects, the State/Province object is also characteristic of the X.500 specification, but again is not commonly used within NDS. It is mentioned here because it is an available container object in NDS. Like an Organizational Unit object, it can hold your network resources but is generally not used in practice.

State, or *Province*, *objects* can be created beneath a C=, O=, OU=, of even another Locality object.

LEAF OBJECTS

Leaf objects will be the most commonly used objects in your Tree. Leaf objects have an abbreviation, or an attribute type (in NDS terms), of *CN=*, where CN stands for common name. *Leaf objects* represent the users and resources (printers, file servers, and so on) these users access on your network. Leaf objects are not container-class objects because leaf objects cannot contain other objects. All leaf objects can be created beneath O=, OU=, Locality, or State/Province objects. Only an Alias leaf object can be created beneath the [Root]. Only Alias and SLP Directory Agent objects can be created beneath the C=.

Table 5.1 represents some of the common container and leaf objects found in the NDS base schema.

TABLE 5.1 COMMON NDS OBJECTS IN THE BASE SCHEMA

AFP Server	Organizational Unit
Alias	
Application	Print Queue
Computer	Print Server (Non NDPS)
Directory Map	Printer (Non NDPS)
Group	Profile
Locality	SLP Directory Agent
	SLP Scope Unit
	Template
	User
NetWare Server	Volume
Organizational Role	

Note

This list might be slightly different from what you see in NWAdmn32 depending on the products you chose to install during the NetWare 5 installation. For example, if you chose to install NDPS, you will see three NDPS leaf objects for this product. The NetWare 5 base schema includes approximately 34 objects, but Table 5.1 only displays some of the more common ones.

Notice this list in Table 5.1 does not contain leaf objects for the following:

- Policy Package
- Workstation
- Workstation Group

These objects will be created when the schema is extended while installing ZENworks (see Figure 5.3). (ZENworks is discussed in Chapter 23 "Server Console Utilities." The schema is discussed in the next section.)

SCHEMA

The *NDS schema* is the "rules" that make up what can be in NDS, how NDS objects can be named, and where NDS objects can be placed in the Tree.

Novell ships a "base" schema that gets installed on every NetWare 5 server (as partially shown in Table 5.1). A base schema includes the most common objects and their properties. You might, however, want to "extend" the base schema to incorporate objects and properties unique to your company. For example, you might want to extend the User object to include a Photograph property or even a Social Security Number property. Or you might want to add a new object in NDS to represent fax machines on your network. This is possible because NDS is an extensible Directory.

Figure 5.3
An NDS Tree, showing parts of the Directory Tree just discussed.

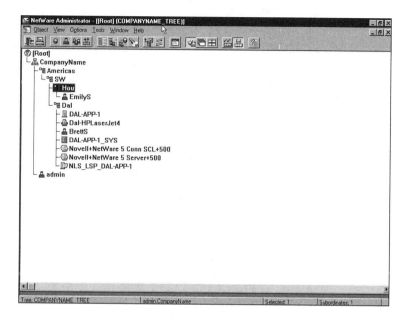

A third-party product from Netoria, called ScheMax, makes extending the NDS schema very easy, even for non-programmers. Netoria can be reached at www.netoria.com.

Additionally, Novell ships a Schema Manager utility (accessible through NDS Manager). However, this utility requires more programming knowledge than Netoria's ScheMax.

Currently, in the majority of cases, the schema is automatically extended when you install additional products that leverage NDS, for example, Novell's ZENworks and NDS for NT. These products add additional leaf and container objects to the base schema, giving NDS more capabilities than the base schema supplies.

STORING INFORMATION ABOUT OBJECTS: NDS PROPERTIES

As discussed earlier, NDS objects have properties. Depending on the object, you will see different properties are available (see Figure 5.4).

Notice that the User object has many more properties than a Printer object.

PART

II

CH

5

Figure 5.4
User properties versus Printer properties.

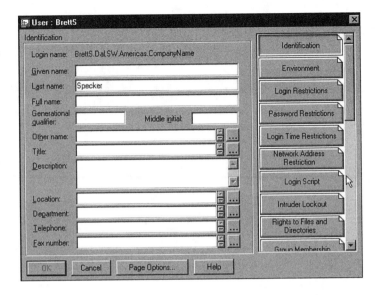

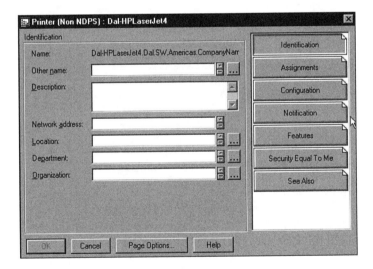

Other facts about NDS properties include the following:

- Some properties are required, for example, the Last Name property when creating a User object.

- Other properties are optional, for example, the Phone Number property on a User object. Optional properties add value to NDS (if they are filled in) in that an NDS lookup tool can then be used to discover a person's phone number.

■ Some properties are single-valued, for example, Full Name property on a User object.

■ Some properties are multi-valued, for example, the Phone Number property on a User object.

In any case, the schema controls all these rules and the Novell utilities will not let you violate these rules, that is, NWAdmn32.EXE will not allow you to create a User object until the Last Name property is filled in.

UNDERSTANDING NDS CONTEXTS

There are two different types of NDS contexts you need to be familiar with:

■ Every container and leaf object in NDS has a location in the NDS Tree. This location is referred to as the object's context. Simply stated, *context* is an object's location in the Tree, relative to the [Root].

Referring to Figure 5.3, BrettS's context is `.dal.sw.americas.companyname` while EmilyS's context is `.hou.sw.americas.companyname`.

■ Additionally, every user logged in to the network has a *current context*, which is the container in the NDS Tree the logged-in user is currently in. A default current context can be set with the Novell Client software for a user's convenience.

In Chapter 14, "Logging in to and Navigating Around the Novell Directory Services Tree," you will see why it is important to understand an object's context and a user's current context.

THE FUTURE OF NDS

Novell has recently announced its next release of NDS, called *NDS 8*. NDS 8 is the next generation of NDS that extends NDS into the Internet and Enterprise Directory market.

Some of the enhancements to NDS 8 include the following:

■ Increased NDS capacity for millions of objects per server, billions of objects per Tree, and hundreds of thousands of objects per container.

■ Increased performance for Directory reads, writes, and searches.

■ ConsoleOne management (truly moving towards one single management utility).

■ Batch utility for adding, modifying, and deleting NDS objects.

For more information on NDS 8: `www.novell.com/products/nds`.

PART

II

CH

5

TROUBLESHOOTING

Sometimes when using NWAdmn32 to view the objects in your Tree, you see objects represented with a question mark icon instead of the normal icon for that object. This does not necessarily mean that NDS is corrupt. Rather, it generally means that you are running the NWAdmn32 utility from a NetWare server that does not have the appropriate snap-ins installed. Snap-ins are DLLs that get "snapped-in" to NWAdmn32 so that NWAdmn32 can properly display the object's icon and you can edit the object's properties. Snap-ins are now located in the SYS:PUBLIC\WIN32\snapins directory. If you ever get in this situation, you can remedy it by reinstalling the product and just selecting the option for installing NWAdmn32; this places the appropriate snap-in DLLs on the file server and the object will now be displayed properly after you restart NWAdmn32.

## CHAPTER 6

DESIGNING THE NOVELL DIRECTORY SERVICES TREE

In this chapter

WHAT MAKES A GOOD TREE?

There are a number of factors that ensure a good NDS Tree design, including the following:

- A solid Tree structure, top and bottom levels
- Good NDS naming standards
- A properly partitioned and replicated NDS database
- An effective time synchronization configuration

> **Note**
>
> The first three are covered in this chapter. Chapter 7, "Time Synchronization," covers the latter.

The end result of a good NDS design is a solid Directory that meets the company's business needs and reduces the cost of managing the network. It is also a Tree that can easily accommodate increased growth and facilitate implementation of additional products that leverage NDS, such as ZENworks.

TREE STRUCTURE

Although no two NDS Trees are ever exactly the same, nor is there only one way to design an NDS Tree, all good Tree designs do share common characteristics. NDS Tree design is split into two parts: the top-level design and the bottom-level design. The overall Tree design takes the shape of an inverted Tree with the [Root] object on top and is shaped like a pyramid, smaller at the top and wider at the bottom. Generally speaking, most Trees will be between four and six levels deep, although levels greater than this are appropriate in large companies. A deep Tree structure may take you (or the Help Desk staff) longer to navigate in NWAdmn32 to get to the resources you need to manage.

> **Tip #37 from**
> *Sally*
>
> The NetWare code (such as the Application Programming Interface, or API) puts a 256-character restriction on an object's Distinguished Name (which is the object's complete name from the object itself up to the [Root], including all containers in between). This is another reason to keep the Tree "shallow" (especially if you are using longer names to represent NDS container and leaf objects). If you reach the 256-character limit on an object's Distinguished Name, the utilities for viewing and managing NDS can have problems.

NDS Tree design is a "logical" design; however, it is recommended that this logical NDS design match your "physical" network environment, especially at the top levels as discussed next.

THE TOP LEVEL

The top level refers to the layers of the Tree which should represent your WAN infrastructure and typically includes the Organization (O=) object and the first or second levels of Organizational Unit (OU=) objects. The Admin user object is automatically created at the Organization level (during the first NetWare 5 server installation). Besides this Admin user, only a few users and network resources should be placed at the top levels in the Tree.

The top level of the Tree is the most important functionally because it serves as the foundation for the rest of the Tree. Changes to the top level of the Tree impact a lot of objects at lower levels, so you don't want to have to adjust this top level too often to accommodate changes or growth.

THE BOTTOM LEVEL

The bottom level refers to all layers below the representation of your WAN layers (top level) and typically represents workgroups, departments, or some other depiction of users and resources in your company. Changes to the bottom level of the Tree do not impact as many objects. You can move users, resources, or even complete departments (OUs) without too much impact on the Tree.

> **Note**
>
> It is easy to move and rename NDS containers at any level in the Tree. However, the biggest challenge to an NDS redesign is changing each user's NAME CONTEXT statement (although you can automate this procedure). A lesser challenge is changing any batch files, menus, login scripts, and so on that reference a specific container that is now in a different location of the Tree. The higher up in the Tree these moves/renames are made, the more objects at lower levels that are affected; for example, changing the Tree Name or Organization object name affects every object in the Tree whereas changing a lower-level OU= affects only those objects directly below that OU=.

A SAMPLE TREE DESIGN

To understand the concepts I have just discussed, a sample Tree design will be created for a fictional company called *CompanyName*. CompanyName is a U.S.-based company with locations in 11 North American cities. CompanyName is expected to grow in the next couple of years, adding new sites that need access to NDS. This growth will be in the U.S and internationally; currently CompanyName has no international sites. All the design decisions made for CompanyName are proven design decisions from real-world companies successfully using NDS.

The inputs you use to design the top levels of the Tree include your company's LAN/WAN diagrams and an understanding of your company's expected future growth. Using these inputs, you create an OU= for each physical site. Figure 6.1 shows an appropriate top-level NDS Tree design for CompanyName.

PART
II

CH
6

Figure 6.1
Top-level NDS design.

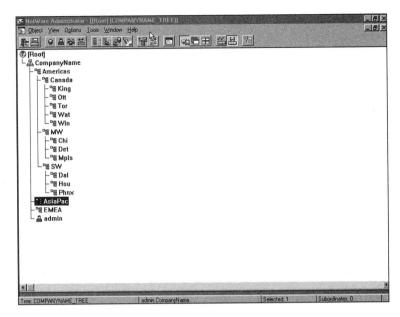

RATIONALE FOR THE TOP-LEVEL TREE DESIGN

The rationale for the top-level Tree design for CompanyName is as follows:

- One Tree was created for the entire company, allowing for single sign-on and centralized administration as discussed in Chapter 5, "Novell Directory Service Tree Basics." Again, the Tree is created during installation of the first NetWare 5 server.

- No Country objects were used, even though CompanyName will become an international company with offices in other countries. Instead, OUs were used to represent countries. Remember from Chapter 5 that Country objects are recommended only in strict X.500 environments.

- One Organization object was used for the entire company. You could deviate from this in a situation where one company has two distinct business operations within it (and will be managed as two distinct companies), while sharing the same LAN/WAN infrastructure. In this case, create two O=s for the two unique business operations (however this is rare and is seldom used in practice). Again, the one required Organization object is created during installation of the first NetWare 5 server. Additional Organization objects (if necessary) are created using NWAdmn32.EXE.

- Organizational Units were used to represent the 11 North American cities that CompanyName is currently located in.

At this point, you should notice that these 11 OUs representing physical sites were not created directly beneath the Organization object. The reason for this is because, due to CompanyName's expected growth, it is possible that CompanyName could have sites in over 100 locations. Current NDS guidelines recommend that you have between 30 and 75 OUs on one given level.

Note

This 30–75 number is due to Subordinate References, which are discussed later in this section. These guidelines will likely be increased when NDS 8 (mentioned in Chapter 5) is available.

What was done, then, to compensate for CompanyName's expected growth was to create *placeholder OUs*. Placeholder OUs are simply a term for an OU= that was created in order to keep the Tree in a pyramid shape and to ensure that no one level goes beyond the 30–75 OU= recommendation. Placeholder OUs were created to represent these geographic areas:

- Americas, AsiaPac, and EMEA, which are considered to be Global Placeholder OUs; and

- MW and SW, which are considered to be Regional Placeholder OUs, dividing the (implied) United States into regions because this is where the majority of growth is expected. An OU=US container could have been created at a parallel to OU=Canada (giving the Tree further definition); however, because this is a U.S.-based company, eliminating this layer (to keep the Tree shallow) was chosen.

The last layer of your top-level design should represent the physical sites in your company (generally speaking these are cities or campuses). In CompanyName's case, the last layer of the top level is King, Ott, Tor, Wat, Win, Chi, Det, Mpls, Dal, Hou, and Phnx.

Note

The CompanyName example assumes a large company. However, if you understand how to design a large Tree, you can scale down to design smaller Trees.

Now that the top level of CompanyName's Tree has been designed, you can move on to the lower-level design.

The inputs you use to design the bottom levels of the Tree include organizational charts and an understanding of the way the network resources are accessed by users in your company, the latter probably being more appropriate. Using these inputs, you create appropriate OUs beneath each site OU=. Figure 6.2 shows a portion of the bottom-level NDS Tree design for CompanyName.

PART

II

CH

6

Figure 6.2
Bottom-level NDS
design.

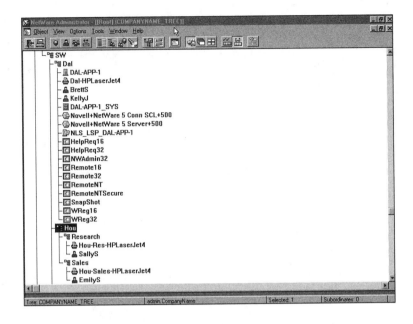

RATIONALE FOR THE BOTTOM-LEVEL TREE DESIGN

The rationale for the bottom-level Tree design for CompanyName's Houston and Dallas sites is as follows. Similar conventions should be used for the other sites in the Tree:

- Organizational Units were created for Houston's Research and Sales departments because these are two distinct departments in Houston that each have their own separate resources. No departmental OUs were created for the Dallas site because all users in Dallas (regardless of the department they are in) share the same resources.

Tip #38 from *Sally*	As a general rule, you should place users in the same container with the resources they access the most, ensuring that users are not accessing these resources across a WAN link. Creating resource-specific containers to hold the different types of NDS leaf objects on your network is not recommended. For example, do not create a container to hold all your printers, another container to hold all your servers, and so on. There is one exception to this, which will be discussed in Chapter 24, "ZENworks."

The key points for designing the bottom levels of the Tree are to make accessing resources easier for the user and managing resources easier for network administrators or help desk staff. You can see, then, that the bottom levels of the Tree are specific to each company whereas the top levels of most Trees should be specific to the WAN infrastructure in any company's case.

NDS NAMING STANDARDS

Good object naming is fundamental to NDS because it provides a definition of the objects in the Tree as well as their relationship to other objects in the Tree. Naming standards need to be meaningful for users and administrators (for information lookup and management) and easy to follow when non–company technical support parties are assisting or troubleshooting. Additionally, standard naming conventions make searching NDS easier which is especially important as new applications continue to leverage NDS.

The rationale for the naming conventions for CompanyName is as follows:

- Used the company's name and appended "_Tree" to it; the schema does not allow any spaces in the NDS Tree name. If you look at the top bar in Figure 6.1, you see that the Tree ([Root]) has been named CompanyName_Tree.

Tip #39 from *Sally*	The reason for naming the Tree this way is because the NDS Tree advertises its name on the network. If you use the IPX protocol, the Tree name is advertised via the Service Advertising Protocol (SAP) and is seen when using the console command DISPLAY SERVERS. If you use the IP protocol, the Tree name is advertised via the Service Location Protocol (SLP) and can be seen by using the console command DISPLAY SLP SERVICES. Having the word *Tree* in the Tree name makes it easier to identify when troubleshooting network problems.

- Used the company's name for the Organization object.
- Used a generally recognized name or abbreviation for global placeholders, for example, Americas, AsiaPac, EMEA.
- Used a generally recognized name or two-character abbreviation for regional placeholders, for example, Canada, MW, SW (for *Midwest* and *Southwest*).
- Although not used in the MyCompany example, using two-character (post office) abbreviations for states would be an appropriate layer between the regional placeholder and the city layers—for example, ON, IL, TX.
- Used three- to four-character abbreviations for cities, for example, King, Ott, Chi, Det, Dal, Hou.
- Servers were named by a combination of where they are located and what function they serve, for example, Dal-App-1, for the first application/file server in Dallas, or Chi-PS-1, for the first print server in Chicago.

There are many variations to these naming standards. The key point is to devise and document meaningful naming standards for your company. This will make it easier for users and for network administrators. Additionally, remember to keep the names short to avoid the 256-character limitation mentioned in an earlier Tip.

PART

II

CH

6

NDS PARTITIONING AND REPLICATING

As mentioned in Chapter 5, the NDS database is a distributed and replicated database, meaning that the database can be partitioned (broken up into smaller parts) and replicated or *distributed* to multiple servers. This means that NDS can be "scaled" to accommodate large NDS environments. If a database is not scaleable, it cannot be partitioned and replicated to share the database load. In these cases, the entire database must be stored on each server or a select number of servers, resulting in possible performance degradation and even inability to log in or access network resources.

WHAT IS A PARTITION?

Partitions are simply logical "breaks" in your NDS database, allowing NDS to be scaleable. (Remember the NDS database is a set of files stored in SYS:_NETWARE). A good analogy for partitioning is taking a three-ring binder that has page after page of product information in it and placing index tabs to section off the various product literature within the binder. This way, you can quickly go to the Printers index tab (as an example) and find all of your printer information there. Without these index tabs, you would have to page through the entire binder until you found the information you were looking for.

WHAT IS A REPLICA?

Whereas partitions are "logical" breaks in your NDS database, *replicas* are "physical" copies of partitions that you place on NetWare servers. Replicas provide the following:

- Fault tolerance for the NDS database
- Faster access to network resources, which are stored in the NDS database
- Support for Bindery Services, if necessary (Bindery Services is discussed in Chapter 16, "Managing NDS Rights, Partitions, and Replicas")

Building on the partitioning analogy above, a good analogy for replicating is making a copy of the information in the Printers section and placing it in another three-ring binder. Now, you have a duplicate copy ("fault tolerance") or an extra copy in your home office for "faster access" when you are working at home.

There are four types of NDS Replicas:

- **Master replica**—A Master replica is created when a partition is first created. There can only be one Master replica for each partition at a given time. This is because the Master replica "locks" a partition during partition operations, therefore ensuring partition integrity. All partitioning operations are performed off of the Master replica.

Tip #40 from
Sally

You must ensure that the server holding the Master replica of a partition is up in order for partitioning operations involving that replica to successfully complete.

- **Read Write replica**—This is the most common type of replica because there can be any number of them per partition (although the recommendation is to have three, as discussed later in this section).

  Master and Read Write replicas are sometimes called *writeable* replicas. This is because users can log in and get authenticated off of a server holding either a Master or a Read Write replica. When a user logs in, three User object properties change, that is, Network Address, Login Time, and Last Login Time; therefore, user login must occur off of a server holding a writeable replica in order to write these changes to NDS.

  Similarly, network administrators can make changes to NDS off of a server holding either a Master or a Read Write replica. When a network administrator adds objects to NDS or changes properties of objects in NDS using NWAdmn32 they are writing to the NDS database; therefore, this must occur off of a server holding a writeable replica.

  In fact, the only real difference between a Master and a Read Write replica is that the Master must be up in order for partitioning operations to successfully complete. Other than that, the two replicas are functionally the same.

- **Read Only replica**—A Read Only replica is not a writeable replica, as its name implies. Therefore, a user can't log in off of a server holding a Read Only replica nor can an administrator make changes off of a server holding a Read Only replica. For these reasons, Read Only replicas are seldom used in practice. They are in NDS to conform to the X.500 Directory Service specification.

> **Note**
>
> Any of these three types of replicas can be manually changed to another type, generally at any time. The process for doing this and for managing partition and replica operations is discussed in Chapter 16.

- **Subordinate Reference (replica)**—Although the first three replicas mentioned previously can be manually created by the network administrator, subordinate references (replicas) are automatically created when a server holds a replica of a parent partition, but not of this parent partition's child partition(s). Subordinate references are essentially the glue that binds your partitioned NDS database together.

All four of these replica types participate in the replica synchronization process (discussed in Chapter 16). In fact, this is the reason for the recommendation of 30–75 OUs at any one level of the Tree: to minimize too many subordinate references, thus minimizing replica synchronization traffic. Subordinate references are not "bad"; in fact, they are a necessary component of a partitioned NDS environment. However, a good design (as discussed previously) will ensure that subordinate references are kept to a minimum.

PARTITION GUIDELINES

If your company's network has WAN links, you need to create partitions. I'll use CompanyName's NDS Tree as an example. If you did not partition CompanyName's Tree, servers would hold the entire NDS database (from the [Root] object down) which contains objects that are *physically* located in Dallas, Houston, Toronto, and so on. When a network administrator adds a new user to, say, the OU=Dal container, that change is sent to all servers holding the non-partitioned NDS database—and these servers will likely be located across WAN links. This could be a very slow process depending on the speed of CompanyName's WAN links. The replica synchronization process could even fail to complete if CompanyName has unreliable WAN links that were not always up, resulting in possible NDS database inconsistencies until the WAN link comes back online.

Additionally, consider the fact that every time a user logs in the NDS database gets updated and these changes need to be replicated! You should now understand why partitions are needed in a WAN environment. With that said, you should partition in the following three cases:

- At each physical site OU=, which is why it is recommended to design the top layer of your NDS Tree around the WAN infrastructure. This assumes that each physical site OU= has a NetWare server; if not, there is no reason to partition that site, except for the following point.

- When the number of objects in a partition reaches 5,000–10,000, regardless of whether or not this partition contains a NetWare server.

- The [Root] object should be partitioned (this is then referred to as the *[Root] partition*). The [Root] partition should remain small and typically include only the [Root] object and the O= container.

Note
Chapter 16 shows you how CompanyName's Tree should be partitioned because it includes placeholder objects not necessarily conforming to the preceding three cases.

In summary, these are the general partitioning guidelines:

- Base partitions on the WAN infrastructure.

- Do not create a partition that spans any WAN link, for example, don't partition the Chi and Det sites together, because a WAN link physically connects the two sites together (assuming your logical NDS design matches the physical network environment). In other words, don't "Span the WAN" with your partitions. The example discussed at the beginning of the "Partition Guidelines" section explained why.

- Partition around the local servers in each geographic area.

- Split the NDS database into partitions that contain the information needed by a central set of users. These partitions will then be replicated on servers physically close to these users.

PARTITION MANAGEMENT

A couple of utilities can be used for managing NDS partitions: NDS Manager (NDSMgr32.EXE) and DSREPAIR.NLM, both of which are discussed in Chapter 16.

REPLICA GUIDELINES

After an NDS Tree is partitioned, copies, or *replicas*, of these partitions need to be placed on strategic NetWare servers for fault tolerance, speed of access, and (possibly) Bindery Services purposes.

These are general replication guidelines:

- Three replicas of the [Root] partition, because the [Root] partition is considered the most important partition. These three [Root] replicas can be placed on three servers at one central location, preferably the center of your WAN which is probably at your headquarters location.

- Three replicas of every other partition for fault tolerance, speed of access, and Bindery Services (if appropriate) purposes. If you follow the NDS design and partitioning guidelines already discussed in this chapter, you would partition CompanyName's OU=Dal container and place three replicas of OU=Dal on three servers in Dallas. This is referred to as "replicating locally."

- If there are not three servers in a physical site, consider using a Replica Server. *Replica Server* is simply a term for a server dedicated to storing replicas. This type of configuration is common in a Branch Office Environment, typical of the banking industry where there is only one NetWare server per physical site (branch). This Replica Server would be placed at a central site in your WAN, so that other servers needing to communicate with this Replica Server are a short number of "hops" away.

- Maximum of 10–20 replicas of any one partition (this larger number is generally to support Bindery Services and is not intended to be used for increased fault tolerance). Three replicas (as discussed previously) are sufficient for fault tolerance.

- Maximum of 20–40 replicas stored on any one server, where this number is increased to 60–120 if this server is acting as a dedicated Replica Server.

Note

Chapter 16 shows you replica placement for CompanyName's Tree.

PART

II

CH

6

Throughout this section, all the guidelines given were in a range, for example, 5,000–10,000 objects per partition. The low end of this range assumes the following NetWare 5 server hardware configuration:

Minimum 300 MHz, 128MB RAM

The high end of this range assumes the following NetWare 5 server hardware configuration:

Minimum 400 MHz, 256MB RAM

REPLICA MANAGEMENT

The same two utilities used for partition management are also used for replica management: NDS Manager (NDSMgr32.EXE) and DSREPAIR.NLM, both of which are discussed in Chapter 16.

FINAL PARTITIONING AND REPLICATING SUGGESTIONS

In addition to the partitioning and replication guidelines just discussed, the following are some worthwhile suggestions for your company:

- Changes and additions to network infrastructure should be communicated to the appropriate person responsible for partitioning and replication, in order to ensure the appropriate strategy is still being used.

- Document your final partitioning and replication scheme, as it is transparent to most backup applications should a complete restore from tape ever be necessary.

PROJECT: DOCUMENT A SCHEME

Using CompanyName's Tree as an example and what you have learned in this chapter, document the partitioning and replication scheme you would use for CompanyName. Then, check your results with Chapter 16.

CHAPTER

7

TIME SYNCHRONIZATION

In this chapter

WHAT IS TIME SYNCHRONIZATION?

Another step in the NDS design process is to determine a proper time synchronization configuration.

Time synchronization is the capability of NetWare servers to coordinate and maintain consistent time among other servers in the NDS Tree—or even with servers that are in different NDS Trees. Time synchronization is necessary to ensure that each NDS event (for example, creating a new user, deleting a print queue, and so on) receives an accurate time stamp.

> **Note**
>
> By *accurate*, I mean a time stamp that is consistent with the time on other servers. Although NDS alone does not require the "correct" time, it does require that all servers agree on the same time. Even though NDS might not require the correct time, other applications running on the network might (such as personal organizer software used to trigger appointment and meeting times), so setting the correct time on your file servers is strongly recommended.

Without an accurate time stamp, objects created or deleted on one server might not be able to replicate to another server because of time differences. In essence, then, time synchronization is needed due to the distributed and replicated nature of NDS (as discussed in earlier chapters).

The console command TIME is used to determine if a NetWare server's time is synchronized to the network's time. Additionally, this command will show you the current time zone settings for the NetWare server, which should be set up properly (especially if you are using time-sensitive applications on this server).

HOW IS TIME SYNCHRONIZATION IMPLEMENTED IN NETWARE 5?

There are two NetWare Loadable Modules (NLMs) in NetWare 5 that provide time synchronization: TIMESYNC.NLM and NTP.NLM. TIMESYNC.NLM is a Novell proprietary time synchronization service available for NetWare versions 4 and higher. NTP.NLM is an Internet standards time protocol (RFC 1305), where *NTP* stands for *Network Time Protocol*. NTP is an Internet standards–based way to share time among different operating systems—for example, Windows NT, Macintosh, UNIX, NetWare, and so on. Novell started shipping NTP.NLM with NetWare 5 because this was Novell's first release of NetWare that was moving to open standards, such as NTP for time and IP (versus IPX) for network communications.

However, since the initial release of NetWare 5, Novell has decided to place the functions of NTP into their own TIMESYNC.NLM and are recommending that TIMESYNC.NLM be used instead of NTP.NLM. This chapter, therefore, was written assuming the use of TIMESYNC.NLM; it will not address using NTP.NLM. Remember, though, you can still get NTP functions by using TIMESYNC.NLM, which will be discussed in this chapter.

NetWare servers use `TIMESYNC.NLM` to coordinate and maintain the server's time with Universal Time Coordinate (UTC), which is the world time standard and is the number of seconds elapsed since January 1, 1900. UTC used to be known as GMT (Greenwich Mean Time).

Note

> You should ensure that you are using at least `TIMESYNC.NLM` version 5.08, especially if you want to implement NTP. This section assumes you are using at least `TIMESYNC.NLM` version 5.08.

If you are familiar with time synchronization in NetWare 4, there are only a couple of differences now:

- With NetWare 4, `TIMESYNC.NLM` only runs over the IPX protocol and, therefore, uses Service Advertising Protocol (SAP) for discovering time servers. With NetWare 5, `TIMESYNC.NLM` still runs over IPX (and uses SAP) but additionally can run over the IP protocol with Service Location Protocol (SLP) for discovering time servers. Note: This dynamic discovery with SLP will not be available until a future NetWare 5 Support Pack. Because `TIMESYNC.NLM` runs over both IP and IPX, time can be synchronized between NetWare 4 servers running IPX and NetWare 5 servers running IP.

Tip #41 from
Sally

> If you have a network comprising both pure IP and pure IPX servers, time can flow from IPX to IP (and vice versa) as long as at least one server is running both IP and IPX to bridge the two sides. You do not need the Migration Gateway solution for this purpose because `TIMESYNC.NLM` now runs over IPX and IP. However, if a pure IP server needs to obtain time from a pure IPX time provider server by using the time provider's server name, Compatibility Mode Driver (CMD) is required to resolve the IPX name. You'll learn more about Migration Agents and CMD in Chapter 9, "Pure IP, Compatibility Mode, and Service Location Protocol (SLP)."

- NetWare 4 does not support NTP.

Besides these two exceptions, there are no other major differences between NetWare 4 and NetWare 5 time synchronization. Functionally, they are equivalent.

DEPLOYMENT OF TIME SYNCHRONIZATION AMONG NETWARE SERVERS WITHOUT NTP

The design and configuration of time synchronization is easily and quickly established for any size NetWare network. When time has been configured, there is very little additional activity required to maintain this function. Time synchronization configuration is based on the physical location of your servers—not on your NDS Tree design.

PART

II

CH

7

Tip #42 from
Sally

Determining and documenting your time synchronization plan and having it available for your installers should make that portion of the NetWare 5 installation trouble-free!

Every NetWare server in your Tree must participate in the time synchronization process. There are four types of time servers with NetWare—three Time Providers and one Time Receiver:

Time Providers	**Time Receiver**
Single Reference	Secondary
Reference	
Primary	

You set your servers to one of these four types, depending on which of the two time configuration methods (discussed next) that you choose to use. If changes are later required, changing the time server type is easily done with console commands or from within the MONITOR.NLM utility.

> **Note**
>
> A number of SET parameters used to customize the NetWare time environment are listed throughout this chapter. You can use either console command SET TIMESYNC parameters or MONITOR.NLM for modifying these parameters (this chapter generally uses the console command format). In either case, the changes you make are automatically written to SYS:SYSTEM\TIMESYNC.CFG, which is where these time synchronization settings need to be placed.

There are two different methods for configuring time:

- Default Time Configuration
- Custom Time Configuration

For each time configuration method I've mentioned, there are two different ways for time servers to find each other and communicate time with one another:

- Service Advertisements (default configuration)
- Configured Lists (custom configuration)

DEFAULT TIME CONFIGURATION

This is the default time configuration method used when you install NetWare 5 on a server. With this method, the first NetWare server installed in the NDS Tree is automatically set up as the Single Reference time provider; subsequent servers that are installed into the same Tree are automatically set up as Secondary time receivers. This method is generally left in place for small networks that have fewer than 30 file servers on a LAN-only network (that is, no WAN links).

Reference and Primary servers are not used with the default configuration. In fact, if you try to manually change a Secondary to either a Reference or Primary while there is a Single Reference server, error messages will be generated at the file server console stating that a Single Reference cannot exist with another time provider. This is because a Single Reference server is the unquestioned, authoritative source of time; all other servers must take time from the Single Reference; a network can only have one Single Reference server; and the Single Reference does not accept time from any other server. For these reasons, this default time configuration is sometimes referred to as *Forced Time Synchronization*.

The Single Reference server can get time from either its internal clock (which is the default) or it can be configured to get time from an atomic clock (with additional third-party software such as Cadence) or from an NTP time provider with no additional third-party software required (as discussed later in this chapter).

The default time configuration method is simple to administer, because it requires no custom configuration files. Rather, Secondaries discover the Single Reference time provider through either SAP (if the servers are running IPX) or SLP (if the servers are running IP). When discovered, Secondaries ask for time from the Single Reference server.

Tip #43 from *Sally*	As mentioned earlier, TIMESYNC.NLM does not support automatic discovery of a time provider over IP/SLP until a future NetWare 5 Support Pack. Until then, if you are using IP, each Secondary server needs to be explicitly configured to take time from the Single Reference server using the Secondary's SYS:SYSTEM\TIMESYNC.CFG file (discussed later in this chapter). If this is not done, the Secondaries report that they are out of sync.

The Single Reference server does introduce a single point of failure because it can be the only time provider on the network (see Figure 7.1). Therefore, if it goes down (and will be down for an extended period of time) you should manually promote one of the Secondaries to ensure that your network still gets consistent time. A network can survive short periods of time while the Single Reference server is down.

Service Advertisements

The service advertisement method is generally used with the Default Time Configuration method and not with the Custom Time Configuration method (where WAN links are involved). This is especially true if you are using IPX because SAPs are very frequent (every 60 seconds), consuming valuable WAN bandwidth. A time-providing server using IPX will use SAP 0x026B to advertise its presence.

On the other hand, SLP advertisement is performed only when TIMESYNC.NLM starts up or when TIMESYNC.NLM has to reregister when the SLP Service / Directory Agent goes down. Advertisement traffic over IP (when this feature is available in a future NetWare 5 Support Pack) is expected to be significantly less than the SAP-based advertisement traffic in IPX.

Figure 7.1
Default Time
Configuration
example.

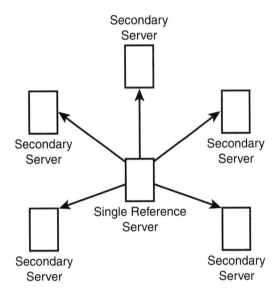

The service advertisement method requires no manual configuration as new NetWare servers are added to the network (except if using IP/SLP as mentioned in an earlier Tip).

To set up the network in Figure 7.1 if running IPX, ensure the following two things:

- The Single Reference advertises its service by setting this console command on it:
  `SET TIMESYNC SERVICE ADVERTISING = ON (this is default)`

- All Secondaries use discovery to obtain a time source by setting this console command on all Secondaries:
  `SET TIMESYNC CONFIGURED SOURCES = OFF (this is default)`

  This command is simply used as a precaution to ensure against misconfiguration of the Secondaries.

To set up the network in Figure 7.1 if running IP (as is currently necessary until a future NetWare 5 Support Pack), perform the following on all Secondaries:

```
SET TIMESYNC CONFIGURED SOURCES = ON (default is OFF)
    SET TIMESYNC TIME SOURCES = <ip address of Single Reference;>
```

The current `TIMESYNC.NLM` (version 5.08) does not yet understand DNS names. This will be resolved in a future Support Pack. For now, you must use the dotted decimal IP address in the `TIMESYNC.CFG` file.

Tip #44 from	Use the console command DISPLAY ENVIRONMENT to see the current settings for all SET parameters (including time). Use the console command SAVE ENVIRONMENT <filename.txt> to write these parameters to a text file. If you do not specify a directory location in the file name, the file will be created in SYS:.
Sally	

In both configuration cases I've mentioned, a Secondary server will completely accept time from the Single Reference. If the Secondary discovers differences between its time and that of the Single Reference, it corrects its clock to gradually synchronize to that of the Single Reference.

CUSTOMIZED TIME CONFIGURATION

This method is for networks that have more than 30 file servers or for networks that have WAN links. With this method, you set up one Reference server and at least two Primaries; a Single Reference is not (and cannot be) used. The Reference and Primaries make up what is called a Time Provider Group (TPG), because it is composed only of time providers. The TPG "votes" with each other to provide the agreed-on network time to Secondaries.

A Reference server is generally placed at a company's headquarters location, simply for ease of access. The Reference server can get time from either its internal clock (which is the default) or it can be configured to get time from an atomic clock (with additional third-party software such as Cadence) or from an NTP time provider with no additional third-party software required (as discussed later in this chapter). If there are other NetWare servers at the headquarters location, they should be set up as Secondaries getting their time from the Reference server.

Primary servers should be placed at each WAN site where there are a large number of NetWare servers. This way, only the Primary at the site comes across the WAN to vote for network time with other members of the TPG and then gives this time to Secondaries at that site (as opposed to all Secondaries coming across the WAN to get time from a time provider). If there are a small number of NetWare servers at a site, you can consider setting them up as Secondaries, realizing that they will all come across the WAN to get time from a time provider.

Tip #45 from	Most companies have stable time environments by using 7–10 members in their TPG. The greater the number in the TPG, the greater the amount of time synchronization traffic that is generated.
Sally	

Because the Custom Time Configuration has multiple time providers, you are protected against failures in any one of the time providers (see Figure 7.2). If the Reference server goes down, the Primaries are fully capable of maintaining and providing consistent time to the Secondaries, until the Reference comes back online.

PART

II

CH

7

Figure 7.2
Custom Time
Configuration
example.

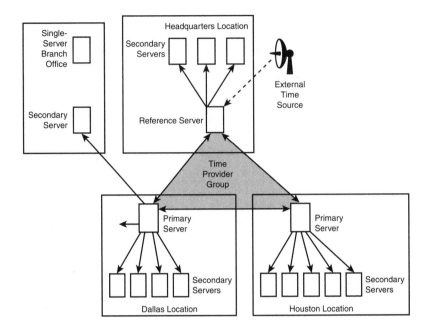

CONFIGURED LISTS

This is generally the method used with the Custom Time Configuration for time servers to find each other and communicate time with one another.

With this method you generally do not use service advertisements (although you can for fallback purposes). This method requires a special configuration file (SYS:SYSTEM\TIMESYNC.CFG) for *every* server specifying exactly which servers should be contacted for voting purposes and for receiving time. Configured lists give you complete control of the time synchronization hierarchy in that you specify which servers to contact for time.

To set up the network in Figure 7.2 to use configured lists, follow these steps:

1. On the Reference and all Primaries, set the following:
   ```
   01SET TIMESYNC CONFIGURED SOURCES = ON (default is off)
   SET TIMESYNC SERVICE ADVERTISING = OFF (default is on)
   SET TIME SYNC TIME SOURCES = <SAP name or IP address of each server in the
   TPG>
   ```

   This list needs to be separated with semi-colons.

Tip #46 from

Sally

You can create this TIMESYNC.CFG file once and copy to the Reference and all Primaries. A time provider will ignore its own name in the list. Each member of the TPG should contact all other members of the TPG, so all time providers should be listed in the TIMESYNC.CFG file.

2. On all Secondaries, set the following:

```
SET TIMESYNC CONFIGURED SOURCES = ON (default is off)
SET TIMESYNC TIME SOURCES = <SAP name or IP address of the time provider
     physically closest to it>
```

Consider putting multiple time providers in this list (separated by semi-colons), with the physically closest time provider at the top of the list. A Secondary starts at the top of the list trying to contact a time provider. It continues down the list until it finds one. Even though there are multiple time providers in the list, a Secondary gets time from only one of the time providers.

DEPLOYMENT OF TIME SYNCHRONIZATION WITH NTP

TIMESYNC.NLM 5.08 or later can work with NTP. This means that TIMESYNC.NLM can both obtain time from an NTP time source and serve time to NTP clients.

SETTING UP A NETWARE SERVER TO OBTAIN TIME FROM AN NTP TIME SOURCE

The configuration is similar to obtaining time from a NetWare time provider (as discussed previously in the Default and Custom Time Configuration sections):

1. Identify the time provider servers in the network. If you have used the Default (Single Reference-Secondary) method, the Single Reference server is the time provider. If you have used the Custom (Reference-Primary-Secondary) method, the Reference and Primary servers are the time providers.

2. Update the time providers to get time from the NTP time source by setting the following:

```
SET CONFIGURED SOURCES = ON
SET TIMESYNC TIME SOURCES = <ip address of NTP source>:123;
```

Here, :123; is added to the IP address because 123 is the NTP port used by TIMESYNC.NLM.

Because the entire network looks to the time providers for time, this process ensures that the entire network gets time from the NTP time source.

SETTING UP A NETWARE SERVER TO PROVIDE TIME TO AN NTP CLIENT

This service is provided through the UDP port 123. So, for example, if you want your UNIX machines to take time from a NetWare server, set up NTP on your UNIX machines with the IP address of the NetWare server in the UNIX box's NTP configuration file.

DEFINITIONS FOR SET TIMESYNC PARAMETERS

The previous examples discussed the required time sync parameters for different configurations. The following list shows some of the other time sync parameters available with NetWare 5, including a definition and some options for their use:

PART

II

CH

7

- **Service Advertising = OFF (Default = ON)**—A setting of OFF means that the Time Providers will not send out or advertise using SAP or SLP. In this case, configured lists communication must be used.

- **Configured Sources = ON (Default = OFF)**—A setting of ON tells the server to rely on the configured list in TIMESYNC.CFG first, using service advertisement as a fallback if it is left on. If service advertisement is left on, the time-providing servers that are discovered will be added (in memory) to the bottom of the TIMESYNC.CFG file. Using both configured lists and SAP as your communication method will add extra traffic. However, the combination provides fault tolerance in case the configured list method fails.

- **Timesync Time Sources**—This is a list of servers to contact to vote on time or to receive time.

- **Directory Tree Mode = ON (Default)**—A setting of ON tells the server to listen to service advertisements for time synchronization only from servers in the same NDS Tree. This parameter is set to OFF when merging two NDS Trees, as discussed in Chapter 16 "Managing NDS Rights, Partitions, and Replicas."

- **Hardware Clock = ON (Default)**—Reads hardware clock for time. This setting should be turned off if getting time from an atomic clock or NTP.

- **Polling Interval = n, where the default n is 600 seconds [10 minutes]**—When the time synchronization system stabilizes, time synchronization activity occurs according to the value set in this parameter. You can minimize time synchronization traffic by increasing this Polling Interval parameter, when you are certain that time is stable in your network. Generally, it is recommended that you keep this setting at the default of 600 seconds, assuming you keep the number of time providers around 7–10.

- **Polling Count = n, where the default n is 3**—This parameter controls how many time exchanges are sent for each polling interval from each server in the TPG. The reason for sending the request three times by default is to average propagation delay through the network. Therefore, it is not recommended to reduce this value in order to decrease time traffic load. This is especially true with dial-up lines where the first time synchronization packet might have to establish the connection.

Note

From these last two parameters, you should realize that as the number of servers in the TPG increases, so does the amount of traffic per default 10 minutes. The general rule is to have 7–10 servers in your TPG. This is not a "fail" number but rather a guideline. As mentioned earlier, this number works very well for most companies.

- **Synchronization Radius = 2000 (Default)**—This setting is in milliseconds and controls the maximum time a server's clock can vary from network time but time is still considered to be synchronized.

TROUBLESHOOTING

I'm still confused. What exactly is synthetic time?

Synthetic time is NDS's way of protecting NDS objects from receiving future time stamps.

What causes synthetic time?

Changing a NetWare server's time to the future and then back again to the correct time. Any changes made to the NDS database (e.g., user login, password change, object creation) while the time was set ahead will cause a future time stamp to be added to the changed object and will also update the partition's time stamp with this future date. Synthetic time is issued when the partition time stamp is in the future as compared to the server time.

What happens during synthetic time?

The partition time is frozen and only the event count portion of the time stamp is changed. The event count will increment from 0 to FFFF every time a change is made to an object in a partition with synthetic time. Only updating the event count (and not the time stamp) is NDS's way of protecting objects in this partition from continuing to receive future time stamps.

What should I do?

Synthetic time will not hurt NDS as long as the future time stamp is not too far ahead. To determine the future time stamp:

1. Load DSREPAIR from any server in the replica ring generating synthetic time messages.
2. Choose "Advanced Options."
3. Choose "Replica and Partition Operations" and highlight the partition indicating a synthetic time error and press Enter.
4. Choose "Display Replica Information." This will generate a log file. At the top of the log file is a section titled "Partition Information and Servers in the Replica Ring." There are several properties listed; The "Timestamp" property will reference the latest time stamp in your NDS database for this partition. If this timestamp is one hour ahead of the actual network time, NDS will issue synthetic time on this partition for one hour. In this case, you do not have to do anything to "fix" synthetic time.

How do I fix synthetic time?

This is done with DSREPAIR.NLM. Please see TID 2921231 "Correcting Synthetic Time Errors" available at http://support.novell.com for the steps to follow. You should use this only when time stamps are so far into the future that it is not reasonable to wait for the problem to correct itself. If in doubt, contact Novell or a Novell-authorized partner for assistance.

PART III

Installing NetWare 5

## CHAPTER 8

INSTALLING NETWARE 5 ON NEW SERVERS

In this chapter

BEFORE YOU INSTALL

After reading the previous chapters, you now have the necessary grounding about Novell Directory Services. It is time to install your new NetWare 5 server so you can implement your NDS tree design. This chapter presents step-by-step procedures necessary for a successful NetWare 5 server installation. The end of the chapter lists some possible problems and solutions you might encounter during your server installation.

Note	The procedures for installing workstation software can be found in Chapter 13, "Installing Workstation Software."

Before you jump in with both feet installing your new NetWare 5 server, check that you've met the following preconditions:

- If you're installing a brand-new NetWare 5 NDS tree, get your hardware ready and go ahead with the installation.

- If you're installing a new NetWare 5 server into an existing NDS tree that consists of only NetWare 5 servers, put your hardware together and go ahead with the installation.

- If you're installing a new NetWare 5 server into an existing NDS tree that has any NetWare 4.1x servers, you *must* first upgrade the DS.NLM on these NetWare 4.1x servers before introducing your first NetWare 5 server into that tree.

- If you're installing a new NetWare 5 server into an existing NDS tree that has any NetWare 4.0x servers, you must first upgrade the NetWare 4.0x servers to *at least* NetWare 4.10 *and* update the DS.NLM on all your NetWare 4 servers before installing your first NetWare 5 server into that tree.

Caution	I can't emphasis enough the importance of having to upgrade NetWare 4's DS.NLM when you're installing your first NetWare 5 server into an existing NDS tree where NetWare 4 servers exist. If you don't upgrade the DS.NLM on these NetWare 4 servers, your NetWare 5 server might fail to be introduced into the tree and can result in NDS inconsistency in your tree.

→ To upgrade existing pre-NetWare 5 servers to NetWare 5, **see** Chapter 11, "Upgrading an Existing Server," **page 243**.

Tip #47 from *Peter*	Chapter 11 also covers how you "upgrade" from NetWare 5 to NetWare 5—via a hardware upgrade of an existing NetWare 5 server.

Before introducing a new or upgraded NetWare 5 server into an existing NDS tree that has NetWare 4 servers, you *must* update the DS.NLM to version 5.99 or later. The reason is that older versions of NDS do not support the increased functionality available with NetWare 5. DS.NLM version 5.99a for NetWare 4.11 is included on your NetWare 5 CD. You can update all NetWare 4.11 servers to DS 5.99a using one of the two following methods:

Note

The internal version (as reported by NDIR /VER) for the supplied DS.NLM is version 5.99. However, when the NLM is loaded, it reports version 5.99a.

Note

Although completely updating all your NetWare 4.11 servers can take up to several hours, depending on the size of your network, they can be updated without service interruption. Updating DS.NLM also includes an update to DSREPAIR.NLM.

- Update your NetWare 4.11 servers manually as follow:
    1. At the NetWare 4.11 server, mount the NetWare 5 Operating System CD-ROM as a NetWare volume or through a DOS CD-ROM driver.

Tip #48 from
Peter

To mount the NetWare 5 Operating System CD-ROM as a NetWare volume on NetWare 4.11, load the necessary drivers for your CD-ROM drive—for example, if you're using IDE CD-ROM drives, ensure IDECD.CDM is loaded—then load CDROM.NLM. Issue the command CD MOUNT NETWARE5 to mount the CD.

2. Type LOAD INSTALL at the server console.
3. Select Product Options and then choose Install a Product Not Listed.
4. Press F3 and specify the drive letter and the path to NDS version 5.99a for NetWare 4.11; if you've mounted the CD as a NetWare volume, use NETWARE5 as the volume name. (Enter \PRODUCTS\411_UPG\NDS as the path.)
5. INSTALL copies the files to your SYS volume and reloads DS.NLM automatically for the new version to take effect. You'll see a message similar to the following on your server console:

```
DSTrace is set to: *.

 4-20-99   8:29:21 pm:    DSOLD-5.95-30
     Bindery close requested by the SERVER


 4-20-99   8:29:22 pm:    DSOLD-5.95-27
     Directory Services:  Local database has been closed


 4-20-99   8:29:28 pm:    DS-5.99-28
     Bindery open requested by the SERVER
```

```
4-20-99   8:29:37 pm:    DS-5.99-26
     Directory Services:  Local database is open


4-20-99   8:30:22 pm:    SERVER-4.11-3191
     Server NETWARE411_A_____@@pMM@@@@@DàPJ
     address has changed from 0000BEEF:000000000001:4006
     to 0000BEEF:000000000001:422C
     Information came from router at 000000000001
```

Repeat all the previous steps at each NetWare 4.11 server, or update all servers automatically by completing the following steps.

■ You can update all other NetWare 4.11 servers on the network automatically as follows:

1. After updating one of your NetWare 4.11 servers to DS 5.99a as described earlier, log in to this server as user Admin or equivalent from a Windows 9x or Windows NT workstation.

2. Launch the new 32-bit NDS Manager utility. (You can find NDSMGR32.EXE in SYS: PUBLIC\WIN95 and SYS:PUBLIC\WINNT). Make sure you run the NDS Manager utility version 1.25 or later, located in one of these two directories.

3. Select View, Partitions and Servers, and then select the Server object that has the updated NDS.

4. Select Object, NDS Version, Update.

5. The selected server name is shown as the Source for version update (see Figure 8.1).

Figure 8.1
Using NDS Manager to automate DS.NLM updates.

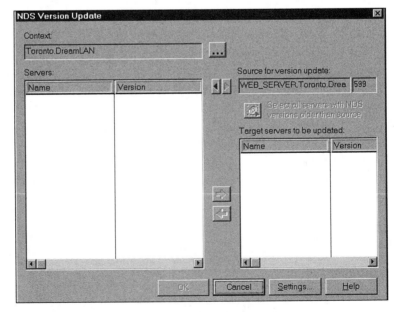

6. Click Settings and change the option for Search for NDS servers to include Entire Subtree (current container and down), as shown in Figure 8.2. Click OK.

Figure 8.2
Changing the NDS version update options.

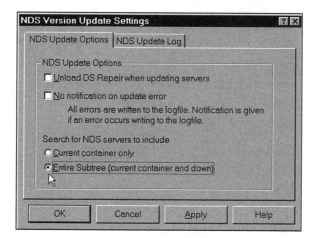

7. Use the Context browser to change the context to [Root] (or a O or OU if you're updating a branch of your tree at a time).

8. Select all other servers that has pre-version 5.99a DS as Target servers to be updated.

9. Click OK.

Tip #49 from
Peter

You also can use NDS Manager to update NetWare 4.10 servers. But you'll need to download the new DS update files from http://support.novell.com to upgrade your initial source server.

When you have your NetWare 4 NDS tree upgraded to use the latest DS.NLM, you can proceed to configure and set up your new NetWare 5 server.

MINIMUM HARDWARE AND SOFTWARE REQUIREMENTS

Compared with previous versions of NetWare, NetWare 5 has a much higher hardware requirement. The following are the minimum system requirements:

- A server-class PC with a Pentium 133MHz or higher processor
- A VGA or higher resolution display adapter (SVGA recommended)
- 550MB of available disk space (50MB for a DOS boot partition, 500MB for a NetWare partition)

SYS Volume Size Requirement

NetWare 5 requires the SYS volume to be at least 350MB in size. Although the NetWare 5 operating system requires only 350MB, volume SYS must be large enough to accommodate all the NetWare products that will be installed. The following table summarizes the size requirements:

NetWare 5 products	Minimum SYS volume size
NetWare 5 operating system	350MB
NetWare 5 with default products	450MB
NetWare 5 with all products	550MB
NetWare 5 with all products and documentation	700MB

- 64MB of RAM (128MB recommended to run Java-based applications)
- One or more network cards
- A CD-ROM drive that can read ISO 9660-formatted CD-ROM disks. Computers with bootable CD-ROM drives must fully support the El Torito specification.

Although a mouse (PS/2 or serial) is not required, it is highly recommended because it makes the installation process much easier and faster.

Tip #50 from *Peter*	The system requirements listed earlier are minimum production-grade requirements. If you're setting up a server for testing or learning purposes, you can get away with less. For example, the server needs only 48MB of RAM for the installation routines to run and NetWare 5 will run on 32MB of RAM with a fast 486 processor (66MHz or faster), if you don't enable Java support.

Tip #51 from *Peter*	You can optimize the server performance by increasing the amount of server memory, disk space, and processor speed. For further information on server performance, see Chapter 26, "Server Tuning for Performance."

Before installing, make sure that you have the following software and information:

- DOS 3.3 or later. A copy of Caldera DR DOS 7.02 is included on the NetWare 5 License disk. *Don't* use the version of MS-DOS that ships with Windows 9x or Windows NT operating systems; they are not standard DOS and can cause your installation process to fail.
- DOS CD-ROM drivers.
- NetWare 5 Operating System CD-ROMs.
- NetWare 5 License disk.
- (Optional) An IP address and subnet mask (if the server will run IP).

- Network card and storage device settings, such as the interrupt and port address. For more information, contact your computer hardware supplier or manufacturer.
- Host adapter modules (HAMs) and custom device modules (CDMs) for your storage devices. (Previous versions of NetWare uses .DSK drivers, but due to the new hardware architecture used in NetWare 5, you now need .HAM and .CDM drivers.)

INSTALLATION OVERVIEW

The NetWare 5 operating system installation process includes the following tasks:

- Meet system and software requirements
- Prepare the network for a NetWare 5 server
- Prepare the computer for server installation
- Begin the installation
- Select the type of installation and regional settings
- Select the platform support module and storage adapter drivers
- Select drivers for storage devices and network boards
- Create a NetWare partition and volume SYS
- Name the NetWare 5 server
- Install the NetWare 5 server file system
- Install networking protocols
- Set the server time zone
- Set up Novell Directory Services
- License the NetWare 5 server
- Select other networking products to install
- Customize your NetWare 5 server installation

These steps are discussed in detail in the following sections.

Note

All examples shown in this chapter are based on the English-language support module (using the US/Canada version of the CD). Dutch, Spanish, French, and Italian language modules also are available. These languages (including English) are shipped as part of NetWare 5 Worldwide Edition (that uses 40-bit security instead of the 128-bit security due to US export laws). Therefore, when purchasing NetWare 5, be sure you order the correct edition.

INSTALLING AND CONFIGURING NETWARE 5

This section assumes that you have fully and correctly installed all necessary hardware and resolved any potential hardware conflict.

PREPARING THE SERVER

There are two components in installing a NetWare 5 server: the DOS component and NetWare itself. Previously, NetWare uses its own boot code but, starting with NetWare 3.0, DOS is used to "bootstrap" NetWare.

Because of the number of files, and their sizes, required by SERVER.EXE during boot, you need to create a bootable DOS partition on your server. Novell recommends a 50MB DOS partition. However, it is best to have a bigger one (100MB to 150MB) so that you have some elbow room for future patches and so on.

Tip #52 from *Peter*	Some people create DOS partitions using this formula: DOS size = amount of server RAM + 100MB. This allows for a "core dump" of memory image in case of server crashes which can be sent to Novell for analysis.

STARTING THE SERVER INSTALL

You need to set up your CD-ROM drive and controller so that the drive can be addressed as a DOS device during the initial installation phase. You can also install from files located on another server on the network. To do this, you need to install the Novell Client for DOS and Windows 3.1x software located on the Novell Client Software CD-ROM.

Installing Novell Client for DOS and Windows

Here's a Quick Start on how to install the Novell Client for DOS and Windows so you can install your NetWare 5 server across the network:

1. Access the Novell Client Software CD-ROM.
2. Change to the PRODUCTS\DOSWIN32 directory, and then execute INSTALL.
3. Press Enter to accept the license agreement.
4. Select the options you want to install on the workstation.
5. Press F10 to continue.
6. Configure the options you are installing. Depending on the options you have chosen, various configuration screens appear. Use the arrow keys to move to a new field and press Enter to edit the field.
7. Press F10 to save your changes and continue.
8. Depending on the type of network board you have installed in the workstation, select the 16-bit or 32-bit LAN driver type.
9. Review the Installation Configuration Summary and make necessary changes by using the arrow keys to move to a new field and pressing Enter to edit the field.

10. Press F10 to continue. Install copies the appropriate files to your workstation and sets up the workstation to run the Novell Client software.

11. Exit Install by pressing Enter to return to DOS or by pressing Ctrl+Alt+Delete to reboot the workstation.

The Novell Client for DOS and Windows 3.1x software loads when the workstation restarts. For an in-depth discussion about client software installation and configuration, see Chapter 13.

Note that HIMEM.SYS is required to run the Novell Client for DOS and Windows 3.1x software.

Tip #53 from

When using Novell Client for DOS and Windows 3.1x to install your server from across the network, make sure you add FILE CACHE LEVEL = 0 to the NetWare DOS Requester section. Otherwise, INSTALL will fail to launch due to insufficient XMS memory.

Tip #54 from
Peter

If your server supports a bootable CD-ROM, you can boot it with the NetWare 5 Operating System CD. You need to make sure that the machine boot order specifies that the CD boots before the hard drive. This ensures that the CD is available for booting and formatting the hard disk.

To boot to the NetWare 5 Operating System CD, the server must have a ROM BIOS that fully supports the El Torito specification—including a hard disk image.

Tip #55 from
Peter

It is to your advantage to use the fastest CD-ROM drive possible for the installation. The faster the drive, the shorter your installation time. As a reference, using a 32x IDE CD-ROM drive on a Pentium P-200 machine with 64MB of RAM, the installation process takes around 30 minutes.

Caution

Make sure that the logical filename of your CD-ROM drive (specified in CONFIG.SYS) is not CDROM or CDINST. If you do, the install process might hang during file copying.

Make sure that the CONFIG.SYS file does *not* load any memory manager (such as HIMEM.SYS), unless you're booting the machine as a workstation first and performing the install across a network using Novell Client for DOS and Windows 3.1x. The following is a set of sample CONFIG.SYS and AUTOEXEC.BAT files that you can use for a CD-ROM based installation:

```
CONFIG.SYS

FILES=50
BUFFERS=30
DEVICE=C:\CDROM\
AOATAPI.SYS
/D:IDECD000
```

```
AUTOEXEC.BAT

PROMPT $P$G
C:\CDROM\\MSCDEX /D:IDECD000
```

Caution

> It is essential that you have at least set the FILES= statement to 30, or else the installation can fail.

To begin the installation, complete the following steps:

1. Insert the NetWare 5 CD-ROM labeled NetWare 5 Operating System into your CD-ROM drive.

2. Change your current drive to the CD-ROM drive. At the CD-ROM drive prompt, type INSTALL. A NetWare 5 splash screen is displayed while some NLMs are loaded in the background. The initial screens of the installation program are displayed in text-based mode whereas the later part of the process are graphical (when having a mouse comes in handy).

3. Accept the License Agreement by pressing F10.

4. Select New Server at the Is This a New Server or Upgrade? prompt (see Figure 8.3) and then select Continue. (New Server is the default selection.)

Figure 8.3
Selecting the type of installation.

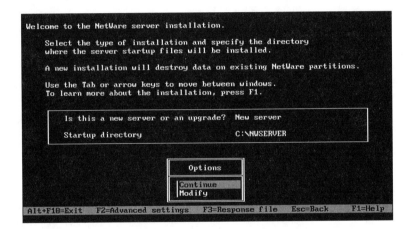

```
Welcome to the NetWare server installation.

    Select the type of installation and specify the directory
    where the server startup files will be installed.

    A new installation will destroy data on existing NetWare partitions.

    Use the Tab or arrow keys to move between windows.
    To learn more about the installation, press F1.


    ┌────────────────────────────────────────────────────────────┐
    │  Is this a new server or an upgrade?   New server          │
    │                                                            │
    │  Startup directory                     C:\NWSERVER         │
    └────────────────────────────────────────────────────────────┘

                    ┌──────────────────────┐
                    │      Options         │
                    ├──────────────────────┤
                    │  Continue            │
                    │  Modify              │
                    └──────────────────────┘

 Alt+F10=Exit    F2=Advanced settings    F3=Response file    Esc=Back    F1=Help
```

Tip #56 from
Peter

> During the text-mode installation phase, you can at any time press F1 to learn more about the displayed options.

Although default settings work for most configurations, you can also use the Advanced Settings option (by pressing F2) to change settings such as server ID number, reboot options, and SET parameters (see Figure 8.4). The NetWare installation screen allows you to change the default settings to settings specific to your networking environment.

Figure 8.4
Changing advanced settings.

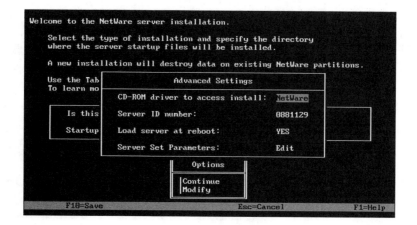

You can change the following settings by pressing F2:

- **CD-ROM driver to access install**—This option allows you select the driver type for accessing the CD-ROM: NetWare or DOS. The default is NetWare as it will be more efficient, thus faster.

- **Server ID number**—A unique server identification number (up to eight hexadecimal digits) identifies the server on the network. The server ID number functions like an internal IPX number. Although a server ID number is automatically created, you can elect to enter a specific server ID number to conform with any numbering system your company is using.

- **Load server at reboot**—Select NO if you do not want AUTOEXEC.BAT to contain the commands to automatically load the server operating system when the computer reboots. If the field is YES (default), the current AUTOEXEC.BAT and CONFIG.SYS files are renamed and saved with a .00*x* extension (such as AUTOEXEC.001).

- **Server Set Parameters**—You might need to modify the SET parameters for some device drivers, such as for network boards and storage devices, in order to complete installation. Select Edit to enter the necessary SET parameters. These SET parameters are saved to the STARTUP.NCF file. Check your hardware documentation for any such requirements.

You're next asked to specify the regional settings which involve choosing the appropriate country, code page, and keyboard mapping for your language and computer (see Figure 8.5). The default setting is what DOS uses.

Figure 8.5
Selecting regional
settings.

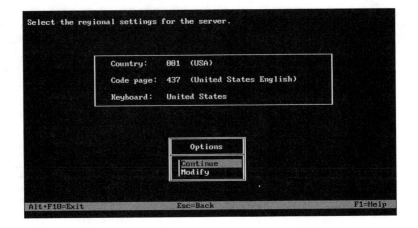

SETTING UP SERVER HARDWARE

The NetWare 5 installation program auto-detects the installed server hardware. In most cases, you should accept the default. If a driver for the existing hardware is not detected, obtain the appropriate driver from the computer manufacturer and follow the instructions to insert the new driver.

Note

The mouse type and video type are not auto-detected by the install program. You must select the appropriate settings for your computer.

To set up the server hardware, complete the following steps:

1. Select the mouse and video type. The NetWare installation program is optimized to display with video display hardware that is VESA 2 compliant. Choose Standard VGA only if your video board does not support 256 colors.

2. Some files are copied to the C:\NWSERVER directory after you select the mouse and video type. You'll see a Copying files... Please Wait message box in the center of the screen. The names of files being copied are shown in the upper-right corner of the screen.

3. Select a platform support module (PSM) if required (see Figure 8.6). This module provides increased performance for multiprocessor computers and some specific hardware configurations. The installation program might auto-detect a PSM. If the installation program does not detect a PSM driver, your computer probably doesn't need one.

Figure 8.6

Selecting hardware support modules and storage adapter drivers.

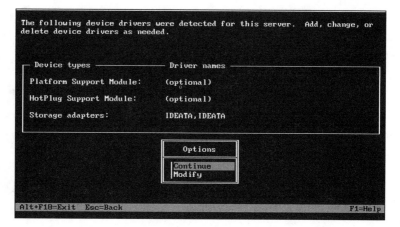

The following device drivers were detected for this server. Add, change, or delete device drivers as needed.

Device types ———————— Driver names ————————

Platform Support Module: (optional)

HotPlug Support Module: (optional)

Storage adapters: IDEATA, IDEATA

Options

Continue
Modify

Alt+F10=Exit   Esc=Back   F1=Help

4. Select PCI HotPlug module, if required. (Computers that support PCI HotPlug technology allow storage adapters and network boards to be inserted and removed while the computer is on; much like the hot-swappable hard drive technology.)

5. Select the necessary storage adapter drivers. The storage adapter requires a driver called a *host adapter module* (*HAM*) to communicate with the computer (host) whereas storage devices require a separate driver called a *custom device module* (*CDM*). Because a single adapter can control more than one type of storage device, your server might require only a single HAM, even though it can have more than one type of storage device—and therefore multiple CDMs (you'll select and configure the CDMs in the next step).

   If your storage adapter is not detected, choose the appropriate driver from the list of available drivers provided with NetWare 5 or add a new driver from a disk. You can obtain HAMs from the storage adapter manufacturer.

6. On the next screen, you need to select and configure the storage device and network cards (see Figure 8.7). This is where you select and configure the CDM drivers for your disks; each type of storage device (such as CD-ROM and hard drives) need its own CDM. Similarly, select and configure a LAN driver for each network card you have installed.

   Some server and network configurations require you to load a NLM before completing the server installation. For example, in a source-route token ring environment, you'll need to load ROUTE.NLM. You can specify that in this screen.

Figure 8.7
Selecting and configuring storage devices and network cards.

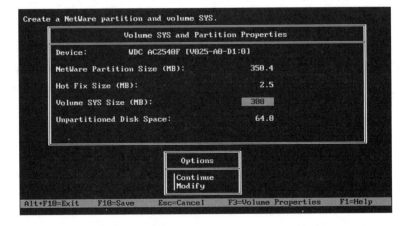

```
The following device drivers were detected for this server.  Add, change, or
delete device drivers as needed.


  ┌ Device types ──────────────┌─ Driver names ──────────────────────────────
    Storage devices:            IDEHD

    Network boards:             PCIODI

    NetWare Loadable Modules:   (optional)



                              ┌─────Options──────┐
                              │ ┌──────────────┐ │
                              │ │Continue      │ │
                              │ │Modify        │ │
                              └─┴──────────────┴─┘

Alt+F10=Exit  Esc=Back                                              F1=Help
```

SETTING UP THE NETWARE PARTITION AND THE SYS VOLUME

When you're finished setting up the LAN and disk drivers, you're ready to set up the NetWare partition and volumes. During the initial stages of installation, the installation program guides you through the steps to create a single NetWare partition containing volume SYS (see Figure 8.8).

Figure 8.8
Creating a NetWare partition and the SYS volume.

```
Create a NetWare partition and volume SYS.
    ┌──────────────────────────────────────────────────────┐
    │         Volume SYS and Partition Properties           │
    │──────────────────────────────────────────────────────│
    │  Device:         WDC AC2540F [V025-A0-D1:0]           │
    │                                                        │
    │  NetWare Partition Size (MB):            350.4         │
    │                                                        │
    │  Hot Fix Size (MB):                        2.5         │
    │                                                        │
    │  Volume SYS Size (MB):                  ▓300▓          │
    │                                                        │
    │  Unpartitioned Disk Space:                64.0         │
    │                                                        │
    └──────────────────────────────────────────────────────┘
                       ┌─────Options──────┐
                       │ ┌──────────────┐ │
                       │ │Continue      │ │
                       │ │Modify        │ │
                       └─┴──────────────┴─┘
Alt+F10=Exit    F10=Save    Esc=Cancel    F3=Volume Properties   F1=Help
```

By default, the NetWare partition uses all available free disk space, and all free space is assigned to the SYS volume. You can manually modify the NetWare partition size as follows:

1. In the Options box, select Modify.
2. Select the appropriate storage device.
3. Select NetWare Partition Size and press Enter.
4. Backspace over the current size, type the new size, and press Enter.
5. Press F10 to save the settings and continue.

Using a similar procedure, you can reduce the size of the SYS volume.

Tip #57 from
Peter

If your storage devices include hardware redirection, you can turn off Hot Fix by setting the Hot Fix size to 0.

Tip #58 from
Peter

Novell Storage Services (NSS) volumes use disk space outside the NetWare partition. Therefore, if you plan to create NSS volumes, remember to reduce the size of the NetWare partition so the appropriate amount of disk space is available for NSS volumes. Details on setting up NSS volumes are discussed in a section later in this chapter and can also be found in Chapter 10, "Disk Management."

Note

At the time of this writing, SYS cannot be placed on a NSS volume due to lack of TTS support by NSS volumes.

Before the SYS volume is actually created, you can change the volume's settings (press Enter on Modify and then press F3), such as block size, file compression flag, block suballocation flag, and data migration flag (see Figure 8.9).

Figure 8.9
Modifying volume
properties.

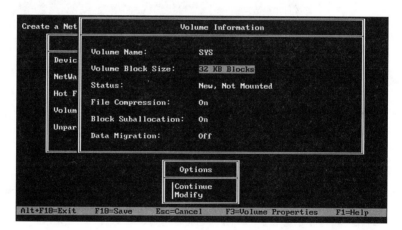

Caution

Note that when a volume is created, volume size, file compression flag, and block suballocation flags cannot be changed unless you re-create the volume.

The data migration flag can, however, be toggled on/off at any time.

Note

The install routine picks a block size that's optimized based on the size of the volume; however, you can change it as per your needs. Typically, a larger block size optimizes the volume for large files and more efficient for file suballocations.

When you've made the all necessary changes, select Continue in the Options box. The sys volume is created, mounted, and then the necessary NetWare system files required for installation are copied to the sys volume (see Figure 8.10). From this point on, the GUI portion of NetWare 5 installation process begins.

Figure 8.10
Copying system files required for installation to the sys volume.

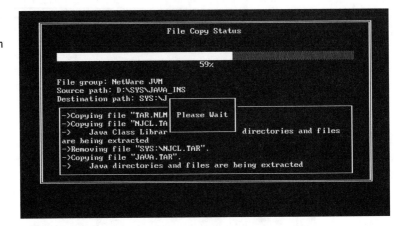

NAMING YOUR NETWARE 5 SERVER

The first of the GUI screens asks you to enter a name for your new NetWare 5 server (see Figure 8.11). The server name *must* be unique from all other servers on the network. The name can be between 2 and 47 alphanumeric characters and can contain underscores and dashes, but no spaces. The first character cannot be a period.

Tip #59 from
Peter

You should not use any periods in the server name. NDS uses a period as delimiter between contexts. Therefore, having a period in the object name (the server's name in this case) makes it difficult to reference the object within NDS.

Figure 8.11
Naming your
NetWare 5 server.

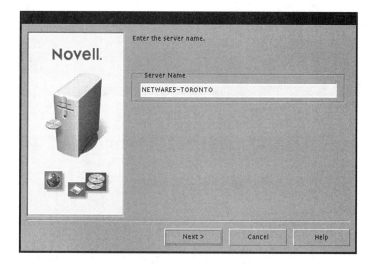

Tip #60 from
Peter

Although unnecessary, the server name should be different from the name you plan to use for the NDS tree to eliminate confusion; it is common practice to append _TREE to the NDS tree name.

Enter a unique server name and click Next to continue.

Keyboard Actions in the GUI Screens

As previously mentioned, a mouse is highly recommended when working with the GUI screens. However, when you lack a mouse, you can use the keyboard commands listed later to navigate through the installation program. Num Lock (number lock) must be on in order for cursor movements to be enabled on the keypad.

Keystroke	Action
Tab	Move focus to next element
Shift+Tab	Move focus to previous element
Enter	Select
Up-arrow (keypad 8)	Move cursor up
Down-arrow (keypad 2)	Move cursor down
Right-arrow (keypad 6)	Move cursor right
Left-arrow (keypad 4)	Move cursor left
Hold Shift while pressing keypad	Accelerate cursor movement
Keypad 5	Select or click an object
Keypad 0	Lock a selected object (for dragging)
Keypad . (period)	Unlock a selected object (to drop)
Keypad + (plus)	Double-click an object
Alt+F7	Move to next window
Alt+F8	Move to previous window

INSTALLING THE NETWARE 5 SERVER FILE SYSTEM

At this point, your NetWare 5 server should have a single NetWare partition and one volume named SYS. If you have space available for creating additional NetWare partitions and volumes, you can create them using this next screen (see Figure 8.12); if you have allocated all available space to volume SYS (as per the default), you will not be prompted for NetWare server file system information.

Figure 8.12
Configuring the file system.

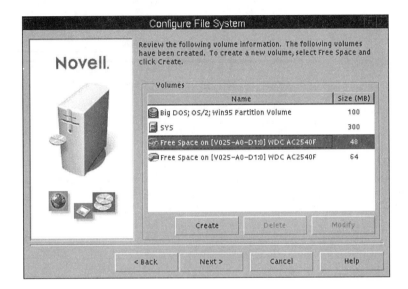

From this screen, you can create two types of volumes: the "traditional" NetWare volume (which supports features such as TTS and suballocation) or the NSS volume (which is the new advanced file system technology). To create a traditional volume, select free space on the screen and click Create. Type the name of the new volume.

Note

Volume names can be between 2 and 15 characters and can contain characters including A through Z, 0 through 9, and the following characters:

_ ! - @ # $ % & ( )

The volume name cannot begin with an underscore or have two or more consecutive underscores.

If you want to allocate only a portion of the free space to the volume, type the amount of space to use, and click Apply to Volume (see Figure 8.13). To make the volume include additional free space, select an additional free space, type the amount of space to use, and click Apply to Volume.

Figure 8.13
Creating additional
volumes.

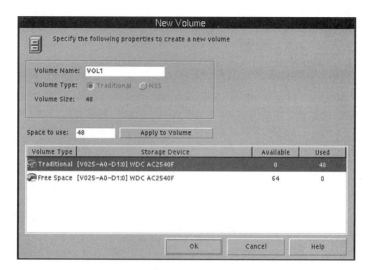

To create an NSS volume, select free space and click Create. (If the Volume Type option is not available, the selected free space is not available for NSS use. In this case, you need to go back to the previous screen and select another free space.) Select Volume Type NSS. Type the name of the volume and click OK. To allocate only a portion of the free space to the volume, type the amount of space to use, and click Apply to Volume. To apply more free space to a volume, select an additional free space, type the amount of space to use, and click Apply to Volume.

Tip #61 from	Unlike traditional NetWare volumes, you can create NSS volumes using unpartitioned free
Peter	space.

Tip #62 from	If you don't set up NSS volumes now, you can create them later following the instructions
Peter	given in Chapter 10.

Click OK to save the volume's setting and return to the Configure File System screen.

If you want to modify a volume's space allocation, select the volume to be modified and click Modify. Using the Configure File System screen, you can also delete any volume you have created, except for the sys volume and the DOS Partition Volume. Keep in mind that when a volume is deleted, any and all data on the volume is lost. To delete a volume, select the volume to be deleted and click Delete.

When you finish with the volumes, click Next to continue. The next screen asks whether the volumes should be mounted immediately or at the end of installation. In order for volumes to be accessed by NetWare, they must be mounted. But because installation files are targeted to the sys volume only, there's no immediate need to mount these new volumes now.

Click Yes to the question Mount All Volumes When the Server Reboots? and then click Next to set up the necessary networking protocols.

INSTALLING NETWORKING PROTOCOLS

A NetWare 5 server can support workstation clients over both IP and the traditional IPX protocols. You can install networking protocols in the following combinations:

- IPX only
- IP only
- IP and IPX
- IP with IPX Compatibility Mode

Tip #63 from
Peter

For more information about IPX Compatibility Mode, see Chapter 9, "Pure IP, Compatibility Mode, and Service Location Protocol (SLP)."

Protocols are assigned to each network card you've installed in the server. Multiple protocols can be assigned to a single network board, which allows the server to communicate using IP and IPX concurrently.

To associate IPX with a network card, click the network board's name and then check the IPX check box (see Figure 8.14). To install IP, click the network board's name, check the IP check box and enter the required IP information (such as IP address, subnet mask, and router address).

Figure 8.14
Configuring networking protocols.

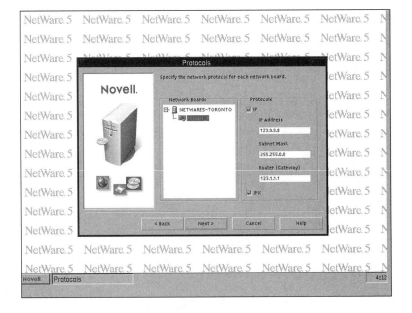

Note

The IP address identifies each device on the network, and, thus, must be unique (just like the server name). The address consists of four eight-bit numbers, which are represented as decimal values separated by periods, such as 123.45.67.89.

The subnet mask allows you to break up your network into smaller networks, and its value depends on how you subdivide your IP network.

The router (also referred to as gateway, in IP parlance) is the address of the router that connects two different IP networks. You can enter a specific router address or you can rely on the network to automatically find the nearest router. If you specify the address, remember that the router must exist on your network segment.

For more information about IP addressing, refer to Chapter 28, "Introduction to TCP/IP."

When IP is selected, Compatibility Mode is automatically enabled to provide service for applications that require IPX. You can use just IP without IPX Compatibility Mode enabled. (Note that when IPX Compatibility Mode is disabled, the server processes only IP packets. Applications that require IPX will not function properly.) To disable Compatibility Mode, see the section, "Customizing the Server Installation," later in this chapter.

When you finish configuring the networking protocols, click Next to proceed to the next step.

SETTING THE TIME ZONE

Because NDS events are time-stamped using UTC time, it is important that you select the correct time zone setting for your NetWare 5 server (see Figure 8.15).

Figure 8.15
Configuring time zone information.

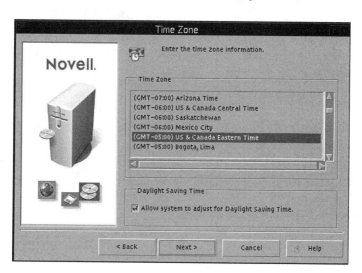

Tip #64 from
Peter

Advanced time synchronization and other settings are available during the customization phase of the installation.

If the time zone you're in observes daylight savings, check the Allow system to adjust for Daylight Savings Time box. Click Next to continue.

SETTING UP NDS

There are two methods in which you can set up NDS on the server (see Figure 8.16): Install the server into an existing NDS tree or create a new NDS tree. If this is the first NetWare 5 server to be installed into an NDS tree with NetWare 4.1x servers, you will be prompted to modify the schema. When prompted, you must provide the administrator name and password for the existing NDS tree. Modifying the NDS schema requires Supervisor rights to the [Root] object of the existing NDS tree.

Figure 8.16
Decide whether you want to create a new NDS tree or install the server into an existing tree.

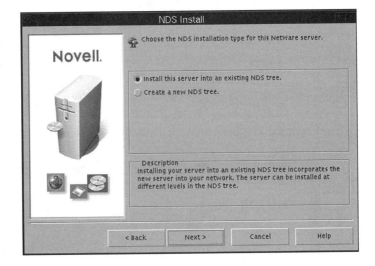

If you selected to install into an existing NDS tree, a screen similar to Figure 8.17 is displayed. The server can be installed in any Organization (O) or Organizational Unit (OU) container in the NDS tree where you have Supervisor rights. You can also create containers during the installation. You will be required to log in and supply the context, username, and password for the user with Supervisor rights to the container.

Tip #65 from
Peter

If you have multiple NDS trees on your network, you can use click the Tree button to locate the desired tree and context for the server.

Figure 8.17
Inserting the current
NetWare 5 server into
an existing NDS tree.
Use the Browse button
to select a tree.

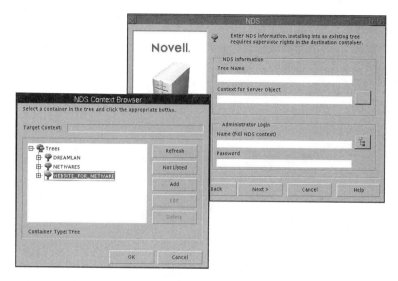

If you elect to create a new NDS tree, a screen similar to Figure 8.18 is displayed. Fill in the tree name and the context in which the Server object will be placed. Each NDS tree must have a name unique from other NDS trees on the network. You're also required to create a user (default name Admin) with Supervisor rights, identify an NDS context in which this Admin user will reside, and assign a password.

Figure 8.18
Creating a new
NDS tree.

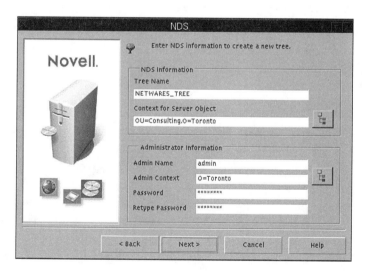

Note The NDS tree name must not be more than 33 characters in length.

Click Next to start the installation of NDS information onto your server. A message about performing a duplicate tree name check is displayed before NDS is installed. When the installation is completed, you'll see a screen similar to Figure 8.19, summarizing the server's NDS information. Click Next to continue.

Figure 8.19
NDS summary.

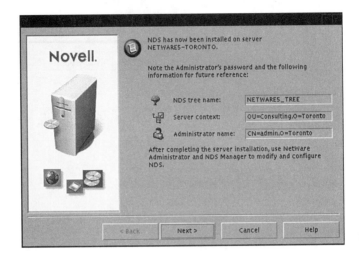

LICENSING THE NETWARE SERVER

Each NetWare server must have a valid (server) license in order to function as a server. You can install the license from the NetWare 5 License disk or browse to a directory that contains NetWare 5 license files. To install the NetWare 5 license from disk, insert the license disk in the server's floppy drive and click Next (see Figure 8.20).

Figure 8.20
Installing NetWare 5 license.

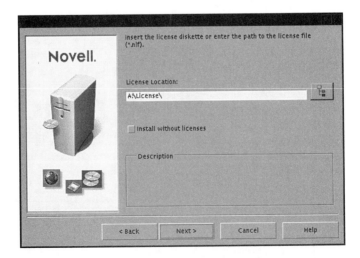

Caution

If your NetWare 5 Operating System CD shows "US/Canada Edition" and your NetWare 5 license has more than eight digits, don't use the GUI to install the license, or you'll hang the process. Instead, check the Install Without Licenses box and use the procedure outlined later in this chapter to install the license later.

If there is more than one license file on the disk, you'll be prompted to select the correct one (see Figure 8.21).

Figure 8.21
Selecting a NetWare 5 license.

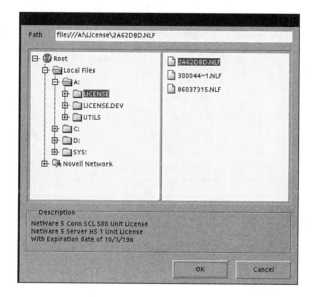

For various reasons (such as the one pointed out in the previous Caution) you might choose to install the server without a license. To do so, check the Install Without Licenses box and click Next to continue. If you do this, however, only two connection licenses will be available. A valid license can be installed after completing the NetWare 5 server installation by using NWAdmin or use the following steps:

1. At the server console, type NWCONFIG.
2. Select License Options and choose Install Licenses.
3. Insert your license disk into the floppy drive, and install the license following the prompts on the screen.
4. Reboot the server when you're finished.

After completing the NetWare server portion of the installation, you can select other networking products (such as LDAP and NDS Catalog Services) to install.

INSTALLING OTHER NETWORKING PRODUCTS AND SERVICES

Other Novell networking products and services can be installed during a NetWare 5 server install (see Figure 8.22).

Figure 8.22
Installing other net-
working products.

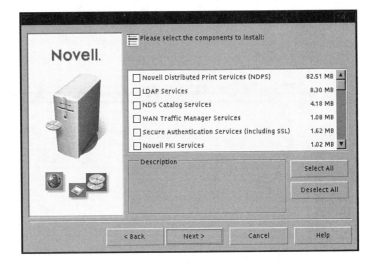

By installing additional products and services, you provide your network with additional networking functions. These services include the following:

- Novell Distributed Print Services (NDPS)
- LDAP Services for NDS
- NDS Catalog Services
- WAN Traffic Management Services
- Secure Authentication Services
- Novell Public Key Infrastructure (PKI) Services
- Novell Internet Access Server (NIAS) 4.1
- Storage Management Services (SMS)
- Novell DNS/DHCP Services

No services are selected for installation by default. Mark multiple products for installation by checking the check box next to the product names. Click Next to go to the summary screen.

Note that you do not have to install any of these products and services at this time. They can be easily installed later using NWCONFIG, as follows:

1. At the server console, load NWCONFIG.

2. Select Product Options and choose Install Other Novell Products.

3. From the resulting GUI screen, select the products you want to install.

Note

If you're not going to install any special products or services during this step, at least install SMS, because that is required by your NetWare 5–aware backup software.

CUSTOMIZING THE SERVER INSTALLATION

After you select the additional products and services to install, the installation program provides a summary screen with a Customize button. Click Customize to customize the installation of each product and service for your networking environment (see Figure 8.23). The following options can be customized:

- NetWare operating system
- File system
- Network protocols
- Novell Directory Services
- Additional networking products or services that you have selected for installation

Figure 8.23
Product customization.

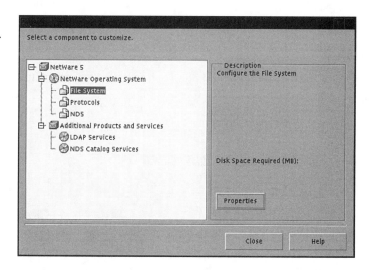

To customize the installation, click Customize on the Summary screen. Choose the product to customize and then click Properties. For example, if you selected the IP protocol earlier but didn't want Compatibility Mode Driver to be loaded, you can customize that here. Click Protocols, click the Properties button, and then click the IPX Compatibility tab. From the resulting screen (see Figure 8.24), uncheck the Load IPX Compatibility check box.

Figure 8.24
Removing IPX
Compatibility Mode
driver.

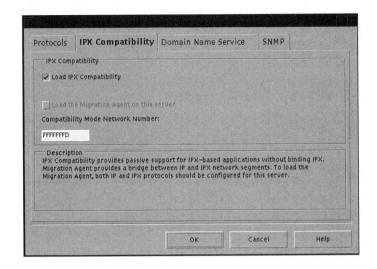

When you're finished, click Close to return to the Summary screen, and then click Finish.

COMPLETING THE INSTALLATION

The NetWare 5 installation program now copies the files for SYS:LOGIN, SYS:PUBLIC, SYS:SYSTEM, and so on, and the selected product files to the server (see Figure 8.25). You are prompted to specify the media path for the CD-ROM. The default path is NETWARE:, and if you're using the DOS CD-ROM drive, enter D:\ (or the appropriate drive letter).

Figure 8.25
Final file copying to
the server.

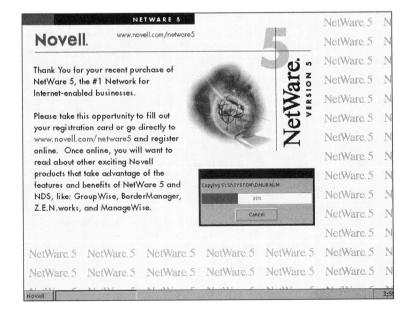

After the files are copied, click Reboot to restart the server so new settings take effect.

POST-INSTALLATION TASKS

To ensure smooth operation of your new NetWare 5 server in the production environment, the following is a list of some of the housekeeping cleanup tasks you should perform after completing the server install:

- Check your AUTOEXEC.BAT to ensure that SERVER.EXE is executed every time the system is rebooted.

- Remove or rename CONFIG.SYS. You don't need to load any DOS device drivers, including CD-ROM, for NetWare to function. As a matter of fact, sometimes they can cause conflict with NetWare. (Although the installation process should do this for you automatically, it doesn't hurt to check just to be sure.)

- Check the STARTUP.NCF file (located in C:\NWSERVER) to ensure any hardware-specific SET commands recommended by the hardware manufacturers are included.

- Verify that the CMOS clock is correct. If the date or time is incorrect, the NetWare server and your workstation clients can inherit the erroneous time.

- If you've set up disk mirroring or duplexing under NetWare, copy the contents of C:\NWSERVER (and its subdirectories) to the DOS partition of the mirror drive—NetWare mirrors only the NetWare partition and not the DOS partition.

TROUBLESHOOTING

Listed in this section are some common problems that you can encounter during your server software installation. Some solutions and workarounds are presented. The list is by no means exhaustive. It is assumed here that you have resolved any possible hardware conflicts.

DISK DRIVER PROBLEM

Given that NetWare 5 requires HAM and CDM drivers, there are some instances where these drivers don't work with older hardware due to the outdated BIOS. Having the same hardware working under NetWare 3 or even NetWare 4 is no guarantee that they work (well) under NetWare 5, due to the architecture change. What's worse, some storage device vendors simply don't write HAM/CDM drivers for their older product lines, forcing you to upgrade.

HARD DISK PROBLEM

Because different manufacturers have different ways of accessing hard drives, especially large capacity drives, it is best not to mix hard drives from different manufactures on the same controller. In some cases, it is also inadvisable to mix drives of different capacities on the same controller, even if they are from the same vendor.

Make sure all shadowing is turned off in your server's BIOS settings and that BIOS is not configured for DOS support for drives larger than 1GB or DOS translation for large drives. These features allow DOS to see larger drives and are incompatible with NetWare.

LAN DRIVER PROBLEM

With the implementation of the Virtual Memory feature in NetWare 5, LAN drivers that assume that logical addresses are equal to physical addresses can cause intermittent data corruption. This problem is most likely to manifest itself in DMA adapters certified before November 1, 1997.

Sometimes LAN drivers for NetWare 4 servers do not work well in the NetWare 5 environment. Check with your vendor for the latest NetWare 5 compatible driver. Under rare conditions, however, a NetWare 4 LAN driver works better than a NetWare 5 driver does.

> **Note**
>
> If your LAN card comes with a certified NetWare 5 driver, use it instead of the one included on the NetWare 5 CD because the vendor-supplied one is likely to be more current.

ETHERNET FRAME FORMAT PROBLEM

Due to the change in default frame format of LAN Ethernet drivers (from ETHERNET_802.3 to ETHERNET_802.2), your NetWare 5 server might not "see" your NetWare 3.*x* and 2.*x* servers but will see your NetWare 4 servers. Make sure that you use the same frame format among all the servers using the CONFIG console command.

> **Note**
>
> During the network protocol installation, NetWare 5's installation program auto-detects the frame types that are present on the wire. However, if you configured your NetWare 5 server in an isolated environment, some frame types might not be included in your AUTOEXEC.NCF file. You can manually add more LOAD and BIND commands as needed.

INSUFFICIENT RAM

Novell recommends 64MB of RAM for a NetWare 5 server. However, if you're running third-party applications (such as a backup utility) or plan to use Java on the server, a *minimum* of 128MB is recommended. There are known instances where a server abends due to insufficient RAM (or when the server is underpowered).

INCOMPATIBLE NLMs

Not all NetWare 3 and NetWare 4 NLMs will run (correctly) on a NetWare 5 server. Check with your vendor to see whether a newer version is required and available. Unfortunately, there is no *comprehensive* published document on certified NLMs for the NetWare 5 platform. At best, the NLM will not load. At worst, it will abend your server.

Tip #66 from
Peter

If you're unsure whether your NLM-based application is NetWare 5 certified, check at `http://developer.novell.com/npp`. The site contains a list of applications that vendors have submitted to Novell for certification and passed.

UNABLE TO BOOT FROM CD-ROM

In order to boot from the NetWare 5 Operating System CD for your installation, the server must have a ROM BIOS that fully supports the El Torito specification—including a hard disk image. Booting on a machine where the specification is not supported might result in hangs after starting Caldera DR DOS or messages such as "No operating system found".

LOG FILES

During a standard installation, a log file (`C:\NWINST.LOG`) is created. `CONLOG.NLM` is used to create this log file. With a normal installation, this file will be 0 bytes because the file is only written when `CONLOG` is unloaded (which doesn't happen during a normal install). If you unload `CONLOG` (from the system console) before rebooting the server, this file will be a screen capture of everything that happened during installation.

Also, a temporary directory, `C:\NWINST.TMP`, is created. This is for storing configuration files and some installation NLMs. If there are problems during installation, you can look for error log files in this directory. One that might be created is the `BOOT$LOG.ERR` file.

These log files can help you to determine the cause of your installation failure.

PURE IP, COMPATIBILITY MODE, AND SERVICE LOCATION PROTOCOL (SLP)

In this chapter

NETWARE PROTOCOLS

Versions of NetWare prior to NetWare 5 used the internetwork packet exchange (IPX) and sequenced package exchange (SPX) protocols for communications. Novell created IPX and SPX based on the Xerox network system (XNS) protocol, which was developed in the 1970s. Open standards were not the norm when Novell developed IPX/SPX—that is, many companies chose to use their own protocols to manage their own systems, making integration with other systems challenging.

As the networking world started moving towards standards-based protocols, Novell came out with a product called NetWare/IP (which runs on NetWare 3 and NetWare 4). NetWare/IP uses the TCP/IP protocol (TCP/IP is discussed in Chapter 28, "Introduction to TCP/IP"); IPX, however, is still required because IPX is actually being encapsulated in an IP (UDP) datagram. The reason that IPX is needed is because prior to NetWare 5, the NetWare Core Protocol (NCP) was tied to IPX.

Note

NCP is NetWare's Core Protocol (at the Application layer of the OSI model, which was discussed in Chapter 4, "Networking Data Flow") that allows communications between Novell clients and servers.

Then, as the Internet (with its TCP/IP protocol) became more popular for doing business, Novell decided to decouple NCP from IPX with NetWare 5. Now, NetWare 5 provides its NCP services over the TCP/IP protocol natively (without any IPX encapsulation). Additionally, NetWare 5 can still run NCP over IPX. In the simplest sense, then, Pure IP is NCP running natively over the IP protocol without any encapsulation or tunneling.

NetWare 5's Pure IP uses a variety of protocols in the TCP/IP protocol suite—for example, Service Location Protocol (SLP), which is discussed later in this chapter. The Pure IP capability in NetWare 5 is one of the main reasons that companies are upgrading to NetWare 5, to get to standards-based protocols and the luxury of maintaining just one protocol (IP) on the wire.

WHICH PROTOCOL SHOULD I USE?

With the introduction of Pure IP to NetWare 5, there are now four different "modes" in which NetWare servers and clients can be set up:

- IPX Only
- Dual Stacks (IP and IPX)
- Pure IP
- IP with Compatibility Mode Driver (CMD)

Which of these four modes you choose depends on your goals for NetWare 5. Although there are many good reasons for upgrading to NetWare 5, such as the enhanced file system (NSS), Java, or improved operating system performance, this chapter assumes one of your goals is to eventually get to a Pure IP environment.

> **Note**
>
> To avoid terminology confusion, this chapter consistently uses the term *Pure IP* to mean no IPX anywhere on the network and, therefore, no capability for running IPX-dependent applications, printing, services, and so on. This distinction will be necessary to avoid confusion between Pure IP and IP with CMD, which gets IPX off the wire but maintains compatibility for IPX-dependent applications. It really boils down to what your definition of Pure IP is. To many, it is simply IPX off the wire but, again, this definition would lead to confusion here between Pure IP and IP with CMD.

The four client and server modes will now be discussed with respect to how they meet the goal of transitioning to Pure IP.

IPX Only

As its name implies, all NetWare servers run only IPX and clients must, therefore, also run IPX. Even though the IP protocol might be on the client for Internet access it cannot be used to connect to NetWare servers running just IPX. An IPX-only NetWare environment would be used in cases where you want to use NetWare 5 for some of its other features but want to continue to use IPX for NetWare communications. At a later date, you could transition to a Pure IP environment. However, installing NetWare 5 with IPX only is not in itself considered a transition path to Pure IP.

Dual Stacks (IP and IPX)

In this case, all NetWare servers run both the IP and IPX protocols. Clients can, therefore, connect to NetWare servers using either IP or IPX. Dual Stacks does not eliminate IPX from the wire until all IPX-dependencies on the network have been eliminated; at this point, you can turn off IPX and have Pure IP.

Tip #67 from
Sally

> You can determine IPX-dependent applications by using `IPXCON.NLM` and looking at the SAP Tables. The SAP tables should give you 90% of your IPX-dependent applications. If there is no SAP for an application, it is NCP-based versus IPX-based. Because NCP in NetWare 5 has been rewritten to run over IP, NCP-based applications will run over IP. For the remaining 10% of applications, check with the vendor to see if and when an IP-based version of the application is available. As a crude approach to seeing whether an application is IPX dependent, try running the application in a lab environment on a server with Pure IP. If it is IPX-based, it will fail!

The following are the benefits of the Dual Stacks approach for transitioning to Pure IP:

- NetWare 4 and NetWare 5 servers can communicate with each other without using Compatibility Mode Drivers (CMDs), thus reducing the planning time and support costs for setting up and maintaining a CMD infrastructure. (CMD is discussed later in this chapter.)

- Servers and workstations do not have to be upgraded at the same time or in any certain order.

- IPX-dependent applications can continue to run on all servers. As IPX dependencies are eliminated, the system simply evolves into a Pure IP environment.

- There is no risk of service interruption because the wire carries both the IP and IPX protocols.

The downsides to this approach are as follows:

- Managing two protocols on the network.

- There will still be IPX's SAP and RIP traffic on the wire, which might not be desirable on WAN links.

Dual Stack is the easiest approach for transitioning to Pure IP. However, depending on how fast your company wants to get IPX off the wire, this might not be the appropriate solution.

> **Note** With Dual Stacks, both servers and clients prefer to use IP for all NCP-based communications. IPX is used for IPX dependencies that are not yet supported over IP.

PURE IP

As its name implies, all NetWare servers run only IP and clients must, therefore, also run IP. There will be no IPX anywhere on the network, which means there can be no applications, printers, services, and so on on the network that rely on IPX.

Pure IP will probably be the eventual goal for many companies (as it is assumed here in this chapter). Realistically, though, the immediate transition to a Pure IP environment is probably only possible in very small networking environments and for environments where there are no IPX dependencies. However, you can get to an IP environment where there is no IPX on the wire, which is generally the goal of most companies. This is accomplished by using IP with CMD (discussed next).

IP WITH CMD (IP/CMD)

As just mentioned, the transition to a Pure IP environment is not something that can happen immediately unless your network has no IPX dependencies at all. Novell realized this and has provided the Compatibility Mode Drivers (for both servers and clients) for backward compatibility with IPX.

CMD is the function in NetWare 5 that allows you to get to IP-only on the wire while still maintaining the capability for servers to run IPX-dependent applications, until they can be migrated to IP-based applications. Again, by this definition, you will not be Pure IP until all IPX dependencies are completely eliminated but you can be IP-only on the wire until that time, by using NetWare 5's CMD.

I already mentioned that Dual Stacks is one way to transition to Pure IP and that it is a gradual transition (because both IP and IPX remain on the wire until all IPX dependencies are eliminated). CMD is the second transition path to Pure IP; it is considered a faster transition path than Dual Stacks because IPX can be removed from the wire immediately (logically and realistically, though, IPX will probably be removed from the wire on a segment-by-segment basis). With the CMD approach for transitioning to IP, however, you must set up and maintain a CMD infrastructure (something you don't have to do with the Dual Stacks approach). Additionally, because CMD requires SLP, you will also need to use SLP when using IP/CMD.

CMD on NetWare 5 servers provides the three features discussed in the following sections.

PART
III
CH
9

BACKWARD COMPATIBILITY FOR IPX-DEPENDENT APPLICATIONS, WHILE ALLOWING JUST IP ON THE WIRE

This feature of CMD is enabled on NetWare servers by loading SCMD.NLM (with no switches).

Tip #68 from	When you load SCMD.NLM (no switches) on a server, IPX can't be bound on that server; if it is, an error message is displayed and SCMD.NLM does not load. Not having IPX loaded on an SCMD server makes sense when you remember its purpose: to allow IPX-dependent applications to be run on an IP (CMD) server. SCMD alone does not put IPX traffic on the wire.
Gally	

You should understand that the only time CMD comes into play is if an application is hard-coded to use IPX; the rest of the NCP-based traffic defaults to the IP stack. SCMD.NLM (no switches) does not in any way provide IPX to IP connectivity; its only purpose is to provide backward compatibility for IPX-dependent applications running on the server. If you want to provide IPX to IP connectivity, use the Migration Agent capability in SCMD.NLM (discussed in the next section).

"BRIDGING" COMMUNICATIONS BETWEEN CONTIGUOUS IPX AND IP SEGMENTS

In this case, CMD is referred to as a Migration Agent (MA) because this functionality is accomplished with the Migration Agent component of SCMD.NLM. The MA component of SCMD is necessary as you start to migrate segments to IP while other segments remain as IPX, waiting to be migrated to IP. In this case, the MAs bridge the IP and IPX segments so that there is no service interruption.

The MA capability is enabled on NetWare servers by loading SCMD.NLM with either the /g (gateway) or the /ma (migration agent) switch (the two switches are identical in function). You can only load SCMD /g or /ma when both IP and IPX are bound, which makes sense when you consider the purpose of the Migration Agent is to bridge contiguous IPX and IP segments.

> **Note**
>
> SCMD.NLM v1.59f or higher (available from scmda.exe at http://support.novell.com) now runs on NetWare 4, in addition to NetWare 5. This was to facilitate migrating from NetWare/IP to IP(CMD).

MAs provide a virtual IPX network in your IP network, allowing an IPX segment to communicate with an IP segment. The default IPX number for CMD is set to hex FFFFFFFD.

> **Tip #69 from**
> *Sally*
>
> This virtual IPX number must be the same on all MAs; therefore, it is recommended that you leave it at this default. However, if there are departments in your company that can bring up NetWare 5 servers on the production LAN/WAN for testing purposes, you should change the production CMD's FFFFFFFD number to avoid possible conflicts. If you do change this number, ensure that it does not conflict with any other IPX network numbers (internal, external, or even another CMD network number).

> **Tip #70 from**
> *Sally*
>
> Using two MAs in the backbone (as shown in Figure 9.1) is recommended for fault tolerance purposes. These two MAs collect SAP/RIP information for clients and servers in Toronto (and any other IPX segments) until these network segments are transitioned to IP/CMD.

Figure 9.1 is an example of how the Migration Agent component of SCMD.NLM bridges the recently converted Dallas (IP/CMD) segment with the Toronto (IPX) segment.

The IP/CMD clients in Dallas can, of course, access the NetWare 5 server in Dallas and run any IPX-dependent applications on it (due to SCMD.NLM). Additionally, the IP/CMD clients in Dallas can access and run applications on the IPX server in Toronto through the Migration Agent in the backbone. The IPX clients in Toronto can, of course, access the IPX server in Toronto. Additionally, the IPX clients in Toronto can access and run applications on the SCMD.NLM server in Dallas through the Migration Agent in the backbone.

"BRIDGING" COMMUNICATIONS BETWEEN NONCONTIGUOUS IPX AND IP SEGMENTS

In this case, CMD is referred to as a Migration Agent with Backbone Support because this function is accomplished with the Backbone Support component of SCMD.NLM. The Backbone Support component of SCMD is necessary if you decide to migrate your backbone to IP first, and then migrate your network segments to IP last, which results in noncontiguous IP and IPX network segments.

Figure 9.1
Migration Agent
example.

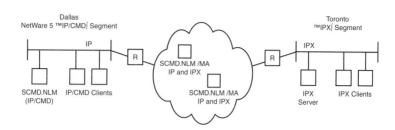

The Backbone Support capability is enabled on NetWare servers by loading SCMD.NLM with the /bs (backbone support) switch. You can load SCMD /bs only when both IP and IPX are bound, which makes sense when you consider the purpose of Backbone Support is to bridge noncontiguous IPX and IP segments.

Note

With the release of the NetWare 5 Support Pack 1, loading /g, /ma, or /bs automatically enables *both* the Migration Agent and the Migration Agent with Backbone Support features. The switches were discussed separately here just to keep the terminology and your understanding of Migration Agent and Migration Agent with Backbone Support clear and concise.

Tip #71 from
Sally

Because Migration Agents and Backbone Support are both enabled when loading /g, /ma, or /bs, Backbone Support also uses the same virtual IPX network as discussed previously and you should, therefore, follow the same tip for determining whether or not to keep this number at FFFFFFFD.

Figure 9.2 is an example of how the Backbone Support component of SCMD.NLM bridges the Dallas and Toronto segments (both running IPX) after the backbone was first converted to IP.

The IPX clients in Dallas can access and run applications on the NetWare 5 server in Dallas which runs both IP and IPX (a requirement of SCMD.NLM /bs). Of course, these clients can also access the IPX server in Dallas, too. Additionally, the IPX clients in Dallas can access and run applications on the IPX server in Toronto through the Migration Agent with Backbone Support servers at both ends of the IP backbone. These IPX clients in Dallas can also access and run applications on the NetWare 5 server in Toronto which runs both IP and IPX (a requirement of SCMD.NLM /bs). This same logic holds true for the clients in Toronto.

Additionally, after the remaining IPX server in Dallas is migrated to IP/CMD the clients in Dallas can also be migrated to IP/CMD.

Figure 9.2
Migration Agent
with Backbone
Support example.

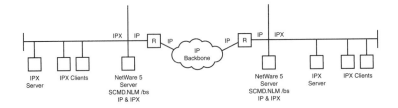

Tip #72 from
Sally

For fault tolerance purposes, you might want to place two Migration Agents with Backbone Support on each network segment.

This section showed you two different methods for getting to Pure IP:

- Dual Stacks
- IP/CMD

With the IP/CMD approach, you can do either of the following:

- Migrate network segments first and the backbone last (in which case you use MAs as shown in Figure 9.1).
- Migrate the backbone first and the network segments last (in which case you use the Backbone Support capability of MAs as shown in Figure 9.2).

SERVICE LOCATION PROTOCOL (SLP)

Every network operating system must have a way to advertise and discover the services available on its network. How this process occurs depends on the protocols in use on the network.

The IPX protocol uses the Service Advertising Protocol (SAP) to advertise its services via broadcast messages; NetWare IPX clients trying to find SAP services send SAP broadcast requests which are answered by IPX (SAP) routers and servers on the network. SAP has the advantage of being plug-and-play, in the sense that you don't have to manually configure SAP. With this advantage comes the disadvantage of the "chattiness" of SAP: It advertises itself every 60 seconds using broadcasts, which are seen by the entire network (by default) and can put excessive traffic on the wire, especially across a WAN.

The IP protocol uses the Service Location Protocol (SLP) to discover services in the IP world. SLP uses multicast messages and unicast messages (and, optionally, can use broadcast messages). Unicast messages cross routers and are only processed by the intended recipient. Multicast messages can be routed (although most companies do not allow multicasts across routers due to traffic considerations). Multicast messages are only processed or received by members of the multicast group—that is, devices running the Internet Group Management Protocol (IGMP). IGMP is a protocol used between clients and multicast routers on a single physical network to establish a client's membership in particular multicast groups. In general, multicast and unicast messages used with SLP are considered less chatty than broadcast messages used with SAP.

There are two principal differences between SAP and SLP:

- SLP alone does not maintain a global database of services as SAP does (assuming there is no filtering).

- SLP assumes that the client can locate the services themselves or a database server representing those services.

SLP is an agent-based protocol and in NetWare 5 is implemented as discussed in the following sections (which is fairly consistent with RFC 2165).

USER AGENTS

User Agents (UAs) are software components that make requests for SLP services. UAs are automatically enabled on every NetWare 5 client and server. You can see that the NetWare 5 client software is now SLP-enabled by looking at the new Service Location property tab in Figure 9.3.

Figure 9.3
SLP-enabled
NetWare Client.

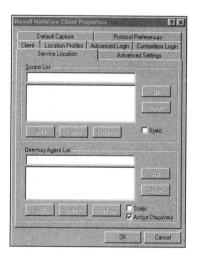

In Figure 9.3, notice that, by default, Active Discovery is enabled and no Directory Agents or Scopes are used (both of which are discussed later in this chapter). UAs, therefore, ask for services available on the network with multicast address 224.0.1.22 (SA General Service Request). This is the multicast address that Novell has registered for a UA to find a Service Agent.

SERVICE AGENTS

Service Agents (SAs) "house" their available IP services and respond to a UA's request for these services. SAs are on all NetWare 5 servers and are enabled with the SLP.NLM and SLPTCP.NLM modules, both of which are automatically loaded when IP is used on a NetWare 5 server.

Note

SAs are enabled on the NetWare 5 client for future use, such as for advertising a workstation-based printer. All SA discussion here assumes an SA is running on a NetWare 5 server.

SAs reply to a UA's multicast request for services via a unicast message. Only the SAs that can hear the multicast request from UAs respond to the UA. (Remember that multicast is generally not supported across routers; therefore, all NetWare 5 servers on the network are not necessarily responding back to the UA.) Additionally, only the SAs that have the service the UA is looking for respond back to the UA. As you should realize now, SAs do not broadcast their available services; rather, they just "wait" for a multicast request for services from a UA then respond with a unicast message if they have the requested service.

The real advantage to the UA-SA communication for finding IP-based services is zero administration and zero configuration, because they are automatically enabled on both NetWare 5 servers and clients. However, the tradeoff is that the more SAs there are on the network, the more multicast traffic there is from the UAs—causing an increase in network utilization on the wire. This is when a Directory Agent can be used to scale the SAs.

Tip #73 from
Sally

A general guideline is to use Directory Agents when there are 20 Service Agents that a User Agent can reach. Again this is a guideline (not a fail number) and really depends on the bandwidth capacity of your links. If your company is WAN-oriented, using SAs without a Directory Agent does not scale very well. In a LAN environment using Ethernet, it scales better than a WAN environment and even better if using Token Ring or FDDI, where the maximum packet size is greater. With SLP Version 1, the maximum SLP packet size is 65KB. When SLP Version 2 is available, the maximum SLP packet size is increased to a 24-bit (16 million) number.

DIRECTORY AGENTS

Directory Agents (DAs) are optional and are not enabled by default on either clients or servers, as SAs and UAs are. A NetWare 5 server becomes a DA when you load SLPDA.NLM on it. DAs can be used for a couple of different scenarios:

- When IP multicasts are not routed and a client on a network segment wants to dynamically discover services across a router (for example, this client wants to use the Windows 95-98 Network Neighborhood to discover, or "see," services on the other side of a router). In this case, a DA is used for dynamic discovery purposes.

- To centralize services so that UAs do not contact all SAs in the multicast group; rather, UAs directly contact a DA, which contains the services forwarded to it by the SAs. In this case, the DA is being used to scale the SAs.

DAs are not needed on all the NetWare 5 servers in your environment. Rather, a DA (or two) is usually placed at each physical site in the network to collect the services on that network segment and provide these services to clients on that network segment. If these services are needed on another network segment, you can use NDS to replicate the SLP Scope Unit container object (which is the container object that holds SLP services as shown in Figure 9.4) to a DA at another site. The RFC for SLP (2165) has no standard for DA-to-DA replication; Novell has used their NDS database for this purpose.

PART

III

CH

9

Figure 9.4
SLP objects in NDS.

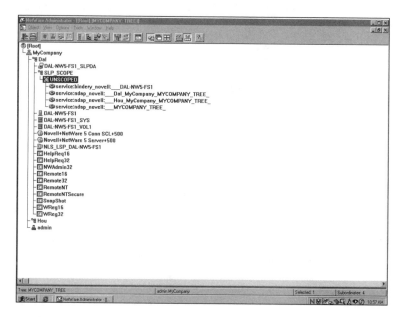

Figure 9.4 shows the default SLP objects created when you load SLPDA.NLM on a NetWare 5 server. Three SLP objects are shown here:

- The SLP Directory Agent (leaf) object, which is represented in Figure 9.4 as DAL-NW5-FS1_SLPDA. The default naming takes the file server name and appends _SLPDA to it. Additionally, this object is created in the same container as the file server on which you load SLPDA.NLM.

- The SLP Scope Unit (container) object, which is represented in Figure 9.4 as UNSCOPED. UNSCOPED itself is a container-class object which was by default created under the OU=SLP_SCOPE container.

- The SLP services known by DAL-NW5_FS1_SLPDA (as forwarded by the SAs), which are represented in Figure 9.4 as the four-leaf objects beginning with service:. Unlike other NDS leaf objects these SLP services cannot be manually created in NWAdmn32; rather, they are created (and deleted) dynamically by the DA as these services become available and unavailable.

DAs announce their presence via multicast address 224.0.1.35 (DA Service Advertisement). This is the multicast address that Novell has registered for a DA to advertise itself. This multicast is done every 10,800 seconds (3 hours) by default and is configurable with the SET SLP DA HEART BEAT TIME parameter.

When SAs see the DA's 224.0.1.35 multicast address, they register their IP services directly with the DA. Additionally, an SA can statically register its IP services with a DA via the SA's SYS:ETC\SLP.CFG file (the sample SLP.CFG file that ships with NetWare 5 shows you the appropriate format). If you want an SA to only use the SLP.CFG to communicate with a DA, use the SET parameter SET SLP DA DISCOVERY OPTIONS = 4, where the available settings are as follows:

1 = Dynamic Discovery

2 = DHCP Discovery

4 = Static file SYS:ETC\SLP.CFG

8 = Disable dynamic discovery when DHCP or static files are present

The default is 15, which is all four options enabled. You simply add each number to enable the DA discovery mode(s) you want.

When UAs see the DA's 224.0.1.35 multicast address, they send *unicast* messages to the DA asking for services (bypassing the multicast request for an SA). A unicast message is a message that is addressed and sent to just the intended recipient (in this case, the DA); therefore, unicast messages generate less traffic than multicast (and broadcast) messages. Additionally, a UA can statically get to a DA via DNS or dynamically via DHCP with Option 78 (which is the option used to give a DHCP client the IP address of a DA).

Tip #74 from
Sally

> Your DHCP Server must support Option 78, as does Novell's DHCP server that ships with NetWare 5 and is discussed in Chapter 30, "Dynamic Host Configuration Protocol (DHCP)."

The DA, therefore, eliminates multicast traffic between UAs and SAs. So what happens if the DA goes down? UAs and SAs will communicate directly using the multicast/unicast mode of communications discussed previously until the DA is back online.

Tip #75 from
Sally

> Having two DAs in your network for fault tolerance would eliminate the falling back on UA-SA multicast communications.

In the simplest sense, DAs become a collection of SLP services on the network containing either all services on the network—if the DA is associated with the Unscoped Scope (as it is by default)—or a localized set of services if the DA is associated with a Registered Scope.

SCOPES

As shown in Figure 9.4, an UNSCOPED SLP Scope Unit (*UNSCOPED Scope*) is created by default when you load SLPDA.NLM. All DAs belong to the UNSCOPED Scope by default; therefore, the UNSCOPED Scope will contain all services on the network.

> **Note**
>
> UNSCOPED Scope is a rather confusing term and will likely be changed in the future. For now, it is best to think of the UNSCOPED Scope as a default scope that contains all services known on the network.

You can scale the UNSCOPED Scope by creating Registered Scope objects. Registered Scopes (for these purposes) are simply scopes that can be created in NWAdmn32; additionally, these Registered Scopes can be partitioned and replicated to sites where other DAs are located. So while DAs scale SAs, Registered Scopes scale the UNSCOPED Scope.

Figure 9.5
Directory Agent example.

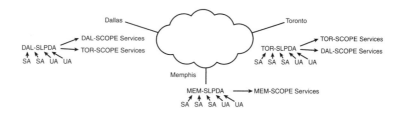

Referring to Figure 9.5, a DAL-Scope object was created in Dallas to house all the IP services from the SAs in Dallas. A TOR-Scope was created in Toronto to house all the IP services from the SAs in Toronto. Additionally, because the Dallas site frequently requires the services in Toronto (and vice versa) the DAL-Scope container was replicated (via NDS) in Toronto and the TOR-Scope container was replicated (via NDS) in Dallas. Memphis is assumed to only need its local IP services. Clients in Memphis can, however, access an IP service in Dallas or Toronto (if needed) by using for example the IP service's DNS name or even its IP address. The UNSCOPED Scope was removed from all three DAs. This configuration shows just one of the many possibilities you have for setting up a Directory Agent environment, depending on your company's needs.

> **Tip #76 from**
> *Sally*
>
> Even if you create Registered Scopes, all services are still registered with the Unscoped Scope. Therefore, depending on your goals for SLP, you might want to remove DAs from their association with the Unscoped Scope.

When a NetWare 5 server starts up, SLP is automatically loaded and services on the server begin registering with the SA on that server itself. The following are common Novell SLP service types. The console command DISPLAY SLP SERVICES shows which ones your NetWare 5 server is advertising:

- BINDERY.NOVELL—This is how a server advertises itself as a NetWare NCP server.
- NDAP.NOVELL—A server advertises this once for each replica of a partition it holds. *NDAP* stands for *Novell Directory Access Protocol* which is the protocol used to access the services in NDS.

- `MGW.NOVELL`—A server acting as a CMD Migration Agent or Migration Agent with Backbone Support advertises this service.
- `SAPSRV.NOVELL`—A server running `SCMD.NLM` advertises this.
- `RMS.NOVELL`—A server running the Resource Management Service of NDPS (Novell Distributed Print Services) advertises this.
- `SRS.NOVELL`—A server running a Novell Distributed Print Services (NDPS) broker advertises this. SRS stands for the Service Registry Service used in NDPS.
- `RCONSOLE.NOVELL`—A server running the Java rconsole advertises this.

Most of the Novell SLP services will end in `.NOVELL`, as in the previous list.

Looking back at Figure 9.4, you can see that the DA has a service listing for an NCP server `DAL-NW5-FS1`, the Tree `MYCOMPANY_TREE`, and two additional replicas (besides the implied `[Root]`) for the partitions `Dal_MyCompany` and `Hou_MyCompany`. If you were to load `SCMD /ma` on `DAL-NW5-FS1`, you would then see the services `service:mgw_novell:<ip_address(es)>` and `sapsrv_novell_<ipx_address(es)>`. Note that in Figure 9.4, `DAL-NW5-FS1` is both the MA and the DA.

Tip #77 from *Gally*	If you are familiar with SAP, you should now start to realize the loose parallels between common advertisements in the SAP and SLP worlds:

Service	SAP Number	SLP Address
Bindery Server	0x0004	`bindery.novell`
NDS	0x0278	`ndap.novell`

PROJECT: FURTHER READING

- Go to `http://support.novell.com` and get TID 2944065 "SCMD Related Documents." This TID contains a compilation of links to Compatibility Mode (CMD) documents and is strongly recommended for further reading on CMD.
- Go to `http://renoir.vill.edu/~ycao/outline.html` for a clear and concise document on how SLP is implemented in RFC 2165. Notice the parallels discussed in this document and in NetWare 5's implementation of SLP, which follows the RFC 2165 specifications.
- Get Novell's April 1999 AppNote "Configuration Parameters for the Compatibility Mode Driver" downloadable from `http://developer.novell.com/research/appnotes.htm`. This AppNote shows you how to configure CMD to get the results needed in your specific environment.
- Get Novell's March 1999 AppNote "Dynamically Discovering Services on an IP Network with SLP" downloadable from `http://developer.novell.com/research/appnotes.htm`.

Tip #78 from
Sally

There are two commands for troubleshooting Client CMD and SLP issues:

```
C:\Novell\Client32\CMDINFO
C:\Novell\Client32\SLPINFO
```

DISK MANAGEMENT

In this chapter

DISK DRIVERS

Your storage hardware consists of two pieces: the storage adapter, which is a fancy way of saying disk controller, and the storage devices themselves, such as disks, CD-ROMs, tape drives, and so on. In NetWare 5, the drivers have changed, and the old .dsk drivers that you are used to no longer work. NWPA, or NetWare Peripheral Architecture, splits up the drivers required into two parts: one for the storage adapter itself, and one for the storage device itself.

Host Adapter Modules, or .HAM drivers, allow the server to communicate with the storage adapter (disk controller). If you have only one controller in the server, you need to load only one .ham driver for it. Always check to make sure that you have the newest .ham drivers from your vendors.

Custom Device Modules, or .CDM drivers, are for the actual storage devices. You load a .cdm driver for each type of storage device you have attached to the controller; for example, if you have a controller with one SCSI disk and one CD-ROM, you load the .ham for the controller, SCSIHD.CDM for the hard disk, and SCSICD.CDM for the CD-ROM (SCSIHD.CDM and SCSICD.CDM are the Novell-supplied .cdm files for the hard disk and CD-ROM, respectively). The .ham and .cdm drivers are loaded in the startup.ncf file, just as you used to do with the .dsk files; nothing has changed there.

DISK UTILITIES

In this section, you will take a quick look at only a few of the utilities used to manage your disk space. I cover the venerable text-based, command-line NDIR, and also take a quick look at vrepair, used to repair disks that will not mount. Space doesn't permit an in-depth look at them all, and one I left out is FILER. FILER is also a command-line executable, but with its familiar character based GUI, it should be pretty straigtforward, even if you have never run it before.

VOLUME STATISTICS

As an administrator, you need to keep an eye on your volume statistics, especially the free space. It's a lot better to know in advance that you are running out of disk space than to find out about it when the warning message pops up! To obtain volume statistics using NetWare Administrator, right-click a volume, choose Details, and then take a look at the statistics page. You will see the information shown in Figure 10.1.

Just about anything you need to know about your volume is summed up for you nicely on the statistics page. The disk space and directory entries are shown graphically, but you can also see the name spaces, the installed features, and statistics on compressed and deleted files.

Figure 10.1

The statistics page for a volume in NetWare Administrator; a wealth of information about the volume is instantly available.

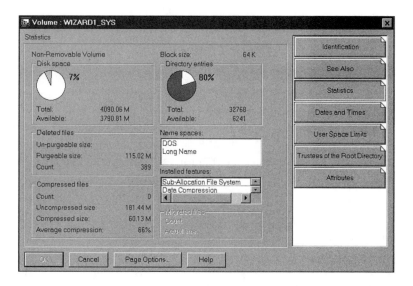

Another graphical interface is the network neighborhood; using network neighborhood gives you the same information, and it is quicker than going in through the NetWare Administrator, browsing to the correct context for the volume you want to see, and so on. If you right-click a volume and then choose Properties, you are presented with the four tabs shown in Figure 10.2, sort of a mini NetWare Administrator.

Figure 10.2

You can easily obtain volume information by right-clicking on a volume in Network Neighborhood and selecting Properties.

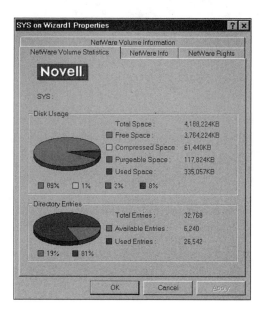

PART

III

CH

10

Of the four tabs shown in Figure 10.2, two are informational only: the Volume Information tab and the Volume Statistics tab. On the NetWare Info tab, you can not only see more volume information, but also set file attributes and, on the NetWare Rights tab, assign and view file-system rights.

But a windows-based utility isn't always the quickest or most convenient, or you might simply still prefer the command line if you are from the old school. At the command line, the venerable NDIR utility is still in existence. The NDIR command has far too many switches for me to cover here, but I will touch on a few of them. To compile your own collection, at the command prompt, enter the command Ndir /? All to pull up all the online help available for the NDIR command.

To see the volume statistics, you can use NDIR /VOL; the output of NDIR /VOL is given here:

```
Statistics for fixed volume WIZARD1/SYS:
Space statistics are in KB (1024 bytes).

Total volume space:                    4,188,224  100.00%
Space used by 26,530 entries:            306,176    7.31%
Deleted space not yet purgeable:               0    0.00%
                                       -----------  --------
Space remaining on volume:             3,882,048   92.69%
Space available to PENCE:              3,882,048   92.69%

Maximum directory entries:                32,768
Available directory entries:               6,238   19.04%

Space used if files were not compressed:  185,344
Space used by compressed files:            61,440
                                       -----------
Space saved by compressing files:         123,904   66.85%

Uncompressed space used:                  362,560

Name spaces loaded: OS/2
```

Tip #79 from
John

> Because NDIR is run from the command line, and the display is just text, you can easily redirect the output to a file. After you have the file, you can grep it, parse it, import it, or even have a mailer email it to you, something you can't do with the GUI interfaces.

A few of the other switches for NDIR are given in Table 10.1, but this is not a complete list. NDIR is a very powerful command-line utility, so by all means, look at the help screens and play around with some of the available options.

TABLE 10.1   SWITCHES FOR THE *NDIR* COMMAND

Switch	Function
/DA	File date information
/R	View filters, rights, and attributes
/MAC	Macintosh file information
/L	Long filenames
/D	Detailed file information
/COMP	Compressed file information
/FO	View files only
/DO	View directories only
/S	Include subdirectories
/C	Continuous output
/VOL	Volume information
/SPA	Directory Space information
/VER or /V	Version information

PART

III

CH

10

VREPAIR

Vrepair is used at the server console to repair the "traditional" NetWare volumes. I say "traditional" because vrepair is not for NSS volumes; NSS, Novell Storage Services, is covered later in this chapter, and NSS volumes have their own rebuild/verify utility. You don't need to worry about making a mistake in this area because vrepair will not even see an NSS volume.

Before you can repair a volume, the volume must be dismounted, as you can see from Figure 10.3.

If you have started vrepair, and then realize that the volume you want to repair is still mounted, you don't have to quit vrepair; you can toggle over to the server console, dismount the volume, and then continue.

Tip #80 from
John

What if the sys volume will not mount when the server comes up? Make sure that you have the vrepair.nlm and all necessary name space support modules (v_long.nlm, v_mac.nlm, and v_nfs.nlm) copied to the server's DOS partition; this way, you can still load and run vrepair even if the SYS: volume will not mount. These files should be on the server's DOS partition by default.

Figure 10.3
Vrepair runs only against unmounted volumes. At this point, you can press Alt+Esc to get to the server console and dismount the volume you want to repair.

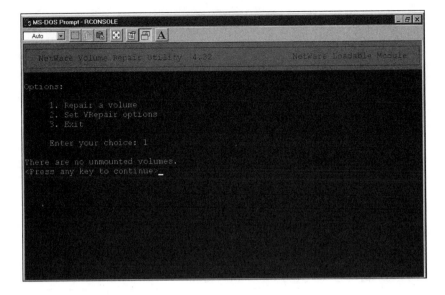

The syntax for vrepair is VREPAIR *<volume name>* *<log file>*. You do not need to specify a volume when loading vrepair; if only one volume is dismounted, that volume will be repaired by default. You don't need to use the log file option either; you can toggle logging on from within vrepair and specify the log filename at that time. If more than one volume is dismounted, you will be presented with a list of unmounted volumes, and you can select the appropriate volume from the list.

Notice the menu choices shown in the main vrepair screen shown in Figure 10.3: Repair a Volume, and Set Vrepair Options. Before you repair a volume, you need to set the options you want to use, as shown in Figure 10.4.

Figure 10.4
You need to set the vrepair options before you begin repairing a volume.

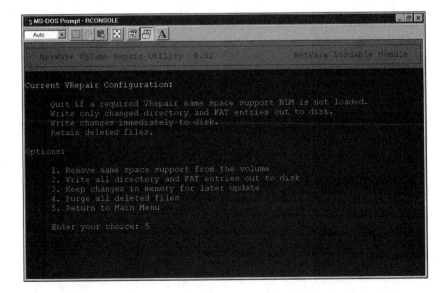

The options listed under Current Vrepair Configuration shown in Figure 10.4 are the defaults; the options are toggle switches. For example, if you selected option 4, the current configuration would change from Retain Deleted Files to Purge All Deleted Files. The vrepair process might delete files for a number of reasons, for example, if a file was found with an invalid DOS filename. If you choose to retain deleted files, they will be named VRxxxxxx.FIL, where x is some number; the files will be created in the directory in which they were found.

After you have set the vrepair options, return to the main menu and select Repair a Volume. If more than one volume is dismounted, select the one you want to repair from the list given. After the volume has been selected, you are ready to begin repairing the volume (see Figure 10.5).

Figure 10.5
Before beginning the repair, you can see the current error settings and can change these with the available options.

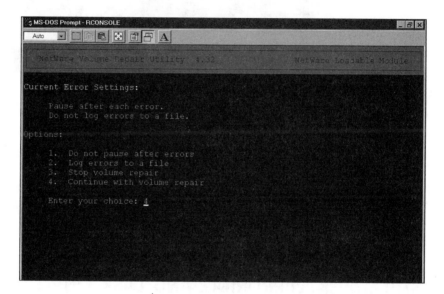

Option 1 toggles the Pause After Each Error. Option 2 toggles the Do Not Log Errors to a File, and when it's enabled, you are asked to supply the name for the log file. If a volume has extensive errors, you might consider turning off Pause After Each Error. Then, after vrepair is finished with the volume, turn on Pause After Each Error and run it again; you shouldn't have to intervene.

In Figure 10.6, you have successfully run vrepair against the Dodge volume. After you select option 4, continue with volume repair; then the necessary name space support modules are loaded and the repair begins. How long a vrepair run takes is related to the number of files and errors found on the volume.

Figure 10.6
Vrepair has been run against the Dodge volume; 0 errors were found and the process took 13 seconds.

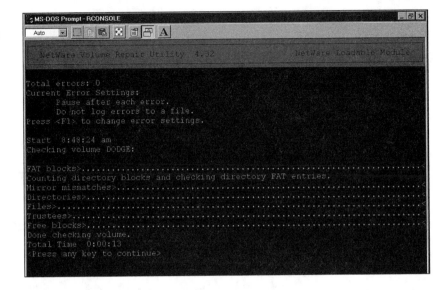

The setting Automatically Repair Bad Volumes will launch vrepair automatically when a volume fails to mount. This setting is on by default. If you do not want vrepair to automatically attempt to repair bad volumes, you need to turn this parameter to Off; changing the system settings is covered in Chapter 23, "Server Console Utilities."

When do you run vrepair? Administrators have differing opinions on this question; some run it as a preventive-maintenance type of thing, whereas others run it only when required. This author falls into the latter school of thinking, and I run it only when a volume fails to mount.

RAID, DISK MIRRORING, AND DISK DUPLEXING

The idea behind RAID, or Redundant Array of Inexpensive Disks, is to take many small disks and make them act as one large disk; to the server, a RAID array will appear as one "logical" disk. Raid can be implemented in either software or hardware. A software implementation is when the operating system itself is responsible for creating and managing the array.

NetWare 5 is capable of a software implementation of RAID-1, or disk mirroring. Disk mirroring is simply writing the same data to a pair of drives. In the event that one drive fails, the server will continue to be available, thanks to the remaining good disk. Writes must go to both drives, or else they would not be in sync; but read operations can be split across each of the drives. Thus, a mirrored pair will improve read access.

Disk mirroring uses only one storage adapter (disk controller) and two or more drives mirrored. This leaves a single point of failure, in that if the storage adapter fails, then even though you still have two perfectly good disks in the server, you cannot access them. Disk duplexing is the same as mirroring, except that more than one controller is used, as shown in Figure 10.7.

Figure 10.7
Disk duplexing is nothing more than disk mirroring, except that more than one controller is used. Make certain that you mirror a drive on one controller to a drive on the other controller.

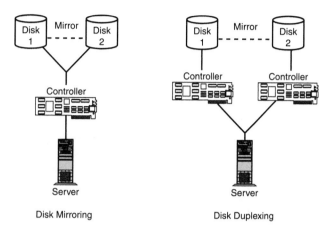

Disk Mirroring

Disk Duplexing

Adding the second storage adapter used by disk duplexing removes the single point of failure that disk mirroring has; you now have two channels to access your disks instead of only one. If a controller fails, you lose access to the disks attached to that controller, but because you are mirroring to the disks attached to the remaining good controller, you have no downtime.

RAID arrays can also be implemented via hardware, as opposed to having the operating system handle the task. In this case, the storage adapter handles setting up and managing the RAID array; all NetWare sees is just one disk. The controller comes with utilities for setting up and managing the array, and these utilities vary from vendor to vendor. Whether to put the additional load of mirroring on the server OS is a matter that will spark debates filled with religious fervor. This author likes to use NetWare's own mirroring, and the reason is simple: it works and it's well-known. After you learn how to mirror disks via NetWare, it's the same wherever you go. Otherwise, you might have a Compaq controller here implementing the array, the next server might be an HP, and in a third you might have a DPT controller; and all three would have different interfaces, terminologies, and capabilities.

RAID-5 is commonly implemented in hardware. Whereas RAID-1 requires only two drives, RAID-5 requires at least three disks. In RAID-5, the data is striped (written) across two of the disks, and parity information is written on the third disk. If one of the disks fails, the missing data can be recovered by use of the parity information. The "parity disk" isn't dedicated (it is in RAID-4), but all the disks take turns when the parity information is written, like this:

	Disk 1	Disk 2	Disk 3
Stripe	J	O	Parity
Stripe	H	Parity	N
Stripe	Parity	P	E
Stripe	N	C	Parity

You can see that the loss of any one disk can be recovered from, because both the data and the parity information are striped across all disks. Costwise, the more disks in the array, the lower your costs. Think about mirroring, or RAID-1; you have two 9GB drives but only 9GB of available space. One of your disks, or fully 50% of your cost, is going to redundancy. Now, think about RAID-5; you have four 9GB drives. If one of them is lost to parity information, that leaves three disks available for storage. In this scenario, you have lost only one disk, or 25%, to redundancy. If there were 10 disks in the array, you would lose only 10%, and so on.

Note

A drive isn't "lost" or dedicated to parity in a RAID-5 array, but you can think of it that way. The parity information has to be written, and even though it is striped across all available drives in the array, the result is the same in terms of space used as if all the parity information had been written to one drive.

PARTITIONS

You can think of a partition as a dedicated slice of your hard disk. A single disk can contain up to four partitions. For example, a typical disk in the server might have a system configuration partition (for the vendor's configuration utilities), a DOS partition to boot from, and a NetWare partition for the sys volume. Each of these partitions is dedicated and has nothing to do with the others. The configuration partition is used only when configuring the machine, the DOS partition is used only by DOS and for booting the machine, and the NetWare partition is used only by Novell.

A NetWare partition can also have a hot fix redirection area (look ahead to Figure 10.9). The hot fix redirection area is "reserved" space; when the operating system encounters a bad block on the disk, it marks the block as bad and redirects it to the hot fix area. So the NetWare partition is generally divided into two areas: a data area for normal writes, and the hot fix area that is used when required. You will want to keep an eye on the number of redirection blocks used, because if this number begins to climb, it's time to replace the disk. To view the hot fix area statistics, load MONITOR, highlight Storage Devices, and press Enter. Select the Hotfixed Partition of the disk you want to view, and press Enter. The statistics are shown in Figure 10.8.

Figure 10.8

The Used Hot Fix Blocks is the number you want to keep an eye on.

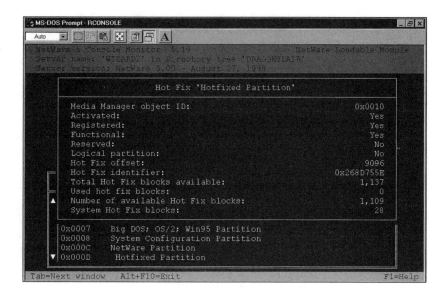

If the number of hot fix blocks begins to climb, keep in mind that you have only so many available; in Figure 10.8, the Number of Available Hot Fix Blocks would begin to drop as the number of hot fix blocks used begins to climb.

> **Note**
>
> If you want to mirror partitions, which I will cover in the next section, all partitions involved in the mirror *must* have a hot fix redirection area.

To create a partition, load NWCONFIG, select Standard Disk Options, and then choose Modify Disk Partitions and Hot Fix. A list of available drives appears. Highlight the drive on which you want to create the partition, and then select Create NetWare Disk Partition from the Disk Options menu. You will be at the Disk Partition Information screen shown in Figure 10.9.

You can enter the size of the partition you want to create in one of two ways: either enter the number of cylinders you want to use on the left, or enter the size in megabytes you want on the right. Entering the size in megabytes has more meaning than entering the number of cylinders, but these two fields are tied together; if you change one, the other naturally changes also.

The Data Area and Redirection Area fields will be filled in automatically when you enter the size, but you can also change them. The defaults should be fine, but if you did not want a hot fix area, or wanted the hot fix area to be larger than the default, you would make the necessary changes here. When you are satisfied, press the F10 key to save the changes, and you are done.

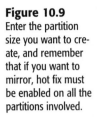

Figure 10.9
Enter the partition size you want to create, and remember that if you want to mirror, hot fix must be enabled on all the partitions involved.

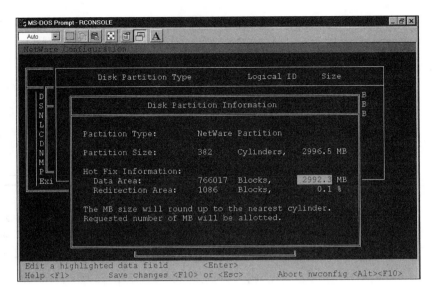

DEVICE NUMBERS

Before I delve into actually mirroring partitions, I need to take a look at device and partition numbering. You will see these strange and arcane numbers later in this chapter, and in utilities such as MONITOR, NWCONFIG, and various console commands such as MIRROR STATUS and LIST DEVICES.

Storage devices and disk partitions are given hexadecimal object numbers by the media manager. The media manager is a database that tracks storage devices and media attached to the server. The object numbers assigned do not have to be sequential, and they are not persistent. If you bring the server down and back up, you might see different object numbers than those you had before. You don't have to worry about assigning the object numbers; that is all automatic. The key, however, is that the object numbers are consistent while the server is up. If a device has an object number of 0x0001 in MONITOR, that device will also be 0x0001 in NWCONFIG, and anywhere else you see object numbers.

Now analyze the output of the console command LIST DEVICES:

```
WIZARD2:list devices
    0x0001: [V500-A0-D0:0] SEAGATE ST410800N rev:0025
    0x0002: [V500-A0-D2:0] SEAGATE ST15150N rev:0011
    0x0003: [V500-A0-D5:0] COMPAQ CD-ROM CR-503BCQ rev:1.1I
```

The first number on each line, the hexadecimal one, is the object number. Partitions have only object numbers, but devices such as disks and storage adapters also have device names, as you can see from the output of the LIST DEVICES command shown previously. You can see that three devices are listed—a CD-ROM and two Seagate disks—but where does the [V500-A0-Dx:0] come from? For that, take a look at the output of the console command LIST STORAGE ADAPTERS:

```
WIZARD2:list storage adapters
   [V500-A0] Compaq Ultra/Fast/Wide SCSI-2 Host Adapter Module
      [V500-A0-D5:0] COMPAQ CD-ROM CR-503BCQ rev:1.1i
      [V500-A0-D0:0] SEAGATE ST410800N rev:0025
      [V500-A0-D2:0] SEAGATE ST15150N rev:0011
```

The command LIST STORAGE ADAPTERS lists the adapters in the system and the devices that the adapter is driving. Here, you see only the one Compaq Ultra/Fast/Wide SCSI-2 controller, and attached to it are the three devices you saw earlier in the output of the LIST DEVICES command. Let me break it down:

- The V500 is the vendor number; this is unique and specific to each vendor.

- The A0 is the instance of the adapter. This is the first one found, so it is A0. The instances of the adapters are unique; for example, if you had three controllers in the system, you would see them as A0, A1, and A2, even if all three controllers were the same make and model.

- The Dx is the device number. For a SCSI device, this will be the SCSI ID. For an IDE device, this will be the number of the bus from the IDE controller.

- Last, the 0 represents the LUN, or Logical Unit Number. Because disk manufacturers seldom use the LUN to identify disks, this one almost always shows up as 0.

Hopefully, by now, the rather cryptic-looking numbers and strings make sense; 0x0001: [V500-A0-D0:0] SEAGATE ST410800N rev:0025 means that the object number is 0x0001 and that this device has a SCSI ID of 0, attached to the first instance of the controller. And don't forget that these numbers will be consistent across all applications; in Figure 10.10, I have loaded MONITOR and then chosen Storage Devices. You can see that the disk in question has the same information that you obtained via the console commands.

Note

You should note that multi-lun support is now disabled by default (at least on the popular ADAPTEC cards). You have to add the LUN_ENABLE option to the driver load line to add multi-lun support. Also, devices that do have multi-lun items don't show it in the device list or list storage adapter.

IMPLEMENTING DISK MIRRORING

Mirroring has come a long way in NetWare 5, baby! Before NetWare 5, you could have only one NetWare partition on a disk. Many times, people would have something like a 2GB drive, and they would plan to upgrade this 2GB drive to a 4GB drive. The question would be "Can I put in the new 4GB drive, and then mirror the two disks, then remove the 2GB drive?"

Figure 10.10
The registered storage objects; this screen shows not only adapters and disks, but also the object numbers of the partitions themselves. For more information on a device listed here, highlight the object and then use the Tab key.

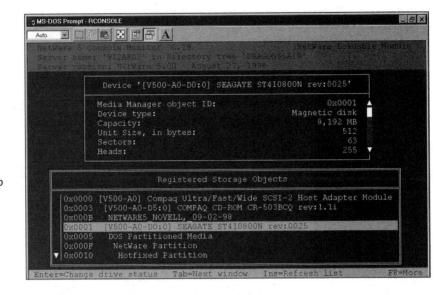

Tip #81 from
John

If you learn nothing else about disk mirroring, learn this: partitions are mirrored, whereas disks are not.

The answer, unfortunately, was no. Partitions are mirrored, not disks. And the partitions had to be the same size. Because you could have only one NetWare partition per disk, you would have to create a 2GB partition on your 4GB drive, and guess what? You just spent the money on a 4GB drive to wind up with 2GB of usable space. Now, with the capability to have more than one NetWare partition on a disk, or by using NSS, such a plan would be feasible, because the remaining space could be utilized.

CREATING THE MIRROR

To mirror a partition, load NWCONFIG and select Standard Disk Options. Then choose Mirror/Unmirror Disk Partitions, and press Enter. A list, the Disk Partition Mirroring Status, appears, as shown in Figure 10.11.

Highlight the partition you want to mirror, the "source" as it were, and press Enter. Your source partition appears in a list by itself. Press the Insert key, and you will see the same list shown in Figure 10.11, minus the partition you have just chosen.

From this list, highlight the "destination" partition and press Enter.

Caution

Be careful when selecting the partitions you are mirroring; if you wind up mirroring two partitions that are on the same disk, you will defeat the entire purpose!

Figure 10.11
In the Disk Partition Mirroring Status, you see existing partitions that are not mirrored, or the status of those that are mirrored.

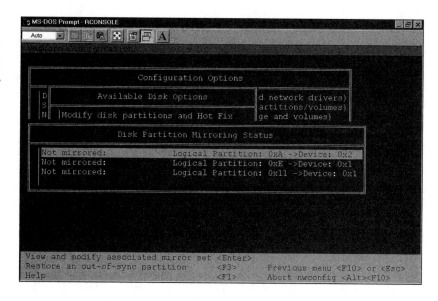

The disk mirroring process begins. Notice that the Disk Partition Mirroring Status window has changed, as shown in Figure 10.12; now, you see not only partitions that are not mirrored, but also those that are.

Figure 10.12
The new mirror now shows up in the Mirroring Status window. Before, three partitions were available; now, only one. You can see that the mirroring process is 29% done.

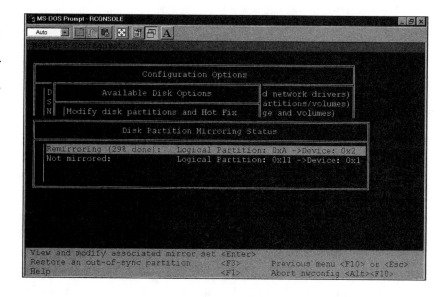

In Figure 10.12, you can see the status of your partitions: two of them are remirroring, and one is not mirrored. There are four possible status "messages" you might see here:

- `Mirrored`—This partition is mirrored.
- `Not Mirrored`—This partition is not mirrored.

- `Remirroring`—This partition is currently being remirrored.

- `Out of Sync`—This partition is mirrored but is currently out of sync with its partner.

Now that you have mirrored partitions, you should take note of a few console commands.

Use the `MIRROR STATUS` command to get a quick look at the mirror status. The syntax and output are shown here:

```
WIZARD2:mirror status
Mirrored object 0x0A is fully synchronized.
Mirror object 0x11 is not mirrored.
```

If the two partitions were in the process of being mirrored, the `MIRROR STATUS` command would also give the percent complete; in this example, that is not shown because the two partitions are fully synchronized.

`ABORT REMIRROR <logical partition number>` would stop mirroring if it was going on. To stop mirroring logical partition `0x000A`, you would enter `ABORT REMIRROR A`.

NetWare automatically remirrors out-of-sync partitions, but if for some reason mirroring has stopped, or you have issued the `ABORT REMIRROR` command, you can force the mirroring to occur via the `REMIRROR PARTITION <logical partition number>` command.

BREAKING THE MIRROR

You might decide that you no longer need a partition mirrored, or might want to break the mirror to remove or change out a disk. Breaking the mirror involves pretty much the same steps you used to create the mirror; start by loading NWCONFIG.

Select Standard Disk Options, and then choose Mirror/Unmirror Disk Partitions. Find the mirrored pair you want to operate on, highlight it, and press Enter. You will be at the Mirrored Disk Partitions screen shown in Figure 10.13.

Select the partition you want unmirrored, highlight it, and press Delete. This is a mirrored partition, so naturally if you have volume information on one, you will have the same volume information on the other. When you press Delete, you will receive a warning (see Figure 10.14).

Press Enter to clear this message, and you are then asked whether you want to salvage the volume information. The volume information is what's referred to in the warning shown in Figure 10.14. If you say no, the data on the partition is destroyed, and the partition is now available again.

If you say yes to salvaging the volume information, you are given a chance to enter a new name for the volume. After you rename the volume, you are back to the Mirrored Disk Partitions screen, but no mirror shows any more.

Figure 10.13
Here is all the information you could need to keep up with a mirrored set of partitions, including the Logical Partition number. You can come to this screen anytime for information; you don't need to be breaking a mirror.

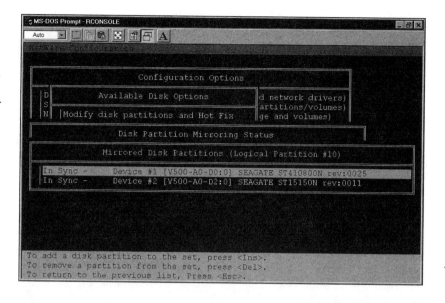

Figure 10.14
Be very careful here. Make the wrong move, and you could wind up losing valuable data.

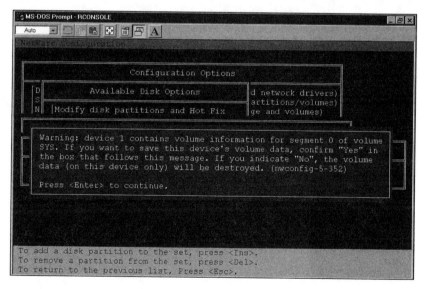

Tip #82 from
John

Always save the volume information; I would suggest naming it the original volume name followed by `old`, such as `sysold` or `dataold`. Odds are that you aren't going to need the salvaged volume, but better safe than sorry. Later, after you are certain that things are OK, you can go back into NWCONFIG under volume options and delete the volume you no longer need.

NOVELL STORAGE SYSTEMS

Novell Storage Systems (NSS) is Novell's new implementation of storage. Using NSS doesn't have to be either/or, meaning that you have to forgo the traditional volumes you are used to. Indeed, you can't lose all of your traditional volumes, because the SYS: volume cannot be on an NSS volume. But instead, you can run NSS and the traditional volumes you are used to side by side, on the same server, and mix and match as your requirements dictate.

Rather than list and define terms such as "provider," I will show you how to actually create and modify an NSS volume in this chapter; by the time you are done, you will have your own understanding of the new terms such as "provider" and "storage groups." Learning by doing beats theory any day!

One NSS volume you will see come and go, depending upon the load status of NSS, is the NSS_ADMIN volume. This is a read-only volume that exists only in RAM and is automatically created; it holds a dynamic list of NSS objects and cannot be deleted or managed, so don't wonder why this strange volume that you did not create suddenly appeared! You can map a drive to the NSS_ADMIN volume and look around if you want, though, for the more curious among us.

Finally, put at least two disks with some free space on them in your test server. Work with NSS and learn it, because there are countless options. After you have a handle on things, implement NSS in your production environment.

Tip #83 from	While you're testing and learning, the most valuable thing you need to know up front is the EXIT parameter for NSS. If you enter the command NSS EXIT at the server's console, it will unload NSS and all of its modules. This is particularly useful for testing the parameters that can be used only when NSS loads, and it's a lot quicker than restarting the server.
John	

THE BENEFITS OF NSS

What are some of the new features and benefits of NSS? One of them is the maximum file size of 8TB. It can be hard to get excited about a file size of 8TB, unless you happen to have that much disk space in your server! A few others are as listed here:

- Large numbers of files. An NSS volume can hold up to 8 trillion files, a number that should last you a while.

- You can have up to one million files open simultaneously.

- Rapid file access. Any size file is opened in the same amount of time.

- Much, much faster volume mounts. NSS volumes appear to mount almost instantaneously.

- The capability to mount the server's DOS partition as a NetWare volume. You can then map a drive to it like any other volume.

- Less memory is required to mount NSS volumes.

- Volume recovery is much faster than vrepair and traditional volumes.

NSS LIMITATIONS

Having sung the glories of NSS in the preceding section, I won't pass over the current limitations of NSS, some of which you might consider show-stoppers:

- File compression.

- Block suballocation. The block size is fixed at 4KB.

- The Sys volume needs to be a traditional NetWare volume.

- TTS (Transaction Tracking System) is not supported, which is one reason the Sys volume would have to be on a traditional volume.

- Disk mirroring or disk duplexing.

Tip #84 from John	Check with the vendor of your tape backup software to make sure that it has no issues with NSS volumes.

CREATING AN NSS VOLUME WITH NWCONFIG

The easiest way to learn about NSS is to jump in and start working with it, so in this and following sections, you are going to create an NSS volume. In this section, you will use NWCONFIG to create your NSS volume. Later, you will see that NSS has its own administration program you can use.

Tip #85 from John	If you use NWCONFIG to create your NSS volumes, an NDS object representing the volume is added to the tree automatically. If you use the NSS Administration utility, NSS volumes you create are not added to NDS automatically; you have to do it yourself via the Directory Services Options menu of NWCONFIG.

Load NWCONFIG and select NSS Disk Options, and the Available NSS Options menu appears. Two choices appear on the Available NSS Options menu:

- **Storage**—The storage option locates your available free space and places it in a pool for NSS to use.

- **NSS Volume Options**—Here, you can create new storage groups and NSS volumes, rename volumes and storage groups, delete volumes and storage groups, and view NSS volumes.

Select the Storage option, and you will be at the menu shown in Figure 10.15.

Figure 10.15
The first thing to do is let NSS gather information about your free space; the Update Provider Information selection does this.

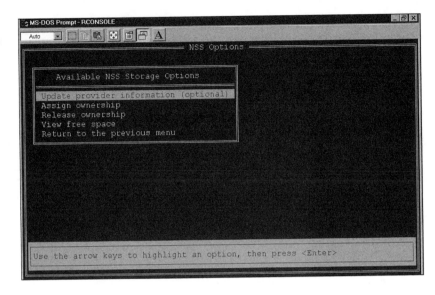

If this is the first time you have worked with NSS, or if you have added new drives, NSS needs to gather information about the available space. Highlight the Update Provider Information option and press Enter. A provider recognizes the free space and deposits it in an object bank. MMPRV is for unpartitioned space, so select it and press Enter. The scan should go very quickly, and you just receive a message to the effect that the scan was successful.

Press any key to continue, and then choose the View Free Space option on the menu; you should see the free unpartitioned space from each of your disks, as shown in Figure 10.16.

Figure 10.16
NSS has found unpartitioned free space on two separate drives.

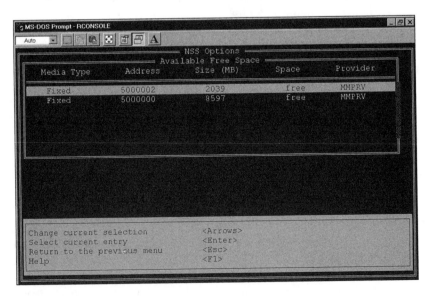

Tip #86 from
John

It would be nice if the information on the Available Free Space screen shown in Figure 10.16 wasn't so cryptic. As far as I can tell, if you look at the Address column, the last digit (2 in the top line, and 0 in the bottom line) of the address given is the SCSI ID of the disk.

Press the Esc key and return to the Storage Options menu, because now that the free space has been found, you need to assign ownership. Select the Assign Ownership option from the menu, and you will see the "pieces" of free space available to you. Press Enter on one, and you have the option to take all the free space or limit the amount you want to take. Either accept the amount shown, which defaults to all the free space, or enter a smaller amount and press Enter. You then need to confirm the action you are about to take; it's a nice red box that should get your attention.

At this point, if you were to view your free space, you would see that the block you just gave to NSS is no longer listed. Furthermore, if you were to look at the disk's partition table, you would see that an NSS partition has been created. For more information on NSS partitions, see the section "NSS Partitions" later in this chapter.

After you have found and assigned the free space, there is nothing left to do in the Storage Options area of the menus. Return to the main NSS options menu, and choose the NSS Volume Options. You are prompted to log in to NDS. (Remember the tip earlier; if you use NWCONFIG to create your NSS volumes, they are added to NDS automatically.) When logged in, you should see the menu shown in Figure 10.17.

Figure 10.17
Now that NSS has been assigned ownership of the free space, you use the volume options menu to create, delete, and modify your NSS volumes.

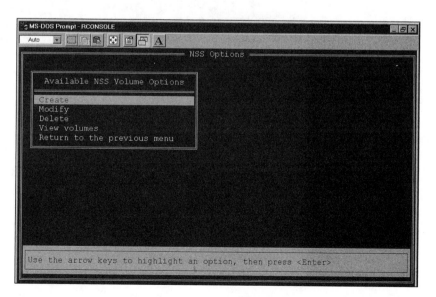

Press Enter on the Create option, and you have two choices: you can create a storage group, or you can create an NSS volume. A storage group is a pool of storage free space that represents logical space owned by NSS. An NSS volume is just what it sounds like; you take some of the NSS-owned space and create an NSS volume. For now, create a storage group; it's more flexible. After you have chosen to create a storage group, you should have a list of the free space owned by NSS (this is the same free space shown in Figure 10.16). Highlight the space you want to use and press Enter; you should see the screen shown in Figure 10.18, where you must confirm your actions.

Figure 10.18

You are assigning 8596MB of space owned by NSS to a storage group. You need to confirm this action.

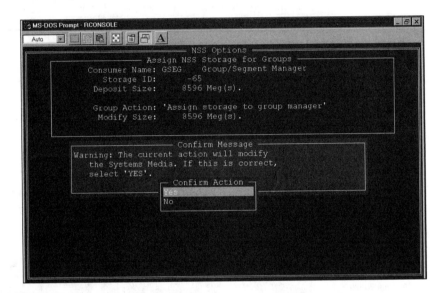

Because you have two areas of space that NSS has taken ownership of, you are going to create two storage groups; the second one will come into play later when you expand your NSS volume by adding the second storage group.

Now that the storage groups have been created, it's time to create the NSS volume. Select NSS Volume from the Create Options menu, and you are again presented with the space that NSS can work with, as shown in Figure 10.19.

Highlight an area of space and press Enter. Either accept the size given, which defaults to all the space, or use less if you want a smaller volume. Change the name from nssvol (the default) to what you want it to be, and again confirm your action. The volume is created and added to NDS automatically, as shown in Figure 10.20.

If you were to go and look at the NDS object in NetWare Administrator, it would appear like any other volume object you are used to; there is nothing about it that indicates it is an NSS volume as opposed to a standard volume.

Figure 10.19
Although this information looks a lot like what is shown in Figure 10.16, there are some major differences. Primarily, this space isn't free but is now of Storage Type Group.

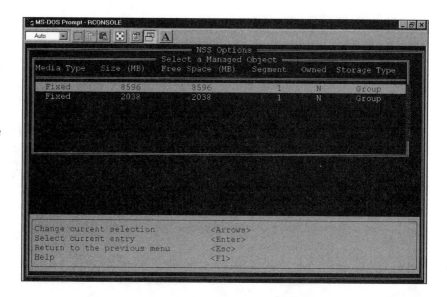

Figure 10.20
You have created an NSS volume, named *NSSVOL1*, with 2038MB of space. This volume was added to NDS automatically because you are using the NSS options of NWCONFIG.

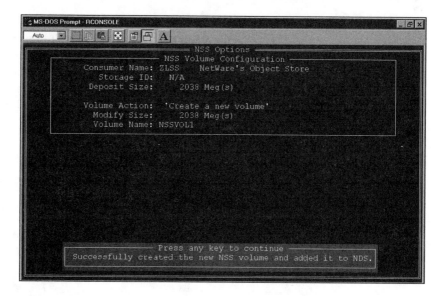

MODIFYING THE NSS VOLUME

Now take a look at some of the flexibility of NSS; you still have another storage group of 8596MB that you haven't used. Now add it to the NSS volume you just created and see whether you can get one volume that is a bit over 10GB (8596MB + 2038MB).

Get back to the Available NSS Volume Options menu, and select Modify. The choices on the Select Modify Option menu are shown in Figure 10.21.

Figure 10.21
You are going to use the option Increase NSS Volume Size and see whether you can add 8GB to your existing 2GB NSS volume.

Select Increase NSS Volume Size, and you will see the existing NSS volume. Press Enter on the volume, and you will see other "free" space—in this case, 8.5GB that has been given to a storage group. Press Enter on the space you want to add to your existing NSS volume, and then either accept the entire size (which is the default) or enter a smaller number to use less space. You are going to add the entire 8.5GB, so you take the default and then confirm. The additional space is added to the volume, giving you an NSS volume with a total size of 10.38GB, as shown in Figure 10.22.

Figure 10.22
You have taken free space on two separate drives and, using NSS, combined them into one large volume.

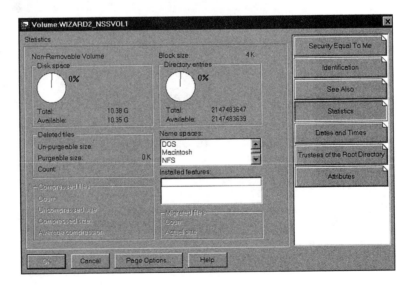

Be very careful with something like this. What you have done is to take the free space on two separate hard drives and combine them into one volume. But NSS does not support mirroring, and the loss of any one disk will take out the entire volume in this case. To those of you familiar with Windows NT Server, this is conceptually the same thing as creating a volume set. Suppose that you wound up with 1GB of free space on each of four disks; you could create four 1GB volumes, but one 4GB volume might be more useful to you. That is when a feature like this would come into play.

CREATING AN NSS VOLUME USING FREE SPACE INSIDE A STANDARD NETWARE VOLUME

NSS can use the free space you have on your traditional, or standard, NetWare volumes. The procedure is the same as creating an NSS volume using unpartitioned free space, except that you need to load another provider. If you look back at the screen shown in Figure 10.16, the only provider shown is MMPRV. MMPRV finds unpartitioned free space; it pays no attention to the free space inside of existing standard NetWare volumes. For NSS to find the free space inside of standard volumes, you need to load the NWPRV provider. Notice in Figure 10.23 that some of the free space found is on NW volumes, provided by NWPRV, and the rest is on fixed disks, provided by MMPRV, which you have already seen.

Figure 10.23
For NSS to see free space inside of traditional NetWare volumes, you need to load the NWPRV provider.

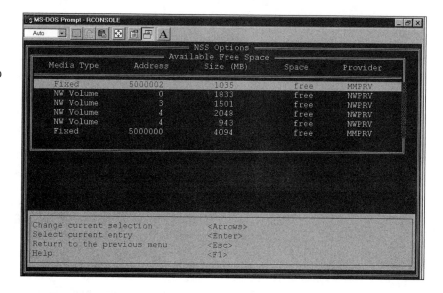

To load the NWPRV provider, simply add NWPRV to the NSS load line, such as NSS NWPRV. But be careful here. Just as with loading DOSFAT, the command NSS NWPRV will keep other modules from loading, and you will not be able to mount your existing NSS volumes. Instead, use the command NSS ZLSS NWPRV. Or, you could issue the command LOAD NWPRV, if NSS is already loaded.

After you have loaded the NWPRV provider, follow the normal procedure of updating the free space available and so forth that you followed earlier to create your NSS volume. When NSS owns the free space inside of a NetWare volume, the traditional NetWare file system recognizes the space owned by NSS as a file. This file will be in the hidden directory $$NSS$$.PRV, as shown by the NDIR command I covered earlier:

```
H:\>ndir $$nss$$.prv /d
WIZARD2/DODGE:$$NSS$$.PRV\*.*
Files:
  DOS:   00510AAC.PRV
  OS/2:  00510AAC.PRV

Rights:
  DOS, OS/2:   Inherited: [SRWCEMFA]
               Effective: [--------]

Owner:  DOS, OS/2:    WIZARD2

Owning namespace:     DOS

Miscellaneous NetWare information:
  Last update:       4-19-99 10:37a
  Last archived:     0-00-00  0:00
  Last accessed:     4-19-99
  Created/Copied:    4-19-99 10:02a
  Flags:             [Rw--HA]  [--P--Ci--RiDcDmDs]  [---]
  File size:         969,932,800


  969,932,800  bytes (969,932,800  bytes of disk space used)
1    File
```

In other words, you have created an NSS volume using the free space on the traditional NetWare volume Dodge. The space available on volume Dodge will shrink, because it recognizes that 969,932,800 bytes are being used by the file 00510AAC.PRV.

There are a few caveats here. One is that to mount the NSS volume, you have to mount the traditional volume first. This also works in reverse; if the traditional volume is dismounted, the NSS volume inside of it will become inaccessible. Another gotcha is one to watch out for: if you delete the traditional volume, the NSS volume it contains is deleted also.

NSS PARTITIONS

If you go under Standard Disk Options and then select Modify Disk Partitions and Hot Fix, you will notice that when NSS claimed ownership of what was your unpartitioned space, it created an NSS partition. Keep this in mind, because if you remember from earlier in the chapter, you can have only four partitions on a disk. In Figure 10.24, you can see that the disk has four partitions—a system configuration, a DOS partition, and two NetWare partitions.

Figure 10.24
This disk has reached its limit of four partitions. NSS will see the 2596.4MB of free space but will be unable to use it.

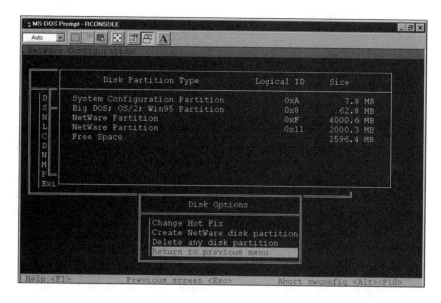

This is not an unlikely scenario; an administrator could have originally created the first NetWare partition for a standard NetWare volume, then later created another NetWare partition for another standard volume, thinking that the free space left could be used by NSS. If you have four partitions and still have free space, NSS will recognize the free space but will not be able to use it, because NSS will be unable to create its own NSS partition. The results are shown in Figure 10.25.

Figure 10.25
Because the disk already had four partitions, NSS was unable to take ownership. This is because NSS was unable to create its own NSS partition.

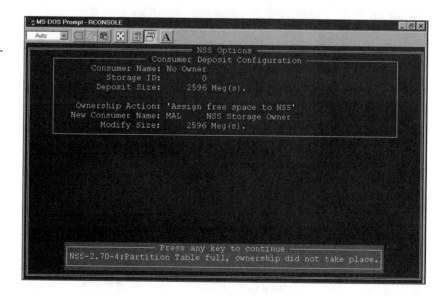

PART

III

CH

10

In a scenario like this, the free space would be wasted forever. Your only choice would be to back up the volumes on the partitions, and delete, re-create, and restore; for NSS to be able to use the space, the maximum number of partitions you can have on the disk is three. The NSS partition created will be number four.

DOSFAT

This has got to be the coolest feature, and one I've wanted in native NetWare for years: the capability to mount the server's DOS partition as a volume! Most administrators are very backup conscious, and religiously check to make sure that the backups are running OK. However, most of them seldom think to back up the server's DOS partition. In a disaster-recovery scenario, having a backup of the server's C: drive will get you back online far faster than having to reinstall NetWare to get the needed files back on C:. Also, if you had to rein-stall, you would lose all updated drivers, patches, and the like that had been applied to the files on the DOS partition.

If you mount the server's DOS partition as a volume, you can map a drive to it like any other, and move, copy, and delete files. Simply copy *.* from the DOS volume to any other volume on the server, and presto, an instant backup of the server's C: drive whenever you like.

Mounting the DOS partition as a volume is simple; merely add the dosfat parameter when loading NSS; for example, NSS DOSFAT. When loaded, any DOS FAT partitions are automatically mounted as volumes. The volume name will be dosfat_<drive letter>, or in this case, DOSFAT_C (see Figure 10.26).

Figure 10.26
You can now mount the server's DOS partition as a volume; it's very nice to have such seamless access to the server's DOS files.

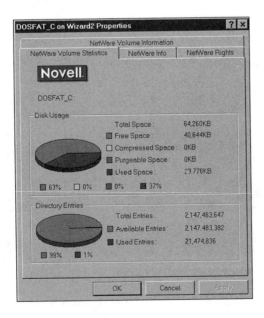

Tip #87 from
John

If you just enter the command NSS DOSFAT, it will mount the server's DOS partition for you with no problem. However, it will also keep you from mounting your other NSS volumes. If you look ahead to the DOSFAT option in the section on options, you'll see that the DOSFAT option loads only the modules needed for DOSFAT support. Also, it can be loaded at startup only, or the first time you load NSS. To make this right, also load ZLSS, such as NSS DOSFAT ZLSS. The ZLSS module provides access to the NSS volume you have created.

THE NSS ADMINISTRATION MENUS

You won't spend a lot of time on the NSS administration menus; the same concepts apply but the interface is different. As you can see from Figure 10.27, not a lot of time was spent polishing the interface of the NSS menus!

Figure 10.27
The NSS menu/administration utility is started by the menu parameter; enter the command NSS MENU.

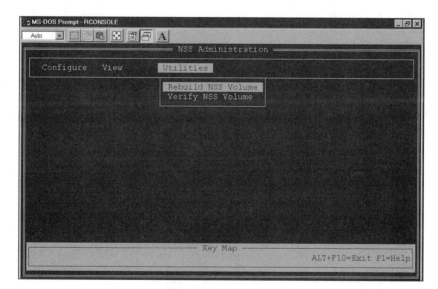

You should keep a few things in mind: one is that if you create your NSS volumes using the menu, they are not automatically added to NDS; you have to do this yourself. And take a close look at the menu choices shown in Figure 10.27: Rebuild and Verify NSS Volume. NSS does not use vrepair, but instead uses the Rebuild option given in the NSS menus. You don't need to worry about inadvertently running vrepair on an NSS volume; vrepair will not even see an unmounted NSS volume.

You can rebuild and verify an NSS volume in two ways. The first method is to load the NSS menu and then use the Rebuild and Verify choices from the toolbar. The second is through the command line:

- NSS /REBUILD shows you a list of NSS volumes that can be rebuilt. After you select a volume, it is rebuilt.

- NSS /REBUILD=*<nss volume name>* rebuilds only the specified volume, bypassing the list of available NSS volumes.

- NSS /REBUILD=*<nss volume name>*, *<nss volume name>* rebuilds the specified volumes. You can do up to five at a time in this fashion.

You can also verify from the command line; the options are pretty much the same:

- NSS /VERIFY puts up a list of all NSS volumes and allows you to choose one to be verified.

- NSS /VERIFY=*<nss volume name>* verifies only the specified volume.

- NSS /VERIFY=ALL verifies all NSS volumes.

Each time you verify an NSS volume, the results are written to a file at the root of the SYS: volume. The file will have the name *<volumename>*.rlf, or in this case, nssvol1.rlf. This file is overwritten each time, so if you want to save it, you will have to move it.

NSS OPTIONS

NSS has a multitude of command-line parameters, as listed in Table 10.2. The description of each parameter is what is returned when you enter the command NSS /? at the server console. The options are not case sensitive, and you can use unique abbreviations; in other words, NSS MOD would give you the same results as NSS MODULES. The syntax is NSS followed by the option, for example, NSS DOSFAT.

TABLE 10.2 NSS OPTIONS

Option	Function
Exit	Unload NSS and all of its modules.
Version	Display version information for NSS.
Modules	Display information about all the modules loaded into NSS.
Help	Display this help information.
/?	Display this help information.
/(No)SkipLoadModules	If specified, skip the auto loading of the NSS support modules. [StartupOnly Value=OFF]
defaultNLMs	If specified, load only default NSS NLMs, and any additional LSS modules specified on the command line. [StartupOnly]
CD9660	If specified, load only those modules essential for CD9660 support. [StartupOnly]
CDHFS	If specified, load only those modules essential for CDHFS support. [StartupOnly]
CDROM	If specified, load only those modules essential for CD9660 & CDHFS support. [StartupOnly]

Option	Function
DOSFAT	If specified, load only those modules essential for DOSFAT support. [StartupOnly]
UDF	If specified, load only those modules essential for UDF support. [StartupOnly]
ZLSS	If specified, load only those modules essential for zLSS support. [StartupOnly]
NoLSS	If specified, do not load any LSS module. [StartupOnly]
AllLSS	If specified, load all the LSS modules. [StartupOnly]
NWPRV	If specified, load NWPRV and specify the LSS you want to load on the command line. [StartupOnly]
Menu	Start the NSS Configuration menu.
Status	Display current NSS status information.
Volumes	Display all the currently available NSS volumes.
/Activate=	Switch the given volumes to the ACTIVE state.
/Deactivate=	Switch the given volumes to the DEACTIVE state.
/Maintenance=	Switch the given volumes to the MAINTENANCE state.
/ForceActivate=	Force the given volumes to the ACTIVE state.
/VerifyVolume=	Verify the specified volume's physical integrity.
/RebuildVolume=	Rebuild the specified volumes.
/VerifyVolume	Select volumes from a menu and VERIFY their physical integrity.
/RebuildVolume	Select volumes from a menu and REBUILD them.
/AutoActivateVolume=	Places specified volumes in ACTIVE state at volume load time.
/AutoDeactivateVolume=	Leave specified volumes in DEACTIVE state at volume load time.
/AutoVerifyVolume=	Verify the specified volume's physical integrity at startup time.
/StorageAlarmThreshold=	Set the threshold (in megabytes) for a low-storage-space warning. [Value=10 Range=0-1000000]
/StorageResetThreshold=	Set the threshold (in megabytes) to reset a low-storage-space warning. [Value=15 Range=0-1000000]
/(No)StorageAlertMessages	Turn ON/OFF sending of low-storage messages to all users. [Value=ON]
/NameCacheSize=	Set the number of Name Cache entries. [StartupOnly Value=2111 Range=3-65521]
/(No)NameCache	Set the name caching ON or OFF. [StartupOnly Value=ON]
/NameCacheStats	Show name-caching statistics.

PART

III

CH

10

continues

TABLE 10.2   CONTINUED

Option	Function
/AuthCacheSize=	Set the number of Authorization Cache entries. [StartupOnly Value=1024 Range=16-50000]
/OpenFileHashShift=	Set the size of the Open File hash table (in powers of 2). [StartupOnly Value=11 Range=8-20]
/ClosedFileCacheSize=	Set the number of closed files that can be cached in memory. [StartupOnly Value=512 Range=1-100000]
/FileFlushTimer=	Set the Flush Time for modified open files in seconds. [Value=10 Range=1-3600].
/MinBufferCacheSize=	Set the minimum number of NSS Buffer Cache entries. [Value=512 Range=256-1048576]
/MinOSBufferCacheSize=	Set the minimum number of NetWare Buffer Cache entries. [Value=1024 Range=1024-1048576]
/BufferFlushTimer=	Set the Flush Time for modified cache buffers in seconds. [Value=1 Range=1-3600]
/(No)CacheBalance	Set the dynamic balancing of free memory for the NSS buffer cache ON or OFF. [StartupOnly Value=ON]
/CacheBalance=	Set what percentage of free memory NSS will use for its buffer cache. [Value=10 Range=1-99]
/CacheBalanceTimer=	Set the Cache Balance Timer in seconds. [Value=30 Range=1-3600]
/CacheStats	Show buffer-caching statistics.
/MailboxSize=	Set the size of the Mailbox. [StartupOnly Value=128 Range=64-256]
/NumAsyncios=	Set the number of Asyncio entries to allocate. [StartupOnly Value=2048 Range=4-65536]
/NumBonds=	Set the number of Bond entries to allocate. [StartupOnly Value=5000 Range=512-2097152]
/NumWorkToDos=	Set the number of WorkToDo entries that can be concurrently executing. [StartupOnly Value=40 Range=5-100]
/Salvage=	Enable salvage of deleted files on the given volumes.
/NoSalvage=	Disable salvage of deleted files on the given volumes.
/(No)STORAGE	Save return address and start the NSS storage options.
/STORAGE=	Save return address and start the NSS storage options. [Value=3489675968]
/(No)VOLUME	Save return address and start the NSS volume options.
/VOLUME=	Save return address and start the NSS volume options. [Value=3489675968]
/MODULEID=	Save return address and start the NSS storage options. [Value=3496409472]

TROUBLESHOOTING

Disks are near and dear to the hearts of network administrators; that's where the data is, and ultimately their jobs, so disk problems generally don't get ignored! First, make sure that the server is patched up to the minimum patch list at http://support.novell.com. Then, make sure that you are using the newest .HAM and .CDM drivers from your vendors.

Don't forget the hardware either. The disks need to be adequately cooled, or they will overheat and generally deactivate. SCSI cables have to be within specs, termination needs to be correct, and you should have no SCSI ID conflicts. All connections should be tight and well seated; over time, as connections heat up and cool down, they have a tendency to work loose, so reseating things is always a good idea.

Keep an eye on the number of redirected blocks, and if you start seeing that number climb, it is time for a new disk. Use vrepair to attempt to repair traditional, or standard, NetWare volumes, and use the NSS rebuild and verify utilities for NSS volumes. Also keep an eye on the amount of free space you have; better to be proactive about this than to find out you are out of disk space when you are actually out of disk space.

As always, refer to the online documentation or Novell's Web site for more detailed information on the various utilities covered here. Time and space did not allow for me to cover all the disk-related utilities, so you might consider looking at Filer, a command-line program with myriad options for manipulating files and directories. Also look into file compression and the options you have there, the command-line FLAG and RIGHTS utilities, and the various file- and directory-manipulation options available from within the NetWare Administrator program.

## CHAPTER 11

UPGRADING AN EXISTING SERVER

In this chapter

METHODS OF UPGRADING

Two methods of upgrading are available to you—in-place and across-the-wire. An *in-place* upgrade is where you keep the same hardware and upgrade only the operating system, say going from NetWare 3 to NetWare 5. An *across-the-wire* migration is used when you have new hardware, and you set up the new server and migrate your users and data across the wire to the new server.

Of the two, you always want to do an across-the-wire migration if possible. The reason for this is because the source is untouched, so that if you encounter problems of any kind, it's no problem; you simply fall back, analyze what went wrong, and then try again later. For example, you have a NetWare 3 server that you want to take to NetWare 5. You do an in-place upgrade, and, true to Murphy's Law, whatever can go wrong, does. You are now faced with reinstalling NetWare 3, reinstalling your tape backup software, and restoring your server from tape...not a good way to end a failed upgrade attempt.

On the other hand, you decide that because NetWare 5 takes more resources than NetWare 3, it would be a perfect time to beef up the server with new hardware. You can put the new server on the wire and install NetWare 5 at your leisure. You can take some time to play with NetWare 5, learn some of the new features, and also give the new box time to burn in. When you are ready to migrate, you are essentially just copying the files and users from the NetWare 3 box to the NetWare 5 box across the wire. If you encounter any show stoppers, it is no problem because the source of the upgrade, the NetWare 3 box, is untouched.

You also will perform hardware upgrades, where you are not changing the versions of the OS, but are simply trying to get the same version of the operating system that you have now running on new and more powerful hardware or a new, larger disk.

When upgrading, the sys volume is generally your main concern; it holds the Bindery in version 3.x, and it holds the NDS database in versions 4.x and 5. Any other data volumes are essentially a matter of just getting the files and trustees over. Because the directory services database is in a constant state of flux, as objects are added and users log in and log out, there needs to be some way to lock down the database in order to copy it to another server or drive. This function is performed by the `dsmaint.nlm` in NetWare 4.1, the `install.nlm` in NetWare 4.11, and by the `nwconfig.nlm` in NetWare 5.

It is imperative that you have test hardware, no matter how small your network. You need to be able to make practice runs of upgrades and get familiar with new operating systems in a nonproduction environment. Do the upgrade in a test setting ten times, if that is what it takes to get comfortable with moving your production system. And keep the test tree around; you need it for service packs, testing third-party NLMs, and so on. If nothing else, get some low-end machines that you would not normally consider servers for your test environment; the test machines do not have to be state-of-the-art, high-speed equipment. And before you start, make sure that you point your browser to `www.novell.com/netware5/upgrade` to see what ideas Novell has on the subject!

NOVELL UPGRADE WIZARD

The Novell Upgrade Wizard allows you to perform an across-the-wire migration; the source server can be either NetWare version 3.x or version 4.x. The previous version of the Upgrade Wizard only worked if the source server was version 3.x, but the new Upgrade Wizard, version 3.0, is now available for download from Novell's Web site. The filename is nuw30.exe; the file size is 8,084,551 bytes. In this section, you are going to upgrade a NetWare 3.12 server to NetWare 5.

To run the Upgrade Wizard, you need a source server running NetWare 3.x and a destination tree. So in a single-server environment, you would install NetWare 5 onto your new hardware, create a new tree, and migrate.

There are a few caveats to using the Upgrade Wizard, but its nicest feature is the ability for you to model the migration—to make a dry run as it were. You set up what you want to happen and have the wizard verify your setup. This lets you solve any errors you encounter at the front end, before the migration starts. When you have the verification process error-free, you can begin the actual migration.

Tip #88 from *John*	Upgrading a server OS is a nontrivial task, Upgrade Wizard or no. Make sure that you have a verified backup of the volume you are going to copy the 3.x file system to, and make certain that you have a current and usable backup of your NDS database.

PART

III

CH

11

INSTALLING THE UPGRADE WIZARD

The first thing to do if you are going to use the Upgrade Wizard is to install it. To install the Upgrade Wizard, run upgrdwzd.exe from the <CDROM>:\PRODUCTS\UPGRDWZD directory, shown in Figure 11.1.

Figure 11.1
Running upgrdwzd.
exe from the \
PRODUCTS\UPGRDWZD
directory launches
the setup for the
Upgrade Wizard.

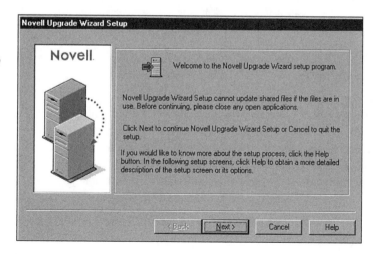

You are prompted to accept the license agreement and then prompted for the folder for the program files. The default folder is C:\Program Files\Novell\Upgrade. When the files are copied, you are ready to run the wizard by selecting Programs, Novell, Novell Upgrade Wizard from the Start menu.

After the setup is complete, there are several points you need to pay attention to prior to running the Upgrade Wizard:

- Update the NLMs on the 3.x server. The setup installs a folder, `C:\Program Files\Novell\Upgrade\products\nw3x`, which has 10 NLMs in it. These are updated NLMs that you need to copy to `Sys:system`. Unless the files you have on your 3.x server are newer than these, you want to overwrite the ones on the server with the updated versions. It is easiest to down and restart the server after this file copy; it is possible to unload and reload NLMs, but often one NLM is being used by another, and trying to manually set things straight is more trouble than a simple restart.

- TSA311 or TSA312 needs to be loaded on the source server; for that matter, TSA500 needs to be loaded on the destination server.

- The Upgrade Wizard can run on either Windows 95/98 or Windows NT. You want to use at least version 3 of the client for the 95/98 platform and version 4.5 for the NT platform. As of this writing, you can upgrade your clients at `www.novell.com/novellsw/brands.html`.

- You need supervisor equivalency on both servers.

- Look for name spaces. If the volumes you are migrating have support for MAC or NFS name spaces, you need to add this support to the destination volumes prior to the upgrade.

> **Note**
>
> *Name spaces* are modules that add functionality to your storage. For example, if you want a Macintosh to be able to save files on the server, you would add the MAC name space to the appropriate volume.

CREATING A PROJECT

When you launch the upgrade wizard, you need to create a project. A project is nothing more than a model of what you want to occur. For example, migrate the bindery from a particular 3.x server to a particular container in the tree, and only move the data volume from the 3.x server to a particular volume in the tree. The first screen you see gives you the option of Creating a new Upgrade Wizard Project, to Open an existing Upgrade Wizard Project, or to open last project. Because this is the first time you have run the wizard, the Create a New Upgrade Wizard Project is selected by default.

Give the project a filename and a location for the files, and then select the source and destination (see Figure 11.2).

Figure 11.2
You need to select a
source server and a
destination tree.

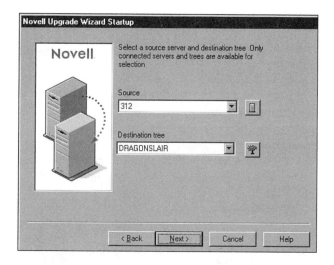

Tip #89 from
John

From the client side, you need to be able to see both the source and the destination. The client defaults to an IP connection to the NetWare 5 server, and this does not work. You need IPX all around for the Upgrade Wizard to work; for the duration of the migration, you might consider disabling IP at the server or having only the IPX protocol at the client.

When connected, you see your source and destination as shown in Figure 11.3.

Figure 11.3
When the source and
destination are speci-
fied, you see two
panes; one is your
3.12 source server,
and the other is the
dragonslair tree,
the destination.

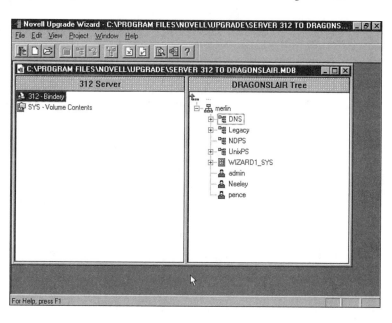

At this point, you want to look over the online help and play around with the menu choices and the icons on the toolbar. You don't have to worry about any changes you make sticking until you actually commit them via the Migrate button, and even then there are numerous opportunities to cancel.

If you are on a container object in the destination, you can click Insert and create a new container; this lets you modify your tree from within the Upgrade Wizard itself (see Figure 11.4). For example, assume you are going to migrate the business server to your new tree. You are going to migrate the bindery, and thus the users and groups, to a new container called `.bus.merlin`. You do not have to create the `.bus.merlin` container and then launch the Upgrade Wizard; instead, you can simply highlight the appropriate container—in this case `.merlin`—click Insert, and create it while in the wizard.

Figure 11.4
From within the Upgrade Wizard, you have created a new container called 312Users and dragged the bindery over to it. You have also created a new folder called 312Disk and dragged the Sys volume over to it.

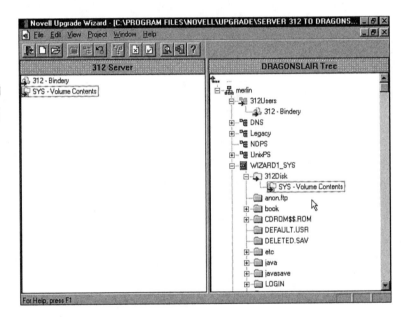

In Figure 11.4, you have created a new container, 312Users, and dragged and dropped the 312 bindery into it. You have done the same thing by creating a new folder, 312Disk, and dropping the Sys volume into it. At this point, you are now ready to verify the project. Verifying checks for conflicts and problems and give you choices on how to handle any conflicts, without actually performing the migration.

VERIFYING THE PROJECT

Verification isn't really necessary because the verify is done again during the migration. However, you do want to verify. This gives you a chance to resolve any errors ahead of time, rather than scramble to fix things when you are on a tight timeline. It's also nice to know that the entire project is ready to go, and all you have to do is to click the Migrate icon!

As part of the verification, you are asked whether you want to migrate the bindery print information to NDS. If you choose to do this, you are asked to provide the volume on which to place the print queues. Next, you have the option of applying a template object to migrated users. If you choose this option, you are asked for the template object you want to apply. Another question you have to resolve is how to handle filename conflicts, as shown in Figure 11.5.

Figure 11.5
You need to decide how to handle duplicate filenames. You can choose to not copy the file, to rename the file, or to copy the file only if it is newer.

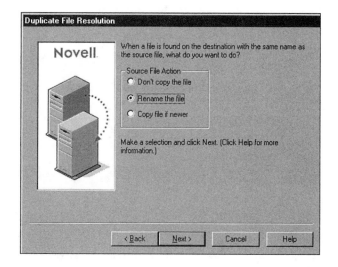

You have three options when dealing with files. You can decide to not copy the file, rename the file, or copy the file only if it is newer. When past this point, you supply the passwords for both the source and destination servers, and answer a few more wizard screens, and the verification begins. Any critical errors have a red circle with an X in it, and you need to resolve these errors before the migration begins. In Figure 11.6, you can see that you have encountered a fatal error—TSA500.NLM cannot be loaded on the destination server.

Figure 11.6
This is your verification results. There is a fatal error here, in that tsa500.nlm could not be loaded on the destination server. You need to correct this before the migration can succeed.

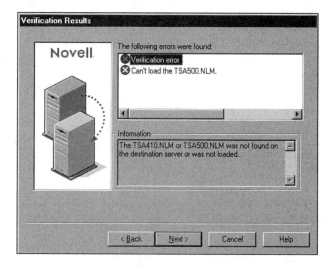

PART

III

CH

11

You can see from Figure 11.6 how nice the verify feature is. As an administrator, you would rather find out about potential upgrade show stoppers at 2:00 in the afternoon, than at 2:00 in the morning when you are actually performing the upgrade.

MIGRATION AND POST-MIGRATION CLEANUP

When all fatal errors have been taken care of, the actual migration is as simple as clicking the Start Migration button. This launches another wizard, and after a few screens, you see the objects as they are migrated, along with a status bar, as shown in Figure 11.7.

Figure 11.7
During the migration, you get to watch animated objects flying from one side to the other. More useful is the status bar showing the elapsed time and the time remaining.

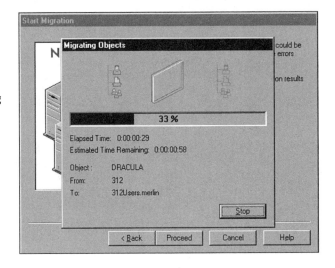

After your successful migration, there are some post-migration steps that you might or might not need to be concerned with:

- **Moving NDS objects**—There is no granularity when moving the bindery, meaning that you can put the bindery into a container, period. You can't put user John in this context and user Peter in a different context. After the users have come across, it is a simple matter to move the users to the correct context via nwadm32.

- **Login scripts**—The login script almost certainly needs to be modified or at least checked. And don't forget that these new users will also run the container login script, if it exists.

- **Files**—Did they all come across, and are the rights and attributes correct?

- **Printing**—If you migrated the print information, here is another area that you almost certainly need to check on. Migrating the print information was one of the choices you had to make when setting up your project. Also, hardware such as an HP JetDirect card needs to be pointed at the new server instead of the old.

- **The user information**—Again, you almost certainly need to check this, including items such as the home directory, any user restrictions, and so on.

Before attending to the post-migration details, the first thing you want to do is to take a look at the success and error logs generated by the Upgrade Wizard.

THE SUCCESS AND ERROR LOGS

The wizard writes both success and error logs, each of which is available via an icon on the Upgrade Wizard toolbar. A portion of the success log is given here. You can see the options that were set up for your project, any warnings that you had before proceeding, and the status of individual aspects, such as user John being successfully migrated:

```
*****************************************************************
Success Log
Project: C:\PROGRAM FILES\NOVELL\UPGRADE\SERVER 312 TO DRAGONSLAIR.MDB
Date :03/26/99  Time: 14:12:18
Operator: SUPERVISOR
*****************************************************************
*****************************************************************
Start migration for Project named 'C:\PROGRAM FILES\NOVELL\UPGRADE\SERVER 312
       TO DRAGONSLAIR.MDB'
Date: 03/29/99  Time: 09:57:29
Operator: PENCE
Source Server: 312
Destination Tree: DRAGONSLAIR
For all partial migrations, please review the error log file for more
       information.
*****************************************************************
```

The following are the project options you selected and warnings that were displayed during verification:

```
You have chosen to migrate print information. The Print Queue volume name is
       WIZARD1_SYS.merlin.

You have chosen not to apply a template to migrated users.

You have chosen not to create a template object.
```

The following warning was encountered during validation:

```
The number of users, besides yourself, still logged in to source server '312'
is 1'. If these users have files open while the migration runs, these files
will not be migrated. It is recommended that all users log out before migrating.
This is the end of the project options and warnings.
*****************************************************************

Complete: Organizational Unit '312Users' was successfully created in NDS
       context 'merlin'.

Complete: Supervisor attributes of bindery object 'SUPERVISOR' were migrated
       to NDS Organizational Unit '312Users' if they didn't already exist in
       the OU.

Complete: Bindery object 'User' named 'GUEST' successfully migrated to NDS
       object 'GUEST'.

Complete: Bindery object 'User' named 'PENCE' successfully migrated to NDS
       object 'PENCE'.
```

```
Complete: Bindery object 'User' named 'SANDRA' successfully migrated to NDS
          object 'SANDRA'.

Complete: Bindery object 'User' named 'PETER' successfully migrated to NDS
          object 'PETER'.
```

A portion of the error log is shown here also. Pay close attention to this log, and note any actions that you need to take, such as giving rights back to user `Pence`:

```
****************************************************************
Error Log
Project: C:\PROGRAM FILES\NOVELL\UPGRADE\SERVER 312 TO DRAGONSLAIR.MDB
Date: 03/26/99 Time: 14:12:18
Operator: SUPERVISOR
****************************************************************
****************************************************************
Project: 'C:\PROGRAM FILES\NOVELL\UPGRADE\SERVER 312 TO DRAGONSLAIR.MDB'
Migration started date: 03/29/99 time: 09:57:29
Operator: PENCE
Source Server: 312
Destination Tree: DRAGONSLAIR
****************************************************************
The Supervisor object is not migrated. The intruder detection information is
    copied to the container where the bindery was dropped. If the container
    already contains intruder detection information, it is left intact.
    Supervisor equivalences will need to be redone after the migration.
The user login script for User SUPERVISOR can't be opened. This may mean that
    there isn't a login script or that access was denied. You will need to
reenter
    the login script for this user.
Object .PENCE.312Users.merlin was security equivalent to Supervisor on the
    source server. You will need to manually assign this object's supervisor
    equivalences.
Object SUPERVISOR was not found in NDS. Object EVERYONE referenced this object
    for property Member. Perhaps the referenced object was not migrated;
    therefore, information has been lost.
File tts$log.err was intentionally not copied wherever it was found on volume
    SYS of server 312. File vol$log.err was intentionally not copied wherever
    it was found on volume SYS of server 312. And the contents of directory
    sys:system were intentionally not copied from server 312.
```

UPGRADING FROM 3.x TO NETWARE 5 (IN-PLACE UPGRADE)

An *in-place upgrade* is when you keep your existing hardware and only change the operating system to the next version. All users and data stay intact, and the only thing that changes is the OS. The main thing to keep in mind when doing an in-place upgrade is your fallback position: if something can go wrong, it will, and what happens if you are left in a position of having to rebuild your 3.x server from scratch? When approaching an in-place upgrade, this is how you have to think. You need to reinstall NetWare 3.x, reinstall your tape backup software, and restore from tape. It would completely ruin your day to find at this point that your tapes cannot be read, or that your backups had not been done correctly, so make certain at the front end!

Tip #90 from _John_	Do not forget to back up the DOS partition on your `C:` drive, specifically `C:\server.31x`. In a multiserver environment, one good way to do this is to use the server as a workstation by loading the NIC driver, running `netx`, and copying the `C:` drive up to the server. This would drastically simplify your life if you needed to restore!

NetWare 5 is going to require more resources than your 3.x server did, so keep this in mind when considering an in-place upgrade. Is your existing hardware sufficient? And never consider an in-place upgrade to a mission-critical server if you can help it; but having said that, there are times when your only option is an in-place upgrade.

The actual upgrade itself is a simple process, no different from a normal installation from scratch. Down the server, and load the drivers necessary for your CD-ROM to work in DOS; then reboot, put in the OS CD, switch to that drive, and run install.

Note	Most newer hardware supports bootable CDs, so if this is your case, you don't need to worry about loading the CD-ROM drivers; the NetWare 5 CD is bootable. Just put it in and go!

Caution	The first screen you are presented with is the Welcome to the NetWare Server Installation screen. On this screen, you select either Is This a New Server or Upgrade From 3.1x or 4.1x. This screen normally defaults to New Server. This is not a good choice for the default because a new installation destroys all your data on existing NetWare partitions. So be careful here.

PART

III

CH

11

Select Upgrade From 3.1x or 4.1x and then continue. On the next screen, choose your mouse type and video mode. The mouse type and video mode are not automatically detected. They seem to be because most people have PS2 mice, and that is what is filled in by default. But again, the mouse and video are not automatically detected. The mouse types available are PS2, Serial Com1, Serial Com2, and No Mouse. The video modes available are Standard VGA and Super VGA.

Next, you select a Platform support module, a HotPlug support module (if needed), and a storage adapter (which is required). These first two choices—the Platform Support Module and the HotPlug Support Module—are optional. The Platform support module is for server hardware that has multiple processors or some other sort of specific configuration. If the installation did not auto-detect this, you probably do not need it. A HotPlug support module provides support for removing and inserting network interface cards and storage adapters while the server is on and powered up. This is referred to as _hot swap_ or _hot swappable_. As in the case of the Platform support module, if the installation did not auto-detect this, you probably do not need it.

On the other hand, there is certainly nothing optional about the storage adapter. The storage adapter connects your computer to your disks; it's a fancy way of saying *disk controller*! The storage adapter is required and is auto-detected by the installation program. If it is not auto-detected, or is detected incorrectly, you need to have the correct drivers on hand from the vendor. The .dsk drivers that you have been used to in NetWare 3.1x are updated to .ham drivers. Ham drivers, or *Host Adapter Modules*, allow the storage adapter to communicate with the server. Each device connected to the adapter requires a .cdm, or *Custom Device Module*. Because you can have more than one drive or device connected to your storage adapter, it is very possible, and likely, that you have only the one .ham driver for your controller, but several .cdm modules loaded for the devices; for example, cpqscsi.ham is the .ham module for a Compaq Ultra/Fast/Wide SCSI-2 controller, while scsihd.cdm and scsicd.cdm are the Novell CDMs for a hard disk and CD-ROM, respectively.

Next, the devices attached to your controller are auto-detected. These are the disks, CD-ROMs, and tape drives. If they are not detected or are detected incorrectly, you need the appropriate drivers from the vendor to add an unlisted driver.

The Sys volume is then mounted, and your network interface cards are auto-detected. Choose the appropriate drivers; then the driver is loaded, and the file copy begins.

Tip #91 from
John

> While installing your new server, go ahead and add IP, even if you do not immediately have plans to use it. This gives you a gradual path to move from IPX to IP, and you can ultimately unload IPX when it is no longer required.

When the file copy is complete, you are in Graphical User Interface land, the graphical portion of the NetWare 5 Installation. The first screen you see allows you to modify, create, and delete disk partitions. Because you are doing an in-place upgrade, you shouldn't need to do anything here. Next is the protocol selection screen; here, you want to make sure that you enable IP. Next is the time zone information and then the NDS install. You either create a new NDS tree or install into an existing tree. If you are in a single-server environment, or if this is the first server moving off of the 3.x platform, create a new tree.

So far, there has been nothing different about the in-place upgrade than a normal, virgin installation of a new server. But you finally get to a 3.x-specific screen, if you choose to install the upgraded server into an existing tree. The installation needs to know at this point how you want to handle conflicts; this is the Bindery Objects Conflicts Resolution dialog box.

For example, you are upgrading from 3.x to NetWare 5 doing an in-place upgrade, and are installing into an existing tree. The installation asks for the context to place the server in, and in this case, you have chosen o=merlin. There is already an NDS user object Pence in o=merlin; there is also a user Pence in the bindery of the 3.x server, so how should this be handled? Your choices are to Merge, Rename, or Delete; these actions are taken against the bindery objects.

NDS is then installed, which could take some time, depending on the size of the NDS database, and the speed of the link between the servers. The final step is licensing; you can either insert the license disk or continue without a license. If you continue without a license, you need to add it later via NWConfig.

In summary, there is very little difference between an in-place upgrade and a brand-new installation. The primary difference is that you are asked how to handle the bindery objects in the event of conflicts.

UPGRADING FROM NETWARE 4.X TO NETWARE 5

There are numerous ways you can get from NetWare 4 to NetWare 5, and I am going to take a look at five possible scenarios here. Three of them entail purchasing new hardware, and the other two are in-place upgrades. New hardware gives you the opportunity to move to NetWare 5, get a more powerful server, and still leave the source server untouched. What are these five methods?

- **Method 1**—In method 1, you are not going to purchase new hardware for the NetWare 5 server, so you will perform an in-place upgrade.

- **Method 2**—This time, you will purchase new hardware for your NetWare 5 server. The idea is to clone your existing server onto the new hardware, and then perform an in-place upgrade to NetWare 5 on the new box.

- **Method 3**—Using method 3, you are also going to be purchasing new hardware for your destination NetWare 5 server. The idea here is to perform an in-place upgrade of your existing server (method 1), and then perform a hardware upgrade (NetWare 5 to NetWare 5), which is covered later in this chapter.

- **Method 4**—This also entails the purchase of new hardware for your NetWare 5 server. In this case, you simply insert the NetWare 5 server into the tree and copy the data over from your NetWare 4 box. Then rename the new server.

- **Method 5**—The accelerated upgrade. This is the same thing as an in-place upgrade, only it essentially runs in unattended mode, speeding things up. Only someone with experience in upgrading to NetWare 5 should try this method.

The pros and cons? Method 1 is the simplest, but it does not leave you with an immediate fallback position. Method 2 seems complex, but it is actually the safest way to go about things. Method 3 does not leave the source server untouched, so the in-place upgrade had better go smoothly. And methods 4 and 5 should be used only by experienced NetWare administrators because there are numerous gotchas that you can be bitten by.

MIGRATING THE DIRECTORY SERVICES

As mentioned at the beginning of this chapter, migrating the Sys volume is where your greatest concerns are because the Sys volume contains the directory services database. And if there is one thing you want to function correctly, it is the directory services synchronization and replication.

The directory services database is loosely coupled, meaning that it is always changing, and the database on one server might not be in the same state as the database on another server. Objects being created and deleted, users logging in and logging out, and other events trigger NDS changes, and all servers need to be aware of what is going on in order to stay in sync. So in order to back up the NDS database, you need some way to freeze it, or lock it, in order to write it to a file.

This is the function of what was originally the DSMaint.nlm. What the DSMaint did, and still does, was to take a "snapshot" of the server's copy of the database; then it locks down directory services. To the other servers, it's as if this server is simply down. This backup.nds file can then be used to bring another server online with an exact copy of the old server's directory services, so from an NDS point of view, all the servers are happy, and things are in sync.

Tip #92 from	dsmaint is for 4.1 servers, and in version 4.11, the functionality of dsmaint was added to
John	the install.nlm. And in NetWare 5, the install NLM was changed to nwconfig.nlm.

Originally, dsmaint was created to move the directory services database from one 4.1 server to another. When IntraNetWare, or NetWare 4.11, came out, the functions of dsmaint were integrated into the 4.11 install.nlm, so dsmaint is not required on a 4.11 server. In NetWare 5, the install NLM was replaced with the nwconfig.nlm, but the directory services backup and restore functions are still there.

Several of the upgrade methods that I am going to outline require you to lock down the NDS database, and copy the resulting file to your new server hardware.

METHOD 1 (IN-PLACE UPGRADE)

If this is the first server you are upgrading in your NetWare 4 tree, your main concern, before thinking about upgrading, is to get all your existing servers patched to the most-current levels. In particular, you are concerned about the DS NLM versions. Go to Novell's Web site, see what DS version your 4.x boxes should be on, and keep in mind that this is a moving target. As bugs are fixed and enhancements are added, newer versions of the DS NLM come around fairly frequently. Also, Novell recommends that the first server you upgrade in your tree be the one that holds the master of the root partition.

All the initial steps laid out in the section on performing an in-place upgrade from 3.x to NetWare 5 are the same when doing an in-place upgrade from 4.x to NetWare 5. You down the server, get your CD-ROM working in DOS, switch to the CD, and run install. The 4.x server is already in a tree, meaning that you have no bindery conflicts to contend with, so it is actually simpler. Because the upgrade process is identical to that of the 3.x in-place upgrade, I will take a quick look; for more detail, see the section on an in-place upgrade from NetWare 3.

After the Novell splash screen, you are presented with the character-based portion of the installation. Accept the license agreement, and then select New Server or Upgrade. As was pointed out earlier, the default is New Server, a bad choice for a default, so be careful here. You need to choose Upgrade from 3.x or 4.x.

Select the correct mouse type and video mode, and again, you should note that the mouse and video type are not auto-detected; they just appear to be. There is a preliminary file copy, and then you select your storage adapter module, Platform support modules, and HotPlug support module. Of these three, only the storage adapter module is required.

The storage devices and network interface cards are detected, and the drivers loaded. If your hardware is not auto-detected, or is detected incorrectly, you need to obtain the correct drivers from the vendor.

Be patient during the GUI portion of the install; it isn't going to run nearly as fast as the character-based portions. Early in the GUI part of the upgrade, you configure your network interface cards for IPX, IP, or both and then finally add a license or install without a license.

Tip #93 from	The GUI installation program cannot handle licenses with more than eight digits. If your license has more than eight digits, choose to install your server without a license. Then, after the upgrade, load NWConfig, select License Options, and install your license then. NWConfig can handle licenses with more than eight digits.
John	

PART

III

CH

11

Finally, you are at the Additional Products and Services menu, where you can choose to install other products such as NDPS, LDAP, NDS Catalog services, and so on. You can always come back to this screen later to add products, so don't worry about needing to install everything now.

MOVING 2 (MOVING TO NEW HARDWARE AND THEN IN-PLACE UPGRADE)

So far, in method 1, you did an in-place upgrade to move from NetWare 4 to NetWare 5. The in-place upgrade is always fraught with peril in a production environment, but it is simple and doesn't bring any new hardware into the picture.

Here is the plan for method 2. You are going to purchase new hardware and want to move to NetWare 5 on the new machine. However, if possible, you would like to leave your source server untouched so that you have an immediate fallback position in the event of problems.

Note	The information in this section is all valid and correct; however, it was written before Novell had an Upgrade Wizard that would work with a version 4.x source server. You could achieve the same results you are after here in a simpler fashion by using the Upgrade Wizard.

So, install the same version of the OS on your new hardware. Use the install NLM to move the directory services database from your old server to the new server. Restore your data to the new server. At this point, you now have the exact setup that you had before, only you are running on new hardware. Now that you have your server running on your new hardware, you can perform an in-place upgrade of the new server, and you will get from NetWare 4 to NetWare 5 without risking your original production server. Here are the steps:

1. Perform a complete, verified, readable backup of your old server. Maybe two!

2. Install the same version of NetWare onto your new hardware. Use the *same* name as your old server and the *same* IPX internal network number. And very important: Install the new server into its own bogus, or temporary, tree. The server doesn't need to be plugged in to the network for you to perform this install, and indeed, it can't be because you are using the same name and number as a current production server. Also, patch this new server to the latest patches available on Novell's Web site.

3. Log in to your old server as user Admin or equivalent. In order for install to make a snapshot of the NDS database, the database needs to be locked. With DS locked, no one can log in. So make sure you log in first before you are locked out!

4. Load install on your old server, select Directory Options, Directory Backup and Restore Options, and choose Save Local DS Information Prior to Hardware Upgrade, as shown in Figure 11.8.

Figure 11.8
The functionality of `Dsmaint`, used in NetWare version 4.1, is built into the `install.nlm` on the IntraNetWare (version 4.11) platform. Here is where you take the snapshot and lock down the directory services database.

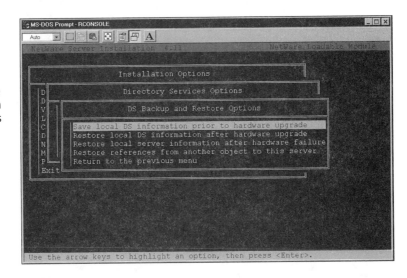

5. Install takes the picture of the NDS database, a file called `backup.nds`, and copies it to `sys:system`. At this time, directory services are locked on your source server.

Tip #94 from

John

Do not attempt to save the `backup.nds` file to the server's A: drive. Your database is almost certainly going to be larger than 1.44MB, and there is no provision for spanning more than one disk!

6. Even though directory services is locked at this point, and no one else can log in, you are okay; you logged in earlier! Copy the `backup.nds` file from `sys:system` to your workstation's hard drive or another location where you can access it later, as you are going to log out of the old server and then shut it down.

7. Shut down your old (source) server.

8. Plug the new server into the network, and log in to the new server as admin or equivalent. Remember, the new server hasn't been cabled into the network because it has the same name and internal IPX number as your original server. Due to the fact that you installed your new server into a bogus tree, the other servers on your real tree do not see the new one, even though it has the same name and number of the one you just took offline. Restoring the directory services database takes care of this.

9. Copy the `backup.nds` file to `sys:system` in the new server. At the console of the new server, load install, choose Directory options, and then remove NDS from this server. Although this sounds drastic, no need to worry; this is the bogus tree, and there is only this one server in it!

10. While still at Directory Options, select Directory Backup and Restore Options, and then choose Restore Local DS Information After Hardware Upgrade. You then supply the path to the file `backup.nds`, in this case, `sys:system`, as shown in Figure 11.9.

PART

III

CH

11

Figure 11.9
It is time to restore directory services on your new hardware. Press F3, and enter the path to `sys:system`.

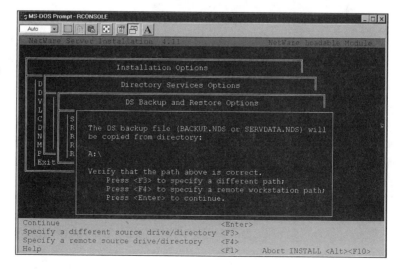

11. At this point, your new hardware should be happily communicating with the other servers in the tree; it should have picked up right where the old server left off. The only thing left to do now is restore your data from the tapes you created in step 1.

12. When you have restored your data, you should have an exact copy of your old server, only up and running on the new hardware.

At this point, your source server, the original production server, is offline and powered down. The new server is online, and you can now perform an in-place upgrade to NetWare 5 on the new server, secure in the knowledge that you have your original server intact, in the event of a failure.

METHOD 3 (IN-PLACE UPGRADE AND THEN MOVING TO NEW HARDWARE)

As in method 2, this time, you will purchase new hardware for your NetWare 5 server. Method 3 is really a composite of an in-place upgrade and a hardware upgrade. In method 2, you went from NetWare 4 to NetWare 4 on new hardware, and then did an in-place upgrade of the new NetWare 4 server. This left your source NetWare 4 server untouched.

In method 3, you do the same thing, only backward; you do an in-place upgrade to get to NetWare 5, and then you perform a hardware upgrade (NetWare 5 to NetWare 5) to get onto your new server hardware.

So, the plan is this:

1. Perform an in-place upgrade of your 4.x server; see the section on performing an in-place upgrade of NetWare 4.x (method 1).

2. When you are certain that the tree is stable, perform a hardware upgrade to get from your NetWare 5 server running on your old hardware, onto your new platform; see the section on hardware upgrade later in this chapter.

The downside to this process is that the very first thing you do is an in-place upgrade of your production server, so if things go wrong, you will be scrambling to recover.

METHOD 4 (INSERT NEW NETWARE 5 SERVER THEN COPY DATA)

This is the simplest of all the upgrade methods when new hardware is being used, but it is also the one you need to be very careful with. The plan here is to simply insert the new server into the tree and copy the user data.

Install NetWare 5 onto your new box, and then insert your new NetWare 5 server into the tree. Remember the cautions I went over regarding DS versions, NetWare 4, and NetWare 5, when discussing the in-place upgrade from 4 to 5? Well, those same cautions still apply. In short, make sure that the 4.x boxes are patched up to the latest available on Novell's Web site (support.novell.com), follow the link to the minimum patch list, and this should put you in good shape.

When the NetWare 5 server is in the tree, and NDS is settled down, you have two concerns:

- **The file server names**—Your old version 4 server and your new version 5 server are both going to be alive on the wire at the same time, so they both cannot have the same name. This is easily handled by renaming the servers after you are finished. Suppose the old file server was named George. You bring the new file server online as Grace. At the end of the process, rename George to OldGeorge. Then rename Grace to George. This has another added bonus; you can keep OldGeorge online for a few days, until you are certain that you did not miss anything during the migration. When you are certain that things are okay, remove OldGeorge from the tree.

- **The files and trustee assignments**—How to get the files and trustees off the volumes of the NetWare 4 server, and onto the volumes of the NetWare 5 server, while maintaining rights? That is the question. To do this, all you need is some sort of file copy utility that maintains rights; ncopy does not do this for you!

Why are you only worried about the files and rights? Well, there is no bindery to worry about; the users already exist in the tree, and your new NetWare 5 server is already a participant. It is important to note that the file rights information is not stored in NDS, but that it is stored as part of the file system, specifically in the Directory Entry Table (DET). So, you need some sort of copy program that is smart enough to move the trustees and rights from the old server to the new server.

And don't forget name spaces. For example, if you have the MAC name space supported on your source, the destination server needs to support the MAC name space. And, the software you use not only needs to be NetWare-aware enough to handle rights, but also the various name spaces.

PART

III

CH

11

There are utilities on Novell's Web site, specifically their toolbox, that you can download to help with this. Or there are third-party utilities available: FSTrust can be found at http://www.jpence.com or http://www.dreamlan.com. Or you can do a backup of the old server and then restore to the new server, as long as you are using an SMS compliant backup, such as the Sbackup program that comes with Novell, or a third-party product, such as Arcserve.

So the procedure is this:

1. Insert the new NetWare 5 server into the tree. Make sure that the tree is healthy, and that all is well as far as directory services is concerned.

2. Using a utility that handles the name spaces in question, along with the file system rights, copy the data you desire from the old server to the new server.

3. Rename the old server. Edit the autoexec.ncf, change the server name, and restart the server. At the console of another server, enter the command RESET ROUTER, and then wait five minutes. Make sure that directory services is happy—that everything is in sync and the old server is seen with its new name. Take your time! Don't do anything else until you are sure that the tree is in sync, and that all processes equal yes.

4. Rename the new server. Same process: Edit the `autoexec.ncf` file, restart, and then wait. Make sure all is in sync.

At this point, you should be able to access your new server with all the old shortcuts, drive mappings, and so on. Check that everything you need comes across okay and that everything is working as it should. Because you haven't done anything to the source NetWare 4 server, if you encounter any show stoppers, all you have to do is put the server names back the way they were, and it is as if you were never there. When you are certain that everything is okay and you are running on the new server with no problems, remove directory services from the old server, and shut it down.

Some things are going to follow the old server, so be careful. For example, assume that your home directory property is set to the `Pence` directory on the user volume on server `ORIGINAL`. Insert your new NetWare 5 server, copy the data, and then start renaming. The first thing you do is rename server `ORIGINAL` to `OLD-ORIGINAL`. You then rename the new NetWare 5 server to `ORIGINAL`. Where is the home directory property going to be pointing if you check in `nwadm32`? It points to the `Pence` directory on the user volume on server `OLD-ORIGINAL`! Why is this? You just changed the name of the server, and that change rippled through the directory; every instance of the old name now reflects the change.

This is the sort of gotcha that method 4 brings to the table; you can copy the data over easily enough and leave the source server unchanged, but you need to watch for this sort of thing. This method might be useful to you, depending on the what the server being upgraded is used for.

METHOD 5 (THE ACCELERATED UPGRADE PROCESS)

The accelerated Upgrade Utility can be obtained from Novell's Web site; the file is `acclupgd.exe`. The utility uses a script file to automate the upgrade process. If you want to learn about script files, track down TID 2944480 from Novell's Web site. The file `cdware.exe` extracts into `cdscript.doc`, which answers any questions you have about scripts and more!

The end result of using the accelerated upgrade process is an in-place upgrade, with all the prompts answered for you. Novell recommends that only administrators with experience at troubleshooting NetWare 5 installations use the accelerated upgrade utility.

There are several neat features here; one is that you can upgrade without a CD-ROM in the server by copying the CD-ROM files to another server or by mounting the CD-ROM as a volume in another server. You can also upgrade a server via `rconsole`! Another rather arcane feature is that the accelerated upgrade process can upgrade a server with only 32MB of RAM, as opposed to the 64MB that is normally required; I say *arcane* because who would expect to run a server with only 32MB of RAM!

Note

The accelerated upgrade utility does not install the IP protocol! You need to go in and manually add IP (and remove IPX if needed) after the upgrade.

There are some other caveats to the accelerated upgrade process, so before you begin, take a close look at the documentation supplied. The file `acclupgd.exe` is a self-extracting file, so to install, make a directory on either the server you mean to upgrade or on any server on the network. Then copy `acclupgd.exe` to this directory and execute the program, which extracts the necessary files.

A source server is the server that has the files extracted from `acclupgd.exe` and also has a complete copy of the NetWare 5 CD-ROM. You can either copy the entire CD-ROM to the source server, or you can simply mount the CD-ROM as a NetWare volume. The source server can be the server you are upgrading; it does not have to be a remote server. For example, you could extract the files to the `Sys` volume of the server you are upgrading, and mount the CD-ROM on the same server if desired. As long as the server being upgraded can access the files, that is all that is required.

You cannot use this utility to upgrade the first server moving to NetWare 5, which means that you already have a mix of versions, NetWare 4 and NetWare 5. As always, make certain that your servers are patched to the latest available from Novell's Web site; specifically, the DS version is the most important to keep the tree healthy.

When you have the source server set up, load NWConfig on the server you want to upgrade; you can either be at the server console, or you can use `rconsole` to access the target server console. When NWConfig is loaded, choose Product Options, and install a product not listed. Enter the path to the directory in which you exploded `acclupgd.exe`, and you see the screen shown in Figure 11.10.

Figure 11.10

These are the choices available to you at the beginning of the accelerated upgrade process. Novell recommends selecting them all, unless you have reason to do otherwise.

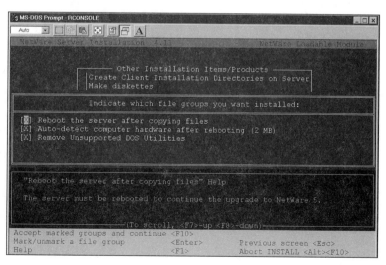

When the upgrade kicks off, read the license and press Esc to continue. Then accept the license agreement, and press Esc to continue, at which time the file copying begins. You are prompted for the location of the NetWare 5 operating system files, and as noted, this can be the CD mounted as a NetWare volume on any server or the files copied from the CD to any server.

From this point on, you can kick back and watch the show. The server reboots, at which time the installation takes over again and run the hardware auto-detection. Finally, the server reboots in its finished state; the one thing you need to do is install the NetWare 5 licenses.

There is a provision to bypass the hardware auto-detection. You might want to do this if you are upgrading numerous identical machines (not likely), or—which would be more useful— the provision can be used to install drivers that are not provided on the CD-ROM. How does this work?

Create a \startup directory in the same directory where you exploded acclupgd.exe. Create or copy the correct startup.ncf file for your hardware to this startup directory, along with the .HAM and .CDM files needed. Then run the accelerated upgrade process as normal.

UPGRADE YOUR HARDWARE

When you purchase a new and more powerful machine, your only interests are in getting an exact copy of your existing server running on your new hardware. You are not going to be upgrading the operating system.

There are two main concerns: your data and rights, and moving the NDS directory correctly from the old machine to the new. To restore your data, it is imperative that you have a NetWare-aware backup program and that you test your ability to restore using it! Your backup program needs to be able to not only handle the file system rights, but also to deal with any additional name space support that you have added.

Tip #95 from
John

When backing up a server, don't forget that having a backup of the DOS partition, specifically C:\nwserver, can be really helpful in getting a dead server back on its feet!

There is one feature about a hardware upgrade that any administrator will love: you are not touching the source of the upgrade, your old server, so you have an immediate fallback position in the event that anything goes wrong. The only thing you are going to do to the source server is lock down its copy of the directory and power it off! So what are the steps? Earlier in this chapter, you saw how it was possible to use the install.nlm to back up the directory of a 4.11 server and then, again using the install NLM, to restore the backed-up copy to a new 4.11 server. You will find the process is identical, except that, in NetWare 5, you will use the nwconfig.nlm, which replaces the install.nlm:

1. Perform a complete, verified, readable backup of your old server. Make sure that you have tested your ability to reload your tape backup software on the server and that you are able to read and actually restore from your tapes.

2. Install the same version of NetWare 5 onto your new hardware. Use the *same* name as your old server and the *same* IPX internal network number. And very important: Install the new server into its own bogus, or temporary, tree. The server doesn't need to be plugged in to the network for you to perform this install, and indeed, it can't be because you are using the same name and number as a current production server.

   A safe bet would be to patch this new server to the latest available on Novell's Web site. And before this new server is put online, now is the perfect time to make sure that you are using the newest NIC and disk drivers available from the vendors of your new hardware.

3. Log in to your old server as user Admin or equivalent. In order for install to make a snapshot of the NDS database, the database needs to be locked. With DS locked, no one can log in. So make sure you log in first before you are locked out!

4. Load NWConfig on your old server, select Directory Options, Directory Backup and Restore Options, and then choose Save Local DS information prior to hardware upgrade; you are presented with the screen shown in Figure 11.11.

Figure 11.11
Read any screens that are presented to you when dealing with Directory services very carefully! Here, the backup.nds file is about to be created; you have a chance to copy it to a location that you specify shortly after this screen.

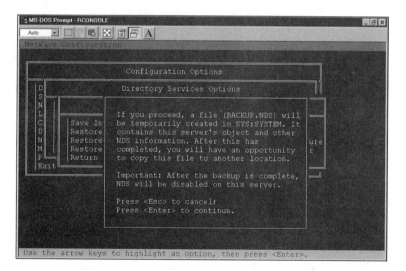

After pressing Enter to continue on the screen shown in Figure 11.11, you need to supply the administrator's name and password. You then have a chance to copy the backup.nds file to a:\.

Caution

Do not attempt to save the backup.nds file to the A: drive. There is no ability for the NWConfig NLM to span multiple floppy disks, and your directory almost certainly exceeds the capacity of one floppy!

The backup is going to be created in sys:system in any case; the copy option isn't really necessary because you have already logged in to the server back in step 3.

5. Install takes a picture of the NDS database, a file called backup.nds, and copies it to sys:system. At this time, directory services are locked on your source server.

6. Even though directory services is locked at this point and no one else can log in, you are okay; you logged in earlier! Copy the backup.nds file from sys:system to your workstation's hard drive or another location where you can access it later because you are preparing to log out of the old server and then shut it down.

7. Log out of the old server, and shut it down.

8. Plug the new server into the network, and log in to the new server as admin or equivalent.

Tip #96 from
John

You have shut down your old server, and to your dismay, you can't find the new server to log in to! Don't forget, you have installed the new server into a temporary tree; you need to use that treename.

Remember, the new server hasn't been cabled into the network because it has the same name and internal IPX number as your original server. Due to the fact that you installed your new server into a bogus tree, the other servers on your real tree do not see the new one, even though it has the same name and number of the one you just took offline. Restoring the directory services database takes care of this.

9. Copy the backup.nds file to sys:system in the new server. At the console of the new server, load NWConfig, choose Directory options, and remove NDS from this server. Although this sounds drastic, there's no need to worry; this is the bogus tree, and there is only this one server in it! You are presented with the screen shown in Figure 11.12.

10. When you answer Yes to remove directory services, you need to supply the administrator's name and password. This isn't the admin and password that you are used to using; this is the admin user, context, and password of the bogus tree that you are still working with! You receive yet another warning (see Figure 11.13). This warning lets you know that you are about to remove NDS from the only server that has a copy of the root. Normally, it would be a great mistake to ignore this, but it is what you would expect; this is a temporary tree with only one server in it.

Figure 11.12
Take the chance to read this screen even though you are not worried about it; it isn't a screen that you see every day, and you soon see that Novell doesn't make removing NDS a task to be taken lightly!

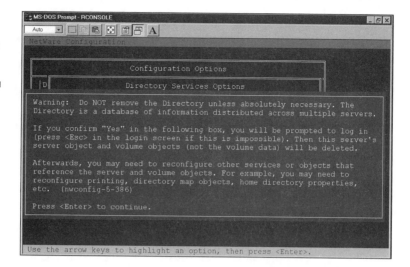

Figure 11.13
This warning is one that you would not normally take lightly! It tells you that you are about to remove the only existing copy of NDS in the tree.

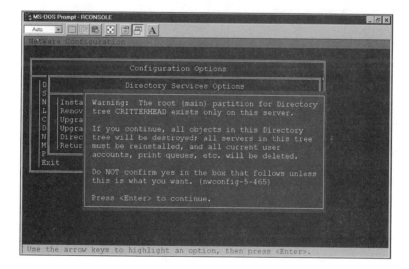

11. When you press Enter at the screen shown in Figure 11.13, you are prompted yet again: Remove Directory Services Anyway? Answer Yes to this question, and you have yet another screen, shown in Figure 11.14. This screen is informational; it tells you that this was a single reference time source and how to handle the possible repercussions of removing NDS from it. You'll notice that Novell has taken steps to ensure that one doesn't lightly remove NDS from a server!

Figure 11.14
In a multiple server environment, removing a Single Reference Time server can have implications. This screen gives you some advice on how to deal with what is about to happen. Because you are still in the bogus tree, and indeed, it is a single server tree, you can ignore it.

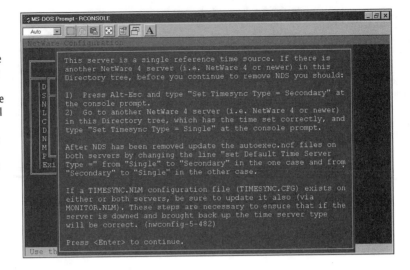

12. While still at Directory Options, select Directory Backup and Restore Options, and then choose Restore Local DS Information After Hardware Upgrade. Press F3 and then supply the path to the file backup.nds, in this case, sys:system. You are prompted for the administrator's name and password; this time, you are going to use your normal admin user, context, and password!

13. With directory services restored, your new hardware should be happily communicating with the other servers in the tree; it should have picked up right where the old server left off. The only thing left to do now is restore your data from the tapes you created in step 1.

When you have restored your data, you should have an exact copy of your old server, only up and running on the new hardware. Are there any files you should not restore? You can restore them all; after all, you are only upgrading the hardware. Is there anything you should not restore? Absolutely; don't restore NDS! You have already taken care of this via the directory backup and restore options of NWConfig.

So in the event of a problem, how do you get back? If you look back over the procedure, you can see that absolutely nothing was done to the source server except to create the backup.nds file in sys:system, thus locking directory services on this server. The server was then shut down.

To get back to your original server, shut down the new one. Bring up the old server, and if you receive any DS-related errors, ignore them; remember, the directory services database is still locked on this server. Load NWConfig, choose the directory backup and restore options, and then select Restore After a Hardware Upgrade. The backup.nds file will still sit there in sys:system! That's it; you are back online with your old server.

Swap Sys Procedure

This process lets you swap the disk containing the sys volume with another disk in the same server, which is very useful for upgrading server hard drives without using tape. Credit for this procedure needs to go to Marcel Cox, one of the Novell Support Connection Sysops, and currently the network manager at the Centre Informatique de l'Etat du Luxembourg (The Luxembourg State Computer Center). There is nothing revolutionary about it; the process uses the Directory Backup and Restore Options of NWConfig, but it's clever; to my knowledge, Marcel is the first one to have thought about using dsmaint to migrate from one disk to another in the same server!

Tip #97 from *John*	Don't try this on a production server until you have done it a few times on your test hardware.

When would you use this procedure? Say that you are on NetWare 5, and your current 2GB sys volume, which seemed like plenty of space at the time, is now full. You have a new 9GB drive to replace this with, but the *only* thing you want to change on your server is the sys volume. You could treat this as a hardware upgrade and start fresh with a black volume, install NetWare 5, and so on, and ultimately restore, but the swap sys procedure is simple and straightforward. It is especially simple when you are using hot swappable drives and can change the SCSI ID merely by changing the slot you place the drive in. What are the steps involved?

1. Install the new drive in the server.

Note	Note that steps 2, 3, and 4 are needed only if the system boots from the disk you are changing out. If your sys volume is not on the same disk as your DOS boot partition, skip to step 5.

2. Using FDISK, create a DOS partition—say, 100MB or even greater; the necessary size of the DOS partition keeps growing with each release.

3. Format the DOS partition with /S to include boot DOS files.

4. Copy all files from the "to-be-replaced" DOS partition over to the new drive with something such as XCOPY C:*.* D:\ /S /E /V (copy every file from C: to D:, include subdirectories, even if they are empty, and verify). Assuming that your sys volume is on the same volume as your boot partition and you have performed steps 2 and 3, you ultimately want your new disk to become your boot disk. If using SCSI, move it to SCSI ID 0, and make sure the DOS partition is marked active.

5. Restart NetWare. NetWare should now be launched from your new drive if you performed steps 2 through 4. How can this be? You copied the files from C: to D:, and then you made what was the D: drive the C: drive, and thus bootable. If your sys volume isn't on the same disk as your DOS boot partition, no worries; simply restart the server so your new disk is online.

PART

III

CH

11

6. Create a NetWare partition on the new drive using the NWConfig NLM. Load NWConfig, Standard Disk Options, Modify Disk Partitions and Hot Fix. Select your new disk; you should see free space (see Figure 11.15).

Figure 11.15
NetWare partitions are created using the NWConfig NLM. On a disk with free space, you can create a NetWare disk partition.

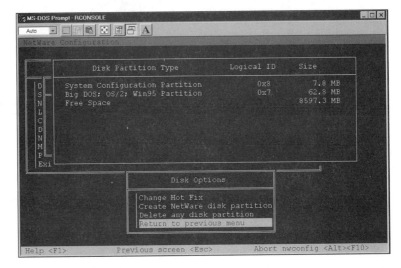

7. Create a newsys volume on the new drive using the free space on your new disk.

8. Copy data from sys to newsys.

   Note that Ncopy does not retain rights. You either need to use something such as Arcserve's copy function, or something such as FSTRust. (FSTrust can be found at http://www.jpence.com or http://www.dreamlan.com.)

   Also, if your sys volume has extra name spaces supported, you need to use some sort of copy function that handles these name spaces.

9. Use the directory backup and restore options of nwconfig.nlm to back up NDS to newsys:system.

10. Make sure that NWConfig is still loaded; NWConfig needs to be loaded now because you are preparing to dismount the sys: volume.

11. Dismount sys and dismount newsys.

12. Using NWConfig, rename sys to oldsys; rename newsys to sys. To rename a volume, select Standard Disk Options, NetWare Volume Options. Highlight the volume in question and press Enter. Then press Enter on the volume name and change it.

13. Mount sys. There's no need to mount oldsys.

14. Use the directory backup and restore options of NWConfig to restore NDS; the backup.nds file is in sys:system. (The current sys volume was formerly the newsys volume, and in step 9 you saved the snapshot of NDS to newsys:system.)

15. If you see a message stating "An older NLS schema extension has been detected. If you have not converted your old licensing data you can do so by running setupnls.nlm," run setupnls to correct this.

TROUBLESHOOTING

The key to a successful upgrade is detailed planning. Plan the upgrade, and then practice it on your test hardware. A normal upgrade window might start at about 2:00 in the morning, and 2:00 in the morning is no time to discover that you have forgotten something. Think it all out, plan it, and write it down. Then follow the plan. A detailed step-by-step procedure of what you are about to do goes a long way toward preventing unpleasant surprises. What areas might you have trouble with? You shouldn't have any trouble with the actual upgrade because you are going to test everything first, but here are a few points to keep in mind:

- **Disk drivers**—Remember, `.dsk` drivers do not work with NetWare 5; you need `.ham` drivers for the storage adapters and `.cdm` drivers for the devices. Make sure you have the correct drivers on hand from the vendors.

- **NIC drivers**—Don't count on your old NIC drivers loading successfully; make sure that you have the newest ones available from the vendor.

- **Frame formats**—Remember, in order for servers and workstations to communicate with each other, they have to run the same frame type. This is especially something to keep in mind if you are moving from the 3.1x version to a later version.

- **Insufficient RAM**—NetWare 5 is going to take more resources than older versions. If you are moving to new hardware, get RAM—the more the better. If you are using an existing server, check to make sure that sufficient RAM is installed.

- **DOS partition size**—Many older servers have been set up with what I would consider very small DOS partitions. These small, 10 or 15MB partitions were more than sufficient in the old days but are not big enough now. If you do not have a large enough DOS partition on C:, the simplest fix would be to add a small D: drive. You can then install to D: but continue to boot from the existing C: drive.

- **Third-party NLMs**—Again, here is an area that you simply have to test prior to upgrading. It would do you no good to upgrade, only to then discover that some of the third-party NLMs that you run no longer work.

## CHAPTER 12

APPLYING PATCHES

In this chapter

FINDING THE LATEST UPDATES

Operating systems are complex by nature and any software has bugs and deficiencies. Despite being one of the best network operating systems available, NetWare 5, like any other software application, contains bugs. Although you might never encounter these bugs in your particular environment, you should keep your NetWare 5 servers up-to-date with patches to prevent unnecessary abends and reduce unwanted downtime. What's more, NetWare 5 updates (known as *Support Packs*) include new product features not included with the shipping product.

Novell maintains on its technical support Web site an online list of current patches and updates to the NetWare operating system, as well as NLM and utility update files. To access the online patch list with download links via the Internet, point your browser to the following URL:

```
http://support.novell.com/misc/patlst.htm
```

The page lists the minimum patch files for each currently shipping and supported products. For example, you'll find Support Packs for NetWare 5 as well as for NetWare 4.11 (see Figure 12.1).

Figure 12.1
Novell product minimum patch list.

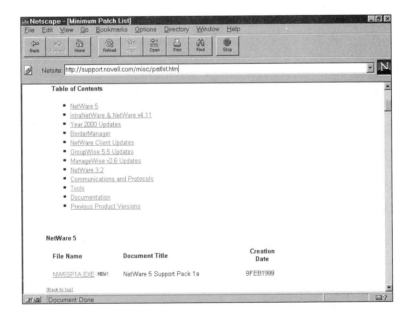

Often, when you contact Novell regarding a server abend issue, the first question you're asked is "Have you applied the latest updates listed on the Minimum Patch List?" Novell Technical Support recommends applying these updates as a baseline.

You should know that Novell divides its updates into a number of levels or categories:

- Internal test patches—These are files for internal testing and use only. These patches are not available to the public.

- Engineering field test patches—These have been successfully used at selected sites outside of Novell to address specific issues. These files are sometimes called *FT files*. These patches are made available at the discretion of Novell Technical Support.

- Beta test patches—When a patch or update file is deemed stabled and is running on more than 50% of the servers within Novell, it is made available to Novell Partners, such as resellers and other support channels, as a beta patch. A beta patch can be made publicly available as an *open beta*.

- Released patch files—After a patch has been running successfully at more than 100 sites outside of Novell, it is deemed fit for release. A released patch is generally available from a number of different channels.

In general, NetWare 5 Support Packs are released once every three months. Any updates or patches released between Support Pack releases are made available separately and are combined into the next version of the Support Pack. So, when you look at the Minimum Patch List page on the Web, you can see the current Support Pack listed along with a number of other files—you need to apply all listed updates in order to stay current.

If you know the name of the patch or update you need, you can locate it by searching the Novell Support Connection Web site at

`http://support.novell.com/search/`

To obtain patch or update files from Novell's FTP server, point your FTP client to

`ftp://ftp.novell.com/pub/updates`

Starting with NetWare 5, because of Java and support for the various languages, the Support Packs have grown fairly large in size. For example, `NW5SP1B.EXE` is 60MB in size! Unless you have a fast link (such as a T1) to the Internet, you should consider using a file download manager to download large files.

Part

III

Ch

12

Tip #98 from
Peter

Because of error detection and correction in the FTP protocol, it is best to use the FTP URL links for file transfers whenever possible, instead of the HTTP links.

Download managers are third-party tools that provide robust file downloading by resuming or scheduling interrupted downloads. I have successfully used Go!Zilla (`http://www.gozilla.com/`) to download `NW5SP1.EXE` from Novell's FTP server over three separate sessions—I deliberately dropped the sessions to simulate interruptions. You can find many of the popular download managers at Download.com (`http://www.download.com/`), using the search words *Resume Download*.

If you have a subscription to the Novell Support Connection CD, you can also find the latest NetWare 5 Support Pack on the CD set. This saves you from having to download the large file over the Internet.

Support Packs are cumulative, so putting on Support Pack 2, for example, is all you need to do; you don't have to first install Support Pack 1. The exception are any updates released after the current Support Pack is made available—they must be downloaded and applied separately, until they are incorporated into the next iteration of the Support Pack.

PATCHING THE SERVER

The following happens during the NetWare 5 Support Pack installation:

- The NetWare 5 Support Pack files are copied to the server. Newer files on the server are *not* overwritten. The installation program checks the version of each file. If two files have the same version, the installation program then checks the date of each file.

- A record is added to the SYS:SYSTEM\PRODUCTS.DAT file in the Installed Products section, and the message SPACK 5.0.1 v1.0 Support Pack for NetWare 5 appears. Any other product installed (such as Oracle for NetWare) and product updates are also listed.

Files in the \MISC directory are not automatically installed by the NetWare Support Pack. You need to manually copy those files to the server.

Before you install the NetWare 5 Support Pack, you must be sure to do the following:

- Have about 150MB of free disk space in order to extract the files from the Support Pack. (This is the requirement for Support Pack 1; later versions might require more disk space.)

- Unload JAVA.NLM and all Java applications on the server in order to update JAVA.NLM and the Java class libraries.

- Load IPXSPX.NLM to install the NetWare 5 Support Pack, if you're running an IP-only environment.

- Have server console operator rights to the server, if you're to use the Config Central software included with the Support Pack.

- Ensure that the NetWare 5 server uses one of the following languages, because the Support Pack contains files for these languages only: English, French, German, Italian, Japanese, Portuguese, or Spanish.

The readme file that comes with the Support Pack describes what has been fixed and included enhancements. Before you apply the patch, *read* over the readme file because it contains Support Pack–specific installation instructions. (For example, in Support Pack 1, because there's an update to fix a problem with the server registry—which keeps track of SET commands—all SET parameters will revert to default NetWare 5 values the first time the server is started after installing the Support Pack.)

The following steps outline the *general* procedures to install the NetWare 5 Support Pack on a single server (Support Pack 1 is used as the example here):

1. Extract the component files from the Support Pack. To explode the file, type NW5SP1 and press Enter. You can explode the file onto any of the server volumes or on a local client that is using RCONSOLE to run the installation.

> **Note**
> The Support Pack file contains directory paths that could exceed the DOS limits. The file must be extracted in a root-level directory on your local drive or to a NetWare volume that accepts longer paths.

2. At the server console prompt, type NWCONFIG and press Enter. (The Support Pack cannot be installed through the GUI installation.)
3. Select Product Options.
4. Select Install a Product Not Listed.
5. Depending on where the NetWare Support Pack files are located, complete one of the following steps:
   - From the local volume SYS:, press F3 and specify the path, including the volume name (for example, SYS:\directory name).
   - From a different server on the network, press F3 and specify the full path including the server name (for example, NETWARE5-B\SYS:\PATCH\NW5SP1). You will be prompted for a login name and password for the other server.
   - From a local drive on a client using RCONSOLE, press F4.

6. Press Enter.
7. Press F10 to accept the marked options (see Figure 12.2) and continue.

PART

III

CH

12

Figure 12.2
Selecting installation options for the Support Pack.

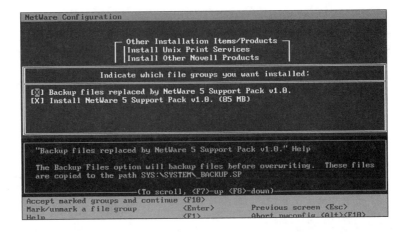

> **Caution**
>
> If you want to be able to uninstall the Support Pack later, you *must* select the option to back up files.

8. Press Enter to end.

9. After files are copied, review the AUTOEXEC.NCF and STARTUP.NCF files for accuracy.

10. At the server console, type DOWN and press Enter. This shuts down the server. Enter the command SERVER to restart the server and completes the installation of the NetWare Support Pack.

> **Caution**
>
> You should *not* simply do a RESTART SERVER; instead use DOWN and then restart the OS. The reason is that the Support Pack contains a new SERVER.EXE which will not get run if you just do a RESTART SERVER, leaving the server in an unstable state.

> **Tip #99 from**
> *Peter*
>
> You can verify whether the Support Pack is installed by checking the SYS:SYSTEM\PRODUCTS.DAT file. At the server console, start up the NWConfig NLM, select Product Options, and then select View/Configure/Remove Installed Products. If a Support Pack was installed, you'll see in the Currently Installed Products section a message similar to SPACK 5.0.1 v1.0 Support Pack for NetWare 5 listed along with any other products.

To install the NetWare Support Pack on multiple servers (English only), repeat the previously mentioned steps. Alternatively, you can use the Config Central Lite (32-bit) application (see Figure 12.3) from a workstation. You'll find the CCNWLITE.EXE file in the NW5SP1 directory.

Figure 12.3
Updating multiple
NetWare 5 servers
using Config
Central Lite.

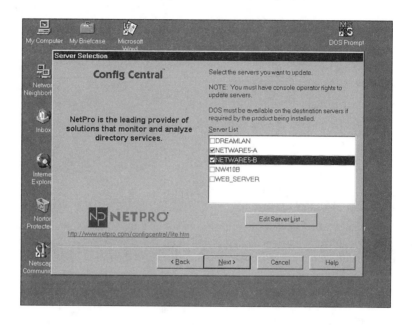

The NetWare Support Pack installation detects the current server configuration and installs the appropriate files. If you change the server configuration, you need to reinstall the NetWare Support Pack for the new configuration.

For example, if LDAP Services for NDS is installed on a NetWare 5 server before Support Pack 1 is installed, the Support Pack 1 installation automatically upgrades LDAP Services for NDS. If LDAP Services for NDS is installed *after* the Support Pack installation, you need to reinstall Support Pack 1 to bring LDAP Services for NDS up to the Support Pack 1 level.

PART
III

CH
12

As mentioned earlier, files in the \MISC directory of the Support Pack are not automatically copied to the server. If you have previously installed the NetWare 5 Netscape FastTrack Web Server, copy the files from MISC\WEBSERV\SYSTEM to SYS:\SYSTEM. These files contain updates to the Web Server product.

BACKING OUT OF THE SUPPORT PACK

If you selected the backup option during installation, which I hope you did, files that are overwritten by the NetWare Support Pack files are backed up to SYS:SYSTEM\BACKSP1\ UNINSTAL, and you can then easily restore the server to its previous state if necessary. If you didn't select the backup option, you can't uninstall the Support Pack.

> **Caution**
>
> You should *not* uninstall the Support Pack if you installed any products or patches after the installation of the NetWare Support Pack because the backed up files might no longer be compatible with the newly installed files.

To uninstall the NetWare Support Pack, use the following procedure:

1. At the server console prompt, type NWCONFIG and press Enter.

2. Select Product Options.

3. Select Install a Product Not Listed.

4. Press F3 and specify the path to the backup files, which is SYS:SYSTEM\BACKSP1\UNINSTAL.

Restart the server after the files from the uninstall directory are placed on your system.

TROUBLESHOOTING

As you have read in this chapter, the steps for installing Support Packs are very straightforward. Should you encounter a problem during installation, you should DOWN the server and restart SERVER.EXE before you attempt another Support Pack installation. This puts the server into a known state before changes are made.

## CHAPTER 13

INSTALLING WORKSTATION SOFTWARE

In this chapter

WHICH CLIENT TO USE?

Both Windows 95/98 and Windows NT ship with NetWare clients; however, unless you seldom access a NetWare server, you will want to install the Novell clients. Although the Microsoft for NetWare clients are, or can be, made somewhat NDS aware, they are not fully NDS aware. And to take full advantage of NDS and ZEN, you will need the Novell client.

Very few shops are pure NetWare, or pure NT, so you will find it common to have the MS client for MS networks installed, right along with the Novell client for Novell Networks. They coexist just fine, allowing seamless access to both Windows and Novell networks. For example, your primary file and print services might be on NetWare servers, but the company's email system might be Exchange. Exchange runs only on NT, so a workstation would need both clients installed to access file and print services, and to email.

If you have previously been using Novell's Macintosh client, take note: Novell no longer has a Macintosh client. Mac support has been farmed out to ProSoft Solutions Inc., at http://www.prosofteng.com. Their current version of the client is 5.12 as of this writing, and there is a closed beta available for testing the NetWare 5 Appleshare services.

MICROSOFT WINDOWS 95/98 CLIENT FOR NETWARE

You would want to run the MS client for NetWare only if you are predominately a Windows shop and seldom need to access a NetWare server, except for the occasional file and print services. For any serious NetWare use, you definitely want the Novell client.

However, the MS client has one excellent feature: it comes with the product. You can install the MS client and then access your NetWare server, from which you can then install the Novell client. When you use the Automatic Client Upgrade process, upgrading to the Novell client happens automatically.

INSTALLATION

To install the Microsoft Client for NetWare Networks, access the Network Configuration panel and choose Add. Select the client for the type of component you want to install, and then choose Microsoft Client for NetWare Networks, as shown in Figure 13.1.

CONFIGURATION

You won't find the configuration of the Client for NetWare Networks a complicated procedure. Highlight the client in the network control panel, and then choose Properties. Your options are somewhat limited, as shown in Figure 13.2.

You can set a preferred server, indicate a first network drive, and specify whether to run the login script. On the Advanced tab, there is only one option, to preserve case.

Figure 13.1
Adding the Microsoft Client for NetWare Networks. After you click OK and then reboot, you are done.

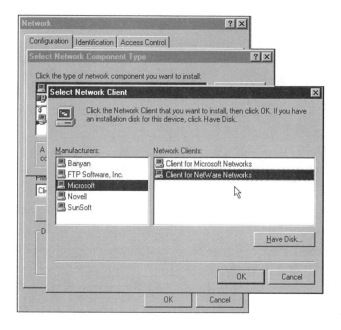

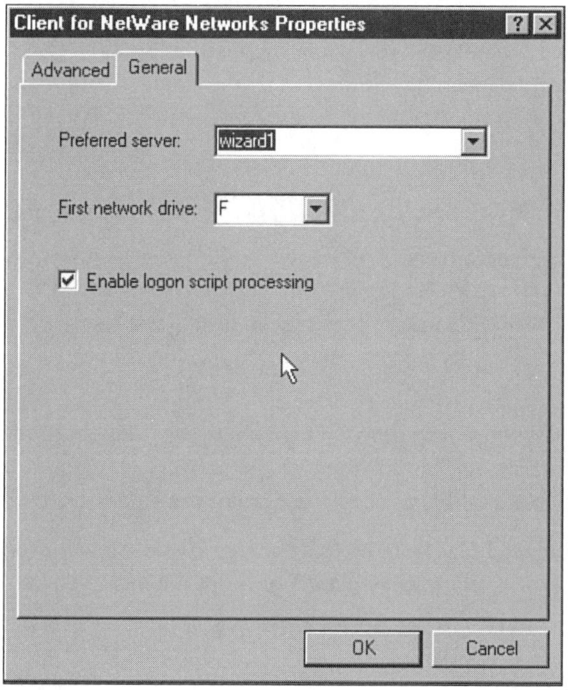

Figure 13.2
There isn't a whole lot of configuring you can do with the Microsoft Client for NetWare Networks.

PART

III

CH

13

NDS SERVICE UPDATE

The MS NetWare client isn't NDS-aware. You can test this by trying to log in as a user that does not exist in a bindery context; you won't be able to. If you are running Windows 95, go to http://www.microsoft.com, search on Services for NetWare Directory Services, and download the appropriate file. To install, follow the instructions in the download. Services for NetWare Directory Services will provide the functionality needed to connect to NDS servers, and make the MS client NDS-aware.

If you are running Windows 98, you already have the NDS service, but you have to add it manually; it isn't part of the client for NetWare installation. To add the NDS service, follow these steps:

1. From the network control panel, click Add to bring up the component list.
2. Highlight Service and click Add to bring up the available network services.
3. Select Microsoft in the manufacturers list, and then highlight Service for NetWare Directory Services from the list.
4. Click OK, and 98 adds the service to the installed network components. No configuration is necessary.

REMOVING THE CLIENT

Removing the client is simply the reverse of the installation; highlight Client for NetWare in the network control panel, click Remove, OK the changes, and reboot. The MS client for NetWare will also be automatically removed by installation of Novell's client.

MICROSOFT WINDOWS NETWARE CLIENT FOR NT

The MS client for NT is somewhat NDS-aware, but you will still want to install Novell's client for serious NetWare access. Again, one possible use for the MS client is to quickly gain access to your network so that you can then install the Novell client.

INSTALLATION

To install NT's NetWare client, right-click the Network Neighborhood icon on the desktop, and choose Properties. This takes you to the network configuration panel; select Services, Add, and then highlight the Client Service for NetWare, as shown in Figure 13.3.

You are prompted for the files from the I386 directory, so you will need the NT installation CD available. After the files are copied and you close the dialog boxes, you must reboot.

CONFIGURATION

To configure the Client Service for NetWare, open the control panel, and there will be a new icon for CSNW. Double-click the CSNW icon, and you will be at the screen shown in Figure 13.4.

Figure 13.3
The Client Service for NetWare is the built-in NetWare client that comes with NT.

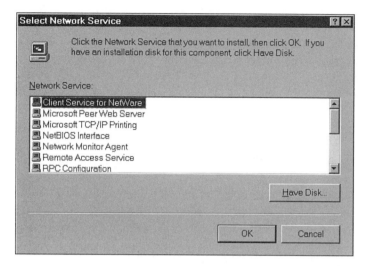

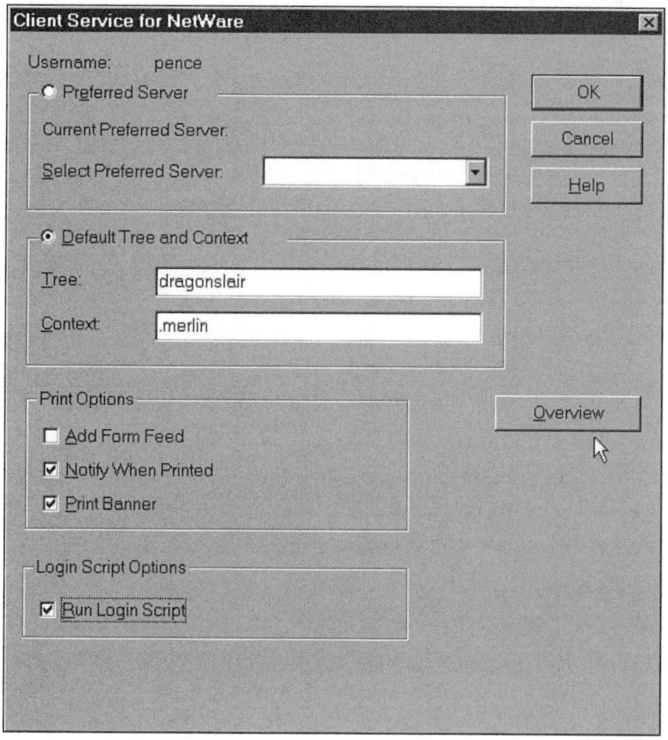

Figure 13.4
Compared to the options available when you're using the Novell client, there isn't a lot here! Be sure to click the Overview button and read the online help.

PART

III

CH

13

Not a whole lot of configuration options are available for the Microsoft Client Service for NetWare. You can specify either a preferred server or a default Tree and context, set a few print options, and specify whether to run the login script. Make sure you click the overview button for what online help is available.

REMOVING THE CLIENT

You remove the Client Service for NetWare just as you would remove any service. Get back to the Services tab; you used the Services tab to install the client. Highlight the Client Service for NetWare and click Remove. Answer Yes to the warning, and then, as always with anything involving Windows, reboot.

NETWARE CLIENT FOR WINDOWS 95/98

Although the Microsoft Client for NetWare Networks ships with Windows 95/98, the preferred client will naturally be Novell's 32-bit client, which is on version three as of this writing. Novell's client is more NDS-aware, is more tightly integrated with the NetWare server, and is required for things like ZENworks. If you have not yet purchased NetWare 5, but still want to test and work with the latest client, you can get it free on Novell's Web site. It is a very sizeable download, so unless you have a very high-speed Internet connection, be prepared to spend a long time online!

INSTALLATION

| Tip #100 from | If you already have the Microsoft Client for NetWare Networks installed, the Novell client |
| John | installation removes it automatically during the installation. There is no need for you to remove the MS client for NetWare before beginning the installation of the Novell client. |

To install the NetWare client for Windows 95/98, insert the CD-ROM, and when the language-selection screen appears, select English. Select the Windows 95/98 Client, and then select to install Novell Client. You need to accept the license agreement, and then need to choose between a typical and a custom installation (see Figure 13.5).

A typical installation sets up the client to use NDS connections over IP or IPX, and adds support for NDPS. NDPS, Novell's Distributed Print System, is covered in Chapter 21, "Network Printing." If you select a custom install, you have the option of adding other services, as you will see later in this section. The next decision you have to make is what protocols to run at the workstation (see Figure 13.6).

When you're selecting protocols, the default, which installs both IPX and IP, is probably a good choice. In a multiserver environment, your migration from an IPX-based network to IP isn't going to happen overnight. You will need to communicate not only with your newer IP-only servers, but also with legacy servers that have not yet been upgraded and understand only IPX.

The protocol choices are self-explanatory, with the possible exception of IP with IPX Compatibility. IP with IPX Compatibility installs IP but also allows the IPX applications to run; this is done by conversion of the IPX packets into IP. You can also communicate with IPX-only servers if a Migration agent has been installed on one of your servers.

Figure 13.5
You need to choose between a typical and a custom installation of the 95/98 client. Also, while at this screen, take advantage of the opportunity to view and print the readme file.

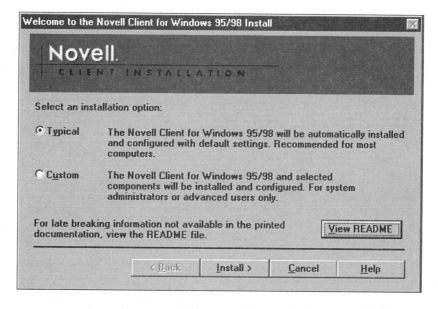

Figure 13.6
You must select the protocols to be installed at the workstation. The default installs both IPX and IP.

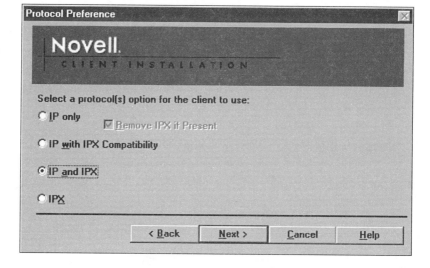

Having chosen the protocols to install, you next select whether you want to establish NDS or bindery connections; you would want to select bindery only if you are still on the NetWare 3 platform. Earlier in the installation, if you chose Custom, you now select the additional components you want to install, as shown in Figure 13.7.

Figure 13.7
A custom installation gives you the opportunity to add other services; Novell Distributed Print Services is checked by default.

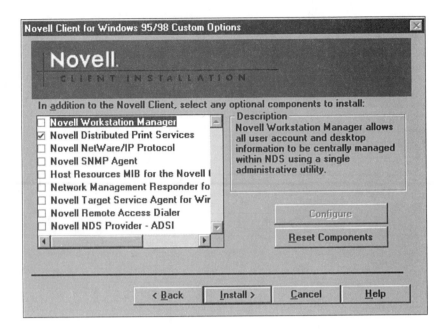

Don't worry that you might miss something here; you can always come back and add these optional components later. What are the additional components?

- **Novell Workstation Manager**—This allows user-account and desktop information to be stored and managed via NDS. On the NT platform, it also eliminates the need for the NT account to exist on the workstation, because the accounts can be created dynamically.

- **Novell Distributed Print Services (NDPS)**—This component is installed automatically if you select a typical installation. If you select custom, it is checked by default. NDPS allows real-time bidirectional communication between the workstation and the printer.

- **Novell NetWare/IP Protocol**—This service encapsulates IPX packets inside IP packets. This allows IPX communication over networks running only IP.

Note

Before NetWare 5, NetWare IP was the only means available to integrate IPX and IP. The servers and workstations used IPX for communication, but before the packet was placed on the wire, it was surrounded by an IP packet. With the advent of NetWare 5 and pure IP, NetWare IP will no longer be necessary.

- **Novell SNMP Agent**—This allows you to monitor the workstation's statistics from a Simple Network Management Protocol (SNMP) console. The agent supports multiple transport protocols.

- **Host Resources MIB for the Novell Client**—This component allows the SNMP console to see workstation-specific information, such as the amount of memory and hard disk space.

- **Network Management Responder for the Novell Client**—This allows an SNMP console to see information about the OS, BIOS, and more.

- **Novell Target Service Agent for Windows 95/98**—This allows communication between a server-based backup, such as Novell's own Sbackup, and the workstation. With the workstation TSA installed, you can back up the workstation's hard disk to the server's tape drive.

- **Novell Remote Access Dialer**—This installs software necessary to connect to a NetWare server that offers remote access services.

- **Novell NDS Provider - ADSI**—This enables an ADSI (Microsoft Active Directory Service Interface) application to communicate with NDS.

The next screen gives you the option to set a preferred tree, server, and context. You can do this now, or you can come back to it later quite easily. If you choose to make the settings now, you will be at the Novell NetWare Client properties screen, the same screen you will use in the future to configure the client; the tabs for the client properties are covered in the next section, "Configuration." Finally, you must reboot; you are then online with your new client.

One of the most obvious changes to your system you will see after the client installation is a system-tray icon that is a big red letter *N*. If you double-click the N, it launches the Network Neighborhood browse window. If you right-click the N, you see the menu shown in Figure 13.8.

Figure 13.8
You access the NetWare services menu by right-clicking on the red N icon in the system tray. Although this method is convenient, some of the selections will strike terror into the hearts of administrators; it is unlikely you'll want them to edit their login scripts!

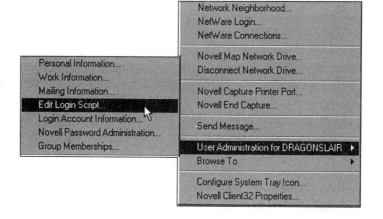

Although the NetWare services menu has many convenient options, the first thing most administrators are going to want to do with this icon is hide it! Odds are, you don't want users messing with drive mappings, connections, and certainly login scripts. We will make it a point to show you how to hide this icon in the configuration section.

CONFIGURATION

Configuring the Novell client is simple; after all, that is what a graphical user interface is for. There are eight primary tabs you can use to configure the client, as shown in Figure 13.9.

Figure 13.9
The options available for configuring the Novell Windows NT client are almost identical to those available for the 95/98 platform.

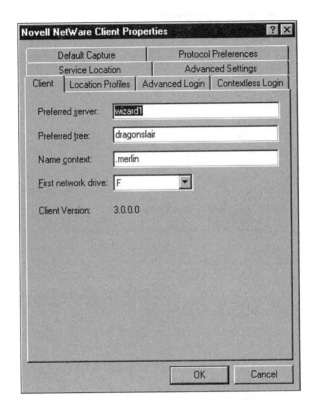

You can access the configuration panes in one of three ways:

- During the client installation, you are asked whether you want to configure settings such as preferred server and NDS tree.

- From the network control panel, highlight the Novell client and click on Properties.

- Using the N icon in the system tray, right-click and then select Novell Client32 Properties from the menu.

A complete run-through of every option on every tab is beyond the scope of this book; it would take a book of its own. Certain things, like the First Network Drive selection shown in Figure 13.9, are obvious, but if you go to the Advanced tab, you might want some help there. In Figure 13.10, we have clicked the Advanced Settings tab, and Close Behind Ticks is highlighted. There is nothing intuitive about understanding the Close Behind Ticks parameter, but there is a brief description of the setting in the Description pane. The Description pane is context sensitive, meaning that the description of whichever parameter you have highlighted shows up in the pane.

Figure 13.10
When you highlight a setting, a brief description of the setting shows up in the Description pane. You can get more-detailed information by right-clicking the setting.

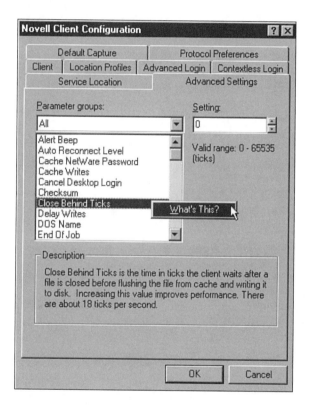

Not a lot of screen real estate is devoted to the descriptions, so they are naturally going to be brief. If you want more detailed information, right-click the parameter, which causes the What's This? button shown in Figure 13.10 to pop up. Click What's This? and more information about the setting appears (see Figure 13.11).

Tip #101 from
John

The file `\novell\client32\prop.hlp` is the context-sensitive help you are accessing in Figure 13.11. You can execute this help file simply by double-clicking it, and then you'll have the help available for reading, printing, and searching without having to go in through the client configuration.

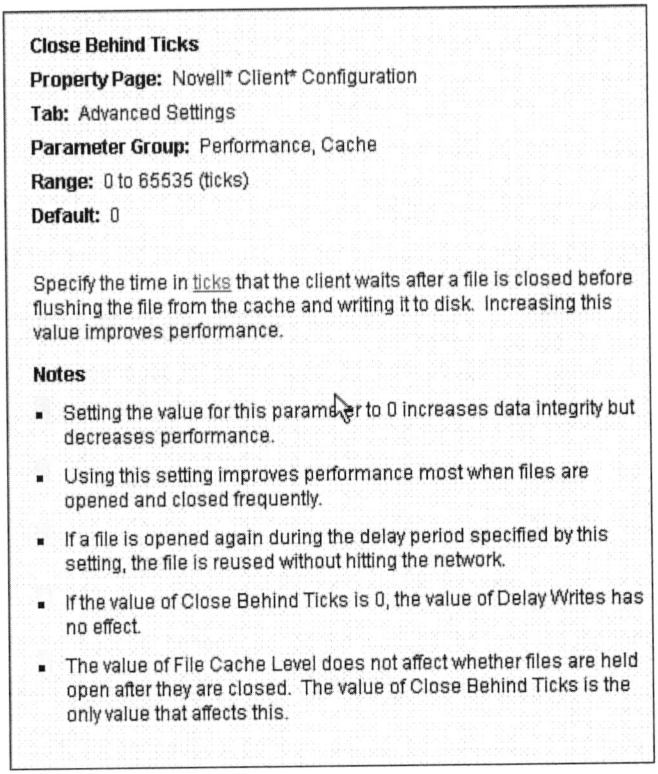

Figure 13.11
The online help for each parameter is far more detailed than the brief description given when a setting is highlighted.

Close Behind Ticks

Property Page: Novell* Client* Configuration

Tab: Advanced Settings

Parameter Group: Performance, Cache

Range: 0 to 65535 (ticks)

Default: 0

Specify the time in <u>ticks</u> that the client waits after a file is closed before flushing the file from the cache and writing it to disk. Increasing this value improves performance.

Notes

- Setting the value for this parameter to 0 increases data integrity but decreases performance.

- Using this setting improves performance most when files are opened and closed frequently.

- If a file is opened again during the delay period specified by this setting, the file is reused without hitting the network.

- If the value of Close Behind Ticks is 0, the value of Delay Writes has no effect.

- The value of File Cache Level does not affect whether files are held open after they are closed. The value of Close Behind Ticks is the only value that affects this.

Don't forget that you also have the online client documentation available for installation, and also the client forums at http://support.novell.com or forums.novell.com if you are using a newsreader. The client sysops are excellent and are right on top of client bugs and configuration issues.

As we pointed out in the installation section, some of the options available to the users via the big red N in the system tray will make administrators run screaming from the room! It is simple enough to hide this icon, but you have to know how to find it. Go to the Advanced Settings tab, and choose the Graphical Interface parameter group from the drop-down list, as shown in Figure 13.12.

At the screen shown in Figure 13.12, you can choose to completely hide the icon, or just control some of the choices available to the user, such as disabling the User Administration menu; this would still enable the users to right-click and have some functionality.

REMOVING THE CLIENT

You might need to remove the client for troubleshooting purposes, or maybe it is no longer needed on a particular machine. You can remove the Novell client in two ways.

Figure 13.12
It is simple enough keep the N icon from showing in the system tray; the Graphical Interface parameter group gives you various degrees of control over the icon or its associated menu options.

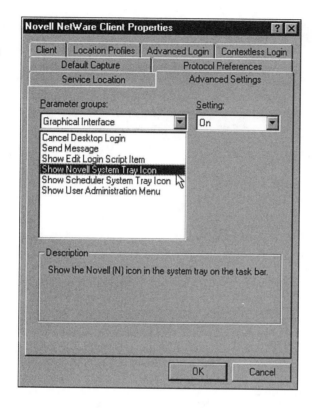

The first method is to access the network control panel; you can get to the network control panel either by right-clicking the Network Neighborhood or via the Network icon in the Control Panel. At the network control panel, highlight the Novell NetWare Client and click Remove.

Tip #102 from
John

When you remove the NetWare client via the network control panel, some of the original configuration remains in the registry. This is why you can re-install the client and see information that was previously set. If you use the Uninstall utility, the client-related registry settings are cleared.

The uninstall utility is not installed on the workstation by default; you have to run or copy it from the client CD-ROM. The file, `unc32.exe`, is located in the `<cdrom>\products\win95\ibm_enu\admin` folder. The icon for `unc32.exe` will have a big red X through it, meaning that you shouldn't do this! Run `unc32.exe`, and if you have any ODI drivers installed, you will have a box you can check if you want them removed; otherwise, you will be at the screen shown in Figure 13.13.

Figure 13.13
Once you've pressed Continue, there is no Cancel button.

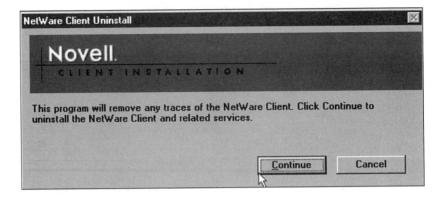

Once you've pressed the Continue button, there is no opportunity to cancel, so you need to be certain that this is what you want at the front end. And if you turn off the workstation in an attempt to stop the uninstall utility, you run the risk of leaving your registry in a corrupted state. If you are interested in more details as to exactly what registry settings and files are removed, either double-click the uninstal.hlp file or search the online documentation. After the client has been removed, you can reboot so that the changes will take effect, or you can return to Windows without rebooting.

AUTOMATIC CLIENT UPDATE

As an administrator, you will think that the automatic client update is the greatest thing since sliced bread. When a user running Windows 95/98 logs in with either an older version of Novell's client or using the Microsoft Client for NetWare Networks, the client is automatically updated to the version that you have in place on the server.

Tip #103 from
John

The automatic client update is kicked off when a user logs in by a command in the user's login script. Don't forget that someone running the MS client without the NDS service will execute a bindery login script.

ACU SETUP

Thea steps involved for setting up automatic client updates are simple:

1. Create a folder on the server, such as sys:acu.
2. Copy the Novell Windows 95/98 client files, along with the windows .cab files, to this folder. If space is a concern, you don't need to copy the windows .cab files, but the user will need to either have the Windows installation CD-ROM available or have the .cab files on their local hard disk. Most Windows installations do have the .cab files on their local disk. Given the size of today's server hard disks, you probably do not need to worry about the amount of space used by the .cab files.

3. Grant the users Read and file scan rights to the folder you created in step 1. Use NetWare Administrator to create a group, give the group rights to the folder, then add users to the group.

4. Modify the login script(s). You can be as granular as you like with this process. You can modify a container login script, which would apply to everyone in that container, or you can modify users' login scripts individually. Use a Universal Naming Convention (UNC) path to point to `setup.exe` in the folder you created in step 1. The UNC syntax is `\\`*servername*`\`*volume*`\`*directory*`\`*file*; for example:

```
\\wizard1\sys\acu\setup.exe /acu
```

The `/acu` switch forces the automatic client upgrade.

Nwsetup.ini AND THE REGISTRY

So what drives the ACU process? The answer is in the `nwsetup.ini` file in your update directory (the directory you created in step 1) and in the workstation's registry. There is a lot in the `nwsetup.ini` file, but you are going to be concerned only with certain portions.

Tip #104 from
John

Check the flags on the `nwsetup.ini` before you jump in and edit it; nothing is more frustrating than having to abandon changes because a file is flagged read-only.

The `nwsetup.ini` file is worth having a look at. It is somewhat self-documenting, and a portion of it is given here:

```
; The following section contains the current version of client software
; and is used for automated upgrade of clients.
;
; The version contains 4 fields. These are:
;
; MajorVersion.MinorVersion.Revision.Level
;
; The major version, minor version, and revision are
; fields supplied by Novell, and refer to the version
; of the client software. These will be updated with
; each new version of the Novell Client.
;
; The level, on the other hand, is a customer/installation
; defined field. It is initially set to 0 by Novell,
; but may be set to any number that is desired by the
; system administrator. This may be used to cause updates
; when the Novell Client software did not actually change,
; but when some other change was made that is desired by
; the system administrator. This field may range from
; 0 to 65000.
;
; The upgrade will take place if any part of the version
; number is greater than that stored in the registry. Thus
; 1.1.1.1 is greater than 1.1.1.0 and 1.1.2.0 is greater
; than 1.1.1.9999
```

PART

III

CH

13

```
[ClientVersion]
Version=3.0.0.0
```

As you can see from the comments pertaining to the [ClientVersion] section of the nwsetup.ini file, you can drive updates by changing the value of the level field. For example, suppose you have updated everyone's computer via ACU to version three of the client. In the workstation's registry, the Major version will have a value of 3, and the minor version, the revision, and the level will all have a value of 0.

Now, as users log in and execute setup /acu, the registry value on the workstation is compared to the value contained in the nwsetup.ini; because they are the same, nothing happens. But if you were to edit the nwsetup.ini file and change the version to 3.0.0.1, then on the user's next login, the client would be "updated"; the acu process will run, even if the client versions (the actual files) are the same as the ones on the server.

If you edit the nwsetup.ini on the server, you will globally force the update process to run, meaning that *all* workstations will be affected. But suppose you want to force the change on only one workstation? You can do that quite easily via the registry; if you down rev the value in the workstation's registry, then the next time the user logs in, ACU will take off. By "down rev," I mean that if the workstation has a value of 3.0.0.1 for example, and you change this to 3.0.0.0, you have backed it down a revision, and will force the update process to occur on that workstation. The pertinent registry keys are shown in Figure 13.14.

Figure 13.14
The Major version, Minor version, Revision, and Level are stored in HKEY_LOCAL_MACHINE\Network\Novell\System Config\Install\Client Version.

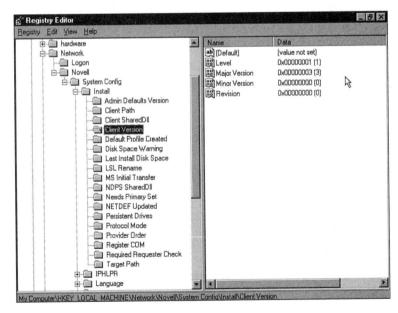

As you can see from the comments (in more of the nwsetup.ini file), [AcuOptions] controls user intervention. The default for DisplayFirstScreen and DisplayLastScreen is No; if you set this to Yes, the user will see the screen shown in Figure 13.15 when the ACU process begins:

```
; ACU Option
; The following section contains settings that will minimize user intervention
; during the automated upgrade of clients.
;
; DisplayFirstScreen
; Setting this to YES will prompt the user whether they wish to continue or
; cancel the automated upgrade.
;
; DisplayLastScreen
; Setting this to YES will prompt the user whether they wish to reboot for the
; changes to take effect or not.

[AcuOptions]
DisplayFirstScreen=No
DisplayLastScreen=No
```

Figure 13.15
If you set `DisplayFirstScreen=YES`, the user has the option of either continuing with the client upgrade or canceling it.

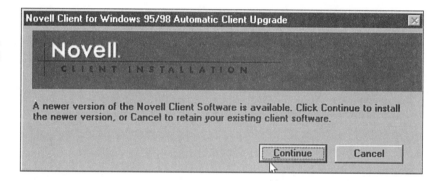

The last screen displayed merely informs the user that the system has changed, and asks the user whether to restart. You can see from the remaining portion of `nwsetup.ini` given here that you also have options for setting the primary network logon and for controlling the protocols installed:

```
; Primary Network Logon
: The following setting is used to determine if the Primary Network Logon
; in the Network Control Panel will be updated.
; Update=YES will cause the update to be performed.
; Update=NO will cause the update to be skipped.

[PrimaryNetworkLogon]
Update=YES

[ProtocolOptions]
DefaultProtocol=IP,IPX

; Default Protocol used by the client
;DefaultProtocol = IP,IPX will cause the client to use IP and IPX
;DefaultProtocol = IPNOCM will cause the client to use IP
;DefaultProtocol = IP will cause the client to use IP with IPX compatibility
;DefaultProtocol = IPX will cause the client to use IPX

; Protocol Detection
```

PART

III

CH

13

```
: The following setting is used to determine if install should detect and use
; the previous client protocol option.  Detecting the previous protocol option
; will override the DefaultProtocol in the [ProtocolOptions] section.
; DetectPreviousProtocol=YES will cause the protocol detection to be performed.
; DetectPreviousProtocol=NO will cause the protocol detection to be skipped.

[ProtocolDetection]
DetectPreviousProtocol=YES
```

ACU SWITCHES

The following are the switches available for the setup program (see Figure 13.16):

- /ACU—Automatically updates the client.

- /NCF—Does not apply the fix to prevent copying the .cab files.

- /RB—Before the upgrade begins, the workstation's current configuration is copied to the \Novell\client32\nwbackup directory. When the workstation reboots at the end of the upgrade, a check is made to see whether a network connection was successfully made. If the connection is successful, the backup is deleted. If the connection is not successful, the backup is used to restore the original configuration.

- /U—Specifies a file with configuration parameters to be applied to the workstation. For example, setup /u:f:\acu\params.txt would use the information in f:\acu\params.txt to configure the client. If you are going to use the /u parameter, you need to create the configuration file via the Novell Client Install Manager.

Figure 13.16
The switches available for the Setup program.

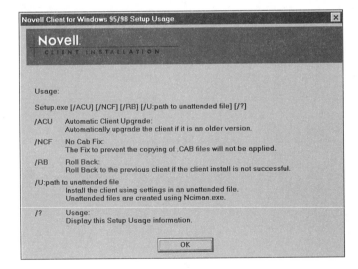

Novell Client Install Manager

The Novell Client Install Manager, `nciman.exe`, is used to create configuration files to "feed" to the ACU process when the /U switch is used. As shown in Figure 13.17, there are two panes.

Figure 13.17
The Novell Client Install Manager, NCIMAN.EXE.

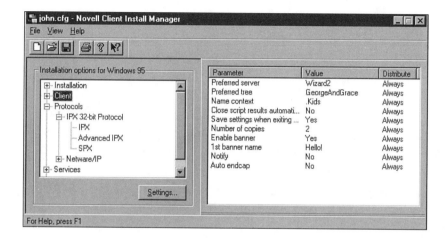

In the left window, you select the option you want to configure and then click the Settings button. Once there, you set the appropriate value, which you will later see on the right. In the example shown in Figure 13.17, we have set various client options, such as setting the preferred tree to GeorgeAndGrace, specifying the name context as Kids, and enabling a banner.

Nciman has a feature you might find useful. You can import the settings from a workstation's registry. Set up one workstation with the configuration you want to distribute. Then, from the File menu, choose Open Registry to import the settings.

After you have the desired configuration set up in nciman, save the file; you can use any filename and extension you desire. The resulting file is simply an ASCII text file, as shown here:

```
[Novell_Client_Install_Manager]
Novell_Client=95

[Novell_Client_Parameters]
Preferred_Server=Wizard2
Preferred_Server_Distribute=Always
Preferred_Tree=GeorgeAndGrace
Preferred_Tree_Distribute=Always
Name_Context=.Kids
Name_Context_Distribute=Always
Close_Script_Results_Automatically=NO
Close_Script_Results_Automatically_Distribute=Always
Save_Settings_When_Exiting_Login=YES
Save_Settings_When_Exiting_Login_Distribute=Always
Number_of_copies=2
```

PART

III

CH

13

```
Number_of_copies_Distribute=Always
Enable_Banner=YES
Enable_Banner_Distribute=Always
1st_Banner=Hello!
1st_Banner_Distribute=Always
Notify=NO
Notify_Distribute=Always
Auto_Endcap=NO
Auto_Endcap_Distribute=Always
```

NetWare Client for Windows NT

As is the case with Windows 95/98, a NetWare client ships with NT. However, you would not run the MS client unless you seldom have a need to access a Novell server. The Novell client is naturally going to be tightly integrated with NDS, and it is required for the good stuff like ZEN (Zero Effort Networking) and Workstation Manager.

The client requires NT 4.0, and SP3 is recommended but not required—but then, no one is running NT 4.0 without at least service pack 3! If you do not have NetWare 5, you can download the client from Novell's Web site; but as is the case with all of today's software, it is a hefty download, so hopefully you have a fast connection to the Internet.

INSTALLATION

Installing the NT client is very similar to the installation of the 95/98 client. From the Winsetup screen that appears when you insert the client CD, select the language and then choose Windows NT Client, Install Novell Client.

You then make the choice between a typical and a custom installation. While on this screen, be sure to print the readme file, winnt.txt, and read it. A typical installation installs the Novell Client for Windows NT, and in addition, Novell Distributed Print Services, Novell Workstation Manager, and ZENworks Application Launcher NT Service.

A custom installation gives you the option to install additional components, as shown in Figure 13.18.

You can also use this screen to prevent services from being installed by clearing the checked boxes. What are the additional components?

- **Novell Distributed Print Services**—Enables real time, bi-directional communications between the workstation and the printer.
- **Novell IP Gateway**—Enables Internet access on IPX or private IP networks when there are Novell IP/IPX gateway servers on the network.
- **Novell Target Service Agent**—Allows you to back up the workstation's hard drive to the tape drive on the server.
- **Novell Workstation Manager**—Allows you to manage and configure workstations via NDS.
- **ZENworks Application Launcher NT Service**—Allows the application launcher to install applications when the user does not have rights to the workstation to do so.

Figure 13.18
A custom installation of the client gives you the option of adding additional services, or preventing the defaults such as NDPS from being installed.

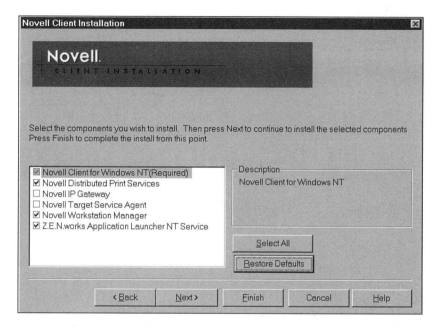

After you have selected the optional components, you need to determine which protocols you want to run. The choices are the same as the ones for the 95/98 platform: IP only, IP with IPX compatibility, IP and IPX, or only IPX.

You then select the connection type to establish, either NDS or bindery, and provide a tree name to be used by the workstation manager. Accept the license, let the installation run, and of course perform the homage necessary to Windows by rebooting to implement the changes.

One of the changes you will notice on NT is that the login screen is changed by the installation of the Novell client. This is because the setup program replaces Microsoft's GINA (Graphical Identification and Authentication) with Novell's own NWGINA. You will also see the same red N icon in the system tray, and on a default installation, you will have an icon for Novell desktop management in the system tray also.

CONFIGURATION

Configuring Novell's NT client is no different from configuring the 95/98 client; highlight the Novell client in the network control panel and select Properties, or right-click the N icon in the system tray. The same eight tabs are available for the NT client as for the 95/98 client (see Figure 13.19).

One item that might be of interest is that you can specify the .bmp file to be used for the welcome screen, along with the caption to be displayed. These two items are configured on the Advanced Login tab.

PART

III

CH

13

Figure 13.19
The protocol preferences.

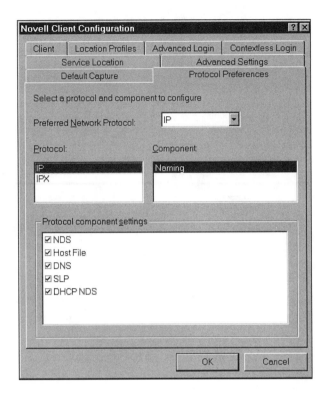

The advanced settings have help you can access in the same manner, by right-clicking the setting in question. Don't forget the online documentation and the support you can obtain from the forums.

REMOVING THE CLIENT

Removing the client is extremely simple. From the network control panel, highlight Novell Client for Windows NT, and then click Remove. If you are installing a newer version of the client, there is no need to remove the existing one first; just proceed with the install of the newer version.

ACCESSING NETWARE FROM LINUX

Linux machines are cropping up all over the place, and they need to be able to access NetWare servers. A Linux distribution from Caldera, NetWare for Linux, has NetWare Client support; the base is Red Hat Linux, and Caldera has added its Network Desktop products. The client gives you full access to NetWare servers, and it includes features such as support for NetWare Directory Services and RSA encryption. You can get more information and details from Caldera's Web site at http://www.caldera.com.

TROUBLESHOOTING

As always, move slowly and ask questions; don't just jump in and start changing things because you can. When you're troubleshooting client issues, the first thing you need to know is if the installation is a new one and has never worked, or if things were OK and suddenly stopped. If the latter situation is true, then track down what has changed.

Check the physical side of things, and make sure that the cabling and connectors are the correct type and have been installed correctly. You can re-install the client without losing any settings, so don't hesitate to try that if all else fails.

In an IP environment, use `ping`, `winipcfg` (for Windows 95/98), and `ipconfig /all` (on Windows NT) to verify that the IP stack is functioning correctly. And don't forget that the problem might lie at the remote end and not be a client issue at all. For example, you can `ping` all workstations on your LAN, and one of the servers on a remote LAN, but you cannot `ping` the second server on the remote LAN. However, users on the remote LAN have no problems connecting.

At first, this might seem like a formidable problem, since there are remote networks, and thus routers, in the picture. But with an understanding of IP, you can probably solve this problem without even leaving your chair. You know that your workstation is OK, because you can see everything except the one remote server. You know that the remote server is up, because the remote users are not having any problems. And you know that the routers are functioning correctly, because you can access one of the remote servers.

But if the server in question did not have a default gateway set, could that not be the issue? To communicate with the users on its own LAN, this problem server would not need a default gateway set. Only when it tries to respond to your requests would the problem show up; since you are remote, it would need to direct the response to its default router, which it does not have.

And above all, don't hesitate to post a question in the client forums. Odds are that others have encountered the same problem you are seeing, and can help you to resolve it.

Managing Your NDS Tree

CHAPTER **14**

LOGGING IN TO AND NAVIGATING THE NOVELL DIRECTORY SERVICES TREE

In this chapter

THE BASICS OF NDS NAVIGATION

There are several different ways to *navigate* (or *browse*) through the NDS Tree in order to find the resources you need to manage or access. One way is by using a command-line utility called CX.EXE, where *CX* stands for *Change Context*. Another way is by using Windows-based utilities—that is, Novell's NWAdmin32 and the Windows Network Neighborhood or Windows Program Manager (depending on the operating system you are using).

Note

This chapter does not discuss the Windows Program Manager, because it is assumed that the majority of people use Windows NT or Windows 95/98 instead of Windows 3.1.

The utilities you use to navigate and browse NDS are a matter of preference. Most people seem to prefer the Windows-based utilities so that they do not have to remember CX's proper syntax or any optional command-line switches. More specifically, because NetWare does not ship with any command-line utilities for creating NDS objects and you cannot create NDS objects with Network Neighborhood, most people tend to prefer NWAdmin32. NWAdmin32 offers "one-stop" functionality in that you can navigate to a container and then create the needed objects in that container, all from within the same utility. Creating objects using NWAdmin32 is discussed in Chapter 15, "Creating and Managing Directory Tree Objects."

Tip #105 from
Sally

NetWare ships with a command-line utility called UIMPORT.EXE (User Import), also discussed in Chapter 15. However, this utility just creates user objects. There is a command-line utility for creating NDS objects called OIMPORT (Object Import); OIMPORT was developed by Novell Consulting but does not ship with NetWare 5. For more information on OIMPORT (and OEXPORT), see http:/consulting.novell.com/products. Also recall that one of the new features in NDS 8 is a batch utility for adding, modifying, and deleting NDS objects.

Before you can navigate NDS, however, you must first successfully log in.

Tip #106 from
Sally

Actually before login you can view the NDS Tree with CX. This is because every user in NDS is a member of the "pseudogroup" object [Public]. And, before login, [Public] is given Browse object rights to the NDS Tree (NDS object rights are discussed in Chapter 18, "Implementing Security"). Using CX before login can be especially helpful if, for example, you forget the container that your user account is in (a valid context is required for a successful login as discussed later in this chapter). To browse the Tree before login, simply cancel out of the Novell Client login screen, shell out to the DOS prompt, and change to F: (which is generally your first network drive). This puts you in the F:\LOGIN directory (the only NetWare directory available to you before login). If you type DIR in F:\LOGIN, you see that CX.EXE is one of the utilities in this directory. Now by typing the command CX /a/r/t (these options are discussed later in this chapter) you can view the entire NDS Tree. This process is not possible using Network Neighborhood.

LOGGING IN TO NDS

Logging in to NDS requires that you "pass" the first level of security—that is, the login/password level of security that governs initial access to the network (as discussed in Chapter 18). A successful login requires that a combination of the following items be "true":

A valid username, including the correct context, is entered.

Note

Entering the correct context is not considered a security issue. The correct context is necessary due to the way that NDS searches for an object, which is discussed later in this chapter.

A valid password is entered.

Any password, network, and time restrictions that can be set for the user are met (these restrictions are discussed in Chapter 18). For example, if time restrictions have been set so that a user can log in only between the hours of 9:00 a.m. and 5:00 p.m., a successful login is only possible between these hours.

I will now discuss the login options available when using the Novell Client for Windows 95/98 (Version 3.10, 2/17/99), as shown in Figure 14.1. The Advanced button was selected here to display the advanced login options that are available. The advanced options are those within the NDS tab (shown in Figure 14.1) and the Script tab (look ahead to Figure 14.2). The username and password are, therefore, not considered advanced options.

Note

It might be that not all the advanced login options that I will discuss are available on the Novell Client for Windows NT, the Novell Client for DOS/Windows, or even different versions of the Novell Client for Windows 95/98. Additionally, if these advanced options are available, they might be located on different tabs of the Novell Client software.

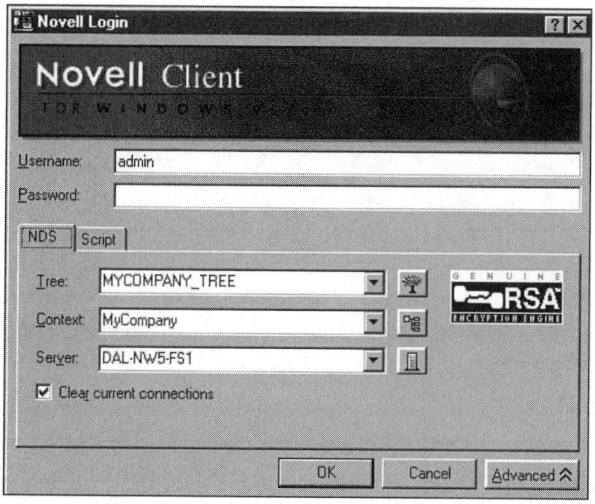

Figure 14.1
Novell Client for Windows 95/98 login screen with advanced NDS options.

GENERAL OPTIONS FOR LOGGING IN TO NDS

The following are the options available on the NDS tab:

Username—This is the username as it has been created in NDS. An NDS username is not case sensitive. The username is also referred to as the *login name*.

Password—Assuming that NetWare passwords are required in your company (which they should be!), this is the password that you have set for yourself or a default password that was temporarily given to you by the network administrator. In the latter case, you should change your password to something different after successfully logging in. NetWare passwords are not case sensitive and NetWare doesn't require the use of a password by default; rather, the network administrator sets up password restrictions to require passwords.

The username and password are generally the only two fields that are (or should be) required for most users to enter. This is because, when the network administrator installs the Novell Client software, he generally sets the remaining advanced options as part of the installation process, as a convenience for users. Also, the username and password options are available on all versions of the Novell Client software since they are required for a successful login.

The advanced login options are discussed next so that you are familiar with their functionality. The options within the NDS tab are discussed first (while referring to Figure 14.1).

ADVANCED OPTIONS FOR LOGGING IN TO NDS

The following are the advanced options on the NDS tab:

Tree—Selecting the down arrow icon (drop-down box) to the right of the Tree name brings up a list of the Trees the workstation has previously been logged in to. Generally speaking a company has just one NDS Tree; however, there are exceptions such as a Tree that was set up for testing purposes. Selecting the Tree icon shows a list of the NDS Trees that are currently advertising on the network. (Remember the NDS Tree advertises itself via SAP or SLP, as discussed in Chapter 6, "Designing the Novell Directory Services Tree"). The Tree name must be set to the Tree where the user account is located.

Context—As mentioned in Chapter 5, "Novell Directory Services Tree Basics," every object in NDS has a context which is simply the container that the object exists in. In order to log in, you must give not only your valid username but also the context (container) that your user object exists in. This is because NDS does not search the entire NDS database looking for objects. Rather, you must guide NDS by pointing to the container where the object (in this case the user) exists. Although this might seem a bit cumbersome, the advantage is the time saved by not having to wait while NDS searches through the entire NDS database looking for referenced objects.

The drop-down box next to Context shows the contexts that have previously been used from the workstation. The OU icon allows you to browse through the NDS Tree to set the context to where your user object is; this is a shortcut to typing in the context name and is especially helpful if you don't know the exact syntax to enter for the context name. Again, the context should be set to the location in NDS where the user object exists.

Tip #107 from *Gally*	Contextless login, which is a feature in NetWare 5, would eliminate the necessity of having to set a context. Contextless login allows NDS to search through the entire Tree (or logically a portion of the Tree) looking for the name specified in the Username field. Where the search starts depends on how the network administrator sets up contextless login. Contextless login currently requires the use of Catalog Services, although this will likely change with NDS 8. For more information see the Technical Information Document (TID) 2940793 "How to Configure Contextless Login in NetWare 5" available from `http://support.novell.com`.

Server—This field is referred to as the user's Preferred Server and should generally point to a local server where the user's home directory is or where the user runs most of his applications. Similar to the Tree and Context fields, the drop-down box shows the servers that this workstation has previously been set to whereas the "server" icon shows the NetWare servers advertising (via SAP or SLP) on the network.

Clear Current Connections—If enabled, this clears any existing connections to NetWare servers.

That covers the advanced login options available from the NDS tab on the Novell Client for Windows 95/98. The following are the advanced login options available from the Script tab (see Figure 14.2):

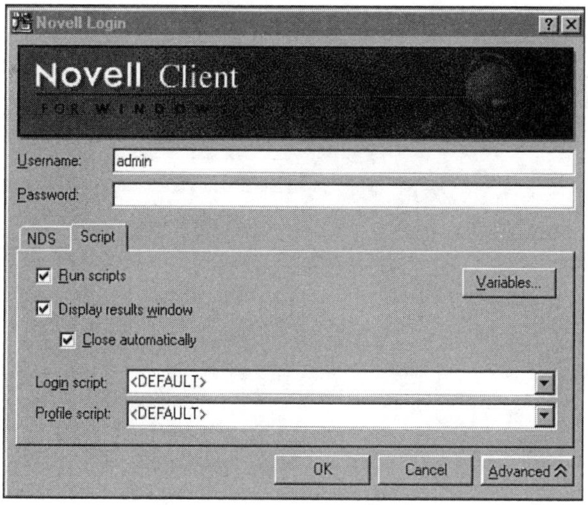

Figure 14.2
Novell Client for Windows 95/98 login screen with advanced script options.

Part

IV

CH

14

Run Scripts—If enabled, all login scripts associated with the user run—that is, Container, Profile, User, or Default. If disabled, none of these four login scripts run.

Tip #108 from *Sally*	It might be beneficial to disable the running of login scripts when you are you are at remote location, which is connected back to your home location via a WAN link. This is because running login scripts across a WAN link can be a very slow process. When you don't run login scripts, you are generally just missing the convenience of having drives automatically mapped for you and then using these drive mappings for saving files. You can still save your files to locations in the file system, though, by using Windows Explorer to navigate to the directory you want to place the file in. It is not recommended that you always disable the running of login scripts because login scripts are sometimes used to automatically install newer versions of the Novell Client software.

Variables—There are four variables (numbered 2–5) that can be filled in for processing a login script, when the login script has been set up to support these variables as input. For example, say that there are users in the company who have both a desktop computer and a laptop computer. Additionally, the login script has been set up to deliver applications via the Novell Application Launcher (NAL) component of ZENWorks (which is discussed in Chapter 24). However, when the laptop computer is used, you don't want these applications delivered. In the login script you could set up a statement similar to the following:

```
IF %2 <> "LAPTOP" THEN #Z:NAL.EXE
```

This statement translates to "If Variable 2 is not equal to LAPTOP, launch NAL.EXE from the Z: drive." When the user uses his laptop computer, he could fill in LAPTOP within the Variable %2 box (see Figure 14.3) and NAL would not be delivered to his laptop computer.

Figure 14.3
Novell Client for
Windows 95/98
Variables dialog box.

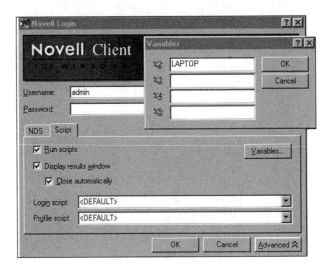

Display Results Window—If this option is enabled, the results of the login script are displayed in a window. If errors occur during the login script process, the Results Window remains open so that you can see these errors, until you select the Close button. If no errors occur during the login script process, the Results Window closes automatically.

Close Automatically—If enabled, the Results Window closes automatically even if the login script did encounter errors.

Login Script and Profile Script—These two fields allow you to enter alternative login scripts to run. When you fill in the Login Script option, the script you specify is the only script executed; no other container, profile, user, or default scripts are run. When you fill in the Profile Script option, any Profile object associated with the user is not executed; rather, the script entered here executes in its place.

FULLY DISTINGUISHED NAMING AND RELATIVE DISTINGUISHED NAMING

Knowing how to reference an NDS object is important for understanding how NDS locates objects in the Tree. There are two different ways to reference an NDS object: by an object's Fully Distinguished Name (FDN) and by an object's Relative Distinguished Name (RDN).

An FDN is an object's complete name, from the object itself up to the [Root]. For example, `.emilys.dal.mycompany` is EmilyS's FDN (an FDN always begins with a leading period). Whereas an object's RDN is simply a portion of the object's FDN, relative to the current context. For example, `emilys` is a valid RDN only when the current context is set to `dal.mycompany` (an RDN never begins with a leading period).

> **Note**
>
> Current context in NDS is roughly equivalent to current directory in the file system. You can have only one current context set at a given time much like you can be in only one directory ("current directory") at a given time. Current context can be set only to a container object just like a current directory can be set only to a directory.

FDN is always an accurate way to reference an NDS object regardless of the current context that is set. However, RDN might not always be an accurate way to reference an NDS object, as you will see in the following example.

Tip #109 from
Sally

> You might want to consider always using an object's Fully Distinguished Name, especially in login scripts, to avoid NDS name resolution problems.

For this example, EmilyS wants to log in and her user account has been created in the NDS container of `dal.mycompany`. Figure 14.4 shows two valid ways that EmilyS can successfully log in.

Figure 14.4
Two different ways to log in.

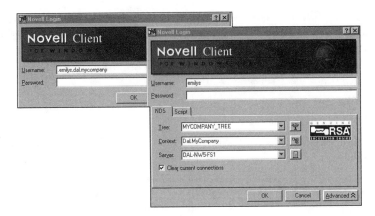

The Login screen on the left shows how EmilyS can use her FDN to log in successfully. The Login screen on the right shows how EmilyS can use her RDN of EmilyS when her context is set to dal.mycompany. If EmilyS changed her context on this right-hand screen to mycompany, the login screen shown on the right would fail; however, the login screen shown on the left (using an FDN) will be valid regardless of the context that is set. It should now be evident why most network administrators set the context for their users as part of the Client installation process. Then a user simply has to enter her username (RDN) to success-fully log in.

It should also now be evident that NDS always uses an FDN to locate an object. The FDN is either entered by the user or built by NDS, from taking the RDN entered by the user and appending the current context to this RDN.

Using the CX command for navigating NDS is now discussed, incorporating the FDN and RDN concepts.

USING CX TO NAVIGATE NDS

CX is a command-line utility to change to another context in the NDS Tree. Additionally, by using some of the options available with the CX command, this utility also allows you to browse the NDS Tree. As you will see, CX is roughly equivalent to the CD command used to change to another directory in the file system. Following are some ways that you can use the CX command to navigate the NDS Tree, assuming this Tree structure:

```
[Root]
  O=MyCompany
    OU=Hou
      OU=Sales
```

Typing CX .sales.hou.mycompany puts you in the sales container by using the FDN for sales. While your current context is set to sales, you could see (browse) the objects in this container by typing CX /a/t which translates to "show all NDS objects in the current con-text and put the output into a tree-structured format."

When your current context is set to the sales container, typing CX . brings you up a level to hou.mycompany. Now that you are in hou.mycompany, typing CX .. brings you up two levels to [Root]. Now that you are in [Root], typing CX mycompany puts you down in mycompany by using the RDN of mycompany.

> **Note**
>
> As shown in the previous examples, entering the attribute types for container objects is not necessary—that is, you do not have to type cx .ou=sales.ou=hou.o=mycompany although this is a valid "typeful" FDN. The previous examples are referred to as "typeless" and are generally used in practice simply because they require less typing.

That should give you a general idea of the options available for navigating and browsing the NDS Tree using CX.

> **Tip #110 from**
> *Sally*
>
> The /? switch brings up the available options for all the NetWare command-line utilities— for example, typing CX /? displays all the available switches for the CX utility.

USING NWADMIN32 TO NAVIGATE NDS

As mentioned at the beginning of this chapter, NWAdmin32 will probably be the primary tool that you use to navigate NDS. More specifically, it will probably be the tool that network administrators use to navigate NDS because they generally use this utility to set up, maintain, and manage NDS (as discussed in Chapter 15). With NWAdmin32, you don't have to worry about typing out lengthy commands as you do with CX; rather, you simply point-and-click to change to another container and automatically you will see the objects displayed in this container. Additionally, the graphical nature of NWAdmin32 makes it easier to see which objects are Organizational Units, users, servers, and so on versus the character-based output you get from CX /a/t.

Figure 14.5 shows a progression of browsing NDS using NWAdmin32. The left-most window shows what you see when NWAdmin32 starts up. By double-clicking MyCompany, you see the Tree structure as represented in the middle window. By double-clicking Dal, you see the Tree structure as represented in the right-most window. It's that easy! There's no typing and no syntax to remember; simply point-and-click.

> **Tip #111 from**
> *Sally*
>
> If you are simply looking for the name of a resource in the Tree, it might be quicker to use the CX /a/r/t option rather than waiting for NWAdmin32 to start up. CX /a/r/t translates to "show all objects from the [Root] of the Tree and display the output on the screen in a tree-structured format." You can also send the contents of the CX command to a text file by typing CX /a/r/t > tree.txt, where tree.txt is a sample filename.

Figure 14.5
Browsing NDS using
NWAdmin32.

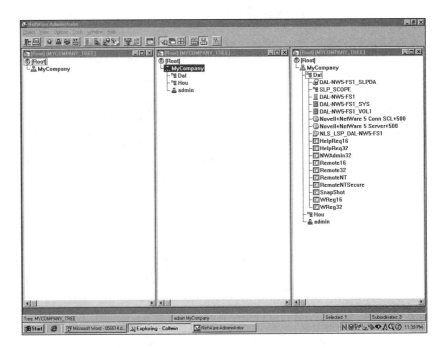

USING NETWORK NEIGHBORHOOD TO NAVIGATE NDS

Whereas network administrators are more likely to use NWAdmin32 to browse NDS, users generally prefer Network Neighborhood. This is possible because the Novell Client software is integrated with Network Neighborhood (and Windows Explorer) after a successful login. You can see that the Novell Client has been integrated with Network Neighborhood by looking at Figure 14.6. Notice the *N* (which stands for *Novell*) next to five of the available options.

When using Network Neighborhood to browse NDS (much like with NWAdmin32) you don't have to worry about typing out lengthy commands as you do with CX; rather, you simply point-and-click. To browse NDS using Network Neighborhood, simply right-click the Network Neighborhood icon on the Windows 95/98 or Windows NT desktop and choose Explore (refer to Figure 14.6). You then see a window similar to the one shown in Figure 14.7.

Figure 14.6
Novell Client integration with Network Neighborhood.

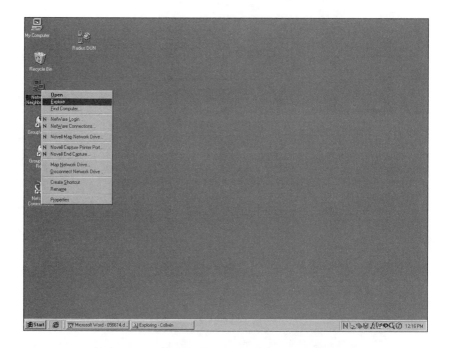

Figure 14.7
Browsing NDS using Network Neighborhood.

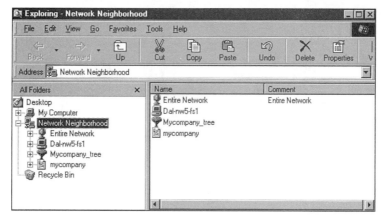

The left pane shows you the NDS resources you either have been authenticated to (no licensed connection) or have licensed connections to. Figure 14.7 shows the results of a client who logged in but did not check the option to Run Scripts. Notice, however, that this client still shows the MyCompany_Tree and DAL-NW5-FS1 server in the left pane. This is because even without any login script, you are NDS-authenticated to both a Tree and a server. The Tree and the server shown in Figure 14.7 are the ones entered on the NDS tab on the Client software (as discussed previously). Additionally, because the user who logged in has his user object in the O=MyCompany container, the icon representing this Organization (mycompany) is also shown in the left pane. If this user logged in again and selected the option to Run Scripts and his login script mapped a drive to DAL-NW5-FS2, this server would also show up in the left pane of Figure 14.7.

To browse NDS using Network Neighborhood, you can use either the left or right pane of the window shown in Figure 14.7. By using the left pane, you can see the entire Tree structure at once, as shown in Figure 14.8. Notice that this shows not only the NDS objects in the Tree but also the volumes and directories on the servers in the Tree. You get to the screen shown in Figure 14.8 by clicking on each plus sign (+) next to the objects starting with the Tree icon.

Figure 14.8
Browsing the entire NDS Tree using Network Neighborhood

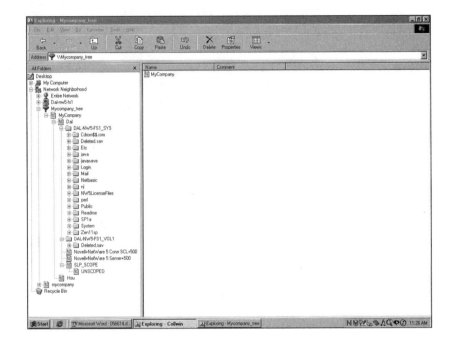

By using the right pane of the window shown in Figure 14.7, you browse the NDS Tree one container at a time. You get to the screen shown in Figure 14.9 by double-clicking the Tree in the right-hand pane, and choosing O=Mycompany, and then OU=DAL. If you look at the top menu bar in Figure 14.9, you will see Exploring - Dal.

Tip #112 from
Gally

If a user browses NDS by using the Network Neighborhood and opens up the DAL-NW5-FS1_SYS volume (shown in Figure 14.9), this causes the user to take a licensed connection to the DAL-NW5-FS1 server, because the user is accessing a resource (the file system) on this server. This, of course, assumes that the user did not already have a licensed connection to DAL-NW5-FS1. This could account for unexplained licensed connections you see on NetWare servers. Also (and logically), this same licensed connection would be taken up if the user used NWAdmin32.

Figure 14.9
Browsing a portion of the NDS Tree using Network Neighborhood

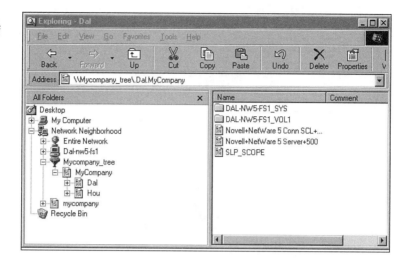

Additionally, from Figure 14.9, a user could create a directory (or folder) on the DAL-NW5-FS1 server's SYS or VOL1 volumes by double-clicking DAL-NW5-FS1_SYS (to open it), right-clicking, and selecting New, Folder—just as he would when creating a folder on his local drive using Network Neighborhood. The user must have the appropriate file system rights to create directories on NetWare volumes; this in no way violates NetWare file system security. At the outset of this chapter, I said that Network Neighborhood could not be used to create NDS objects; remember, though, that the NetWare file system is not part of NDS!

PROJECT: TESTING YOURSELF

Try the following first two exercises to learn two additional ways to navigate NDS. Try the third exercise to determine the version of the Novell Client software you are running:

1. The examples in this section showed you how to use the Network Neighborhood for browsing NDS. You can also browse NDS by using "Explore" from the My Computer icon on the Windows 95/98 or Windows NT desktop. Try this on your own to see how similar it is to using Network Neighborhood.

2. Look for the red *N* icon in the System Tray on your Windows 95/98 or Windows NT workstation. If you right-click this, you see the option Browse To, which is an alternative way to get to either Network Neighborhood or My Computer to browse NDS.

3. Also from this red *N* icon, select the option Novell Client32 Properties. On the bottom of the Client tab, you can see which version of the Novell Client software you are running, which can be helpful for troubleshooting purposes.

PART

IV

CH

14

CHAPTER **15**

CREATING, MANAGING, AND USING NDS OBJECTS

In this chapter

NDS MANAGEMENT UTILITIES

You have several utilities to choose from to create and manage the NDS objects that are necessary for your network environment:

- **NetWare Administrator**—This is the primary utility used for creating and managing NDS. NWADMN32.EXE is a 32-bit Windows utility that enables you to easily create and modify all objects (and their properties) in the NDS Tree. You can use NWAdmn32 to create, delete, modify, rename, move, and get detailed property information about any NDS object in the Tree, provided that you have the appropriate NWAdmn32 snap-ins for creating and managing non–base schema objects (as discussed in Chapter 5, "Novell Directory Services Tree Basics").

- **ConsoleOne**—ConsoleOne is a Java-based utility that will eventually replace NWAdmn32. However, the version currently shipping with NetWare 5 does not yet have the same functionality as NWAdmn32; therefore, ConsoleOne is not currently used in practice much. ConsoleOne is included in NetWare 5 as a glimpse of the future direction of NetWare's administration utilities. In fact, ConsoleOne will eventually be the only administration tool for managing all aspects of NDS, including optional products such as NDS for NT and ManageWise.

  ConsoleOne uses the Novell Java Class Libraries (NJCL) to interface with NetWare; currently, the NJCL relies on the Novell Client software DLLs for NCP calls. The NJCL project is moving toward being 100% Java, at which point it will be possible to run ConsoleOne on any Java platform.

  For now, you can use ConsoleOne to create and manage objects from any Novell Client workstation that is Java-enabled. Additionally, because NetWare 5 ships with the Java Runtime Environment, you can even run ConsoleOne on a NetWare 5 server. This capability is shown in Figure 15.1.

Figure 15.1
ConsoleOne can be used to create and manage NDS objects.

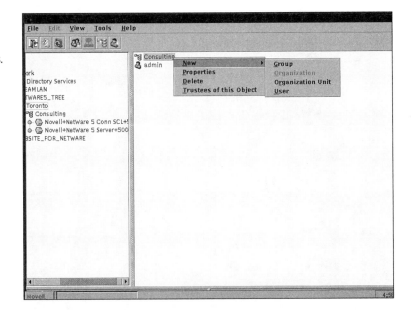

As you can see in Figure 15.1, ConsoleOne currently supports the creation only of Group, Organization, Organizational Unit, and User objects. However, the future capability of being able to manage all aspects of NDS and NDS-related products with one standard utility will make NetWare administration even easier than it is now.

Note

This section does not discuss using ConsoleOne for creating and managing NDS objects, due to its current limited functionality.

- **User Import**—UIMPORT.EXE is a DOS-based, command-line utility that allows you to create and modify user objects and their properties in "batches." UIMPORT is especially useful in school environments, in which students might be created and deleted from NDS every semester or quarter. UIMPORT is discussed later in this chapter.

Regardless of the utility you use, you must always have the appropriate NDS rights in order to create, delete, and modify NDS objects and their properties (NDS rights are discussed in Chapter 16, "Managing NDS Rights, Partitions, and Replicas").

ADMIN USER

Admin is the user account that is automatically created when you install the first NetWare 5 server in the Tree. The Admin account is created in the container you specify during the installation of NDS. There is only one system-created Admin account per Tree (regardless of the number of servers). This Admin account (by default) has all NDS rights and all file-system rights to the entire Tree, making it the "super user" account for NetWare and NDS.

Tip #113 from
Sally

Admin's default rights to manage the entire NDS Tree can be restricted. This capability is discussed in Chapter 16.

The next sections discuss using NWAdmn32 for creating NDS objects and the properties available for these objects. These next sections assume that you are logged in as Admin (or another user that has been given the appropriate rights to create and manage all NDS objects in the Tree) and that you are running NWAdmn32, which is located in NetWare's SYS:PUBLIC\WIN32 directory. You can create all NDS objects within NWAdmn32 by following these steps:

1. Select the container you want to create the object in.
2. Select the Create option from within NWAdmn32's Object menu.
3. Scroll through the New Object list (as shown in Figure 15.2) to select the object you want to create.

Note

Since all NDS objects can be created by following these three steps, they will not be repeated for each object discussed in this section.

Figure 15.2
This is a partial listing of the NDS objects that can be created using NWAdmn32.

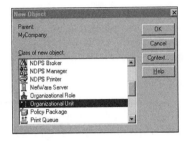

Tip #114 from
Sally

If the object you want to create does not show up in the Class of New Object list (shown in Figure 15.2), ensure that you are selecting a container that supports the creation of this object type. Remember from Chapter 5 that the NDS schema allows only certain classes of objects to be created within certain containers. Another possibility is that the schema has not yet been extended to support the object you want to create, or you are running NWAdmn32 from a server that does not have the appropriate snap-ins.

CREATING CONTAINER OBJECTS

Container objects are used to organize the resources in the NDS Tree and give NDS its hierarchy. Most of your container objects will be Organizational Units, because it is generally recommended that most companies have just one Organization object (as discussed in Chapter 5).

The following three options are available when you're creating an Organizational Unit (see Figure 15.3).

■ **Organizational Unit Name**—This is the name of the Organizational Unit as it will appear in NDS.

Tip #115 from
Sally

Follow your NDS Design (as discussed in Chapter 6, "Designing the Novell Directory Services Tree") to determine the proper placement and naming for all of your NDS objects.

■ **Define Additional Properties**—If enabled, this option automatically brings up the property screen (look ahead to Figure 15.4), allowing you to fill in detailed property information immediately after creating the Organizational Unit.

■ **Create Another Organizational Unit**—If enabled, this option automatically brings up another dialog box, allowing you to create another Organizational Unit in the same context.

Figure 15.3
The only required property for an Organizational Unit is its name.

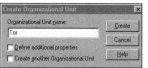

After the Organizational Unit (or any NDS object, for that matter) has been created, you can see all the object's available properties (or "details," as they are referred to in NWAdmn32) by following these steps:

1. Select the object.

2. Right-click it.

3. Select Details.

You are now presented with the Organizational Unit's property screen, as shown in Figure 15.4. These properties are the same for Organization objects too.

Figure 15.4
The properties available for an Organizational Unit are functionally organized within property "tabs."

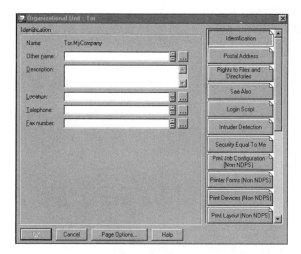

Notice that in Figure 15.4, not all the available properties are displayed; therefore, you must use the scrollbar (directly to the right of the property tabs) to see the others.

PROPERTIES FOR CONTAINER OBJECTS

This section discusses container properties so that you can become familiar with their functionality. The properties you choose to implement depend upon the NDS products you have installed and how you choose to leverage the capabilities available with NDS. These are the container object properties:

- **Identification and Postal Address**—Both of these properties are informational only, meaning that they do not impact how NDS functions.

Tip #116 from *Sally*	You could fill in the Telephone property of the person responsible for managing this container. Additionally, you could add that person's User object to the Other Name property. If there were problems with this container, you would then know whom to contact.

- **Rights to Files and Directories**—This property is discussed in Chapter 18, "Implementing Security." When rights to files and directories are given to a container, these rights apply to all users in that container and any subcontainers.

- **See Also**—This is a multivalued property that allows you to list other objects related to this object. The list has no functional purpose; it is for reference only.

Tip #117 from *Sally*	You could use the See Also property to list another container object that is set up the same as this one, as a reference or a checkpoint for which properties should be enabled.

- **Login Script**—This property is discussed in Chapter 22, "Configuring User Environment Using Login Scripts." When a login script is created for a container object, the login script executes for all users in that container but *not* for users in any subcontainers.

- **Intruder Detection**—This property is discussed in Chapter 18. When intruder detection is set on a container, the restrictions apply to all users in that container but *not* for users in any subcontainers.

- **Security Equal to Me**—This property lists the users that have been given *explicit* security equivalence to this container. These users will, therefore, have the same rights that were given to this container (for example, from the Rights to Files and Directories property discussed previously).

Tip #118 from *Sally*	The Security Equal to Me property needs only to list users that are not located in this container. This is because all users in a container have *implied* security equivalence to that container, even if they do not show up in the Security Equal to Me property list. Additionally, security equivalence as a means to giving rights should be used only for temporary rights assignment.

- **Print Job Configuration (Non NDPS)**—A print job configuration is simply a collection of CAPTURE commands. (The CAPTURE command is discussed in Chapter 21, "Network Printing.") Therefore, within a print job configuration you can set the number of copies to print, whether or not to issue a printer form feed, whom to notify when the job has finished printing, and so on (see Figure 15.5).

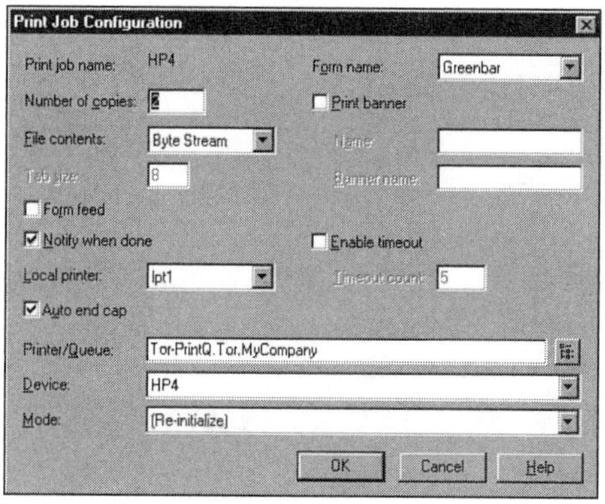

Figure 15.5
A print job configuration is specific to a printer/queue.

If users are using the CAPTURE command to send their jobs to print queues or non-NDPS printers, they can simply reference this print job configuration name in their CAPTURE statement, for example, CAPTURE j=HP4. The CAPTURE statement (and therefore print job configurations) are not used very often, because most people now operate in a Windows environment. Print job configurations defined for a container will be accessible by any user in that container but *not* for users in any subcontainers.

- **Printer Forms (Non NDPS)**—This property allows you to create forms to define special paper sizes for your printer. The printer forms are "referenced from" a print job configuration (see Figure 15.5 and note that the form Greenbar has been created and made a part of this print job configuration).

  Printer forms are not used very often, because most people now operate in a Windows environment and the Windows printer driver handles this functionality. Printer forms defined for a container will be accessible by any user in that container but *not* for users in any subcontainers.

- **Print Devices (Non NDPS)**—This property allows you to define control sequences that are sent to a printer to perform specialized functions, for example, to reinitialize the printer or print in landscape mode. You also have the capability to create *device modes*, which are simply logical "groups" of escape sequences sent to the printer simultaneously. Print devices and device modes are "referenced from" a print job configuration (see Figure 15.5 and note that the print device HP4 and the device mode Re-initialize have been created and made a part of this print job configuration).

  Print devices and device modes are not used very often, because most people now operate in a Windows environment and the Windows printer driver handles this functionality. Print devices and device modes defined for a container will be accessible by any user in that container but *not* for any users in subcontainers.

■ **Print Layout (Non NDPS)**—Setting up traditional queue-based "legacy" printing is briefly discussed in Chapter 21. This property page allows you to graphically see whether the necessary linking has been made among the printer server, printer, and print queue in this container. As shown in Figure 15.6 (in the Organizational Unit:Tor window), all the proper links have been made. However, the exclamation point next to the Print Server indicates a problem. By selecting the Print Server and then clicking the Status button, the Tor-PrintServer window appears, showing that the Print Server is down, meaning that the PSERVER.NLM has not been loaded on the server.

Figure 15.6
The Print Layout property is used for troubleshooting.

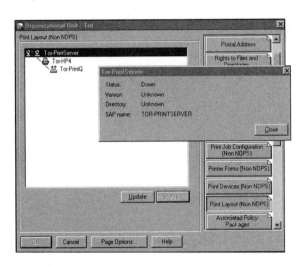

The Print Layout property is only used with PSERVER.NLM and not for any network-connected print servers (for example, JetDirect Cards) or NDPS.

■ **NDPS Remote Printer Management**—Setting up NDPS printing is discussed in Chapter 21. This Remote Printer Management feature of NDPS allows you to install printers remotely (that is, from within NWAdmn32). These printers then are accessible for all users in the container but *not* for users in any subcontainers.

The following seven properties are for ZENworks, which is discussed in Chapter 24:

■ **Associated Policy Packages**—This property shows the ZENworks policy package objects that have been associated with the container and which can, therefore, be used by any user in that container and any sub-containers. This property is also used to associate (assign) policy package objects to the container.

■ **Applications**—This property shows the ZENworks application objects that have been associated with the container and which can, therefore, be accessed by any user in that container and any sub-containers. This property is also used to associate (assign) application objects to the container.

- **Launcher Configuration**—This property configures the application launcher component of ZENworks for users in this container and sub-containers, controlling the applications that appear on a user's desktop.

- **Workstation Registration**—This property shows workstation objects that are registered and ready to be imported into the NDS Tree. This property can also be used to import these registered workstation objects.

- **Workstation Tracking**—This property shows a log of workstation objects that have been moved from, or renamed within, the container.

- **Workstation Filter**—This property is used to control (filter) the workstation objects that can be imported into the container. The filter is based upon a workstation's IPX or IP network address.

- **Workstation Inventory Extract**—This property is used to export the inventory information for a workstation into tab-delimited text files. You can then use these delimited files to create reports using application software such as Microsoft Access. This property will only be available if you have installed the full version of ZENworks, not just the starter pack version of ZENworks that ships with NetWare 5.

As you should now realize, most container properties apply to users in that specific container only. This is why containers are sometimes referred to as "natural groups." A user is implied as security equivalent to its parent container; therefore, this user gets all the property information set on its parent container. There is no way to remove this implied security equivalence (except for removing the user from the container).

You should also see now why it is recommended that you design the bottom layers of your Tree around users: to take advantage of containers as natural groups.

CREATING USER OBJECTS

User objects are the most fundamental (and the most common) leaf objects in NDS. User objects represent the people in your company who need access to the resources available in NDS. As mentioned earlier, the only user account that is automatically created is Admin; all other user accounts must be created by the network administrator.

Every user should have his or her individual user account (that is, it is generally not recommended that users share accounts). Additionally, each user needs only one user account even if there are multiple servers in NDS. This is because NDS is a global database, and after you are logged in to one server in the NDS Tree, you can access other servers in the same Tree through a user-transparent background authentication process. This assumes, of course, that you have the necessary rights to these servers. This background authentication occurs when you map a drive to another server or when you look at a server's directory structure through Network Neighborhood (as just two examples).

When creating a user account, you must fill in two required properties before the user object can be created: Login Name and Last Name (see Figure 15.7).

Figure 15.7
The "Create" button will be grayed-out until you put at least one character in the "Last Name" field.

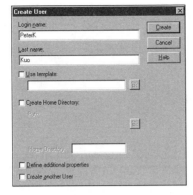

The *login name* is the name of the user leaf object that will appear in NDS and is also the name that the user will log in with. The Last Name property, though required to create a user object, is not a functional property in NDS. It is a required property to conform to the X.500 specification.

As also shown in Figure 15.7, two other options are available when you're creating users: Use Template (which is discussed later in this chapter) and Create Home Directory.

All users should have their own, personal home directory. A home directory is simply a directory on a NetWare volume where users can store their files; additionally, no users (except the owner and the Admin user) should have rights to this home directory. Home directories are usually created in a standardized location on the NetWare file system—for example, VOL1:USERS\<home_directory_name>.

From Figure 15.7, you create a home directory for a new user by following these steps:

1. Select the Create Home Directory check box.
2. Click the Browser button (to the right of Create Home Directory) to "walk" (browse) the NDS Tree. This opens the Select Object dialog box.
3. Select the directory under which the home directory will be created (see Figure 15.8).

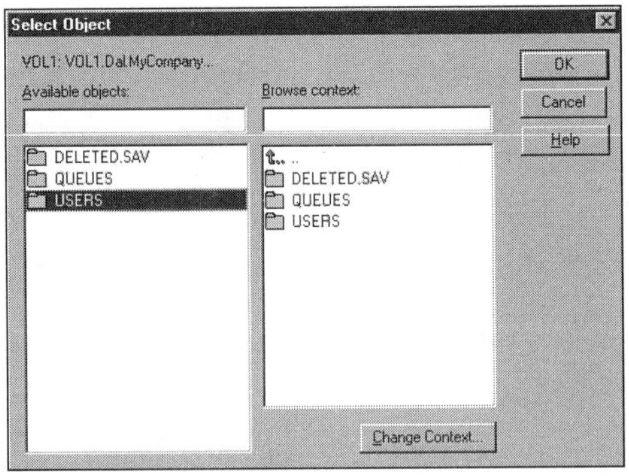

Figure 15.8
These options will create a home directory on the VOL1:USERS directory in the Dal container.

The home directory name that gets created matches the login name, which is a common and recommended practice (see Figure 15.9).

Figure 15.9
The PeterK home directory name was automatically filled in here; it can, however, be changed.

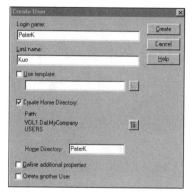

When you create the home directory at the same time that you create the user, the user automatically gets all file-system rights to their home directory (which is recommended). Additionally, the user's Home Directory property automatically gets filled in. Therefore, creating a home directory when you create the user object is recommended to avoid having to do both of these tasks manually.

Tip #119 from
Sally

When the Home Directory property is filled in, you can use the %HOME_DIRECTORY% variable in login scripts or even within macros in the Novell Application Launcher (NAL) component of ZENworks. For example, to map the H: drive to a user's home directory, you could simply place this command in a container login script:

MAP H:=%HOME_DIRECTORY%

PROPERTIES FOR USER OBJECTS

User properties are used when there are unique settings for an individual user (for example a special login script command) that do not pertain to any other users. Because of the extra administration involved with setting up individual user properties, you should try to use them sparingly. Notice in Figure 15.10 that user properties are very similar to container properties; however, user properties apply only to the specific user.

The following are all the user properties available:

■ **Identification**—The fields available in this property provide additional information about the user; however, this information does not impact how NDS functions. Identification information (if filled in) can be used to look up, for example, a user's telephone number from within NWAdmn32.

■ **Environment**—The fields available in this property (shown in Figure 15.11) allow you to customize a user's network environment (as discussed later). This property is not available on a container; however, you can globally set these fields with a Template object (discussed later in this chapter).

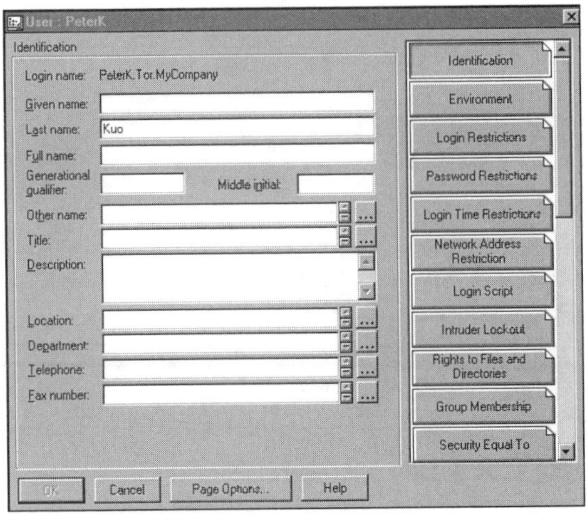

Figure 15.10

The properties available for a user are functionally organized within property "tabs."

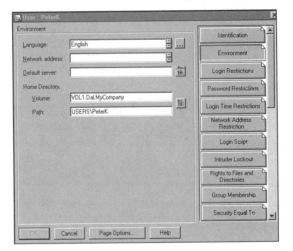

Figure 15.11

The only property you cannot set for a user is their Network Address property.

■ **Language**—If a user runs a utility that checks this property, the text of the utility is displayed in the language specified here. This is a multivalued property so other languages can be listed; if the first language listed is not available, the next one in the list will be used, and so on.

Note

Multivalued properties have the "up and down" arrows to the right of them, as shown in Figure 15.11 next to both Language and Network Address.

■ **Network Address**—This is the address of the workstation the user is logged in from. It is an empty field unless the user is logged in.

■ **Default Server**—This is the server the user is connected to after login, if no server is specified on the Novell Client Software login screen (discussed in Chapter 14, "Logging In To and Navigating Around the Novell Directory Services Tree"). Default Server is also used by the Send utility, which is used to send messages to other logged-in users.

■ **Home Directory**—This property's Volume and Path are automatically filled in when the home directory is created at the same time as the user (as shown here for PeterK). This property needs to be filled in to use the %HOME_DIRECTORY% variable.

■ **Login Restrictions**—This property (discussed further in Chapter 18) lets you set an expiration date for the user account. You can also limit the number of concurrent login sessions the user can have.

■ **Password Restrictions**—This property (discussed further in Chapter 18) lets you implement login password security for the user, such as requiring a password and forcing a periodic password change.

■ **Login Time Restrictions**—This property (discussed further in Chapter 18) lets you restrict the times when the user can be logged in.

■ **Network Address Restriction**—This property (discussed further in Chapter 18) lets you list the network addresses (and protocol) that the user can log in from.

■ **Login Script**—When a login script is created for a user object, the login script executes only for that user. This property is discussed further in Chapter 22.

■ **Intruder Lockout**—This is a status screen showing whether a user account has been locked due to intruder detection (which is set on a container basis). Figure 15.12 shows intruder lockout for PeterK. A network administrator that has the appropriate NDS rights unlocks the account from this property page.

Figure 15.12
The date/time and the network/workstation address where the user lockout occurred is logged in NDS.

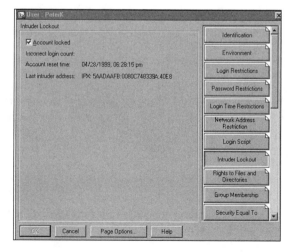

■ **Rights to Files and Directories**—When rights to files and directories are given to a user, these rights apply to that user only (and to any users that are security equivalent to this user). This property is further discussed in Chapter 18.

■ **Group Membership**—This property shows the groups a user is a member of (see Figure 15.13). It is also one way a network administrator can make the user a member of a group (by using the Add button also shown in Figure 15.13).

Figure 15.13
A user's Group Membership property is used to view, add, and delete the groups a user belongs to.

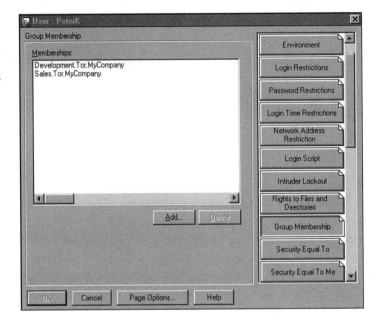

PeterK will have all the rights that were given to both the Sales and the Development groups due to his membership in these two groups.

■ **Security Equal To**—This property lists the objects the user is security equivalent to. In Figure 15.14, PeterK is security equivalent to the Sales and Development groups because he was made a member of both of these groups (refer to Figure 15.13).

Tip #120 from
Sally

If users have the NDS Supervisor or Write property right to the Security Equal To property, they can add the name of the Admin user account here and, therefore, have all rights to the entire NDS Tree.

Figure 15.14
A user's Security Equal To property is used to view, add, and delete the objects a user is security equivalent to.

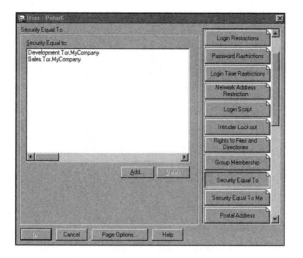

- **Security Equal To Me**—This property lists the users that are security equivalent to this user.

- **Account Balance**—This property lets you set and monitor an accounting balance for a user. With this property, you can also cause the user account to be locked if the user's account balance falls below a specified value. The default is unlimited credit. NetWare Accounting is discussed in Chapter 20, "NetWare Accounting."

- **Print Job Configuration (Non NDPS)**—This is the same property as was discussed previously for a Container object. If set here, however, it applies only to the user.

- **See Also**—This property lets you list other objects related to this object. The list has no functional purpose; it is for reference only.

- **NDPS Printer Access Control**—This property allows you to configure NDPS access control for this individual user.

- **NetWare Registry Editor**—This property is for the older versions of NetWare Administrator that used the Registry to track snap-ins. It can be used with NWAdmn32 to track "non-standard" snap-ins that do not get loaded from the SYS:PUBLIC\WIN32\SNAPINS directory.

The following six properties are for ZENworks, which is discussed in more detail in Chapter 24:

- **Associated Policy Packages**—This property shows the ZENworks policy package objects that have been associated with the user. This property is also used to associate (assign) policy package objects to a user.

- **Effective Policies**—This property shows the individual ZENworks policies within a policy package object that the user will get.

- **Applications**—This property shows the ZENworks application objects that have been associated with the user. This property is also used to associate (assign) application objects to a user.

- **Launcher Configuration**—This property configures the application launcher component of ZENworks for the user and is used to control the applications that appear on the user's desktop.

- **Remote Control**—This property is one of the ways you can take remote control of a workstation. This property will only be available if you have installed the full version of ZENworks, not just the starter pack version of ZENworks that ships with NetWare 5.

- **Associated Workstations**—This property displays the names of all workstation objects associated with the user. You can also view and set details (properties) on these workstation objects.

CREATING MULTIPLE USER ACCOUNTS WITH TEMPLATES

A *template* is an NDS leaf object that is used for creating users with similar property requirements. After you create a Template object, you set up the necessary user properties within the template; essentially, a template contains the same properties as an NDS user object. Then when you create new users, you select the option to Use Template (refer to Figure 15.7). All the properties that were set on the template are now set for the newly created users.

Users that have been created with a template are listed in the template's Members of Template property (see Figure 15.15). You can double-click the template (or any NDS leaf object for that matter) to show its properties.

Figure 15.15
The KimS and MikeB user accounts were created with the Dal-Template.

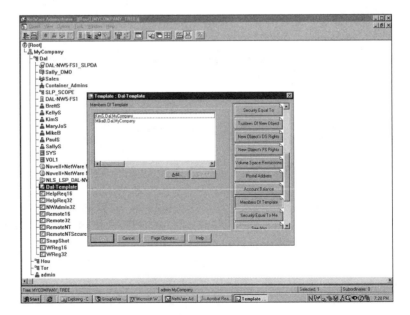

The template uses the Members of Template property for maintaining a link with the user objects that have been created with it. When a change is made to the template's properties (using the Details on Multiple Users option, discussed next), the change will also be made to the associated users' properties. You must use the Details on Multiple Users option for this to work.

You can create as many templates as necessary for users that have similar characteristics (properties).

Tip #121 from
Sally

Create Template objects in each physical site container (or containers beneath them) for the users at these sites. You do not want users to be "members" of a Template object across a WAN link.

WORKING WITH MULTIPLE USER ACCOUNTS

User properties can be modified in two ways with NWAdmn32:

- Individually, in which case some properties, such as Username, Last Name, and Password, can be changed only on a user-by-user basis.

- As a "group," using the Details on Multiple Users option.

To change properties common to multiple users, such as requiring a minimum password length and forcing a periodic password change, select the users and then select Details on Multiple Users from within the Object menu. The Details on Multiple Users dialog box appears, as shown in Figure 15.16.

Figure 15.16
These properties are being set simultaneously for the KellyS, MaryJoS, and PaulS user accounts.

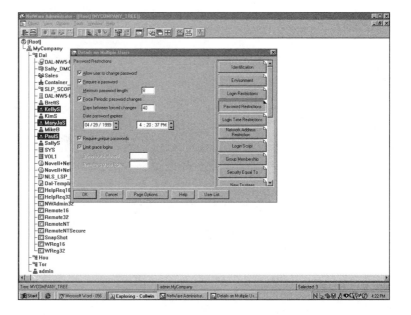

Tip #122 from
Sally

You can also select an Organizational Unit, a Group, or a Template and then use the Details on Multiple Users option to modify properties on the users associated with these objects.

Whereas the Template object allows you to quickly create new users with similar property settings, the Details on Multiple Users option allows you to quickly modify or set properties on existing users.

USING GROUPS

Group objects are NDS leaf objects. Groups are used when container objects (which act as "natural" groups) are too broad of a group classification. Groups, therefore, allow you to create a subset of the users in a container (or even across containers). Groups are generally created to facilitate the assignment of file-system rights or to distribute applications or policies with ZENworks.

Caution

Groups should contain only members that are within the same partition. Having a group contain members that cross partition boundaries results in External References. External References are created in NDS to reference an object that is not physically located on the local server. Although External References themselves are not bad, having External References across a WAN (especially a slow or unreliable WAN) *can* be.

The NDS properties for a group are shown in Figure 15.17. All of these properties were discussed earlier (as they related to either Container or User objects), with the exception of the Members property. The Members property is another way to add users to groups, as also shown in Figure 15.17.

Figure 15.17
PeterK has been made a member of the Sales group.

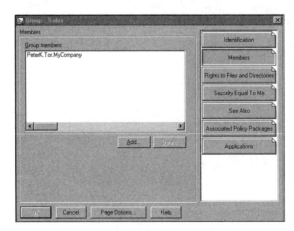

All group properties apply only to the members of the group.

USING ORGANIZATIONAL ROLES

Organizational Roles are NDS leaf objects and are very similar in functionality to groups. In fact, the biggest difference is that groups have a Members property, whereas Organizational Roles have an Occupant property within the Identification property (see Figure 15.18).

Figure 15.18
Users are made occupants of an Organizational Role.

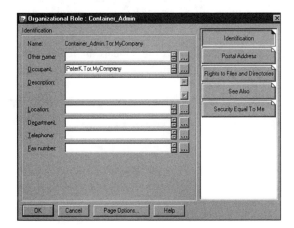

Notice that the other properties shown in Figure 15.18 are similar to the ones available for Container, Group, and User objects. However, you cannot associate ZENworks application objects or policy package objects with an Organizational Role. All Organizational Role properties apply only to the occupants of the Organizational Role.

Tip #123 from
Gally

Due to the similarity between Groups and Organizational Roles, it is a common practice to use Groups for assigning file-system rights and Organizational Roles for assigning NDS rights. Then you can tell by looking at an object in NWAdmn32 what its function is.

USING ALIAS OBJECTS

Alias objects are NDS leaf objects. Alias objects are generally created as a convenience for users or network administrators so that they don't have to navigate throughout the NDS Tree looking for objects they commonly access or manage. An Alias object is simply an object that "points" to the original object.

Figure 15.19 shows the screen used to create an Alias object—the Create Alias dialog box. The alias is required to have a name; additionally, you must browse the NDS Tree to select the object that the alias will point to. As shown in Figure 15.19, VOL1 will be the alias name and will point to ("alias") the original VOL1 object in Dal.MyCompany.

Figure 15.19
Both the Alias Name
and Aliased Object
are required before
an Alias object can be
created.

Notice in Figure 15.20 that the Alias icon is the same as the icon for the original object (in this case the Volume object) but also contains a "mask" icon to designate this as the alias.

Figure 15.20
An alias icon has
been created for the
VOL1 Volume object.

Alias icon ⌐

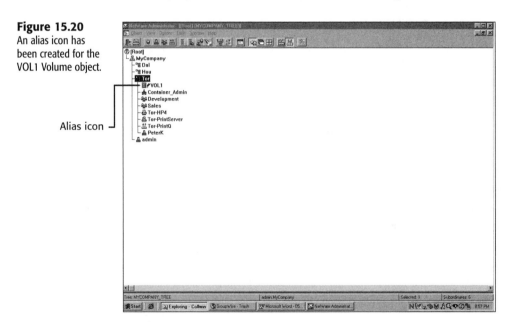

There are mixed opinions on the need for aliases. One opinion is that a good NDS design alleviates the need for the use of Alias objects and that Alias objects just increase the size of the NDS database (although very minimally). The opposing opinion is that they should be used where needed as a convenience for users and network administrators. The one case in which an Alias object is very useful is after NDS containers are moved, which is especially common after NDS Tree Merges are done (discussed in Chapter 16).

Alias objects can reference any other NDS object, including another alias. This process is referred to as *dereferencing*, because if an alias references another alias, the result is that the "aliased" alias still points to the original object.

The properties for an Alias object are the same as the properties on the original object. If you make a change to one of the alias' properties, the change is actually being made to the original object. Again, the alias is simply a pointer to the original object.

CREATING USERS WITH UIMPORT

UIMPORT allows you to create, delete, and rename users in NDS from an existing user database, possibly one that has been created for (or can be exported from) another application. Additionally, UIMPORT allows you to modify user properties.

To use UIMPORT, you must first get the database information into a delimited ASCII text file. The comma is the default delimiter used by UIMPORT. This comma-delimited text file is called the UIMPORT Data File. The following is an example of a Data File:

> **Note**
>
> The spaces have been added between the two records to make this easier to read; you should remove them before running UIMPORT to avoid creating a "blank" record. Also there should be no carriage return between the fields in each record (word-wrap caused the ones below).

```
UIMPORT Data File: DATA.TXT
Specker,Sally,A,1234 Specker Circle,Dallas,
Texas,75222,Senior Consultant,972-555-1212

Barker,Mike,A,4321 Barker Lane,Dallas,
Texas,75444,President,972-555-2345
```

When this Data File is read through UIMPORT, a comma will indicate a new property to be added to the User object in NDS.

Next you must create a UIMPORT Control File. In this Control File, you set parameters to control things such as whether UIMPORT should create new users and the context these users should be created in, or whether UIMPORT should update or delete existing users. The Control File is also where you can change the default comma delimiter to a different character, by using the Separator parameter. Finally, the Control File contains the fields that "match up" with the information in the Data File. Following is an example of a Control File:

```
UIMPORT Control File: CONTROL.TXT
Import control
       Name context=.DAL.MYCOMPANY
       Create home directory=y
       Home directory path="USERS"
       Home directory volume=".VOL1_DAL-NW5-FS1.DAL.MYCOMPANY"
       Import Mode = B
       Separator = ,
Fields
       Last name
       Name
       Skip
```

```
Skip
Skip
Skip
Skip
Title
Telephone
```

After the Data and Control Files have been properly set up, you simply run the UIMPORT utility to create these users in NDS. UIMPORT.EXE is in the SYS:PUBLIC directory. To run UIMPORT for this example, type this at the DOS prompt:

UIMPORT CONTROL.TXT DATA.TXT

Sally and Mike will be the two user objects created (as a result of the Import Mode = B statement in the Control File). Their user accounts will be created in the DAL.MYCOMPANY container (as a result of the Name Context statement in the Control File).

Tip #125 from	Use the Fully Distinguished Name (FDN) for any NDS objects you reference in the Control File, as shown previously for both the Name Context and the Home Directory entries. If you don't use the FDN, the objects will be created in your current context.
Sally	

Home directories will be created for Sally and Mike beneath the DAL-NW5-FS1 file server's VOL1:USERS directory. Middle initial and address information is not required for users in NDS; therefore, Skip was used to ignore these fields in the Data File. Both Sally and Mike's Title and Telephone Number will be entered as User properties in NDS.

The parameters you can use with the Import Mode statement are as listed here:

- B, which updates existing properties of user objects with the values from the Data File. The B value also creates user objects even if there is no corresponding user in NDS.
- C, which creates user objects only. If a user listed in the Data File already exists in NDS, the data in the Data File is ignored for this object.
- R, which removes user objects listed in the Data File.
- U, which updates data only for existing user objects.

For more information on UIMPORT, refer to the Novell documentation.

SEARCHING NDS

This chapter has shown you how to create some of the common objects and these objects' properties in NDS. Now you need a way to search NDS for this information. Both NWAdmn32 and NLIST provide this functionality.

USING NWADMN32 TO SEARCH NDS

As an example, let's say you are concerned with security; specifically, you think that someone has been made security equivalent to the Admin account. You have just learned in this chapter that all users have a Security Equal To property; therefore, you can search NDS for this property to see whether a user in the Tree has this set to the Admin user.

To search for objects, their properties, and the values of these properties in NWAdmn32, simply select the Search option in the Object menu. Then select the appropriate search criteria (see Figure 15.21).

Figure 15.21
Searching NDS to find users who are security equivalent to Admin.

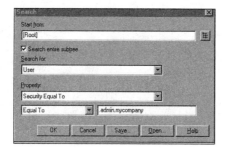

In Figure 15.21, the search will start from the [Root] and search the entire Tree looking for User objects that have a Security Equal To property with the value of .admin.mycompany. Notice that the browser icon next to Start From allows you to browse the NDS Tree to select the container you want to start the search from. Additionally, the "drop-down boxes next to Search For and Property allow you to pick the object and property from a list.

> **Caution**
>
> Searching the entire NDS Tree from the [Root] down will cause this search to go across your company's WAN links, assuming that your NDS database is partitioned and replicated to other sites.

In Figure 15.22, the Search window in the middle is the result of the search settings from Figure 15.21. When BrettS is double-clicked in this middle window, the User window on the right immediately brings up property information for BrettS. From this window, you can now remove Admin from his Security Equal To property.

USING NLIST TO SEARCH NDS

NLIST.EXE (in the SYS:PUBLIC directory) is a command-line utility that also has searching capabilities. With NLIST (as with any command-line utility) you must type in the proper syntax in order for the search to be successful versus using the drop-down lists available with NWAdmn32. This is how you would use NLIST for the example previously illustrated:

```
CX /r
NLIST user where "security equal to" = .admin.mycompany /s
```

/r changes context to the [Root] and /s searches all subcontainers.

Figure 15.22
NWAdmn32 allows you to see and change the search results.

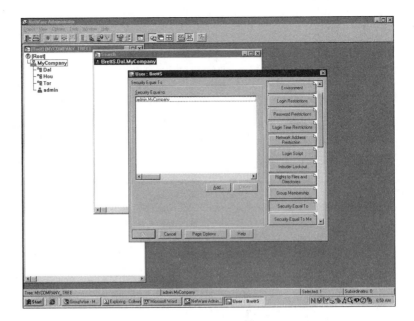

The output is shown here:

```
Object Class: User
Current context: Dal.MyCompany
User name= The name of the user
Dis      = Login disabled
Log exp  = The login expiration date, 0 if no expiration date
Pwd      = Yes if passwords are required
Pwd exp  = The password expiration date, 0 if no expiration date
Uni      = Yes if unique passwords are required
Min      = The minimum password length, 0 if no minimum


User Name                               Dis  Log Exp Pwd  Pwd Exp Uni Min
-------------------------------------------------------------------------
BrettS                                  No  00/00/00 No  00/00/00 No   0
One User object was found in this context.

One User object was found.
```

You would now need to use NWAdmn32 to remove BrettS's security equivalence to Admin, because NLIST does not have this capability.

PROJECT: EXPERIMENT WITH NWADMN32 AND NLIST

When you have a grasp on this chapter, try the following projects:

- Experiment with the searching capabilities in NWAdmn32 to see how easy it is to get information on objects and their properties.

- Type `NLIST /?` to see the other options available for using the NLIST utility. A nice feature of NLIST is that you can send the output to a text file, such as

  `NLIST USER /s > users.txt`

  which lists all user objects from your current context and below and places the output in a file called `users.txt`. Remember to do a `cx /r` if you want this search to start from the [Root] of the Tree.

- If you like the functionality within UIMPORT, take a look at Novell Consulting's OIMPORT/OEXPORT (Object Import and Object Export) utilities that are available for purchase from `http://consulting.novell.com/products/oimport/index.html`.

## CHAPTER 16

MANAGING NDS RIGHTS, PARTITIONS, AND REPLICAS

In this chapter

CONTROLLING ACCESS TO OBJECTS AND THEIR PROPERTIES

In Chapter 15, "Creating, Managing, and Using NDS Objects," you learned how to create objects and modify these objects' properties using NWAdmn32. Obviously, you want to ensure that only the appropriate users (designated as NDS administrators) have the rights to do this type of NDS administration. Additionally, you might want to control specifically what these NDS administrators can and cannot do in NDS. All of this is accomplished with NDS rights.

Although this chapter discusses only NDS rights, it is important that you understand the other three levels of NetWare security and the order they are implemented in, which are as follows:

- Login level of security (discussed in Chapter 18, "Implementing Security")
- NDS level of security (discussed in this chapter)
- File System level of security (discussed in Chapter 18)

As an example, let's say that a user wants to use NWAdmn32 to add a user object in NDS. They must first log in with a valid user account and password, and meet any login restrictions that might have been placed on their account. After a successful login, this user account must have the appropriate file-system rights to run NWAdmn32.EXE. And finally, a user must have the appropriate NDS rights to create objects in NDS. This example should help you understand the relationship between the three levels of security.

Although NDS and File System security are two discrete systems that are discussed separately in this book, the concepts and terminology used in both of them are very similar. NDS rights, however, generally are given to a smaller population of users than file-system rights are. This is, of course, because you don't want all users to be able to manipulate the NDS database, whereas most users need access to the data and applications stored on a NetWare volume.

Tip #126 from	All users will be able to execute NWAdmn32 due to their default file-system rights of Read and File Scan to SYS:PUBLIC; however, what users can and cannot do with NWAdmn32 is strictly governed by their NDS rights.
Gally	

NDS contains objects and these objects have properties. NDS security is very granular in that you can control what users can do with these objects (via NDS object rights) and what users can do to these objects' properties (via NDS property rights). Table 16.1 shows the NDS object rights and a description of what they do.

TABLE 16.1   NDS OBJECT RIGHTS

Right	Description
Supervisor (S)	Grants all rights to an NDS object. Additionally, this right grants all rights to all properties of an NDS object.
Browse (B)	Grants the right to see NDS objects.
Create (C)	Grants the right to create NDS objects. This right can be given only to container objects.
Delete (D)	Grants the right to delete NDS objects.
Rename (R)	Grants the rights to rename NDS objects.
Inheritable (I)	NDS object rights will flow down the Tree even without this right, so this right is currently ineffective. This right can be given only to container objects. This right is automatically assigned when you grant any of the preceding five object rights.

PART

IV

CH

16

Tip #127 from
Sally

The Create object right gives the rights to create *any* NDS object in a container; that is, there is currently no way with NWAdmn32 to give the rights to create just a specific type of object.

Object rights are usually assigned in combinations to give appropriate access to NDS objects. For example, if EmilyS is granted the Browse and Create object rights to the HOU.MYCOMPANY container, EmilyS would be able to browse (see) all objects and create new objects in HOU. Additionally, because object rights flow down the Tree, EmilyS's Browse and Create object rights will apply to any subcontainers and objects beneath HOU. With this rights assignment of just Browse and Create, the only objects EmilyS will be able to delete or rename will be the ones she created herself.

Tip #128 from
Sally

After a user creates an object, the user has all object and property rights to that object.

Whereas object rights control what you can do to NDS objects, property rights control what you can do to objects' properties. Property rights alone do not give the user any object rights. Table 16.2 shows the NDS property rights and a description of what they do.

TABLE 16.2 NDS PROPERTY RIGHTS

Right	Description
Supervisor (S)	Grants all rights to NDS properties.
Compare (C)	Grants the right to compare the value of NDS properties with another value.
Read (R)	Grants the right to read the value of NDS properties.
Write (W)	Grants the right to enter or change the value of NDS properties.
Add Self (A)	Grants the right to add yourself as a member of NDS properties.
Inheritable (I)	This right is automatically assigned when you grant any of the preceding five property rights using All Properties; however, as with NDS object rights, rights assigned to All Properties will flow down the Tree even without this Inheritable right. This right is not automatically assigned when you grant any of the preceding five property rights using Selected Properties but can be manually set so that individual property rights will flow down the Tree. This right can be given only to container objects.

Property rights are also usually assigned in combinations to give users appropriate access to NDS properties. In fact, if you give a user just the Read right, the Compare right is implied (given). Additionally, if you give a user just the Write right, the Add Self right is implied (given).

With property rights, you can give rights to All Properties of an object, or you can give rights to Selected Properties of an object.

For example, if EmilyS is given the Read and Write All Property rights to the HOU.MYCOMPANY container, EmilyS will be able to see and change all property information at HOU. Because the Compare property right is implied with Read, EmilyS will be able to use an NDS search utility (for example, NWAdmn32 or NLIST, as discussed in Chapter 15) to query (compare) an NDS property with a value and then see (read) the results of this query. Additionally, because All Property rights flow down the Tree, EmilyS's Read and Write property rights will apply to any subcontainers and objects beneath HOU.

Caution

The Write property right to All Properties is a very powerful rights assignment because the user can now change all properties on objects. The user can also make themselves (or another user) security equivalent to Admin with the Security Equal To property discussed in Chapter 15. Additionally, the Write property right to a File Server object gives the user all file-system rights for every volume that is physically located on that server. As such, you need to be very cautious with the Write property right.

If you want to give EmilyS the ability to see and modify just a specific property—for example, all user login scripts—you would use the Selected Properties option. If EmilyS is given the Read, Write, and Inheritable property rights to HOU.MYCOMPANY's login script property, EmilyS will be able to see and modify all user login scripts beneath HOU.

Tip #129 from *Sally*	The Inheritable property right for Selected Properties is a new feature with the DS.NLM in NetWare 5. This feature allows users to perform container role-based administration—for example, just the necessary rights to modify login scripts (as just discussed previously) or to change user passwords. Selected property rights cannot be inherited with the DS.NLM in NetWare 4.

TRUSTEE ASSIGNMENTS

The previous examples discussed giving NDS rights to a user object. Actually, though, many types of objects can be granted rights. Objects that have been granted NDS rights are referred to as *trustees*, and the rights themselves are referred to as *trustee assignments*. In the first example given previously, then, it would be appropriate to say that EmilyS is a trustee of the HOU.MYCOMPANY container with the trustee assignment of Browse and Create object rights.

Granting individual user rights might not be the most efficient way to administer the network and definitely does not take advantage of the power of NDS containers, groups, and organizational roles. Therefore, when you make trustee assignments, try to start with the broadest categorization of users possible that needs the rights, and then work your way down as follows:

- **[Public]**—[Public] is a special type of NDS object that can be viewed only when granting rights. You will not see this object when browsing the Tree with NWAdmn32. [Public] would be used when NDS rights are needed for *every* user in the Tree. There is no way to exclude a user from inheriting the rights of [Public], so this method of granting rights should be used with caution.

- **Container Objects**—Trustee assignments can be given to any container object in the Tree (including the [Root]). When container trustee assignments are given, users in that container (and potentially all users in any subcontainers) will get the trustee assignment. The higher up in the Tree container assignments are made, the greater the number of users that can (potentially) get the rights assignment, thus making NDS rights administration easier to manage.

- **Groups or Organizational Roles**—Trustee assignments can be given to groups or organizational roles when a container-based trustee assignment is too broad. In this case, any user who is made a member of a group (or an occupant of an organizational role) will get the trustee assignment given to these objects. If a user is a member of two or more groups, their rights are cumulative; the same is true if a user is an occupant of two or more organizational roles.

Tip #130 from *Sally*	Previous versions of NDS had a limitation that a user could be a member of only 64 groups; in this case, the 65th and higher group memberships were not recognized by NDS. This limitation has been removed in NetWare 5.

- **Individual Users**—Trustee assignments can be made on a user-by-user basis.

- **Security Equivalence**—Another method that can be used to grant NDS rights is *security equivalences*. Security equivalences are not transitive; that is, if UserA is security equivalent to UserB, and UserB is security equivalent to UserC, UserA is *not* security equivalent to UserC. Also, security equivalences are not commutable; that is, if UserA is security equivalent to UserB, UserB is *not* security equivalent to UserA. Finally, if the only way a user is getting their NDS rights is through a security equivalence and the account that the user is security equivalent to gets deleted, all the user's rights will be immediately lost. It is for these reasons that security equivalence should be used only for temporary, short-term purposes.

Tip #131 from
Sally

If you want to have a second (backup) user account to manage the entire NDS Tree (which is recommended), do not make this account security equivalent to Admin. The Admin account can be deleted and its rights can be restricted. Rather, give this account a trustee assignment of all five object and property rights to the [Root].

DEFAULT NDS RIGHTS

Before assigning any NDS rights, you should recognize the default NDS rights that are automatically assigned. You can view trustee assignments for an object in NWAdmn32 by selecting that object, right-clicking, and selecting Trustees of This Object. In Figure 16.1, this process was followed to show the default NDS rights given at [Root].

Figure 16.1
These are the default NDS object rights assigned at [Root]; no default NDS property rights are assigned at [Root].

As you can see in the left screen of Figure 16.1, [Public] is granted the Browse and Inheritable object rights to [Root]; therefore, all users can see the entire NDS Tree. This default NDS rights assignment will be sufficient for most users on the network. You might need to assign additional NDS property rights depending on the NDS objects that users will need to access. For example, a user needs the Read property right to the Path property on a Directory Map object and the Read property right to the Login Script property of a Profile object.

Tip #132 from
Sally

If you want to ensure that all users in the Tree have the necessary rights to use all NDS objects, give [Public] the Read All Properties rights to the [Root].

As you can see in the right screen of Figure 16.1, the system-created Admin account is given the Supervisor and Inheritable object rights to [Root]; therefore, this account has all NDS object and property rights and all file-system rights to all volumes on all file servers.

Tip #133 from
Sally

Although NDS and File System security are two separate systems, there is one overlap between the two: When the Supervisor object right is given and flows down the Tree, this Supervisor object right will be inherited by all File Server objects in the Tree. When this happens, the Supervisor object right "spills over" into the file system, giving all file-system rights to all volumes on these servers. Therefore, use caution when assigning the Supervisor object right. If you assign all other object rights (that is, Browse, Create, Delete, and Rename), this will give the same effective NDS rights but will not have the "spill-over" effect into the file system. There are no file-system rights that will automatically give NDS rights.

When a user object is created, that user is given rights to itself. As you can see in the left screen of Figure 16.2, a new user is given Read to its All Properties; additionally, as you can see in the right screen of Figure 16.2, a new user is given Read and Write to its Login Script property.

Figure 16.2
A user by default gets these NDS property rights to itself.

Note

A new user is also given Read and Write to its Print Job Configuration property, although this is not shown in Figure 16.2. Also notice in Figure 16.2 that to show the rights given to individual NDS properties, you must select the radio button next to "Selected Properties" and then scroll through the list of properties. A check-mark will appear next to individual properties that have been given rights.

With these default property rights, users can see all of their own property information and can write (make changes) to their own login script and print-job configurations. Essentially, the Read property assignment made to All Properties was "overwritten" by the two specific individual property assignments of Read and Write to login script and print-job configuration only; all other properties for the user are just readable.

When a container is created, it will receive Read property rights to both its login script and its print-job configuration properties. Because the users in this container are security equivalent to the container, these users can read and run the login script and any print-job configurations set on the container.

CALCULATING EFFECTIVE RIGHTS

Users' *effective rights* to an object are what they can do to that object. You can calculate effective rights to an object by using NWAdmn32 and selecting that object, right-clicking, and selecting Trustees of This Object. From this window, click the Effective Rights button and use the browse button (next to Object Name) to walk the Tree and select the user (or other) object you want to calculate effective rights for. In Figure 16.3, this process was followed to show the effective rights that NewUser has to its parent container of HOU.MYCOMPANY.

Figure 16.3
A user by default has these effective NDS object and All Property rights to its parent container.

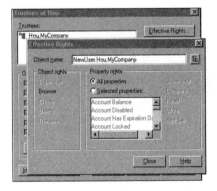

NewUser's effective Browse right to HOU.MYCOMPANY comes from NewUser's implied membership in [Public], which, as was shown in Figure 16.1, automatically gets the Browse and Inheritable object rights to the [Root]. Therefore, NewUser has its Browse effective rights due to NDS inheritance. Although not shown in Figure 16.3, NewUser by default also has effective Read and Write property rights to HOU's login script and print-job configuration properties.

Users can get their effective NDS rights in two ways:

- **NDS Inheritance**—This is the process whereby a user inherits rights that were given to a container object that is higher in the Tree than its user object. NDS inheritance was just demonstrated with the example used in Figure 16.3.

- **A Direct Trustee Assignment**—A direct trustee assignment is an explicit assignment made to an NDS object, as shown in Figure 16.4.

Figure 16.4
EmilyS is a direct trustee of HOU.MYCOMPANY with the Supervisor and Inheritable object rights.

There is one slight difference between NDS inheritance and a direct trustee assignment. The difference is that a direct trustee assignment will always equal the user's effective rights at the container where the direct trustee assignment was made. For example, in Figure 16.4, EmilyS's effective rights to HOU.MYCOMPANY will be the Supervisor object right that she was explicitly given here.

However, EmilyS's effective rights to the subcontainers of HOU.MYCOMPANY (that is, SALES AND TESTING) may not necessarily be Supervisor object rights. This is because every container object (and leaf object) in NDS has an Inheritable Rights Filter (IRF) property. By default, this IRF allows all rights to "flow through" and be inherited beneath. You can view the IRF on an object by selecting that object, right-clicking, selecting Trustees of This Object, and clicking the Inherited Rights Filter button. The default IRF for the SALES.HOU.MYCOMPANY container is shown in Figure 16.5.

Figure 16.5
The down arrows and the check-marks next to all rights show that this IRF allows all rights to be inherited.

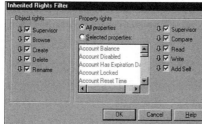

Since all object and all property rights are allowed to be inherited at the SALES.HOU.MYCOMPANY container, EmilyS's effective rights at SALES.HOU.MYCOMPANY will be the Supervisor object right that was granted to her at HOU.MYCOMPANY.

If you look at Figure 16.6, the Supervisor object right has been filtered at the TESTING.HOU.MYCOMPANY container. Therefore, EmilyS will lose the Supervisor object right that she was granted at HOU.MYCOMPANY. However, EmilyS will still have her Browse object right (from [Public]) to see this TESTING container, because the IRF allows the Browse object right to be inherited here.

Figure 16.6
The Supervisor object right has been blocked with an IRF; therefore, this right cannot be inherited at this container.

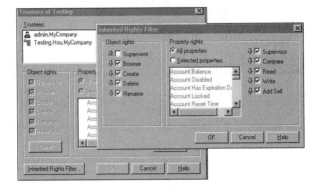

Caution

Actually, in this case, Admin will also lose its Supervisor object right that was granted at [Root]. This is because an IRF is not specific to an individual user; rather, an IRF blocks all rights that are being inherited by any user, including Admin.

If you look again at Figure 16.6, you will see that I have protected the Admin account from being affected by this IRF by making Admin a direct trustee of TESTING.HOU.MYCOMPANY. Although not shown in Figure 16.6, Admin was given a direct trustee assignment of all five object rights and all five property rights. This direct trustee assignment, then, gives them all rights at TESTING regardless of the IRF that was set here. A direct trustee assignment supersedes the IRF, and a direct trustee assignment always equals the effective rights for that container. As its name implies, an IRF filters rights that are being inherited; an IRF does not filter a direct trustee assignment.

Tip #134 from
Sally

Although the Supervisor NDS object and property rights can be blocked with an IRF, the Supervisor file-system right cannot be blocked with an IRF.

There is another (and potentially less dangerous) way to block EmilyS's Supervisor object right at the TESTING.HOU.MYCOMPANY container instead of using an IRF. This is by giving EmilyS a direct trustee assignment to TESTING.HOU.MYCOMPANY of just the Browse object right. EmilyS's effective rights to TESTING (and any subcontainers) will, therefore, be just Browse.

ASSIGNING NDS RIGHTS

You assign NDS rights with NWAdmn32 by selecting the object you want to give the rights to, right-clicking that object, and selecting Trustees of This Object. The Trustees of dialog appears (see Figure 16.7). From this screen, click the Add Trustee button, which enables you to walk the NDS Tree to select the user (or other object) that will receive rights to the selected object.

Figure 16.7
Giving a user a direct trustee assignment to a container.

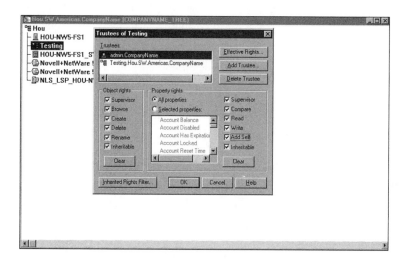

Tip #135 from
Sally

You can select an object and drag it on top of the object you want to give it rights to. This presents you with the same dialog box shown in Figure 16.7. Although there is no command-line utility from Novell for assigning NDS rights, the NDSRight utility available from `http://www.dreamlan.com` was written for this purpose.

In Figure 16.7 the Admin user has been made a direct trustee of TESTING with all object and property rights. If you want to remove this assignment, you simply select the Admin account and then click the Delete Trustee button.

WORKING WITH PARTITIONS AND REPLICAS

Although the primary tool for setting up and managing NDS is NWAdmn32, the tool used for creating NDS partitions and replicas is NDS Manager (NDSMgr32.EXE). NDSMgr32 is a standalone, 32-bit Windows utility located in the SYS:PUBLIC\WIN32 directory.

Tip #136 from
Sally

NSDMgr32 can also be run as an NWAdmn32 snap-in. To do this, simply copy the NMSNAP32.DLL from SYS:PUBLIC\WIN32 to SYS:PUBLIC\WIN32\SNAPINS. The next time NWAdmn32 is launched, NDS Manager will be accessible from the Tools menu.

→ For more information about partitions and replicas and the guidelines for using them, **see** Chapter 6, "Designing the Novell Directory Services Tree," **p. 135**

Tip #137 from	Ensure that partitioning and replication operations are performed from only one workstation at a time. This helps to better regulate partition actions.
Sally	

Only NDS container objects can be partitioned. And, you need the Supervisor object right to the container where you want to create the partition (this container is referred to as the *partition root object*); having just the Browse, Create, Delete, and Rename object rights will not allow you to create a partition. Additionally, you need the appropriate file-system rights to be able to create (place) a replica on a server, because ultimately you are writing information to the SYS:_NETWARE directory when you place a replica on another server.

Before we discuss how to partition a Tree, you should recognize the partitions and replicas that are automatically created.

AUTOMATICALLY CREATED PARTITIONS AND REPLICAS

The first server installed (not upgraded) into NDS will create the [Root], Organization, and any subsequent container objects defined during installation. The NDS database at this point is referred to as having just the [Root] partition, containing all objects within it. Assuming that you don't partition the [Root] any further, the second and third servers installed into this Tree will receive Read-Write replicas of the [Root]. Any additional servers installed will not automatically receive any replicas.

Now let's assume that a Tree has been partitioned. Even in this case, the same logic holds true as stated previously; that is, the first server installed (not upgraded) into an existing partition receives a Master replica of that partition, and the second and third servers installed into that partition receive Read-Write replicas. Any additional servers installed into this partition will not automatically receive any replicas.

You can see, then, that the NetWare installation utility "guides" you toward the three-replica rule discussed in Chapter 6, "Designing the Novell Directory Services Tree."

Now, if a server is upgraded from NetWare 3 and placed into an NDS Tree, this server will always contain a replica of the partition in which it is installed in order to support Bindery Services (discussed later in this chapter). This is true even if there are already three replicas of this partition.

Note	Bindery Services is the number-one reason for over-replication. After upgrading NetWare 3 servers into the Tree, you should revisit partitioning and replication to ensure that the appropriate scheme is being implemented.

If a server is upgraded from NetWare 4 to NetWare 5 and already contains replicas, this server will keep these replicas.

PARTITIONING AND REPLICATING NDS

The NDS Tree that was designed for CompanyName is shown in Figure 16.8 (this was created in Chapter 6). Notice that NDSMgr32 shows only container and server objects in the Tree (and not any other leaf objects). This is because you can partition only container-class objects. Additionally, NDSMgr32 shows the SLP Scope and NLS objects because these are container-class objects (although they generally do not need to be partitioned).

PART

IV

CH

16

Figure 16.8
NDSMgr32 shows how an NDS Tree is partitioned.

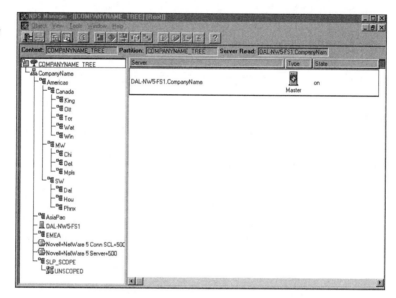

As shown in Figure 16.8, there are no other partitions except for [Root] (the green-and-yellow icon preceding the COMPANYNAME_TREE is the icon used to represent an NDS partition). Figure 16.8 also shows that the Master replica of [Root] is stored on the DAL-NW5-FS1 server.

Following the guidelines discussed in Chapter 6, the CompanyName_Tree should be partitioned at each of the 11 city sites: King, Ott, Tor, Wat, Win, Chi, Det, Mpls, Dal, Hou, and Phnx. This is because these 11 sites are physically connected to each other via WAN links.

To create a partition in NDSMgr32, select the container object from the left pane shown in Figure 16.8, right-click, and then select Create Partition. Figure 16.9 shows the result of these steps for the DAL container.

Figure 16.9
The DAL container is
partitioned.

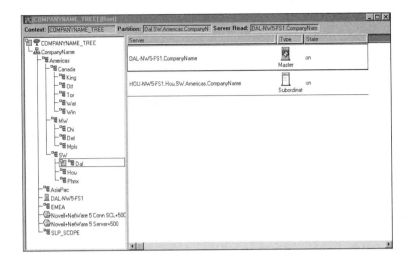

Notice in Figure 16.9 that a Master replica of DAL was placed on the DAL-NW5-FS1 file server. A Master replica was created because this was DAL's first partition. Additionally, this replica was placed on the DAL-NW5-FS1 server because this is the server that holds the parent partition (that is, [Root]) of DAL. Also notice in Figure 16.9 the icon is now in front of DAL, indicating that DAL is a partition.

In Figure 16.9, also notice that the HOU-NW5-FS1 server holds a subordinate reference replica of DAL. Subordinate references are created on servers that hold a replica (either Master, Read-Write, or Read-Only) of a parent partition but not a replica of a child partition. In this case, the HOU-NW5-FS1 has a Read-Write replica of [Root] but does not have a replica of [Root]'s child partition, DAL. Therefore, HOU-NW5-FS1 automatically gets a subordinate reference replica to DAL. Subordinate references are necessary to "glue" together the partitioned NDS Tree.

The remaining 10 city containers for CompanyName should now be partitioned.

After the partitioning has been completed for each site connected by a WAN link, the proper replica placement needs to be determined. In the "perfect" scenario, each city will have three servers to house the recommended three replicas for their site (one Master and two Read-Writes). However, if there were just two servers in a city, the three-replica guideline could be overlooked and one server could hold the Master while the second held the Read-Write. You will still have two copies of the partition (not including your backup of NDS). Two replicas for a partition are generally adequate (the exception being that there should always be three replicas of [Root]). However, if you are uncomfortable with just two replicas, you can place the third replica across a WAN link on another server.

Now let's consider the single-server cities. You should never have just one copy of a partition; therefore, a second (and optionally third) copy could be placed across a WAN link on another server. If you have many single-server cities, you will probably want to consider using a Dedicated Replica Server.

DEDICATED REPLICA SERVER

As discussed in Chapter 6, a *Dedicated Replica Server* is simply a NetWare server that holds replicas; it is not generally a server accessed by users on the network for running applications or storing their files. Dedicated Replica Servers should be placed at a central location in your WAN infrastructure and optimally at a location where network support personnel are available to administer them, if needed.

There are differing opinions on whether to place the Master replicas on the Dedicated Replica Server or on the respective local server at each site. Although there is no "wrong" approach, there are some issues to consider. If all Master replicas are placed on one Replica Server and this server goes down (or worse yet, crashes and needs to be reinstalled), it is a more difficult NDS recovery process when this server contains all Master replicas. Of course, this impact can be offset somewhat if you have two Dedicated Replica Servers with the Master replicas split among them.

PART

IV

CH

16

> **Note**
>
> Although you could restore NDS from backup, this information will probably not be as up-to-date as the NDS information contained in the current replicas. Ideally, with the proper NDS partition and replication scheme, you will never have to rely on an NDS backup.

The "pro" opinion for having Master replicas on one (or two) Dedicated Replica Servers is that partitioning operations will (theoretically) be completed faster. However, partitioning operations are generally not done on a day-to-day basis.

You will need to weigh the disaster recovery versus the speed of partitioning operations to make the proper decision on where to place your Master replicas when using Dedicated Replica Servers.

One other notable factor to consider is that the ZENworks Remote Control feature (discussed in Chapter 24, "ZENworks") will be performed off the Master replica holding the Workstation object you are remote-controlling. In this case, the remote control process will probably be faster when this Master replica is local.

You can see, then, that partitioning is a fairly clear-cut process, whereas the replication scheme depends on the number of servers you have at each site. Just remember that the goal is to replicate locally (where possible) to avoid NDS synchronization traffic across WAN links. Any change you make to NDS must be synchronized with all other servers holding a replica of the partition where this change was made (this list of servers holding a common replica is referred to as a *replica ring*). In addition, all servers in a replica ring will perform a "heartbeat" (by default every 30 minutes) to ensure partition integrity with the servers in the replica ring (including subordinate reference replicas). It is for these reasons that you should try to keep the replica ring local, thereby reducing traffic on your WAN links.

Tip #138 from
Sally

WAN Traffic Manager is an NLM (WTM.NLM) that ships with NetWare 5. WAN Traffic Manager is a policy-based service that allows a network administrator to control NDS traffic in a WAN environment. You can control communications based on time, traffic type, destination of traffic, and other configurable settings. For more information, see TID 2942079, "What is and how to configure WANMAN in NW5," available from http://support.novell.com.

If you want to see the replicas a server holds, simply select that server from the left pane, as shown in Figure 16.10.

Figure 16.10
Viewing the replicas on the DAL-NW5-FS1 server.

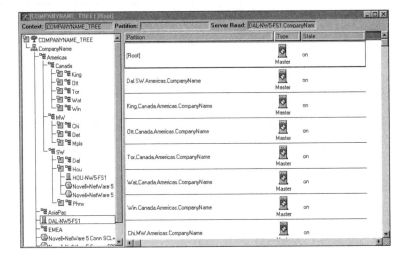

In Figure 16.10, you can see that DAL-NW5-FS1 holds the Master replicas for the [Root] and all the 11 partitions that were just created.

If at any time you need to change the replica placement, simply right-click the partition and select Add Replica. You will then be presented with the screen shown in Figure 16.11.

You would use the browser button next to Server Name to walk the NDS Tree and select the server (in this case HOU-NW5-FS1) you want to place this replica on.

To change the replica type, select the server from the left pane, right-click the replica you want to change, and then select Change Type.

Figure 16.11
Placing a Read-Write replica of the HOU partition on the HOU-NW5-FS1 server.

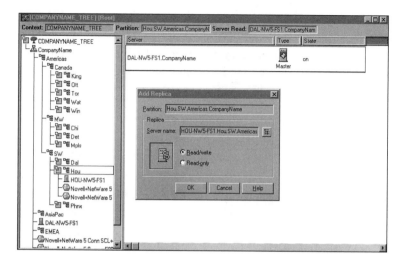

Tip #139 from
Gally

You cannot change a Master to a Read-Write; rather, you will have to select the Read-Write and then change it to a Master, which will automatically demote the existing Master to a Read-Write because you can have only one Master replica per partition.

After the 11 lower-level city containers have been partitioned, the [Root] partition contains the remaining non-partitioned container objects as shown in Figure 16.12.

Figure 16.12
The [Root] partition for CompanyName Tree now contains just the container objects in black, which denotes they are not partitioned.

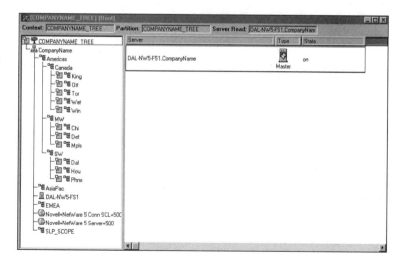

In Figure 16.12, the [Root] partition primarily contains just the placeholder OUs that were created to keep this Tree in a pyramid shape. Because these placeholder OUs have no objects in them, you can keep them as part of the [Root] partition. Another option would be to partition the placeholder OUs and replicate them on servers in site locations to facilitate Tree-walking. For example, if a user in PHNX always needs to access resources in HOU, this user gets to the resources in HOU by Tree-walking up to SW and then back down to HOU. As shown previously in Figure 16.12, the SW container is part of the [Root] partition stored on the DAL server. Therefore, this user in PHNX would Tree-walk through the server in Dallas to get to the server in Houston. In this case, you could consider partitioning SW and placing a replica on a server in HOU.

Although this type of granularity is not always needed when you're partitioning and replicating, it should give you a good idea of the available options. This type of fine-tuning is dependent on user access needs to other resources and the speed and reliability of your WAN links. Changes like this can be made at any time in NDSMgr32, so it is not something that has to be immediately decided—or permanently left in place. Partition and replica placement can be made on an as-needed basis as your network/NDS Tree grows.

REPAIRING THE NDS DATABASE

DSREPAIR.NLM ships with NetWare 5 and is the utility used to diagnose and repair problems with the NDS database on a single server. DSREPAIR does not correct problems on NDS databases on other remote servers.

Tip #140 from
Sally

> NDS errors are numbered as -6xx or -7xx. The LogicSource for NDS, available from Novell, contains complete documentation on what these error codes mean and possible solutions for resolving them. If you are ever unsure about the appropriate way to resolve an NDS problem, it is best to contact Novell Technical Support or another authorized Novell partner for assistance.

Many times, you become aware of NDS errors while using the utilities for managing NDS (that is, NWAdmn32 or NDSMgr32). These two utilities generally display the error code and the probable cause for the error (see Figure 16.13).

In this case, a partition operation was attempted before another partition operation was completed. This problem generally resolves itself if you give NDS time to complete the first partition operation. A DSREPAIR is probably not necessary here; also, do not down the server until this operation is completed.

Other errors might not resolve themselves (even if given enough time). In these cases, DSREPAIR can be run on the server that is generating these errors. If you look at the upper-right screen in Figure 16.13, you will see that NDSMgr32 reports the server that is being read. This would be the appropriate server, then, to run DSREPAIR on.

Figure 16.13
NDSMgr32 reporting
NDS error message
-654.

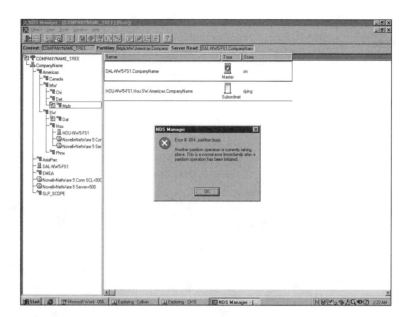

Tip #141 from
Sally

Ensure that you are using the appropriate DSREPAIR.NLM for your version of NDS
(DS.NLM). Generally, when a new DS.NLM is available, a new DSREPAIR.NLM is included
with it.

Since DSREPAIR is an NLM, it must be run from the file server console itself or through
RCONSOLE (which is discussed in Chapter 23 "Server Console Utilities"). Simply type the
command DSREPAIR which brings up the menu shown in Figure 16.14.

Figure 16.14
The DSREPAIR.NLM
main menu.

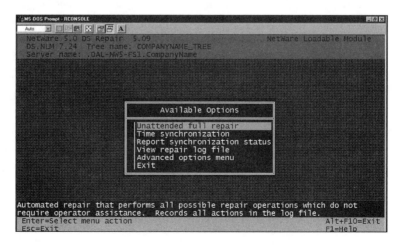

An Unattended Full Repair performs all repair operations (specifically all operations that do not require operator intervention) for the NDS replicas stored on this server only. After you run this option, the total number of errors will be reported in the upper-right portion of the screen. You should run this option until the number of errors is zero, because sometimes DSREPAIR.NLM cannot resolve all errors on the first pass. If you consistently get the same number of errors each time you run this utility, check the repair log by selecting View Repair Log File. This log file lists the NDS -6xx and -7xx errors, allowing you to pinpoint the possible problem (see Figure 16.15).

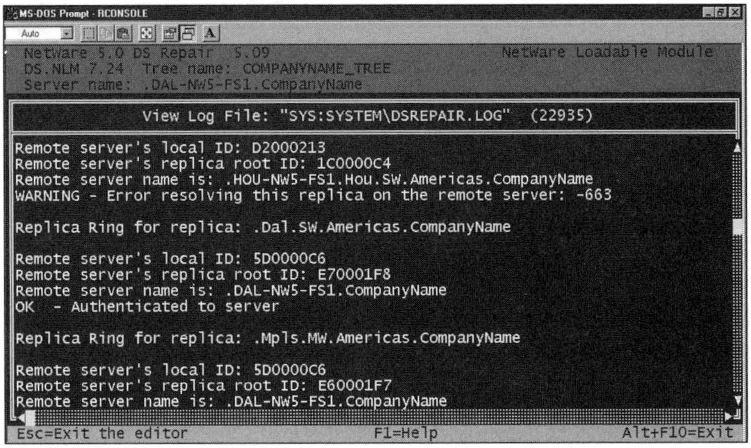

Figure 16.15
The DSREPAIR log file
(DSREPAIR.LOG) is
stored in SYS:SYSTEM.

In Figure 16.15, the Remote Server Name Is line indicates that the DAL server (on which DSREPAIR was run) could not communicate with the HOU-NW5-FS1 server during the repair process. This error was generated on the DAL server because it contains a replica of the HOU server. The error -663 beneath this line indicates that Directory Services is locked on the HOU-NW5-FS1 server. This error message could indicate that this server is busy with a partitioning operation or that this server's NDS database is currently locked because it is also performing a DSREPAIR function (as it was for this example).

Tip #142 from
Sally

Running an Unattended Full Repair locks the NDS database on that server. DSREPAIR displays a message alerting you to this fact.

Many times, the error messages you see after running a repair are -625 (Transport Failure). Such -625 errors indicate that a server tried to contact another server to synchronize to and was never able to reach the server. This problem could be as simple as a mismatch on the two protocols used between the servers or a problem with the server's LAN driver. The -625 error is probably the most common NDS error message.

The Time Synchronization option (refer to Figure 16.14) gathers time-synchronization information for all servers known to the local NDS database. If a replica of the [Root] partition is contained on the server, all servers in the Directory Tree are contacted for their time-synchronization information.

Tip #143 from *Gally*	When you're troubleshooting time-synchronization problems, it is recommended that you run the Time Synchronization option from a server that holds a replica of [Root], because [Root] will be able to contact all other replicas in the Tree. Again, DSREPAIR looks only at the servers known to its local database.

The output from the Time Synchronization option is shown in Figure 16.16, indicating that time is in sync between these two servers.

Figure 16.16
DSREPAIR time synchronization status is reported in the DSREPAIR.LOG file.

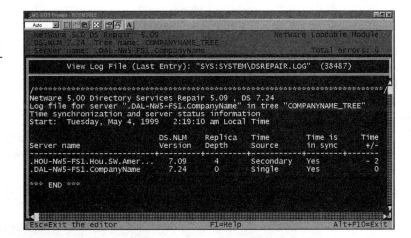

Notice in Figure 16.16 that the Time Synchronization option also shows the DS.NLM version that is running on these servers.

Tip #144 from *Gally*	NDSMgr32 has the capability to remotely update the DS.NLM on servers in the same NDS tree without having to visit that server or RConsole into that server to reload the new DS.NLM. This is done by selecting a server that contains the latest DS.NLM and then selecting Object, NDS Version, Update. A dialog box is then displayed allowing you to select the servers to receive this DS.NLM. The Object, Preferences, NDS Update Options should be set to Entire Subtree for this process to work as documented here.

> **Note**
>
> If the DS.NLM is included as part of a Support Pack, then the DS.NLM should be installed with that Support Pack, as there may be dependencies. NDSMgr32 is used to update a standalone DS.NLM, as discussed in the above Tip.

The Report Synchronization Status option looks at each partition on this server and at which servers hold replicas of these partitions (giving you, then, the Replica Ring information for this partition). Any NDS synchronization errors on the Replica Rings are reported. Additionally, this option shows the last time that all servers in the replica ring were synchronized. You can also obtain similar information when using NDSMgr32 by selecting a partition, right-clicking, and then selecting Information or Check Synchronization.

The View Repair Log File option tracks all actions performed by, and the results of, any repair operations. The default log file is SYS:SYSTEM\DSREPAIR.LOG. You can configure options for the log file by accessing Log File and Login Configuration in the Advanced Options menu.

The Advanced Options (shown in Figure 16.17) allow you to perform more detailed repair and analysis if the Unattended Repair option was not successful or if the output you received from the Unattended Repair option indicated that further troubleshooting was necessary.

Figure 16.17
DSREPAIR advanced options.

The following text discusses some of DSREPAIR's advanced options.

The Log File and Login Configuration option allows you to customize the size, name, and location of the DSREPAIR.LOG file. Additionally, you can select the name and password to be used when accessing some of the other Advanced options available within DSREPAIR.

The Repair Local DS Database option allows you to specify actions to occur when DSREPAIR is running—for example, whether to pause when errors are encountered and whether to exit DSREPAIR automatically after completion.

The Servers Known to This Database option indicates the servers that were found in the local NDS database, therefore representing the servers that will be contacted when DSRE-PAIR options are being used. From this main menu, you can see the file-server names and whether these servers are up or down. Additionally, selecting one of the servers in this list brings up another menu allowing you to perform server-specific operations, such as repairing network addresses to ensure that the servers in your network are broadcasting correct addresses. You can also choose Repair Network Addresses in NDSMgr32 within the Partition Continuity option.

Replica and Partition Operations lists all the replicas stored on this server, including the Replica Type and the state that the replica is in (that is, up, down, merging a partition, deleting a partition, and so on). Within this option, you can also change a replica type. These same operations can also be seen and performed in NDSMgr32.

PART

IV

CH

16

Tip #145 from	The main difference between DSREPAIR.NLM and NDSMgr32 is that DSREPAIR allows you
Gally	to perform operations only on that one server, whereas NDSMgr32 allows you to view the entire Tree, selecting the server or partition you want to perform the operation on.

The Global Schema Operations option is used during an NDS Tree Merge (discussed later in this chapter).

The Create a Database Dump File option creates a compressed file of an NDS database. You can either diagnose the damaged database yourself or send this dump file in to Novell Technical Services for analysis, if necessary.

Tip #146 from	Executing DSREPAIR -a will add items to the Advanced menu for further troubleshooting,
Gally	such as declaring a new time epoch. Some of these advanced options are needed when following the TIDs on Novell's support.novell.com Web site.

BINDERY SERVICES

For you to understand Bindery Services, a little NetWare history is in order. NetWare 3 (and NetWare 2, for that matter) did not use NDS as a data store for the resources available on the network. Rather, these versions of NetWare used the bindery. The *bindery* is a flat-file database and is not shared among other NetWare servers as NDS is. Rather, the objects in the bindery are server-specific, and any user that needs access to these resources must have a user account on that server. As an example, if there are eight NetWare 3 servers that a user needs access to, this user would require eight separate user accounts on these eight servers.

When NetWare 4 was released, Novell replaced the bindery with NDS. However, Novell realized that companies were running applications that were written to assume the existence of a NetWare bindery (including, at that time, Novell's own NETX Client software, which is not NDS-aware). Therefore, Bindery Services was "built in" to NDS for backward compatibility with bindery-dependent applications.

You can loosely compare the issues surrounding the use of Bindery Services with the issues discussed in Chapter 9, "Pure IP, Compatibility Mode, and Service Location Protocol," for moving to a Pure IP environment. In Chapter 9, you learned that moving to a Pure IP environment requires that there be no IPX-dependent applications on the network. Similarly, when NetWare 4 (with the introduction of NDS) first came out, moving to an all-NDS environment required eliminating any bindery-dependent applications. Because NDS has been available since the 1993 timeframe, chances are you can run applications that are now NDS-aware; if not, that is when you use Bindery Services.

Bindery Services must be set to the container where the bindery-dependent application (or the objects used by the application) exists. For example, if your tape-backup software is bindery based, the objects used by your tape-backup software would need to be placed in a container where Bindery Services has been enabled. This container is then referred to as the *bindery context*.

Tip #147 from	If your tape-backup software is not NDS-aware, you will not be able to back up the NDS database. Any bindery-dependent application should be replaced with an NDS-aware version as soon as possible so that you can fully leverage NDS.
Sally	

You set the bindery context on a server with the console command of SET BINDERY CONTEXT =, where you place the names of the containers you want to support Bindery Services after the =. A single NetWare server can support up to 16 containers running in Bindery Services mode. Bindery Services does not in any way impact the functioning of any NDS objects in these containers. So in the preceding example, if your tape-backup software placed objects in the O=MYCOMPANY container, you would type the following command on your NetWare 5 server:

```
SET BINDERY CONTEXT = .MYCOMPANY
```

Tip #148 from	A server must hold a Master or Read-Write replica of the container you set with the BINDERY CONTEXT command.
Sally	

To verify that the bindery context has been properly set, type the console command CONFIG. Do not rely on the output you receive after issuing the SET BINDERY CONTEXT console command. Figure 16.18 shows a server with multiple bindery contexts set.

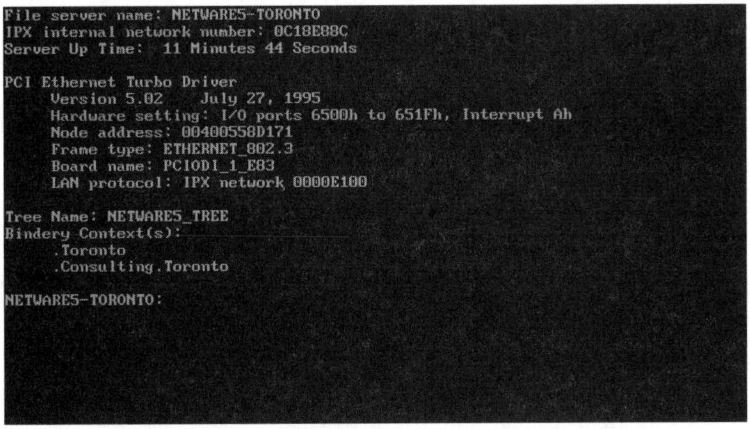

Figure 16.18
A server's bindery context is displayed by typing the console command CONFIG.

```
File server name: NETWARE5-TORONTO
IPX internal network number: 0C18E88C
Server Up Time:  11 Minutes 44 Seconds

PCI Ethernet Turbo Driver
     Version 5.02    July 27, 1995
     Hardware setting: I/O ports 6500h to 651Fh, Interrupt Ah
     Node address: 00400558D171
     Frame type: ETHERNET_802.3
     Board name: PCIODI_1_E83
     LAN protocol: IPX network 0000E100

Tree Name: NETWARE5_TREE
Bindery Context(s):
          .Toronto
          .Consulting.Toronto

NETWARE5-TORONTO:
```

Tip #149 from
Sally

The bindery context list is searched similar to the way that a DOS PATH statement is; that is, if Bindery Services encounters an object in the first context set, it does not search any other containers in the list. Although NDS object names can be the same as long as they are in different containers (because NDS always builds a fully distinguished name for every object), this is not true of the bindery. When two bindery contexts are set on a server, all objects in both of these contexts are seen together. Therefore, if you rely heavily on Bindery Services, you should ensure that these object names are unique across containers supporting Bindery Services.

Again, Bindery Services is not used much any more because most applications have been rewritten to support NDS, including Novell's Client software. A notable exception would be any print servers you might have that are not yet NDS-enabled.

SUPERVISOR ACCOUNT

When Bindery Services is enabled on a server, a Supervisor account is also available for this server. Supervisor is the name of the system-created "super user" account in the bindery. This Supervisor account is server-centric (unlike the Admin account, which is the super user account for the entire NDS Tree).

The Supervisor account is available for applications that require the Supervisor (and not the Admin) user privileges. For example, earlier versions of MONITOR.NLM locked the file-server console with a password. If this password was forgotten, it was the Supervisor (not Admin) password that could also be used to unlock the console. The Supervisor password on a server is the same as the password used to install NetWare 5 on that server (usually this is the Admin password). However, if Admin's password is later changed, that does not change the Supervisor password.

Tip #150 from	Document or make a note to change Supervisor passwords when you change the Admin
Gally	password. Or remember the original password used to install your NetWare 5 servers. Although this Supervisor account will probably not be needed, it is a good precaution to have this information documented.

MERGING NDS TREES

If your company merges business operations with another company that uses NDS, an NDS Tree Merge might be appropriate so that the combined company can share resources and management tasks throughout just one NDS Tree. NetWare 5 ships with a utility called DSMERGE.NLM for this purpose—that is, merging two NDS Trees together.

In the simplest sense, DSMERGE takes a "source" Tree and pushes it into the "target" Tree, the result being that all the objects in the source Tree will then be a part of the target Tree. The one exception to this is that the Tree Name from the source Tree will be gone.

The first thing to determine when doing a DSMERGE is which Tree will be the source and which Tree will be the target.

Tip #151 from	If one Tree is smaller than the other, this smaller Tree should be chosen as the source,
Gally	because there will then be fewer objects to push in and synchronize to the target Tree. Or if there are users in one Tree that make use of the Preferred Tree statement, this Tree could be the target (remember, the source Tree's name will be gone after the merge process).

After you have determined the source and target Trees, there are some prerequisites that must be met before an NDS Tree merge can be undertaken. These prerequisite requirements are discussed here to get you more familiar with what occurs during the DSMERGE process:

- Optional: You might want to make the O= in the source Tree its own partition, to shorten the merge time. If there is more than one O= in the source Tree, make each its own partition. This is the largest part of the merge and can save a lot of time. Essentially, Tree merges occur at the O= level.

- The Tree names must be unique in both Trees. A Tree can be renamed with the DSMERGE.NLM. If this is necessary, rename the source Tree because this Tree name will be gone after the DSMERGE process anyway.

- The O= in each Tree must have a unique name, because every O= in the source Tree will become O= in the new (target) Tree.

- All servers in both Trees should have the latest DS.NLM, DSREPAIR.NLM, and DSMERGE.NLM.

Tip #152 from
Sally

> If you are merging a NetWare 4 and a NetWare 5 Tree, the Master replica of [Root] in both Trees must hold the latest and the same NetWare 5 DS.NLM. Therefore, upgrade the server in the 4.11 Tree that holds the Master of [Root] to NetWare 5. NetWare 5 extends the schema and propagates all schema updates in this Tree by using an across-and-down "trickle" approach.

- Both NDS Trees should be healthy before the Tree merge is performed; that is, NDS should be properly synchronizing and no DS errors should be shown when you're running SET DSTRACE = ON. Run DSREPAIR.NLM on all servers in both Trees to check NDS's health.

- The schema on both Trees must be identical; that is, if ZENworks has been installed in one Tree, these schema extensions must be in the other Tree for the DSMERGE process to complete. The DSMERGE.NLM will notify you if the schemas do not match.

  In this case, rebuild the operational schema on the servers holding the Master of [Root] in both Trees. You do this by using DSREPAIR's Advanced options menu, Global Schema Operations, Import Remote Schema. Again, this should be run on the servers in both Trees that contain the Master of [Root].

- Optional: You can also create an NDS database dump file for both Trees. A simple way to do this is LOAD DSREPAIR -RC; or use DSREPAIR's Create a Database Dump File option as discussed previously. This creates an archive of the SYS:_NETWARE directory. If there was a serious problem, Novell could dial in and put you right back where you were before you started. You should create this database dump file on the two servers in each Tree that hold the Master replica of [Root].

- The servers in your source Tree should be getting time from the time providers in the Target tree so that the new objects receive a consistent time stamp from the target Tree. The options for setting time providers are discussed in Chapter 7, "Time Synchronization."

PART

IV

CH

16

Most Tree merges complete successfully, as long as things are working properly before you start. See TID 2912750, "DSMerge - Merging two trees together," available from http://support.novell.com, for information on using the DSMERGE.NLM to merge two Trees. Additionally, it is strongly recommended that you run through DSMERGE in a lab environment to become familiar with the process.

After two Trees have been merged, users will be able to access the resources as usual; the only things that will not be valid are any Preferred Tree statements that were being used by the users in the source Tree. Other than this, the DSMerge process will be transparent to users on the network.

Network administrators will, however, want to clean up the Tree after the merge process. Remember that there will now be at least two occurrences of O= in the new Tree. NDSMgr32 can be used to move containers; NDSMgr32 is used and not NWAdmn32 because a container move is considered to be a partition operation. In fact, a container must be partitioned before you can move it. To move a container (partition), select the partition in NDSMgr32 and then select "Move" from the Object menu. When you move a container with NDSMgr32, you can create an alias to the original container (see Figure 16.19).

Figure 16.19
Moving an NDS container (partition).

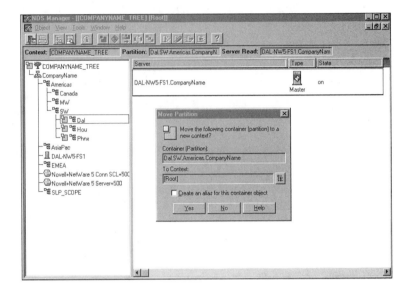

Creating an Alias to the original container allows you to use the alias container's login script to update a user's NAME CONTEXT statement to the new location after the container move. Follow these steps:

1. Use REGEDIT to find the following key:

   ```
   HKEY_LOCAL_MACHINE\Network\Novell\System Config\NetWare DOS Requester\
   ÂName Context
   ```

2. With the NAME CONTEXT folder highlighted, select Registry, Export Registry File from the menu bar.

3. Save it to SYS:PUBLIC (or somewhere the users have rights) as the following:

   ```
   SYS:PUBLIC\NAMECON.REG (or some other descriptive name)
   ```

4. Edit NAMECON.REG to reflect the new name context.

5. From the Login Script, enter the following:

   ```
   IF LOGIN_ALIAS_CONTEXT = "Y" THEN BEGIN
       MAP INS S1:=servername/SYS:PUBLIC
       #REGEDIT /S NAMECON.REG
       MAP DEL S1:
   END
   ```

Note

> The /S switch places REGEDIT in Silent Mode, suppressing the dialog box stating that the operation was successful.

Additionally, NDSMgr32 should be used to view the partitions and replicas that were automatically created during the DSMERGE process. Then you should make the necessary changes to be consistent with your company's documented partitioning and replication scheme.

Caution

> The Admin account from the source Tree will have all privileges to the target Tree after a DSMERGE; that is, you will see this Admin account as a Trustee of the [Root] with Supervisor object rights. You will want to determine the appropriate security strategy to deploy after a DSMERGE.

PROJECT: BECOMING PROFICIENT

The more you understand NDS, the more efficient your NDS Tree will be and the more quickly you will be able to resolve any NDS problems that might occur. You can learn about NDS through experimenting in a test environment and through seminars and computer-based training. Some good options include the following:

- Using NWAdmn32, experiment with giving rights to an object by selecting that object first, right-clicking, and then choosing Rights to Other Objects. Notice that the result is the same as with the approach documented in this chapter; however, you have to navigate through more windows using this method.

- If you want to become more proficient with NDS troubleshooting, consider attending a Novell Technical Services's Mastery Training Series session on this topic. Information on this and other sessions are available from
  http://support.novell.com/additional/advtt/.

- If you want to become more proficient with NDS internals and error messages, consider obtaining the LogicSource for NDS (available on CD from Novell).

PART V

NETWORK OPERATIONS

## CHAPTER 17

ORGANIZING AND ACCESSING INFORMATION ON THE NETWARE SERVER

In this chapter

NetWare's Directory Hierarchy

The primary function of a file server is to provide data storage and retrieval services. Therefore, you need to organize the information in a logical manner that makes it easy for you to manage and painless for your users understand and to access. It is important for you to know how NetWare organizes its files on the server, because this knowledge is essential for many network management tasks you perform, including granting user access rights to files and directories, configuring shared printers, and securing your server from unwanted access.

NetWare organizes its files in a *tree structure*, much the same way DOS, Windows 9x/NT, and other common desktop platforms do. This is so that to a user, the data will be presented in a consistent manner, making it easy to access. On the desktop, the topmost part of the tree is a drive letter corresponding to a partition on the hard disk—c:, for example. On the NetWare server, however, the top most level of a tree is called a *volume*. Recall from Chapter 8, "Installing NetWare 5 on New Servers," that a NetWare volume is a logical entity that consists of a fixed amount of physical space on one or more hard disks.

Tip #153 from	A CD-ROM can also be mounted as a NetWare NSS using CDROM.NLM.
Peter	

Mounting CD-ROM as a NetWare Volume

In NetWare 5, mounting CD-ROMs is done automatically when CDROM.NLM is loaded. The CD-ROMs are mounted as read-only NSS volumes. (Treat the CD-ROM as a read-only volume. Do not enable block suballocation or use file compression on the volume.) The NetWare 5 version of CDROM.NLM is a simple NetWare module that loads the following and does not stay in memory:

- NSS.NLM
- CD9660.NSS
- CDHFS.NSS

You can load NSS.NLM, CD9660.NSS, or CDHFS.NSS separately if preferred.

After these drivers are loaded, any CD-ROM disks inserted are automatically detected and mounted. You'll see messages similar to the following:

```
Moving ISO9660 CD volume '08NW8030' to active state
Activating volume "08NW8030"
  Mounting Volume 08NW8030
** 08NW8030 mounted successfully
```

You can verify that your CD-ROM is mounted as a NetWare NSS volume using the VOLUMES console command:

```
NETWARE5:volumes
Mounted Volumes          Name Spaces                Flags
  SYS                    DOS, LONG                  Cp Sa
  NSS_ADMIN              DOS, MAC, NFS, LONG         NSS
  08NW8030               DOS, MAC, NFS, LONG         NSS

3 volumes mounted
```

A NetWare server is divided into one or more volumes. The first network volume is named SYS and is created during NetWare installation. Using NWConfig, you can create a new volume on any hard disk that has a NetWare partition.

> **Note**
>
> Each NetWare server *must* have a SYS volume, or you don't have a functional server. If the SYS volume is not mounted or failed, you will be unable to access any resources on this server.

In a NetWare environment, the complete NetWare name of a file is similar to its DOS counterpart, with a few different parts. The following shows the components of the complete NetWare path for a file:

```
server_name/volume:directory\subdirectory\filename.extension
```

Note that a forward slash (/) separates the server name from the volume name and that a colon (:) follows the volume name. Backslashes (\) separate directories, subdirectories, and filenames.

> **Note**
>
> Although you can use either forward slashes or backslashes in the naming, the "correct" syntax is what's shown above.

PART

V

CH

17

THE SYS VOLUME

If you've worked with previous versions of NetWare, you'll find that NetWare 5's system-created directories are similar, but that it has a number of new directories. During installation, NetWare automatically creates the following directories and files on the SYS volume:

- CDROM$$.ROM—Contains index for mounted CD-ROM. This is a hidden directory.
- DELETED.SAV—Contains deleted files which have not been purged from directories that have been removed. This is a hidden directory.
- ETC—Contains sample files to help configure the server for TCP/IP protocols.
- JAVA—Stores Java support-related files.
- JAVASAVE—Contains Java-related files.
- LOGIN—Contains the programs necessary for logging in.
- MAIL—Might or might not contain subdirectories or files. This directory and a hex-numbered subdirectory are automatically created when a bindery client logs into this server.
- NDPS—Contains Novell Distributed Print Services.
- NETBASIC—Contains NetBasic support files.
- NI—Contains NetWare installation files.
- PERL—Stores Perl script–related files.
- PUBLIC—Holds the NetWare commands and utilities available to network users.

- README—Holds README files.
- SYSTEM—Stores files used by the NetWare operating system or by the network adminis-trator. The SYSTEM directory holds NLMs and files specific to the NetWare server.
- TEMP—Holds temporary files used by NetWare.

Depending on what products were selected for installation when you set up your server, not all your servers will have the directories and files mentioned earlier. However, the following system directories must exist on each server:

- DELETED.SAV
- ETC
- JAVA
- JAVASAVE
- LOGIN
- NETBASIC
- NI
- PERL
- PUBLIC
- README
- SYSTEM

Caution

Directories created by NetWare are used to maintain normal server and network opera-tions. These directories should not be deleted, moved, or renamed.

If you delete a system-created directory, you could have severe operational problems with NetWare. You need restore the deleted files from your backup or use NWConfig to recopy the lost files.

You *must* have one, *and only one*, volume called SYS. You can have other volumes (up to 64 for legacy-formatted volumes and up to 255 for NSS-formatted volumes, subject to hard-ware limitations) and call them whatever names you want.

SUGGESTIONS ON SYS VOLUME USAGE

Because the SYS volume is where the NDS database is kept, it is generally (strongly) recom-mended that you try to leave as much free volume space on this volume as possible. If SYS fills up, your NDS database on this server will stop being updated; also if SYS fills up, TTS will shut down and, as a result, NDS (on this server) will also be shut down, rendering your server inaccessible.

As you'll find out later in this book many of the new NetWare products, such as ZENworks and DHCP, make heavy use of NDS for storing data; therefore, maintaining sufficient free space on SYS is vital. Also, from my experience learned from server disaster recovery, upgrade, and migration projects, keeping the SYS volume uncluttered by third-party application files and user files will make these tasks much easier.

The following are some recommendations for keeping your SYS volume mean and lean:

- Allow for 500MB of free space if possible. At the very minimum, leave 250MB free for NDS growth and Support Pack file updates.
- Don't install any applications on the SYS volume whenever possible.
- Don't put any user directories and files on the SYS volume.
- Don't create any queue directories on the SYS volume.

Tip #154 from	Keep an eye on the amount of available free space on SYS to prevent NDS and TTS from shutting down.
Peter	

SUGGESTIONS ON ORGANIZING THE FILE SYSTEM

As network administrator, you need to create efficient directory structures for your network environment. I recommend that you set up a separate volume (call it DATA, for example) for non-NetWare system files and use the following types of directories to organize individual files in the directory structure:

- Home directories
- ZENworks profile directories
- Application directories
- Shared data directories

Use descriptive names for directories so that their purpose and content are easy to determine, especially by your users.

HOME DIRECTORIES

You should provide each user with a "home directory" in which to store individual user-created files. The home directory is often named after the user's login name for uniformity and ease in creating login scripts.

→ For more information about automatically setting up user-to-home-directory association, **see** Chapter 22, "Configuring User Environment Using Login Scripts," **p.509**

Usually, you'll grant full access rights for individual users to their own home directories so that they can manage (create, delete, and so on) their own files. However, you should *not* give the Access Control right for user home directories because that can lead to potential security risks.

→ For more details about file system security, **see** Chapter 18, "Implementing Security," **p. 405**

To facilitate easier backup and security management, you should create a parent directory, such as the USERS directory in the Figure 17.1, to hold all the user home directories.

Figure 17.1
Suggested directory structure.

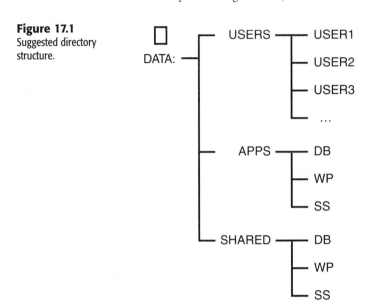

ZENWORKS PROFILE DIRECTORIES

Windows NT saves desktop settings and other information related to your user name as a *profile*. Settings saved in the user profile include taskbar settings, control panel settings, Explorer settings, and so on. The user profile can exist either as a local profile or as a roaming profile. Local profiles are maintained on a single NT workstation. They allow different users to log in to the local machine and receive their customized desktop setup. Roaming profiles are stored on a server and allow the user to move from one NT workstation to another and receive the same profile information.

Using the new workstation client software, you can save the NT user profile to a NetWare server. Although it makes sense to save the user profile in each user's home directory, it is best to save the profile in a separate profile directory. The reason is that users tend to delete files in their own home directories if they didn't create them or don't know what the files do. So, if you keep the NT user profiles in the user home directories, you run the risk of them being deleted unknowingly, resulting in unnecessary support calls.

Note

In order to save NT user profiles on a NetWare volume, you must ensure the volume supports long names (see the "Name Space Support" section later in this chapter).

Application Directories

Application directories should contain only the application program files (.EXE, .BAT, and .COM files). In general, all you need is to give users Read access to these directories. However, some applications require their configuration files to be located in the same directory, making security assignments more difficult. Unless an application requires it, no user-created data files should be stored here—users' home directories can store user-created files. You could also create various data directories for data files.

Similar to user home directories, you should create a parent directory, such as the APPS directory (refer to Figure 17.1), to hold all the subdirectories containing individual applications.

Shared Data Directories

Shared data directories should be created so that groups of users can share information. The type of security access to shared data directories varies widely depending on the purpose of the directories and the group sharing them. For example, a group might simply need to read weekly update reports and only one person in that group needs to update the files. Therefore, you need to grant Read access rights for the group in general, and full rights to the person responsible for the file updates.

Part V
Ch 17

General Guidelines

Directory structures vary depending on individual and organizational needs. There are few absolute right or wrong directory structures. Instead, when considering the directory structure for your NetWare 5 server, answer to yourself the following questions:

- Is it easy to use? That is, would your users, without much coaching from you, be able to find the files they need?

- Is it easy to administer? If you have a pretty flat directory structure, making NetWare security rights assignments would take more work because you can't easily take advantage of the right inheritance feature.

- Does the organization of files and directories make sense? That is, can you easily navigate from one data directory to another without too many keystrokes?

In addition, a directory structure often mirrors the type of information kept on the system. You should create each level of the directory structure after considering what information users need, and group them logically.

Tip #155 from
Peter

I recommend that you evaluate several (but not too many!) potential directory structure designs before creating one for your organization. You should not spend more than 30 minutes, however, to come up with your final working design.

USING VOLUME OBJECTS

In NDS, each volume on a NetWare server is represented with a Volume object. When you create a volume with the NWConfig utility, NWConfig automatically creates a Volume object in the same context as the NetWare server within the NDS tree. However, should you need to, you can easily move the Volume objects to a different context using NetWare Administrator.

By default, NWConfig names the Volume object

servername_volumename

For example, the volume object of the SYS volume on a NetWare server called NETWARE5 is called NETWARE5_SYS.

> **Note**
>
> If you need to rename a volume, change the volume name on the server using the NWConfig utility (Standard Disk Options, NetWare Volume Options), and then change the volume object's name in the NDS using NetWare Administrator so that the two names match.

There are a number of uses of the Volume objects. You can use them to store information as well as for managing file system security. For example,

- In the Volume object's properties, you can store information about the physical volume, such as the owner, space use restrictions for users, or a description of its use (see Figure 17.2).

Figure 17.2
A Volume object's identification data.

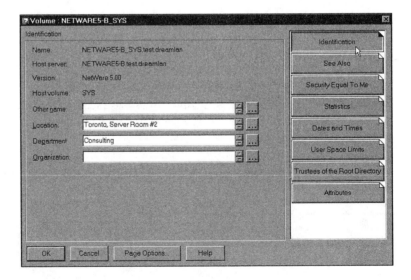

- You can also view statistical information on disk space availability, block size, directory entries, name space support, and so on (see Figure 17.3).

Figure 17.3
Volume statistics
information.

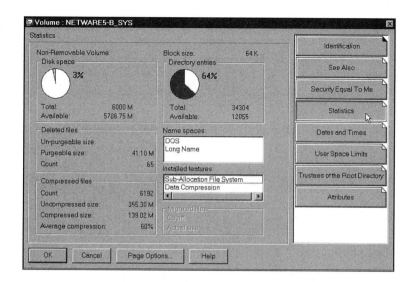

- Although the information is stored not in NDS, but in NWAdmin, you can easily manage the file systems from a central location (see Figure 17.4).

Figure 17.4
By opening the
Volume object, you
can get a list of files
and directories locat-
ed on this volume.
And through the (file
or directory) object's
properties, you can
manage its settings.

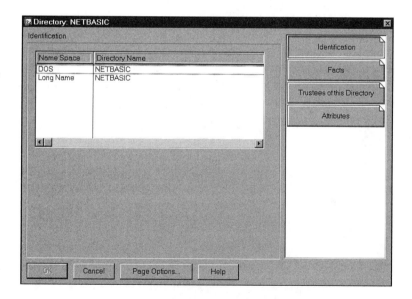

Note

Files and directories on a volume don't have a corresponding NDS object and are *not* stored in NDS. But NWAdmin will show them because these are resources on a NetWare server, and offers you a centralized method to manage them.

Instead of specifying a server name and volume name for the complete NetWare path of a file, you can use a Volume object instead. For example, instead of the following:

```
NETWARE5/SYS:PUBLIC\WIN32\NWADMN32.EXE
```

you can instead use the following:

```
NETWARE5_SYS:PUBLIC\WIN32\NWADMN32.EXE
```

You can further simplify reference to a file by using Directory Map objects.

USING DIRECTORY MAP OBJECTS

A Directory Map object represents a particular directory in a file system. You can create Directory Map (DM) objects to point to directories that contain frequently used files such as applications. In a way, a DM is like an alias so that you can reference a directory using a much shorter name.

DM objects offer you two advantages. First, you can use them to provide descriptive and simple names that users can easily understand and use, instead of having to remember complicated NetWare directory paths. The "Using the MAP Command" section in this chapter explains how you can use DM objects to access files.

Secondly, DM objects also offer you a way to assign an unchanging name to programs and data that can change location. For example, if you need to move a database application from SERVER1 to SERVER2, using DM objects, the users don't have to know about the changes as long as they use the DM object name to locate the files; you simply change the database's DM object definition to point to the program's new location (and grant appropriate user access rights).

You can create DM objects using NWAdmin. Note that you need to have the Create object right to the container where the DM object will be created. The following outlines the procedure:

1. In NWAdmin, select the Organization or Organizational Unit object where you want to create the DM object.
2. Choose Create from the Object menu.
3. Choose Directory Map from the New Object dialog box.
4. Choose OK.
5. Enter the name for the Directory Map object in the space provided.
6. In the Volume field, enter the name of the volume this Directory Map object will point to (see Figure 17.5). You can type the complete name of the Volume object, or you can choose the browser button to the right of the Volume field to browse for the Volume and directory path.

Figure 17.5
Creating a Directory
Map object.

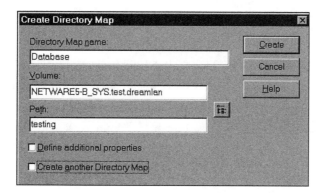

7. If you did not use the Browse button, enter the path of the directory this Directory Map object will point to. If the Directory Map object will point to the root of the specified volume, leave the Path field blank.

8. (Optional) To define additional properties immediately after creating the Directory Map object, choose Define Additional Properties.

9. (Optional) To create another Directory Map object immediately after this one, choose Create Another Directory Map.

10. Choose Create.

PART

V

CH

17

> **Note**
>
> Steps 8 and 9 are mutually exclusive.

If you chose Define Additional Properties (step 8), the identification screen appears. If you chose Create Another Directory Map (step 9), the Create dialog box appears.

> **Caution**
>
> Don't use the Rights to Files and Directories option of the DM object to assign access rights to the directory—it will *not* give your users access rights to the directory pointed to by the DM object. Make users and groups trustees of the directory instead, using the procedure outlined in Chapter 18.

USING THE MAP COMMAND

When working with files on a PC, you use drive letters to reference different hard drives installed in your workstation. The drive letters also serve as shortcuts to directories to avoid having to enter long pathnames. Similarly, you use drive letters to reference NetWare paths.

From the command-line prompt of your workstation's operating system, you can use the MAP command to map drives to volumes, directories, or a directory map object. You can also use the MAP command in login scripts (see Chapter 22) to establish search drives. Search drives are inserted into the PATH statement which the OS uses to find executable files.

The following is the basic command syntax:

```
MAP [[ option] drive:= [ volume:path]]
```

The following is a brief explanation of each portion of the command syntax:

- `Option`—Replace with any option `MAP` option as discussed later in this chapter.
- `Drive`—Replace with a letter from A to Z.
- `Volume:path`—Replace with any acceptable NetWare server/volume:directory name. This could be the Volume object name or the physical name.

For example, to map the `SYS:NETBASIC` directory on server `NETWARE5` as the F drive:

```
MAP F:=NETWARE5/SYS:NETBASIC
```

The following four methods for mapping drives are discussed in this section:

- Mapping drives to volumes
- Mapping drives to directories
- Mapping network search drives
- Mapping drives to directory map objects

In the "Using Windows GUI Tools" section later in this chapter, you'll find out how to map drives using the GUI tools.

MAPPED DRIVES

A mapped network drive is simply a pointer—an alphabet letter that points to a particular directory on a NetWare server. To create a mapped drive, use the following syntax:

```
MAP letter:=netware_path
```

where the *netware_path* optionally consists of a server name, volume name, and directory path. If you have only one server on your network, you don't need to include the server name in the path; you need to always specify the volume name, even if you have only the `SYS` volume.

When you map a drive with just the volume name, it automatically points to the root of the volume. For example, the following

```
MAP F:=SYS:
```

maps F: to point to the root of `SYS`. If F was previously mapped to, say, `DATA:ORACLE8`, its assignment will be changed to the root of the `SYS` volume. Therefore, you should be careful when you make new drive mappings, or else you can overwrite existing assignment causing applications to stop functioning. You can get a list of the currently mapped drives using the `MAP` command by itself:

```
F:\DATA>map
```

```
Drives A,B,C,D,E map to a local disk.
Drive F: = NETWARE5_SYS.Consulting.Toronto.North_America.: \
```

```
Drive G: = NETWARE5_DATA.Consulting.Toronto.North_America.: \
          -----    Search Drives    -----

S1: = S:. [NETWARE5_SYS.Consulting.Toronto.North_America.: \SDK\NLM\NOVBIN]
S2: = Z:. [NETWARE5_SYS.Consulting.Toronto.North_America.: \PUBLIC]
S3: = C:\NWDOS
S4: = D:\NOVELL\CLIENT32
S5: = C:\UTILS
S6: = D:\BIN
S7: = D:\LWP5\BIN

F:\DATA>
```

If you don't care what letter is used in the mapping, you can use the MAP NEXT (or simply MAP N) option, such as:

```
MAP NEXT VOL1:USERS
```

to grab the next available alphabet from the top of the list (that is, from A down). For example, if your first network drive is set to be F (as configured in the workstation client software), and you already have F and G mapped to other network directories, the MAP NEXT command will assign H to the USERS directory on VOL1.

PART

V

CH

17

Tip #156 from
Peter

> You can map multiple letters to the same volume but have the letters point to different directories and subdirectories on the volume. This can greatly facilitate directory and file access.

You can map drives using NDS Volume and DM objects. For example, to map a drive to the DATABASE directory on the APPS volume on server NETWEARE5, enter

```
MAP I:=NETWARE5_APPS:DATABASE
```

assuming the Volume objects in your current NDS context. If the object is in a different object, specify the NDS path accordingly. For example,

```
MAP I:=.NETWARE5_APPS.Toronto.ACME_University:DATABASE
```

You can use either relative or full distinguish name, typeless or typeful naming syntax. Alternatively, if you have a DM object that points to the volume and directory, you can use it instead:

```
MAP I:=DATBASE_DM
```

Note that a trailing colon is not required.

To remove a currently mapped drive, use the MAP DELETE (or MAP REMOVE) command. For example, the following

```
MAP DEL I:
```

will delete the drive mapping assignment for I.

Note

Drive mapping assignments are not permanent. They are deleted after you log out of the network. Therefore, to retain the same set of drive mappings, you should set up a login script as outlined in Chapter 22. Alternatively, you can set up permanent drive mappings (that get reconnected after you logged in to the network) through the desktop's operating system, if the feature is supported.

MAP-ROOTED DRIVES

Many applications must be run from the root of a drive, so when you want to install such an application to a NetWare volume it can greatly mess up your carefully planned directory structure. Fortunately, the ROOT option for the MAP command allows you to map a drive to a subdirectory that functions as a root directory.

If a drive has been mapped to a subdirectory using the MAP ROOT (or simply MAP R) command, you can't move any higher in the file system using that drive mapping than the subdirectory that the drive was mapped to. For example, the following

```
MAP ROOT I:=APPS:DATABASE
```

makes any subdirectories under the DATABASE directory to *appear* as though they are off the root of the I drive (for example APPS:DATABASE\DB-V2 will appear as I:\DB-V2).

Tip #157 from
Peter

If you map-rooted your users' home directory drive letter, they will be unable to use DOS commands, such as CD, to switch to directories above their home directories. This helps the users to access their own home directory and not someone else's.

Caution

Many GUI tools, such as Windows Explorer, do not respect map-rooted drives. Therefore, they will still show the full path starting from the root of the volume down.

SEARCH DRIVES

You can also use the MAP command to set up search drives. Search drive mappings function just like PATH settings, which enable the system to locate a program even if it isn't located in the directory the user is working in.

NetWare supports a maximum of 16 search drives. Note that you can't map a search drive and a regular network drive to the same letter. When you map a search drive, use a search drive number (an S followed by a number). This search drive number assigns the next available drive letter to the mapping, starting with Z and working backwards through the English alphabet. For example,

```
F:\DATA>map

Drives A,B,C,D,E map to a local disk.
```

```
Drive F: = NETWARE5_SYS.Consulting.Toronto.North_America.: \
       -----     Search Drives     -----

S1: = Z:. [NETWARE5_SYS.Consulting.Toronto.North_America.: \PUBLIC]

F:\DATA> map s2:=sys:utils

S2: = Y:. [NETWARE5_SYS.Consulting.Toronto.North_America.: \UTILS]
```

The letter assigned to the search drive is put into your workstation's PATH environment. If you already have search drives in the PATH statement, the command MAP S1: *overwrites* the first one in the path. To prevent search drive assignments from overwriting existing PATH settings, use the INSERT option when assigning search drives, such as the following:

MAP INS S16:=*path*

To ensure that users can access NetWare utilities and applications, you should consider mapping search drives so that the first search drive (S1:) maps to the SYS:PUBLIC directory, which contains the NetWare utilities for DOS and MS Windows workstations.

The order in which mappings are listed is important because the order of items in the list is the order in which the directories are searched. The system searches, following the numerical order of the search drives, until the program file either is found or can't be located. The list can include a combination of local and network directories.

Tip #158 from
Peter

To avoid inadvertently changing the order of any search drives that must be mapped to a specific drive letter, you can map all remaining search drives with the number S16:, which assigns the next lowest search number available each time it is used.

If you have an application that requires a particular drive letter, you can use the following command to map the search drive, replacing drive with the drive letter:

MAP S16:=*drive*:=*path*

If you map a search drive using a number already assigned to a search drive, NetWare makes the old search drive a network drive. The letter assigned to the old search drive remains assigned as the converted drive mapping. The new search drive takes the next unused letter in the alphabet.

Finally, you remove a search drive the same way you delete a mapped drive. For instance, the following

MAP DEL S1:

will remove the first search drive mapping, and any remaining search drive mappings will be moved up by one; that is, S2 becomes S1, S3 becomes S2, and so on. Therefore, care should be taken when you're deleting multiple search drives, as you might inadvertently delete a wrong one from the list because of the order change.

PART
V

CH
17

USING WINDOWS GUI TOOLS

With the popularity of GUI desktop operating systems, such as Windows 9x and Windows NT, you and your users are not likely to use the command line–based MAP command discussed earlier. If you're using Windows 9x or NT, you should use the GUI tools to access the file system.

The NetWare workstation client, Client32, for Windows 9x and NT are tightly integrated with My Computer, Windows Explorer, and the Network Neighborhood. However, the NetWare clients adds some extensions, so in the following discussion it is Client32-specific; the overall concept, however, is also applicable if you use Microsoft's Client for NetWare Networks.

EXPLORING NETWARE VOLUMES

You can easily browse for NetWare Volume objects using My Computer, Explorer, or Network Neighborhood. The easiest way, however, is to use Network Neighborhood.

Tip #159 from *Peter*	When browsing your NetWare 5 network, Network Neighborhood will also show NDS printers, whereas My Computer will not).

Use the following steps to browse for Volume objects:

1. Open Network Neighborhood. If you're not already authenticated to the network, only the Entire Network icon is shown. If you're authenticated, you'll see the Entire Network icon, a list of NDS trees (that you're authenticated to), a list of NetWare servers, and an icon (which looks like a piece of paper with a dog-eared upper-right corner) that represents your current NDS context.

2. To start browsing from the [Root] of the tree down, double-click a tree name. You're presented with a list of containers as you drill down the tree. To start browsing from the current name context down, double-click the icon that represents your current context. As you walk the tree, you'll see containers, Printers, Print Queues, and DM and Volume objects in a given context, as shown in Figure 17.6; you'll not see User, Group, or Server objects.

Note	Network Neighborhood doesn't distinguish between a Volume object from a DM object. Both are shown with a folder icon suggesting they are Volume objects.

Figure 17.6
Container, Printer, and Volume objects in an NDS context.

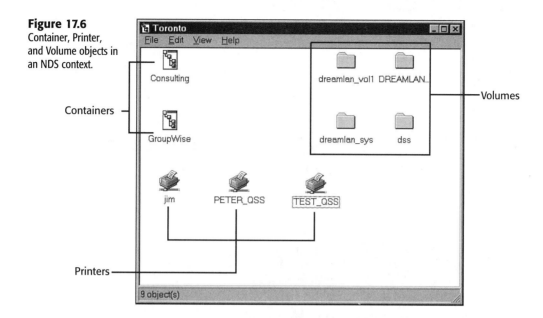

3. Double-click a Volume object to obtain a list of files and directories. And you can continue drilling-down the layers of directories.

You can also retrieve volume- and file-related information, like you could using NWAdmin. For example, highlight a Volume object, right-click to bring up the context menu and select Properties. You get a number of volume-related data, such as statistics and security assignments (see Figure 17.7).

Figure 17.7
Volume statistics.

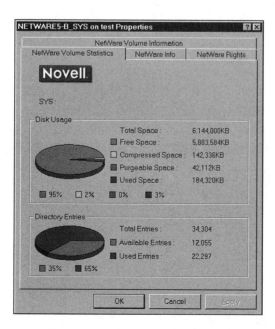

Another way to view and walk the tree is to right-click the tree and select Explore from the context menu to bring up Explorer. Open the NetWare Servers branch to see a list of server. From there, you can open a server to see a list of volume names, and you can open a volume name to see a list of files and directories, starting at the volume's root, as shown in Figure 17.8. Note too that you can use the Explorer to explore network printers and logical drives (as created by NetWare drive mappings) as though they were local devices.

Figure 17.8
Exploring a NetWare volume.

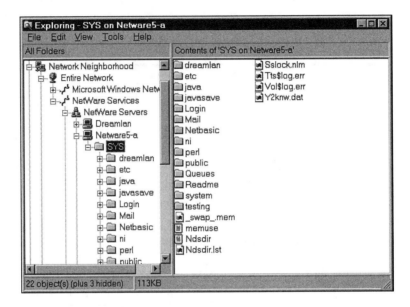

<table>
<tr><td>Tip #160 from
Peter</td><td>The new Client32 software also gives you the ability to salvage, purge, and copy files through the context menu, instead of you having to start up NWAdmin or other tools.</td></tr>
</table>

MAPPING A NETWORK DRIVE

You can easily map a network drive using either Explorer or Network Neighborhood. To try this, follow these steps:

1. Locate the directory you want to map using either Explorer or Network Neighborhood.

2. Right-click the directory icon and select Map Network Drive from the context menu to display the Map Drive dialog box, shown in Figure 17.9.

3. Use the Device drop-down list to select the drive letter you want to use.

4. If you want the drive to be reconnected at logon, activate the Reconnect At Logon check box. (This is known as creating a "permanent" drive mapping.)

Figure 17.9
Use this dialog box to
map a network drive.

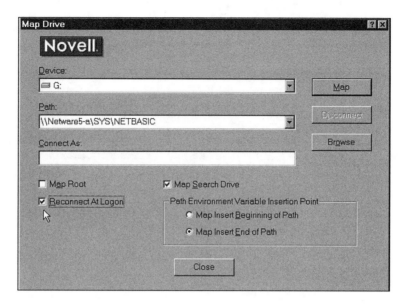

5. If you want the drive to be map-rooted, activate the Map Root check box.

6. If this is to be a search drive, activate the Map Search Drive check box and select the appropriate Path Environment Variable Insertion Point setting.

7. Click OK and the mapped drive shows up as a networked drive icon (a disk drive attached to a network cable).

Or, if you're using the latest Client32 workstation software, there's a NetWare Services icon in the system tray. Right-click the red N symbol and then select the Novell Map Network Drive option on the context menu to bring up the Map Drive dialog box. You can then use the Browse button to locate the directory you want to map to, and follow Step 3 in the preceding list.

RELEASING A MAPPED NETWORK DRIVE

When you no longer need a network drive, you should release it—generally referred to as "deleting the drive mapping." There are several ways to do this; here are two of them:

- Open My Computer, right-click the network drive icon, and then select Disconnect from the context menu.

- Right-click the red N symbol in the system tray, and click the Disconnect Network Drive option in the context menu. Highlight the drive you want to release in the Disconnect Network Drive dialog box and then click OK (see Figure 17.10).

PART
V

CH

17

Figure 17.10
Releasing a previously mapped network drive.

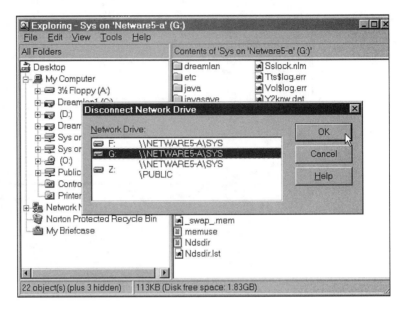

NAME SPACE SUPPORT

NetWare supports a number of different file-naming format, including the long names used by Windows 9x/NT and OS/2, as well as NFS file structure. This is done through the use of name space modules, which are NLMs with the name extension .NAM. All NetWare volumes support the DOS name space; by default, the SYS volume also supports the long-name name space (LONG). The following steps illustrates how to add long-name name space support to your existing volumes:

1. At the server console, type LONG.NAM (or LOAD LONG.NAM).

2. Add the name space to the volumes by entering the following command (in which *volumename* is the name of the volume for which you want the name space):

   ADD NAME SPACE LONG TO *volumename*

3. Repeat step 2 for each volume you want to have long filename support.

4. Edit your STARTUP.NCF file and include the LOAD LONG.NAM command in the file.

You need to perform these tasks only once. The changes are made permanently to the volumes.

If for any reason you need to remove the name space support, use the VREPAIR.NLM that is shipped with NetWare to delete the name space. However, you can't delete the DOS name space support.

FILE MANAGEMENT TOOLS

From a user's point of view, storing and accessing files on a NetWare volume is just like accessing files locally. However, because NetWare uses its own disk and partition structure that is different from a PC's, traditional file management tools such as DOS's Undelete and Norton Utilities can't be used against a NetWare volume. Instead, you need to use a NetWare-specific version of the tools.

RECOVERING DELETED FILES

On a NetWare volume, files are not removed right away when they are deleted. Instead, like many other operating systems, such as DOS and Windows NT, NetWare retains deleted files until the disk space they occupy must be reused. Therefore, if your volume has ample free space and has relatively light disk write activity, chances are good that you can recover deleted files, going back a number of days.

Like DOS, deleted files are stored invisibly. Because a NetWare volume's structure is different than those used by the common desktop operating systems, such as Windows NT, you can't use tools such as Norton Utilities for Windows NT to undelete deleted files from a NetWare volume. Instead, you use either FILER or NWAdmin, both of which are included with NetWare.

The following procedure outlines how to salvage a deleted file using NWAdmin; the general principal also applies to FILER, a DOS-based utility:

1. Start NWAdmin and locate the directory in which the deleted file was stored, by drilling down on the Volume object into its subdirectories.
2. Highlight the desired directory.
3. From the pull-down menu, select Tools, Salvage. A screen similar to Figure 17.11 is displayed.

Figure 17.11
Working with deleted files in NWAdmin.

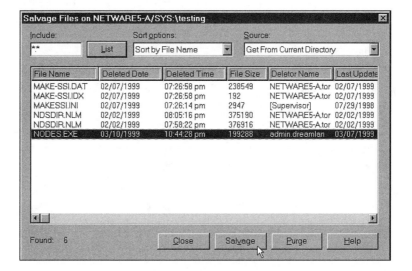

4. Start by selecting the file name pattern for NWAdmin to use to search for deleted files; the default is all files (*.*). Then select your desired sort option using the pull-down list. Finally, choose to salvage files from either the current directory or from deleted directories.

5. Press List to display the files that match your selection criteria. This list displays each file's name, the date and time the file was deleted, the size of the file, and so on. The most important piece of information, as asked in many cases, the user ID that deleted the file.

6. To recover one or more files, highlight the names of the file you want to recover and click Salvage.

7. Click Close when you're finished.

If you try to salvage a file for which a file with the same name already exists in the same directory, you'll be prompted to enter a new name for the recovered file.

Tip #161 from
Peter

You can salvage files by right-clicking a NetWare directory in Explorer and select the Salvage Files option from the context menu, if you have the latest Client32 software installed.

Note

If you salvaged files from deleted directories, they will be stored in the DELETED.SAV directory off the root of the volume. You will need to manually move the recovered files to their final location. Bear in mind that DELETED.SAV is a hidden directory and can be accessed only by users with Supervisor (file system) rights.

Caution

By default, a NetWare 5 server is set to purge all deleted files *immediately*. However, you can change this using the server console SET to change Immediate Purge of Deleted Files from On to Off. See Chapter 23, "Server Console Utilities," for more details about console SET commands.

REMOVING DELETED FILES

There are instances you might want to make sure NetWare erases the deleted files so they can't ever be salvaged. You can do this by purging the deleted files. Follow the same procedure as outlined for salvaging files, but at step 6, instead of clicking on the Salvage button, click Purge instead.

You can also purge files from the command-line using the PURGE utility. Using this utility, you can purge files selectively using a filename pattern, such as PURGE .BAK, or purge all files by simply entering PURGE; the default file name pattern is *.*.

You can also use FILER to purge deleted files.

Tip #162 from
Peter

You can purge deleted files by right-clicking a NetWare directory in Explorer and select the Purge Files option from the context menu, if you have the latest Client32 software installed.

Tip #163 from
Peter

If you want a specific file to be purged automatically when it is deleted, assign the Purge attribute to the file. Similarly, if you want any file within a specific directory to be automatically purged after it is deleted, assign the Purge attribute to the directory. Refer to Chapter 18 for more on administrating file system rights.

COPYING FILES

Why do you need to know how to copy files? Everyone knows, right? Well, yes and no. There's a right way to copy files in NetWare, and a not-so-right way. Typically, when you need to copy a file from one directory to another, you'll use COPY from the command-line or through Explorer. These methods are fine when you're copying files from one local device to another. They are not so efficient when you're copying files from one NetWare location to another, especially if you're copying a large amount of data.

Here's what happens when you use a standard copy application. As illustrated in Figure 17.12, when User1 issues a COPY command, the data first goes from the server to the user workstation and *back* to the server. However, when an NCOPY command is used instead, because it is a NetWare utility, rather than bring the data down to the workstation and back out, NCOPY simply asks the *server* to copy the data from DATA1: to DATA2: on behave of the client! As you can clearly determine, when copying large amounts of data, NCOPY would be much more efficient and takes less network bandwidth than COPY or similar non-NetWare aware utilities.

Figure 17.12
Data flow of COPY versus NCOPY.

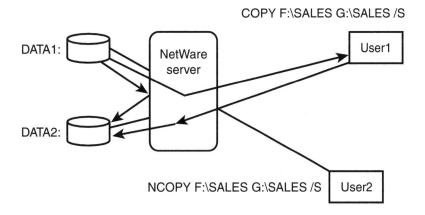

The command syntax of NCOPY is very similar to that of COPY. For a list of NCOPY options, type NCOPY /?.

PART
V

CH
17

Tip #164 from *Peter*	You can NCOPY files by right-clicking a NetWare directory in Explorer and select the NetWare Copy option from the context menu, if you have the latest Client32 software installed.

DEFRAGMENTING NETWARE VOLUMES

For many operating systems, there's a frequent need to defragment the disk drives in order to maintain good disk access performance. Novice administrators often ask how someone would go about doing that on a NetWare server and how often. The answers are "You don't" and "Never," respectively.

NetWare makes heavy use of server RAM for caching, both for disk reads and writes, because RAM access speed is much faster than disk access speed. By keeping the most recently read files in RAM, user read requests can be quickly serviced without accessing the (slower) disk. And first writing the client data to RAM (and then later writing to disk in the background) instead of disk also speeds up client write performance. Couple file caching with advanced disk seek algorithms, a NetWare volume need never be defragged.

Should you ever need to "defrag," or defragment, a NetWare volume, you need to back up the data, delete the volume, re-create it, and restore the files. However, benchmark tests have been done in the past, even back in the NetWare 2.1x era; a fragmented NetWare volume performs just as well as a refreshed restored NetWare volume, under heavy I/O load.

PROJECT: WHICH TOOL IS MORE EFFICIENT?

Because every network is unique in its own way (such as hardware, network topology, and so on), the following exercise will help you to determine which of COPY, NCOPY, or Windows tools is more efficient in copying large files on your network.

There are a number of ways to determine data throughput on a network. The easiest is to simply copy a known amount of data across the network and time it. Follow these steps and fill out the table at the end of this section:

1. Create a directory on a NetWare volume called SOURCE.

2. Create a directory on the same NetWare volume (or another one if you have more than one) called TARGET.

3. Copy the files from SYS:PUBLIC into the SOURCE directory.

4. Use PKZIP, WinZIP, or similar utility to create three ZIP files using the files from SYS:PUBLIC. The ZIP files should be of different sizes, ranging from 1MB to 10MB.

5. Use COPY to copy these files from SOURCE to TARGET. Don't time this copy process. (This first time will cause these three ZIP files to be cached in server RAM so all subsequent copies are served from RAM. If you don't do this step, the first copy will take a penalty as it will be served from disk.)

6. Now use COPY, NCOPY, and Explorer to copy the ZIP files from SOURCE to TARGET and time each copy. Use the following table to log the time in:

	1 MB	5 MB	10 MB
DOS COPY command			
NCOPY.EXE			
Windows Explorer			

In general, you'll find that COPY and perhaps Explorer are more efficient when copying small files (less than 5MB in size) and NCOPY is much more efficient when copying large files.

## CHAPTER 18

IMPLEMENTING SECURITY

In this chapter

COMPONENTS OF NETWARE SECURITY

Many organizations depend heavily on their computer networks for mission-critical applications. Thus, it is paramount that network data and resources are secured against unauthorized access and tempering.

A simple definition of network security is the process of protecting a network from danger or risk of loss—making it safe from intruders, loss of data, and errors. There are many forms of network security, including file and directory security, password protection, virus protection, and physical security of workstations and file servers.

In the early stages of designing NetWare, Novell recognized that customers wanted to be able to easily implement secured networks without much overhead on the operating system. Therefore, NetWare 5 includes a number of different levels of security that control who can access the network, which resources users can access, and how they can use those resources. These levels include the following:

- Login/password security
- NetWare Directory Services security
- File system security
- File server console security

Login/password security controls initial access to the network. When initial access is granted, NDS security controls which objects (such as User and Directory Map objects) in the NDS users can access. File system security controls which files and directories users can access on the NetWare volumes, and what can be done with them (such as read and write). And, lastly, file server console security controls who can access the file server console.

With the enhanced support included in NetWare 5 for Internet services, an additional layer of communication-related security has been added. This layer is responsible for establishing a secured client-to-server connection over TCP/IP, using industry standard protocols.

LOGIN/PASSWORD SECURITY

Login/password security is the outermost layer of your security measure that you can surround your network with. It governs who can access the network and when. To most network administrators and users, this level of security seems quite simplistic: Each user has a unique login ID and password and that's that. However, it is not as simple as it leads you to believe. The login process often times is considered the easiest link in network security. Because of this, it is important that you fully understand the significance of this level of security.

Several things can cause security breaches during the login process. These include password breaking using techniques such as wire tapping, Trojan horse attacks (such as installing a fake login program to capture your username and password), and brute force attacks (by simply guessing at username/password combinations). These security breaches can be easily overcome by establishing and enforcing security policies and educating users on the importance of passwords and their use. NetWare 5 includes features that prevent unauthorized access during the login process. These features include a sophisticated public-key cryptosystem, digital packet signatures, and other login-level security options.

Public/Private Keys

NetWare 5 uses a public/private key algorithm for password authentication, and this is based on a public-key cryptosystem technology developed by RSA Data Security, Inc. This system ensures that every request for login or attachment to a NetWare server passes the following tests:

- The sender of the login or attachment request is a valid network client
- The sender's station actually created the request
- The request originated at the workstation where the authentication data was created
- The request pertains to the current session
- The message or request has not been tampered with

Note

Public-key cryptosystems use two keys: a public key and a private key. The *public key*, analogous to a user's telephone number, is published to a directory—anyone can look it up. The *private key* is known only to the decrypting object—the owner of that telephone number. To send a message, the sender encrypts the message by using the destination object's public key. The receiver then decrypts the message by using its private key.

When a user requests login or attachment to a NetWare server, the client workstation software transmits the user's ID and encrypted password to NDS. NDS verifies the password against the stored, encrypted version in NDS. If they match, NDS then generates a public and private key for that user, encrypting the private key with the user's password. The encrypted password is then sent back to the user and is decrypted by the workstation software. It is important to note that neither the private key nor the password ever cross the network in an unencrypted format.

The workstation client software then builds a unique digital signature for the user's current session using information that's unique to this user, such as the network station address and the time of login or attachment request. This digital signature is then combined with the private key for the user to form a *credential*. When this credential is formed, the user's private key is removed from the workstation's memory.

Finally, when the credential is built, the workstation client transmits this along with "proof" back to NDS for login or attachment authentication. The proof consists of encrypted contents from the original login packet. If the credential and proof are correct, the user is granted access. Therefore, you can surmise here that a lot goes on after you supplied your user ID and password and pressed Enter at the login prompt!

BACKGROUND AUTHENTICATION

One advantage of the global nature of NDS is single login. You no longer need to supply a user ID and password for each file server you need access to. In a NetWare 5 environment, you provide your user ID and password once during the initial login, and a *background authentication* process grants you access to additional resources on the network, as long as you have the appropriate rights to access those resources.

The background authentication uses the credential and proof created during the initial login. The only difference is that background authentication takes place automatically, transparent to the user. Figure 18.1 summarizes the background authentication process.

Figure 18.1
NDS's background authentication process.

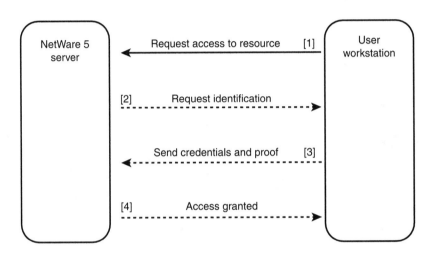

NCP PACKET SIGNATURES, SAS, AND PKIS

NetWare 5 has an optional security feature called NetWare Core Protocol (NCP) Packet Signature, that prevents forged packets from being accepted. Forged packets are a potential security breach in high-security environments. Without NCP Packet Signatures, it is possible that an NCP request could be injected into the privileged session (such as one logged in by Admin) to grant access to a network intruder. By enabling NCP Packet Signatures, a digital signature is added to each NCP *packet*, preventing unauthorized NCP requests from being accepted by the server for processing. These digital signatures are based on the RSA MD4 message digest algorithm.

To enable NCP Packet Signatures, configuration at both the server level and the client workstation level. There are four different NCP Packet Signature settings:

- Level 0—Don't sign packets (that is, disabled)
- Level 1—Sign packets only if the workstation requires them
- Level 2—Sign packets if the client can; don't sign if the client can't support it
- Level 3—Always sign packets

Figure 18.2 shows how you can change the NCP Packet Signature level setting on the file server using MONITOR. At the workstations, NCP Packet Signature settings are part of the client properties settings (see Figure 18.3).

Figure 18.2

Setting server's NCP Packet Signature level through MONITOR.

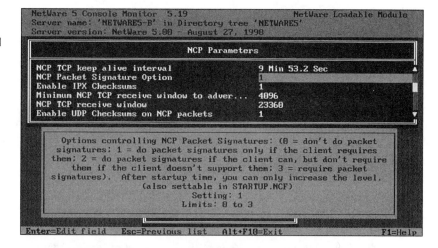

Figure 18.3

Setting client's NCP Packet Signature level.

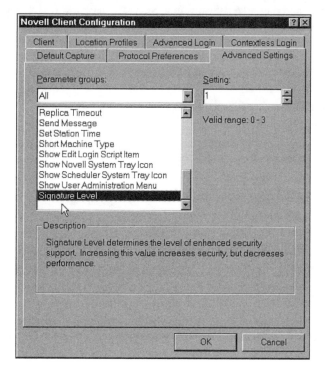

> **Caution**
>
> Enabling packet signatures can put additional processing overhead on both your servers and workstations.

In addition to NCP Packet Signatures, NetWare 5 also introduced Secure Authentication Services (SAS) and Public Key Infrastructure Services (PKIS) to address additional network security requirements.

NetWare 5 takes what the networking industry considers the best security to the next level by providing the next generation of authentication services named *Secure Authentication Services* (SAS). SAS is designed to provide support for new and evolving industry authentication mechanisms. The SAS design also includes a framework for distinguishing between authentication mechanisms of various qualities, as well as support for the introduction of third-party authentication services. SAS also provides server-based user applications with controlled access to files and NDS objects based on the user's SAS authentication. NetWare 5's SAS supports Secure Socket Layer (SSL) and uses the SAS API set to establish encrypted SSL connections—the ability to establish encrypted SSL connections is an essential requirement in commerce applications on the Web.

The *Public Key Infrastructure Services* (PKIS) are a set of services that enable the use of public key cryptography and digital certificates in a NetWare network. PKI services for NetWare 5 enable administrators to establish a Certificate Authority (CA) management domain within NDS. This CA is used by administrators to perform certificate and key management activities that enable certificate-based security services such as SSL security for LDAP servers. Like SAS, PKIS plays an important role in e-commerce applications.

OPTIONAL LOGIN SECURITY FEATURES

NetWare 5 includes a number of optional login security features that you can choose to implement on a global or a user-by-user basis. These features include the following:

- Login restrictions
- Password restrictions
- Login time restrictions
- Network address restrictions
- Intruder detection

LOGIN RESTRICTIONS

Through login restrictions, you can easily control how users can use the network. Through this feature, user accounts can be disabled, given an expiration date, or limited to a number of concurrent logins.

When a user account is disabled or has expired, that user can't log in to the network, even with a valid user ID and password. Disabled or expired accounts can be reenabled by the network administrator at any time, without any loss of data. Disabling the account denies the user access to the network without requiring you to delete the user account. For example, if a user leaves the company, you can simply disable the account and later reenable (and rename) it after a employee is hired. That way, the new user has access to all the old information.

Tip #165 from
Peter

> Account expiration is often used by schools to automatically cut off access at the end of an academic term. Also, many organizations use this feature to set up accounts for contractors.

Another useful login restriction feature is limiting concurrent user logins. This places a limit on the number of times a user can be logged in to the network simultaneously from different workstations. A good rule of thumb is to give each user two concurrent connections. Giving them only one connection can create more administrative work than necessary.

The way NetWare tracks user connections is by examining the number of entries in the Network Address attribute of the user object in NDS; every time you log in, the network address of your workstation is recorded in NDS. The entry is removed when you log out. However, if a user is forced to reboot his or her workstation without a proper logout from the network, the NetWare server might still hold the user's connection open, thus NDS is not updated. When this occurs, if the user is configured with only one concurrent connection, access to the network is denied until NetWare releases the original connection and the Network Address attribute updated.

Note

> It is a known issue that sometimes the Network Address attribute is not updated when a user logs out properly. In most situations, the cause has been traced to an outdated LAN driver on the server. However, in those cases where server LAN drivers are up to date, it suggests a bug in NDS.
>
> Novell is aware of this problem and has been working on it. But because it is not a high-priority issue, it might be some time yet before it gets resolved. The problem dates back to early versions of NetWare 4. Therefore, if you're going to pose a concurrent login limit, allow for at least two connections.

Figure 18.4 shows the Login Restrictions screen in NWAdmin where you can set the various parameters.

PART

V

CH

18

Figure 18.4
The user login restrictions screen in NWAdmin.

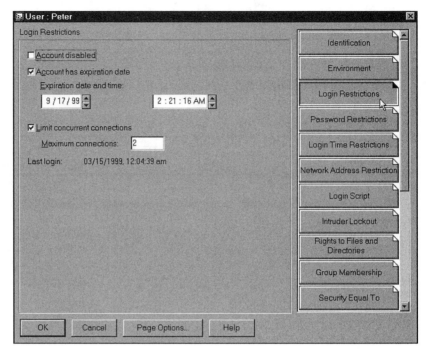

PASSWORD RESTRICTIONS

You can impose *password restrictions* to help enforce certain guidelines set for user passwords. These guidelines include requiring user passwords, minimum password lengths, password expiration dates, requiring unique passwords, and allowing grace logins.

Requiring user passwords is a *must* in every network, regardless of the level of security you want to accomplish. User accounts that have no passwords leave the network wide open for every type of security breach possible. Unfortunately, requiring a password is not a default option in NetWare. Because of this, setting the Require a Password property is the first thing that should be done when each user account is created. Not only should passwords be required, a minimum password length of five or more characters should be assigned. This prevents users from using their initials or something similar as their password. Simple precautionary measures such as these make it difficult for hackers to break into the network.

Tip #166 from
Peter

You can preset these parameters for the new users to be created using Template objects. Refer to Chapter 15, "Creating, Managing, and Using NDS Objects," for more about Template objects.

Because users often provide their current password to other users, it's also important to force periodic password changes. Normally, accepting the NetWare default of 40 days between password changes is sufficient. However, forcing password changes doesn't do any good unless *unique passwords* are required as well. Requiring unique password prevents users from using the same password over and over again. NetWare 5 keeps track of the last 10 passwords a user has used.

Note

The password must have been in use for more than 24 hours before it's considered for tracking by the unique passwords feature.

When a user's password expires, he or she is given the option to change the password right away or to change it later. Limiting the number of grace logins limits the number of times the user can use the old password after it expires. If a user exceeds the set number of grace logins, the account is locked and must be released by the network administrator.

Figure 18.5 shows the user password restrictions screen in NWAdmin. Notice you can also use this screen to change the user's password. In order for a regular user to change a password, the original password must be provided (and that the user has sufficient NDS rights) before a new password can be assigned. Network administrators can change user passwords without entering the old password first.

Tip #167 from
Peter

In order for one user to be able to change another user's password, this user must have Read and Write access to the Password Management NDS attribute of the target user.

PART

V

CH

18

Figure 18.5
The user password restrictions screen in NWAdmin.

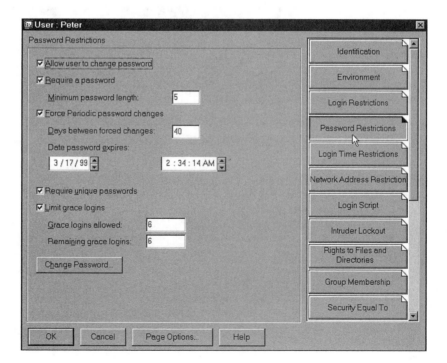

LOGIN TIME RESTRICTIONS

Login time restrictions enable the network administrator to restrict users from logging in to the network during specific times of the day. A common usage of this option is to ensure that all users are logged out before backups are performed. Many times, users leave for the day and fail to exit their applications and log off the network. When this occurs, the open files are skipped during the backup. Setting a time restriction just prior to the backup time not only prevents new users from logging in but also clears the connections of any users who forgot to log out. This ensures that all files are closed when the backup runs. Users still logged in when a time restriction approaches are sent warning messages that a time restriction is approaching. If the warnings are ignored, the user is automatically logged out by the system and the connection is cleared.

Tip #168 from
Peter

To address the issue of being unable to back up open files, many vendors offer an open file manager agent for their backup solutions. This agent allows the backup software to take a snapshot of the open file and back that up.

Figure 18.6 shows the time restriction screen in NetWare Administrator. By default, user's login times are unrestricted; by blocking out an area of time, a restriction is made. The example shows the user is restricted from logging in during all hours on the weekend and from midnight to 6 a.m. during weekdays.

Figure 18.6
The user login time restrictions screen in NWAdmin.

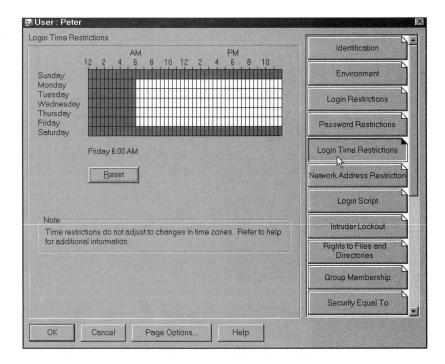

NETWORK ADDRESS RESTRICTIONS

Network address restrictions enable administrators to define specific addresses from which users can log in. This is useful when you want to prevent users from logging in from other people's workstations. In order to make a network address restriction, the network administrator needs to know the network address and the node ID of the workstation from which the user will be logging in. The *network address* is a software address assigned to a network segment when the network protocol is bound to the LAN driver. The *node ID* is the unique physical hardware ID on the network interface card of each workstation. The easiest method to find this information is to use the NetWare NLIST command, as follows:

NLIST USER /B /A

This returns a display that shows the network addresses and node IDs of all currently logged in users (both bindery and NDS). For example, the following output shows Admin is logged in on network E100 and the node ID of the workstation is 0020187168F2 (leading zeros are not shown by NLIST and each node ID consits of 12 hex digits):

```
Object Class: User
Known to Server: NETWARE5-A
Conn       = The server connection number
*          = The asterisk means this is your connection
User Name  = The login name of the user
Address    = The network address
Node       = The network node
Login time = The time when the user logged in

Conn *User Name                    Address       Node      Login Time
-------------------------------------------------------------------------
   1  .NETWARE5-A.toronto.dreaml  [  402418][            1] 03/11/99 06:38:08 pm
   2  .SAS Service - NETWARE5-A.  [  402418][            1] 03/11/99 06:38:08 pm
   4  .NETWARE5-A.toronto.dreaml  [  402418][            1] 03/14/99 10:09:08 pm
   5  .NETWARE5-A.toronto.dreaml  [  402418][            1] 03/11/99 06:38:08 pm
   7  .NETWARE5-A.toronto.dreaml  [  402418][            1] 03/11/99 06:38:08 pm
   8  .NETWARE5-A.toronto.dreaml  [  402418][            1] 03/13/99 01:12:08 pm
  10  .NETWARE5-B.test.dreamlan   [      5B][            1] 03/14/99 01:14:08 pm
  12  .NETWARE5-A.toronto.dreaml  [  402418][            1] 03/14/99 01:09:08 am
  13  .NETWARE5-A.toronto.dreaml  [  402418][            1] 03/11/99 07:09:08 pm
  15  .NETWARE5-B.test.dreamlan   [7B377B37][            0] 03/14/99 01:19:08 pm
  16  .NETWARE5-B.test.dreamlan   [      5B][            1] 03/14/99 02:14:08 pm
  17 *.admin.dreamlan             [    E100][  20187168F2] 03/11/99 08:17:08 pm
A total of 12 User objects was found on Preferred Server NETWARE5-A.
```

Note

> NLIST counts all server connections as *user objects*, regardless of whether the connection was actually made by a user or a service (such as SAS).

Figure 18.7 shows the network address restriction screen in NetWare Administrator.

PART

V

CH

18

Figure 18.7
The user network address restrictions screen in NWAdmin.

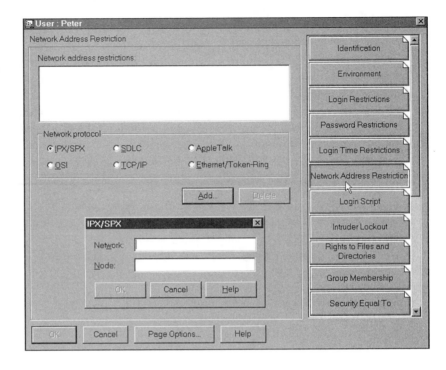

INTRUDER DETECTION

You can enable the *Intruder Detection* security option to detect and lock out intruders on the network. When a user attempts to log in to the network using a valid username but an invalid password, intruder detection is activated. Then, based on the intruder detection parameters, the user account is temporarily locked if the thresholds are exceeded.

Intruder detection is set at the container level in NDS. When it is enabled, the network administrator configures the number of incorrect login attempts allowed in a specific period of time, and whether or not to lock the account after detection of an intruder. For example, the NetWare defaults for intruder detection shown in Figure 18.8 lock an account if three incorrect login attempts are made on a single user account in 3.5 hours. When the account is locked, it is disabled for one day and 15 minutes and then automatically released by the system. In addition, a message is displayed at the file server console and logged in the file server's error log, indicating the account that was locked and the network address the lock out occurred from. This enables the administrator to easily track any lock outs that occur on the network.

Figure 18.8
Setting up intruder
detection using
NWAdmin.

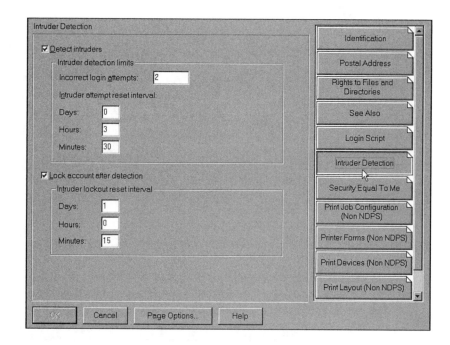

Tip #169 from
Peter

Some organizations set the lock account after detection time to be a very large value (more than 60 days). This is to force the offending user to contact the network administrator to have the account reset. Otherwise, if the lockout period is short, an intruder might not be noticed because the account was reset when the legit user logs on.

If an account is locked through intruder detection, you can release the account before the system releases it. This is done through the Intruder Lockout property of the user, as shown in Figure 18.9.

Tip #170 from
Peter

If the Admin account is locked through the intruder detection feature, it can be immediately released using the ENABLE LOGIN command at the file server console that reported the intruder lockout message. This does *not* unlock any other user accounts, however.

NOVELL DIRECTORY SERVICES (NDS) SECURITY

When you pass the hurdles associated with the login security, NDS security takes effect. It is the second level of NetWare security. NDS security controls who can access and manage the objects in the directory tree.

Figure 18.9
Unlocking intruder
detection using
NWAdmin.

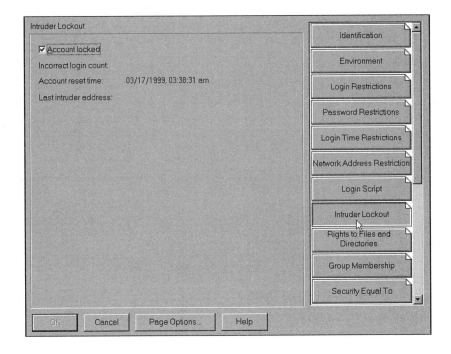

As you have previously learned in Chapter 16, "Managing NDS Rights, Partitions, and Replicas," a user's NDS rights determine what object the user can see in the Directory tree and what actions they can perform on other NDS objects. By default, you'll be able to see all objects in the tree but would not be able to change them in any way, unless you're Admin.

Every time you make a reference to an NDS object, such as trying to do a drive mapping using a Directory Map object, your NDS privilege is checked to see whether you can have access to that DM object before the map operation takes place. Therefore, NDS security governs what network resources you may have access to.

FILE SYSTEM SECURITY

One main reason for installing file servers is to store data on them and make them available to different users. However, some type of security must be implemented or one user might be able to read someone else's files when he is not supposed to, or someone can update a file when she is not authorized to.

NetWare implements fairly tight default file system security—in order for users to access the files and directories of network volumes, they *must* be given the appropriate file system security access. The default NetWare file system security—users have no access to any files and directories on NetWare volumes—is opposite to that of the default NDS security.

File system security in NetWare 5 consists of two components:

- **Directory and file rights**—These determine which type of access a user has to a directory or file, such as whether the user can write to particular files or view them. Without a rights assignment, a user can do nothing, not even view files or a directory.

- **File attributes**—Attribute security assigns special properties to individual directories and files that may override rights a user's rights assignment.

DIRECTORY AND FILE RIGHTS

As mentioned previously, directory and file rights give users access to the files and directories of network volumes. NetWare 5 makes no assumptions when it comes to giving users file system rights. Only the user Admin has rights to files and directories by default. Rights to access files and directories *must* be explicitly granted to users by the network administrator.

Table 18.1 shows a list of file system rights in NetWare 5. These rights can be granted at the directory or subdirectory level or at the individual file level.

TABLE 18.1   FILE SYSTEM RIGHTS

Right	Description
Supervisor (S)	Grants all rights to a file or directory. When granted, cannot be blocked in subsequent subdirectories by an inherited rights filter.
Write (W)	Grants the right to open and write to files.
Create (C)	Grants the right to create new files in a subdirectory.
Erase (E)	Grants the right to delete files or subdirectories.
Modify (M)	Grants the rights to rename or change the attributes of files and subdirectories.
File Scan (F)	Grants the rights to view files and directories.
Access Control (A)	Grants the right to control who has access to a file or directory. Allows the granting of new rights (except Supervisor) as well as changing attributes.

Often times, these rights need to be used in combinations in order to give users appropriate access to a particular file or directory. For example, if a user is required to create new files in a directory, granting the Create right alone will only enable him to create new files but not view or modify the files after creation.

To make it easier to determine which combinations of rights to give users, determine which of the following categories a user fits into and grant them the rights indicated:

- Users who need to create and write to files ([RFWCEM])
- Users who need to view or copy files only ([RF])

■ Users who need to run network application ([RF])

■ Users who can perform administrative functions ([RFWCEMA])

Caution

You should take note when granting user Access Control right to a file or directory; that user can in turn give file system rights to other users. Therefore, the unchecked use of Access Control can lead to security breaches.

When you use NWAdmin to create the home directory for a new user, NWAdmin automatically assigns the Access Control right to that user. You should revoke that right assignment.

TRUSTEE ASSIGNMENTS

As you learned in Chapter 16, with NDS rights there are many different types of objects that can be granted rights. Objects with file system rights are referred to as *trustees* (just the same as in NDS security) and the rights themselves are known as *trustee assignments*. The most obvious type of trustee is an individual User object. In most cases, however, users share common data and common network resources and require common rights. When this occurs, granting individual user rights might not be the most efficient way to administer the network. The following objects can grant users trustee assignments to files and directories:

■ **Groups**—Group objects can be granted rights to directories and files on volumes any where in the directory tree. Any user who is made a member of the group will inherit the groups rights. Users can be made members of multiple groups and the rights inherited from those groups are cumulative.

Tip #171 from
Peter

Although it's rarely encountered, you should be aware that there is an NDS limitation that a user can be members of only 64 groups. The 65th and higher assignments can be made but NDS will not realize the user is a member of those groups. This can result in users not getting the file system rights assigned through those groups. This has been fixed in NetWare 5.

■ **Container Objects**—When a container object is granted rights to files and directories, those rights will flow down to all the objects (both container and leaf) below that container. If rights are granted to the [Root] object all objects in the entire tree inherit those rights.

■ **[Public]**—This is a special type of NDS object that can be viewed only when granting rights. [Public] is used to grant rights to every user on the network to a particular file or directory. There is no way to exclude a user from inheriting the rights of [Public], so this method of granting rights should be used with caution.

Another method that can be used to grant users file system rights is *security equivalences*. By making an NDS user security equivalent to another user, you are giving that user the same rights as the other user.

Note

Security equivalence (SE) assignments are not transitive. That means when UserA is made SE to UserB, and UserB is made SE to UserC, UserA is *not* SE to UserC.

Also, SE assignments are not commutable. That is to say if UserA is SE to UserB, UserB is *not* SE to UserA.

FILE SYSTEM RIGHTS INHERITANCE

Whether a user receives trustee rights from an explicit user trustee assignment, through a group membership or from a container object, any directory or subdirectory level right will flow down to the files and subdirectories below—just as is the case with NDS trustee assignment, discussed in Chapter 16. For example, consider the file system directory structure in Figure 18.10.

Figure 18.10
File system rights flow down the directory structure.

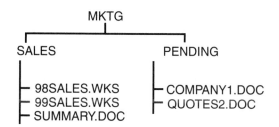

MKTG
SALES   PENDING
├ 98SALES.WKS   ├ COMPANY1.DOC
├ 99SALES.WKS   ├ QUOTES2.DOC
├ SUMMARY.DOC

If Sally is granted the [RFWCEM] rights to the directory MKTG, she will have those same rights at the subdirectories SALES and PENDING and their files. Rights will continue to flow down the file system directory structure until another explicit assignment is given at a lower level or until an Inherited Rights Filter (IRF) blocks the rights.

If Sally is to be given the access to view but not to change the contents of the SALES subdirectory, the network administrator can grant Sally an explicit trustee assignment of [RF] to SALES, overriding her previous assignment.

If rights flowing from parent directories need to be blocked for all users, an IRF can be used. An IRF in the file system, similar to the IRF discussed in the NDS rights section, filters rights flowing from parent directories. When a file or directory is created the IRF is set to allow all eight rights [SRFWCEDM], to flow down. To block rights flowing from parent directories, the network administrator removes rights (except for S, which can't be blocked) from the IRF using NWAdmin or FILER.

Note

The one difference between how IRF works in NDS and how it works in file system is that you can block Supervisory right from flowing down the tree, but *you can't block S right in the file system*.

To illustrate how an IRF works, consider the preceding directory structure once again.

Assume that the group MARKETING has been granted [RF] to the MKTG subdirectory, giving them the capability to view all subdirectories and files below MKTG. Because the file QUOTES2.DOC contains confidential pricing information, the network administrator wants to prevent all unauthorized users from seeing the file. By setting the IRF of the file to [S], all users with rights other than Supervisor will be blocked from the file.

Inherited Rights Filters only block rights that are being inherited from parent directories; they do not block explicit trustee assignments. In other words if the user Sally from the previous example (who is a member of the MARKETING group) needs the ability to view the contents of the QUOTES2.DOC file, you can grant her [RF] explicitly at the file level. Because it is an explicit assignment and the rights are not being inherited from a parent directory, the IRF has no effect on Sally's rights.

ATTRIBUTE SECURITY

As you just learned, to determine a user's total rights to a file or directory you first must check to see whether the user has an explicit trustee assignment for that file or directory. If there is not an explicit assignment, you need to check to see whether rights are being inherited from parent directories. If they are, you then need to take into account the IRF to see whether all rights are allowed to filter through. The result is the user's *effective* rights to that file or directory.

Effective rights do not always determine what a user can do in a file or directory because you have not yet considered the final level of file system security: *attribute security*.

Attributes are special properties that can be added to a file or a directory. Attribute security can actually override a user's effective rights. For example, if the user's effective rights give the permission to write to a file, and the file has the Read Only attribute assigned, the user will be denied write access.

Attributes can be assigned at both the file and directory level. Table 18.2 shows a list of the available attributes and a brief definition of each.

TABLE 18.2   FILE SYSTEM ATTRIBUTE

Attribute	Description
Archive Needed (A)	Indicates file has been modified since last backup. Cleared when file is backed up. Can be assigned to files only.
Copy Inhibit (CI)	Prevents Macintosh users from copying DOS files. Can be assigned to files only. Has no effect to non-Mac clients.
Don't Compress (DC)	Prevents the file from being compressed even if the server-defined thresholds are reached. Can be applied to both files and directories.
Delete Inhibit (DI)	Prevents the file from being deleted, even if the trustee has been granted the Delete right. Can be assigned to both files and directories.

Attribute	Description
Don't Migrate (DM)	Prevents the file from being migrated to a secondary storage device if data migration is enabled. Can be assigned to both files and directories.
Immediate Compress (IC)	Forces immediate compression of the file without waiting for the server-defined file compression thresholds to be met. Can be applied to files only.
Execute Only (X)	Indicates that the file can be only executed. Files marked with this attribute cannot be copied or backed up and some applications cannot execute these files properly. Can only be assigned by Admin and should be used with caution. Can be applied to files only.
Hidden (H)	Prevents file from being viewed with the DOS DIR command. NetWare's NDIR command allows the viewing of Hidden files. Also prevents files from being deleted or copied. Can be applied to both files and directories.
Purge (P)	Indicates that the file should be purged immediately after deletion. Purged files cannot be salvaged. Can be applied to both files and directories.
Read Only (RO)	Indicates that the file cannot be deleted, modified, or renamed. Files not flagged Read Only are automatically Read Write. Can be applied to files only.
Read Write (RW)	Indicates that the file can be deleted, modified, or renamed. All files not flagged Read Only are automatically Read Write. Can be applied to files only.
Rename Inhibit (RI)	Prevents the file from being renamed, even if the trustee has been granted the Access Control right. Can be assigned to both files and directories.
Shareable (Sh)	Allows a file to be used by more than one user at a time. Files not flagged Shareable are automatically Non-Shareable. Can be applied to files only.
System (Sy)	Marks files used by the operating system. Files flagged system cannot be viewed with the DOS DIR command. NetWare's NDIR can view System files. Also prevents files from being deleted or copied. Can be applied to files and directories.
Transactional (T)	Shows that a file is protected by the Transaction Tracking System (YYS). Transactional files cannot be deleted or renamed. Can be applied to files only.

File attributes can be administered in three ways. From Windows, the NWAdmin utility can be used. Through DOS, FILER or the FLAG command can be used. Procedures for assigning file attributes are outlined later in this chapter.

→ For more on FILER, **see** "Using FILER," page **425**

ADMINISTERING FILE SYSTEM RIGHTS

NetWare 5 provides a number of different methods of granting rights to files and directories. The method chosen depends largely on whether you, as the network administrator, prefer to work in a Windows GUI environment or a DOS text-based environment. In a Windows environment, the NWAdmin utility is used. The main benefit to administering rights through NWAdmin is that the "point-and-click" and "drag-and-drop" methods commonly used in Windows applications makes administering rights fast and easy. The benefit of DOS utilities is their efficiency.

USING NETWARE ADMINISTRATOR

File system rights can be administered using two techniques through NWAdmin. One way is by selecting the Rights to Files and Directories property in a user's Details page. The Details page is accessed by selecting the object and choosing Details from the Object menu or by double-clicking the object.

Tip #172 from
Peter

When you right-click an object, the context menu includes the Details option as well as other useful options.

When the Rights to Files and Directories property is selected, a form appears that enables you to administer file system rights. Figure 18.11 shows an example of this form. Rights are granted to a directory or file by clicking the Add button and then browsing the tree for the volume and directory or file to which you want to grant rights. Rights are then granted by clicking the box to the left of the permission.

An alternative method is to use the Volume objects. After drilling down the volume, locate the desired directory or file, right-click it, and select Details. When the Trustees of this Directory (or Trustees of this File) property is selected, a form appears that enables you to administer file system rights (see Figure 18.12). Rights are granted to a directory or file by clicking the Add button and then browsing the tree for the object which you want to be a trustee. Rights are then granted by clicking the selections under the Access rights column.

Tip #173 from
Peter

Using the second technique, you can also manage the file/directory attribute by selecting the Attribute property.

Figure 18.11
File system rights are granted through NWAdmin by selecting Rights to Files and Directories in a user's Details.

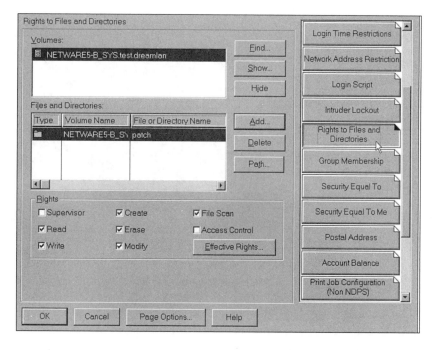

Figure 18.12
Assigning trustees to a file/directory.

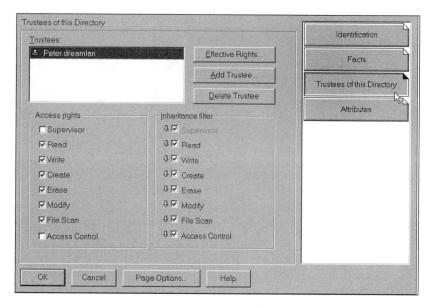

USING FILER

Rights to files and directories can also be administered using the FILER utility. The text interface, known as *C-Worthy*, is using FILER. Figure 18.13 shows the FILER main menu.

Figure 18.13
You can "walk the file systems" using FILER's Manage files and directories option, even to volumes on other servers, without exiting FILER.

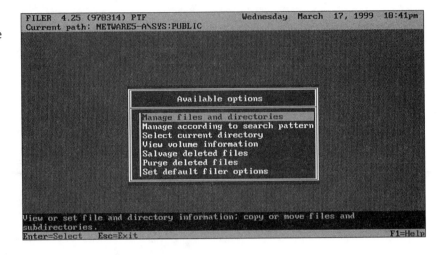

To grant rights, select Manage Files and Directories from the FILER main menu. Use the arrow keys to scroll through the directory list and press Enter to select a directory. When you locate the subdirectory or file you want, press F10 to access the Subdirectory or file options. A menu, as shown in Figure 18.14, is presented.

Figure 18.14
Granting file system rights through FILER.

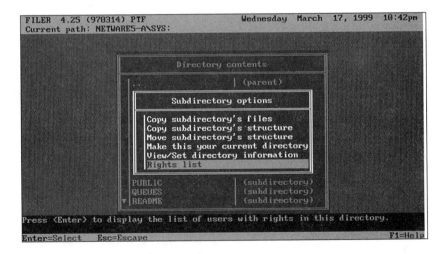

Selecting Rights list enables you to view a list of existing trustees of this directory. Selecting View/Set directory information enables you to view or change information, such as directory attributes, the IRF of this directory, or the Trustees (see Figure 18.15). You can add a trustee assignment by first selecting Trustees from this menu and using the Insert key to add the name of the trustee.

Figure 18.15
Directory information enables you to administer directory attributes, the IRF, and trustees of a directory.

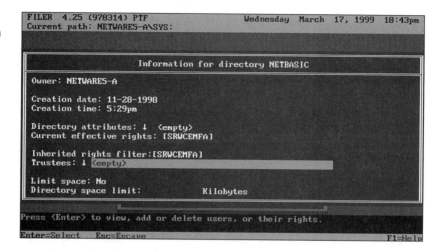

USING THE RIGHTS COMMAND

Probably the most difficult method NetWare 5 provides for granting rights to files and directories is the RIGHTS command. Type RIGHTS /? from the DOS command line to show a general help screen for the RIGHTS command (see Figure 18.16).

Figure 18.16
Help screen for RIGHTS.

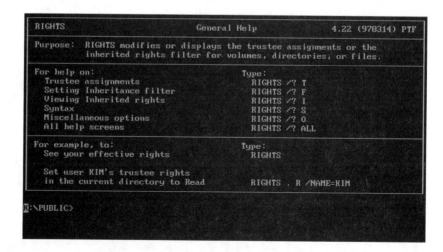

You can get more detailed help for using the RIGHTS command. For example, typing RIGHTS /? T gives you help on setting or viewing trustee assignments and RIGHTS /? F provides more information setting the IRF.

If you choose to use the DOS command line to grant rights to users, use the following syntax:

RIGHTS *Path Rights List* /NAME=*object*

For example, to grant Sally the Read and File Scan rights to the SYS:MKTG\SALES directory, type the following:

```
RIGHTS SYS:MKTG\SALES RF /NAME=SALLY
```

This assumes Sally exists in your current NDS context. If the user object Sally is not in the current context, it would be necessary to provide the NDS object name in either full distinguish name or relative distinguish name syntax, as in the following example:

```
RIGHTS SYS:MKTG\SALES RF /NAME=.Sally.Consulting.Dallas
```

To change the inherited rights filter of a file or directory using the RIGHTS command, use the following syntax:

```
RIGHTS Path Rights List /F
```

So, if you want to restrict all rights except users with Supervisor rights to the file system from being inherited from parent directories to the QUOTES2.DOC file, you can use the following syntax to set the IRF:

```
RIGHTS SYS:MKTG\PENDING\QUOTES2.DOC S /F
```

USING THE FLAG COMMAND

For those of you who prefer the DOS command line, you can use the FLAG command to assign file or directory attributes. Display the FLAG syntax by typing the following:

```
FLAG /? SYNTAX
```

Figure 18.17 shows the FLAG syntax help screen.

Figure 18.17
The FLAG syntax help screen.

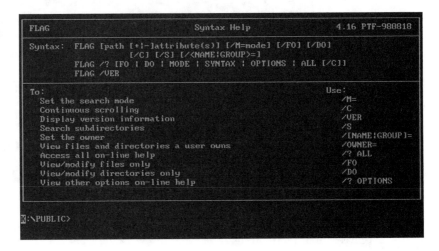

Suppose that you want to flag the file SALES99.WKS in the SYS:MKTG\SALES directory as Read Only. The syntax is as follows:

```
FLAG SYS:MKTG\SALES\SALES99.WKS RO
```

Tip #174 from
Peter

Using FLAG, you can set *all* the files in a given directory branch to have the same attribut- es. For example, FLAG *.* RO /S /C sets all files in the current directory and all its sub- directories to be Read Only; the /S tells FLAG to transverse all subdirectories, and /C means don't pause the screen display. Such a task is not possible using NWAdmin or FILER.

FILE SERVER CONSOLE SECURITY

The final level of NetWare security is file server console security. File server console securi- ty protects your file server from unauthorized access. To keep your file server secure, you need to prevent unauthorized users from being able to do the following:

- Loading or unloading NLM
- Changing the file server's date and/or time
- Dismounting a volume
- Downing the file server

The easiest way to protect your file server is to lock it up. Any time your file server is stored in a location that people have general access to, you're asking for trouble. Generally, a file server is just sitting there with not a lot going on on its screen. So, an unknowing user walks up and decides he wants to use the floppy drive. When the user can't get to the A: drive, he or she decides to turn the machine off and back on again. There goes your file server.

Note

In any networking environment, physical security is your first line of defense. Without physical security, no matter how many restrictions you implement using the features avail- able in the operating system, it would be pointless should someone physically remove your server!

Another issue to be aware of is the file server's date and time. In NetWare 5, changing the date and time at the file server console can very likely disrupt times synchronization on the network, especially if the server is one of Single Reference, Reference, or Primary time server. Times synchronization is important to successful synchronization of NDS. If times synchronization on the network is off, synchronization of your NDS replicas cannot take place. If your server console can be accessed by anyone, it is very easy to use the TIME com- mand to change the date and time.

Also, if your server is in a common area just about anyone can load or unload NLMs. NLMs can be loaded from the SYS:SYSTEM directory, the DOS partition, or from a floppy drive. Without proper security, it would be very easy for someone to unload a critical NLM, such as a LAN or disk driver, or worse yet, load a rogue NLM. Rouge NLMs are NLMs that either intentionally or unintentionally cause problems on your network. Some "grow" as time goes on, using more and more memory. Others attempt to break into the system, breaching security. Some might even attempt to introduce a virus to the network.

So, the easiest way to prevent a situations such as these is to store your file server in a location where unauthorized users can't access it. Lock it in a closet if you have to. Remember, most of the administration in NetWare 5 is done from a workstation, and RCONSOLE can manage the server console remotely, so don't worry about it being easily accessible for administration, unless you have a need to run Java applications on the server.

Note

At the time of this writing, it is not possible to access the GUI screens on the NetWare 5 server remotely.

Following are two other ways to protect your server console:

- Use SCRSAVER.NLM to lock the console.
- Use the SECURE CONSOLE command.

Prior to NetWare 5, the console locking function was provided through the MONITOR.NLM main menu. However, in NetWare 5, this function has been removed from MONITOR and is implemented using the SCRSAVER.NLM.

SCRSAVER allows a software lock to be placed on the server. When it's set, a valid user/password combination must be provided before anything can be done at the server. Figure 18.18 shows an example of a locked file server console.

Figure 18.18
SCRSAVER.NLM can be used to place a software lock on the server.

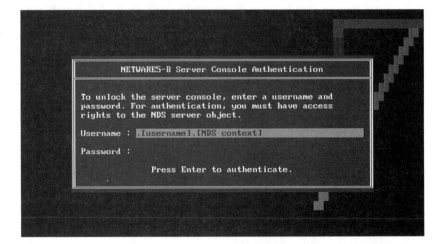

Tip #175 from
Peter

SCRSAVER requires that the User object have Supervisor rights to the Server object for the unlocking. This might not be possible in all cases. An alternative console locker/screen saver, SSLock for NDS, can be found at http://www.dreamlan.com/sslock.htm. With SSLock, shown in Figure 18.19, you can define a group of users that can unlock the console and a different group of user that can unlock the console or unload the NLM; Supervisor rights to the Server object are not required.

SCRSAVER doesn't work on NetWare 4.1x but SSLock does.

Figure 18.19
SSLock for NDS doesn't require the user to have Supervisor right to the Server object.

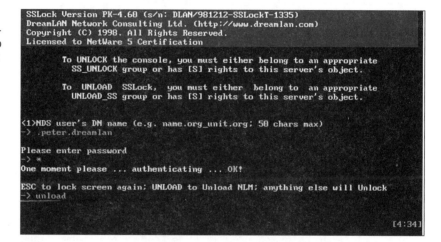

```
SSLock Version PK-4.60 (s/n: DLAN/981212-SSLockT-1335)
DreamLAN Network Consulting Ltd. (http://www.dreamlan.com)
Copyright (C) 1998. All Rights Reserved.
Licensed to NetWare 5 Certification

      To UNLOCK the console, you must either belong to an appropriate
        SS_UNLOCK group or has [S] rights to this server's object.

      To UNLOAD SSLock, you must either belong to an appropriate
        UNLOAD_SS group or has [S] rights to this server's object.

<1>NDS user's DN name (e.g. name.org_unit.org; 50 chars max)
-> .peter.dreamlan

Please enter password
-> *
One moment please ... authenticating ... OK!

ESC to lock screen again; UNLOAD to Unload NLM; anything else will Unlock
-> unload

                                                                  [4:34]
```

The SECURE CONSOLE command can also be used to protect your file server. If you enter SECURE CONSOLE from the server console, you provide the following added security:

- Prevents NLMs from being loaded from any path not specified in the server's SEARCH paths.

- Removes DOS from the servers memory preventing NLMs from being loaded from C: or A:.

- Prevents entry into the OS debugger. The OS debugger enables developers to directly access the server's memory from the server console. Unauthorized or uneducated access to the OS debugger could potentially cause serious problems (such as file corruption) to your file server.

As you can see, protecting your file server console is not a difficult task. Consider using not just one but all the techniques mentioned earlier to protect your server. In the long run, you'll be glad that you did.

TROUBLESHOOTING

Because there are many ways a user can obtain file system rights (from direct trustee assignments, groups belonged to, and even from NDS containers), it is not always easy to determine or troubleshoot a scenario in which a user has full file system rights. The following procedures outline the steps you can take in order to track the cause.

At the root of the volume type RIGHTS /T to see if there was an explicit rights assignment granted to the user or any group or container the user is a member of. If so, revoke that assignment and see if that resolves the problem.

If there is no explicit assignment, the user has most likely inherited the rights from NDS. That means somewhere the user, container, and so on was granted at least [W] property right to the file server object's Object Trustees (ACL) property. They can get this by via one or more of the following assignments:

- Having [S] object rights
- Having [S] or [W] right to All Properties
- Having [S] or [W] to the Object Trustees (ACL) property

One way to track the above assignments down is to select Trustees of this Object for the [Root] object, and then select Effective Rights and see what the User's effective rights are. Then if they have excessive rights, find the object in the Trustees of this Object list that was granted the excessive rights. Then work your way down the tree branch by doing the same thing for each container between the [Root] and the server object, including the server object. At some point you will see that the user's effective rights are more than the default (only [B] object rights and [RC] All property rights). It is then at this level in the tree that the assignment was made.

## CHAPTER 19

AUDITING

In this chapter

THE NEED FOR AUDITING

As discussed in Chapter 18, "Implementing Security," there are various methods of implementing security. Password protection, login restrictions, and locked server consoles are a few such security measures. Each level of security is important and provides a solution for one aspect of network security; however, these levels do not address the most vulnerable part of a network—the user.

The biggest threat to a network's data is the user. Users are human and make mistakes. When a user gets disgruntled and attacks what he or she thinks is the company's weakest point, the network, the avenues available for that user to corrupt, delete, or change network data make him or her the single largest threat to the security of your network data.

Networks and their hardware components (computers, network cards, cables, and so on) were not designed with security in mind. Thus, network security features offered by the network operating system must be properly enabled and configured to maintain system confidentiality, security, and reliability.

Today, nearly everyone in the business world uses some form of network computing. The use of network computing technology is not without danger. The environment in which information is being retrieved, processed, transmitted, and stored daily, is not inherently secure. As mission critical business applications come to networks, the need for internal controls, security, and auditing capabilities grow, especially now that network operating systems are fulfilling an ever-increasing role of the business. This increasing role of the network increases reliance on data communications systems.

Because of this reliance, network administrators need to ensure network access is as secure as possible. One method of ensuring the confidentiality of the data on your network is to perform auditing.

> **Note**
>
> Auditors should not be network administrators and should not have Admin rights or the equivalent. Otherwise, the purpose behind performing an audit is negated.
>
> Auditors can track events and activities on the network. This form of security not only aids in creating a more secure environment, but also helps to guarantee that data has not been tampered with or altered.

NetWare 5's auditing features enable you to monitor and record networkwide events for any designated network resource (both NDS and file system). By auditing network resource usage, you can verify the network is properly set up and secure. It also helps to ensure company's security policies and procedures are adhered to.

The principle behind using NetWare 5's auditing functions is based on creating an independent auditor, who is responsible for auditing past and present transactions on the network. This network user, the auditor, can monitor and record designated events but cannot (and should not) access any resource other than the audit reports.

In fact, to be most effective an auditor should act independently of the network administrator. This creates a checks-and-balances system that can help ensure that network records are accurate and confidential information is secure.

Businesses might want to perform an audit for several reasons. For example, an internal auditor would verify that things such as regulatory requirements or processes are being followed. You can perform an audit to determine whether there are opportunities for improvement or simply to measure compliance with company policy. It is common for external auditors, especially in the accounting profession, to perform an audit, and it is likely that this type of audit will find its way into the realm of computing. The exact approach and procedures an auditor employs depends on the objective of the audit.

Another purpose of an audit is to detect activities that might compromise the security of the system. For example, an audit would aid in determining unauthorized access or attempted access to sensitive data or areas of the network. Audits with a type of objective could be categorized as *security audits*. During a security audit you should consider the following:

- Creation of users
- Changes to a user's properties or rights
- Granting of Admin security equivalences
- Authenticating users
- Access system areas
- Changing the configuration of the system
- Installation and deletion of program software
- Modifications made to accounts
- Deleting or copying sensitive files

After you establish the level of security you want, you need to continually perform audits because security tends to deteriorate over time and weakens with the complexity and flexibility of the particular network environment.

Typically, the factors that contribute to the degradation of a systems security are the following types of actions:

- Installation of new software
- Employee turnover
- Changes in employee responsibilities
- Temporary employee accesses (that are not revoked)
- New applications updates
- Regular security monitoring
- Periodic security audits

PART

V

CH

19

Tip #176 from
Peter

One of the biggest factors adding to the possibility of a security breach is the failure of a network administrator to perform regular security audits.

Regular monitoring of a network's security should be part of the administrator's responsibility.

Periodic security audits should be performed by someone other than the network administrator. The frequency of a security audit depends on the size of the security risk.

The following policies enable the system administrator to control network security that can be implemented at the Directory Services, network, server, and file system levels to determine the following:

- Who can access the network
- Which resources (such as file system directories and files) users can access
- How users can utilize the resources
- Who can perform tasks at the server console

The auditing function of NetWare 5 helps increase the integrity of network data by tracking network events. Auditing data can be used to determine whether procedures are being followed and who is performing tasks at the NetWare server level.

The transactions and events that can be monitored through NetWare 5's auditing console are as follows:

- Logins and logouts
- Trustee modifications
- File creations, deletions, reads, and writes
- Requests to manipulate queues
- Directory Services object creations, deletions, reads, and writes
- Events directly related to Directory Services objects
- Events directly related to users

With NetWare 5, auditors also can track Directory Services events, which include the creation or deletion of an object or of an object's properties. Auditing functions also are available for the file system, which includes the access or use of a server's volume or files.

Note

Auditing is enabled at the volume level for file system auditing. It is enabled at the container level when auditing Novell Directory Services events.

When an auditor designates certain network resources for auditing, the auditing information is kept in audit files, which are automatically created—that is, when a volume or container has had auditing enabled. These auditing files are similar to the records that are kept for the system error logs, except that a password can be assigned to the log file, which protects the contents from being altered.

| **Tip #177 from** *Peter* | It is vital that you establish procedures for clearing the auditing files. These files continue to accept information until the volume is full. You should at least limit the size of the audit files and regularly view and migrate the files to a secondary source of storage.

See the "Working with Audit Files" section later in this chapter for information on managing audit files. |
|---|---|

To access the audit reports, you need to use AUDITCON. The AUDITCON program and files are automatically installed on the network when you install or upgrade to NetWare 5; however, by default, auditing is not automatically initiated. For more information on initiating the auditing function in NetWare 5, see the "Setting Up Auditing" section of this chapter.

Note	By installing all the auditing files and utilities during installation, all the network auditor has to do is enable the auditing process. This separates the network administrators' roles and the auditing functions, allowing the person elected to be the auditor to perform auditing responsibilities and functions without having to perform network administrator tasks.

UNDERSTANDING NETWARE AUDITING

NetWare auditing uses the server to provide protected mechanisms to record audit information in a protected audit trail. Individuals known as auditors can then review this information or configure the server to collect other information.

An NetWare audit trail consists of the following:

- An NDS Audit File object
- A sequence of audit data files

The Audit File object and its Novell Directory Services properties define the audit configuration and the rights of other NDS entities to access the Audit File object and its audit files. The sequence of audit data files include the current audit file (where data is currently being recorded), up to 15 old online audit files, and a sequence of offline audit files.

Note	AUDITCON creates the Audit File object when you enable auditing, and the Audit File object is transparently checked by the server for access rights each time a user attempts to access the audit trail.

The complete audit trail consists of a sequence of audit records that potentially extends from the first audit event recorded on an offline audit file to the last audit event recorded on the current audit file. Each audit file includes a creation timestamp that determines the (time) position of each audit file in the sequence.

> **Note**
>
> Each audit record is time-stamped with the originating server's local time; therefore, it is important that you set the server's time zone information correctly. Events on different servers are synchronized by NDS time synchronization mechanisms, which usually maintain times on multiple servers to within a second of each other.

Audit records can logically be divided into two types:

- Audit history records, which record such management actions as examining or configuring the audit trail
- Audit event records, which record user actions that were audited by the NetWare server or an external client

Audit history and audit event records are physically stored together in audit data files. However, AUDITCON provides separate facilities to examine the two types of records.

Audit history records are always recorded if auditing is enabled; you can't use preselection (advance specification of the events, users, and files to be audited) to avoid recording audit history records.

Three types of audit trails are maintained by a NetWare server:

- **Volume audit trails**—A volume audit trail is associated with a single volume on a single server. The audit data is stored in the volume on that server. The volume audit trail contains audit history events for the volume audit trail, plus security-relevant events recorded by the OS (volume mounts and file opens, for example). The audit configuration (rules for generating audit events and other items) can specified on a volume-by-volume basis, so that auditing can be enabled for one volume and disabled for another volume.

  Volume audit events can be preselected based on event type, user identity, and (for certain file system events) on filename.

  In addition to the events that can be recorded in each volume audit trail, the SYS: volume audit trail can also record events detected by OS. These include console events, such as loading NLMs and defining SET parameters. Because the server does not provide a mechanism for logging in administrators at the server console, console auditing must be supported by a manual log that identifies which administrator is using the server console.

- **Container audit trails**—Container audit trails record security-relevant NDS events performed in the associated NDS container object, as well as audit history records for the audit trail. Because NDS is a distributed database, container audit trails are associated with the distributed NDS container object and not with any specific server (as with volume audit trails). Container audit trails (but not necessarily all events in the audit trail) are replicated to each server holding the audited container object. The audit configuration is specified separately for each audited NDS container object.

   Preselection of container audit events can be configured in one of two ways: event only (this is the default) or audit by user as well as by event.

   Auditing of a particular container object (an Organization object, for example) does not imply auditing of subcontainers within the audited container (its Organizational Unit objects, for example).

- **External audit trails**—The server provides external audit trails that can be used by trusted clients to store audit data on the server. External audit trails also contain audit history records. Preselection of client-generated audit records is performed by the client before submission of audit records to the server. The NetWare server sees the external audit information as a stream of uninterpreted data; interpretation of the audit events is performed solely by the client.

SETTING UP AUDITING

The first step in setting up auditing is to establish a set of procedures and guidelines. Given the flexibility of today's networks, as well as the various methods of implementing and using networks, it is virtually impossible to define an exact set of auditing procedures and practices that are a one-size-fits-all approach. However, there are methods you can use to help define the appropriate auditing principles and practices, regardless of network implementation or size.

The best approach for determining the auditing needs of your particular network implementation is to take a component-by-component approach. That is, look at each component of your network and determine its exact function, as well as who should have access to that particular function. The awareness of the access to the component's function, or the regularity of an audit on that given component, should directly correlate with the importance of that component's function to operation of the overall network.

PART
V

CH
19

Tip #178 from
Peter

When setting up security and auditing, keep asking yourself this one simple question: "Why should I audit a particular network component?" This often helps to answer the question, "Do I need to audit this network component?"

During the process of determining your company's auditing guidelines, you should also pay close attention to the objectives of an audit by asking yourself the following questions:

- What is the purpose of the audit?
- What are the objectives?
- What functions should be audited and why?
- Are there any company policies or standards that deserve special attention?
- Should management and users be informed of the audit process?

Tip #179 from
Peter

If the audit's purpose is to determine whether your users adhere to company policies, you would most likely not inform them that an audit is being considered. However, you should discuss this with the proper high-level managers and perhaps even with Human Resources to ensure you're not crossing any lines, such as privacy policies.

- Has the physical security of the network been forgotten?

Tip #180 from
Peter

After considering who should have access to specific network components and defining the objectives of the audit, you should be well on your way to implementing company audit policies and procedures. Before completely defining company policy, however, you should also consider the security of the network.

There usually is ample information about implementing the security of the network, passwords, rights, and so on; but often, the physical security of vital network components is overlooked. In other words, critical network components, such as your servers, should be placed behind lock and key. You also should ask yourself the following questions:

- What is the status of the system security and controls?
- Is sensitive data protected and well backed up?
- Are there company procedures in place?
- In case of a disaster, are procedures for continuing operation in place?
- Have all continuing operation plans been tested?

In the past, most communications devices were designated for a particular function; however, this is no longer true. Equipment on local area networks interoperate and act as an exchange for many applications, allowing virtually any user access to any part of the system—transparently and around the world.

To compound network security risks, networks are usually geographically dispersed, are constantly growing, and are globally accessible. The auditing process should support, not hinder, this real-time user need for flexibility.

Therefore, auditing in the network computing environment must provide you with the capability to monitor, collect, and review user activities, systemwide options, NDS, individual servers, and the resources that each of these network components provide.

AUDITCON is a DOS utility that allows auditors to specify the parts of the system to be monitored and provides functions for outputting auditing data for management review. AUDITCON also monitors the activities concerned with identification, access, and modification of network resources.

The role of the network administrator is to set up the auditor's environment or the network and enable auditing for the appropriate NDS container or volume. When this is complete, the network administrator gives the auditing password to the auditor, who assumes responsibility for auditing. The auditor changes the auditing password to ensure that the auditing data is secure. The auditor configures the auditing environment, sets the events to be audited, and manages the auditing data.

The reporting capability of AUDITCON provides reassurance to management and other parties interested in the security and integrity of the network. Each company should know that a user's access to and use of network resources is appropriate and authorized and that the system is operating appropriately.

When you've decided on your guidelines, you're ready to enable auditing on your NetWare 5 network.

Preparing to Enable Audit

Before the actual initiation of the auditing functions, you should perform several tasks which will provide the auditor with the rights and accesses needed to perform an audit. The following describes these processes as well as describes the actual implementation of the auditing function:

- **Create a directory in the file system for the auditor to use**—The auditor needs space to store audit reports. Create a directory, as you did for other users (that is, if your policy is to create a directory for each user account).

- **Give the auditor file system trustee rights to the directory you created**—Similar to the case of user home directories, you should grant the auditor all rights except for the Supervisor and Access Control rights to the directory.

- **Create the auditor as a User object and grant NDS rights**—If the auditor will audit NDS events, assign him or her the Browse object right in the container objects to be audited.

Tip #181 from

Peter

The administrator can create the auditor User object in any container in the NDS tree. However, for increased isolation from administrative users, you might want to request the administrator to perform the following additional steps:

1. Create a separate NDS container to hold auditor User objects.

2. Create an auditor User object who has all rights to the container. Subsequently, this auditor will perform all administrative functions (such as adding other auditor User objects, setting rights, and deleting auditor objects) in the auditor container.

3. Set an IRF for the auditor container object to filter out all inherited rights. This prevents administrators (other than the auditor created in step 2) from accessing the auditor container object.

4. Enable auditing for the auditor container object. This helps to keep track of changes made to this container.

   The administrator must run AUDITCON to enable auditing. This creates the Audit File object in the tree. The administrator must then give the auditor rights to this object.

5. Edit the ACL for the Audit File object associated with the container to remove the administrator (other than the auditor created in step 2) as a trustee of the Audit File object.

6. Edit the ACL for the container object to remove the administrator (other than the auditor created in step 2) as a trustee of the container.

These steps help to isolate auditor accounts from non-auditor administrative users, but do not protect auditor data from administrative users. Look ahead to the "Controlling Access to Audit Data" section in this chapter on how to limit access to your audit information.

Event Selection Considerations

NetWare provides two general methods of tracking users' accesses to protected resources:

- *Post-processing* is a method of filtering an existing audit trail to present only the events that are of interest. AUDITCON provides menus to define post-processing filters for volume, container, and external auditing.

- *Preselection* is a method of causing the server to record selected event types (such as file opens), specific users, or specific resources (such as files or directories) to the current volume trail. For volume auditing, you can preselect by event types, users, and files.

   For container auditing, you can preselect by users and event types. The server does not provide any preselection for external auditing.

You can't generate audit reports for events that are not preselected for auditing when the event occurs (as there will be no records of those events in the audit trail). For example, if you want to review which files were opened by a user two weeks ago, but you didn't have file opens preselected at that time, you will not be able to generate an audit report that lists the files.

Consequently, you must balance your need for certain audit information with the resources required to audit those events.

ENABLING VOLUME AUDITING

If you have different data that will be monitored by different auditors, you should create a separate volume for each set of data. For example, you might not want someone in Human Resources to have access to the company financial information. For this type of situation, you can create separate volumes of each data set. Then each auditor could be given the appropriate rights for the data that they are suppose to audit.

Note

You must have the Read right to the Volume object's Audit File Link attribute. This is necessary for AUDITCON to determine the existence of an Audit File object for the volume.

If an Audit File object does not already exist for the volume, you must have the Write right to the Volume object's Audit File Link attribute to modify the volume's Audit File Link to point to the Audit File object.

If an Audit File object does not already exist for the volume, you must have the Create object right to the container object where the Volume object is located.

To enable auditing on a volume, complete the following steps:

1. Log in to the network as Admin or equivalent.

2. Start AUDITCON and your current server and volume are displayed at the top of the screen. To select a different server or volume to audit, select the Change Current Server or Change Current Volume option.

3. Select the desired server or volume.

4. Select Enable Volume Auditing from the Available Audit Options menu, as shown in Figure 19.1. (This option is available only when auditing is not already enabled for the volume.)

Figure 19.1
Enabling volume auditing.

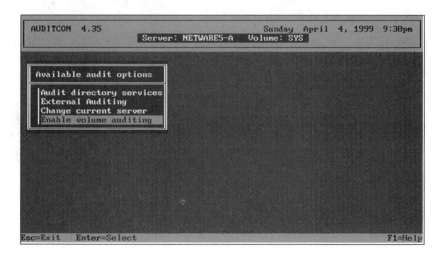

Caution

If there are NetWare 4.1x servers in the same tree as your NetWare 5 servers, ensure you've upgraded DS.NLM on all the NetWare 4.1x servers to the latest version *before* you enable auditing. Of particular note is NetWare 4.11 servers must be running DS.NLM v6.0 or higher.

Failure to upgrade your NetWare 4's DS.NLM can cause DS lock ups when auditing is enabled.

Tip #182 from
Peter

If the volume does not have an Audit File object (for example, auditing was not previously enabled for this volume), AUDITCON creates an Audit File object in the NDS container where the volume is stored. The name of the Audit File object is AFO*id_volumename*, where *id* is a counter (starting at zero) used if there is already an object with the desired name, and *volumename* is the name of the volume.

For example, if the volume name is NETWARE5_SYS.Company, the Audit File object is named AFO0_NETWARE5_SYS.Company; or if that object already exists, AFO1_NETWARE5_SYS.Company.

Therefore, by looking for the existence of AFO*id_volumename* objects, you can determine whether volume auditing is or was enabled for a given volume.

5. AUDITCON enables auditing for the volume and returns to the main menu. The main menu now has additional selections, as shown in Figure 19.2.

Figure 19.2
Main menu of
AUDITCON after
volume auditing is
enabled.

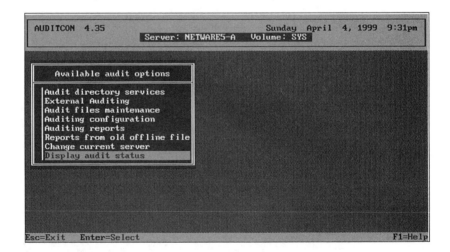

After volume level auditing is enabled, the independent auditor assumes control of the process.

Tip #183 from

Peter

Unlike NetWare 4 where the auditing information is password-protected, NetWare 5 protects its audit data through either NDS security or password (as is the case in NetWare 4). See the "Controlling Access to Audit Data" section later in this chapter for more information.

Enabling Directory Services Auditing

NetWare 4 also enables you to audit the use of its Directory Services. Just as with volume auditing, NDS level auditing must be enabled should you want to track changes made.

Note

When you enable auditing for a container object (Organization or Organizational Unit), it does not enable auditing for subordinate container objects.

As an auditor, you will only "see" those containers to which you have been given the NDS Browse right. If you do not see the container you want to audit, contact the network administrator.

To enable Directory auditing for a specific container, follow these steps:

1. Start AUDITCON and your current server name and volume are displayed at the top of the screen.

2. Select Audit Directory Services from the Available Audit Options menu. Your current context is displayed at the top of the screen.

3. Select Audit Directory Tree from the Audit Directory Services menu.

4. Locate the container where you are enabling auditing by pressing Enter to move around in the NDS tree.

5. Select the container you want, press F10, and then select Enable Container Auditing from the Available Audit Options menu.

6. Enter a password as prompted.

PART

V

Cн

19

Tip #184 from

Peter

As in the case of volume auditing, if the container doesn't have an Audit File object (for example, auditing was not previously enabled for this container), AUDITCON creates an Audit File object inside the NDS container. The name of the Audit File object is AFO*id_containername*, where *id* is a counter used if there is already an object with the desired name, and *containername* is the name of the container.

Therefore, by looking for the existence of AFO*id_containername* objects, you can determine whether NDS auditing is or was enabled for a given container.

7. AUDITCON enables auditing for the container and returns to the main menu. The Available Audit Options menu now has additional selections, as shown in Figure 19.3.

Figure 19.3
The Available Audit Options menu of AUDITCON after NDS auditing is enabled.

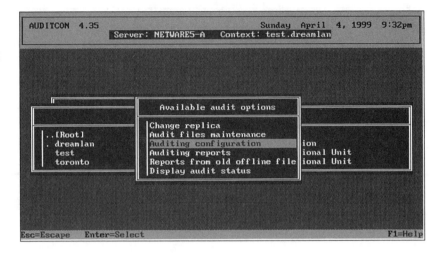

CONTROLLING ACCESS TO AUDIT DATA

NetWare 5 servers provide two separate methods for controlling access to online audit configuration data and recorded audit files:

- **Via NDS security**—NDS provides an Audit File object for each audit trail that defines the access rights to the audit configuration and audit data. The server checks the Audit File object's NDS rights when you try to access an audit trail or make changes to the Audit File object properties. If this check succeeds, the user can access the audit trail. This is the default approach for NetWare 5 servers.

- **Via password-protection**—For compatibility with previous releases, NetWare 5 also supports an optional password-based access control method. This option is enabled on individual servers by setting the ALLOW AUDIT PASSWORDS console parameter. If audit passwords are enabled at the server console, the single-level audit password controls access to all aspects of the audit trail.

  You can also configure the audit file to use dual-level passwords, where the first-level password is required to view the audit data and the audit configuration, and a second-level password is required to change the audit configuration.

The default value for ALLOW AUDIT PASSWORDS is OFF, meaning that access to the audit data is controlled solely by the Audit File object's object property rights.

However, you can configure servers to permit the use of audit passwords. Such configuration is done on *a server-by-server* basis, so that mixed configurations are possible—some servers using the Audit File object rights-based access controls and other servers using audit passwords.

When AUDITCON creates an Audit File object, the server gives the creator (the user) Supervisor right to the [Entry Rights] of the Audit File object (the S right to the object itself). AUDITCON assigns additional rights. The following rights are assigned to the creator (the NetWare server) of the Audit File object:

- Read and write rights to the `Audit:Policy` property
- Read right to the `Audit:Contents` property

These rights enable the auditor who created the Audit File object to read audit files, change the audit configuration data, and assign access rights to other auditors. If you work in a single-auditor environment, this might be sufficient for your needs. You (or any other user with the Supervisor right (or Write right to the Audit File object's ACL attribute) can use NWAdmin, for example, to define rights for other auditors.

> **Note**
>
> To exclude Admin and equivalent users from access audit data, either remove/block their NDS rights to the Audit File objects or enable password restrictions.

You can have three logical groupings of rights. These rights groupings are conceptual; you can organize rights any way you find convenient. The groupings are as follows:

- **Audit Viewers**—These people are responsible for reviewing audit trails, looking for anomalies, and generating reports.
- **Audit Administrators**—These people are responsible for the tasks of Audit Viewers and are also responsible for configuring the audit subsystem and performing audit data backup and recovery.
- **Audit Sources**—These are objects (such as a volume) that append audit records to server-recorded audit trails.

Shown in Table 19.1 are the rights required for each of these three groups.

TABLE 19.1   AUDITOR RIGHTS AND ACCESS PROFILES

Auditor type	NDS-based access	Password-based access
Audit Viewer	R to Audit File object's Audit: Policy attribute	Level 1 password
	R to Audit File object's Audit: Contents attribute	

continues

PART

V

CH

19

TABLE 19.1   CONTINUED

Auditor type	NDS-based access	Password-based access
Audit Administrator	R to Audit File object's Audit: Policy attribute	Level 2 password
	W to Audit File object's Audit: Policy attribute	
	R to Audit File object's Audit: Contents attribute	
Audit Source (a specific volume, container, or external source)	W to Audit File object's Audit: Contents	N/A
	R to Audit File object's Audit: Path	

The server checks whether you have the appropriate rights when performing each action and refuses to perform the action if you don't have those rights. If you revoke access rights to an auditor who is already accessing an audit file, these changes do *not* take effect until the auditor tries to reestablish access to the volume or container audit trail.

Tip #185 from
Peter

Do not give any untrusted users (individuals who are not auditors or administrators) any rights to the Audit File object (or its properties) except the Browse right.

USING AUDITCON

As mentioned previously, AUDITCON is a DOS utility that allows auditors to specify the parts of the network to be monitored and provides functions for outputting auditing data for management review. AUDITCON also monitors the activities concerned with identification, access, and modification of network resources.

Note

By default, the AUDITCON program and Unicode files are located in the SYS:PUBLIC and SYS:PUBLIC\NLS directories, respectively.

Note

Because significant changes have been made to the auditing system in NetWare 5, if you have a NDS tree with a mix of NetWare 5 and NetWare 4 servers, you must replace any previous versions of AUDITCON in your network with AUDITCON version 4.35.

To keep your audit information secure, it is suggested that as the auditor you perform the following tasks before you begin auditing:

- Immediately change the auditing password (if password-protection is enabled) given to you by the network supervisor.
- Log in to the volume or container using the new password.
- Set your preferences for the auditing environment.

From this point on, you can select what you want to audit and create reports based on the audit records you collect. Using AUDITCON, you also can create reports about the activities of the items you are auditing, as well as the auditor's activities.

Tip #186 from _Peter_	As an auditor, (if password-protection is enabled) you can set an additional level of security for your audit records by enabling a second-level password. If you set this option, a second password is required before any changes to the audit configurations or report filters can be made.

To start AUDITCON, log in to the network as a user that has been given auditing rights, and then type AUDITCON. After starting the auditor console, you will be given the following options as shown earlier in Figure 19.2.

Tip #187 from _Peter_	With auditing enabled, you will notice that the very last option changes from Enable Volume Auditing to Display Audit Status (compare Figure 19.1 to Figure 19.2).

Selecting the Audit directory services option displays a list of NDS containers that you can access. You can't see a container unless you have access (Browse rights). You need to have the administrator provide you with rights to all containers you want to audit.

Note	The only options that appear are the ones that are valid for the volume or container that you are currently logged in to.
	To change to a different context, highlight a container or object and press Enter. This moves you up one level in the tree.
	To perform an audit on a container, highlight the container and press F10.

The next section covers the more important volume and DS audit options found in AUDITCON.

Tip #188 from _Peter_	The existing AUDITCON utility described in this section does not provide a means for correlating multiple volume and container audit trails, or for correlating the servers' audit trails with clients' external audit trails. Correlation of multiple audit trails must be performed manually. One way is to generate individual printed audit reports for each desired volume or container, and then merge or sort the various reports into a single trail.

PART
V

CH

19

> **Note**
>
> In addition to auditing volumes and NDS containers, AUDITCON can also be used to maintain "external audit trails" that contain client audit records and client audit history generated by client workstations. Any workstation that uses the server's external audit trail must have its own workstation-based audit management tool to configure and manipulate the external audit trail.
>
> Consequently, AUDITCON can manage external audit trails, but can't generate reports or view the events stored in those audit trails (except for audit history events). Because external audit trails are heavily vendor-specific, their discussion are beyond the scope of this chapter. If you use the external audit trails feature, you need to refer to the vendor's documentation provided with your client workstation for information on the specific utilities for viewing external audit data.

CONFIGURING AUDITING

As an auditor, you are required to create reports on past and present network incidents. The auditor configuration screen allows you to select which network functions to be traced. The Audit Configuration menus (there's a separate menu for volume and NDS auditing) enable you to change or select the following container auditing settings:

- Audit by DS events
- Audit by file/directory
- Audit by user
- Audit options configuration
- Change audit password
- Display volume auditing
- Display audit status

Following is a brief description of each configuration option.

AUDIT BY DS EVENTS

Selecting Audit by DS Events displays a list of Directory Services events to audit.

To select a DS event to audit, or configure for auditing, choose the desired option and press Enter. You then see a list of events that can be turned on or off. By default, most of the events are turned off, or not audited. If you want to turn on, or audit, an event, highlight the event and press F10 to toggle that particular event. If you want to toggle all the events, press F8.

Figure 19.4 shows the Change ACL event has been toggled to on or, in other words, turned on for auditing.

Figure 19.4
Audit by DS Events
options menu. The
Change ACL events
are being tracked.

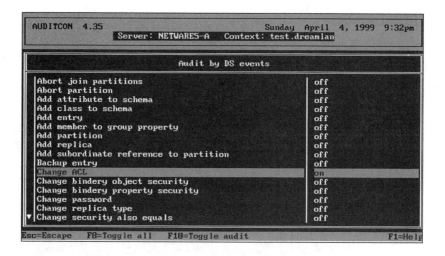

```
AUDITCON  4.35                              Sunday  April  4, 1999  9:32pm
                 Server: NETWARE5-A    Context: test.dreamlan

┌──────────────────────── Audit by DS events ────────────────────────┐
│ Abort join partitions                              │ off │
│ Abort partition                                    │ off │
│ Add attribute to schema                            │ off │
│ Add class to schema                                │ off │
│ Add entry                                          │ off │
│ Add member to group property                       │ off │
│ Add partition                                      │ off │
│ Add replica                                        │ off │
│ Add subordinate reference to partition             │ off │
│ Backup entry                                       │ off │
│ Change ACL                                         │ on  │
│ Change bindery object security                     │ off │
│ Change bindery property security                   │ off │
│ Change password                                    │ off │
│ Change replica type                                │ off │
│▼Change security also equals                        │ off │
└─────────────────────────────────────────────────────────────────────┘
Esc=Escape   F8=Toggle all   F10=Toggle audit                    F1=Help
```

Caution

The more events that are audited, the more performance degradation the server will experience. Also, the more audited events that are toggled to on, the larger the disk space requirement is for storing the auditing file.

AUDIT BY USER

This option enables you to turn auditing on or off for user objects.

After you select the Audit by User options, a NDS Browser screen appears. This screen lists all the objects that are located in the current directory context.

Tip #189 from
Peter

Your current context is displayed at the top of the screen.

To select a user, move the highlight bar to that particular user object and press F10. An on status appears to the right side of the screen.

When a user is selected, all the user's transactions in this container are recorded in the Audit Data file.

Tip #190 from
Peter

If the user object you want to audit is not listed, you need to change to the correct context. To change contexts, browse the tree by moving the highlight bar and selecting a container by pressing the Enter key.

When you have marked the selected users, press the Escape key and then answer Yes to the dialog box that appears (to save the changes.)

PART

V

CH

19

AUDIT OPTIONS CONFIGURATION

Selecting the Audit Options Configuration option enables you to set basic audit parameters, such as data file size, auditor login requirements, and error recovery options. When this option has been selected, you are given the Audit Configuration options box (Figure 19.5).

Figure 19.5
Audit Configuration menu.

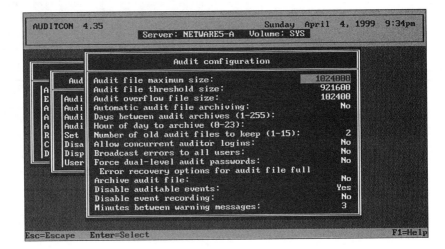

This option box is divided into three different sets of options. The first set of options allows you to specify the maximum audit file size and threshold. The middle set of options enable you to configure the automatic audit file archiving. The final set of options deals with the error recovery options when the audit file does become full. This section briefly covers the most important options; the ones that are not covered are self-explanatory.

The audit file maximum size, as its name implies, enables you to specify the maximum audit file size. This function is important, because the audit file continues to grow until it reaches this limit.

The default audit file size is 1,024,000 Bytes (or 10MB), and is the same for any size disk; this default size is not based on the available disk space or the size of the disk.

Each environment requires a different size auditing file. The best way to determine the appropriate file size is to determine how much or how long you want to audit any particular set of transactions. For example, you will want the file size set large enough to track activities for the appropriate amount of time: a day, two weeks, a month, and so on.

It is helpful to note that you can keep a total of 15 different old audit files online. These files can be migrated or kept on the disk drive. The benefit of segmenting or keeping multiple files on the drive is simply to let you view multiple versions for comparison.

One option discussed later in this section is the capability to have the volume dismount when the audit file is full. This option can be used for the ultimate in data protection. For example, you can create an audit sequence that looks at the access of certain information or attempts to access information from a specific user. As you create this audit sequence, you can set the audit file small enough that one incident of the action by a suspected user would cause the volume to dismount. This example might seem extreme, and probably is, but it also demonstrates the power available to an effective audit.

Tip #191 from *Peter*	If a volume is dismounted because the Audit Data file reached its maximum size limit and the Dismount Volume Option is set, the network supervisor must remount the volume and enable auditing again. To remount the volume, complete the following steps: 1. At the console, mount the volume by typing MOUNT *volume_name* <Enter> 2. An "Audit file full" error message appears on the server console screen and you are prompted to mount the volume with auditing disabled. 3. At the server console, enter the current auditing password for the volume. (This is the password the auditor assigned to the volume.) 4. Reenable auditing.

Another option related to the maximum file size is the file threshold. Setting the threshold size helps ensure that this doesn't happen. The Audit file threshold size is a function that alarms you when the file approaches the maximum threshold size. The threshold size is by default set to 90% of the audit file size.

When the file reaches the maximum size, you have the option to delete it, rename it, or dismount the volume (to continue auditing, one of the options must be performed).

You also can elect to have the file automatically achieved (default setting). This provides a no-hands-on backup of your audit data and audit history files. For each archived file, however, disk space is required.

From this options menu, you also can specify whether you want to provide multiple auditors concurrent access to the same container or volume, which gives them access to the same audit information.

PART

V

CH

19

Tip #192 from *Peter*	Auditors that need access to the same volumes and containers must have knowledge of the same passwords.

If you plan to use multiple auditors and don't want them to have access to each other's auditing information, you need to implement your volume and directory structure accordingly. For example, if you want an auditor to have access to the companies accounting information but not to the payroll data, you need to be sure to set these different data sets on separate volumes.

Another option in the configuration screen that you might want to note is the ability to force dual-level auditing passwords. This option requires one password to be able to audit activities on the network, and a second password to configure or change the auditing parameters.

CHANGE AUDIT PASSWORD

As its name implies, this option enables you to change the AUDITCON password. The process required to change the audit password is as follows:

1. Select the Change Audit Password option.

2. Enter the current auditor password for the volume or container.

3. Enter a new auditor password for the current volume or container.

4. Confirm the change by reentering the password when prompted.

> **Note**
>
> If you enter the incorrect auditing password, access to change to a new password is denied.

> **Note**
>
> The Change Audit Password option is available only on servers that has ALLOW AUDIT PASSWORDS set to ON.

DISABLE CONTAINER AUDITING

Auditors can disable auditing, but supervisor rights are required to enable auditing.

> **Caution**
>
> Be careful! This is not the same as exiting out of AUDITCON.
>
> If you disable network auditing, you can't audit the network. To reenable auditing you have to contact the network administrator or someone with administrative rights.
>
> Furthermore, if auditing is disabled, the auditing file is reset, and the information contained in the original file is moved to the old audit data file.

DISPLAY AUDIT STATUS

Selecting this option provides you with a screen similar to Figure 19.6, which enables you to view basic information about the audit files.

> **Note**
>
> The information presented on the Audit Status screen is for the current volume or container.

After configuring any of the audit events or configurations, press the Escape key. After pressing the Escape key, a dialog box appears asking whether you want to save the changes.

Figure 19.6
Audit Status screen.

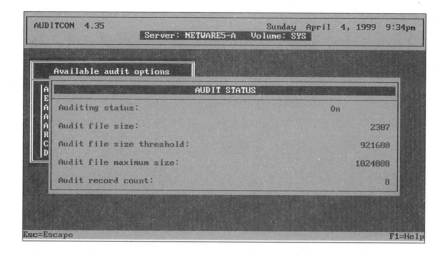

AUDITING REPORTS

The Auditing Reports option enables you to select and view data to be extracted from the audit data file that was created during the audit process. If there is information that you want, but it is not contained in the report, you will have to reaudit and make the appropriate configuration changes.

To create an audit report, complete the following steps:

1. Select Auditing Reports from the Available Audit Options menu, which brings up a menu with a list of options as shown in Figure 19.7.

Figure 19.7
The Auditing Reports menu.

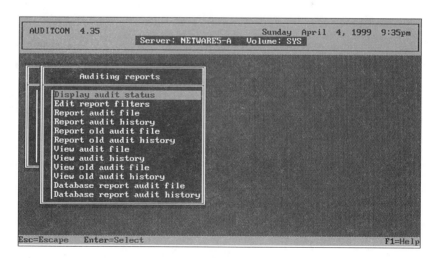

PART

V

CH

19

2. From this list of options, select Report Audit File, and specify where you want the file to be sent by completing one of the following steps:

Caution

> If you send reports to a network directory, a user with Supervisor rights in the file system can see the file. If you want to secure your reports, you should send them to a local drive or a floppy drive on your workstation.

- Press Enter to copy the report to a file in your default directory. (The default filename is AUDITDAT.TXT.)
- Enter the directory path and filename where you want the file to be sent, and then press Enter.

Note

> AUDITCON does not create a file for you. You must specify an existing directory path and filename.

3. Select a filter from the Select Filter list and press Enter. To create a report without a filter, select no_filter. To create or edit a filter, complete one of the following steps:

- To edit a filter in the list, press Enter.
- To create a filter, press Insert.

Note

> The list item no_filter can't be edited.

The following is a brief definition of the available report options.

Specify how you want the filter to be used by completing one of the following steps:

- To save the filter changes, select Save filter Changes.
- If it is a new filter, enter a name (maximum of eight characters).
- To use the filter once without permanently changing the filter, select Use Filter Without Saving Changes.

The report is generated with the new filter settings, and then the filter reverts to its original settings.

Tip #193 from
Peter

> New filters are not saved.
> To discard filter changes, select Discard Filter Changes.
> Edited filters revert to the original settings. New filters are deleted.

You are returned to the Auditing report menu, where you can now select the View Audit file option to view the report. Or, the filtered report is sent to the directory and file you specified and can be viewed with a DOS text file format editor.

To use the View audit file option, complete the following steps:

1. Select View Audit File from the Auditing Reports menu.

2. Select a filter from the Select Filter list and press Enter. To see a report without a filter, select no_filter from the list.

Tip #194 from *Peter*	As mentioned previously, to edit a filter in the list, press Enter. And to create a filter, press Insert. Remember that the no_filter list item can't be edited.

Specify how you want the filter to be used by completing one of the following steps:

1. To save new changes to the filter, select Save Filter Changes.

2. If you created a new filter, enter a name. The name should be eight characters or fewer.

3. To use the filter for this report only, select Use filter without saving changes. The report is generated with the new filter settings, and then the filter reverts to its original settings.

Note	If you define any new filters for This Report Only, they are not saved for future use.

4. To discard filter changes, select Discard Filter Changes.

Tip #195 from *Peter*	Edited filters revert to the original settings. New filters are deleted.

PART
V
CH
19

When the report is loaded, you can use the arrow keys to scroll through the report. To exit, press Esc and answer Yes at the Exit View prompt. On long reports, you might want to use a DOS text editor, or a word processor.

WORKING WITH AUDIT FILES

AUDITCON automatically creates audit files when it is enabled. Each volume or container using AUDITCON has its own audit files. The audit data file keeps records of all audited transactions. The auditing configuration you set determines which type of records are entered into the data file.

This file operates like a system log or error file, in that records are automatically entered into the file whenever an audited event occurs.

When you audit container objects for Directory Services events, the audit history information is combined with audit data into this file.

THE AUDIT HISTORY FILE

The audit history file keeps a record of the auditor's activities in a volume, such as auditing configuration changes and auditor logins and logouts.

In Directory Services, the auditor's activities are recorded in the audit data file. There is no separate file for this information.

You can, however, use the menu options, such as View Audit History, to see auditor records, just as you would if you were auditing a volume.

RESETTING THE AUDIT DATA FILE

When the auditor resets an audit file, existing records are moved to an old audit data or old audit history file. The original audit file continues to function as it did before.

To reset the audit data file, complete the following steps:

1. Select Audit Files Maintenance from the Available Audit Options menu.
2. Select Reset Audit Data File from the Audit Files Maintenance menu.

> **Note**
>
> A warning message appears on screen to notify you that the current contents of the file will be moved to the old audit data file. If you already have data in the old file, it will be deleted.

3. Select Yes to reset the file.

The remaining options are self-explanatory and perform the following functions:

- **Audit Report Filters**—Enables you to edit an existing filter or create a new filter.

> **Note**
>
> You can create filters to extract specific data from the audit data file. Filtered information can then be copied to a separate file or viewed on screen.

- **Report Audit File**—Enables you to send a report from the audit data file to a specified file or directory.
- **Report Audit History**—Enables you to send a report from the audit history file to a specified file or directory.
- **Report Old Audit File**—Enables you to send a report from the old audit data file to a file or directory.

- **Report Old Audit History**—Enables you to send a report from the old audit history file to a specified file or directory. This option applies to volume auditing only.

- **View Audit File**—Enables you to see the current audit data file on your screen.

- **View Audit History**—Enables you to see the current audit history file on your screen. This option applies to volume auditing only.

- **View Old Audit File**—Enables you to see the old audit data file on your screen.

- **View Old Audit History**—Enables you to see the old audit history file on your screen. This applies to volume auditing only.

DISPLAY AUDIT STATUS

The Display Audit Status screen shows the following information about the auditing files on the current volume or container:

- **Auditing Status**—Indicates whether auditing has been enabled for the current volume or container.

- **Audit File Size**—This is the current size of the Audit Data file.

- **Audit File Size Threshold**—When the Audit Data file reaches the size shown here, a warning message is sent to the console and the system log file.

- **Audit File Maximum Size**—This number is the maximum size allowed for the Audit Data file.

CHANGE SESSION CONTEXT

After selecting the Change Session Context, a prompt appears enabling you to type the context to which you would like to change.

Tip #196 from *Peter*	If you can't see the container you want to audit, use Change Session Context to move to a different area of the Directory tree.
	If auditing is not turned on, select the container you want to enable auditing on, and you have one option: Enable Container Auditing. Press Enter to enable the auditing.

CHANGE CURRENT SERVER

If the volume you want to audit is not on this server, you can select a different server by choosing the Change Current Server option. After selecting this option, a dialog box appears from which you can select the desired server. If the server is not listed, press the Insert key. To remove a server from the list press the Delete key.

From this location, you also can log in under a different username, by pressing the F3 or Modify key. You then are given the option to type the username and appropriate password.

AUDIT FILES MAINTENANCE

The Audit Files Maintenance option is available only after you have gained access to auditing. After logging in to auditing, you can use the Audit Files Maintenance menu to select the following options:

- **Close Audit File**—For security and system reasons, files containing audit data remain open. This option will allow old audit files be accessed outside of AUDITCON. This also means that the file may be accessible by users other than the auditor.

- **Copy Old Audit File**—This option enables you to copy an old audit data file to another location. This can be useful for putting old audit files in a location where they can be compressed; this function also enables you to leave the file as nonreadable. To copy an audit data file in readable report format, select Report Old Audit File from the Auditing Reports menu.

- **Delete Old Audit File**—This option enables to you delete old audit data files, without having any effect on your current audit data file.

- **Display Audit Status**—This selection enables you to view information about the audit files.

- **Reset Audit Data File**—To create a new audit data file, select this option. From this option you also can rename the current file.

- **Reset Auditing History**—Select this option to delete Audit File Information, without completely deleting the file. Deleting audit file entries will clear the file, allowing you to store new information. (This is true for auditing volumes only.)

LICENSE MANAGEMENT

Other than keeping track of accesses to your network resources, such as data files on a NetWare volume, you should also keep a tab on your NetWare license usage. NetWare tells you when you've used up all your licenses, but it doesn't tell you when you're constantly underusing your licenses—but, why purchase more licenses than you really need?

NetWare 5 keeps its licensing information in NDS and a history of license usage is kept in NDS as well. Using NLS Manager (NLSMAN32.EXE) you can easily generate a report of your license usage. Shown in Figure 19.8 is the Quick View of licensing usage. From this screen, you can quickly determine your current license usage. By switching into the tree view mode, you can obtain a list of users that are currently using the licenses (see Figure 19.10), much like you can using the Connections option from MONITOR.NLM.

Figure 19.8
The Quick View of your current license usage.

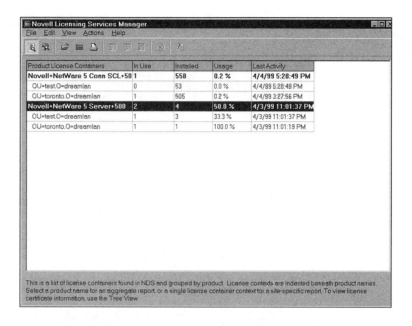

Figure 19.9
Highlight the license object to get a list of current users of that license object.

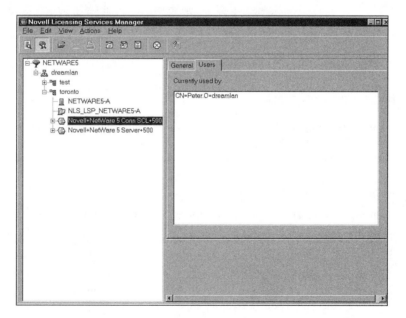

By double-clicking one of the rows in the table, you obtain a License Usage Report in graphical format for that license container, as shown in Figure 19.9. By changing the start and end dates, you can generate usage reports for different time periods. And by examining closely the peak usage versus the installed license counts, you can then have a handle on if your current number of installed licenses is underused or not.

Figure 19.10
Sample license usage
graph.

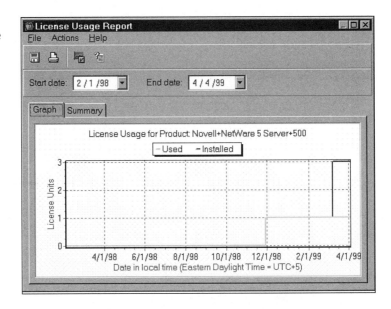

TROUBLESHOOTING

This section describes solutions to potential volume and container audit problems. These problems include audit trail overflow, synchronization of the container audit files to other NDS partitions, as well as recovery from catastrophic failures.

CATASTROPHIC FAILURE RECOVERY

There are two major catastrophic failures possible for volume audit:

- **Loss of all copies of the Audit File object describing the volume audit trail**—If all copies of the Audit File object are lost (for example, because there was no replica copies of the NDS partition, and the server it was on suffered a disk failure), you might be able to recover the Audit File object from a backup of your Directory tree (presuming you have backed up your Directory tree). If so, you will be able to regain access to the existing online audit data. If not, no access is possible to the online audit data. You must re-create the volume audit trail (including selecting events, audit full actions, and so on) using the procedures in the "Enabling Volume Auditing" section in this chapter.

■ **Loss of a volume (for example, because of a disk failure)**—Because volume audit files are stored in an inaccessible directory (_NETWARE on the respective volume) which can't be directly backed up, loss of a volume means that the online audit files (both the current audit file and any old audit files) are lost. You should use AUDITCON to perform regular backups of audit data to avoid loss of online audit data.

In the case of NDS auditing, there are also two major catastrophic failures. The first is the loss of all copies of the Audit File object describing the container audit trail. The recovery steps here is the same as the situation in volume auditing. The second scenarios is the loss of volume SYS: on any server containing the container audit data.

Because container audit files are stored in an inaccessible directory (SYS:_NETWARE) which can't be backed up, loss of volume SYS: means that the online audit files (both the current audit file and any old audit files) are lost. You should use AUDITCON to perform regular backups of audit data to avoid loss of online audit data.

If there is at least one other server with a copy of the container, when the failed server comes back online it is automatically updated, and container auditing automatically resumes. If there are no other servers with copies of the container, you must restore the container from an NDS backup and recreate the container audit trail using the procedures described in the "Enabling Directory Services Container Auditing" section in this chapter.

Tip #198 from *Peter*	If you have multiple servers on your network, you should follow the Novell-recommended guideline that each partition should have at least three replicas for fault-tolerance.

AUDIT TRAIL OVERFLOW

If your volume or NDS audit trail overflows, the only option that prevents the loss of audit events (from audit overflow situations) is to first disable auditable events and then recover from this overflow state.

Caution	In the NDS audit trail overflow state, any event that is preselected for auditing is disabled. For example, if logins are preselected for auditing, any attempt to log in to an object in the container (*except* for attempts by auditors of the container) would fail.

To recover from an audit trail overflow state, an auditor (with the Write right to the volume Audit File object Audit Policy property) must reset the current audit trail as follows:

1. If volume SYS: overflows, the server allows an auditor to perform a "read-only" login to reset the audit file.

Tip #199 from
Peter

> To perform a read-only login when volume SYS: overflows means to run the login utility from the workstation's local hard drive. To make things simple, it is best to use Windows 9x or Windows NT Workstation because Client32 (including the login components) are installed to the workstation.

2. If you want to save the oldest audit file, and you haven't already backed it up, copy the oldest old audit file to offline storage (for example, a file in the server or workstation or removable media).

3. Reset the current volume audit file, as described in the "Reset Audit Data File" section earlier in this chapter. This rolls over the current audit file (to an old audit file), deleting the oldest old audit file, and initializes a new audit file.

4. If you want to save any audit files that you haven't already saved (including the newest of the old audit files), copy those audit files to offline storage.

CONTAINER AUDIT FILE REPLICATION

Container audit files are replicated by NDS to the servers that hold replicas of the container object. That is, if container Consulting.Company is replicated by NDS onto three different servers, the audit file for that container is also replicated onto the same three servers. Replication of container audit files is automatic, and there is no way that you can tell the server to not replicate the audit file, other than to not replicate the audited container.

On the other hand, because NDS audit file information is replicated by the NDS synchronization processes, any failure in NDS synchronization causes the copies of the audit files to be inconsistent. Therefore, if you notice any discrepancy in your container audit files, check using DSTrace that NDS is synchronizing correctly without any errors.

→ For information on dealing with NDS problems, **see** Chapter 27, "Troubleshooting common Problems," **p.685**

CHAPTER **20**

NetWare Accounting

In this chapter

ESTABLISHING AN ACCOUNTING STRATEGY

The accounting feature in NetWare appears to be a carry-over from the mindset of main-frame computer management. Due to the enormous cost of mainframes, many potential users of computing services were unable to afford one of their own. This dilemma gave rise to the practice of two or more companies jointly purchasing one mainframe computer and sharing it, or one company making the purchase and charging users of the system within another company to defray the cost. In either case, it was necessary to have the capability to account and charge for use of the system. Although the costs of the first local area networks still didn't compare with those of mainframes, the capital outlay was sufficient to spawn some sharing of server resources early on. Thus, NetWare accounting.

> **Note**
>
> NetWare accounting and auditing are completely separate functions within NetWare. Accounting is defined earlier in this chapter. Auditing is a new feature first introduced with NetWare 4 and is concerned with the security of the network versus financial accountability. The two features cannot even be managed by the same person, conceptually, because the network administrator manages accounting, and one of the main functions of the "auditor" is keeping the network administrator honest. Auditing is covered in more detail in Chapter 19, "Auditing."

Although accounting was intended to distribute the costs of operating the network, it has not been widely used for that purpose, primarily for two reasons. First, the vast majority of local area networks are each owned and operated by one entity, such as a company or institution, versus being jointly owned, so the need to charge others for use of the network isn't really there. Second, the accounting feature was not initially, nor is it yet, developed to an extent to be useful, so even those few who would use it for its intended purpose or those many more who would have undoubtedly found new uses for it weren't provided the functionality to do so.

> **Note**
>
> One other reason why NetWare accounting isn't popular in NDS environment is that the accounting feature is bindery-based, thus is servercentric. As you'll read later, to enable accounting on a server, the server needs to have Bindery Servcies enabled, meaning it needs to have a writeable copy of a replica. If you have many servers in your tree, it is not feasible to enable account on all servers due to the number of replicas required.

TRACKING LOGINS AND LOGOUTS

Most of the networks that implemented accounting only used it to track users logging in and out, in case they ever needed to know whether "Bob was logged in at 2:00 a.m. last night." No one using accounting for its primary, financial purpose, and although there was a good amount of emerging NetWare 5 users, no one was really using accounting for what it was originally designed for.

PREPAID NETWORK USAGE

In a "pay-as-you-go" type of environment, such as student labs at colleges and universities or other public access sites, a user can pay for a certain amount of usage, maybe as "connect time," in advance. The network administrator sets the user's account balance commensurate with the prepaid amount, and the user is logged out by the system when his account balance was depleted, and prevented from future logins until he pays to increase his account balance. More information on setting account balances is covered later.

Tip #200 from *Peter*	Even though you might not charge for LAN usage, billing for connect time helps to ensure fair use of workstations that are shared among a number of users.

RESOURCE UTILIZATION

If few are using accounting, does that mean that there are no uses for it? Not quite. In addition to the need for Novell to develop accounting to at least a minimally functional level, it seems that the accounting feature would be better if renamed to *Resource Utilization*. This new name reflects a usage of this function that would be valuable to most versus only a few. Although few network administrators need to charge their users for network services, all of them can benefit from historical, statistical data on who uses the network how much. This data could be used to project, prepare for, and help justify financially increases in network capacity. For that reason alone, accounting can be usefully installed on servers, even in its current state of development. Aggregate network use information can be accessed through the use of the ATOTAL utility. Although Novell doesn't provide anything else for the standard network administrator to make use of the resource utilization data stored in NET$ACCT.DAT, there are a few free third-party tools to help out.

ENABLING ACCOUNTING

Unlike many other NetWare 5 features, activating NetWare accounting is more akin to turning on a light switch in terms of simplicity than to an "installation," per se. The following steps outline the procedure:

1. Use NWAdmin to select the desired server (server object) on which you want to install accounting.

Note	Because NetWare Accounting is a bindery-based feature, the server must have Bindery Services enabled.

2. Double-click the Server object to bring up the object information window. The categories of information on the right side of the window, such as Identification and Error Log, stop with Costs. The accounting resource tabs appear below Users after installation.

3. Click the Accounting button at the bottom of the window.

4. Answer Yes to Do You Want to Install Accounting? (see Figure 20.1).

Figure 20.1
Accounting installation dialog box.

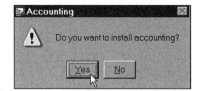

Now if you look at the selection tabs on the right side of the window, you'll find the extra accounting-related ones such as Blocks Read and Blocks Written. There are five categories in all:

- Blocks Read
- Blocks Written
- Connect Time
- Disk Storage
- Service Requests

> **Note**
>
> One drawback of NetWare Accounting is the lack of print accounting. In many companies, especially law and accounting firms, tracking the number of pages printed per client account is important. Fortunately, there are available third-party solutions to this need. If you have this requirement, search the listings available at
> `http://developer.novell.com/npp`.

If those tabs now appear, you've successfully activated accounting. Now you need to configure it for charge data to accrue.

> **Note**
>
> The Costs tab is not part of Accounting; it is for the WAN Traffic Manager.

Tip #201 from
Peter

If you don't see all these five tabs, click the Page Options button and check to see whether they are marked as Active Pages.

Tip #202 from
Peter

> The only maintenance related specifically to the accounting function concerns the accounting data collection file, NET$ACCT.DAT (located in the SYS:SYSTEM directory). This file grows rapidly and can't be cropped. When the data in the file has outlived its usefulness or the file becomes too large, unlike audit data where you can easily save histories, your only option with the accounting data is to rename or delete it. A new NET$ACCT.DAT file is created the next time accounting information needs to be saved to disk by NetWare.

CONFIGURATION

Accounting picks up its functionality from the assignment of "charge rates" for the five different services, or "resources," and user account balance settings.

RESOURCE TYPES

The five resources are blocks read, blocks written, connect time, disk storage, and service requests. Following are explanations for these resources:

- **Blocks Read**—The charge is per disk block. During installation of NetWare 5, the volume block size is automatically determined depending on the size of the volume. Therefore, if your USERS volume is set to 64KB block size, the user will be charged per 64KB block.

- **Blocks Written**—Same as Blocks Read.

- **Connect Time**—The charge is per minute of time that a user is logged in.

- **Disk Storage**—The charge is per "block-day." That means that you can charge a user only once a day for file storage space used on the server. As a matter of fact, when assigning charge rates in the Disk Storage window, the assignment feature prevents rate assignment for more than one 30-minute period per day, as shown in Figure 20.2.

- **Service Requests**—Each time the workstation requests any service from the server, the user is charged. A request is not defined as simply as the use of any of the four preceding resources types. A service request is equivalent to an NCP, or Network Core Protocols, request. The simple act of logging in generates literally hundreds of service requests. This might be the most confusing resource type to charge for, and explain to users, and so can easily be left unused, that is, "No Charge" assigned.

PART
V

CH
20

Figure 20.2
The highlighted time specifies when the charge is calculated.

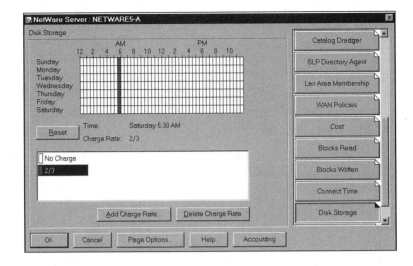

CHARGE RATES

After enabling Accounting, the amount of "resource units" (or fraction of one unit) to charge for the use of each resource needs to be determined. For illustration's sake, suppose that one resource unit equals one cent. Using Blocks Read, if a charge rate of 2/1 is assigned, two *resource units* or two cents is charged for each block read. Conversely, 1/2 is one-half cent for each block. The first or top number is called the *multiplier* and the second or bottom number, the *divisor*. Use of the term *resource unit* is not a technicality. It was mentioned earlier that assigning actual money amounts to be charged is impossible. NetWare accounting keeps track of resources used and users' account balances in resource units. After the number of units used is known, theoretically, a value can be manually assigned to each unit and a bill prepared.

ADDING AND REMOVING CHARGE RATES

To assign or *add* a charge rate, select the desired accounting resource type, such as Connect Time, from the Server Object information window. The default charge rate is No Charge, which reflects throughout the Day and Time Grid and in the Charge Rates list box. Click the Add Charge Rate button, type the desired multiplier and divisor, and choose OK.

Tip #203 from
Peter

Partial resource unit charge rates cannot be entered with decimals, such as 2.5/1. You must use whole numbers. In this case, multiply the multiplier and divisor by 10 (or enough factors of 10 to eliminate the decimal from the multiplier), and use 25/10 to achieve the same result.

The charge rate appears, color coded, in the Charge Rates list box (see Figure 20.3). You have no control over the colors assigned to each rate. The colors are assigned by the order of creation, not the actual charge rate, and likely vary among resource types.

Figure 20.3
Multiple charge rates has been configured for Connect Time.

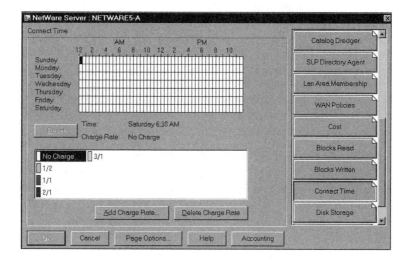

The standard recommendation is to set a charge rate for all five resources of 1/1 and give all users an unlimited account balance when you first install accounting, for a test period of time. This procedure allows a common reference, 1/1, to monitor and analyze network usage without the management challenge associated with regularly depleting account balances. Realistic charge rates and account balances can be set later when the network administrator has determined what they should be.

Tip #204 from
Peter

Do not define more rates than are to be assigned immediately. Any charge rates (with the exception of No Charge) defined in the Charge Rates list box, but not assigned in the Day and Time Grid, are deleted as soon as you choose OK and exit. Any charge rate can be added back just as it was defined originally.

In order to delete a charge rate, highlight the desired charge rate in the Charge Rates list box and click the Delete Charge Rate button. Realistically, deleting a charge rate is really unnecessary. When you stop using a given charge rate in the Day and Time Grid, it automatically is deleted on selecting OK and exiting from that window.

Note

You can't delete a charge rate if it's still in use anywhere in the Day and Time Grid.

MANAGING USER ACCOUNT BALANCE

When Accounting is enabled, you should assign each user either an unlimited account balance or a specific account balance as one of the properties of the User object. Account balance information is also a part of the new user creation template, and can be set there initially. If granted an unlimited balance, the user may continue using network services as a negative balance accrues. If using a specific balance, the user is given a five-minute warning to log out just after the balance has been depleted and then will be automatically logged out in five minutes, after one additional one-minute warning, if not already logged out by then.

Users should be encouraged to log themselves out versus having their connections terminated, because a forceful termination can damage any open files and results in the loss of any unsaved data or documents.

If the user prepays for network usage, the administrator can reset his or her account balance when more services are paid for in advance. If the user is paying on credit, the network administrator can reset the balance when each usage period is billed or as the bill is paid. For credit balance users, the balance should be set at least high enough to get a user through a normal billing period, such as one month or one quarter, plus a reasonable bill payment period. To assign or modify a user account balance, select the user (User object) from the main NWAdmin window. The User Identification window will appear. Scroll down the categories on the right side of the window and select Account Balance. You will see the window shown in Figure 20.4.

Figure 20.4
Account Balance window.

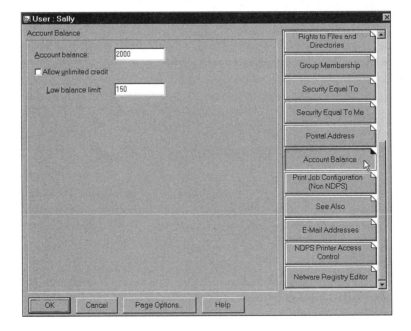

The current account balance, for a given user, is displayed in the top box or *field*. Replace the number in this field with the desired balance if purposely limiting the user. If the user is to be given *unlimited credit*, toggle that setting on by selecting, and thus placing an *x* in, the box to the left of Allow Unlimited Credit. The Low Balance Limit is active only if a user does not have unlimited credit. Although the number in this field can be changed, the default setting of 0 is best for normal use.

DISABLING ACCOUNTING

Removal of accounting is as easy as, and nearly identical to, its installation. The following steps outline the procedure:

1. Use NWAdmin to select the desired server (server object) on which you want to remove accounting.
2. Double-click the Server object to bring up the object information window.
3. Click the Accounting button at the bottom of the window.
4. Answer Yes to Do You Want to Remove Accounting?

Now check for the Accounting resource categories on the right side of the window, such as Blocks Read and Blocks Written. If those categories are gone, you've successfully deactivated or removed Accounting.

Caution

The NET$ACCT.DAT file is unaffected by the removal of accounting and remains in SYS:SYSTEM, but no additional accounting data is stored in it. However, removal of accounting deletes all charge rate definitions and assignments, all of which have to be re-created if accounting is reinstalled.

REPORTING TOOLS

NetWare 5 includes only one utility to make use of the collected accounting data. This limitation considerably detracts from the usefulness of the accounting function. There are a few third-party utilities which can extract accounting data and produce various reports much better than the Novell-supplied tool.

NOVELL'S ATOTAL UTILITY

The sole utility provided with NetWare 5 for accounting purposes is ATOTAL.EXE or the Accounting Services Total Utility, a DOS-based program. The information provided by ATOTAL lacks usefulness in that it is for the entire server, versus by user or group, and includes all information because accounting was originally installed instead of a selectable period. With this in mind, it seems realistically impossible to prepare bills for network usage without going into NWADMIN or NETADMIN to check each user's account balance manually. Following is an edited, sample ATOTAL report:

```
ACCOUNTING SERVICES TOTAL UTILITY
   Reading accounting records, please wait...
03/31/1999:
   Connect time:        597     Server requests:      54839
   Blocks read:        6254     Blocks written:        1981
   Blocks/day:          744
(( Some days omitted for demonstration purposes ))
Totals for week:
   Connect time:       2597     Server requests:    2554839
   Blocks read:       32254     Blocks written:       51951
   Blocks/day:        45076
```

This report includes a daily total for each of the five resource types and a similar weekly summary. As all information because the installation of accounting is included each time the report is generated, the compilation time and the report itself can be quite long.

NOVELL's PAUDIT UTILITY

Included with NetWare 3 and previous was a utility called PAUDIT. It can be used to generate on a per-user basis accounting statistics. However, because it is a bindery-based tool, Novell did not include it with NetWare 4 and higher. But due to customer demand, you can download it from Novell Support Connection's Web site at `http://support.novell.com`. Use the File Finder and search for 402PA1.EXE.

Tip #205 from	To use this tool, you'll also need the `NET$REC.DAT` file, which is not included with
Peter	`402PA1.EXE`. You can find a copy this file in the `SYS:SYSTEM` directory of a NetWare 3 or NetWare 4 server. `NET$REC.DAT` is a template file used by PAUDIT to read the `NET$ACCT.DAT` file.

The following shows a sample output from PAUDIT:

```
F:\SYSTEM\>paudit

4/1/99 5:31:29  File Server NETWARE5-A
   CHARGE: 155 to User SALLY for File Server services.
   11173 disk blocks stored for 1 half-hour periods.
```

THE PAUDIT2 UTILITY

PAUDIT2 is a public domain utility written by Wolfgang Schreiber of Novell Developer Support, Germany. While Novell's PAUDIT allows only a global view of accounting data, PAUDIT2 gives a more comfortable compact overview and additionally allows searching for specific information. Some advantages of PAUDIT2 are the following:

- Several criteria to select data from the audit file
- Higher speed, only 10% of PAUDIT's Network load
- Selectable input file
- Read/recover damaged `NET$ACCT.DAT`
- Optional database formatted or Btrieve output

For example, PAUDIT2 can generate a report on certain users or groups between certain dates. The following sample syntax generates a usage report on members of the Consulting group for the first quarter in 1999:

```
PAUDIT2 GROUP=Consulting BEFORE=<1.4.99> AFTER=<31.12.98>
```

PAUDIT2 can be found on many NetWare-related Web sites on the Internet, including the homepage for Wolfgang at

```
http://www.geocities.com/SiliconValley/Vista/5577/index.html.
```

THE ACCOUNT UTILITY

Another public domain utility developed by Wolfgang is ACCOUNT.EXE. This handy tool allows you to look up or modify a user's account balance. The following shows its usage syntax:

```
ACCOUNT.EXE    Utility to modify user accounts  v1.01   (Wolfgang Schreiber)
Syntax:        ACCOUNT username¦SELF [[option] amount]

               - Charging can be done by anyone, setting/viewing by SVs
               - Use "SELF" instead of <username> to refer to own account

   ACCOUNT BALANCES can be viewed
           e.g.:  ACCOUNT guest
   ACCOUNTS can be charged by using the parameter "ch[arge]"
           The optional comment will be stored in NET$ACCT.DAT
           e.g.:  ACCOUNT SELF charge 25 [comment]
   ACCOUNT HOLDS can be set by using the parameter "h[old]"
           e.g.:  ACCOUNT guest hold 25
   ACCOUNT BALANCES can be set by using the parameter "s[et]"
           e.g.:  ACCOUNT guest set 25
   ACCOUNT NOTES can be written to NET$ACCT.DAT by using the parameter "N[ote]"
           The comment will be stored in NET$ACCT.DAT  (see PAUDIT2)
           e.g.:  ACCOUNT guest note  Tried to start SECRET.EXE
   CREDIT LIMITS can be set by using the parameter "L[imit]"
           unlimited credit can be set by "un[limited]" as amount
           e.g.:  ACCOUNT guest limit 25    or    ACCOUNT guest credit unlimited
```

For example, to look up Sally's account balance (assuming Sally's User object is in the server's bindery context):

```
F:\>ACCOUNT SALLY
SALLY:  Account Balance: 14534    Credit Limit: 15000
```

ACCOUNT.EXE can be found in ACCT.ZIP on Wolfgang's homepage and many NetWare-related Web sites.

TROUBLESHOOTING

Three common issues are frequently encountered when running Accounting. If ATOTAL is run within a short time after installation of accounting (even up to a few hours later), it will likely abort and give the following error message:

```
ATOTAL-4.1-912: The specified file cannot be found: SYS:SYSTEM\NET$ACCT.DAT.
```

The message suggests that an invalid filename was specified or the file is not in the path. This is, however, misleading. First, neither of these potential problems are accounting configuration settings—you can specify neither the directory path nor the filename used by Accounting. Second, checking for the existence of the file in SYS:SYSTEM shows that it *does* exist there.

The creation of a NET$ACCT.DAT file to store accounting information happens immediately on installation of accounting but it is not written to right away. It is because the accounting data initially is cached in server memory until the operating system decides to move it to disk; only then is the NET$ACCT.DAT file updated.

Secondly, this caching behavior also explains why NetWare's reporting of a user's account balance or the date/time of NET$ACCT.DAT doesn't always update immediately on logout.

Thirdly, because NetWare Accounting is bindery-based, many reporting tools, such as PAUDIT, sometimes report that a user has been deleted when in fact the user has not—the User object simply isn't in the bindery context.

CHAPTER 21

NETWORK PRINTING

In this chapter

OVERVIEW OF LEGACY NETWARE PRINT SERVICES

Before the advent of Novell Distributed Print Services (NDPS), in order to print, at a minimum you needed a print queue, a print server, and a printer. If you have upgraded to NetWare 5 from an earlier version of NetWare, your printing environment should be in place and functioning; you should investigate the new features of NDPS. If you prefer the old queue-and-capture method, or require it for some reason, it's all still there.

Legacy printing involves two components: a print-server nlm that runs at the server, and the client piece that runs on the workstation and talks to the print server. The capture command is used to "capture" a parallel port, and the data that is sent to the captured port is actually redirected to the specified queue. After it's in the queue, the print server's job is to send it to the correct printer.

Legacy, or queue-based printing, requires you to create a print queue, a printer, and a print server, along with necessary associations between them. Workstations print to a print queue via the capture command. After the job is in the print queue, the print server is responsible for sending the print job to the appropriate printer. On the server side, the print server nlm is pserver.nlm. On the client side, you load nprinter for DOS and nptwin95 for the Windows platform. Nptwin95 acts as the middleman between pserver.nlm and the printer attached to the workstation.

SETTING UP LEGACY PRINTING

The easiest way to get up and going is to select Print Services Quick Setup (Non NDPS) from the Tools menu of nwadmn32. In any case, you will need a print server, a print queue, and a printer; the nice thing about the quick setup is that it makes the necessary associations for you. After making the selection, you will be looking at the screen shown in Figure 21.1.

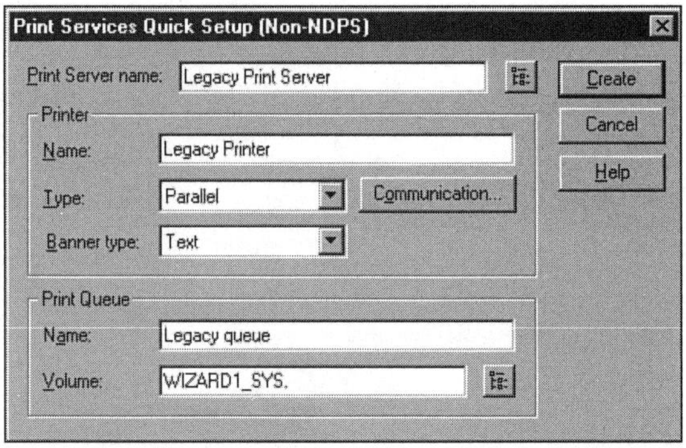

Figure 21.1
Print Services Quick Setup requires only a print server name, a queue name, and a printer name. The quick setup makes all the necessary associations for you.

The only things you need to enter are the name for the print server, the printer name and type of connection, and the print-queue name and volume.

Tip #206 from	If possible, you should not use your sys volume as the volume for your print queues; having the sys volume run out of space because of print jobs is a bad idea!
John	

The key is that the quick setup makes the necessary associations for you; you could achieve the same results by manually creating the server object, the printer object, and the queue object, and then linking them yourself. What are the associations? If you look at the details of the three NDS objects that have been created, on the Assignments page, you can do the detective work yourself. A printer has a queue assigned to it, and the print server has the printers assigned to it.

After you have created your printer, queue, and server, it's time to load them. There are two pieces to the puzzle, one on the server, and the other on the client. To activate your print server, you need to load pserver.nlm at the server console. You can simply enter the command pserver, and then browse to the correct context, highlight the print server you have configured, and press Enter. But because you will need the print server running, it is best to add the necessary load statement to your autoexec.ncf file; the syntax is <load> pserver .server.legacy.merlin. Of course, you need to replace the name of the print server and context with your own.

At the initial print server console screen, there aren't a lot of choices; in fact, there are only two. You can select either Printer Status or Print Server Information. If you select Print Server Information, you'll get various detail information about the version, advertising name, and so on, but the only useful thing here is the current status. By highlighting the current status, you can unload the print server, or unload it after the active print jobs. If you select Printer Status from the main menu, you are presented with a list of printers; highlight the printer in question and press Enter, and you will have the printer control screen shown in Figure 21.2.

At the printer status and control screen, you can abort print jobs, start and stop the printer, add or delete print queues, and more. You can do all of this from within nwadmn32, but having the functionality available at the server console is often quite convenient.

Certain devices are available, such as the JetDirect card from Hewlett-Packard, that can act as print servers; they let you take the load off the server. These third-party devices come with their own configuration utilities; some allow you to create the required NDS objects from within the vendor's utility, whereas others require that you create the objects yourself from nwadmn32 and then merely point the box at them.

PART

V

CH

21

Figure 21.2
After you highlight a printer from the Printer Status menu, you can control it from the console.

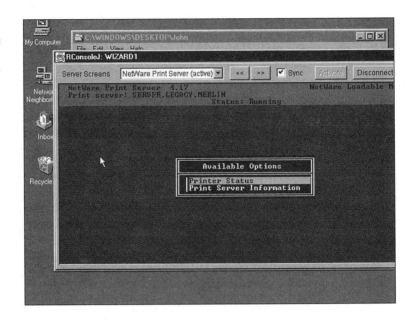

Tip #207 from
John

If you get a third-party print server, make sure that it is NDS aware.

After you have pserver.nlm up and running, it is time to move on the client side, where you will load nprinter or nptwin95.

NPRINTER/NPTWIN95

You can configure a printer as Auto Load (Local to Print Server) and have a shared, or networked, printer attached to the file server. However, this is seldom done anymore in the real world; the file server should be in a secure location, so even if you did connect a printer, no one could get to it. More realistically, you will have two types of printers: the ones that are directly attached to the network, via boxes such as the HP JetDirect, or those that are attached to users' workstations.

For configuring a JetDirect or some other brand of box to act as a print server, you will need to read the vendor's documentation. However, Novell provides the capability to share users' printers right out of the box; this is done via nprinter.exe in DOS, or nptwin95.exe on the Windows side. There are two pieces to this puzzle. You have already taken care of the server side by loading pserver.nlm; now, loading nptwin95 will let the print server print through the workstation to the workstation's printer. In essence, nptwin95 acts as the middleman between the print server and the printer attached to the workstation.

The first time you run nptwin95, which is in sys:public\win95, you will see the screen shown in Figure 21.3.

Figure 21.3
The NetWare Nprinter Manager. Here, you select the printer you have already defined in NDS.

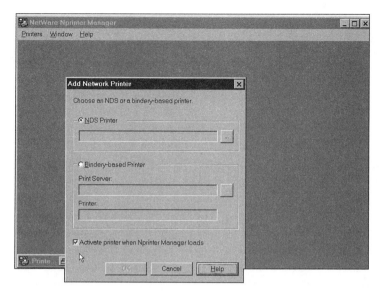

If you are selecting an NDS printer, browse to the correct context and choose the printer; if you are selecting a bindery-based printer, you need to choose a print server and a printer. Only the print servers that are advertising themselves on the wire show up in the list. To activate this printer whenever Nprinter Manager loads, check the box for that purpose.

You can add nptwin95 to the startup folder so that it will load automatically; if nptwin95 isn't loaded on the workstation, the printer is not available to other workstations. Create a shortcut and add it to the startup folder; if you add the /exit parameter to the shortcut, the Nprinter Manager will load silently, without displaying the window.

The Nprinter Manager does not need to be kept running; you can exit the manager, and your currently activated nprinters will remain active. Figure 21.4 shows the status of nptwin95.exe successfully communicating with pserver.nlm; you should also be able to highlight this same printer from the Printer Status menu of pserver (at the file-server console) and see its current status as waiting for a job.

THE Capture COMMAND

By now, you have pserver loaded at the file server, and nptwin95 loaded at the workstation; that leaves the question of how other workstations print to your new network printer. The answer is the capture command. The capture command is used to redirect the data being sent to the LPT port, and to send it instead to the appropriate print queue. When the data is in the queue, the print server will take over and get it to the right printer.

PART
V

CH
21

Figure 21.4
Nptwin95 has successfully loaded and is communicating with *pserver.nlm*.

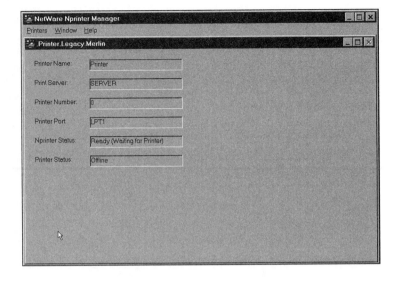

A typical `capture` statement might look like `capture q=business l=1 nb nff nt ti=4`. Capture is a command-line program, and it has far more switches than I will attempt to cover here; some of the more common ones, however, are given in Table 21.1. The preceding example would capture lpt1 and redirect the output to the business queue. It would send no banner, no form feed, and no tabs (byte stream), and it would have a timeout of four seconds. The `timeout` parameter is used to close the print job; for example, if you are printing and no data has entered the queue in the preceding four seconds, the job will be closed at that time and begin printing.

TABLE 21.1 CAPTURE COMMAND SWITCHES

Switch	Function
Q=	Specify the print queue
Ec	End capture
/?	Access online help
sh	Show the current capture settings
c=	The number of copies
l=	The parallel port to capture
Nb	No banner
NFF	No form feed
Nt	No tab expansion
Ti=	In seconds, how long to wait after the last data is received; then close and print the job

The `capture` command is generally added to the user or container login script, and as with any external command, you need to preface it with the #, for example:

```
#capture q=business l=2 nb nff nt ti=4
```

Of the switches, one of the most useful is `sh` (show), which instantly gives you the status of where the parallel ports are pointing. The output of `capture /sh` is shown here:

```
LPT1  Capturing data to print queue queue.legacy.merlin
  Notify:              Disabled
  Automatic end:       Enabled
  Timeout count:       2 seconds
  Name:                (None)
  Form feed:           Disabled
  Banner:              (None)
  Keep:                Disabled
  Copies:              1
  Tabs:                No conversion
  Form:                Unknown
  User hold:           Disabled

LPT2  Capturing is not currently active.

LPT3  Capturing is not currently active.
```

To really dig into the `capture` command, enter the command `capture help all`, and you will get several screenfuls.

MANAGING THE QUEUES

The print queue object has a Job List page that, when selected, shows you the jobs currently in the queue (see Figure 21.5).

Figure 21.5
The Job List page of the print queue object shows you the jobs currently in the queue; from here, you can pause, resume, or delete jobs.

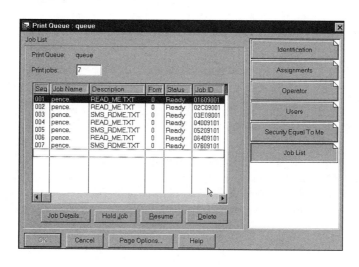

From the Job List page, you can see the job's sequence in the queue, the name of the job, the filename, the status, and more. If you highlight a job and click the Job Details button, you will be at the Print Job Detail screen shown in Figure 21.6, where you can obtain even more information and control over the job.

Figure 21.6
There are numerous options for controlling the job in the Print Job Detail dialog box, including deferring it to print later.

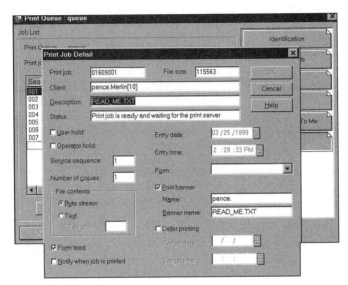

There are many options for controlling the job in the Print Job Detail dialog box: you can change the banner, the form feeds, the notify, the bit-stream type, the sequence, and more. One feature that might be of interest is the capability to defer printing until a target date and time; using this feature, you could let the user go ahead and print that enormous mail-merge job, but you could defer it from printing until that night when everyone had gone home. Otherwise, the printer would be tied up all day and it would do no one else any good.

OVERVIEW OF NOVELL DISTRIBUTED PRINT SERVICES (NDPS)

Novell Distributed Print Services is nothing like the old queue-and-captures you are used to. Using legacy printing, to get printed output, you needed to create a print server, a print queue, and a printer. Then you had to capture one of the ports at the workstation. In Novell Distributed Print Services, the printer agent takes the place and function of the print server, queue, and printer. NDPS was co-developed by Novell,HP and Xerox. It is not a Novell-only development.

There are four main pieces of the puzzle that this section covers. Don't get wrapped around the axle trying to fit these pieces together from the "theoretical" discussion; when you start actually implementing NDPS, the pieces will all fall together, and you'll have a much clearer understanding. The following sections focus on getting NDPS up and running; later in the chapter, I will come back to some more theory and strategies.

These are the four important pieces of the puzzle:

■ **The NDPS Broker**—The broker provides three services: the Service Registration Service, the Event Notification Service, and the Resource Management Service.

The Service Registration Service (SRS) allows printers to register themselves. One primary advantage to the SRS is that it eliminates the need for Service Advertising Protocol (SAP). Historically, print servers advertised their presence via SAP packets, which can create excessive network traffic if many printers are involved. Now, a printer will register itself with SRS, and the Service Registration Service can be queried to locate printers.

The Event Notification Service (ENS) allows printers to access various means of notifying users and administrators about printer events. There are several options, ranging all the way from pop-up windows to logs, email, and more.

The Resource Management Service (RMS) enables you to keep resources, such as printer drivers, on the server, and then download them as required. The RMS also makes automatic printer-driver downloading possible.

You have to create a broker object and then load the broker at the server. The creation of the broker object is done via nwadm32, and the NLM to load the broker is, not surprisingly, `broker.nlm`.

■ **The NDPS Manager**—The manager is used to create, start, stop, configure, and delete printer agents. Like the broker object, the manager is created via nwadm32, and then the NDPSM nlm must be loaded at the server.

■ **The Printer Agent**—The printer agent receives and processes printer and job requests, and it provides a consistent interface to you, no matter what type of printer is being represented. Ideally, the printer would be NDPS-aware and would have the printer agent embedded in its firmware. Because you are not going to have any NDPS-aware printers, the agent is an instance of software running at the server to represent the printer—a "front end" for the printer, as it were. You create printer agents from within `nwadmn32.exe` or at the NDPSM console screen.

Printer agents can be either public or controlled. Public printer agents are available to anyone on the network and are not represented by an NDS object. Because there is no NDS object, there is no access control. Controlled printer agents are represented by NDS objects, and access can be controlled via the NDS object and Nwadmn32.

■ **Gateways**—If the printer was NDPS-aware, you could communicate directly with it, and as NDPS printers become available, you will not need the gateways. But until then, it is the job of the gateway to talk NDPS-speak on one side and then translate the NDPS-speak out the other side into printer-specific language the printer can understand. This works because when you configure the gateway, you select a specific printer type. Three gateways are available: the Novell Printer gateway, the Hewlett-Packard IP/IPX Printer Gateway, and the Xerox Printer Gateway. Gateways are not created but are a part of configuring a printer agent.

But enough theory; the best way to learn about Novell Distributed Print Services is to get started and get it going. I will follow these six steps to get you up and going with NDPS:

1. Do a server-side install; file copy and schema extended.

2. Do a client-side install; add NDPS support.

3. Create and load the NDPS Broker.

4. Create and load the NDPS Manager.

5. Create a printer agent.

6. Use the printer agent you have created to explore the features of NDPS.

GETTING STARTED WITH NDPS

I will start with no NDPS support installed on the server, and no NDPS support installed on the client, completely from scratch. With no NDPS support on either the server or the client, if you go to run nwadmn32, you will receive the message shown in Figure 21.7.

Figure 21.7
If you receive this warning when starting nwadmn32, then the client, the server, or both were installed without support for NDPS.

If you are getting this error message, it is safe to assume that the server, the client, or both have been installed without NDPS support; it does take two to tango. After you install NDPS, you should not receive this message anymore. To get rid of this error message, start by installing NDPS on the server and seeing what that does.

THE SERVER

To install NetWare Distributed Print Services, first mount your installation CD-ROM as a volume, either on the server itself or as a volume on another server.

Load NWConfig at the server console prompt, and then select product options. Choose Install Other Novell Products, as shown in Figure 21.8.

Figure 21.8
When you press Enter on Install Other Novell Products, it is off to GUI land!

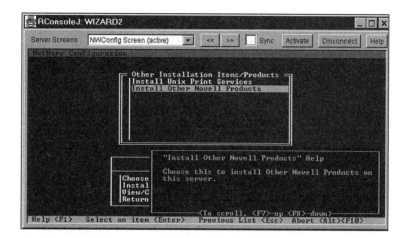

When you press Enter on Install Other Novell Products, it is off to GUI land, so be patient! Reference the screen shots in Chapter 8, "Installing NetWare 5 on New Servers," and you will remember that at one point in the GUI portion of the installation, you were presented with a menu of Additional Products and Services. On this menu, you could select the products you wanted to have installed, such as NDPS. Via nwconfig, which is going to launch the GUI, you wind up back at this menu; select NetWare Distributed Print Services and click Next.

After the files are copied and the schema is extended by the installation, you are done on the server side. The installation will create the NDPS broker object for you, if this is the first time NDPS has been installed in the tree.

Tip #208 from _John_	As always, take note that you need supervisor rights at the root of the tree in order to extend the schema.

Is the missing dll installed? Before the installation, if you had looked into the sys:public\win32\snapins directory for ndpsw32.dll, it would not have been there. Now, you should find that ndpsw32.dll has been added to the sys:public\win32\snapins directory. You can see from the error message in Figure 21.7 that the file in question is ndpsw32.dll, so hopefully, having this file in place will make the error message go away.

THE CLIENT

Now that you have taken care of the server portion of the install, run nwadmn32 again and see whether you still have the error when it launches; after all, you know that the NDPSW32.DLL is there. Not surprisingly, if you run nwadmn32, you still receive the error. This is because the client needs to be made NDPS-aware also, not just the server.

If you originally installed the Novell client using the typical install, support for NDPS is installed by default. If you chose custom when installing, and unchecked the box for NDPS, all is not lost. You can add Novell Distributed Print Services to a machine you have previously installed without it.

Right-click Network Neighborhood; choose Properties, Add, and then double-click Service. Choose Novell, and then select Novell Distributed Print Services, as shown in Figure 21.9.

Figure 21.9
You can easily add Novell Distributed Print Services to workstations that were installed without it. You need to have the client CD-ROM available.

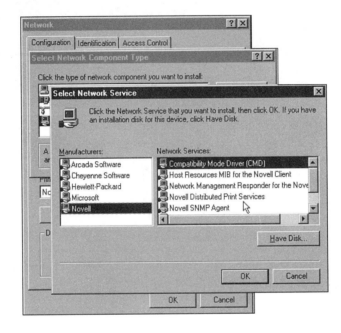

When you're asked for the location of the necessary files, point the installation to `<cd-rom>:\products\win95\imb_enu`. Replace the `win95` used in the example with the correct product; you can browse the product's directory on the CD-ROM to see what is available.

After restarting, you should be able to launch nwadmn32 and should not receive any errors. Also, on the Create menu, you will see some new choices: NDPS Broker, NDPS Manager, and NDPS Printer.

CREATING AND LOADING THE NDPS BROKER

Now that you have copied the files and extended the schema via the server-side installation, and you have installed NDPS support on the client, you are ready to create the broker object. If this is the first time NDPS has been installed in the tree, the broker object is created automatically for you; in this case, you will still want to read this section, but you will not need to create a broker object at this time.

On a large network with many servers, you will want to create more than one broker object; Novell recommends having a broker no more than three router hops away from the printer agent. You would definitely want more than one broker if slow WAN links are involved, a broker running on each side of the WAN link.

When running nwadmn32, you create the NDPS Broker like any other NDS object, either via File, Create from the nwadmn32 toolbar, or by pressing the Insert key on the appropriate container. The Create NDPS Broker Object dialog box appears, as shown in Figure 21.10.

Figure 21.10
The Create NDPS Broker Object dialog box.

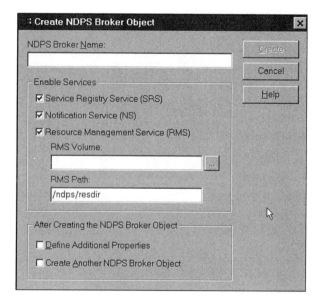

The NDPS Broker Name is simply the NDS object name. You can also enable or disable the SRS, ENS, and RMS services at this point. If you enable RMS, you need to specify a volume and path for the RMS files.

The RMS directory is pretty interesting; the server-side install will take care of you initially, by creating the RMS directory for you on the server where you perform the installation. But if you later create another broker to run on another server, this path must exist and must already contain resources. The solution is to copy the resources from another server; the catch is to make sure that you give the broker object supervisory rights to the new RMS resource directory; otherwise, nwadmn32 will say that the directory doesn't exist, even though you know it does!

If you remember from earlier in the chapter, the broker will provide three services to the network: Service Registry Service (SRS), Event Notification Service (ENS), and Resource Management Service (RMS):

PART

V

CH

21

- **Service Registry Service**—The SRS keeps a list of all registered printers on the network. When you need to print, you contact the SRS to retrieve a list of available resources. Because printers are registering themselves, there is no need for them to use SAP, and this cuts down on network traffic.

- **Event Notification Service**—The ENS lets you configure various types of event notifications, such as sending a print operator any significant printer events.

- **Resource Management Service**—The RMS lets you keep resources, such as printer drivers, in a central location for downloading to the clients.

After the broker object is created, you can manage it like any other NDS object, as shown in Figure 21.11.

Figure 21.11
Five tabs are available for managing the broker object: Identification, Access Control, Service Registry (SRS), Event Notification (ENS), and Resource Management (RMS).

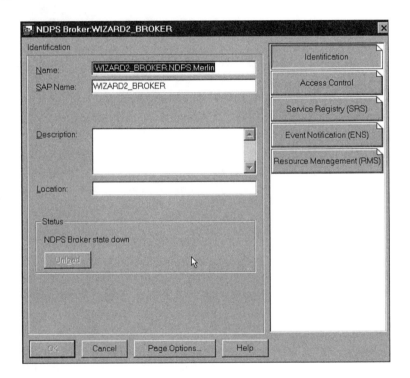

Now that you have created the NDPS broker object, you need to start the broker running on the server, and the easiest way to do this for the first time is to simply enter the command broker at the server console prompt. You can then browse and select to the correct NDS context of the broker object, highlight it, and press Enter.

After it's successfully loaded, you should see the NDPS broker console, as shown in Figure 21.12. From here, you can enable or disable the three services provided by the broker: Service Registry Service, Event Notification Service, and Resource Management Service. You can also see the five most recent events on this screen. To look at a complete list of the broker events, take a look at the sys$log.err file in sys:system; it is an ASCII text file. There isn't much you will do with the broker console other than leave it alone.

Figure 21.12
The five most recent events are displayed.

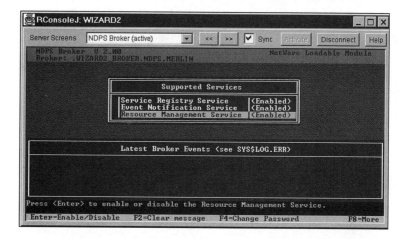

Loading the broker via browsing for the correct context, though simple, is certainly not automated! You will want to add the command broker to the server's autoexec.ncf file, and for that, you need to give the correct syntax:

```
LOAD BROKER "WIZARD2_NDPS_BROKER.ndps.Merlin"
```

It goes without saying that you need to replace the name of the leaf object and the context with your own data. Practice loading it a few times at the command line until you get it right. The broker.nlm will also accept several command-line switches, and the complete syntax of the broker nlm is

```
broker <broker_name> </p=password> /noui /noipx /noip
```

where /noui means no user interface, to run silently as it were. The /noipx parameter disables the broker from using the IPX protocol, and the /noip parameter disables the broker from using the IP protocol. Needless to say, you would not use both the noipx and the noip parameters at the same time, else there would be no protocols left to use!

CREATING AND LOADING THE NDPS MANAGER

Having created and loaded the broker, you now need to create the NDPS Manager. The manager, if you remember, manages the printer agents, and stores information used by the NDPSM.NLM. The NDPSM nlm is what you will be loading on the server later in this section to start the manager running.

The manager is created from within Nwadmn32 like any other NDS object. Choose Insert at the container level; or choose File, Create from the toolbar, and choose NDPS Manager. You will see the Create NDPS Manager Object dialog box, as shown in Figure 21.13.

PART

V

CH

21

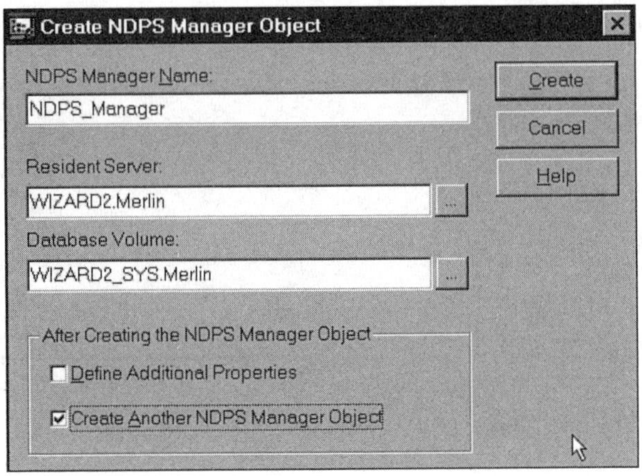

Figure 21.13
Here you choose the NDS name, the resident server, and the database volume for the manager.

The choices aren't exactly legion here; you need to specify the NDS object name for the manager, the resident server, and the volume to hold the NDPS Manager database. After it's created, it is time to load NDPSM at the server console.

As with loading the broker nlm, the easiest way to load NDPSM.NLM for the first time is to simply enter the command NDPSM at the server console and then browse to the correct context, highlight the NDPS manager object, and press Enter. When it's loaded, you should see the NDPS Manager console screen, as shown in Figure 21.14.

Figure 21.14
From here, you can see and manage the printer agent list and the NDPS Manager itself.

But, again, there is nothing automated about having a human stand there and browse for the right context just to highlight an object and press Enter, so you will want to add a load command for NDPSM in the autoexec.bat of the server. Here's the syntax:

```
load ndpsm .ndps_manager.ndps.merlin
```

Of course, you need to replace the NDS object name of the leaf object and context with your own data. For now, you can just leave the NDPSM console screen alone and move on to creating a printer agent in the next section. You are now ready to create a printer agent and test the setup, and to start exploring the features of Novell Distributed Print Services. If you must delve into the NDPSM console screen and what you can do here, skip ahead to the section "Managing at the NDPSM.NLM Console Screen."

CREATING PRINTER AGENTS

Now that the broker object and the manager object are created, and both are loaded, create a simple public printer to see whether things are working.

In this scenario, you are going to connect a printer directly to the server's parallel port. Now, you normally wouldn't connect a shared printer to your file server, and if you did, only administrators would have rights to use it. But what you want to know is, "Is what I've done so far working?" After all, you have run an install on the server, run an install on the client, and then created NDS objects and loaded NLMs. After you see that the system is working, you can move on to more "complex" scenarios. Your test printer will also act as your guinea pig for exploring all the neat features of NDPS; you can always delete this test printer later, either at the NDPS console or from within NWAdmn32. After all, if you can make things work with one printer agent, you can make NDPS work with more than one.

You create a printer agent from within NWAdmn32 by double-clicking the NDPS Manager Icon, choosing the Printer Agent page, and then selecting New. The Create Printer Agent dialog box appears (see Figure 21.15).

Figure 21.15
The Create Printer Agent dialog box is the first step in creating a printer agent; here you name the printer agent, select the manager, and choose the gateway.

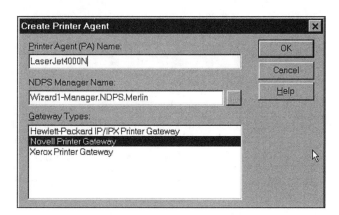

The Create Printer Agent dialog box is only the first step in the chain; the dialog boxes just keep on going! At the Create Printer Agent dialog box, you need to supply the NDS object name, supply the NDPS manager name, and select the type of gateway. Remember, the gateway is going to serve as a "translator" between NDPS and the printer itself. After the

PART
V

CH
21

NDPS agents are embedded in the printer's firmware, the gateways will no longer be needed. Because you are going to connect the printer directly to the server, select the Novell Printer Gateway. After you OK your selections, you select the printer type, as shown in Figure 21.16.

Note

The gateway speaks to you on one side using NDPS-speak, and it talks to the printer on the "other" side using the printer's language; so it is important that it speak the correct language. If you select an Epson dot matrix for the gateway to use but the printer is actually a Laserjet, the gateway will be sending Epson codes and formats to the Laserjet printer, and the results won't be pretty!

Figure 21.16
It is important that you select the correct printer type; otherwise, the gateway will send documents and control codes to the printer that the printer will not understand.

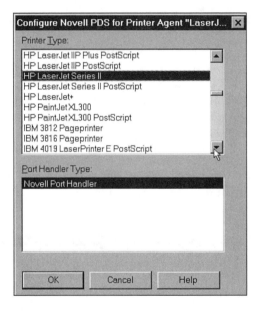

The next two screens you encounter are the configuration panels for the port handler. The job of the port handler is to make certain that the print-device subsystem can communicate with the printer, regardless of what type of connection is being used. To set up your test printer, choose Local (Physical Connection to Server), as shown in Figure 21.17.

Here is where you select the type of connection: Local, Remote (Rprinter on IPX), Remote (LPR on IP), or Forward Jobs to a Queue. The subsequent screens and dialog boxes you'll see are dependent on the connection type. For example, if you have chosen to forward jobs to a queue, you are asked for the queue name; if you have chosen LPR, you are asked for the host IP address; and so on.

Because you have chosen Local on LPT1, the next dialog box, shown in Figure 21.18, prompts you for the controller type and interrupt of the parallel port.

Figure 21.17
The port handler makes sure that the print-device subsystem can communicate, no matter what type of connection is being used.

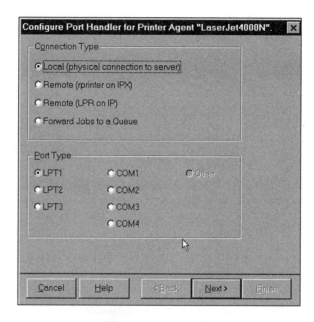

Figure 21.18
A local connection on LPT1 has been selected; next, you select the controller type and the interrupt of the parallel port.

Only one step remains in the creation of the printer agent, and that is to select the printer drivers to be downloaded when your printer is installed. As you can see from Figure 21.19, there are tabs for Windows 3.1, Windows 95/98, and Windows NT 4.

Figure 21.19
The last step in creating your printer agent is to select the printer drivers that will be used by the clients.

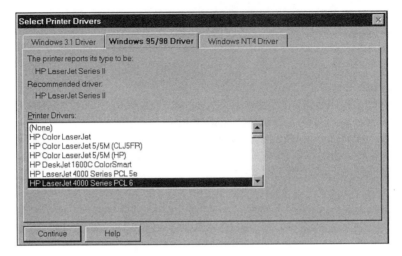

These tabs are independent of each other; for example, the drivers you choose to have downloaded to the Win 95/98 machines do not have to be the same as the ones for NT. You might download HP Series II drivers for 95, yet choose to download HP LaserJet 4000 Series for NT.

Having waded through the numerous dialog boxes, you finally will see your creation in the printer agent list, and it should have a status of idle. Now for the test. If you browse Network Neighborhood, you should see a new folder titled NDPS Public Access Printers. Open this folder, and you should see your newly created public-access printer. Double-click on it, and the message shown in Figure 21.20 appears.

Figure 21.20
The public printer is alive on the network and ready to be installed.

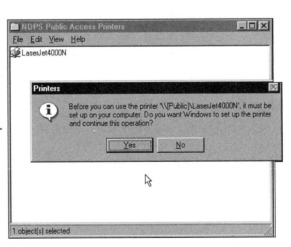

HP LaserJet 4000 PCL 5e

Your new public printer is alive and is ready to be installed. Installation is as simple as responding Yes to the message shown in Figure 21.20; the Add Printer Wizard is launched, and you are in business.

If you now go and look at your NDS tree, you will not see an NDS object that corresponds to your new printer agent; it exists only in the list of printer agents that the NDPS Print Manager is keeping. Only controlled-access printer agents have NDS objects, and by using the access control list of the NDS object, that is how you limit access to the printer.

The conversion from public to controlled is covered later in this chapter. Notice that at no time in the creation of your printer agent were you given a choice as to public or controlled. Going in through the printer agent list creates only public-access printers; to created a controlled one, you need to create an NDPS printer.

CREATING A PRINTER AGENT USING AN HP JETDIRECT CARD

Now that you have created a test printer and printed to it, you know that your entire installation is correct. All agents are created the same way; the primary difference is in the choice of the gateway and its configuration. HP JetDirect cards are both popular and prevalent, so in this section, you will create a printer agent for a network attached printer, a scenario you are likely to encounter in the real world, far more so than having the printer locally attached to the server.

The steps for creating a printer agent always begin the same, so open your NDPS Print Manager object from within Nwadmn32 and select New on the printer agent list. This time, you will not choose the Novell Gateway, but rather the Hewlett-Packard IP/IPX Printer Gateway. This will take you to the Configure HP Printer Gateway dialog box (see Figure 21.21).

Figure 21.21
The configuration for using an HP JetDirect card over IP is done here. Specify the printer type and its address; that's it!

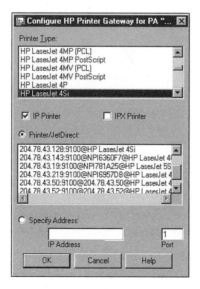

Configuring the HP gateway is a joy; the printers existing out on the network are automatically filled in for you. Choose the printer type, choose the protocol, and specify the address of the printer, and you are done. The only remaining step will be to select the printer drivers, and that works the same as in the previous example, when you set up the locally attached printer.

You will find a new screen on your server after this adventure, the Hewlett-Packard NDPS Gateway Console, as shown in Figure 21.22.

Figure 21.22
Here is a new console that magically appeared when the printer agent for the network attached printer, the one with the JetDirect card, was brought online.

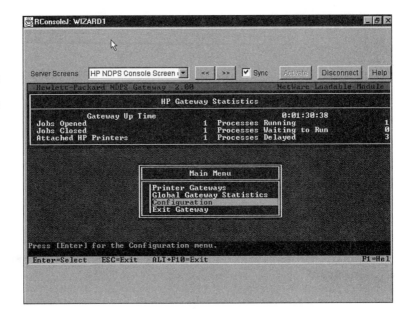

The HP Gateway console was brought online by the HPGATE.NLM getting auto-loaded. The hpgate nlm will accept numerous parameters; you can view the syntax of the command by entering hpgate /? at the server console prompt. The HP gateway will let you configure gateway settings, view statistics, and manipulate public-access printing for any HP printer connected with either an internal or an external JetDirect card. You can select statistics for individual printers, or you can look at global statistics, add, delete, and so on. Browse through the various screens and use the F1 help key for more information on the HP Gateway Console.

CREATING AND MANAGING AN NDPS PRINTER

So far, you have created two public printers: one attached to the server, and one attached to the network using an HP JetDirect card. But what if you do not want the printer to be public? What if you want to control the access?

You can go about this in two ways. You can create a public printer agent and then convert it to controlled printer, something I will cover later in this chapter. This is an extra step if you are after a controlled-access printer from square one; a more efficient method would be to create an NDPS printer. Unlike public-access printers, which do not have NDS objects, NDPS printers *are* represented by NDS objects. To create an NDPS printer object, select it from the Create menu, and you will be at the Create NDPS Printer dialog box (see Figure 21.23).

Figure 21.23
Here, you select the NDS object name, and you use an existing printer agent, create a new printer agent, or use an existing NDPS printer object.

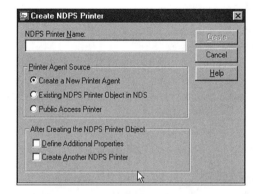

If you choose to create a new printer agent, you will be taken to the Create Printer Agent dialog box you have already seen. If you choose to use a public-access printer, you will get a warning that converting the public-access printer will cause all instances of that printer to need to be re-installed; see the section in this chapter on converting from public to controlled access, "Converting Public-Access Printers to Controlled."

After the printer object is created, you can manage access via the Access Control page. You can also control the printer by using the Printer Control page (see Figure 21.24).

Figure 21.24
The Printer Control page of an NDPS printer object.

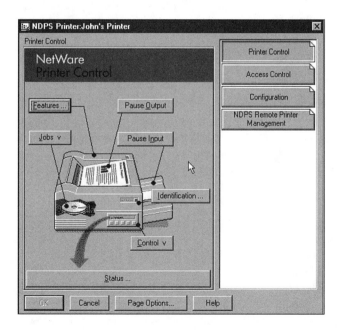

INSTALLING THE PRINTER

You can install printers on the workstation manually, or you can automate the procedure with remote printer management.

MANUAL NDPS PRINTER INSTALLATION

You can either use the Windows Add Printer wizard from Start, Settings, Printers, Add Printer, or use the Novell Printer Manager. The Novell Printer Manager, nwpmw32.exe, is in sys:public\win32, so your users can also access this program. To use the Windows Add Printer wizard, proceed as you normally would, but when it is time to browse for the printer, browse to the NDPS Public Access Printers folder and select the printer from there.

To add a printer using Novell Printer Manager, launch nwpmw32, and select Printer, New, Add. The Novell Printers installation dialog box shown in Figure 21.25 appears.

Figure 21.25
You can add, delete, and manage printers via the Novell Printer Manager, which is
sys:public/win32/nwpmw32.exe.

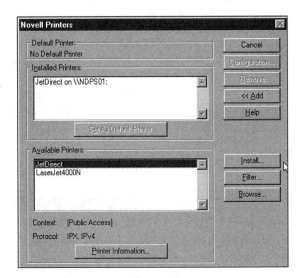

Figure 21.25 shows you the installed and available printers. Simply highlight one of the available printers and then click the Install button, and you are done. From within the Novell Printer Manager, you can also set up notification, customize printer configurations, manage print jobs, and do much more.

REMOTE PRINTER INSTALLATION AND MANAGEMENT

Remote printer installation has got to be the neatest thing since sliced bread. Say the business department has had an old IBM 4019 that is on its last legs; they get a nice new HP printer, which you cable directly into the network via the JetDirect card. The printer is up and available, but no one in the business department can use it. You have to make the rounds and install the new printer on each workstation, and at the same time, remove the old 4019. It would be nice to automate this task and do it all remotely, without getting out of your chair, and that is what the remote printer management feature of NDPS will let you do.

How do you start remote printer management? There are numerous ways, but the simplest is to select NDPS Remote Printer Management from the Tools menu in nwadmn32. Other methods are from the Details page of the container object or from the Details page of the printer itself. Or from the Printer Control page of a printer, you can select Remote Printer Management. The Remote Printer Management screen that appears is shown in Figure 21.26.

Figure 21.26
From here, you select printers to be automatically removed or installed.

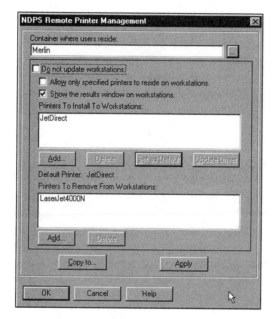

Following are the options in the Remote Printer Management dialog box:

- **Container Where Users Reside**—The changes you apply take effect at the container level; here, you select the container of the users whose workstations you want to update. If you look at the container object, you will see the NDPS Remote Printer Management page referenced earlier.

- **Do Not Update Workstations**—This disables remote printer management. You might check this box while setting up and testing.

- **Allow Only Specified Printers to Reside on Workstations**—With this option checked, the users are allowed only printers you specify. They can install other printers after they are logged in, but their new installations will not stick; the next time they log in, their new installations will be removed.

- **Show the Results Window on Workstations**—If you check this option, then after the updates are applied, there will be a small results window, showing which printers were added or removed.

- **Printers to Install to Workstations**—Here you select the printers you want to add. Use the Add button to add and the Delete button to remove, and you can also set the user's default printer with the Set as Default button.

- **Printers to Remove from Workstations**—This is just like the Printers to Install box, except that it removes the selected printers from the workstations.

- **Copy To**—This button copies your configuration to another container. In other words, if you want the same setup to be applied to another container, you do not have to go in and do this all over again; just click Copy To.

- **Apply**—This button applies your changes.

When someone logs in, the client checks its container for any remote printer configuration information. There is a time stamp on the workstation and in the configuration that is compared, and if the workstation's time stamp is different, the changes are applied. This is not done on a user-by-user basis, but on a machine-by-machine basis. In other words, if you set up a printer to be installed remotely, and George logs on to the workstation, the printer is installed. If George then logs out and Grace logs in, the printer is not re-installed; it's already there.

A log file is kept at the workstation of the changes made by remote printer management; the file is dprpmlog.txt, and it has the following format:

```
Printer JetDirect:  Installed
Printer LaserJet4000N:  Removed
-----------
Printer NewPrn:  Installed
Printer JetDirect:  Removed
```

As you might have noticed, the dprpmlog.txt file isn't very exciting. This file is limited to 5KB by default, which would make for a large number of changes. If you want to disable logging, you should run regedit, find HKEY_LOCAL_MACHINE/SOFTWARE/NDPS/RPM, and set the value of ErrorLog to 0 instead of 1.

> **Note**
>
> While you are in HKEY_LOCAL_MACHINE/SOFTWARE/NDPS/RPM disabling the creation of the dprpmlog.txt file, you'll find a time-stamp variable that might be interesting to play with. This is the time stamp, as far as I can tell, used to see whether the remote configuration changes need to be applied. Setting it to some smaller value and logging back in will force the changes.

MANAGING AT THE NDPSM.NLM CONSOLE SCREEN

Unlike with the broker console screen, which you pretty much leave alone, you can do several things at the NDPSM console screen. There are two choices other than Exit: the Printer Agent List, and the NDPS Manager Status and Control.

You aren't going to get totally wrapped around the axle on the features of the NDPS console screen, because most of your management will be done from within nwadmn32. But it is sometimes more convenient to be able to manage things at the server, especially if you are already in the server room.

THE PRINTER AGENT LIST

The printer agent is an instance of software that represents a local or remote printer, or one that is attached directly to the network. The printer agent list lets you create, delete, and manage the printer agents.

To create a new printer agent, use the Insert key. To delete a printer agent, highlight it and press Delete. The F3 key lets you rename a printer agent, and the F2 key toggles from the printer agent list to the NDS printer object list.

If you highlight a printer agent and press Enter, you will be at a control screen very much like the old pconsole. From here, you can delete jobs, look at statistics, pause and resume the printer, and more (see Figure 21.27).

Figure 21.27
From the NDPSM console, you can control the printer agents, as well as create and delete them.

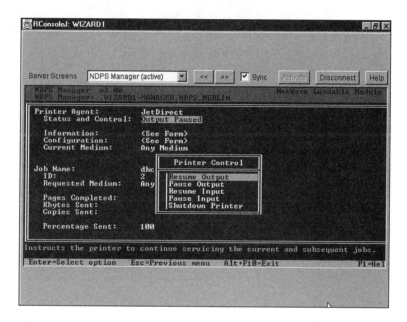

NDPS MANAGER STATUS AND CONTROL

If you select the NDPS Manager Status and Control from the Available Options of the NDPS Manager (refer to Figure 21.14), then you are taken to the NDPS Manager Status and Control Screen. Your options here are the status of the NDPS manager and Database Options.

The status will give you several unload options, which you will be familiar with from the old pserver nlm. You can choose Cancel Unload, Unload Immediately, Unload After Active Print Jobs, and Unload After All Print Jobs.

If you choose Database Options, you are given the Database Options screen shown in Figure 21.28.

Figure 21.28
You get here by selecting NDPS Manager Status and Control from the main NDPS menu, and then selecting Database Options.

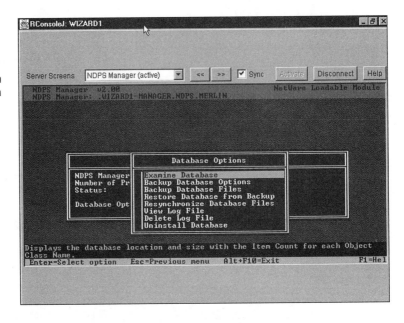

The NDPS Manager database has an index file and a data file, and it contains information about printers, jobs, media, and more. The choices on the database options are as listed here:

- **Examine Database**—Here, you see the database statistics and the number of objects in each object class within the database.

- **Backup Database Options**—You can set backup options here, such as enabling auto backup, setting start hours, and specifying days between backups.

- **Backup Database Files**—This option does exactly what the name implies, makes a copy of the database.

- **Restore Database from Backup**—This option replaces the existing database with the last backup.

- **Resynchronize Database Files**—This option rebuilds the index file by using the data file. A log file is kept whenever the database is resynchronized; the log is in sys: system\dprepair.log and will have the following format:

```
/*************************************************************************/
Database repair for NDPS Manager ".WIZARD1-MANAGER.NDPS.MERLIN"
Start time: Monday, March 22, 1999  11:30:41 am


Action: CATEGORIZE DATABASE
Database objects found: 40
Deleted records found: 1

Action: RECORD CONSISTENCY CHECK
Errors found: 0
```

```
Action: REBUILDING DATABASE FILES
Deleted records purged: 1

Database repair complete 0 errors found
```

| **Tip #209 from** | In the heat of battle, don't confuse the `dprepair.log` with the `dsrepair.log`—they |
| *John* | have only one character's difference in their names. |

- **View Log File**—You can view the log file from here or look for it in `sys:system`; it is an ASCII text file.
- **Delete Log File**—This option does exactly what its name implies.
- **Uninstall Database**—This option removes the existing NDPS Manager database and its supporting directories.

CONVERTING PUBLIC-ACCESS PRINTERS TO CONTROLLED

As I have already pointed out, when you create a public-access printer, there is no NDS object associated. The printer is simply there, available for anyone on the network to use. This might be fine for your configuration, but you might have printers you want to control access to, such as a color printer used by the Marketing department.

Converting a printer from public access to controlled access creates an NDS object; and you use the NDS object to control access, just as you would for any other object, such as a volume. To convert a printer from public, launch NWAdmn32 and choose NDPS Public Access Printers from the Tools menu. You are presented with a list of public-access printers. Select the printer you want to covert, and from the Object menu choose Convert to NDPS Printer Object (see Figure 21.29).

You will receive the warning `Converting a Public Access Printer to an NDPS printer object in NDS will require every client installation of this printer to be reinstalled. Do you want to convert this Public Access Printer?` In this case, you did and answered OK. You then browse to the appropriate context for the new NDS object, supply a name for the new NDS object, and click Create. You will immediately see the printer you have converted vanish from the list of public-access printers, and if you collapse and expand the container where you created the NDS object, you will see an NDS printer object.

Because this conversion entails the re-installation of the printer to all the workstations, you might tread warily here. If you are after a controlled-access printer, either create the public one and immediately convert it, or start with a controlled NDPS object in the first place; see "Creating and Managing an NDPS Printer," earlier in this chapter.

PART

V

CH

21

Figure 21.29
To convert a public-access printer to controlled, highlight the printer in question and select Convert to NDPS Printer Object from the Object menu.

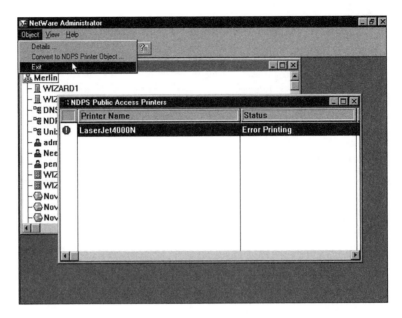

NDPS SUMMARY

With all the new NDPS features, it's hard to find a way to not manage your printers! On the NDS side of the picture, the only NDS objects you will have will be controlled-access printers, or NDPS printer objects, and the NDPS Print Manager object. You can double-click to manage these like any other NDS objects; the printer objects will have a printer control page, and the only thing you will need to do with the Print Manager object is to manipulate the printer agent list.

To view the public printers, select NDPS public-access printers from the Tools menu of Nwadmn32. There is also the Novell Printer Manager, which I covered briefly under "Manual NDPS Printer Installation," earlier in this chapter. And the fact that you can manage the printer agents from the NDPSM console screen is yet another management tool.

NDPS, or Novell Distributed Print Services, is the next generation of printing offered by Novell. The printer agent combines the functions of the print queue, print server, and printer. Printer agents can be in the firmware of an NDPS-aware printer, but as of this writing, it is more common to implement them at the server in software, and have them talk to a non-NDPS-aware printer via a gateway. The gateway is also software, which talks both NDPS-speak and the printer's natural language. The gateway acts as an interpreter for the printer and translates the NDPS-speak into commands the printer can understand.

A broker is required for NDPS; the broker provides three new services:

- **The Service Registration Service, or SRS**—This provides a place for printer agents to register themselves and eliminates the need for printers to SAP.

- **The Event Notification Service, or ENS**—This provides several methods for users to be notified of printer events.
- **The Resource Management Service, or RMS**—This allows for storing and downloading printer drivers from a central location.

A Print Manager is also required for NDPS; the Print Manager is used to create and manipulate the printer agents. Both the broker and the manager are represented by NDS objects, and both must be loaded at the server console. The nlm to load the broker services is `broker.nlm`, and the nlm to load the manager is `ndpsm.nlm`. Both of these nlms have console screens; you won't do much with the broker console except to leave it alone, but the NDPSM console screen can be used to manage printer agents.

Printer agents can be either public or controlled. Public printers have no means by which access can be controlled, and they do not have NDS objects; they exist only in the list of printer agents maintained by the Print Manager. Controlled printers do have NDPS print objects in NDS, and access to the printer is managed here, via the Access page of the NDS object. It is possible to convert public printers to controlled-access printers, but doing so requires the re-installation of what had been the public printer.

NDPS also has the capability to provide you with remote printer management, a totally cool feature. Using remote printer administration, you can automatically add and remove printers from the user's workstation, thus eliminating the need to make a trip out on the floor.

NDPS contains many other features that I haven't covered in detail, such as the new queuing methods (first-in-first out like the old way, but also by small-size jobs first). There is also the capability to control how much data can be queued up (ie, size limits on the queues). And remember, the theory behind NDPS is to get the NetWare server out of the picture. Once the agents are in the printers, clients will talk directly to the printer instead of going through a queue. Also, NDPS is desinged to provide much more feedback to the user, and gives you the ability to move a job once it is submitted to a different queue instead of having to reprint.

TROUBLESHOOTING

Probably the most common cry for help you hear from your users relates to some sort of printing problem. The first thing to do is to make sure that they are sending the data to the printer formatted correctly. You see, there are two main issues to sending a print job to a network printer. The first is, "Where is the print going?" and the second is, "How is the print job formatted?" If your word processor thinks it is printing to an HP Laserjet, but in reality, the job winds up going to a dot matrix printer, the dot matrix printer is going to choke and start printing strange garble, generally only a few characters per page. So it is not enough simply to redirect to another printer: you also need to keep in mind that the job must be formatted correctly for this other printer.

You can see that this book continually stresses keeping the server patched and using the newest nic and disk drivers from the vendor(s). Well, printing is the same, if not even more important. Assuming that the job is going to the correct printer and that it is formatted correctly, the next most common problem is going to be with the printer drivers. It is almost a given that the ones that ship with the printer are outdated by the time you get them, so hit the manufacturer's Web site first thing in order to get the newest version.

If things have been working and suddenly stop or if the printer starts putting out garble, reset the printer before jumping in and changing things. The printers can lock up, and this is more likely than capture statements rearranging themselves! If the printer is directly attached to the network, such as one with a JetDirect card, cabling and connector issues apply, just as they would with a workstation. A loose or poorly made cable connection will cause the printer to drift on and off the network or possibly lose data.

Make sure that you have the appropriate NLMs loaded on the server: pserver for for legacy printing, and the broker and ndpsm NLMs loaded for NDPS. For legacy printing, you also need to make sure that the client piece, nprinter, or nptwin95 is loaded correctly on the workstation. When troubleshooting a network printer, the first question to ask is whether the problem is specific to one user. If so, something is wrong with the configuration of that workstation. If everyone has problems or no one can see the printer, the problem is most likely on the server side of things.

And don't forget the printer cable itself. Most newer printers want or need a bidirectional printer cable and may be more susceptible to the length of the cable. The old printer might have worked fine with that 20-foot parallel cable, but when you slap the new printer into the same location, it quits working!

## CHAPTER 22

CONFIGURING USER ENVIRONMENT USING LOGIN SCRIPTS

In this chapter

WHAT IS A LOGIN SCRIPT?

Login scripts are commands used both by the administrator and the user to set up the network computing environment. Upon login, depending on the user's configuration, these login scripts can be executed. Like an AUTOEXEC.BAT under DOS, a login script can be used to establish path settings or drive mappings for applications, as well as to provide a mechanism for executing a file (such as CAPTURE.EXE for printing). They also can be used to display information for all users, groups of users, or even a particular user.

TYPES OF LOGIN SCRIPTS

NetWare 5 uses three types of login scripts, and you should become familiar with them as an administrator:

- **System Login Script (or Container Login Script)**—This script is used to set up general network computing environments for users within a certain organization or organizational unit. Upon the initial login, this script is executed first.

- **Profile Login Script**—This script is used to set up a general network computing environment for users, much like a system login script, but at the groups level. The difference between the Profile and System Login Script is that multiple profile scripts could exist within an organization or an organizational unit. One of the profile scripts could be assigned to multiple users and another to other users. The rule is that only one profile script can be assigned per user. This is ideal for groups that may want to have control over a specific general script, without letting them have control of the System Login Script. If a profile script is assigned to a user, it will be executed after the System Login Script finished execution.

- **User Login Script**—This script is specific to a user. It is used to customize the environment for each user. It is executed after the Profile Login Script.

Within the code of LOGIN.EXE and Client32, a default login script is used for users without any scripts. It contains the essential commands needed (drive mappings to NetWare) for a login from a user without any scripts (such as Admin upon initial login). The default login script cannot be modified. As an administrator, you do not need to be overly concerned about this script, but you should be aware that it exists.

As an administrator, you'll want scripts that are easy to maintain. The fewest number of modifications as possible should be the ultimate goal. The following sections describe the different types of login scripts and provide brief examples of what each script type might contain.

CONTAINER LOGIN SCRIPT

The Container Login Script, or System Login Script as it is sometimes referred to (as a holdover from the NetWare 3 days), is executed by all the users that reside within that container. This script is used to set up the general working environment for a "department" or "division" of users and should include the following:

- Drive (search) mappings to applications, such as word processor and email
- Drive mappings for data, such as to the user's home directory
- Login Script greetings
- General displayed messages
- Default printer capture statements

Profile Login Script

After establishing the general working environment for the users using the Container Login Script, you can further customize the environment for particular groups of users with the use of Profile Login Scripts. You may consider Profile Login Scripts as "group" login scripts. You should include the following in your Profile Login Scripts:

- Specific group application mappings
- Group messages
- Group printer capture statements
- Group environment settings

User Login Script

Often, the use of Container and Profile Login Scripts are sufficient to set up the proper working environment for a user. But if you need further customization, down to the individual user level, you can use User Login Scripts. In general, User Login Scripts contain the following:

- Personal drive mappings to local and network drives
- Personal messages (such as reminders)
- Capture statements to specific printers

Remember that NetWare login scripts are very flexible; you can do it any way you want to. If you can, keep most (global) commands and setups in the Container Login Script and then the Profile Login Script. This should help minimize administration time.

> **Note**
>
> Frequently, the use of Container Login Scripts is sufficient.

> **Tip #210 from**
> *Peter*
>
> Whenever possible, avoid using User Login Scripts. When you start customizing environments at that level, things can very quickly get out of hand as far as manageability goes. Imagine the problems if you have to maintain the User Login Scripts for 200 users. The other problem with User Login Scripts is that they can be modified by the users. Therefore, the potential exists of users changing their script without notifying you, which can result in the users not receiving certain drive mappings (because they overwrote it with their own mappings). When that happens, it can be difficult to troubleshoot problems.

CREATING, COPYING, AND MODIFYING LOGIN SCRIPTS

To create, copy, and modify login scripts in NetWare 5, you use the NWAdmin utility. If you have a NetWare 4 server on your network, you can also use NETADMIN (not included in NetWare 5) to create, copy, and modify login scripts.

> **Note**
>
> It is possible to use NETADMIN from NetWare 4 to manage users and groups. However, because NETADMIN doesn't know about the new enhancements made to NDS in NetWare 5, you can't take full advantage of the new features, such as NDS's new rights inheritance.

For those of you that have a NetWare 3 background, it is important to note that if you use the SYSCON utility that was provided with NetWare 2.x or 3.x to modify a system or user login script, those changes will not appear in Directory Services and are not available to users logged in under the NDS mode. The scripts created by SYSCON are for bindery clients and are stored as files in SYS:PUBLIC (System Login Script) and in SYS:MAIL (User Login Scripts). Therefore, if you have a mixture of NDS and bindery clients, you need to maintain two sets of scripts.

> **Tip #211 from**
> *Peter*
>
> Instead of maintaining two sets of system login scripts, you can just maintain the bindery System Login Script and in your Container Login Script, insert the statement INCLUDE SYS:PUBLIC\NET$LOG.DAT. See the "Login Script Commands" section later in this chapter for more information.

The following is a list of the different login scripts and their association with objects found in Directory Services. When creating, copying, or modifying scripts, you will need to go to the login script property associated with the respective objects:

System Login Script	This script is a property of the Organization or Organizational Unit objects.
Profile Login Script	This script is a property of the Profile object.
User Login Script	This script is a property of the User object.

Next, we'll take a look at the mechanics of working with these login scripts.

CREATING AND MODIFYING A LOGIN SCRIPT

The NetWare Administrator (NWAdmin) is a graphical-based utility that can be used to manage login scripts. To manage login scripts, you will need to have the Write property write to the Login Script attribute of the objects that contain the login scripts. To create and modify login scripts, follow these steps:

1. Start NWAdmin, and using the Browser, select the object whose login script you want to modify or create.
2. Right-click and select Details from the context menu.

3. Click the Login Script option button on the right side of the displayed menu (see Figure 22.1).

Figure 22.1
The Login Script tab of a container object.

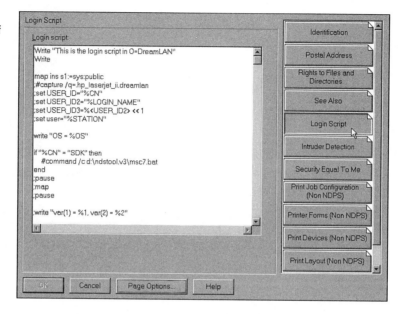

4. A login script text box appears, where can you add or delete login script commands and variables.

5. After you make the changes you want, choose OK to save the login script. If you have created a login script, you should read the next section to learn more about using this script.

ASSOCIATING A PROFILE SCRIPT TO A USER

If you created a profile script (defined through a Profile object) that must be associated with a user, you will need to assign and give the user rights to the Profile Login Script. To ensure that a user will execute the Profile Login Script, follow these steps:

1. Using the Browser, select the User object to which you will be assigning the profile script.

2. Right-click and select Details from the context menu.

3. Click the Login Script option button.

4. Enter the name of the Profile object you want to assign in the Default Profile field. If you want, you can search for the Profile by clicking the Browser button next to the Default Profile field (see Figure 22.2).

Figure 22.2
Assigning a Profile
Login Script to a user.

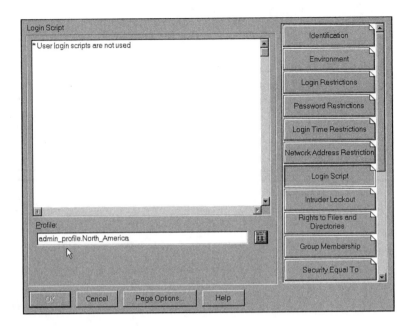

5. After you make your changes, choose OK to save the changes.

   The next few steps explain how to give the user sufficient rights to use the login script.

6. Using the Browser, select the Profile object you wish the user to have rights to.

7. Right-click and select Trustee of this Object from the context menu.

8. Select Add Trustee.

9. Enter the name of the User object that will be using this Profile object. You can use the Browser button to search for User object, if needed.

10. Make sure that the Browse object right and the Read property right are checked.

11. Click OK.

COPYING A LOGIN SCRIPT

Copying login scripts can help save time, especially when many of the System and Profiles Login Scripts are very similar throughout the network. You should log in to Directory Services as a user with sufficient rights to make changes. To copy login scripts, follow these steps:

1. Use NWAdmin's Browser to select the object whose login script you want to copy.

2. Right-click and select Details from the context menu.

3. Select the Login Script option button.

4. Within the Login Script text box, highlight the text you want to copy.

5. Press Ctrl+Ins (or Ctrl+C) to copy the highlighted text into a buffer in memory.

6. Click OK to exit the login script.

7. Using the Browser, select the object whose login script you want to paste in the text.

8. Right-click and select Detail from the context menu.

9. Select the Login Script option button.

10. Within the Login Script text box, place the cursor where you want to paste the text and press Shift+Ins (or CTRL+V).

11. Click OK to save the modified login script.

LOGIN SCRIPT COMMANDS

The login script commands are very useful in automating the creation of the users environment during their logging in to the network. The environment may consist of messages, drive mappings, and DOS environment settings. With each command, an explanation, a command format, and a brief example are given on how you can use a login script. A later section provides full examples of login scripts.

In the following sections, the various login script commands are listed in alphabetical order. The syntax for the command and an example is given where appropriate.

Login Script Command Syntax Explained
Before going into detail about the various commands, an explanation of the command format syntax can help you determine what is mandatory or optional:

[ ]	Square brackets indicate that the enclosed item is optional.
|	The vertical bar is used to show that either the item to the left of the bar or to the right of the bar can be used. You cannot use both items.
[option]	Options or parameters are listed with the command.
[[]]	The nested square brackets indicate that all enclosed items are optional. However, if the items within the innermost brackets are used, then you must use the items within the outermost brackets.

THE # COMMAND

This command (#) is used to execute an external command (which can be a DOS or Windows application) from within the login script. This is especially useful when you want to capture a user to a particular printer on the network through the login script. The following is the command format that you can use:

```
# [path] filename [parameter]
```

The *path* variable represents the full DOS path where the file you want to execute is located; NetWare path specification (such as SYS:UTILS) may be used.

The *filename* variable represents the name of the file you want to have executed from the login script.

> **Note**
>
> The login script processing stops and waits until the named external program finishes running before continuing with other login script commands.

> **Caution**
>
> You should not use this option to load any TSR programs because that can cause memory fragmentation in the workstation.

The *parameter* variable represents file parameters that may be executed with the file.

Workstations may not have enough memory to execute the LOGIN utility and the external command, so the LOGIN utility will "swap" out of conventional memory and place the LOGIN into available higher memory or onto the disk. If you want to swap LOGIN out of conventional memory every time you execute an external command, you can place the SWAP command in the login script before the # command.

If you do not want to temporarily swap to higher memory, you may use the NOSWAP command. (The NOSWAP command is discussed later in this section.)

For example, if you wanted a user to capture to PRINT_Q upon login, you may place the following line inside the login script:

```
#CAPTURE Q=PRINT_Q NB NFF TI=10
```

THE @ COMMAND

This command (@) functions in much the same way as the # command previously discussed. However, it is specific to the Microsoft Windows environment; you can't use this with a DOS login. In addition, this command executes a program that is external to the login script and then continues with the script (similar to the Startup Group).

For example, if you wanted a user to capture to PRINT_Q upon login, you may place the following line inside the login script:

```
@CAPTURE Q=PRINT_Q NB NFF TI=10
```

THE ATTACH COMMAND

The ATTACH command is used to connect to bindery-based NetWare servers (NetWare 2.x and/or NetWare 3.x) or to NetWare 5/4.x server using bindery emulation. The command format is:

```
ATTACH [server[/username[;password]]]
```

> **Note**
>
> When users attach to a NetWare 5 server for resources via the NDS mode, they automatically have access to any resources in the tree to which they have rights. Rights to resources are verified through background authentication and no ATTACH command is necessary.

The *server* variable represents the actual server name to which you are requesting a connection.

The *username* variable represents the login name you want to use when connecting to the specified server.

The *password* variable represents the password of the login name specified. If the password used to log in to NDS is the same as the password on the target bindery server, no password information needs to be specified.

For example, if you wanted to attach to a bindery-based NetWare server called NW32_ACCT as user SALLY with the same password used when logging into NDS, you would add the following line to the login script:

```
ATTACH NW32_ACCT/SALLY
```

THE BREAK COMMAND

The BREAK command is used to control the user's capability to use the Ctrl+C or Ctrl+Break to terminate the execution of the login script. If BREAK ON is placed in the login script, a user can terminate the execution of the login script. BREAK OFF is the default setting. The command format is:

```
BREAK [ON ¦ OFF]
```

> **Note**
>
> Including BREAK ON in a login script does not affect the DOS Ctrl+Break check. For more details, see DOS BREAK later in this section.

THE CLS COMMAND

The CLS command is used to clear the display within the login process. This can be especially helpful when you want to clear the screen before displaying a message. The following is the command format:

```
CLS
```

> **Note**
>
> This command is valid for DOS and OS/2 workstations. It is unnecessary in Windows 95/98 and NT because a separate login script dialog box exists.

The COMSPEC Command

The COMSPEC command is used to specify the location of a DOS user's command processor (COMMAND.COM). Some users on the network set their COMSPEC to a local drive. In the case, where multiple DOS versions are available on your network, you will need a separate directory for each version. Later in this section when variables are discussed, an example of setting up multiple DOS versions is given. The command format is as follows:

```
COMSPEC = [path]COMMAND.COM
```

The *path* variable represents the full DOS path needed to find the command processor, COMMAND.COM.

If your users are running OS/2, do not include the COMSPEC variable in the login script. In the case where OS/2 users use a virtual DOS session, you will need to make sure the COMSPEC statement is in the CONFIG.SYS.

For example, if your users have a DOS directory as a second search drive (S2:, which will map to drive Y:) in the login script, you would place one of the following commands in the login script:

```
COMSPEC=S2:COMMAND.COM
COMSPEC=Y:COMMAND.COM
```

The CONTEXT Command

The CONTEXT command is used to set the user's current context in the Directory Services tree. The command format is

```
CONTEXT context
```

The *context* variable represents the full context of where you want the users context set to.

For example, if you want to switch a user's current context to the Sales Organization Unit, within the Consulting Organization you would put the following line in the login script:

```
CONTEXT .Sales.Consulting
```

Note

It is important to include the leading period in the preceding command. If you leave it out, LOGIN will try to change context to Sales.Consulting relative to your current context. This may or may not be what you want.

Tip #212 from
Peter

You can type a single period instead of a container name to indicate that you want to move up one level. To move up two levels, enter two periods, and so forth.

THE DISPLAY COMMAND

The DISPLAY command is used to display the content of a text file, much like the DOS TYPE command. This can be helpful for displaying certain messages upon login. If a file was saved in a word processor format, the codes used by the word processor may appear as garbage when being displayed. To display a file that was created and saved in a word processor format, use the FDISPLAY command, which is described later in this section. The command format is as follows:

DISPLAY [path]filename

The path variable represents the full DOS path of where the file you want display is located.

The filename variable represents the actual file name of the context you want displayed.

For example, to display a message upon login that is contained in the file BULLETIN.TXT in SYS:PUBLIC\SYSNEWS directory, put the following in the login script:

DISPLAY SYS:PUBLIC\SYSNEWS\BULLETIN.TXT

Tip #213 from *Peter*	Make sure you put the file in a directory where the users will have Read access. Because all users have Read and File Scan to SYS:PUBLIC, SYS:PUBLIC or one of its subdirectories is a good location in which to put the message file.

THE DOS BREAK COMMAND

The DOS BREAK command is used to control the Ctrl+Break level of DOS. If you place the DOS BREAK ON statement within the login script, you will allow users to terminate programs (other than the login script) by using the Ctrl+Break key sequence. This command is different than the BREAK command, discussed earlier, in that the BREAK command allows users to terminate login script execution. The command format is

DOS BREAK [ON ¦ OFF]

By default, DOS BREAK is set to OFF.

For example, for users wanting to use the Ctrl+Break key sequence to terminate programs, place the following statement in the login script:

DOS BREAK ON

THE DOS SET COMMAND

The DOS SET command (much like DOS's SET command) is used to set DOS or OS/2 environment variables to specified values. For the OS/2 workstation, the DOS SET environment variable remains valid only during the execution of the login script. The command format is

DOS SET name = "value"

The name variable represents the actual name of the environment variable.

The `"value"` variable represents the value to which you want the environment variable set.

For example, to set a TEMP environment variable pointing to the TEMP directory under the user's home directory, place the following in the login script:

```
DOS SET TEMP = "F:\USERS\%LOGIN_NAME\TEMP"
```

THE DOS VERIFY COMMAND

The DOS VERIFY command is used to verify data that the workstation copied to its local drive, using the DOS COPY command, can be read after the copy. Users using the NetWare NCOPY utility to copy data will not need to use this command. The command format is:

```
DOS VERIFY [ON ¦ OFF]
```

The default for DOS VERIFY is OFF.

For example, to ensure the data integrity copied to a local drive using the DOS COPY command, place the following in the login script:

```
DOS VERIFY ON
```

THE DRIVE COMMAND

You use the DRIVE command to change your default drive. The command format is

```
DRIVE [drive: ¦ *n:]
```

The *drive* variable represents the local or network drive letter you want to make as your default.

The *n* variable represents the drive number you want as your default; that is, *2 means the second *network* drive.

For example, to have the user exit the script to drive G:, place the following in your script:

```
DRIVE G:
```

THE EXIT COMMAND

You use the EXIT command to terminate the execution of the LOGIN utility; however, this is not supported in OS/2. This command also enables you to execute a file when exiting the script, which could be useful for putting a user in an application or menu. The command format is

```
EXIT ["filename"]
```

The `"filename"` represents the name of the file to which you want to exit; the quotes are required.

The length of information between the quotes is not limited in Microsoft Windows. However, the length of information between quotes is limited in DOS; the length of information between quotes can't exceed your keyboard buffer length minus 1 (commonly 15−1=14 characters).

For example, to have Windows automatically start up after a user executes upon login, place the following in the login script:

```
EXIT "WIN"
```

Tip #214 from
Peter

You can use this (exit-to-program) feature to load TSRs.

Note

Any program started via the EXIT option does not hold the login script open, such as in the cases when you are using # and @.

Caution

When the EXIT command is encountered, the login script interpretation/execution process is terminated. Therefore, if you place EXIT in your Container Login Script, Profile or User Login Scripts are *not* executed.

Tip #215 from
Peter

As discussed at the beginning of this chapter, it is generally not a good idea to use User Login Scripts unless you have no other choice. By placing EXIT in your Container or Profile Login Scripts, you can prevent any User Login Scripts from being executed.

This command can add more functionality when used in an IF...THEN statement, which is discussed later in this section.

THE FDISPLAY COMMAND

FDISPLAY (filtered display) is used to display text of a word processed file during the login procedure. It ignores control characters placed in the file from the word processor and only displays the text. The command format is

```
FDISPLAY [path]filename
```

The *path* variable represents the full DOS path of the file that contains the text message.

The *filename* variable represents the actual file name that contains the text message.

For example, to display a message in word processed file named BULLETIN.TXT in the SYS:PUBLIC\SYSNEWS directory, use the following in the login script:

```
FDISPLAY SYS:PUBLIC\SYSNEWS\BULLETIN.TXT
```

THE FIRE PHASERS COMMAND

You use the FIRE PHASERS command to cause a phaser sound at the workstation upon login. This can be useful for getting the user's attention when displaying an important message in the login script. The command format is

```
FIRE [PHASERS] n [filename]
```

The n variable represents the number of times you want the phaser sound to go off.

Under Windows, you can specify a .WAV sound filename as part of the command; the default .WAV filename is PHASERS.WAV (installed on the workstation).

For example, to fire phasers three times upon login, use the following in the login script:

```
FIRE 3
```

THE GOTO COMMAND

You use the GOTO command to execute a portion of the login script out of sequence. The command format is

```
GOTO label
```

The label variable is used to refer to the login script portion you want executed next.

For example, if you want users in a group called SKIP_THIS to bypass all or a portion of the login script, use the GOTO statement to bypass all or portions of the script, as in the following:

```
IF MEMBER OF "SKIP_THIS" THEN GOTO BYPASS_SCRIPT
     ... other script commands
BYPASS_SCRIPT:
```

In this example, if the user is a member of the group SKIP_THIS, the GOTO statement will skip all commands between it and the label.

> **Caution**
>
> Do not use the GOTO command in nested IF...THEN statements because it does not work correctly.

THE IF...THEN...ELSE...END COMMAND

You use the IF...THEN...ELSE...END command when you want the script to perform certain actions if the conditions are met. The command format is

```
IF conditional [AND ¦ OR [conditional] THEN commands
[ELSE commands]
[END]
```

The conditional variable can be replaced with identifier variables. The identifier variables are discussed later in this chapter.

The commands variable represents login script commands (such as MAP, DRIVE, DOS SET, and so on).

A conditional statement can be used to find out if a variable is equivalent to a value, such as the following:

```
IF MEMBER OF "USERS"
```

The preceding statement tests to see whether the user is a member of the USERS group; it assumed the object is in the current NDS context.

Conditional statements can derive a relationship between the variable (%LOGIN_NAME) and its value (JOHN) by using the following symbols:

Symbol	Definition
=	Equals
<>	Does not equal
>	Is greater than
>=	Is greater than or equal to
<	Is less than
<=	Is less than or equal to

For example, the following line shows how you could set up a search drive mapping to SYS:SYSTEM for your administrators:

```
IF MEMBER OF "LAN_ADMIN" THEN MAP INS S1:=SYS:SYSTEM
```

Note

If you need to execute more than one command after the THEN, the BEGIN and the END commands are required.

THE END COMMAND

You use the END command in conjunction with IF...THEN...BEGIN, when more than one command will be included in the IF block. If you wanted to display a weekly Friday meeting reminder, you could place the following in the script:

```
IF DAY_OF_WEEK = "FRIDAY" THEN BEGIN
     CLS
     WRITE "Reminder for weekly staff meeting at 3:00 PM today!!!"
     PAUSE
END
```

Tip #216 from
Peter

You don't need to indent the commands between the IF...THEN...BEGIN...END, as shown in the above example. However, indentations make them stand out and easier to read.

THE INCLUDE COMMAND

You use the INCLUDE command to execute login script commands stored in a file or another NDS object's login script as a subscript of the login script. This could be useful for groups or users that want to customize their own scripts, without having rights to change the main script. Only valid login script commands and variables can be used. The command format is as follows:

```
INCLUDE [path] filename
```

or

```
INCLUDE objectname
```

The *path* variable represents the full path needed to find the subscript file. This can either begin with a drive letter or a full directory path beginning with the NetWare volume name.

The *filename* variable represents the actual subscripts file name. Remember, if users are going to modify this subscript file, they must have Read and Write rights to this file. Those using the file must have Read rights.

Tip #217 from
Peter

As mentioned earlier in this chapter, you can use the INCLUDE command to maintain one set of login scripts for both bindery and NDS users—in your Container Login Script, insert `INCLUDE SYS:PUBLIC\NET$LOG.DAT`.

The *objectname* variable represents the name of the object whose login script you are going to execute.

For example, if a group called SUPPORT wanted to execute a subscript they created called UTILS.TXT in the VOL1:UTILS\SCRIPTS directory, you would put the following in the script:

```
IF MEMBER OF ".Support.Network.Gemini" THEN
     INCLUDE VOL1:UTILS\UTILS.TXT
END
```

Or, if you wanted to have a login script execute another Organizational Unit's login script, you could place reference in the INCLUDE command to the objects name. If the Organizational Unit is named Sales.Consulting, for example, you would put the following in the login script:

```
INCLUDE .OU=Sales.O=Consulting
```

Note

As mentioned earlier, the inclusion of the leading period in the object name may be required.

THE LASTLOGINTIME COMMAND

You use the LASTLOGINTIME command to display the user's last login time. The command format is

```
LASTLOGINTIME
```

THE MACHINE COMMAND

You use the MACHINE command to set the DOS machine name for the workstation; for example, IBM_PC, COMPAQ, HEWPAC, and so on. The MACHINE command is not used by NetWare but is necessary for some programs (such as NetBIOS) written to run under PC-DOS. The following is the command format:

```
MACHINE = name
```

The *name* variable represents the name of the actual machine name. The name can be up to 15 characters. Names longer than 15 characters are truncated.

> **Note**
>
> The name doesn't have to be a brand name. It can be any name. Some sites use location names, such as FRONT_DESK, as machine names.

The value set using the MACHINE command can be used by some programs (such as NETBIOS) written to run under PC DOS. The name can include such identifier variables as STATION.

For example, to set the MACHINE name to COMPAQ, place the following command in the login script:

```
MACHINE=COMPAQ
```

> **Note**
>
> This command is for DOS and Windows 3.x machines only.

THE MAP COMMAND

You use the MAP command to view and establish drives to network directories. The command format is

```
MAP [option] [drive:=path]
```

The *drive* variable can be replaced with the actual drive letter that you want associated with the directory path.

The *path* variable can be replaced with a drive letter, a full directory path (which may include a server name or a Volume object name), or a Directory Map object.

Tip #218 from Peter	In a multiserver environment, mapping drives to directories on a server should include the Volume object name or a server name. This ensures that the mapped drive points to the correct server.

You'll find many of the options for the MAP command are similar to the ones available for MAP.EXE—the MAP command in the login script does not, however, rely on the MAP.EXE program. Some of the support options are as follows:

- **DISPLAY ON|OFF**—Determines whether drive mappings are displayed on the screen when the user logs in. The default setting is ON. This option is valid only in login scripts.

Tip #219 from Peter	Add the MAP DISPLAY OFF command at the beginning of the login script, and when all drive map assignments have been completed, add the line MAP DISPLAY ON and MAP to your login script. This sequence provides a cleaner display for users as they log in.

- **ERRORS ON|OFF**—Determines whether MAP error messages are displayed when the user logs in. MAP ERROR OFF must be placed before MAP commands in the login script. The default setting is ON. This option is valid only in login scripts.
- **INS**—Inserts a drive mapping between existing search mappings.
- **DEL**—Deletes a drive mapping, making that drive letter available for other mapping assignments.
- **ROOT**—Maps a fake root. Windows NT and OS/2 are always mapped to the root.

Tip #220 from Peter	The Windows NT native environment forces a map root on all drives. To prevent a forced map root in a Windows NT environment, put DOS SET MAPROOTOFF="1" as the first line of the login script. This would globally force all NT workstations using the login script not to map root drives except for explicit map root drives.

- **C (Change)**—Changes a search drive mapping to a regular mapping, or a regular mapping to a search drive mapping.
- **P (Physical)**—Maps a drive to the physical volume of a server, rather than to the Volume object's name. It is possible to have a Volume object name that conflicts with a physical volume name. (For example, object ACCT is an Accounting volume, but there is also an ACCT that is a physical volume.) Therefore, if you prefer to map a drive to the physical volume name, use MAP P.
- **N (Next)**—When used without specifying a drive number or letter, it maps the next available drive.

For example, set up a search map to SYS:PUBLIC\WIN32 for all network administrators so they can easily access NWAdmin and NDS Manager:

```
MAP INS S1:=SYS:PUBLIC\WIN32
```

Caution

You should always ensure that there's a search map to SYS:PUBLIC where the common NetWare utilities are located.

THE NO_DEFAULT COMMAND

The NO_DEFAULT command can be used from a system or profile script to prevent execution of the default user login script (which is built into the LOGIN program, both the DOS and the GUI versions). The command format is

```
NO_DEFAULT
```

In the case where you do not want to create user login scripts, and you do not want the default User Login Script to be executed, you would place this command in the Container or Profile Login Script.

Tip #221 from
Peter

Alternatively, you can place an EXIT command at the end of your Container or Profile Login Script and achieve a similar result. The only difference is that with NO_DEFAULT, the User Login Script will be executed if one exists.

THE NOSWAP COMMAND

The NOSWAP command is used to prevent the (DOS) LOGIN utility from swapping out of conventional memory into available higher memory or from swapping to disk, in the case where a workstation runs out of memory while executing an external command (#). The command format is

```
NOSWAP
```

This command could save the workstation time by skipping the normal process of having LOGIN attempt a swap.

THE PAUSE COMMAND

The PAUSE command is used to pause the executing login script until the user presses a key, the same as the DOS PAUSE command. This is helpful when displaying messages to the user via login script, allowing the user to read the message before it scrolls off the screen. The command format is

```
PAUSE
```

If you include PAUSE, the message Strike any key when ready... appears on the workstation screen. The LOGIN utility then waits for a key to be pressed before it executes the rest of the login script.

THE PCCOMPATIBLE COMMAND

The PCCOMPATIBLE command is used to enable the EXIT login script command to work on workstations whose names are not IBM_PC. The command format is

PCCOMPATIBLE

If a workstation had a long machine name that was not set to IBM_PC (such as HEWPAC, COMPAQ, and so on) in the NET.CFG for DOS) or in the Client32 properties (under Advanced Settings, Long Machine Type, in Windows 9x/NT), you need to include this command in the login script to allow the EXIT command to work.

For example, if you had a Compaq computer with the long machine name of COMPAQ in the NET.CFG and you wanted the workstation to exit to a menu upon login, you would place the following in the login script:

PCCOMPATIBLE
EXIT "WIN"

> **Note**
>
> This command does not apply to OS/2 workstations.

THE PROFILE COMMAND

The PROFILE command in a container script can be used to set or override a user's assigned or command line-specified profile script. This is useful when defining a group profile. The command format is

PROFILE *profile_object_name*

For example, to override the profile script assigned to John, and to cause John to execute a Profile Login Script called magic_profile in the Network.Gemini container, include the following commands in the Container Login Script:

IF "%1" = ".John.Network.Gemini" THEN
     PROFILE .Magic_Profile.Network.Gemini
END

THE REM AND REMARK COMMANDS

You use the REM or REMARK commands to insert explanatory text into the login script. Text used with this command in front of it will not be displayed to the screen nor executed. The command format is one of the following:

REM [ARK] [*text*]

* [*text*]

; [*text*]

The *text* variable is replaced by the explanatory text.

Tip #222 from Peter	When troubleshooting, you can also use the command to temporarily prevent certain login script commands from executing.

Tip #223 from Peter	A common use of remarks is to document changes made in the login scripts. Include a date and the user ID of who made the changes and when. Perhaps include a short sentence to explain why the change was made.

The following are some sample usage with the REMARK command and its variants:

```
Remark " This is an example login script
Rem Don't map root drive F:
; but drive G: must be map rooted
* in order for NODES-1 to work properly.
```

THE SCRIPT_SERVER COMMAND

You use the SCRIPT_SERVER command to set a home server from where the bindery login script is read for NetWare 2 and NetWare 3 users. This command has no effect on NDS users. The command format is

```
SCRIPT_SERVER server_name
```

THE SET COMMAND

The SET command (much like DOS's SET command) is used to set DOS or OS/2 environment variables to specified values. For OS/2 workstations, the SET environment variable only remains valid during the execution of the login script. The command format is

```
[TEMP] SET name = "value"
```

The name variable represents the actual name of the environment variable.

The "value" variable represents the value to which you want the environment variable set. The quotes are required.

Tip #224 from Peter	If value ends in a \" (backslash-quote), these two characters are interpreted as an embedded quote preceded by an escape character. To avoid this problem, use two backslashes before the ending double quotes (\\").

To change the environment for the login script, but not for the workstation itself after the login script has finished executing, use the optional keyword TEMP. Because all variables set in the login script for an OS/2 workstation affect the environment only while the login script is running, all variables are considered TEMP with OS/2 workstations.

For example, to set a DOS prompt to display the current directory path (such as F:\HOME\SALLY>) rather than just the drive letter, place the following line in the login script:

```
SET PROMPT="$P$G"
```

THE SET_TIME COMMAND

The SET_TIME command is used to set the workstation time equal to the time on the NetWare server to which it first attaches. The command format is

```
SET_TIME ON ¦ OFF
```

The default value is ON.

> **Note**
>
> The default value is based on the Client32's SET STATION TIME advanced property setting; the default is ON. If you include SET_TIME OFF in the login script, the workstation time does not update to the server's time.

THE SHIFT COMMAND

The SHIFT command is used to change the %n identifier variable used in the login script. This command could allow the users to enter other parameters (command-line arguments) with the LOGIN utility to change the user's environment mappings. The command format is

```
SHIFT [n]
```

The n represents the number of places you want to shift the command line variables. You can use positive and negative numbers to move the variable in either direction. For example, SHIFT 2 would move the % variable two positions to the right; the default is 1.

When users log in, they can specify parameters with the LOGIN command. The login script then interprets these parameters as instructions to perform certain login script commands. When the login script parser interprets the login script, it sees any percent sign (%) followed by a number in a command as corresponding to a parameter used when the LOGIN executes. The numbers can range from 0 to 10 (for DOS); the GUI login interface supports only 0 to 5. The parameters in the command are given the value of %0 corresponding with the server name, %1 as the user name, and so on.

(With the GUI login interface, you can specify only %2 through %5.)

The following DOS LOGIN command line:

```
LOGIN NETWARE5/SALLY ORACLE8 LAPTOP
```

would have the following corresponding variables:

```
%0 = NETWARE5
%1 = SALLY
%2 = ORACLE8
%3 = LAPTOP
```

To manipulate these variables in the login script, you can use an IF...THEN statement to see whether a certain condition is met, and then a command can be executed. For example, if specified at the LOGIN command line, the following script command could determine which version of the Oracle database Sally wants to use:

```
SET ORA_VER = "ORACLE_V7"
```

```
IF "%2" = "ORACLE8" THEN SET ORA_VER="ORACLE_V8"
SHIFT 1
SET WS_TYPE = "WORKSTATION"
IF "%2" <> "" THEN SET WS_TYPE = "%2"
```

In this example, the login script parse will test to see whether Sally specified ORACLE8 and/or a workstation type after her name. Note that with this sample login script, the order of the parameters are important.

THE SWAP COMMAND

The SWAP command is used to swap the LOGIN utility out of conventional memory into higher memory (if available) or to disk when executing external commands (using the # parameter) in the login script. The command format is

```
SWAP [ path]
```

The *path* variable can be replaced with the NetWare volume name and path or with a drive letter and path. Make sure the user has sufficient rights to the path.

THE TERM COMMAND

You use the TERM command in conjunction with Novell Application Launcher (NAL) scripts. Because NAL supports only Windows platforms, this command does not apply to DOS or OS/2 workstations. The command format is

```
TERM nnn
```

Replace *nnn* with an error level. Any error level between 000 and 999 is valid.

The TERM command is used in a login script to stop the login script and return an error code. You can also use TERM in an IF...THEN statement, so that the login script stops and an error code is returned only if an IF statement is true (that is, a certain condition exists). If the IF statement is false (that is, a condition doesn't exist), the login script skips the TERM command and continues executing.

| Tip #225 from | Because TERM stops the login script execution (just like the EXIT command), be sure to put |
| Peter | this command either at the end of the login script or at a point within the script where you intend execution to stop. |

THE TREE COMMAND

The TREE command can be used to attach to another NDS tree within your network and to access its resources. The workstation needs to be running Client32, which supports multiple NDS tree attachments. The command format is

```
TREE tree_name[/complete_name[;password]]
```

Replace *tree_name* with the name of the NDS tree that you want the user to attach to.

Replace *complete_name* with the user's complete name (Distinguished Name) for the NDS tree that the user is attaching to. The complete name establishes your context in the tree. If you do not include the complete name, the user is prompted for a complete name when the TREE command is executed from the login script.

Replace *password* with the correct password for that user and tree. If the username and password are the same as the primary login username and password, you can omit the password and not be prompted for it.

Tip #226 from *Peter*	For security reasons, it is best not to include any passwords in login scripts.

Caution	The TREE command changes the "focus" of your login script so that all NDS object references in subsequent script commands (for drive mappings, print captures, and so on) apply to the NDS tree named in the TREE command. However, you can use multiple TREE commands within a login script to switch the login script's "focus" back and forth between different trees.

For example, to attach the user, Sally, to the test tree during login, add the following lines to the login script:

```
IF "%1"= ".Sally.Sales.Consulting" THEN
    TREE TEST_TREE/.Sally.Consulting
END
```

If Sally's password in the TEST_TREE is not the same as the current tree's, she'll be prompted for the password.

THE WRITE COMMAND

You use the WRITE command to display messages to the workstation upon login. The command format is

```
WRITE "[text][%identifier]" [;][identifier]
```

The *text* variable can be replaced with the text you want to display on the workstation's screen upon login.

The *identifier* variable can be replaced with a NetWare login script variable (discussed later in this chapter), such as a greeting time or a user's name. This command also enables you to use special characters to enhance the functionality. The following is a list of the characters, with an explanation:

Character	Meaning
\r	Invokes a carriage return
\n	Starts a new line of text
\7	Makes a beep sound
\"	Displays a quotation mark

The following is an example of how you would display a message to users:

```
IF DAY_OF_WEEK = "FRIDAY" THEN
     WRITE "Time cards are due today!!! \7"
     PAUSE
END
```

Notice the \7 that will cause a beep sound.

Following is an example of how you could use the WRITE command with login script variables:

```
WRITE "Good %GREETING_TIME %LOGIN_NAME!!!"
```

Note

When a login script variable is used in the WRITE command, a percent sign (%) precedes the variable name. And when the variable is referenced within quotes, its name must be all uppercase.

Details about login script variables can be found in the next section.

LOGIN SCRIPT VARIABLES

In this section, login script variables that can be used in conjunction with the login script command discussed above are covered. The identifier variables are broken down into nine categories, as described in the following sections.

DATE IDENTIFIER VARIABLES

You can obtain or display date information in a number of ways. Seven different date-related identifier variables are listed below:

DAY	Day number (01 through 31)
DAY_OF_WEEK	Day of the week (Monday, Tuesday, Wednesday, and so on)
MONTH	Month number (01 through 12)
MONTH_NAME	Month name (January, February, March and so on)
NDAY_OF_WEEK	Weekday number (1 through 7; 1=Sunday)
SHORT_YEAR	Last two digits of a year (91, 92, 93, and so on)
YEAR	Four digits of a year (1991, 1992, 1993, and so on)

For example, to display a date in a WRITE statement, you could use the following:

```
WRITE "Today is %DAY_OF_WEEK, %MONTH_NAME %DAY, %YEAR"
```

The login script would display the following statement upon login:

```
Today is Friday, March 12, 1999
```

Tip #227 from *Peter*	Given the possible confusion of the Y2K problem, it is best to use YEAR instead of SHORT_YEAR.

TIME IDENTIFIER VARIABLES

Using the time identifier variables below, you can obtain or display time-related information:

AM_PM	Day or night (a.m. or p.m.)
GREETING TIME	Time of day (morning, afternoon, or evening)
HOUR	Hour (12-hour scale; 1 through 12)
HOUR24	Hour (24-hour scale; 00 through 23; 00 = midnight)
MINUTE	Minutes (00 through 59)
SECOND	Seconds (00 through 59)

For example, to display the time in a WRITE statement, you could use the following:

```
WRITE "Good %GREETING_TIME, the time is %HOUR:%MINUTE:%SECOND %AM_PM!!"
```

The login script would display the following upon login:

```
Good Morning, the time is 8:03:15 AM!!
```

USER IDENTIFIER VARIABLES

Often, you want to customize the messages so your users have a "personal touch" feeling. This can be achieved using the user identifier variables:

CN	User's common name in NDS.
FULL_NAME	User's unique username. It is the value of the FULL_NAME property for both NDS and bindery-based NetWare. Spaces are replaced with underscores.
LAST_NAME	User's last name (surname) in NDS, or full login name in bindery-based NetWare.
LOGIN_ALIAS_CONTEXT	Is "Y" if the value of the REQUESTER_CONTEXT is an Alias.
LOGIN_CONEXT	NDS context where the User object resides.

LOGIN_NAME	Users unique login name (long names are truncated to eight).
MEMBER OF "group"	Group object to which the user is assigned.
NOT MEMBER OF "group"	Group object to which the user is not assigned.
PASSWORD_EXPIRES	Number of days before the password for the user expires.
REQUESTER_CONTEXT	Context when login started.
USER_ID	Unique hex. number (8 digits) assigned to each user.

The following is one way you could use a couple of these identifier variables:

```
WRITE "Good %GREETING_TIME, %FULL_NAME"
WRITE "Warning: You have %PASSWORD_EXPIRES days before your password expires \7"
```

NETWORK IDENTIFIER VARIABLES

Two network identifier variables can help you to determine the name of the server you are logged in to as well as the IPX network address you are on:

FILE_SERVER	NetWare server name
NETWORK_ADDRESS	Network number of the cabling system (8-digit hex. number)

For example:

```
WRITE "Good %GREETING_TIME. You're attached to server %FILE_SERVER"
```

WORKSTATION IDENTIFIER VARIABLES

You can extract workstation information, such as the version of DOS, using workstation identifier variables and make use of them in the logins script:

MACHINE	Type of computer (IBM_PC, and so on) (non-OS/2); refer to your DOS manual for more information.
NETWARE_REQUESTER	Version of the NetWare Requester for OS/2 and VLM.
OS	Type of DOS on the workstation (DR DOS, MS-DOS).
OS_VERSION	Version of DOS on the workstation (3.30, 4.00, and so on).
P_STATION	Workstation's node address (12-hex digits).

PLATFORM	Workstation's operating system platform: DOS, OS2, WIN (Windows 3.1), WNT (Windows NT), or W95 (Windows 95).
SHELL_TYPE	Version of the workstations DOS shell (1.20, and so on); this variable is supported under 2.x and 3.x shells and the NetWare 4.x Requester for DOS (VLM).
SMACHINE	Short machine name (IBM, and so on) (non-OS/2).
STATION	Workstation's connection number.
WINVER	Version of workstations' Windows operating system

You can use these variables to map out the DOS directory, as in the following:

```
MAP S2:=SYS:PUBLIC\%MACHINE\%OS\%OS_VERSION
```

If you were using IBM_PC as the MACHINE type, MS-DOS as the OS type, and you had version 6.22 of DOS, you would get the following result:

```
SEARCH2:=.Y:=[ACCOUNTING\SYS:PUBLIC\IBM_PC\MSDOS\V6.22]
```

NetWare Mobile Variables

If your workstation has the NetWare Mobile client installed, you can make use of the following two variables:

DIALUP	0 = Not using dialup; 1 = Using NetWare Mobile Client dialup profile
OFFLINE	0 = Not offline; 1 = disconnected

DOS Environment Identifier Variables

You can also make use of DOS environment variables from within the login script, using the following syntax:

<variable>	Any DOS variable can be used in angle brackets (< >). If you use a DOS environment variable in a MAP command, add a percent sign (%) in front of the variable.

For example, you could MAP a search drive to the path environment variable:

```
MAP S16:=%<path>
```

Miscellaneous Identifier Variables

The following are some miscellaneous identifier variables that you may find useful in controlling the execution of the login script:

ACCESS_SERVER	This is used to show whether the server you are logging in to is an access server (TRUE = functional, FALSE = not functional).

| ERROR_LEVEL | An error number (0=No errors). |
| %*n* | Replaced by parameters the user enters at the command line with the LOGIN utility |

OBJECT PROPERTIES IDENTIFIER VARIABLES

Under NetWare 5 (also in NetWare 4), it is possible to make use of information that is stored in the NDS. In the login script, you can make use of the different attributes associated with a user object. The syntax for referring to an NDS attribute is

| %*property name* | Properties of the NDS objects can be used as variables. The property's name can be used like any other variable. If the property name includes a space, enclose the name in quotation marks. |

For example, to map drive F: to the user's home directory, you can use the following command:

```
MAP F:=%HOME DIRECTORY
```

Note that the attribute name is preceded by a percent sign and must be in uppercase.

WINDOWS REGISTRY KEYS

The Client32 v3.0 and 4.5 clients include a new login script command called REGREAD. The syntax is as follows:

```
REGREAD "HIVE,KEY,VALUE"
```

Hive is one of HKLM, HKCU, HKU, and so on.

Key is the path to the value, for instance Software\Novell\Login\History\Contexts.

Value is the name of the value you want to read, if other than default. To read the default value, leave it blank.

> **Caution**
>
> Case is important and there cannot be any spaces after the commas.

For example, the following will read the data from the Value Name 0, instead of the default:

```
REGREAD "HKLM,Software\Novell\Login\History\Contexts,0"
```

The data read will be placed in the variable %99. The value can then be used in subsequent login script logic.

SAMPLE LOGIN SCRIPT

The following is an example of a Container Login Script that made use of some of the login script commands and identifiers discussed in earlier sections of this chapter:

```
; Container login script for OU=Sales.O=Consulting
;-----------------------------------------------------------
;
; History:
;     Jan 13/1999. PCK. Initial script.
;     Jan 14/1999. PCK. Added drive G: for GroupWise.
;     Jan 17/1999. SAS. Removed search map to VOL1:DATABASE\SQL
;                       and added search map to VOL1:DATABASE\ORACLE
;
; Drive mapping information:
;     1. Drive G: needs to be mapped to Email directory
;     2. Do not change the search drives 1, 2, and 3 -
;        for specific uses.
;     3. Drive M: is reserved for database
;
;-----------------------------------------------------------

WRITE "Good %GREETING_TIME, %FULL_NAME!"
WRITE "Welcome to server %FILE_SERVER!!"
WRITE "Today is %DAY_OF_WEEK, %MONTH_NAME %DAY, %YEAR."
WRITE "The time is %HOUR:%MINUTE %AM_PM"

MAP DISPLAY OFF
MAP G:=EMAIL:GW55
MAP S1:=SYS:PUBLIC
IF MEMBER OF ".LAN_ADMIN.SALES.CONSULTING"THEN MAP S2:=SYS:SYSTEM
SET PROMPT = "$P$G"

IF MEMBER OF ".WORD_PRO.CONSULTING" THEN BEGIN
     MAP S3:=.WP.SALES.CONSULTING
END

IF MEMBER OF ".ACCOUNT_PAYABLE.BEANIES.CONSULTING" THEN BEGIN
        DISPLAY SYS:PUBLIC\SYSNEWS\ACCTNEWS.TXT
        PAUSE
        SET USER = "%LOGIN_NAME"
        MAP L:=VOL1:DATABASE\ACCDATA
        MAP S16:=VOL1:DATABASE\ORACLE
END

IF MEMBER OF ".LASER_PRINT.CONSULTING" THEN BEGIN
        #CAPTURE Q=.LASER.PRT.CONSULTING TI=10
END

IF MEMBER OF ".COLOR_PRINT.CONSULTING" THEN BEGIN
        #CAPTURE Q=.COLOR.PRT.CONSULTING NB NFF TI=10
END

MAP DISPLAY ON
MAP
```

This login script first greets the user, then informs the user of the name of the server logged on to, followed by date and time information. The script then sets up some drive mapping depending on the group the user belongs to, and it sets up a CAPTURE command so the print job will be routed to the correct printer.

TROUBLESHOOTING

A majority of the problems you encounter in login scripts deal with mapping drives and capturing printers. Usually, these problems can be attributed to syntax and spelling errors. Correcting spelling errors and using variables in the right way (such as putting quotes around a login name being tested in an IF...THEN condition) resolve many problems.

The best way to troubleshoot the above mentioned problems is to do one or more of the following:

- Set MAP DISPLAY and MAP ERRORS to ON in the login script. Many administrators set these parameters to OFF so that users are not bothered by the login process. However, these settings also hide any mapping errors which may occur during login script execution. By setting them to ON, the errors will display, often providing clues as to why a certain command did not execute as expected. After seeing that the login script performs all map commands without error, the MAP DISPLAY and MAP ERRORS parameters can be returned to the OFF setting.

- Use the WRITE or MAP commands together with the PAUSE command prior to the script command which doesn't work as expected. For example, if the login script didn't seem to be getting into an IF...THEN statement, put both a WRITE and a PAUSE statement immediately before the IF...THEN statements to verify that the script executed to that point. Then, place a WRITE and PAUSE inside the IF...THEN to see if it gets past the IF correctly. It would also be helpful to have the WRITE statement give the value of the variables being tested to make sure that the variables are correct going into the script (*e.g.* WRITE "This is the login name: %LOGIN_NAME"). Similarly, you can use the MAP command with a PAUSE to troubleshoot drive mapping problems. This is useful to determine when and where a certain mapping was made in a login script.

- Make a test login script file either on the local drive or a network drive using any text editor. Test this script file by using the /S parameter for LOGIN.EXE (*e.g.* LOGIN /S <drive>:\<filename> <servername>/<username>); in the Windows 9x/NT environment, specify the name of the test script file in the Script tab of the GUI. If this login script works correctly, start cutting and pasting the statements in this login script into the login script that doesn't seem to be working correctly. This way, problems in login scripts can be dealt with by elimination.

The following is a list of some other commonly found login script problems and their resolutions:

- **Losing PATH settings after login**. After each login, the user would lose a part of the path specified in the AUTOEXEC.BAT. The user had PATH statement in AUTOEXEC.BAT and then had mapped some search drives in the system login script (MAP S1:= MAP S2:=). PATH statements are set up as search mappings when logged onto the network starting with S1, S2, and so on. When you specifically MAP (S1:=), then you *overwrite* the existing search mapping (PATH). The fix is to use MAP INS on the search drives instead. It will push the existing statements down the line without overwriting. Furthermore, using MAP INS S16:= will append the mapped drive to the end of the PATH without overwriting those at the beginning.

- **Could not execute external command <COMMAND>.** This error occurs when trying to run external commands or applications from inside a login script, such as CAPTURE.EXE. To troubleshoot this problem, make sure a search drive to where the utility is located has been established before the command is used.

- **Login script behavior is unpredictable**. Make sure there are no viruses on the workstation. Computer viruses can cause numerous strange problems with login scripts that have previously executed or should now execute correctly. Also, temporarily remove any unnecessary drivers, such as those for sound cards, to eliminate any possible conflicts.

  Using the ATTACH login script command to create an attachment to another NetWare 4 or NetWare 5 server in the same NDS tree can also cause unexpected results such as intermittent premature termination of the login script. The ATTACH command makes a bindery connection which causes any previous NDS connections to that server to be destroyed. Using CAPTURE with the Server parameter will also cause a bindery attachment to occur.

In summary, login script problems are generally fairly easy to isolate and fix. You just need a little patience with your troubleshooting procedures.

CHAPTER **23**

SERVER CONSOLE UTILITIES

In this chapter

THE SERVER CONSOLE

UNDERSTANDING THE CONSOLE

The *console* is where you start or stop the server, load and unload NLMs, set server configuration parameters, and more. You will encounter several interfaces at the server console. The first is simply the command line, and it shows the server name followed by a colon, such as WIZARD1: <command is entered here>. The next interface is the character-based menus that all NetWare users are familiar with, such as the MONITOR.NLM that you will see later in this chapter. And finally, new in NetWare 5, there is the Java-based GUI.

Tip #228 from
John

> One important point to keep in mind is that without physical security, there is no security, so you should restrict access to the server console. You can also restrict keyboard access via the console command SECURE CONSOLE and the locking feature that has been moved from MONITOR.NLM to the SCRSAVER.NLM, which is covered later in this chapter.

Theree can be more than one screen available at a time on your server, because it is a multitasking engine. There are two ways to switch between screens. The first method is to use the key combination Alt+Esc, which toggles you from one screen to the next, very much like Alt+Tab does in Windows. The second method has a more user-friendly interface; the key combination Ctrl+Esc pops up a menu of all the current screens, as shown in Figure 23.1. You can then choose (by number), the screen that you want to view.

Figure 23.1
The key combination Ctrl+Esc pops up a menu of the current screens available at the server and allows you to choose by number the screen you want to go to.

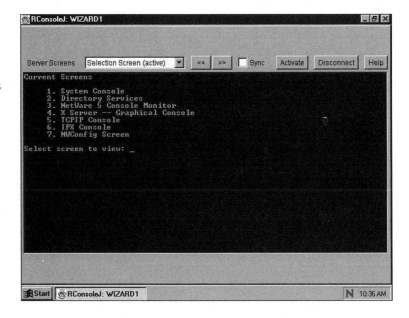

In Figure 23.1, there are seven screens available, and to switch to the IPX console, for example, you would choose 6. Using the Ctrl+Esc menu can potentially save you from a lot of Alt+Escs!

Server Console Commands

The following is a list of the server console commands as reported by issuing the HELP command at the server console. The HELP command displays a list of valid console commands; for more information on a particular command, enter HELP <command>. For more in-depth information on some of these commands, search the online documentation.

\# specifies the line as a comment (used in NCF files). For example,

```
#This NCF file will initialize the server
```

; specifies the line as a comment (used in NCF files). For example,

```
;This NCF file will unload and reload the lan driver
```

ABORT REMIRROR

Stops the remirroring of the specified partition.

Syntax: ABORT REMIRROR partition_number

Example: ABORT REMIRROR 3

ADD NAME SPACE

Allows non-DOS files to be stored on a volume. The name space module must be loaded before this command can be used.

Syntax: ADD NAME SPACE name_space [TO [volume_name]]

Example: ADD NAME SPACE mac TO sys

ALERT

Command Descriptions:

EVENT: Generate Event BIT(s)

LOG: Log to File BIT(s)

EVERYONE: Send to Everyone BIT(s)

CONSOLE: Display on Console BIT(s)

BELL: No Ring the Bell BIT(s)

ID: Display ID BIT(s)

LOCUS: Display LOCUS BIT(s)

ALERT: `No Alert BIT(s)`

NMID: `No Display nmID BIT(s)`

ALL: `Toggle (LOG,BELL) BIT(s)`

Syntax: `ALERT nmID {Commands} {ON ¦ OFF}`

ALIAS

Uses the specified alias to execute the specified command.

Syntax: `ALIAS alias command`

Example: `ALIAS v volume`

APPLET

Java AppletViewer

Syntax: `APPLET [-debug] [-J<runtime flag>] url¦file`

APPLETVIEWER

Java AppletViewer

Syntax: `APPLET [-debug] [-J<runtime flag>] url¦file`

BIND

Links a specific network board to a communication protocol. Packets received by a LAN adapter will be discarded unless it has been bound to a protocol. The LAN driver and protocol stack modules must be loaded before this command can be used.

Syntax: `BIND protocol [TO] LAN_driver¦board_name [driver_parameter...]`

Example: `BIND ipx TO ne3200 [slot=3, frame=ethernet_ii] net=12345678`

BINDERY

Adds or removes a bindery context to or from the list of all bindery contexts for this server.

Syntax: `BINDERY ADD¦DELETE [ CONTEXT ]=`

Examples:

`BINDERY ADD CONTEXT=OU=Division.O=Corporation`

`BINDERY DELETE CONTEXT=OU=Division.O=Corporation`

BROADCAST

Sends a message to all users logged in or attached to a file server or to a list of users or connection numbers.

Syntax: BROADCAST "*message*" [[TO] *username¦connection_number*] [[and,] *user¦ connection_number*...

Example: BROADCAST "Please delete unneeded files to free disk space"

CLEAR STATION

Syntax: CLEAR STATION *station_number* or CLEAR STATION ALL

Removes all files server resources allocated to a specific station. Use with caution.

Example: CLEAR STATION 3

CLS

Clears the console screen.

Example: CLS

CONFIG

Displays configuration information.

Example: CONFIG

CPUCHECK

Displays processor information.

Syntax: CPUCHECK

CSET

Views or sets parameters by category.

Syntax: CSET *category name*

Example: CSET MEMORY

DISABLE LOGIN

Prevent users from logging in.

Example: DISABLE LOGIN

DISABLE TTS

Manually disables NetWare Transaction Tracking System (TTS). Primarily used only by application developers for testing purposes.

Example: DISABLE TTS

DISMOUNT

Allows volume maintenance or repairs while the file server is up by making a volume unavailable to users.

Syntax: DISMOUNT *volume_name*

Example: DISMOUNT sys

DISPLAY ENVIRONMENT

Displays current settings of the set parameters.

Syntax: DISPLAY ENVIRONMENT

DISPLAY INTERRUPTS

Displays interrupt handler and interrupt statistics information.

Syntax: DISPLAY INTERRUPTS [*I# I# I#* ¦ ALL] [PROC ¦ REAL] [ALLOC]

Examples:

DISPLAY INTERRUPTS—Displays interrupts currently in use.

DISPLAY INTERRUPTS 3 10—Displays interrupts 3 and 10.

DISPLAY INTERRUPTS ALL—Displays all interrupts.

DISPLAY INTERRUPTS PROC—Displays per processor interrupt information.

DISPLAY INTERRUPTS ALLOC—Displays allocated interrupts.

DISPLAY INTERRUPTS REAL—Displays interrupts which occurred while the OS was in real mode and were reflected back to protected mode for servicing. When a processor is taken OFFLINE or when an interrupt handler is removed, the detailed statistics pertaining to that processor interrupt handler are, by default, removed from memory. To retain per-processor interrupt handler statistics for OFFLINE processors or to retain the total interrupt contribution from a previously loaded handler, change the set parameter Set Auto Clear Interrupt Statistics to OFF.

DISPLAY IPX NETWORKS

Displays all IPX network numbers (including hops/ticks) the IPX internal router is aware of.

Example: DISPLAY IPX NETWORKS

DISPLAY IPX SERVERS

Includes * wildcard characters. Displays all IPX servers (including hops) the IPX internal router is aware of.

Syntax: DISPLAY IPX SERVERS or DISPLAY IPX SERVERS [*Server Name*]

Examples:

```
DISPLAY IPX SERVERS

DISPLAY IPX SERVERS NOV*
```

DISPLAY MODIFIED ENVIRONMENT

Displays the set parameters that have been modified, showing both current value and the default value.

Syntax: `DISPLAY MODIFIED ENVIRONMENT`

Part

V

Ch

23

Tip #229 from John	This is an excellent one to keep in mind; you can instantly see which set parameters have been changed, and depending on the problem you are troubleshooting, a changed parameter might quickly lead to the solution.

DISPLAY PROCESSORS

Display processor status.

Syntax: `DISPLAY PROCESSORS [P# P#]`

Examples:

`DISPLAY PROCESSORS`—Displays the status of all processors.

`DISPLAY PROCESSORS 1 3`—Displays the status of processors 1 and 3.

DOWN

Ensures system and data integrity before turning of file server power.

Example: `DOWN`

ECHO OFF

Disables displaying of commands executed from NCF files.

Example: `ECHO OFF`

ECHO ON

Enables displaying of commands executed from NCF files.

Example: `ECHO ON`

ENABLE LOGIN

Allows users to log in or enables a `SUPERVISOR` account that has been locked out by intruder detection.

Example: `ENABLE LOGIN`

ENABLE TTS

Manually enables NetWare Transaction Tracking System (TTS).

Example: ENABLE TTS

Tip #230 from *John*	The ENVSET command and other Java-related commands are displayed by the console HELP command only if you have Java loaded.

ENVSET

Displays, sets, appends, and removes global environment variables.

Syntax: ENVSET—Displays all environment variables.

ENVSET *variable*—Displays specified environment variable.

ENVSET *variable*=—Removes specified environment variable.

ENVSET *variable*=<string>

ENVSET *variable*=$<variable><string>—Appends string value to environment variable.

FILE SERVER NAME

Sets the file server name (set in the AUTOEXEC.NCF file).

Syntax: FILE SERVER NAME *file_server_name*

Example: FILE SERVER NAME superserver

HELP

Displays a list of commands or the usage and description of a specific command. HELP ALL displays descriptions for all valid commands.

Syntax: HELP [*command*] or HELP ALL

Example: HELP BIND

IPX INTERNAL NET

Sets file server's internal IPX network address (set in the AUTOEXEC.NCF file).

Example: IPX INTERNAL NET 99aabbcc

JAR

Java Archive Tool

Syntax: JAR {ctx}[vfm0M] [*mainfest-file*] *files* ...

JAVA

Java Runtime

Type JAVA -HELP or java -nwhelp to get help on options

Syntax: JAVA [-*options*] class [*class options*]

JAVA-RMI.CGI

Java RMI CGI

Syntax: JAVA-RMI.CGI

JAVAC

Java Compiler

Syntax: JAVAC [-g][-depend][-nowarn][-verbose][-classpath path][-nowrite][-peprecation][-d dir][-j<*runtime flag*>] file.java...

JAVADOC

Java Documentation Generator

Syntax: JAVADOC " + *program* +" *flags** [*class* ¦ *package*]*

JAVAH

C Header and Stub File Generator

Syntax: JAVAH [-v] [-*options*] *classes*

JAVAKEY

Digital Signing Tool

Syntax: JAVAKEY <*options*>

JAVAP

Class File Disassembler

Syntax: JAVAP [-v -c -p -h -*verify* -*verify-verbose*] *files*

LANGUAGE

Syntax:

LANGUAGE—Displays current NLM language.

LANGUAGE *list*—Displays list of available languages.

LANGUAGE *name*¦*number*—Sets preferred NLM language by name or number.

LANGUAGE *add number name*—Adds a new language name and number.

LANGUAGE *ren number new_name*—Renames the language specified by number.

Example: LANGUAGE spanish

LIST DEVICES

Lists all the physical storage devices on the system.

Example: LIST DEVICES

LIST STORAGE ADAPTERS

Lists all the storage adapters and their associated devices.

Syntax: LIST STORAGE ADAPTERS

LIST STORAGE DEVICE BINDINGS

Lists all the filters and HAMs bound to a specified storage device. A Host Adapter Module (HAM) is the driver that will allow the storage adapter to communicate with the server. The device number is the first number displayed on LIST DEVICES.

Example: LIST STORAGE DEVICE BINDINGS 2

LOAD

Links a loadable module with the operating system.

LOAD [*inheritance*] [*protection*] [*path*]loadable_module [*parameter...*]

Example: LOAD monitor

INHERITANCE OPTIONS

-a[*=name*]—Loads module into an application.

Examples:

LOAD -a=application some.nlm

LOAN -a protected some.nlm

PROTECTION OPTIONS

PROTECTED—Loads module in a protected address space.

RESTART—Flags address space as restartable.

ADDRESS SPACE = *AS_NAME*—Loads this module in the address space specified by AS_NAME.

The PROTECTED option is not necessary if either RESTART or an address space name are supplied on the command line.

Examples:

```
LOAD PROTECTED clib
```

```
LOAD ADDRESS SPACE = GroupWise restart clib
```

LOADSTAGE

Loads the stage specified by x or loads all stages that have not been loaded.

```
LOADSTAGE x
```

```
LOADSTAGE ALL
```

MAGAZINE INSERTED

Acknowledges the insertion of the specified media magazine in response to the Insert Magazine console alert.

Example: `MAGAZINE INSERTED`

MAGAZINE NOT INSERTED

Acknowledges that the insertion of the specified media magazine was *not* performed.

Example: `MAGAZINE NOT INSERTED`

MAGAZINE NOT REMOVED

Acknowledges that the removal of the magazine was *not* performed.

Example: `MAGAZINE NOT REMOVED`

MAGAZINE REMOVED

Acknowledges the removal of a magazine from the specified device in response to the Remove Magazine console alert.

Example: `REMOVE MAGAZINE`

MEDIA INSERTED

Acknowledges the insertion of the specified media in response to the Insert Media console alert.

Example: `MEDIA INSERTED`

MEDIA NOT INSERTED

Acknowledges that the insertion of the specified media was *not* performed.

Example: `MEDIA NOT INSERTED`

MEDIA NOT REMOVED

Acknowledges that the removal of the media was *not* performed.

Example: MEDIA NOT REMOVED

MEDIA REMOVED

Acknowledges the removal of the media from the specified device in response to the Remove Media console alert.

Example: MEDIA REMOVED

MEMORY

Displays the amount of server RAM.

Example: MEMORY

MEMORY MAP

Displays a map of server RAM.

Example: MEMORY MAP

MIRROR STATUS

Displays the status of NetWare-mirrored partitions.

Displays the status of specific NetWare-mirrored partitions.

Syntax: MIRROR STATUS or MIRROR STATUS [*partition number*]

Example: MIRROR STATUS or MIRROR STATUS 0

MODULES

Includes the * wildcard. Displays a list of loaded modules including the address space that the module is loaded in.

Syntax: MODULES or MODULES [*module name*]

Example: MODULES or MODULES mon*

MOUNT

Makes a volume available to users.

Syntax: MOUNT *volume_name* or MOUNT ALL

Example: MOUNT sys

NAME

Displays the server's name.

Example: NAME

NATIVE2ASCII

Native-to-ASCII Converter

Syntax: NATIVE2ASCII <filename>

NCP ADDRESSES

Displays NCP NetWork Service Addresses.

NCP DUMP

Dump the NCP standard deviation statistics to a specified file.

Syntax: NCP DUMP filename.ext

NCP STATS

Displays NCP statistics on income NCP requests. Command can also reset counters.

Syntax: NCP STATS {RESET}

NCP TRACE

Decodes incoming NCP packets to the screen or to a file that is specified.

Syntax: NCP TRACE ON {filename.ext} or NCP TRACE OFF

OFF

Clears the console screen.

Example: OFF

PAUSE

Waits for a key to be pressed before continuing. Used in NCF files.

Example: pause

PROTECT

This console command is used when you have an existing NCF file that is used to load NLMs and you would now like to load them in a protected address space.

Syntax: PROTECT (NCF file name)

Example: PROTECT Grpwise

PROTECTION

Displays information about the protected memory address spaces in the system. Also provides a means of enabling you to disable the restart feature for a protected address space.

Syntax: `PROTECTION [[[NO] RESTART] address space name]`

Examples:

```
PROTECTION
```

```
PROTECTION ADDRESS_SPACE1
```

```
PROTECTION RESTART ADDRESS_SPACE1
```

```
PROTECTION NO RESTART ADDRESS_SPACE1
```

PROTOCOL

Views registered protocols and frame types.

PROTOCOL REGISTER

Registers additional protocols and frame types.

Syntax: `PROTOCOL REGISTER protocol_name framd id_number`

Example: `PROTOCOL REGISTER ip ethernet_ii 800`

PSM

Executes a Platform Support Module (PSM) console command. To display a list of supported PSM commands type: `PSM?`

PSM Commands:

`PSM?`

`PSM SHOW PIC`

REGISTER MEMORY

Manually registers memory above 16MB with the operating system.

Syntax: `REGISTER MEMORY start_address length`

Example: `REGISTER MEMORY 1000000 1250000`

REM

Specifies this line as a comment (used in NCF files). This NCF file loads and initializes the database.

Example: `REM`

REMIRROR PARTITION

Attempts to start the remirror of the specified partition.

Syntax: `REMIRROR PARTITION partition_number`

Example: `REMIRROR PARTITION 4`

REMOVE STORAGE ADAPTER

Removes an instance of a storage adapter.

Example: `REMOVE STORAGE ADAPTER A0`

RESTART SERVER

Restarts server execution after downing the server

Syntax: `RESTART SERVER options`

Options:

`-ns`—Do not use the startup NCF file.

`-na`—Do not use the autoexec NCF file.

`-d`—Break into the internal debugger.

Example: `RESTART SERVER`

RMIC

Java RMI Stub Converter

Syntax: `RMIC [-g][-O][-debug][-depend][-nowarn][-verbose][-classpath path]`
`[-nowrite][-d dir][-dskel dir][-show][-keepgenerated] classname...`

RMIREGISTRY

Java Remote Object Registry

Syntax: `RMIREGISTRY <port>`

SCAN ALL

Scans all the LUNs on SCSI adapters.

Examples:

`SCAN ALL`—Scans all LUNs on all SCSI Adapters.

`SCAN ALL A0`—Scans all LUNs on adapter 0.

SCAN FOR NEW DEVICES

Causes the OS Storage device drivers to look for and add new storage devices on the system.

Example: SCAN FOR NEW DEVICES

SEARCH

Tells the operating system where to look for loadable modules and NCF files. By itself it displays the current search paths.

The default is SYS:system.

Syntax: SEARCH [ADD [number]] path or SEARCH DEL number or SEARCH

Examples:

SEARCH ADD 3 c:\nlms

SEARCH DEL 1

SECURE CONSOLE

Adds the following security features:

Allows loading loadable modules *only* from the current SEARCH paths. Allows *only* the console operator to modify the date and time. Prevents keyboard entry into the internal debugger.

Example: SECURE CONSOLE

SEND

Sends a message to all users logged in or attached to a file server or to a list of users or connection numbers.

Syntax: SEND "message" [[TO] username¦connection_number] [[and¦,] username¦ connection_number...]

Example: SEND "Your deleted files have been restored" TO jack and jill

SERIALVER

Serial Version Command

Syntax: SERIALVER [-show] [classname...]

SET

Views or sets current operating system parameters. Most parameters do not need to be changed; however, they can be configured to fit your situation.

Type HELP SET [TIME ¦ TIME ZONE] to display specific help.

Syntax: SET [parameter_name] [= parameter_value]

Example: SET replace console prompt with server name = off

SET TIME

Sets the file server date and time.

Syntax: SET TIME [*month/day/year*] [*hour:minute:second*]

Example: SET TIME 9 October 2000 5:25:00 pm

Tip #231 from *John*	Be careful with this one. When you go to use it, you will receive the warning that "Time Synchronization is active on this server. Are you sure you want to change the time?". It's easy to get synthetic time issued if you make a mistake.

SET TIME ZONE

Displays or sets the file server time zone.

Syntax: SET TIME ZONE or SET TIME ZONE *zone* [*hour* [*daylight*]]

Example: SET TIME ZONE mst7mdt

SPEED

Displays processor relative speed. Some machines have an AUTO or COMMON speed mode that can reduce the processor speed to as little as 6MHz.

Example: speed

SPOOL

Creates, changes, or displays spooler mappings.

Syntax: SPOOL *spool_number* [TO] [QUEUE] *queue_name*

Example: SPOOL 1 to queue laser

START PROCESSORS

Syntax: START PROCESSORS [*P# P# P#...*]

Examples:

START PROCESSORS—Starts all secondary processors.

START PROCESSORS 1 3—Starts secondary processors 1 and 3.

STOP PROCESSORS

Syntax: STOP PROCESSORS [*P# P# P#...*]

Examples:

STOP PROCESSORS—Stops all secondary processors.

STOP PROCESSORS 1 3—Stops secondary processors 1 and 3.

SWAP

Adds or removes the swap file from a volume and sets MIN, MAX and MIN Free. If no parameters are given, displays swap file information.

Syntax: SWAP [ADD¦DELETE *volume_name*]

All values are in millions of bytes.

MIN or MINIMUM—Minimum swap file size. (default = 2)

MAX or MAXIMUM—Maximum swap file size. (default = Free volume space)

MIN FREE or MINIMUM FREE—Minimum free space to be preserved on a volume outside the swap file; this controls the maximum size of the swap file on this volume.

(default =5)

Examples:

```
SWAP

SWAP ADD vol2

SWAP ADD vol3 min = 5 max = 100 min free = 10

SWAP DELETE vol3

SWAP PARAMETER vol2 min = 2
max = 1000 min free = 100
```

TIME

Displays the file server current date and time.

Example: TIME

TRACK OFF

Disables the router tracking screen.

Example: TRACK OFF

TRACK ON

Enables the router tracking screen.

Example: TRACK ON

UNBIND

Unlinks a specific network board from a communication protocol.

Syntax: UNBIND *protocol* [FROM] *LAN_driver*¦*board_name* [*driver_parameter*...]

Example: UNBIND ipx from ne3200 [slot=3,frame=ethernet_ii]

UNLOAD

Unlinks a loadable module from the operating system that was previously linked to the operating system with the LOAD command. An address space can also be specified with the unload command to unload a module from a specific address space. If an address space is specified without a module, all the NLMs in that address will be unloaded.

Syntax: UNLOAD loadable_module

Examples:

UNLOAD MONITOR

UNLOAD ADDRESS SPACE = Groupwise or

UNLOAD ADDRESS SPACE = Groupwise clib

VERSION

Displays the file server version information and copyright notice.

Example: VERSION

VMDISMOUNT

Allows volume maintenance or repairs while the file server is up by making a volume unavailable to users.

Syntax: VMDISMOUNT *VolumeName* or *VolumeNumber*

Example: VMDISMOUNT sys or vmdismount 0

VMMOUNT

Makes a volume available to users.

Syntax: VMMOUNT *VolumeName* or *VolumeNumber*

Example: VMMOUNT sys or vmmount 0

VMVOLUMES

Displays a list of currently mounted volumes including number, status, and name.

Example: VMVOLUMES

VOLUME

Displays a list of currently mounted volumes or the information about a specific volume.

Syntax: VOLUME or VOLUME [*name*]

Example: VOLUME or VOLUME sys

OBTAINING SERVER INFORMATION

There are several useful console commands and utilities that you can use to obtain information about the server and its configuration. The ones listed here are some of the more common, and, like MONITOR, are always used. You might consider installing the online documentation to obtain information on other utilities and a more in-depth look at some of the ones covered here.

THE CONLOG COMMAND

It is often convenient to be able to print what you see onscreen, as in when you use the CONFIG command, when an NLM loads and things flash by too quickly, or when you receive errors during some aspect of system initialization. If you load CONLOG, it logs what happens on the console to sys:etc\console.log. You can then go back and print, edit, and review this file at your leisure.

The syntax is as follows:

```
[LOAD] CONLOG [FILE=log filename] [SAVE=backup filename] [ARCHIVE=YES]
[ENTIRE=YES] [MAXIMUM=max filesize] [NEXT=hh:mm:ss] ¦ HELP
```

The output shown in the next section of the CONFIG command was obtained using CONLOG. Use the online documentation for a detailed explanation of the various command line parameters for CONLOG. Assuming you have installed the online documentation (and if you haven't, you are going to, right?), select Reference on the home page, then Utilities Reference.

THE CONFIG COMMAND

The CONFIG command is very useful. The syntax is CONFIG at the server console. You get the network numbers, the bindings, the frame types, the protocols, and more. Also, at the end, the tree name and bindery contexts are displayed. The output of the CONFIG command is shown here:

```
IPX internal network number: 0833FE37
Server Up Time:  9 Days 21 Hours 2 Minutes 29 Seconds

AMD PCNTNW
     Version 4.10    May 12, 1998
     Hardware setting: Slot 10002, I/O ports 7000h to 701Fh, Interrupt 3h
     Node address: 00805F92C218
     Frame type: ETHERNET_II
     Board name: PCNTNW_1_EII
     LAN protocol: ARP
     LAN protocol: IP Address 204.78.43.68 Mask FF.FF.FF.0(255.255.255.0)
                   Interfaces 1

Compatibility Mode Driver
     Version 1.04c   August 13, 1998
     Hardware setting: I/O Port A55h
     Node address: 7E01CC4E2B44
     Frame type: CMD
```

```
Board name: CMD Server
LAN protocol: IPX network FFFFFFFD

Tree Name: DRAGONSLAIR
Bindery Context(s):
     .Merlin
```

THE MONITOR UTILITY

Anywhere there is a NetWare server, you will find MONITOR.NLM running on it. Historically, MONITOR was how the famous "NetWare worm," or screensaver, was activated, so it was almost always left running. Monitor is an NLM that will display an incredible amount of information and statistics about your server, and also let you change the SET parameters.

In NetWare 5, the screensaver function has been moved from the Monitor NLM to the SCRSAVER.NLM, as you will see later in this chapter, but the information about your server is still found in MONITOR. The syntax to load MONITOR is simply MONITOR, or LOAD MONITOR, and the main screen appears as shown in Figure 23.2.

PART

V

CH

23

Figure 23.2
The Tab key moves you between the General Information section and the Available Options section.

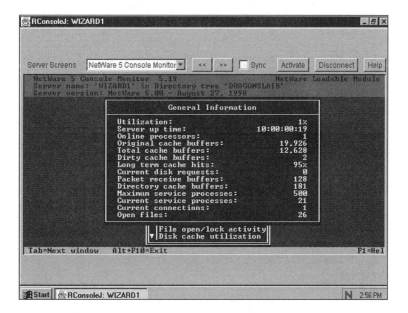

The general information screen gives you a look at some of the key statistics that you will want to keep an eye on, such as Cache Buffers, Packet Receive Buffers, and more. The Tab key moves you from the general information screen to the available options menu, where you can "drill down" to obtain detailed information on a variety of choices. For online help, use the F1 key on any screen.

CONTROLLING ACCESS TO THE SERVER

The main point about securing your server has been mentioned previously, but is repeated here: Without physical security, there is no security. This is especially true with the hot swappable drives in many servers; someone could simply remove the drive, walk out, and then work on retrieving the data later at his or her leisure.

DISABLE LOGIN/ENABLE LOGIN

There are times when you do not want anyone to access the server; for example, you might be updating an application or backing up a database. To do this, you need to use the console commands DISABLE LOGIN and ENABLE LOGIN. The syntax is just that; at the console prompt, enter the command DISABLE LOGIN or ENABLE LOGIN.

The command DISABLE LOGIN does just that: no one will be able to log in. Make sure that you log yourself in first though! Otherwise, it's a trip back to the computer room. After you disable logins, you can clear connections to the server as necessary using either MONITOR.NLM or the CLEAR STATION command. When you are finished, and to allow users to once again log in, enter the command ENABLE LOGIN.

CLEAR STATION

The console command CLEAR STATION can be used to clear a workstation's connection. Use this command lightly; if the user is in the middle of saving a file or some other sort of transaction, she will not take lightly to having the rug pulled out from underneath her!

The syntax is CLEAR STATION <station number> to clear a specific connection, or CLEAR STATION ALL to close all connections. You can use MONITOR to obtain the connection number; choose connections from the available options menu. Or, you could use the less-friendly NLIST command from a command prompt at a workstation.

And don't forget that the new Novell clients auto-reconnect, so if you are trying to get everyone off using CLEAR STATION, you need to use it in conjunction with the DISABLE LOGIN command.

SCRSAVER.NLM

The famous NetWare worm, the screensaver, used to be kicked off by loading MONITOR.NLM, and MONITOR also gave you the ability to lock your console. These features have been moved to the new SCRSAVER.NLM.

SCRSAVER has several command-line options. More than one option can be used at a time; simply separate the parameters with semicolons. To make sure that the screensaver and console locking are available, you might want to use NWCONFIG to edit the AUTOEXEC.NCF file and place the SCRSAVER command and your options there.

The syntax is scrsaver <option>; <option>; option. The options and their meanings appear next, as shown at the server console when using the command SCRSAVER HELP.

```
WIZARD1:scrsaver help
The following SCRSAVER commands are available:
    ACTIVATE
    AUTO CLEAR DELAY
    DELAY
    DISABLE
    DISABLE AUTO CLEAR
    DISABLE LOCK
    ENABLE
    ENABLE AUTO CLEAR
    ENABLE LOCK
    NO PASSWORD
    HELP
    STATUS
```

Multiple commands, separated by semicolons, can be entered on the same line. For example:

```
SCRSAVER ENABLE; DELAY=2; DISABLE LOCK
```

Type SCRSAVER HELP [command] to obtain help on a specific command:

- WIZARD1:scrsaver HELP activate

  SCRSAVER ACTIVATE

  Activates the screensaver immediately, overriding the normal delay.

- WIZARD1:scrsaver HELP auto clear delay

  SCRSAVER AUTO CLEAR DELAY

  Sets the number of seconds to wait for input before clearing the unlock portal. The limits are from 1 to 300. The default is 60, or 1 minute.

  Example: SCRSAVER AUTO CLEAR DELAY=40

- WIZARD1:SCRSAVER HELP DELAY

  SCRSAVER DELAY

  Sets the number of seconds of keyboard inactivity to delay before activating the screensaver. The limits are from 1 to 7200. The default is 600, or 10 minutes.

  Examples: SCRSAVER DELAY 60 or SCRSAVER DELAY=120

- WIZARD1:SCRSAVER HELP DISABLE

  SCRSAVER DISABLE

  Disables the screensaver, preventing the screen from being saved.

- WIZARD1:SCRSAVER HELP DISABLE AUTO CLEAR

  SCRSAVER DISABLE AUTO CLEAR

  Disables the automatic clearing of the portal used to unlock the console. When this feature is disabled, the unlock portal remains on the screen until cleared by user input.

PART

V

CH

23

- WIZARD1:SCRSAVER HELP DISABLE LOCK

  SCRSAVER DISABLE LOCK

  Disables the console locking feature. When this feature is disabled, the screensaver restores the saved screen without requiring the name and password of a console operator.

- WIZARD1:SCRSAVER HELP ENABLE

  SCRSAVER ENABLE

  Enables the screensaver. When enabled, the screen will be saved after the keyboard has been inactive for the number of seconds specified via the SCRSAVER DELAY command.

- WIZARD1:SCRSAVER HELP ENABLE AUTO CLEAR

  SCRSAVER ENABLE AUTO CLEAR

  Enables the automatic clearing of the portal used to unlock the console. When this feature is enabled, the unlock portal is automatically cleared from the screen after the number of seconds of keyboard inactivity set via the SCRSAVER AUTO CLEAR DELAY command.

- WIZARD1:SCRSAVER HELP ENABLE LOCK

  SCRSAVER ENABLE LOCK

  Enables the console locking feature. When this feature is enabled, the screensaver requires the name and password of a valid console operator before restoring the saved screen.

- WIZARD1:SCRSAVER HELP NO PASSWORD

  SCRSAVER NO PASSWORD

  Unlocks the console without asking for a password when NDS is unavailable.

- WIZARD1:SCRSAVER HELP STATUS

  SCRSAVER STATUS

  Displays the current status of the screensaver features.

REMOTE.NLM

REMOTE.NLM is loaded at the server to allow remote access to the server console. In larger environments, being able to physically walk up to the server console might not be possible; the server might be in another city! With REMOTE, you can access the server console as if you were sitting in front of it.

Tip #232 from
John

Although you might be able to access the server console as if you were sitting there, you won't be able to switch to any of the Java/GUI screens, only to the character-based menuing applications and the console prompt.

There are two pieces to this puzzle—the client application, rconsole that communicates with the server side, the remote NLM. The client side, RCONSOLE, is covered later in this chapter.

The syntax is REMOTE <password> ¦ -E <Encrypted password>.

For example, REMOTE john loads the REMOTE NLM with a password of john. If you simply load REMOTE with no password, the system prompts you for one.

It is possible to load REMOTE with an encrypted password. To encrypt the password, load REMOTE with a password as you would normally. Then, use the command REMOTE ENCRYPT. For example,

```
remote john
REMOTE ENCRYPT
```

The system prompts you to Enter a password to encrypt. When you enter a password, the system displays the encrypted password and asks Would you like this command written to sys:system\ldremote.ncf? If you answer *yes*, the LDREMOTE.NCF file is created and you can use this NCF file to load REMOTE with the encrypted password. In other words, you would simply have to use the command LDREMOTE.

Tip #233 from	Important! REMOTE is for the IPX/SPX protocols, not IP. If you are using only IP, you need RCONAG6, covered next. When REMOTE is loaded, you need to load RSPX to allow communications via SPX, used with a direct LAN connection. You can also run a remote session via modem; see the online documentation for information on REMOTE console sessions over a modem.
John	

When REMOTE is loaded, you can use three parameters: LOCK OUT, UNLOCK, and HELP.

REMOTE HELP displays a help screen. REMOTE LOCK OUT disables anyone from making a new remote connection. And finally, REMOTE UNLOCK allows new remote connections to be made to the server.

RCONAG6

Just as the REMOTE.NLM is the server-side piece for remote access when using SPX, the RCONAG6 NLM is the server-side piece that allows remote access over IP. The client side of the puzzle when using IP is RCONSOLEJ, as opposed to RCONSOLE that is used with REMOTE.

The RCONAG6 NLM is almost identical to the REMOTE NLM in terms of options and the loading procedure. The syntax is RCONAG6 <password> ¦ <encrypted password> TCP Port SPX Port.

If you simply enter RCONAG6, the system prompts you for a password. You are then prompted for the TCP port number to use; the default is 2034. You are then prompted for the SPX port number; the default is 16800.

Tip #234 from *John*	Why would RCONAG6 need an SPX port, when I am talking about remote access using IP? The SPX port is the port number RCONAG6 uses to listen to a proxy server. A proxy server runs both IP and IPX and allows RCNSOLEJ to communicate through the proxy server with a target server using only IPX.

To disable listening on either the TCP port or the SPX port, enter a value of ×1 when prompted for the port number. For example, in a pure IP environment, you would enter ×1 for the SPX port number when asked.

RCONAG6 varies a bit from the process you used with REMOTE.NLM to encrypt the password. Use the command RCONAG6 ENCRYPT. The system prompts you for a password, the TCP port, and the SPX port and then asks whether you want to write the syntax to the sys:system\LDRCONAG.NCF file. If you answer yes, the LDRCONAG.NCF file is created, and you can use this to load RCONAG6; that is, instead of using the command RCONAG6, you simply enter LDRCONAG.

ACCESSING THE NETWARE CONSOLE FROM A WORKSTATION

So far, you have only seen the server side of the remote console picture. This section covers the client, or *workstation*, side.

RCONSOLE

RCONSOLE, found in sys:public, talks to the remote NLM loaded on the server and gives you a remote console. As you have already seen when discussing REMOTE.NLM, RCONSOLE is for SPX connections to the server. If you are using IP, you will run RConsoleJ, covered next. The first thing you will see when executing RCONSOLE will be the dire warning shown in Figure 23.3.

Although it's not reassuring, that message has been around for years. I've not had any problems running RCONSOLE from a command box in either Windows NT or Windows 95/98. After you press Enter to continue, you are presented with a screen listing the available servers, as shown in Figure 23.4.

Figure 23.3
When executing RCONSOLE in a DOS window, you always receive the warning shown in Figure 23.3. RCONSOLE must have caused some real problems in its day to warrant the warning still being around!

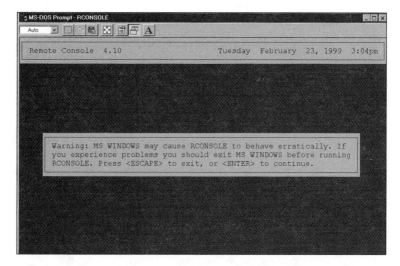

Figure 23.4
RCONSOLE presents you with a screen of available servers. Highlight the server you want to connect to and press Enter.

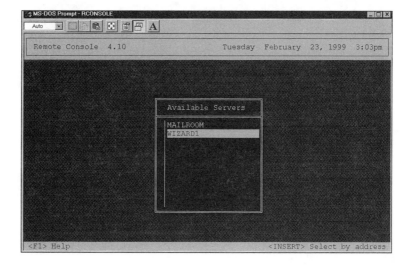

Highlight the server in question, press Enter, supply the password, and you are "sitting" at the server console.

There are a few key combinations you need to know in order to navigate through the available screens:

- **Alt+F2**—Exit RCONSOLE.
- **Alt+F3 or Alt+F4**—Toggle from screen to screen; equivalent to the Alt+Esc key sequence that is used at the actual console.
- **Alt+F1**—Access the available options menu.
- **Alt+F5**—Show the address of the workstation you are using.

RCONSOLEJ

RConsoleJ is the client piece you use to connect to a server over IP. RConsoleJ is going to talk to the RCONAG6.NLM you have previously loaded at the server. To run RConsoleJ, execute RCONJ.EXE found in sys:public, and you are presented with the initial screen shown in Figure 23.5. Another way to start RConsoleJ is to select Tools, Pure IP Remote Console from NWAdmin32.

Figure 23.5
The initial screen of RConsoleJ. Similar to RCONSOLE, it is where you select the server you want to connect to.

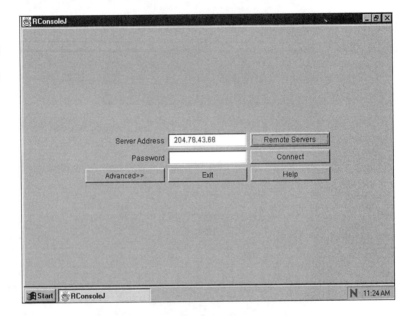

The initial RConsoleJ screen is similar to what you saw when you first started RCONSOLE; you fill in the information about the target server, supply the password, and then use the Connect button. The GUI makes navigating the available screens a bit easier than the Alt+function keys of RCONSOLE. As you can see in Figure 23.6, there is a drop-down menu of available server screens.

At the server itself, you can run RConsoleJ in one of two fashions; if you are running ConsoleOne, select Myserver, Tools, RConsoleJ. The other option at the server is to enter RCONJ at the console prompt. RCONJ is an NCF file located in sys:system.

Figure 23.6
Navigating the available screens can be done with the drop-down menu. You can still use the Alt+F2 or Alt+F3 to cycle between screens if you desire.

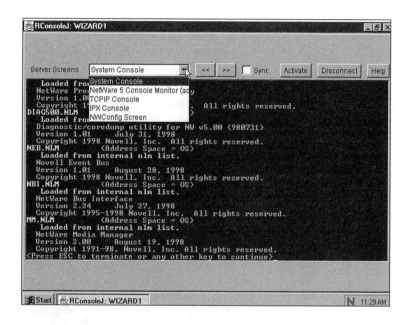

SERVER SET PARAMETERS

Novell has set the default parameters to be optimal for most servers. However, you might need to change certain values to optimize your system. There are 16 categories of parameters that you can set:

- Communications
- Memory
- File caching
- Directory caching
- File system
- Locks
- Transaction tracking
- Disk
- Time
- NCP
- Miscellaneous
- Error handling
- Directory services
- Multiprocessor
- Service location protocol
- Licensing services

New in NetWare 5 is the fact that the server parameters stick, or are *persistent*. If you make a change, the change is still there after the server is restarted. There are two ways to change the server parameters: the first one is by using the SET command at the server console, as shown in Figure 23.7.

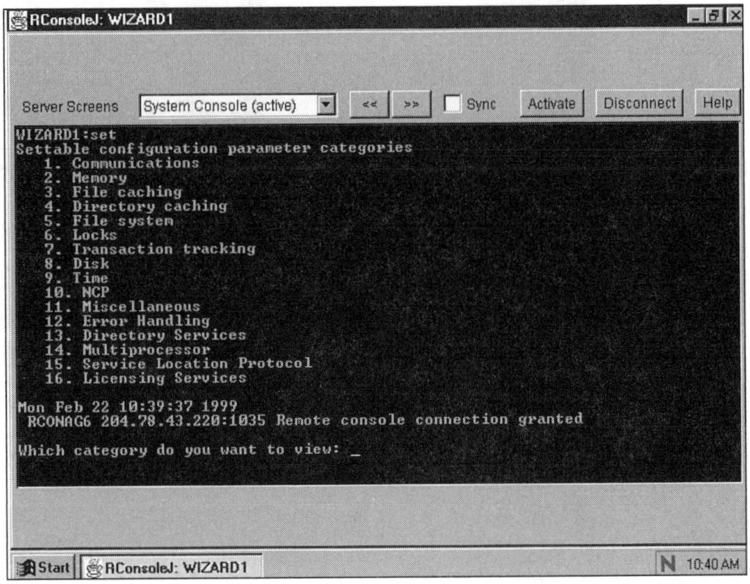

Figure 23.7
The Server Parameters can be viewed and changed at the server console using the *SET* command.

Entering the command SET at the server console displays the menu shown in Figure 23.7, and you are prompted to choose a category to view. When you select a category, the parameters are displayed one screen at a time. To stop on a particular screen, press Esc. To continue, simply press any key.

If you type SET <some parameter>, the current value, the limits, and a description are displayed. If you type SET <some parameter> = <some value>, the parameter is changed. For example, SET nds trace to screen shows the current setting, whereas SET nds trace to screen = on changes the value of NDS TRACE to screen to on.

The other method of viewing and changing the server parameters is via MONITOR. Load MONITOR and choose Server Parameters from the Available Options screen, as shown in Figure 23.8.

Figure 23.8
Server Parameters from the console monitor can also be used to view and change values.

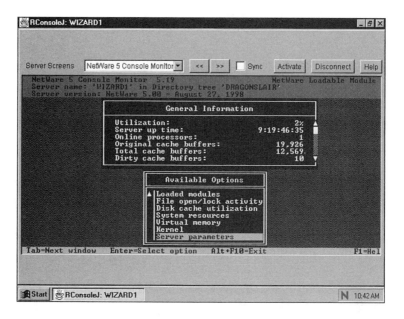

When you choose Server Parameters, the same 16 categories are displayed. Use the up and down arrows to highlight the category you are interested in, and then press Enter. In Figure 23.9, the Communications categories have been chosen. As you scroll up and down the list, the current setting is shown along with an explanation, and you have the option of changing it.

Figure 23.9
The Communications parameters have been chosen, and you can scroll up and down to view and configure the server parameters.

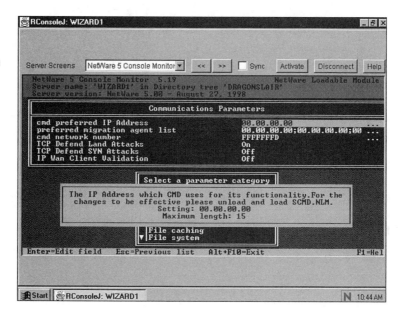

One very nice feature that using MONITOR gives you is the ability to document your current system settings. Select Server Parameters and press F3 in order to write to a file. The default filename is sys:system\setcmds.cp, and it is simply an ASCII text file that has the following format (note that only a small piece of this file is being shown here):

```
Allow IP Address Duplicates = Off
IPX Router Broadcast Delay = 0
Reply To Get Nearest Server = On
IPX NetBIOS Replication Option = 2
Use Old Watchdog Packet Type = Off
Number Of Watchdog Packets = 10
Delay Between Watchdog Packets = 59.3
Delay Before First Watchdog Packet = 296.6
```

There are also two new commands you can use to check parameter values, the DISPLAY ENVIRONMENT and DISPLAY MODIFIED ENVIRONMENT. DISPLAY ENVIRONMENT shows the server's search path and the current values of the settable parameters. The DISPLAY MODIFIED ENVIRONMENT command is very useful; it shows only the settings that have been modified from the original defaults, along with the default value. Very handy for troubleshooting, as you can instantly get a handle on what SET commands have been issued, as opposed to scrolling through various screens in MONITOR.

Tip #235 from	Don't change the server's set parameters because you can; make sure that you know why you want to change a setting. And keep in mind that many of the settings are interrelated, and a change made to one has a ripple effect. There might be other settings affected or that need to be changed also.
John	

The following are the set parameters as displayed at the server console using the SET command. On some of these parameters, more detailed information can be obtained by searching the online documentation. Search for Utilities Reference and choose set.

COMMUNICATIONS

The communication settings control packet receive buffers, watchdog settings, packet sizes, and so on; any of the communications-related settings are under this category. The settings, and a brief description of each one, are given here. The brief description is what is returned by using the SET console command and looking at the parameters available.

CMD PREFERRED IP ADDRESS: 00.00.00.00

Maximum length: 15

Description: The IP Address which CMD uses for its functionality. For the changes to be effective, unload and load SCMD.NLM.

PREFERRED MIGRATION AGENT LIST:

00.00.00.00;00.00.00.00;00.00.00.00;00.00.00.00;00.00.00.00/

Maximum length: 80

Description: List of Preferred Migration Agents (Maximum = 5) separated by semicolons and ended by / which this node will be using. For the changes to be effective, unload and load SCMD.NLM.

CMD NETWORK NUMBER: FFFFFFFD

Maximum length: 8

Description: The virtual IPX network number which Compatibility Mode Driver uses. For the changes to be effective, unload and load SCMD.NLM

TCP DEFEND LAND ATTACKS: ON

Can be set in the startup NCF file.

Description: Defend against Land Attacks. Default: ON

TCP DEFEND SYN ATTACKS: OFF

Can be set in the startup NCF file.

Description: Defend against SYN Attacks. Default: OFF

IP WAN CLIENT VALIDATION: OFF

Can be set in the startup NCF file.

Description: Start or Stop IP WAN Client Validation for remote client dialing through NetWare Connect. By default, IP WAN Client Validation is OFF.

ALLOW IP ADDRESS DUPLICATES: OFF

Can be set in the startup NCF file.

Description: TCPIP.NLM will not allow you to bind IP addresses that conflict with other nodes in the network. If you want to bind the IP address even if it conflicts with another node on the network, set this variable to ON.

IPX ROUTER BROADCAST DELAY: 0

Limits: 0 to 2

Can be set in the startup NCF file.

Description: How long the IPX router should delay between SAP/RIP broadcast packets. 0 = adjust delay to size of SAP/RIP tables; 1 = delay 1 tick; 2 = delay 2 ticks.

REPLY TO GET NEAREST SERVER: ON

Can be set in the startup NCF file.

Description: Does this server respond to GET NEAREST SERVER requests from workstations that are attempting to locate a server?

IPX NetBIOS REPLICATION OPTION: 2

Limits: 0 to 3

Description: How the IPX router deals with NetBIOS replicated broadcasts:

- 0 = don't replicate them
- 1 = replicate them using the OLD algorithm (which causes duplicate broadcasts when there are redundant routes)
- 2 = replicate them using the NEW algorithm(which squelches duplicate broadcasts but doesn't go as far)
- 3 = same as method 2, but doesn't replicate to WAN links

USE OLD WATCHDOG PACKET TYPE: OFF

Description: Use type 0 instead of type 4 for watchdog packets. Some old router hardware filters out type 4 IPX packets which can cause a client to lose its connection to the server when it sits inactive for a few minutes.

NUMBER OF WATCHDOG PACKETS: 10

Limits: 5 to 100

Description: The number of times the server asks an inactive workstation whether it is still attached to the file server before terminating the workstation's connection if no response has been received.

DELAY BETWEEN WATCHDOG PACKETS: 59.3 SECONDS

Limits: 9.9 seconds to 10 minutes, 26.2 seconds

Description: Amount of time the server waits for an inactive workstation to reply to a watchdog packet, before asking the workstation again whether it is still attached to the file server.

DELAY BEFORE FIRST WATCHDOG PACKET: 4 MINUTES 56.6 SECONDS

Limits: 15.7 seconds to 14 days

Description: Amount of time the server waits, without receiving a request from a workstation, before asking the workstation whether it is still attached to the file server.

CONSOLE DISPLAY WATCHDOG LOGOUTS: OFF

Description: Display an alert on the console when the watchdog logs out a user because of a connection failure.

MAXIMUM PACKET RECEIVE BUFFERS: 500

Limits: 50 to 4294967295

Can be set in the startup NCF file.

Description: Maximum number of packet receive buffers that can be allocated by the server.

MINIMUM PACKET RECEIVE BUFFERS: 128

Limits: 10 to 4294967295

Can be set in the startup NCF file.

Description: Minimum number of packet receive buffers allocated by the server.

MAXIMUM PHYSICAL RECEIVE PACKET SIZE: 4224

Limits: 618 to 24682

Can only be set in the startup NCF file.

Description: Size of the largest packet that can be received by an MLID.

NEW PACKET RECEIVE BUFFER WAIT TIME: 0.1 SECONDS

Limits: 0.1 seconds to 20 seconds

Description: Minimum time to wait before allocating a new packet receive buffer.

MAXIMUM INTERRUPT EVENTS: 10

Limits: 1 to 1000000

Description: Maximum number of interrupt time events (such as IPX routing) allowed before guaranteeing that a thread switch has occurred(when maximum reached switch to thread time processing of events).

IPX CMD MODE ROUTING: ON

Can be set in the startup NCF file.

Description: Whether IPX CMD Mode Routing is ON or OFF.

MEMORY

The settings that affect memory, such as protection and garbage collection, are given here, along with a brief description. The brief description is what is returned by using the SET console command and looking at the parameters available.

AVERAGE PAGE IN ALERT THRESHOLD: 2000

Limits: 1 to 4294967295

Can be set in the startup NCF file.

Description: If the average page INs for the VM system reach this level you send an alert to the console.

MEMORY PROTECTION NO RESTART INTERVAL: 1

Limits: 0 to 60

Can be set in the startup NCF file.

Description: Don't restart a user address space if the address space is faulting more than once during the specified number of minutes. A value of 0 disables this set parameter. If a memory protection violation is attempted in a restartable address space, the offending address space and its loaded NLMs are removed and their resources are returned to the system. A new user address space with the same name is created and the NLMs are reloaded. The restart feature is disabled if the user address space was restarted more recently than the interval specified by this set parameter.

MEMORY PROTECTION FAULT CLEANUP: ON

Can be set in the startup NCF file.

Description: Clean up after user address space memory protection faults. If an NLM loaded in a user address space attempts to violate memory protection and this parameter is set to ON, the offending user address space and its loaded NLMs are removed and their resources are returned to the system. If an NLM loaded in a user address space attempts to violate memory protection and this parameter is set to OFF, no effort is made to handle the fault and the situation is left to the abend recovery mechanism.

GARBAGE COLLECTION INTERVAL: 5 MINUTES

Limits: 1 minute to 1 hour

Can be set in the startup NCF file.

Description: Maximum time between garbage collections.

ALLOC MEMORY CHECK FLAG: OFF

Can be set in the startup NCF file.

Description: Do corruption checking in Alloc memory nodes.

RESERVED BUFFERS BELOW 16 MEG: 300

Limits: 8 to 2000

Can only be set in the startup NCF file.

Description: Number of file cache buffers to be kept for device drivers unable to access memory above 16MB.

PART

V

CH

23

FILE CACHING

The settings that affect file caching, a brief description of each, and their defaults are given here. The brief description is what is returned by using the SET console command and looking at the parameters available.

READ AHEAD ENABLED: ON

Description: As long as sequential file access is occurring, do background reads to get the blocks that will be requested soon into the cache in advance.

READ AHEAD LRU SITTING TIME THRESHOLD: 10 SECONDS

Limits: 0 seconds to 1 hour

Description: If the Cache LRU sitting time is below this threshold, read ahead will not take place.

MINIMUM FILE CACHE BUFFERS: 20

Limits: 20 to 2000

Description: Number of file cache buffers to be left by the server (not allocated for other uses).

MAXIMUM CONCURRENT DISK CACHE WRITES: 750

Limits: 10 to 4000

Description: Maximum number of concurrent writes of dirty disk cache buffers.

DIRTY DISK CACHE DELAY TIME: 3.3 SECONDS

Limits: 0.1 seconds to 10 seconds

Description: Minimum amount of time the system waits before writing a not completely dirty disk cache buffer.

MINIMUM FILE CACHE REPORT THRESHOLD: 20

Limits: 0 to 2000

Description: How close the number of cache buffers has to get to the minimum before a warning is issued.

DIRECTORY CACHING

The settings that affect directory caching are given here, along with a brief description and the default value. The brief description is what is returned by using the SET console command and looking at the parameters available.

DIRTY DIRECTORY CACHE DELAY TIME: 0.5 SECONDS

Limits: 0 seconds to 10 seconds

Description: Minimum time the system waits before writing a dirty directory cache buffer.

MAXIMUM CONCURRENT DIRECTORY CACHE WRITES: 75

Limits: 5 to 500

Description: Maximum number of concurrent writes of directory cache buffers.

DIRECTORY CACHE ALLOCATION WAIT TIME: 2.2 SECONDS

Limits: 0.1 seconds to 2 minutes

Description: Minimum time to wait between new directory cache buffer allocations.

DIRECTORY CACHE BUFFER NONREFERENCED DELAY: 5.5 SECONDS

Limits: 1 second to 1 hour

Description: Normal time to wait after a directory cache buffer was referenced before reusing it.

MAXIMUM DIRECTORY CACHE BUFFERS: 500

Limits: 20 to 200000

Can be set in the startup NCF file.

Description: Maximum number of directory cache buffers that can be allocated by the system.

Minimum Directory Cache Buffers: 150
Limits: 10 to 100000

Can be set in the startup NCF file.

Description: Minimum number of directory cache buffers to be allocated by the server before delaying.

Maximum Number Of Internal Directory Handles: 100
Limits: 40 to 1000

Can be set in the startup NCF file.

Description: The maximum number of directory handles retained for NLMs using connection zero. This facilitates rapid acquisition of access rights in a given directory.

Maximum Number Of Directory Handles: 20
Limits: 20 to 1000

Can be set in the startup NCF file.

Description: The maximum number of directory handles retained per connection to facilitate rapid acquisition of access rights in a given directory.

File System

The settings that affect the file system are given here, along with a brief description of the setting and its defaults. The brief description is what is returned by using the SET console command and looking at the parameters available.

Minimum File Delete Wait Time: 1 minute 5.9 seconds
Limits: 0 seconds to 7 days

Description: Minimum time to wait after a file is deleted before purging it.

File Delete Wait Time: 5 minutes 29.6 seconds
Limits: 0 seconds to 7 days

Description: Normal time to wait after a file is deleted before purging it.

Automatically Repair Bad Volumes: ON
Can be set in the startup NCF file.

Description: When a volume fails to mount, automatically run VRepair to fix it.

PART

V

CH

23

ALLOW DELETION OF ACTIVE DIRECTORIES: ON

Description: Allows the deletion of a directory when another connection has a drive mapped to it.

MAXIMUM PERCENT OF VOLUME SPACE ALLOWED FOR

Extended Attributes: 10

Limits: 5 to 50

Can be set in the startup NCF file.

Description: Percent of volume space allowed for Extended Attributes storage.

MAXIMUM EXTENDED ATTRIBUTES PER FILE OR PATH: 16

Limits: 4 to 512

Description: Allowable number of extended attributes for files or paths.

FAST VOLUME MOUNTS: ON

Can be set in the startup NCF file.

Description: Relax when checking less important fields for faster volume mounts. This is not recommended unless the volume was dismounted normally the last time.

MAXIMUM PERCENT OF VOLUME USED BY DIRECTORY: 13

Limits: 5 to 85

Description: Maximum percentage of each volume that can be allocated for the directory.

IMMEDIATE PURGE OF DELETED FILES: OFF

Description: Purge all files immediately upon deletion.

MAXIMUM SUBDIRECTORY TREE DEPTH: 25

Limits: 10 to 100

Description: Maximum depth of subdirectories.

VOLUME LOW WARN ALL USERS: ON

Description: Send volume low warning to all users.

Limits: 0 to 100000

VOLUME LOW WARNING RESET THRESHOLD: 256

Description: The number of disk blocks above the volume low warning threshold where the warning trigger is reset.

Limits: 0 to 100000

VOLUME LOW WARNING THRESHOLD: 256

Limits: 0 to 1000000

Description: Threshold where a warning is issued that the volume is getting low on disk space (number is in disk allocation units).

TURBO FAT REUSE WAIT TIME: 5 MINUTES 29.6 SECONDS

Limits: 0.3 seconds to 1 hour 5 minutes 54.6 seconds

Description: Minimum time to wait before reusing a closed Turbo FAT.

COMPRESSION DAILY CHECK STOP HOUR: 6

Limits: 0 to 23

Can be set in the startup NCF file.

Description: The hour (0 = midnight, 23 = 11pm) when the file compressor ends scanning each enabled volume for files that need to be compressed (if Compression Daily Check Stop Hour is equal to Compression Daily Starting Hour, start checking every day at Compression Daily Starting Hour and run as long as necessary to finish all files meeting the compressible criteria).

COMPRESSION DAILY CHECK STARTING HOUR: 0

Limits: 0 to 23

Can be set in the startup NCF file.

Description: The hour (0 = midnight, 23 = 11pm) when the file compressor starts scanning each enabled volume for files that need to be compressed.

MINIMUM COMPRESSION PERCENTAGE GAIN: 20

Limits: 0 to 50

Can be set in the startup NCF file.

Description: The minimum percentage a file must compress in order to remain compressed.

ENABLE FILE COMPRESSION: ON

Can be set in the startup NCF file.

Description: Allow file compression to occur on compression enabled volumes. If disabled, no compression takes place. Requests are queued until compression is allowed.

MAXIMUM CONCURRENT COMPRESSIONS: 2

Limits: 1 to 8

Can be set in the startup NCF file.

Description: The number of simultaneous compressions allowed by the system (simultaneous compressions can only occur if there are multiple volumes).

CONVERT COMPRESSED TO UNCOMPRESSED OPTION: 1

Limits: 0 to 2

Can be set in the startup NCF file.

Description: What to do to the uncompressed version when the server uncompresses a file (0 = always leave compressed version, 1 = if compressed file is read only once [within the time frame defined by "Days Untouched Before Compression"], leave the file compressed (on second access leave uncompressed), 2 = always change to the uncompressed version).

DECOMPRESS PERCENT DISK SPACE FREE TO ALLOW COMMIT: 10

Limits: 0 to 75

Can be set in the startup NCF file.

Description: The percentage of disk space on a volume that is required to be free in order for file decompression to permanently change the compressed file version to uncompressed, which prevents newly uncompressed files from entirely filling up the volume (compressed files that are written to are always left uncompressed).

DECOMPRESS FREE SPACE WARNING INTERVAL: 31 MINUTES 18.5 SECONDS

Limits: 0 seconds to 29 days 15 hours 50 minutes 3.8 seconds

Can be set in the startup NCF file.

Description: The time interval between displaying warning alerts when the file system is not permanently changing compressed files to uncompressed files due to insufficient free disk space (setting the display interval to 0 turns off the alert)

DELETED FILES COMPRESSION OPTION: 1

Limits: 0 to 2

Can be set in the startup NCF file.

Description: How to compress deleted files (0 = don't, 1 = compress next day, 2 = compress immediately).

DAYS UNTOUCHED BEFORE COMPRESSION: 14

Limits: 0 to 100000

Can be set in the startup NCF file.

Description: The number of days to wait after a file was last accessed before automatically compressing it.

ALLOW UNOWNED FILES TO BE EXTENDED: ON

Can be set in the startup NCF file.

Description: Controls whether or not an unowned file can be extended.

LOCKS

The settings that deal with file and record locks are given here, along with their defaults and a brief description. The brief description is what is returned by using the SET console command and looking at the parameters available.

MAXIMUM RECORD LOCKS PER CONNECTIONS: 500

Description: Maximum number of record locks per connection (physical, logical & semaphores).

MAXIMUM FILE LOCKS PER CONNECTION: 250

Limits: 10 to 1000

Description: Maximum number of file locks per connection (including open files).

MAXIMUM RECORD LOCKS: 20000

Limits: 100 to 400000

Description: System wide maximum number of record locks (physical, logical, and semaphores).

MAXIMUM FILE LOCKS: 10000

Limits: 100 to 100000

Description: System-wide maximum number of file locks (including open files).

TRANSACTION TRACKING

The Transaction Tracking System (TTS) settings are given here, along with a brief description and the default. The brief description is what is returned by using the SET console command and looking at the parameters available.

AUTO TTS BACKOUT FLAG: ON

Can be set only in the startup NCF file.

Description: Automatically do TTS backouts on reboot (skip the prompts).

TTS ABORT DUMP FLAG: OFF

Description: Enable dumping of data from aborted transactions to a log file.

MAXIMUM TRANSACTIONS: 10000

Limits: 100 to 10000

Description: System-wide maximum number of concurrent transactions.

TTS UNWRITTEN CACHE WAIT TIME: 1 MINUTE 5.9 SECONDS

Limits: 11 seconds to 10 minutes 59.1 seconds

Description: Maximum time a cache buffer write can be delayed by TTS.

TTS BACKOUT FILE TRUNCATION WAIT TIME: 59 MINUTES 19.2 SECONDS

Limits: 1 minute 5.9 seconds to 1 day 2 hours 21 minutes 51.3 seconds

Description: Minimum time to wait before truncating the TTS backout file.

DISK

The disk related settings, along with a description and their defaults, are given here. The brief description is what is returned by using the SET console command and looking at the parameters available.

SEQUENTIAL ELEVATOR DEPTH: 8

Limits: 0 to 4294967295

Can be set in the startup NCF file.

Description: Set the maximum elevator depth for sequential requests. Media Manager sends the number of sequential requests up to this value to the same device. When the device contains this number of requests and another device in the mirror group is empty, Media Manager begins sending requests to the idle device.

ENABLE IO HANDICAP ATTRIBUTE: OFF

Can be set in the startup NCF file.

Description: Drivers and applications can set an attribute to inhibit or handicap read requests from one or more devices. Setting this parameter to ON enables the attribute to function. Setting this parameter to OFF allows NetWare to treat the device as any other device. Do not set this parameter to ON unless instructed to do so by a device manufacturer.

MIRRORED DEVICES ARE OUT OF SYNC MESSAGE FREQUENCY: 28

Limits: 5 to 9999

Can be set in the startup ncf file.

Description: Sets the frequency in minutes where NetWare will check for Out Of Sync devices.

REMIRROR BLOCK SIZE: 1

Limits: 1 to 8

Description: Sets the remirror block size in 4K increments (1=4K, 2=8K,...8=32K).

CONCURRENT REMIRROR REQUESTS: 32

Limits: 2 to 32

Description: Sets the number of remirror requests per mirror object.

IGNORE DISK GEOMETRY: OFF

Can be set in the startup NCF file.

Description: Ignore Disk Geometry when reading or writing the disk partition. Turning this setting on while modifying or creating partitions allows the creation of nonstandard and unsupported partitions. CAUTION: This can adversely affect other filesystems on the disk.

ENABLE HARDWARE WRITE BACK: OFF

Can be set in the startup NCF file.

Description: Allows drivers to use hardware Write Back if supported. IO write requests can be cached and succeeded before data is actually committed to the media. Write performance is typically increased. (Excludes Transaction Tracking requests).

ENABLE DISK READ AFTER WRITE VERIFY: OFF

Can be set in the startup NCF file.

Description: Read back all data written to disk and verify correctness.

TIME

The settings that pertain to time are listed here, along with a brief description of each and their defaults. The brief description is what is returned by using the SET console command and looking at the parameters available.

TIMESYNC CONFIGURED SOURCES: ON

Description: When ON, this server does not listen to advertising time sources. Instead it only contacts sources explicitly configured with the TIMESYNC Time Sources option.

TIMESYNC DIRECTORY TREE MODE: ON

Description: Controls the use of SAP packets in conjunction with the directory services tree structure. The default, ON, causes time synchronization to ignore SAP packets which do not originate from within the tree to which this server belongs. The default installation puts a SINGLE time source at the root of every directory tree, which causes confusion because there should only be one SINGLE time source on the entire network. Setting this parameter to OFF allows this server to receive SAP packets from any time source on the network.

TIMESYNC HARDWARE CLOCK: ON

Description: Controls Hardware clock synchronization. When set to ON, a SINGLE or REFERENCE server reads the hardware clock at the beginning of each polling loop. A PRIMARY or SECONDARY server sets the hardware clock, instead of reading it.

TIMESYNC POLLING COUNT: 3

Limits: 1 to 1000

Description: Polling count. How many time packets to exchange while polling.

TIMESYNC POLLING INTERVAL: 600

Limits: 10 to 2678400

Description: In seconds. Long polling interval. Maximum is 31 days.

TIMESYNC RESET: OFF

Description: When set to ON, the TIMESYNC NLM resets selected internal values and clears the configured server list. The flag automatically resets to OFF.

TIMESYNC RESTART FLAG: OFF

Description: When set to ON, the TIMESYNC NLM restarts. The flag automatically resets to OFF.

TIMESYNC Service Advertising: ON

Description: When ON, this time source advertises using SAP. However, secondary time sources never advertise.

TIMESYNC Synchronization Radius: 2000

Limits: 0 to 2147483647

Description: In milliseconds. Maximum adjustment allowed while still considered to be synchronized.

TIMESYNC Time Adjustment: None Scheduled

Maximum length: 98

Description: Schedule a time adjustment. Can only be issued from a SINGLE, REFERENCE, or PRIMARY type server. The format is [+¦-]hh:mm:ss [AT [date and time]]. Default date and time is six polling intervals or one hour (whichever is larger) from now. Using the word CANCEL instead of a date cancels a previously scheduled adjustment. SINGLE and REFERENCE servers do not accept adjustments from PRIMARY servers.

TIMESYNC Time Sources: ;

Maximum length: 149

Description: Sets the servers to contact in the configured list. It is delimited by ;. At least one ; must be in the list for this value to change. For example: ; (clears list) or MyServer;137.65.120.2;.ServerName.NDSContext

TIMESYNC Type: SECONDARY

Maximum length: 22

Description: The type of time source. Choose from SINGLE reference, REFERENCE, PRIMARY, or SECONDARY.

New Time With Daylight Savings Time Status: OFF

Description: Indicates whether daylight savings time is in effect (ON) and that the daylight savings time offset should be used in time calculations. The default is OFF. The difference between this call and Set Daylight Savings Time Status is that this call also automatically adjusts the local time by adding or subtracting the daylight savings time offset.

Daylight Savings Time Status: OFF

Can be set in the startup NCF file.

Description: Indicates whether daylight savings time is in effect (ON) and that the daylight savings time offset should be used in time calculations. The default is OFF. Changing the status does not change the local time.

DAYLIGHT SAVINGS TIME OFFSET: +1:00:00

Can be set in the startup NCF file.

Description: The offset applied in time calculations when daylight savings time is in effect. The default is +1:00:00 (one hour). Issuing this command causes UTC time to be recalculated from local time.

END OF DAYLIGHT SAVINGS TIME: (OCTOBER SUNDAY LAST 2:00:00 AM)

Maximum length: 78

Description: Local date and time when the switch off of daylight savings time should occur. Formats include a simple date and time or rules introduced by a (. For example, October 31 1993 2:0:0 am, (October 31 2:0:0 am), (October Sunday <= 31 2:0:0 am), or (October Sunday last 2:0:0 am). Only rules cause rescheduling for the next year. You must set both the start and end dates before either will be scheduled.

START OF DAYLIGHT SAVINGS TIME: (APRIL SUNDAY FIRST 2:00:00 AM)

Maximum length: 78

Description: Local date and time when the switch onto daylight savings time should occur. Formats include a simple date and time or rules introduced by a (. For example, April 4 1993 2:0:0 am, (April 4 2:0:0 am), (April Sunday >= 1 2:0:0 am), or (April Sunday First 2:0:0 am). Only rules cause rescheduling for the next year. You must set both the start and end dates before either will be scheduled.

DEFAULT TIME SERVER TYPE: SECONDARY

Maximum length: 49

Can be set in the startup NCF file.

Description: The default time synchronization server type. Choose from SECONDARY, PRIMARY, REFERENCE, or SINGLE. Can be overridden by separate time synchronization parameters. Default is SECONDARY.

TIME ZONE: CST6CDT

Maximum length: 79

Can be set in the startup NCF file.

Description: Time zone string indicating the abbreviated name of the time zone, the offset from Universal Time Coordinated (UTC), and the alternative abbreviated time zone name to be used when daylight savings time is in effect. The default is <<NO TIME ZONE>>. Issuing this command causes UTC time to be recalculated from local time.

TIMESYNC CONFIGURATION FILE: SYS:SYSTEM\TIMESYNC.CFG

Maximum length: 254

Description: Selects a configuration file path. This file is automatically updated when the TIMESYNC parameters are changed, using either MONITOR.NLM or SET parameters from the command line. TIMESYNC reads from this file when TIMESYNC Restart Flag is set to ON.

NCP

The settings that pertain to NCP are listed here, along with a brief description of each and their defaults. The brief description is what is returned by using the SET console command and looking at the parameters available.

NCP TCP KEEP ALIVE INTERVAL: 9 MINUTES 53.2 SECONDS

Limits: 0 seconds to 15 hours 59 minutes 53.6 seconds

Can be set in the startup NCF file.

Description: Set the delay before TCP keep alive closes idle NCP connections; 0 = never time out idle connections

MINIMUM NCP TCP RECEIVE WINDOW TO ADVERTISE: 4096

Limits: 256 to 16384

Can be set in the startup NCF file.

Description: Set the minimum receive window to advertise on NCP connections

NCP TCP RECEIVE WINDOW: 23360

Limits: 1400 to 65535

Can be set in the startup NCF file.

Description: Set the advertised receive window on NCP connections

ENABLE UDP CHECKSUMS ON NCP PACKETS: 1

Limits: 0 to 2

Can be set in the startup NCF file.

Description: Enable checksumming of NCP UDP packets (0 = no checksums; 1 = checksum if enabled at the client; 2 = require checksumming)

NCP PACKET SIGNATURE OPTION: 1

Limits: 0 to 3

Can be set in the startup NCF file.

Description: Options controlling NCP Packet Signatures: (0 = don't do packet signatures; 1 = do packet signatures only if the client requires them; 2 = do packet signatures if the client can, but don't require them if the client doesn't support them; 3 = require packet signatures). After startup time, you can only increase the level.

ENABLE IPX CHECKSUMS: 1

Limits: 0 to 2

Can be set in the startup NCF file.

Description: Enable checksumming of IPX packets (0 = no checksums; 1 = checksum if enabled at the client; 2 = require checksumming).

NCP PROTOCOL PREFERENCES: TCP UDP IPX

Maximum length: 126

Description: Set the preferred protocol order of the loaded transports. The NCP engine supports the following transports: IPX, TCP, UDP. Example: SET NCP PROTOCOL PREFERENCES = TCP IPX

NCP FILE COMMIT: ON

Description: Allow applications to flush all pending file writes to disk.

DISPLAY NCP BAD COMPONENT WARNINGS: OFF

Can be set in the startup NCF file.

Description: Display NCP bad component alert messages

REJECT NCP PACKETS WITH BAD COMPONENTS: OFF

Can be set in the startup NCF file. Description: Reject NCP packets which fail component checking.

DISPLAY NCP BAD LENGTH WARNINGS: OFF

Can be set in the startup NCF file.

Description: Display NCP bad length alert messages.

REJECT NCP PACKETS WITH BAD LENGTHS: OFF

Can be set in the startup NCF file.

Description: Reject NCP packets which fail boundary checking.

MAXIMUM OUTSTANDING NCP SEARCHES: 51

Limits: 10 to 1000

Description: Maximum number of simultaneous NCP directory searches that a connection can have.

ALLOW CHANGE TO CLIENT RIGHTS: ON

Can be set in the startup NCF file.

Description: Allow a Print or Job server to assume the rights of a queue job's submitter as it services that queue job.

ALLOW LIP: ON

Can be set in the startup NCF file.

Description: Allow Large Internet Packet support.

MISCELLANEOUS

The miscellaneous settings do not fall nicely into any of the other categories, so they wind up with one of their own! The miscellaneous settings are given here, along with a brief description and their defaults. The brief description is returned by using the SET console command and looking at the parameters available.

DISPLAY INCOMPLETE IPX PACKET ALERTS: ON

Can be set in the startup NCF file.

Description: Display alert messages when IPX receives incomplete packets.

ENABLE SECURE.NCF: OFF

Can be set in the startup NCF file.

Description: ON causes SECURE.NCF to be executed during server boot.

ALLOW AUDIT PASSWORDS: OFF

Description: Allow audit password requests to be used.

COMMAND LINE PROMPT DEFAULT CHOICE: ON

Can be set in the startup NCF file.

Description: Specifies the default input for the ? (conditional execution) console command as ON = 'Y' and OFF = 'N'. Note that the default can be overridden if a 'Y' or an 'N' follows the ? command. The format for the ? command is ?{Y or N} {"prompt text"} command, where {} denotes optional parameters.

PART

V

CH

23

COMMAND LINE PROMPT TIME OUT: 10

Limits: 0 to 4294967295

Can be set in the startup NCF file.

Description: Amount of time in seconds that the Command Line ? command prompt will wait before the default answer is used. If 0 seconds is used, the prompt does not time out.

SOUND BELL FOR ALERTS: ON

Description: Sound the bell when an alert message is displayed on the console.

REPLACE CONSOLE PROMPT WITH SERVER NAME: ON

Can be set in the startup NCF file.

Description: Replace the console prompt with the server name.

ALERT MESSAGE NODES: 20

Limits: 10 to 256

Can be set in the startup NCF file.

Description: The number of preallocated Alert Message nodes.

WORKER THREAD EXECUTE IN A ROW COUNT: 10

Limits: 1 to 20

Description: Number of times in a row the scheduler will dispatch new work before allowing other threads to run.

HALT SYSTEM ON INVALID PARAMETERS: OFF

Can be set in the startup NCF file.

Description: Halt system when an invalid parameter or condition is detected rather than displaying a system alert and continuing.

DISPLAY RELINQUISH CONTROL ALERTS: OFF

Can be set in the startup NCF file.

Description: Display alert messages when a process does not relinquish control frequently.

DISPLAY OLD API NAMES: OFF

Can be set in the startup NCF file.

Description: Display the names of old API routines that a module is using when the module is loaded.

CPU Hog Timeout Amount: 1 minute

Limits: 0 seconds to 1 hour

Can be set in the startup NCF file.

Description: Time in seconds to wait before terminating a process that has not relinquished control of the CPU. A value of 0 disables this option.

Developer Option: OFF

Can be set in the startup NCF file.

Description: Enable options associated with developer environment.

Display Spurious Interrupt Alerts Threshold: 200

Limits: 1 to 1000000

Can be set in the startup NCF file.

Description: Sets the minimum number of spurious interrupts per second that must be detected before a spurious interrupt alert message is displayed on the system console. Set Display Lost Interrupt Alerts must also be set to ON.

Display Lost Interrupt Alerts Threshold: 10

Limits: 1 to 1000000

Can be set in the startup NCF file.

Description: Sets the minimum number of lost interrupts per second that must be detected before a lost interrupt alert message will be displayed on the system console. Set Display Lost Interrupt Alerts must also be set to ON.

Display Spurious Interrupt Alerts: OFF

Can be set in the startup NCF file.

Description: Display alert messages when a spurious hardware interrupt is detected. A NetWare spurious interrupt is defined as an interrupt which is not serviced, or not claimed, by any of the interrupt service routines hooked to that interrupt.

Display Lost Interrupt Alerts: OFF

Can be set in the startup NCF file.

Description: Display alert messages when the interrupt controller detects a lost hardware interrupt. A NetWare lost hardware interrupt occurs when, at interrupt acknowledge time, there are no interrupt request bits set in the programmable interrupt controller hardware. When this happens the programmable interrupt controller delivers an appropriate interrupt vector to the processor signaling the occurrence of the lost interrupt.

PSEUDO PREEMPTION COUNT: 40

Limits: 1 to 4294967295

Description: Number of times to allow the threads to make file read or write system calls without relinquishing before forcing a relinquish (Pseudo Preemption is either enabled globally or for threads created by specific NLMs).

GLOBAL PSEUDO PREEMPTION: ON

Description: Cause all threads to use Pseudo Preemption.

MINIMUM SERVICE PROCESSES: 100

Limits: 10 to 500

Description: Number of Service Processes that can be allocated without waiting; configured as New Service Process Wait Time.

MAXIMUM SERVICE PROCESSES: 500

Limits: 50 to 1000

Description: Maximum number of request servicing processes.

NEW SERVICE PROCESS WAIT TIME: 2.2 SECONDS

Limits: 0.3 seconds to 20 seconds

Description: Minimum time to wait before creating a new request servicing process.

ALLOW UNENCRYPTED PASSWORDS: OFF

Description: Allow unencrypted password requests to be used.

ERROR HANDLING

The error handling parameters, along with a brief description and the defaults, are listed here. The brief description is what is returned by using the SET console command and looking at the parameters available.

VOLUME LOG FILE STATE: 1

Can be set in the startup NCF file.

Description: Action to take if the VOL$LOG.ERR file size grows larger than size limit (0 = take no action; 1 = delete the log file; 2 = rename log file).

VOLUME TTS LOG FILE STATE: 1

Limits: 0 to 2

Can be set in the startup NCF file.

Description: Action to take if the TTS$LOG.ERR file size grows larger than size limit (0 = take no action; 1 = delete the log file; 2 = rename log file).

VOLUME LOG FILE OVERFLOW SIZE: 4194304

Limits: 65536 to 4294967295

Can be set in the startup NCF file.

Description: Maximum size for the file VOL$LOG.ERR.

VOLUME TTS LOG FILE OVERFLOW SIZE: 4194304

Limits: 65536 to 4294967295

Can be set in the startup NCF file.

Description: Maximum size for the file TTS$LOG.ERR.

SERVER LOG FILE STATE: 1

Limits: 0 to 2

Can be set in the startup NCF file.

Description: Action to take if the SYS$LOG.ERR file size grows larger than size limit: (0 = take no action; 1 = delete the log file; 2 = rename log file).

SERVER LOG FILE OVERFLOW SIZE: 4194304

Limits: 65536 to 4294967295

Can be set in the startup NCF file.

Description: Maximum size for the file SYS$LOG.ERR.

BOOT ERROR LOG FILE STATE: 3

Limits: 0 to 3

Can be set in the startup NCF file.

Description: Action to take if the BOOT$LOG.ERR file size grows larger than size limit (0 = take no action; 1 = delete the log file; 2 = rename log file; 3 = Start a new log file every time the server is started).

BOOT ERROR LOG FILE OVERFLOW SIZE: 4194304

Limits: 65536 to 4294967295

Can be set in the startup NCF file.

Description: Maximum size for the file BOOT$LOG.ERR.

BOOT ERROR LOG: ON

Can be set in the startup NCF file.

Description: This parameter determines whether the error messages from the console are saved in BOOT$LOG.ERR. If this is set to ON then all error messages that go to the console are saved in BOOT$LOG.ERR. If this is set to OFF then only the error messages that are displayed during the boot procedure will be saved to this file.

HUNG UNLOAD WAIT DELAY: 30 SECONDS

Limits: 0 seconds to 1 minute 58.3 seconds

Can be set in the startup NCF file.

Description: The amount of time to wait for an NLM that is hung to unload before prompting the user about whether to shut down the address space that the NLM was loaded in. (This only applies to NLMs that are loaded in a protected memory space.)

AUTO RESTART AFTER ABEND DELAY TIME: 2

Limits: 2 to 60

Can be set in the startup NCF file.

Description: Time in minutes that the server waits before automatically going down and restarting when an abend occurs.

AUTO RESTART AFTER ABEND: 1

Limits: 0 to 3

Can be set in the startup NCF file.

Description: This settable parameter controls what the server does after an abend. The values 0–3 have the following behavior:

- 0—Do not try to recover from the abend.
- 1—(default) For software abends, NMIs, and Machine Check Exceptions: attempt to recover from the problem, down the server in the configured amount of time, and then restart the OS. For other Exception Abends, suspend the faulting process and leave the server up.
- 2—For all software and hardware abends, attempt to recover from the problem, down the server in the configured amount of time, and then restart the OS.

- 3—For all software and hardware abends, do an immediate restart of the server. Note that when the server abends, detailed information is logged to the ABEND.LOG file in SYS:SYSTEM. Also note that abends indicate that the server is in an invalid state, and therefore recovery is not always possible. This option is disabled when the developer option settable parameter is turned on.

DIRECTORY SERVICES

The parameters that pertain to directory services are documented here, along with a brief description and their defaults. The brief description is what is returned by using the SET console command and looking at the parameters available.

NDS EXTERNAL REFERENCE LIFE SPAN: 192

Limits: 1 to 384

Description: Specifies number of hours unused external references are allowed to exist before being removed.

NDS INACTIVITY SYNCHRONIZATION INTERVAL: 60

Limits: 2 to 1440

Description: The interval in minutes after which full synchronization of replicas is performed following a period of no change to the information held in NDS on the server.

NDS SYNCHRONIZATION RESTRICTIONS: OFF

Maximum length: 131

Description: OFF allows synchronization with any version of DS. ON restricts synchronization to version numbers you specify as parameters. Example: ON, 420, 421

NDS SERVERS STATUS: UP/DOWN

Maximum length: 7

Description: Marks the status of all server objects in the local namebase as UP or DOWN.

NDS JANITOR INTERVAL: 60

Limits: 1 to 10080

Description: Sets the interval in minutes at which the NDS janitor process is executed.

NDS DISTRIBUTED REFERENCE LINK INTERVAL: 780

Limits: 2 to 10080

Description: Sets the interval in minutes at which NDS distributed reference link consistency checking is performed.

NDS BACKLINK INTERVAL: 780

Limits: 2 to 10080

Description: Sets the interval in minutes at which NDS backlink consistency checking is performed.

NDS TRACE FILE LENGTH TO ZERO: OFF

Description: Clears the NDS trace file. When cleared, parameter resets itself to OFF. To use this parameter, you must also set the NDS trace to file parameter to ON.

NDS BOOTSTRAP ADDRESS

Maximum length: 129

Description: If this server does not hold a replica, this value specifies the address of a remote server with which it can perform tree connectivity operations.

BINDERY CONTEXT: .OU=XXX.O=YYY

Maximum length: 2047

Can be set in the startup NCF file.

Description: The NetWare Directory Services container where bindery services are provided. Set multiple contexts by separating contexts with semicolons.

NDS TRACE FILENAME: SYSTEM\DSTRACE.DBG

Maximum length: 254

Description: Sets the path and name of the NDS trace file on the SYS volume.

NDS TRACE TO FILE: OFF

Description: Trace DS Events to the NDS trace file on SYS volume.

NDS TRACE TO SCREEN: OFF

Description: Enable DS trace screen.

MULTIPROCESSOR

The few settings that pertain to servers with multiple processors are listed here, along with the defaults and a brief description. The brief description is what is returned by using the SET console command and looking at the parameters available.

SYSTEM THRESHOLD: 1536

Limits: 0 to 102400

Can be set in the startup NCF file.

Description: Controls the main value used in calculating thread shedding for load balancing.

AUTO CLEAR INTERRUPT STATISTICS: ON

Preferably set in the startup NCF file.

Description: When a processor is taken OFFLINE or when an interrupt handler is removed, the detailed statistics pertaining to that processor or interrupt handler are, by default, removed from memory. To retain per processor interrupt handler statistics for OFFLINE processors or to retain the total interrupt contribution from a previously loaded handler, change the set parameter Set Auto Clear Interrupt Statistics to OFF. Default is ON.

AUTO START PROCESSORS: ON

Preferably set in the startup NCF file.

Description: When ON, secondary processors are automatically started when the Platform Support Module (PSM) is loaded. When OFF, the console command START PROCESSORS must be used to activate secondary processors. Default is ON.

SERVICE LOCATION PROTOCOL

The SLP (Service Location Protocol) parameters are listed here, along with the defaults and a brief description. The brief description is what is returned by using the SET console command and looking at the parameters available.

SLP SCOPE LIST

Maximum length: 184

Can be set in the startup NCF file.

Description: A comma-delimited string specifying a scope policy list.

SLP CLOSE IDLE TCP CONNECTIONS TIME: 300

Limits: 0 to 86400

Can be set in the startup NCF file.

Description: An integer value describing the number of seconds before idle TCP connections should be terminated.

SLP DA HEART BEAT TIME: 10800

Limits: 0 to 65535

Can be set in the startup NCF file.

Description: An integer value describing the number of seconds before sending the next DA heartbeat packet.

SLP DA EVENT TIMEOUT: 15

Limits: 0 to 120

Can be set in the startup NCF file.

Description: An integer value describing the number of seconds to wait before timing out DA packet request.

SLP EVENT TIMEOUT: 3

Limits: 0 to 120

Can be set in the startup NCF file.

Description: An integer value describing the number of seconds to wait before timing out multicast packet request.

SLP SA DEFAULT LIFETIME: 3600

Limits: 0 to 65535

Can be set in the startup NCF file.

Description: An integer value describing the default lifetime on service registers.

SLP RETRY COUNT: 3

Limits: 0 to 128

Can be set in the startup NCF file.

Description: An integer value describing the maximum number of retries.

SLP DEBUG: 0

Limits: 0 to 65535

Can be set in the startup NCF file.

Description: Enables SLP debug mode. BIT 0x01=COMM, 0x02=TRAN, 0x04=API, 0x08=DA, 0x10=ERR, 0x20=SA. These bits can be ORed together for multiple values.

SLP Rediscover Inactive Directory Agents: 60

Limits: 0 to 86400

Can be set in the startup NCF file.

Description: The minimum time period (seconds) that SLP waits to issue service requests to rediscover inactive DAs.

SLP Multicast Radius: 32

Limits: 0 to 32

Can be set in the startup NCF file.

Description: An integer describing the multicast radius.

SLP DA Discovery Options: 7

Limits: 0 to 8

Can be set in the startup NCF file.

Description: BIT 0x01 = Use dynamic DA advertisements, 0x02 = Use DHCP Discovery, 0x04 = Use static file SYS:ETC\SLP.CFG, 0x08 = Scopes Required. These bits can be ORed together for multiple values. Zero disables all DA discovery.

SLP MTU Size: 1450

Limits: 0 to 24682

Can be set in the startup NCF file.

Description: An integer describing the maximum transfer unit size.

SLP Broadcast: OFF

Can be set in the startup NCF file.

Description: Use broadcast packets instead of multicast packets.

SLP TCP: OFF

Can be set in the startup NCF file.

Description: Use TCP packets instead of UDP packets when possible.

Licensing Services

The few settings that pertain to licensing are listed here, along with the defaults and a brief description. The brief description is what is returned by using the SET console command and looking at the parameters available.

DIRTY CERTIFICATE CACHE DELAY TIME: 1 MINUTE

Limits: 1 minute to 1 hour

Can be set in the startup NCF file.

Description: Minimum time the licensing services wait before writing a dirty certificate cache to DS.

NLS SEARCH TYPE: 0

Limits: 0 to 1

Description: 0 = Stop upward search for license certificate at tree root. 1 = Stop upward search at partition root.

MANAGING NLMs

You can think of an *NetWare Loadable Module (NLM)* as an executable that runs on the server. When loaded, the system allocates memory to the NLM and dynamically links it to the operating system. When the NLM is unloaded, the memory is freed and given back to the system.

Some NLMs, such as TCPCON or NWCONFIG, you might load, do something with the utility, and then unload. Other NLMs such as disk and LAN drivers need to be loaded all of the time. There are six types of NLMs:

- LAN drivers, which have a .LAN extension. LAN drivers allow communication between the OS and the NIC. You can load and unload the LAN drivers, but when unloaded, no communication is possible with the server.

- Server applications, which have a .NLM extension. Examples of these would be Monitor, TCPCon, IPXcon, NWConfig, and so on. You load these to change or monitor the system, and they can be loaded and unloaded as needed.

- Name space support modules, which have an extension of .NAM. These allow support for non-DOS filenames on the server. For example, if you add name space LONG to a volume, you can save files with names such as This is my resume done in February.doc instead of simply RESUME.

- Platform support modules, which have a .PSM extension. A .PSM module would provide support for multiple processors.

- NetWare Peripheral Architecture modules (NWPA), which have extensions of .CDM and .HAM. These provide support for disks and CD-ROMs.

- Files used to support the NSS (Novell Storage Services) file system, which have .NSS extensions.

THE MODULES COMMAND

The console command MODULES is used to display information about NLMs that are loaded. The syntax is simply MODULES. One nice thing about the MODULES command is that it supports the asterisk (*) as a wildcard. Because the list of modules can be quite long, you might have to keep pressing a key to continue, and it is easy to miss the information about the one NLM you are interested in. By using the wildcard, you can limit the display just like the DOS dir command. Here, you have entered modules sc* to see information only about NLMs beginning with the letters sc:

```
WIZARD1:modules sc*
SCSIHD.CDM      (Address Space = OS)
  Novell SCSI Fixed Disk Custom Device Module
  Version 1.34k    July 29, 1998
  1995-98 Novell, Inc. All Rights Reserved.
SCSICD.CDM      (Address Space = OS)
  Novell SCSI CD-ROM Device Custom Device Module
  Version 1.34k    July 29, 1998
  1995-98 Novell, Inc. All Rights Reserved.
SCMD.NLM        (Address Space = OS)
  Compatibility Mode Driver
  Version 1.04c    August 13, 1998
  Copyright 1993-1998 Novell, Inc. All rights reserved.
SCRSAVER.NLM    (Address Space = OS)
  NetWare 5 Screen Saver
  Version 1.02    June 19, 1998
  Copyright 1997-98, Novell, Inc.  All rights reserved.
```

Shown is the name of the NLM, the address space it is loaded in, a description, the version and date, and a copyright notice. If you have a color monitor, the colors indicate how the NLM was loaded, for example, light blue shows loaded from internal nlm list, whereas red shows Loaded from startup device.

THE LOAD AND UNLOAD COMMANDS

To load an NLM, simply enter the name of the NLM at the console prompt, such as WIZARD1:monitor, which would load MONITOR. To unload an NLM, use the UNLOAD command, such as WIZARD1:UNLOAD monitor to unload the MONITOR.NLM.

The loader has been changed in NetWare 5. In previous versions, you always needed to use the syntax LOAD <nlm name>; you had to use the LOAD command. In NetWare 5, you can do without using the word LOAD, and use the name of the NLM.

PART

V

CH

23

Tip #236 from	However, if you have created any .NCF files with the same name as NLMs, you need to use the LOAD command, otherwise, the .NCF file is executed. In other words, if you create a MONITOR.NCF file and you enter the command MONITOR, the .NCF file is executed. In order to load MONITOR.NLM, you would need to use the keyword LOAD, as in LOAD MONITOR.
John	

For more detailed information on the LOAD command, such as loading a module into a protected address space, search the utilities reference for the LOAD command.

THE SEARCH COMMAND

Just like a workstation, the server has a path it follows to look for NLMs. You use the SEARCH command to add, delete, and view the current search path:

- SEARCH by itself displays the current search path:

```
WIZARD1:search
Search 1: [Server Path] SYS:SYSTEM\
Search 2: [DOS Path] (default directory)
Search 3: [Server Path] SYS:\JAVA\BIN\
Search 4: [Server Path] SYS:\JAVA\NWGFX\
Search 5: [Server Path] SYS:\NI\BIN\
Search 6: [Server Path] SYS:\SERVERI\
```

- SEARCH ADD *<path>* adds the new directory to the path. For example, SEARCH ADD sys:magicnet appends sys:magicnet to the path.

- SEARCH ADD 3 sys:magicnet inserts sys:magicnet as the third directory to be searched.

- SEARCH DEL 3 removes the third directory from the path.

THE SECURE CONSOLE COMMAND

The SECURE CONSOLE command disables you from adding or removing search paths. This prevents users from adding their own directories to the search path, thus enabling them to load their own modules. When the console is secure, NLMs can be loaded only from the existing search paths, only the console operator can modify the date and time, and using the keyboard combination Shift+Shift+Alt+Esc to break into the debugger is disabled.

The only way to unsecure the console is to down the server and bring it back up.

CONSOLEONE

ConsoleOne is a Java application for managing the network. Having said that, forget it. ConsoleOne currently has very limited functionality, and it is a real resource hog. As of this writing, you should consider ConsoleOne more a "proof of concept" than a useful utility. You still need to manage your network by using NWAdmin32 and NDSManager32 found in the sys:public\win32 folder.

To run ConsoleOne at the server, either choose Novell, ConsoleOne at the GUI toolbar, or use the command C1START at the console prompt. C1START is an NCF file located in sys:system.

> **Note**
> An *NCF file* is like a batch file for the server. You can take valid console commands, and save them in an ASCII text file as `FILENAME.NCF`. Entering the command filename at the server console will run the commands. An example would be the traditional `AUTOEXEC.NCF` file.

You can also run ConsoleOne on your workstation. Go to the `sys:public\mgmt` folder and execute `CONSOLE1.EXE`. The ConsoleOne screen is shown in Figure 23.10.

Figure 23.10
The ConsoleOne screen. This is the Java based application which will (someday?) replace the existing management utilities such as Netware Administrator.

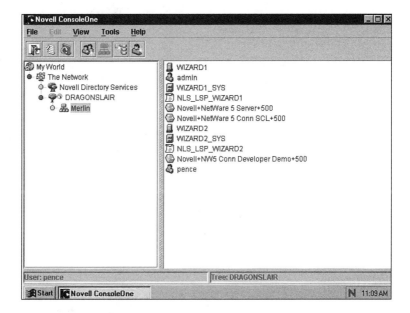

TROUBLESHOOTING

What can go wrong at the server console? NLMs failing to load is one thing; either the NLM or some of its dependencies are not on the server's search path, so the server's path would be something to check. One good tool I discussed in this chapter is `conlog`; you can load `conlog`, and try to load the troublesome NLM. The statements about failing to find this or that public symbol normally go by too fast for you to read, but with `conlog`, you are capturing all of this to the `console.log`, and can read it at your leisure.

Another problem with loading NLMs is not that the dependencies aren't on the path, but that they are the wrong version. You could be using either newer or older versions of NLMs required by the one you are trying to load, and thus the load fails.

Make sure you have the servers configuration documented; that is as important as documenting the network. No matter how obvious a setting seems right now, two years from now at 3 a.m., it won't be! Keeping a log by the servers console is an excellent idea; write down everything you do to the server, no matter how trivial. This is often helpful when pondering server problems; you think "I never had this problem until about two or three weeks ago." Then you look at the server's log, and realize that at about that time, you changed three settings in an attempt to tune the server, and the log leads you to the solution.

And don't forget to keep a close eye on the General Information screen of Monitor. Here are the statistics that you most likely want to watch, which is why they are shown on the main screen.

CHAPTER 24

ZENworks

In this chapter

WHAT IS ZENWORKS?

ZENworks (Zero Effort Networks) is an NDS-enabled software bundle you can use to manage the NetWare clients on your network from one central location—that is, with NWAdmn32. ZENworks enables you to deliver a standard desktop appearance and workstation configuration to all NDS users. Two different sets of the ZENworks product are available: The *ZENworks Full Pack* and the *ZENworks Starter Pack*.

The Full Pack is a purchasable product from Novell and includes the following components:

- **Novell Application Launcher (NAL)**—NAL is the server-to-client software distribution piece in ZENworks that enables you to distribute software applications, service packs, or any other set of files, including registry settings, to a workstation.

- **Software Metering**—This component enables you to meter NAL-delivered applications to comply with software licensing agreements or simply for application capacity planning.

- **Remote Control**—Enables you to remote control workstations securely through NDS, using NWAdmn32.

- **Hardware Inventory**—Workstations can send their hardware information into the NDS database. You use NWAdmn32 to view and print this information. Additionally, you can export the hardware information for use with another application (as mentioned in Chapter 15, "Creating, Managing, and Using NDS Objects").

- **Help Desk**—This feature enables users to send trouble tickets or an electronic mail message to the help desk. Additionally, users have a client utility that, when launched, gives information about the workstation they are logged in from—that is, their user context and the name of their workstation object as it appears in NDS.

- **User and Computer System Policies**—These policies control things such as removing the Run command or the Control Panel applet from the Start menu. These policies contain the Microsoft Default User and Default Computer policies, which have been implemented into NDS.

- **Desktop Preferences**—This allows you to control things such as the color scheme and wallpaper that users have on their desktops. These desktop preferences are essentially Microsoft's Profiles, which have been implemented into NDS.

- **Printer Drivers**—Can automatically be distributed to either users or workstations.

- **Novell Client Software Settings**—These can be added, removed, or customized for workstations.

- **Check 2000**— A software program from a company called Greenwich Mean Time. Check 2000 assesses and resolves your Year 2000 risks. A five-user license is provided.

The Starter Pack is a set of free components that ships with NetWare 5 and contains everything in the Full Pack except for Remote Control, Hardware Inventory, Help Desk, and Software Metering.

PART

V

CH

24

> **Note**
>
> This chapter discusses the ZENworks Full Pack components. Additionally, this chapter refers to ZENworks 1.1. Although ZENworks 2.0 is scheduled to release shortly, you will find that the majority of ZENworks 1.1 setup, configuration, and usage will pertain to ZENworks 2.0. ZENworks 2.0 is simply adding more features to ZENworks 1.1, such as server-to-server software distribution and software inventory.

Because ZENworks is NDS-enabled, you can take advantage of NDS containers to deliver a common desktop appearance and workstation configuration for all users in a container. Or, if containers are too broad of a categorization, you can use NDS groups for this delivery.

ZENworks is supported on NetWare versions 4.11 and later; additionally, ZENworks supports Windows NT, Windows 95/98, and Windows 3.1x workstations.

INSTALLING ZENWORKS

The ZENworks installation is very straightforward and uses an InstallShield Wizard to guide you through the installation steps as follows:

1. ZENworks ships on an auto-running CD, which means when you insert the CD the ZENworks installation program automatically starts up (see Figure 24.1).

Figure 24.1
The ZENworks CD also ships with the Novell Client software that is required for ZENworks.

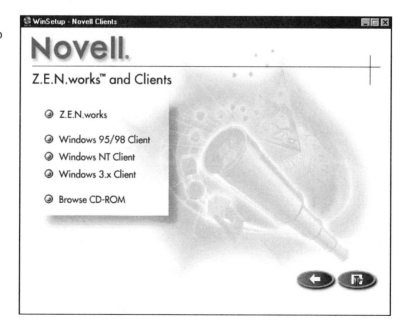

> **Note**
>
> Novell recently changed this product's name from Z.E.N.works to ZENworks. Although the installation screens for ZENworks 1.1 still use the older spelling, this chapter refers to the product as *ZENworks*.

The minimum Novell Client software version required for ZENworks 1.1 is the following:

Windows 3.1x:	2.6+
Windows 95/98:	3.02+
Windows NT 4.0:	4.51+

Specifically, these versions are required when you want to use a component of ZENworks that uses an imported workstation object.

2. From Figure 24.1, you select ZENworks, which then brings up the screen shown in Figure 24.2.

Figure 24.2
Software Metering has a separate installation process. Additionally, the Check 2000 tool is installed from within the Third-Party Products option.

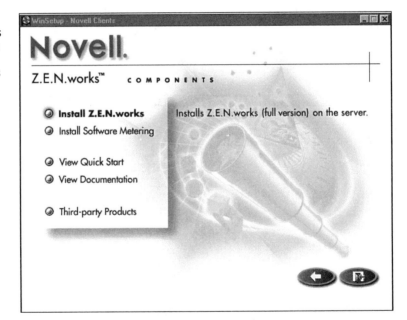

3. From Figure 24.2, select Install ZENworks.

You are now prompted to exit any Windows programs that are running and to read the ZENworks software licensing agreement. After accepting the terms of the ZENworks licensing agreement, you are presented with screen shown in Figure 24.3.

Figure 24.3
There are three options for installing ZENworks.

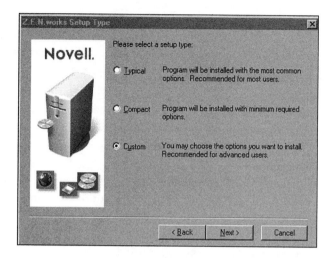

I would recommend you select the Custom installation option so that you see the available ZENworks components and you can select the servers they will be installed on. Additionally, the Custom option is what you would select if, at a later time, you wanted to install just the ZENworks NWAdmn32 snap-ins to another file server or if you needed to just reinstall the ZENworks schema extensions.

4. From Figure 24.3, select Custom, which brings up the screen shown in Figure 24.4.

Figure 24.4
The ZENworks custom installation is broken up into individual product components.

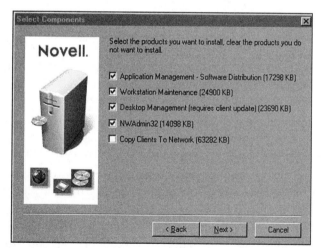

As mentioned earlier, ZENworks is a software bundle that allows you to manage NetWare client workstations. As such, you can choose the specific product components (from Figure 24.4) that you want to install and subsequently implement as follows:

- **Application Management-Software Distribution**—Selecting this option will install the NAL components.

- **Workstation Maintenance**—Selecting this option will install the components of ZENworks that do not require a workstation object—for example, desktop preferences, user system policies, and the help desk feature.

- **Desktop Management**—Selecting this option will install the components of ZENworks that make use of workstation objects—for example, computer system policies, remote control, and workstation inventory. Notice in Figure 24.4 that the Desktop Management component specifically requires the client versions referenced earlier.

- **NWAdmin32**—Selecting this option will install the necessary ZENworks snap-ins on a file server so that the ZENworks objects can be created and managed in NWAdmn32. These snap-ins will only be placed on the servers that you specify (look ahead to Figure 24.6).

Note

The previous four product components are selected and installed by default. If you are unsure which of these four components to install, select them all. This way, you can implement any of the ZENworks features. Remember that Software Metering and Check 2000 have separate installation utilities.

- **Copy Clients to Network**—Selecting this option will place the Novell Client software on a NetWare volume so that the client software can be updated (or installed) "across-the-wire." Installing the Novell Client software is discussed in Chapter 13, "Installing Workstation Software." The Copy Clients to Network option is not selected by default.

5. After you have selected the product components to install, select Next (from Figure 24.4), which brings up the screen as shown in Figure 24.5.

   If this is the first time you are installing ZENworks in the NDS Tree, select and install all components in Figure 24.5. The following discusses what these components are:

- **Files**—This option must be selected to install the ZENworks product files (selected in Figure 24.5). These ZENworks files will be copied to the servers specified in Figure 24.6.

- **Schema Extensions**—This option must be selected to install the schema extensions necessary to support the creation of ZENworks objects. Schema extensions will be propagated to *all* servers in the Tree that is specified in Figure 24.6.

Figure 24.5
The ZENworks custom installation allows you to specify the files that you need to install.

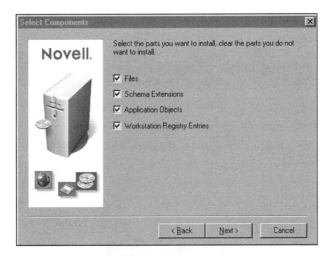

Caution

ZENworks will extend the NDS schema; therefore, you must be logged in as a user that has Supervisor object rights to the [Root] of the NDS Tree. Additionally, the server holding the Master replica of [Root] must be up to properly extend the NDS schema for ZENworks. Your NDS Tree should be "healthy" before installing any product that extends the schema—that is, there should be no NDS errors when running the console command SET DSTRACE=ON. If necessary, you can stop the ZENworks installation process at this point to ensure that NDS is properly synchronizing in the Tree.

- **Application Objects**—Selecting this option will install sample Application objects that can be used to deliver the client components of ZENworks.

6. After you have selected the components to install, select Next (from Figure 24.5), which brings up the screen as shown in Figure 24.6.

Figure 24.6
The NDS schema will be extended on this Tree and the product component files will be installed on this server.

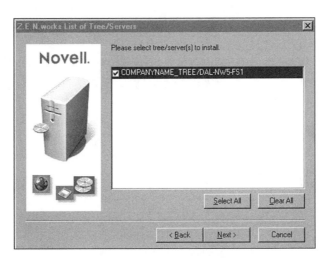

The list displayed in Figure 24.6 shows the NDS Tree and servers that you currently have a connection to. If you need to install the product component files on a server not listed here, just map a drive to that server and run the ZENworks custom installation at a later time, selecting just the necessary components to install on this server. You do not have to reinstall the Schema files for any other servers.

7. After you have selected the components to install, select Next (from Figure 24.6).

You are now prompted to select the language you want to install ZENworks in. After selecting the appropriate language, a summary screen is displayed showing the ZENworks components that have been selected for installation. Select Next from this summary screen to start copying the ZENworks program files. When the file copying process is complete, you are presented with the screen shown in Figure 24.7.

Figure 24.7
Preparing the NDS Tree for workstation registration.

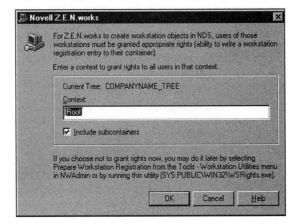

Figure 24.7 is necessary to prepare the NDS Tree so that users have the appropriate NDS container property rights for the workstation registration process (discussed later in this chapter). The default option (shown in Figure 24.7) gives these NDS property rights to all containers from the [Root] down. It is recommended that you leave this setting at its default so that workstation registration can occur at any container in the NDS Tree.

8. Select OK in Figure 24.7 to prepare the NDS Tree for workstation registration. At this point, the ZENworks installation is complete.

SAMPLE APPLICATION OBJECTS

The sample application objects that were created during the ZENworks installation can be viewed in NWAdmn32 (see Figure 24.8).

Figure 24.8
The 10 sample application objects were created in the same container as the server specified in Figure 24.6.

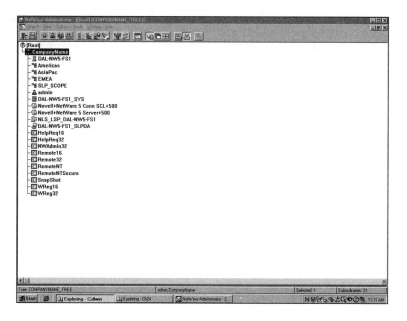

Although these objects are referred to as "sample," they are in fact fully functional application objects that can be used to deliver the remote control agent and workstation registration software (both of which will be discussed later in this chapter).

ZENWORKS POLICY PACKAGE OBJECTS

All ZENworks components (with the exception of NAL) are implemented with a policy package object, which is simply an NDS leaf object created in NWAdmn32. To create a policy package object in NWAdmn32

1. Select the container you want to create the policy package object in.

2. Select Create from the Object menu.

3. Select Policy Package from the Class of New Object list.

This brings up the screen as shown in Figure 24.9.

Note

This same three-step process is used to create all policy package objects that are needed. Therefore, these steps will not be repeated throughout this chapter.

Figure 24.9
Policy package objects are created with a wizard.

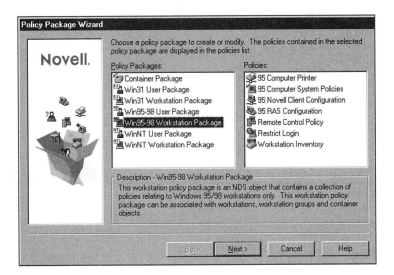

There are two types of policy package objects: user policy package objects and workstation policy package objects. Additionally, there are three different user and workstation policy package objects, one for each operating system that ZENworks supports (see Figure 24.9). Notice there is also a container package, which will be discussed later in this chapter.

The options available within each policy package object are referred to as policies. It is important that you realize that policy package objects contain individual policies within them. It is these policies that implement the majority of ZENworks features discussed at the beginning of this chapter. Also, when a policy package object is associated to a container (or another object), all policies that are enabled within the policy package object become the policies for those users or workstations. Figure 24.9 shows the policies available for a Windows 95/98 workstation policy package object.

Note

This chapter discusses the Windows 95/98 policy package objects, which are very similar in functionality to the Windows NT policy package objects. The Windows 3.1x policy package objects have limited functionality compared to Windows 95/98 and Windows NT.

REMOTE CONTROL

Assume that you want to deploy the remote control feature of ZENworks. The first thing to determine is the operating systems that need to be remote controlled, which will determine the types of policy package objects that need to be created. If you will remote control Windows 95/98 and Windows NT workstations, you will need to create both a Windows 95/98 and a Windows NT policy package object. The next thing to determine are the users (ultimately their workstations) that need to be remote controlled and where they exist in the NDS tree.

In this example, we assume that all users to be remote controlled run Windows 95/98 on their workstations and that these users are all located in Toronto. The remote control policy in ZENworks is enabled from within either a workstation or a user policy package object.

Tip #237 from
Sally

Use the remote control policy within a workstation policy package object; then, if exceptions are needed for an individual user, you can implement them with the remote control policy within a user policy package object. When "effective" policies are calculated, it is the one closest to the user that "wins." A user's effective policies can be determined from its "Effective Policies" property in NWAdmn32.

Therefore, we will create a Windows 95/98 workstation policy package object in the TOR.CANADA.AMERICAS.COMPANYNAME container. Selecting the Next button shown in Figure 24.9 brings up the screen as shown in Figure 24.10.

Figure 24.10
These two fields must be filled in to create a policy package object.

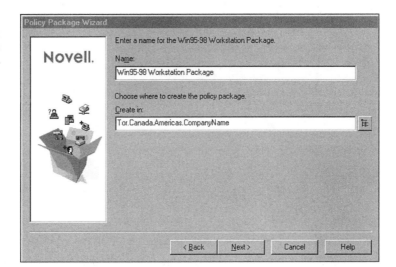

You should establish standard naming conventions for your policy package objects, making the names general (as shown in Figure 24.10). If you name this policy package object "Remote Control" and then at a later time decide to implement the workstation inventory policy, the name would be meaningless (although it could be renamed). You should create the policy package objects close to the users who will be accessing them.

Tip #238 from
Sally

Do not have users access a policy package object across a WAN link. Like other NDS leaf objects, policy package objects should be placed close to the users who need access to them and in a partition local to the users.

Selecting Next in Figure 24.10 will bring up a screen asking you which policies you want to enable within the policy package object. In this case, you would select the remote control policy. You can use NWAdmn32 later to change or add additional policies to this policy package object. The next screen that is brought up is shown in Figure 24.11.

Figure 24.11
A policy package object by default will be associated with the container that you create it in.

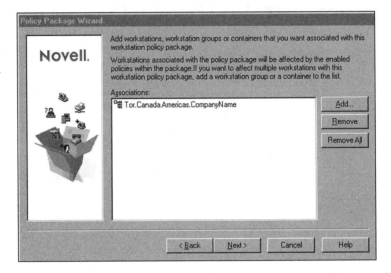

Workstation policy package objects can be associated with containers, workstation groups, or individual workstation objects. You can change the association from within Figure 24.11, or you can later use NWAdmn32 and make these associations through the workstation policy package object's "Associations" property.

Selecting Next from Figure 24.11 brings up a summary screen, showing the selections you have made. Select Finish from this summary screen to create the policy package object.

After the policy package object has been created, you double-click it to bring up its properties; then you double-click the remote control policy to bring up its properties (see Figure 24.12).

The default is that the users are prompted for permission before their workstations can be remote controlled, and users see a visible signal flashing on their screens the entire time their workstations are being remote controlled. For our example here, the Prompt User for Permission to Remote Control was disabled (refer to Figure 24.12).

Tip #239 from
Sally

The "Display Remote Control Agent Icon to User" checkbox shows the user that the remote control agent software is running. If you want to make sure that the user cannot unload the remote control agent software (which, of course, means that the workstation cannot be remote controlled), disable this option.

Figure 24.12
There is only one property tab for customizing a remote control policy.

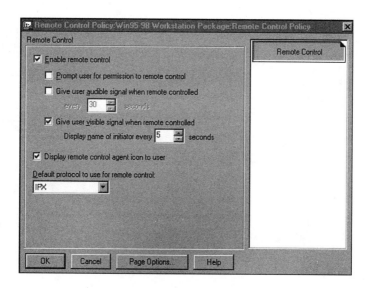

Now that the remote control policy has been set up and its workstation policy package object associated with the TOR container, the next step is to deploy the remote control agent software to the users' workstations. This software is required before a workstation can be remote controlled:

- WUSER.EXE is the Windows 3.1 Remote Control Agent software. It can be delivered via NAL (discussed later in this chapter) with the sample application object of Remote16 (refer back to Figure 24.8).

- ZENRC32.EXE is the Windows 95/98 Remote Control Agent software. It can be delivered via NAL with the sample application object of Remote32.

- NTSTACFG.EXE is the Windows NT Remote Control Agent software. It can be delivered via NAL with the sample application object of RemoteNT.

Tip #240 from
Sally

If a workstation currently has remote control agent software installed, you must remove this before deploying the remote control agents from ZENworks. The exception is that the remote control agent software from ManageWise 2.6 is compatible with ZENworks.

IMPORTING WORKSTATION OBJECTS

Any of the policies within a workstation policy package require that the workstation be imported into NDS. To import a workstation object, a user policy package must be created, with a workstation import policy enabled within it. You can follow the three steps discussed earlier for creating this policy package object, which will get you to the wizard as shown in Figure 24.13.

PART
V

CH
24

Figure 24.13
A workstation import policy will be created so that workstation objects can be imported into NDS.

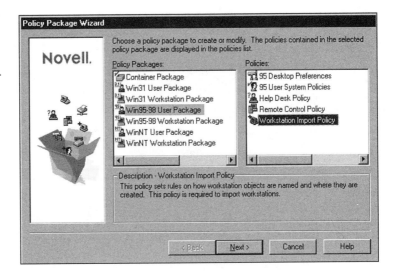

The following are the properties available for a workstation import policy (see Figure 24.14):

Figure 24.14
There are three property tabs for customizing a workstation import policy.

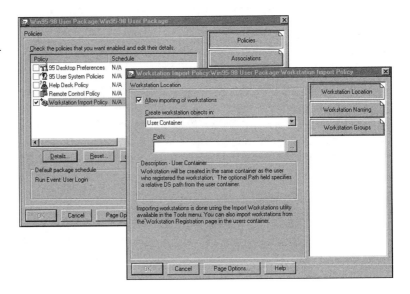

- **Workstation Location**—As shown in Figure 24.14, imported workstation objects are placed in the same container as the users (by default). Although creating containers dedicated to holding specific types of NDS leaf objects is generally not recommended, for workstation objects it is a good idea for the following reasons:

- The number of workstations imported will match the number of users. By keeping the workstations in a separate container, you can easily partition off this container if it exceeds the recommended number of objects per partition.

- Security can be easier. For example, you can easily give help desk people only the rights to remote control workstations in a dedicated Workstations container.

- Users do not need access to workstation objects (which is generally the reason it is recommended that you put resources in the same containers as users). Instead, the Novell Client software and network administrators (or help desk people) will access the workstation objects.

Therefore, for this example, we will set the workstation location property to the OU=Workstations container in Toronto (see Figure 24.15).

Figure 24.15
Workstation objects will be created (imported) in this selected container.

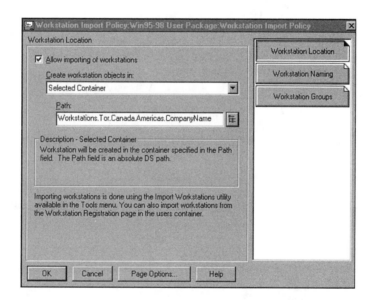

- **Workstation Naming**—The default name for an imported workstation object is the workstation's computer (NetBIOS) name and the workstation's network address (either the IPX or IP address, depending on the protocol being used).

Tip #241 from
Sally

Devise a standard naming scheme for your workstations' NetBIOS computer names. You can use NAL or another automated method to push this down to the workstations' registry. For example, you can use an asset tag number or some other number (or name) that uniquely identifies a workstation on the network. This will make it easier for help desk people to recognize the workstation object by name in NWAdmn32. Imported workstation objects can be renamed from within NWAdmn32; however, if the workstation object ever needs to be reimported, it will pick up the computer name as it is set in the workstation's registry. Also, before you reimport a workstation object, you must delete the existing workstation object first.

■ **Workstation Groups**—This is an NDS leaf object that is similar in functionality to normal group objects, except workstation groups have imported workstation objects as members. In the example we're discussing here, a workstation policy package object (with the remote control policy) was created and associated with TOR, which means it will apply to all workstations in TOR and subcontainers. If you need to create separate workstation policy package objects/remote control policies for different workstations in TOR, you could create workstation groups and associate with them.

Tip #242 from
Sally

> If you associate a policy package object with a workstation group, don't associate the same policy package object with the container. If you do, a workstation could get the policies in the package from both the container and the workstation group. In this case, no easy way exists to control which policy is the effective one.

After the workstation import policy has been set, you associate its user policy package object with the container where the users exist (in this example the TOR container). User policy package objects can be associated with containers, groups, or users. You make these associations through the user policy package object's Associations property.

Before the workstations can be remote controlled, a three-step workstation registration/import process must occur:

1. Workstation registration information gets recorded in NDS. This can happen in the following two ways:

● Users log in to the network, and the desktop management scheduler on their workstation is set to automatically run WSREG.DLL at login time. This is the default and is shown in Figure 24.16.

Figure 24.16
The desktop management scheduler runs the workstation registration agent by default each time the user logs in.

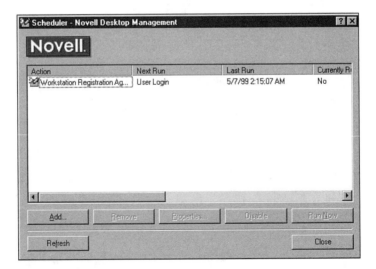

> **Note**
>
> Desktop management is a component of the ZENworks client and can be accessed from its icon in the Windows system tray (the icon is the calendar with the clock and pencil overlaid, as shown in Figure 24.16).

- If users will not have the desktop management component of ZENworks, you can run the workstation registration program from a login script: WSREG16.EXE (for Windows 3.1) or WSREG32.EXE (for Windows 95/98 or Windows NT). Another option is to use NAL to deliver the workstation registration program by using the sample application object WReg16 for Windows 3.1 or WReg32 for Windows 95/98 and Windows NT.

  Figure 24.17 shows PeterK's workstation object ready to be imported into NDS.

Figure 24.17
A workstation object is listed here after it has been registered in NDS.

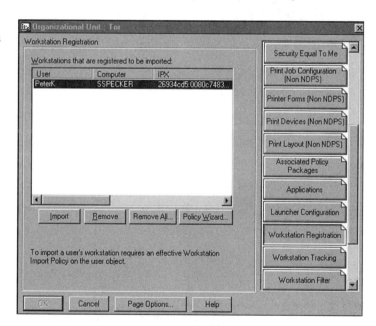

2. An administrator now imports the workstation into NDS. You can either select the Import option (shown in Figure 24.17) or use NWAdmn32's Tools, Import Workstations option. Additionally, the workstation import utility (SYS:PUBLIC\ WSIMPORT.EXE) could be placed into a login script.

> **Tip #243 from**
> *Sally*
>
> Sometimes a workstation fails to register properly (in the previous step 1) because it has already been registered in another tree. To unregister a workstation, run UNREG16.EXE or UNREG32.EXE at that workstation. This will clear out the "old" information in the registry under HKLM/Software/Novell/Workstation Manager/Identification. You will not be able to import a workstation until the registration in step 1 has been completed properly.

3. Allow workstations to re-register in the NDS tree. This second registration will automatically happen based on the method chosen in step 1. Workstations must register this second time so that NDS can discover the physical workstation represented by the workstation objects.

After this three-step process has been completed, workstation objects will appear in the tree (see Figure 24.18).

Figure 24.18
Workstation objects cannot be created with NWAdmn32; rather, they must be imported into NDS.

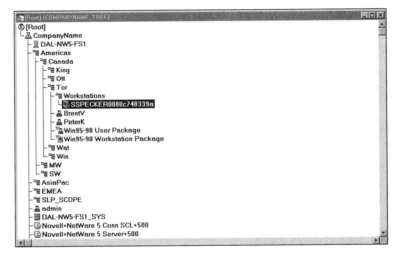

Notice that the workstation object for PeterK is confusingly named SSPECKER, which is why it was recommended that you set the NetBIOS computer name to something meaningful. Also notice that the workstation object was placed into the Workstations container because of the user import policy we created for it.

To remote control this workstation, simply select the workstation object and use the Tools, Remote Control option within NWAdmn32.

WORKSTATION OBJECT PROPERTIES

Workstation objects, like other NDS leaf objects in the Tree, contain properties that give these objects additional functionality. You will recognize many of these workstation object properties, because they are the same ones available for other NDS leaf objects. To see these properties, you simply double-click the workstation object. Some of the properties on a workstation object include the following:

■ **Operators**—A list of users that have rights to modify this workstation object, including the ability to remote control this workstation. The user that registered the workstation object (in step 1 of the three-step registration process discussed above) is automatically listed as an operator.

Tip #244 from
Sally

For security purposes, ensure that only the appropriate users are listed as workstation object operators.

- **User History**—A list of the last 10 users who have logged in from this workstation. This field is updated when the workstation registration program is run (discussed earlier).

- **Registered Time**—Shows the date and time that the workstation registration program was last run on this workstation.

- **Workstation Inventory**—Shows the hardware information for this workstation object, if it is associated with a workstation inventory policy.

POLICY PACKAGE OBJECTS DESIGN

PART

V

CH

24

The goal of ZENworks is to provide desktop standardization for users from the policies enabled within a policy package object. Ideally, then, one user and/or workstation policy package object should be created and associated with each physical site container. This way, one set of standard policies is delivered to all users at that site. At times, however, different policy settings are needed by different groups of users (therefore requiring different policy package objects).

So before deploying ZENworks, you should classify your users into "categories," corresponding to the policies and policy settings they require. Additionally, you should try to keep the number of categories to a minimum. As the number of categories increases, so does the management of these objects; at the same time, the goal of desktop standardization decreases.

For example, you could have a Group A category, comprising 80% of the users getting the same policies with the same settings. Group B could be for super users who need less restrictive policies. Group C could be for admin-type users who may get no restrictions at all. Three to five categories should be sufficient for the majority of companies.

Tip #245 from
Sally

If you use the ZENworks user or computer system policies to lock down a desktop (for example, to disable the Control Panel applet), it is important that your admin and possibly help desk users have a nonrestrictive policy. This is so that when they log in to a workstation to troubleshoot, their nonrestrictive policy overrides the registry settings (in this case to hide the Control Panel applet) that have been made on this workstation from a restricted policy. The Control Panel is something that the help desk will probably need to troubleshoot problems on workstations.

CONTAINER POLICY PACKAGE OBJECTS

A container policy package object contains just one policy—a search policy. The purpose of the search policy is to minimize WAN traffic by controlling how far the Novell Client desktop management component searches for associated policy packages (Search Level). A search policy can also control the order in which policies are searched; the default search order is object (user or workstation), group, and then container (Search Order).

You can follow the three steps discussed earlier to create container policy package objects. You should create and associate container policy package objects at each of your physical locations or site containers. When a container policy package object has been created, you can double-click this object in NWAdmn32 to bring up the search policy properties (see Figure 24.19).

Figure 24.19
There are two property tabs for customizing a search policy.

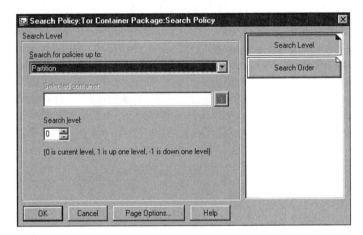

If your partitioning scheme follows your WAN links (as recommended in this book), you can then set the Search for Policies Up To option to Partition to avoid unnecessary traffic on WAN links, as shown in Figure 24.19. The default for this setting is to search to the [Root].

Also in Figure 24.19, the Search Level of 0 (which is the default) searches to whatever is specified in the Search for Policies Up To field—in this case, the Partition Root. A setting of 1 searches one level above the current level, where the current level is the level set in Search for Policies Up To. 2 searches two levels above the current level, and so on, and -1 limits the search up to, but not including, the current level.

For the example here, the container policy package object at the TOR container ensures that all users in Toronto do not cross WAN links searching for associated policy package objects.

IMPLEMENTING OTHER ZENWORKS POLICIES

When you use any of the other policies within ZENworks, you can follow a similar process to the one described above for setting up remote control. Remember that any policies within a workstation policy package object require you to follow the above steps for importing workstation objects. Now all you need to do is experiment with ZENworks policies and implement the ones specific to your environment!

NOVELL APPLICATION LAUNCHER (NAL)

NAL is the server-to-client software distribution component in ZENworks. NAL allows network administrators to create application objects (which are simply leaf objects in the NDS Tree) that represent the software applications (such as Corel WordPerfect or Microsoft Word for Windows) to be distributed to users. One application object should be created for each software application to be distributed. Within the application object, you set up the application's dependencies, such as the following:

- A drive mapping or UNC path to the application's executable file
- The operating systems that can run the application
- The minimum RAM or hard drive space needed to run this application
- Any registry or INI settings necessary to run the application
- The actual program files necessary to run the application

All these dependencies are implemented with an application object's properties, and, as you will see in this section, many other properties can be set to customize how an application is distributed to users.

After application objects are set up, the network administrator simply associates these application objects to the appropriate NDS container, group, or user. When a user logs in, these applications are distributed based on the associations made.

NAL completely leverages NDS, meaning that all the information associated with an application object (such as the dependencies listed above, with the exception of program files, are stored within the NDS database). Additionally, all NAL administration is done within NWAdmn32.

NAL allows you to "pull" or "push" software to workstations. Pull distribution surfaces an application icon on the user's desktop. Clicking this icon either launches the application or installs the application on the workstation only (depending on the property you set on the application object, which will be discussed later in this section).

Push distribution does the same as pull distribution except that it is done without user intervention. In NAL terminology, this is called a "Force Run." This works well in scenarios where certain software needs to reside on workstations, such as operating system patches, client-side electronic mail software, and so on. It is also useful when you want a certain application to automatically be run on a user's workstation after login.

A user can use two utilities to see and launch NAL-delivered applications: the NAL Window (SYS:PUBLIC\NAL.EXE) or the NAL Explorer (SYS:PUBLIC\NALEXPLD.EXE).

The NAL Window only displays NAL-delivered applications in a window, whereas the NAL Explorer can display NAL-delivered applications in a window, the Start menu, the Windows Desktop, or the Windows system tray (or any combination of these four).

Which of these two user interfaces you choose to use is a personal preference decision and is also dependent on the client operating system; that is, the NAL Explorer can be run only on Windows 95/98 or Windows NT 4+ workstations. You generally would not use both on the same workstation. Many network administrators prefer the NAL Explorer because it allows you to distribute applications to a user's Start menu, from where Windows 95/98 and Windows NT users are used to launching their applications.

Tip #246 from _Sally_	To automatically bring up the NAL Window or NAL Explorer for users, place #NAL.EXE or #NALEXPLD.EXE in the container or user login script.

USING NAL TO DISTRIBUTE A SIMPLE APPLICATION

After ZENworks is installed, you are ready to start distributing applications to users. For this example, we will distribute the Novell Filer utility, which is a "simple" application— that is, an application that does not require any registry changes, INI file changes, or DLLs to be present at the workstation in order to run the application. To create an application object in NWAdmn32, complete the following steps:

1. Select the container you want to create the application object in.
2. Select Create from the Object menu.
3. Select Application from the Class of New Object list.

This brings up the screen as shown in Figure 24.20.

Figure 24.20
A simple application object requires no AOT (Application Object Template) file.

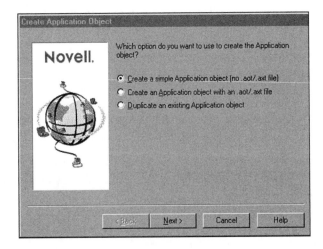

From Figure 24.20, select the Create a Simple Application Object option. This brings up the screen shown in Figure 24.21.

Figure 24.21
These are the only two required properties needed for creating an application object.

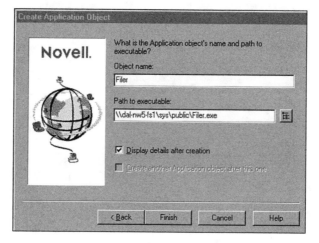

Use standard naming conventions for your application objects. Use UNC naming for the path to the executable file so that the user does not need a drive mapping to execute this application.

After the Filer application object has been created, the only other thing that must be done is to associate this application object to the users that need it. Associations is a property of all application objects. As with other leaf objects, the properties of an application object can be displayed by simply double-clicking the object in NWAdmn32. For our example here, we will associate the Filer application object with the TOR container. Now, when any user in the TOR container (or containers beneath) logs in, they will get the Filer application, as shown in Figure 24.22.

Figure 24.22
This is how NAL-delivered applications appear in the NAL Window.

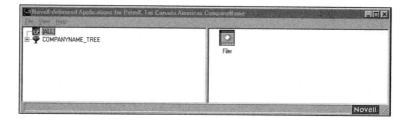

APPLICATION OBJECT PROPERTIES

An application object has 24 properties, which can be customized for additional application functionality. Double-click the Filer application object to see its available properties, which are shown in Figure 24.23.

PART
V
CH
24

Figure 24.23
This shows a partial listing of an application object's properties.

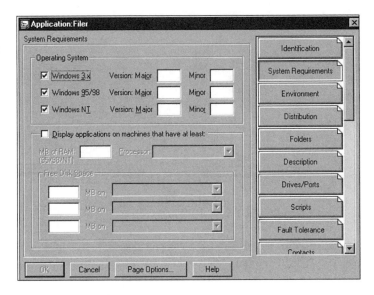

The following are some of the more common application object properties (and suggestions for their use):

- **Identification**—Contains properties controlling what the user sees and how an application is distributed. Application Icon Title shows the application object name as it will appear to the user in the NAL Window or NAL Explorer. The default is the name you used when you created the application object; however, this can be changed and can be different from the name of the application object in the tree.

- **Path to Executable File**—Points to where an application's executable is located. This can be edited if you later move the application to another location. Additionally, this option will distribute any registry settings, INI settings, and so on that are part of the application the first time the user launches this application; subsequent launches will simply execute the application. Install Only is mutually exclusive with Path to Executable File. This option is used when there isn't an application to execute—for example, installing a service pack on a workstation.

- **Run Once**—Run Once, which needs to be installed only once. When this option is set, the application object disappears from the NAL Window or NAL Explorer after it has been run once. In this scenario, you might also consider setting this service pack application object up as a "Force Run" (from the Associations property) so that it runs once without user intervention.

- **System Requirements**—Controls the operating system on which the NAL-delivered application appears (such as Windows 3.1x, Windows 95/98, and/or Windows NT). This property can also control application delivery based on the type of processor, the amount of physical RAM (on Windows 95/98 and Windows NT only), and free disk space.

Tip #247 from
Sally

> System Requirements is a good property to check out for troubleshooting purposes if a NAL-delivered application is not appearing on a certain workstation.

- **Environment**—Controls how the application is launched. Command Line Parameters can be used for special startup switches for the application's executable, and Working Directory sets the path to the application's working directory. Enable Error Logging to File allows you to see applications that failed to launch or install. No status is tracked here except for errors (although this will be enhanced with ZENworks 2.0). Clean Up Network Resources cleans up resources allocated, such as drives mapped, printer ports captured, and connections made to file systems for accessing the application. In essence, NAL is cleaning up licensed connections when the application is exited.

- **Distribution**—Enables you to control what happens during distribution of the application. Reboot enables you to control if and when a workstation reboot should occur after an application has been installed. Version Stamp is a tool to assist with upgrading applications. This stamps the workstation with a text string (in the registry) which represents the version of the application that was distributed (this text string may or may not have anything to do with the actual version of the product).

  For example, you could type in 1.0 to coincide with the first distribution of this application. Then, if you later change some property of the application object, you could enter a different string (such as 2.0). Because the 2.0 version stamp will not match the 1.0 stamp previously entered in the workstation's registry, a new distribution will occur the next time the user launches the application. This process would not need to be used if the application was set up as Distribute Always. Distribute Always forces a distribution, along with any registry or INI settings, every time a user launches the application, as compared to only the first time they launch an application. Distribute Always is useful when you want to ensure that certain registry or INI settings are present or updated every time an application is run, not just the first time.

- **Drives/Ports Property**—Any drive mappings or printer ports captured here are set when a user launches the application, and they are automatically cleaned up when a user exits the application, assuming the Clean Up Network Resources option (discussed above) is on. This is useful for eliminating unnecessary licensed connections after an application is exited.

- **Administrator Notes Property**—An informational text field (not viewable by users) that can be used to track changes made to the application object or any other special requirements that are necessary for proper functioning of this application.

- **Registry Settings Property**—Contains the registry settings that will be made when this application is distributed to workstations. snAppShot (discussed later in this section) automatically fills in the necessary registry settings required for an application. You can, of course, customize these at any time. Also, if a registry setting is needed by all workstations in the network, you could use NAL to distribute it by using this property.

- **INI Files Property**—Contains the INI files that will be customized when this application is distributed to workstations. snAppShot (discussed later in this section) automatically fills in this property if an application requires INI settings.

- **Application Files Property**—Contains a list of the files required to run the application. snAppShot (discussed later in this section) automatically fills in the necessary files required by an application.

- **Macros**—A very powerful NAL feature that enables you to customize and "generalize" the information that gets distributed to users. For example, if you were distributing an application with NAL and the 200 files necessary to run this application were located on the DAL-NW5-FS1 server, you could create a macro called "Install_Dir," where the value of this macro was `\\dal-nw5-fs1\vol1\apps`. Each of the 200 files to be distributed (in the Application Files property just discussed) would then contain the `Install_Dir` macro name as part of its complete filename—instead of using the complete "DOS-type" filename. Then, if you moved these 200 application files from the DAL-NW5-FS1 server to DAL-NW5-FS2, you would simply change the value of the `Install_Dir` macro to point to this new server. You would not need to manually change the filename on all 200 application files.

- **Text Files Property**—Contains settings for files such as `CONFIG.SYS` and `AUTOEXEC.BAT` (discovered by snAppShot). As with the four previous properties just discussed, you can manually edit or create the settings in this property.

- **Icons/Shortcuts Property**—Lists the icons (discovered by snAppShot) that will be created at the workstation when this application is distributed.

Tip #248 from *Sally*	You should remove any icons or shortcuts to ensure that users do not run an application outside of NAL. This is especially important if you are using Software Metering, which currently only meters NAL-delivered applications.

DISTRIBUTING A COMPLEX APPLICATION

A complex application is one that needs to have registry or INI settings enabled, DLLs present, and so on before the application can successfully launch. The majority of Windows-based applications (such as Word or Excel) fall into this category. If you are very familiar with your application and know which settings need to be enabled and which files need to be distributed, you can simply create the application object (as just discussed in the "simple" application distribution example above) and manually add this information to the object's appropriate property settings. However, most people will not want to do this manually, which is why the snAppShot utility is provided with ZENworks.

The snAppShot utility (`SYS:PUBLIC\SNAPSHOT\SNAPSHOT.EXE`) will do the following when executed:

- Take a snapshot of the machine you're running snAppShot on (a "before" picture).

- Ask you to install the application you want to distribute. During this process, you can make any other changes necessary to customize this application for users. Because the snAppShot utility is running, it will "capture" these changes you are making.

- Take another snapshot of the machine to discover the changes made by the application's installation program and any manual changes you may have made (an "after" picture).

- Generate an Application Object Template (AOT) with the changes between the before and after snapshots. An AOT is simply a file that is read and edited when you make any property changes to this application object in NWAdmin32.

This snAppShot-generated AOT file is then used when creating the application object in NWAdmin32 (see Figure 24.24).

Figure 24.24
To create a complex application object, select the Create an Application Object with an .aot/.axt option and then select the path to where this .aot/.axt file is located.

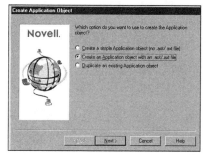
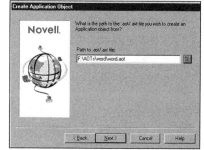

All the snAppShot-discovered application dependencies (for example, registry settings, INI file entries, DLLs, and application files) become part of the application object (as discussed previously). In addition, you can set any of the other properties as appropriate. The only difference between a simple and a complex application is the latter uses an AOT file (generated from snAppShot) to assist you in creating the application object.

Tip #249 from
Sally

You should set up a dedicated, "clean" workstation (that is, one that has never had the application installed on it) for using snAppShot. Additionally, you should thoroughly test this process in a lab environment before actual implementation.

NAL DESIGN CONSIDERATIONS

As with any other NDS object resource in the tree, you should place application objects close to the users who will be accessing them, ideally in a partition local to the users. It is not recommended that users access application objects across a WAN link. If you create an application object that you want users in 10 containers to access, you can use the Duplicate an Existing Application Object option to copy the application object to these 10 sites (refer to Figure 24.20).

Tip #250 from
Gally

The Duplicate an Existing Application Object feature does not copy the association's property. In addition, this option will not copy the application files (which are stored on the NetWare volume specified during the snAppShot process). You will need to copy these files to the appropriate volume and reset any other application properties that reference this location. ZENworks 2.0 will make this process easier by virtue of server-to-server software distribution.

The Launcher Configuration property (on containers and users) can be used to control how far the application launcher (either `NAL.EXE` or `NALEXPLD.EXE`) looks for launcher configuration settings and how far it looks for container-associated application objects. This functionality is similar to the search policy within a container policy package object discussed previously, which controls how far to look for policy package objects.

For each of your site containers (representing a partition), you should set the launcher configuration property of Top Object to this site container. This Top Object setting ensures that the application launcher does not go above this setting when looking for launcher configuration settings on other containers. As shown in Figure 24.25, the Top Object has been set to the TOR container.

Figure 24.25
Launcher configuration is a property on container and user objects.

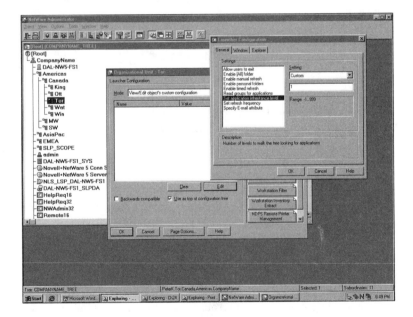

If containers are present beneath TOR, you could also set their Top Object to TOR (for centrally managing launcher configuration settings) or you could have these subcontainers use their own unique launcher configuration settings by setting the Top Object to that subcontainer. The key is to not set a container's Top Object to a container across a WAN link, which can dramatically slow down the loading of the application launcher.

The Set Application Inheritance Level value (also shown in Figure 24.25) determines how far the application launcher searches for container-associated applications; it currently does not control the searching for user- and/or group-associated application objects. In Figure 24.25, the TOR container was set with a value of 1 (the default), meaning the application launcher will look at the immediate container for container-associated application objects. A value of 0 means that the application launcher will not look for any container-associated application objects; a value of 2 means that the application launcher looks at the container up two levels; a value of 3 looks up three levels, and so on. A value of –1 means the application launcher looks up to the [Root] for any container-associated application objects.

Tip #251 from	Use the –1 (search to top of tree) setting sparingly. It should realistically be set just in LAN-only networks. Also, if a container-associated application object is not showing up at a workstation, ensure that the application inheritance level setting is properly defined.
Sally	

Four other launcher configuration property settings (shown in Figure 24.25) can be used to control how the application launcher searches:

- **Enable Manual Refresh**—The default setting is Yes; therefore, if a user presses the F5 (Refresh) key, the application launcher will look for user- and group-based associations up to the [Root]. However, the application launcher looks for container-based associations based on the setting in Top Object. Again, no way currently exists to restrict the searching for user-based associations up to [Root], except by eliminating user-based associations altogether or by disabling this Manual Refresh feature. You can eliminate the group searching completely by using the following setting.

- **Read Groups for Applications**—The default is Yes, meaning that the application launcher will search for group-associated application objects up to the [Root]. This setting can (and should) be turned off only if you are not using group-associated application objects. Again, no way currently exists to restrict how far up the tree the application launcher looks for group-based associations, so you may want to restrict group associations altogether.

- **Enable Timed Refresh**—The default is No and it is recommended that you leave this setting disabled.

- **Set Refresh Frequency**—The default is one hour (3600 seconds). This setting is effectively disabled when the Enable Timed Refresh setting above is left at its default of No.

Tip #252 from	It is very important that you appropriately set the Top Object and Set Application Inheritance Level values. Without these settings, the application launcher can be slow to launch.
Sally	

Also notice in Figure 24.25 that three tabs are present on the launcher configuration:

- General (which applies both to the NAL Window and NAL Explorer)
- Window (which applies just to the NAL Window)
- Explorer (which applies just to the NAL Explorer)

NAL also adds an Application Launcher Tools option to the Tools menu in NWAdmn32. With these NAL tools, you can do things such as export an entire application object, or parts thereof, to an AXT file. An AXT file converts the AOT (which is only readable by NWAdmn32) into a text file that can be edited and later reimported into NDS.

A network administrator can also highlight a user in NWAdmn32 and then select the Show Inherited Applications option from within Application Launcher Tools to see what applications a user will receive via NAL.

SOFTWARE METERING

Before discussing Software Metering, we need to discuss Novell Licensing Services (NLS). NLS is used to monitor and manage license usage for NLS-aware applications, such as NetWare 5. The Licensing Service Provider (LSP) is enabled on a server by loading NLSLSP.NLM. NLSLSP.NLM runs on NetWare 4.11 (with Support Pack 6) and later servers and when loaded, creates an object in NDS—for example, NLS_LSP_HOU-NW5-FS1 (look ahead to Figure 24.26). LSP takes requests for a license (or release of a license) from NLS-aware applications. The NLS responses to license requests are typically either "Yes, there is a license for you," or "No, there are no licenses for you." The NLS client library passes the responses from NLS to the NLS-aware application, which determines if the application can be run.

Note | NetWare 5 licenses are tracked with NLS. However, even though NLS is available for NetWare 4.11 servers, it does not track NetWare 4.11 license usage; rather, it is used for tracking NLS-aware applications such as BorderManager or Software Metering with NAL.

ZENworks Software Metering leverages NLS to allow you to manage and monitor the usage of any non–NLS-aware application that is distributed through NAL. NAL is the NLS-enabled application that sends the license requests to NLS prior to launching software-metered applications; depending on the response back from NLS, NAL either launches or denies access to launch the application. Software Metering uses the same NLSLSP.NLM that is running on NetWare 4.11 and later servers.

CREATING A METERED CERTIFICATE

Software Metering uses a *metered certificate* NDS object to track license usage for NAL-delivered applications. These objects are created in NWAdmn32 by selecting Tools, Install License, Create Metered Certificate. The Create Metered Certificate dialog box appears (see Figure 24.26).

Tip #253 from
Gally

The Install License Certificate and Install Envelope options available from NWAdmn32's Tools menu allow you to license your NetWare 5 server from within NWAdmn32.

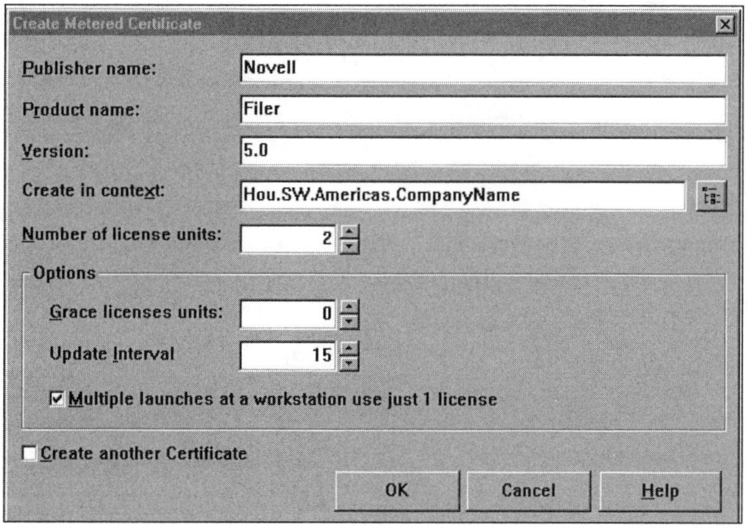

Figure 24.26
Creating a metered certificate to license the Filer application object in HOU.

PART

V

CH

24

In Figure 24.26, Novell is the publisher of the product Filer Version 5.0. If a period (.) is used as part of the version number, the Product License Container object (which is automatically created and contains the metered certificate object) will add a backslash to its NDS name. The metered certificate for Filer will be created in the HOU.SW.AMERICAS. COMPANYNAME container. This copy of Filer will be licensed only for two concurrent usages with no grace license units allowed; however, if the same user launches Filer from a single workstation, this will only count as one license unit. LSP will poll this metered certificate every 15 minutes to see if there have been updates to it. If you set the Update Interval to 0, LSP will not poll the metered certificate at all.

The Filer metered certificate now appears in its Product License Container object, as shown in Figure 24.27.

The last thing that needs to be done is to bring up property information for the Filer application object. When Software Metering is installed, all application objects will have a property called Software Metering. From this property, enable the checkbox next to the Use Novell Licensing and Metering for this Application option and use the browser to select the metered certificate Novell+Filer+5\.0 created in the previous example.

Now when a user executes the NAL-delivered Filer, the usage information will be tracked in NDS, and users will be bound to the license limits set on the metered certificate for Filer.

Figure 24.27
A Product License
Container object is
automatically created
to hold the metered
certificates you create.

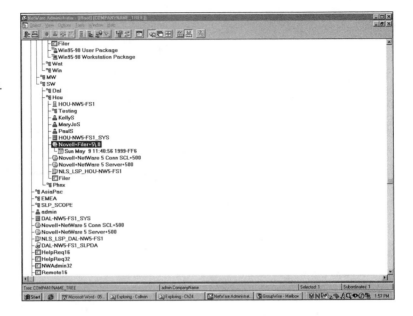

MONITORING USAGE ON A METERED CERTIFICATE

To monitor the usage of a metered certificate, simply double-click the metered certificate object in NWAdmn32 to bring up its five properties. From here you can get general information on the certificate, such as the number of licenses installed. You can also see the users who are currently using the metered software and who the owner of the certificate is (that is, the user who created it). You can also make a file server assignment to this metered application. After you make file server assignments, only those objects that have been assigned to the license certificates can use the license. Lastly, you can see general policy information on this certificate.

Tip #254 from
Gally

If you want to increase the license count on a metered application, create another metered certificate for the application with the same name. After this is done, you will see two metered certificates in the product license container, and their license counts will be cumulative.

The properties available on the product license container allow you to see historical information on the metered software, such as the highest number of licenses used as of a certain date and time. This information is stored in the NDS database for 15 months and then "recycled" on a first-in, first-out basis. Additionally, the NLS Manager utility (SYS:PUBLIC\WIN32\NLSMAN32.EXE) can be used to generate reports and view information on all licensed products in the NDS Tree (see Figure 24.28).

Figure 24.28
Licensing Usage
Report.

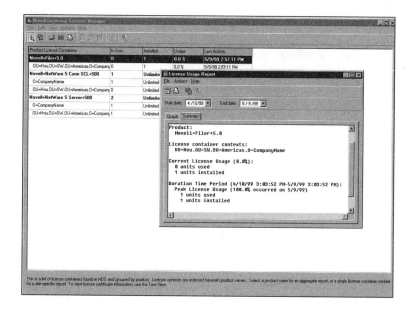

Finally, NLS is enabled for the Simple Network Management Protocol (SNMP) via the NLSTRAP.NLM. Therefore, an SNMP-based management console (such as ManageWise) can receive alerts (traps) when a license count has been exceeded, among other NLS traps that are available.

NLS DESIGN CONSIDERATIONS

To make use of Software Metering, users must either attach to an LSP server or the LSP server object must exist in a context higher in the tree than their user object. Because all NetWare 5 servers provide licensing services, a user connected to a NetWare 5 server will have the necessary access to NLS.

You can set up a fault-tolerant NLS system simply by making sure users have a connection to one or more of the LSP servers.

The location of an application's executable file is not important to ZENworks Software Metering. An application can be launched locally from a workstation or from a file server and still be metered. The key for Software Metering is that an application is delivered to the user through NAL.

With little effort on your part, NLS and ZENworks Software Metering can help you to keep track of the software licenses scattered around your network. Additionally, Software Metering can also help you monitor use of software applications for which license-usage tracking is not required.

PROJECT: RESEARCH THE NET

ZENworks is a powerful and full-featured product. To learn more about ZENworks, in your Internet browser, bookmark the site `http://www.novell.com/coolsolutions/zenworks`, which contains a wealth of articles, FAQs, tips, tricks, and ideas for using all aspects of ZENworks. Specifically check out these articles that relate to the topics discussed in this chapter:

- `http://www.novell.com/coolsolutions/zenworks/basics.html`.

  Two articles are in the "Back to Basics" section: "NDS Design for ZENworks" and "How to Register a Workstation."

- `http://www.novell.com/coolsolutions/zenworks/vault.html`.

  Many articles are listed in "The Vault" about the Application Launcher, Application Objects, the ZENworks Client, Using Macros, snAppShot, and so on.

- `http://developer.novell.com`

  Refer to the January 1998 AppNote, "A Practical Guide to using Novell Application Launcher (NAL) 2.01." Although slightly outdated, much of the information here can be applied to ZENworks 1.1 (NAL 2.7). This AppNote goes into depth on using the snAppShot utility; the only difference is that the interface for snAppShot has changed slightly with ZENworks 1.1.

Also, look at the properties that were set for the sample application objects in NWAdmn32, especially the macros. This should give you a good idea about how macros are implemented.

Maintenance and Troubleshooting

CHAPTER **25**

DATA ARCHIVING AND BACKUP

In this chapter

DATA ARCHIVING REQUIREMENTS

Data is one of the most valuable assets of any computerized organization. In fact, much of what these organizations do today is represented by computer data: financial transactions, research and development, manufacturing, inventory, materials ordering systems, accounting, taxes, artwork, literature, music, graphics, telephone records, and so on. Computer data has become the lifeblood of many modern organizations. The value of this data to an organization cannot be overemphasized.

To preserve the lifeblood of your computerized company, you need to understand the basic data archiving and retrieval requirement of your NetWare 5 server. The data backup system must be capable of backing up and restoring NetWare data including the NDS, the file system, and its associated information. It is best if you have a system that performs the backup without human intervention. Even these basic requirements require some fairly sophisticated technology. Beyond the basic requirements, however, are many options that might be appropriate for your organization.

THE NETWARE FILE SYSTEM

Archiving and restoring data from a NetWare 5 server is not as simple as it sounds. The NetWare file system—the formats and methods NetWare uses to order and update file data—is very complex. Such complexity is the result of NetWare's support for different file formats, including DOS; Macintosh; UNIX; long names used by OS/2, Windows 9x, and Windows NT; and also the result of NetWare's multiuser, multitasking file access routines.

Any archiving system you use to back up and restore data from a NetWare server must be aware of the intricacies of the NetWare file system and must handle these intricacies, plus errors and other conditions that might arise during the normal use of the file system. NetWare-specific items, featured by archiving systems (for both backup and restoration operations), include the following:

- Support for NetWare-specific file attributes
- Support NetWare name spaces—non-DOS file formats such as UNIX, Macintosh, OS/2 HPFS, NT, and so on
- Awareness of file concurrence issues, including file and record locking
- Support for NetWare 5 background file compression and the capability to handle compressed files
- Awareness of NetWare 5 data migration system, and the capability to recognize migrated files

One additional consideration for NetWare 5:

- Does the backup solution support the new Novell Storage Services (NSS) format?

Many archiving systems on the market today that are certified for NetWare 5 handle most, if not all, of the items listed previously. However, many archiving systems on the market today are not designed for use with NetWare at all. For example, if you attempt to archive NetWare 5 data using a backup program written for DOS, you will not only experience errors backing up file system data, but you could corrupt existing files when you attempt to restore archived data. The same thing can happen if you apply a backup program written for UNIX, Macintosh, or any other workstation operating system, to a NetWare 5 file system.

NetWare-Specific File Attributes

Every file stored on a NetWare server contains 32 bits of file attributes. These file attribute bits are a superset of the 8 bits of DOS file attributes you might be familiar with. In other words, NetWare has three times the number of file attribute bits as DOS. Many of these extra file attribute bits are used internally by NetWare and are invisible to users. However, some of the file attribute bits that are visible to users include the Execute Only bit, the Immediate Purge bit, and so on. A back-up system written for DOS recognizes the DOS-specific file attributes of a NetWare file, but remains ignorant of the other NetWare file attribute bits, some of which are critical to security implementation of NetWare.

In addition, NetWare files have more information associated with them than DOS files. This extra information includes the owner of the file, users with access privileges to the file (trustee list), the last access data for the file, and so on. Much of this additional information is useful to the archiving process. However, to make use of the full range of information NetWare associates with a file, the archiving system must be written specifically for NetWare.

Name Space Support

Name spaces are duplicate directory entries that contain non-DOS file format information. For example, UNIX name space directory entries contain the long UNIX filename, UNIX file attribute bits, and other information required by the UNIX file format. Macintosh name space entries contain the long Macintosh filename, Finder information (the Finder is the desktop used by the Macintosh graphical interface), and a pointer to the Macintosh file's resource fork.

> **Note**
>
> Mac files have two portions—the data fork and the resource fork. The data fork, as the name implies, is where the actual data is stored. The resource fork contains information such as the icon that represents the file type.

Because of the way name spaces work, a file's data is stored on the NetWare file system *only once*. However, that file has a separate directory entry for each file format supported. On a NetWare 5 server with the UNIX and Macintosh name spaces loaded, for example, every file has three directory entries: the standard NetWare (DOS) directory entry, a UNIX directory entry, and a Macintosh directory entry.

An archiving system which does not support name spaces is capable of backing up and restoring all the files on a NetWare server supporting multiple name spaces. However, all the information stored in the name space directory entries will be lost. This means, for example, that DOS clients will not notice anything missing, but Macintosh and UNIX clients will see a truncated name for each restored file and that any special file attributes native to Mac and UNIX are lost.

Another reason to be extremely cautious of backup systems that are not NetWare aware is binary (compiled) or executable files. Binary files with file formats other than that of your backup system are completely unusable when restored. The backup system used records these files in its own binary form and restores them again in that form. The files are then completely corrupt and unusable. For example, if a Macintosh application file for Microsoft Word is backed up to a DOS floppy disk using the DOS BACKUP command, the file would be unusable on restoration. Although some applications are available for both Mac and DOS, the Macintosh application files are not necessarily identical in their binary forms.

It is critical then, that any archiving system you purchase support all the name spaces supported by your NetWare 5 server. Currently, NetWare 5's list of supported name spaces includes DOS, AFP (Macintosh), UNIX, and long names used by OS/2 HPFS and Windows 9x/NT.

AWARENESS OF FILE CONGRUENCY ISSUES

File congruency issues include how NetWare handles file and record locking, file sharing, file opening and closing, and file reading and writing. The NetWare file system is designed to enable many users to open the same file concurrently. This means that NetWare must control the order in which users having a file open are allowed to read information from and write data to that file. NetWare provides extensive programming interfaces to the file system that allow an archiving system to finish its job, even when other users have files open and are reading from and writing to such files.

An archiving system that is aware of file congruency issues can do the following:

■ Archive opened files
■ Prevent users from disrupting the archiving process by opening files that are in the process of being backed up
■ Archive system files, including NDS information
■ Archive online databases

Without awareness of NetWare's file congruency controls, an archiving system will be incapable of performing any of the tasks listed previously. In the old days, many archiving systems required that you down the NetWare server and close its bindery before performing a back up. There is no reason why you should have to put up with that kind of trouble today.

> **Note**
>
> You'll generally find that the capability to back up open files is not part of the core features of a backup utility but is available as an add-on option. Therefore, when evaluating a backup solution for your network, if you don't see open-file backup as a feature, check to see whether the vendor has an "open file manager" agent add-on. The same is true for backing up databases, such as Oracle–a database-specific agent is required.

AWARENESS OF FILE COMPRESSION

NetWare 5's background file compression process raises some interesting problems for archiving systems. For instance, when archiving a compressed file, does the backup software store the file in its compressed form or its uncompressed form? (And conversely, when restoring a file.) When scanning compressed files for archiving, does the backup software know the size of such files when they are uncompressed? Does the backup software know when a file is compressed or uncompressed? These and other questions must be answered in order for the archiving system to work correctly with the NetWare 5 file system.

Tip #255 from
Peter

You can find out which files–you have on a NetWare volume–are compressed using the NDIR or the FLAG NetWare utility. In the output, compressed files are flagged with the lowercase letters *co*, such as shown in this sample output from the FLAG utility:

```
F:\JAVA> flag
Files          = The name of the files found
Directories    = The name of the directories found
DOS Attr       = The DOS attributes for the specified file
NetWare Attr   = The NetWare attributes for the specified file or directory
Status         = The current status of migration and compression for a file
                 or directory
Owner          = The current owner of the file or directory
Mode           = The search mode set for the current file

Files                   DOS Attr NetWare Attr         Status Owner          Mode
- - - - - - - - - - - - - - - - - - - - - - - - - - - - - - - - - - - - - - - - - - -
COPYRI~1                [Rw---A] [----------------]          .[Supervisor]  N/A
LICENSE.TXT             [Rw----] [----------------] Co       .[Supervisor]  N/A
README.TXT              [Rw----] [----------------] Co       .[Supervisor]  N/A

Directories             NetWare Attr    Owner
- - - - - - - - - - - - - - - - - - - - - - - - - - - - - - - - - - - - - - - - - - -
BIN                     [-----------] .[Supervisor]
LIB                     [-----------] .[Supervisor]
BEANS                   [-----------] .[Supervisor]
CLASSES                 [-----------] .[Supervisor]
NWGFX                   [-----------] .[Supervisor]
README                  [-----------] .[Supervisor]
```

Tip #256 from	You can get a list of all compressed files on a NetWare volume using NDIR *.* /FO /COMP /S; and if the volume has non-DOS name spaces, add /LONG or /MAC as appropriate.
Peter	

Most archiving systems on the market today that are designed for NetWare handle NetWare 5 compressed files in the following manner:

- Backup software identifies compressed files by inspecting the NetWare file attribute bits.
- Backup software (optionally) decompresses files before archiving them.
- When restoring files that were compressed, the backup software restores the file in an uncompressed state, and then causes NetWare to compress the file.

Caution	With many backup software programs, when compressed files are restored to a NetWare volume, that volume must support compression, or else the files will not be restored.

One issue to consider is how much space the files take up when you restore them in an uncompressed form. Some backup systems today that support NetWare 5 are not yet aware of data compression. They simply read the file the same way any NetWare user would read it. You might find that the 1GB of data (as stored on the NetWare volume) you archived consumed 1.7GB of tape space. This can be a real problem when it comes time to restore if the total volume space you have available is only 1.5GB. At a minimum it causes you to spend a great deal of time doing the restore. At the worst the program could decompress each file before it archives it and could leave it in that expanded form after the copy is obtained. This action alone would fill your hard drive very quickly.

If you enable compression on your NetWare volumes, how your backup solution handles compressed file should be high on your list of concerns when evaluating a backup solution.

AWARENESS OF FILE MIGRATION

The NetWare 5 Data Migration feature is a mechanism whereby files can reside on secondary offline or near-line storage media, yet still remain available via the standard NetWare file system. For example, a large database file resides on a specially formatted optical disk, yet appears as a standard NetWare file when users issue the DIR command. When a user attempts to open the database file, the Data Migration system retrieves the file from the optical drive and copies the file's data to the NetWare volume. NetWare then opens the file and provides the user with access to the graphical image. When the user is finished with the file, NetWare copies the database file back to the optical drive and removes the file from the NetWare volume, but retains the file's directory entry. As a result, the file remains accessible to users in the standard fashion (albeit a little more slowly), even though the file is stored on a specially formatted optical drive.

The Data Migration system consists of special NetWare file attributes and a low-level programming interface. Developers provide specially formatted offline or near-line media (such as optical, tape, CD-ROM, magneto-optical, and so on.) and NLMs for controlling the movement of data between the NetWare file system and the specially formatted media. Data Migration is designed specifically for multimedia image databases, but also has applications for leading-edge data archiving, journalized file systems, and very large databases.

An archiving system for NetWare 4.x must be aware of the following issues regarding the Data Migration system:

- How to recognize migrated files
- How to gain information about the media storing migrated files
- When archiving migrated files, how to detect and recover from migration-related errors
- When storing migrated files, how to detect and recover from migration-related errors

Novell released the Data Migration programming interface to third parties prior to the release of NetWare 4.0. However, the concept was not widely embraced. Hence, it is possible for an archiving system on the market right now to not support Data Migration. However, you should inquire of the archive system's vendor whether they are working with Novell to support Data Migration in the future.

When this form of data storage is available you should keep in mind the same file considerations where necessary for compressed files. It follows that if you must move a file to a volume, in order to back it up, you must have sufficient space available.

CAPABILITY TO BACKUP WORKSTATIONS AND REMOTE SERVERS

Through the use of Target Service Agents (TSAs), Storage Management Services (SMS)–compatible backup solutions are capable of not only backing up and restoring files that reside on the server on which the backup is running, but also backing up any remote devices (such as workstations and other servers) that run a supported TSA. For example, by loading TSA500.NLM on all your NetWare 5 servers, you need only one copy of the backup software—it can back up the files stored locally as well as all other servers across-the-wire. Of course, the disadvantage of the cost savings of using only one copy of the software is lost in performance due to the prolonged time necessary to back up all servers.

Note

For more about Storage Management Services and Target Service Agents, refer to Chapter 1, "Features of NetWare 5."

If you have mixed operating systems on your network, such as UNIX and Windows NT servers, you should check whether your backup solution has agents for these platforms so you can consider backing up these servers across-the-wire (if the amount of data is relatively small) to your NetWare server.

NETWARE CERTIFICATION

Because of the intricacies of the NetWare 5 file system and changes from previous versions of NetWare, you should only consider purchasing archiving systems that have been certified for use with NetWare 5. Novell Labs, based in Provo, Utah, runs a certification program. When an archiving system vendor achieves certification for its product, Novell guarantees that the certified product works correctly with NetWare. Vendors achieving certification are allowed to display a copyrighted symbol (Yes! Tested & Approved) indicating that the product has been certified for use with NetWare (see Figure 25.1).

Figure 25.1
Novell's Yes! logo.

Note, however, that "NetWare certification" by itself does not guarantee success when using the certified product with NetWare 5. The product must be *specifically* certified for use with NetWare 5. Many products on the market today are certified for use with NetWare 3 and NetWare 4. However, certification for NetWare 4 does not guarantee successful results when the product is applied to NetWare 5 (even though they both use NDS). The product must be certified specifically for use with NetWare 5—and for the particular version or revision of NetWare 5 you are using—it's been known that due to changes introduced by Support Packs, software certified for one revision of NetWare might not function correctly when a new Support Pack is applied. This is especially important for archiving systems, because they are insurance for your lifeblood.

ARCHIVING METHODS

There are two basic types of archiving methods used by archiving systems to back up and restore data: image and file-by-file. From these two types of backup methodologies, you will find that administrators use one or a combination of the following several methods for backing up their data:

- Rotating media
- Journalized archive
- Perpetual archive

IMAGE BACKUP

An image backup is simply a copy of the NetWare server's magnetic media, sector-by-sector. Image backup ignores the NetWare file system completely in the sense that it does not back up files per se. Rather, it backs up the magnetic image of the server's hard drives.

Image backup has the following disadvantages:

- You can only archive and restore a complete hard drive
- Your backup media must have the capacity to hold the data for the complete drive as spanning an image across multiple tapes (for example) complicates the restore process
- Inability to backup remote workstations and servers
- You must shut down the NetWare server for the duration of an image archive, therefore, not suitable in a 24/7 environment

> **Note**
>
> Some image-based backup systems do allow you to restore selective files, instead of having to restore the full disk image.

Image backup are sometimes used in situations where simple disaster recovery procedure is required (such as in a remote site where there is no dedicated network administrator) and when rebuilding an entire volume, rather than just restoring several lost files, is a viable option.

> **Caution**
>
> Image backups are an extremely precarious form of data archiving. Because of the fact that this type of backup is an image of the current hard drive at the time of the backup you might find that you are unable to restore your data to a new hard drive if yours should fail. Many image backup systems restore only to the exact physical unit (size-wise and geometry-wise) from which they originated. This makes for very bad archiving practice when your failed drive is no longer being manufactured.

FILE-BY-FILE BACKUP AND RESTORE

Files on a NetWare server are logical structures. That is, they provide a logical order of physical data stored randomly on hard drives or other media used as a NetWare volume. Further, logical information is associated with a file, other than simply the file's data. This information includes the creation and last access date of a file, its last archiving data, its owner, and so on.

A file-by-file backup and restore orders data logically in the same manner as the NetWare file system does. This is the opposite of an image backup and restore, which ignores the logical organization of files and simply copies the magnetic image of the hard drive.

A file-by-file archiving system is by far the most commonly used and has the following advantages:

- Backup and restore operations can occur on a per-file basis
- Because file-by-file archiving systems use the logical file structures maintained by the NetWare file system, archiving and restoration can occur while the server is up and running
- Multiple backup devices (such as tape drives) can be used simultaneously to shorten the backup time needed
- Logical information associated with files, such as their owner and creation date, can be included in logs maintained by the archiving system

Clearly, a file-by-file archiving system is more desirable to the image backup method. However, file-by-file archive sessions can take longer to complete than image backup sessions. This performance disadvantage is nullified when you consider that a file-by-file allows you to selectively back up and restore particular files and directories as well as choose the physical hard drive unit you restore to. Archive sessions can actually complete faster under a file-by-file system, because you can eliminate archiving of redundant information, deleted files, and other data used internally by NetWare.

The one major disadvantage of a non-image backup system is the handling of compressed and migrated files, as discussed earlier in the "Awareness of File Compression" and "Awareness of File Migration" sections.

BACKUP METHODOLOGIES

When using the file-by-file backup method, you must decide how much of your data you will back up. Are you going to back up all your data each time you back up, or are you only going to back up those things that have changed? You have some choices. Each of the different variations on this theme has a name and a specific set of rules:

- **Full Backup**—A complete backup of all data on your file server. All files are backed up regardless of the state of the archive bit.
- **Incremental Backup**—A backup of only those files that are new or that have been changed since your last backup of any kind.
- **Differential Backup**—A backup of all those files that have been modified since the last full backup.

You can combine these methods and you must combine at least two for differential. But whatever methods you use, you have some extra items to think about. If you use full backup every time you back up, you gain the capability to find any file on every backup set, but you use more backup media (tapes, disks, optical cartridges, and so on). If you combine a full backup with several incremental backups, you save on backup media, but looking for files to restore can be tougher. Differential backups take up more space than incremental, but still less than continuous full backups.

Tip #257 from *Peter*	There's also the time factor to consider. As servers get larger in storage space, the longer it takes to do a full backup of all the volumes. Often times, administrators of large servers perform a full backup on, say, Friday evening, and incremental backups during the work week. That way, you can quite easily locate files that have been changed during the week.

You clearly have many choices to make and following are some possible combinations of timing and media that can help you decide. Other than choosing the backup methodology, you also need to consider how you're going to handle the backup media.

ROTATING MEDIA

Rotating media simply means that you have a set of media (tapes, magneto-optical cartridges, and so on), using each member of the set for archiving at regular intervals. For example, you have five tape cartridges labeled "A," "B," "C," "D," and "E." One day you use "A" for archiving data; the next day you use "B;" the third day you use "C;" and so on. These schemes usually include either all full backups, or a combination of full and incremental, or full and differential.

Rotation of media serves to protect you against media failure, but it also provides a more extensive data archive. Sophisticated media rotation schemes have been developed using anywhere from one to ten or more media cartridges. Most of these rotation schemes provide you with an extensive data archiving. You can restore data from any number of days, weeks, months, or years in the past.

One such method that allows restoration of data aged from one day to many years is the *Grandfather, Father, Son (GFS)* method. This method requires a total of 20 tapes—8 tapes for the first month and one tape per month after that. In this method you mark the initial 8 tapes as follows:

> MONDAY, TUESDAY, WEDNESDAY, THURSDAY
>
> FRIDAY-1, FRIDAY-2, FRIDAY-3, FRIDAY-4

You begin the cycle on Monday by using the tape marked MONDAY and continue this process with tape TUESDAY, WEDNESDAY, THURSDAY, and FRIDAY-1 on the respective days. On the Fridays that follow, use each FRIDAY-x tape in order. When you reach FRIDAY-4, you can restore from tapes that are 1–6 days old and tapes that are 1–4 weeks old. This method can be extrapolated out by replacing your FRIDAY-1 tape each month and marking the old FRIDAY-1 tape with the month for storage. Keep the tapes from each month and before long you have quite a library of your business records and critical data.

In the early days of networks, most computer managers or technicians had to design and maintain a media rotation scheme manually. This is a lot of work and leaves room for human error. Today, most archiving systems provide software which manages media rotation, and even automates it. This is much more preferable to the old manual methods.

Media rotation is usually used in combination with image backup, file-by-file backup, and journalized archiving systems.

JOURNALIZED ARCHIVE

A *journalized archive* is a special version of the file-by-file archive. Not only does a journalized archive allow you to back up and restore data on a per-file basis, it also allows you to back up and restore files as they existed on a certain day or even at a certain time on a certain day. In other words, a journalized archive system not only archives files as they presently exist, but allows you to view the entire history of files, including the manner in which files were updated over a period of time.

Journalized archive systems are especially useful in environments where documents are the main end product, such as law firms, accounting firms, software engineering houses, publishing houses, and so on. In environments such as these, it might be necessary to evaluate how a document has changed over time. Only a journalized archive system can maintain this information for you.

The only disadvantage of a journalized archive system is that it is media-intensive. In other words, you can use more media cartridges over time to archive the same amount of data. However, when a journalized archive system is used in combination with a very high-capacity media, such as magneto-optical or WORM (Write Once, Read Many), this might not be a concern.

PERPETUAL ARCHIVE

A *perpetual archive* system is one that runs all the time and that archives files in real-time as they are updated. In other words, whenever you close a file after writing to it, the perpetual archive system backs up that file immediately. Perpetual archiving systems eliminate the need to perform periodic backup operations. They also ensure that your data archive is completely up-to-the-minute. With a standard archiving system, you restore data that is several hours to a week old. Even though you have been able to restore your data, you've still lost between several hours and a week's worth of work. With a perpetual backup system, the most work you will ever lose is several minutes worth.

Perpetual archiving systems are fairly new to NetWare. That's because Novell never provided certain low-level programming interfaces needed in order for vendors to develop the software required for perpetual archiving. However, NetWare 5 includes support for these low-level programming interfaces and all you need are vendors to take advantage of them.

ARCHIVING HARDWARE AND SOFTWARE

The data archiving business is generally divided between hardware vendors and software vendors. Hardware vendors manufacture archiving devices, such as tape drives, magneto-optical drives, and so on. Hardware vendors usually do not tailor their products to any specific operation system or hardware architecture. Rather, they manufacture devices capable of working with various hardware architectures and operating systems, given the appropriate device controller and device driver.

Archiving hardware options for NetWare communicate with the CPU by using a disk drive controller card. Different types of drive controllers are available including mostly *SCSI* (*Small Computer Systems Interface*) or proprietary schemes.

SCSI drive controllers are the preferred controller type for use with backup devices because of their high throughput rate. The NetWare disk driver interface has several features that take advantage of advanced SCSI commands. Another bonus is that virtually all manufacturers of archive devices produce SCSI hardware. This provides you with a wider array of hardware options. SCSI controllers are also capable of controlling multiple devices. This allows you to add to the number of backup devices on your server and not limit yourself from growth.

Vendors of archiving software operate in one of two ways. Some software vendors purchase archive hardware and then tailor their software to match the hardware. This tailoring process includes writing NetWare device drivers for the archive hardware. When you purchase an archiving system from one of these vendors, you purchase an entire package—hardware, drivers, and software.

Other archiving software vendors do not tailor their software to any single hardware device. Rather, they construct their software so that it works with most of the popular archiving hardware on the market. When you purchase software from one of these vendors, you receive not only the software, but also device drivers for most of the popular archive devices on the market. You still need to purchase archive hardware separately.

PART
VI

CH
25

ARCHIVING HARDWARE

There's a wide range of archiving hardware available today. Until a few years ago, virtually all archiving hardware used quarter-inch magnetic tape cartridges (QIC), which had a capacity of 40MB to 300MB. These devices were reliable and inexpensive. However, hard drive manufacturers have since dramatically increased the storage capacity of the drives they produce. Multiple 9GB or 18GB hard drives are not uncommon on NetWare servers today. This causes a problem with QIC media because you need to use many QIC tape cartridges to archive a single NetWare volume.

Although it's possible to archive a single volume to multiple QIC tape cartridges, it is problematic to do so automatically, because somebody needs to sit by the tape drive to insert the next cartridge when the previous cartridge fills up. (It is possible today, however, using SCSI-based tape-changers.)

QIC devices are capable of archiving only around 0.5MB per minute. This is no concern if you are archiving only 20MB or so, as was the case when these devices were originally put on the market. However, if you archive several hundred megabytes of data, a QIC cartridge simply doesn't have enough capacity for you.

Today, most people use either 8mm or 4mm magnetic tape to archive their NetWare data. 8mm tape is also popular as a medium for video camcorders; 4mm tape, also known as digital audio tape (DAT), is popular among stereo enthusiasts. Both 8mm and 4mm data-grade tape cartridges are widely available today and relatively inexpensive, given their capacity.

Most archiving devices that use either 8mm or 4mm tape cartridges can store up to 8GB of data on a single cartridge. Moreover, the electronics required for reading from and writing to 8mm and 4mm tape cartridges are more compact than the older QIC electronics. That makes it easier to build multicartridge devices (changers) that can archive 20GB or more of data while running unattended.

8mm and 4mm tape devices can archive up to 5MB per minute. That means you can archive 100MB in 20 minutes. With these devices, it is possible to archive several gigabytes of data overnight. The newer DLT tape drives can easily backup many gigabytes of data in a matter of hours.

Some archiving hardware devices use optical WORM media or magneto-optical read/write media for archiving and restoring data. These devices share the capacity advantages of 8mm and 4mm tape and also have the advantage of providing random access to media sectors, which gives them a performance advantage over tape. Tape remains a less expensive medium to use than WORM or magneto-optical, so most people today use tape as an archiving medium.

ARCHIVING SOFTWARE

Archiving software has become more sophisticated over the past several years. Among today's standard features offered by archiving software are the following:

- Unattended operation
- Configuring and scheduling multiple archive sessions
- Filters that enable you to archive selectively different types of files (based on filenames or file extensions)
- Storage of archive session logs in a database format, allowing quick retrieval of specific historical information
- Management of multiple media cartridges, including media rotation schemes and media directories
- Multiple data restoration options, including restoration by file and date
- Multiserver archiving sessions, where data from many servers is archived to or restored from a central hardware device
- Archiving and restoration of workstation-based data across the network

Several years ago some of these capabilities would have seemed exotic, but now they are fairly standard fare. As NetWare sites have grown, many of which have hundreds of servers, the degree of automation and the spectrum of operations made possible by archiving software has reflected the changes in the way organizations use NetWare.

When selecting archiving systems for your organization, you should evaluate the human resources available for performing data backup. As a rule, the more automated and featured the archiving software is, the less human-intensive the data archiving process will be. With the right software and hardware, a small administration staff can archive an entire organization's data. Also the more automated your backup software is the less likely you are to miss a backup due to human error.

Included with NetWare 5 are two backup utilities that can get your initial backup requirements going while you evaluate the need for a third-party solution. From the server console, you can use SBCON.NLM (formerly known as SBACKUP) to initiate backup and restore operations (see Figure 25.2). From the workstation, you can use NWBACK32, a 32-bit Windows-based application (see Figure 25.3).

Figure 25.2
Main menu of SBCON.NLM.

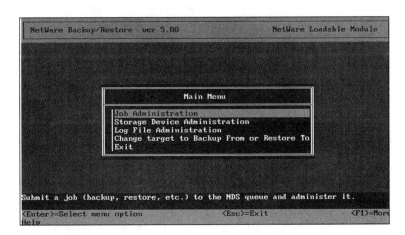

PART

VI

CH

25

The following steps outline how you can use SBCON to back up your NetWare volume (I assume that you have already correctly installed and configured your tape device):

1. Load any drivers necessary for your tape device.

2. Load TSA500.NLM, NWTAPE.HAM, QMAN.NLM, and then load SBCON.NLM. (SMDR will be autoloaded if not already loaded.)

3. From the Main Menu, select Storage Device Administration.

4. From the Select a Device menu, highlight the device you want to use. If the device is an autoloader, press Enter to display a list of loaded media.

Figure 25.3
Quick access dialog
box of NWBACK32.

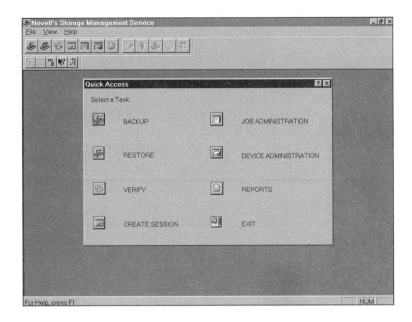

5. Highlight the media you want to use and press Enter to select it.

6. Press Esc to return to the main menu.

7. Select Job Administration.

8. Select Backup from the Select Job menu.

9. Use the Target Service option of the Backup Options menu to select the target server
   (see Figure 25.4). If the selected target server has multiple TSAs, such as TSANDS and
   TSA500, running, you also need to select the appropriate service. To back up the volume, select the appropriate *server_name*.NetWare File System service (for instance, if
   the server is called NETWARE5-A, select NETWARE5-A.NetWare File System).

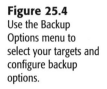

Figure 25.4
Use the Backup Options menu to select your targets and configure backup options.

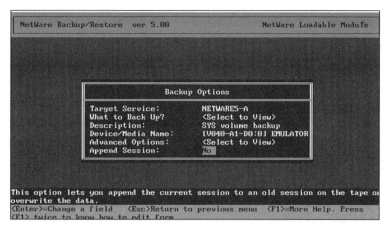

10. You're then prompted for a username and password that has sufficient rights to backup the volume(s); use the *.username.org* naming syntax. On successful login, a message similar to You are connected to target service ... <Press ENTER to continue> is displayed. In the Target Service option, you'll now see the service names listed.

11. Use the What to Back Up? option to select whether you're backing up the whole server, Server Specific Information (SSI), or a volume.

> **Note**
> SSI information is important during a file server disaster recovery process. Refer to the SMS section in Chapter 1, "Features of NetWare 5," for more information. Also, see the "Disaster Recovery" section later in this chapter.

12. If you selected a volume name, press Enter to bring up a list of files and directories that you can select for backup.

13. Repeat steps 11 and 12 to select any other files, directories, or volumes you want to back up.

14. Enter a description (up to 23 characters), such as SYS volume backup, in the Description field.

15. Use the Device/Media Name field to select the tape device that will be used.

16. Use the Advanced Options to schedule when the job will run and if it's a repeating job. You can schedule the job as a run-once or as a recurring job.

17. Finally, use the Append Session option to specify whether the data on the tape is to be appended to or overwritten.

18. Press Esc and select Yes in response to the Do You Want to Submit a Job? prompt. You're then returned to the Select Job menu.

PART
VI

CH
25

> **Note**
>
> The procedure for backing up NDS is similar—you need to load `TSANDS.NLM` instead of `TSA500.NLM`, and in the TSA Service selection, choose *SERVER NAME*.`Novell Directory` instead.
>
> To back up both the NDS and the file system, you need to load both `TSANDS.NLM` *and* `TSA500.NLM`.

The following is a partial list of NetWare 5-certified backup software solutions:

- **ANCHORA Backup Utility**—Anchora S.R.O. (`http://www.anchora.cz/abackup`)
- **ARCserveIT 6.6 for NetWare**—Computer Associates (`http://www.cheyenne.com/storage`)
- **Backup Exec for NetWare Version 8**—Seagate Software, Inc.—Storage Management Group (`http://www.smg.seagatesoftware.com/`)
- **BackOnline 1.0**—Divya, Inc. (`http://divya.com/products/infoBook/`)
- **FDR/UPSTREAM 3.0.0**—Innovation Data Processing (`http://www.innovationdp.com/`)

For the latest up-to-date list, visit `http://developer.novell.com/npp`.

DISASTER RECOVERY

Disaster recovery (also known as *business resumption*) planning is a special science, related to data archiving but entailing much more. Whereas data archiving helps you to recover from data loss, disaster recovery helps you to recover from loss of computers, facilities, communications, and more. Disaster recovery is a good topic to introduce after a discussion on data archiving.

Your organization should have a disaster recovery plan (DRP) in-place as soon as possible after you have your network up and running. A disaster recovery plan addresses the following noninclusive list of topics:

- Procedures for recovering from total hardware system failure (machine breakdown)
- Off-site locations for storage of archived data
- Procedures for loss of power to your building, including backup generators if appropriate
- Emergency evacuation plans
- Procedures for continuing business operations in the event your physical plant is destroyed or unavailable for a time
- A phone number for employees to call in the event of an emergency
- Insurance provisions for recovering from a disaster

Disaster recovery is a subject you and your organization should address seriously before becoming so dependent on NetWare 5 that an interruption of network service could cause serious financial damage to your organization. And DRP should be exercised at least once a year to ensure it's up-to-date and that it's accurate.

From a NetWare 5 server's point of view, losing the SYS volume is in the same category as a server crash—NDS information is lost and must be recovered accordingly. It is beyond the scope of this chapter to go into the great details necessary to recover from a server down problem. However, Novell Research has an excellent article in their October 1996 issue of Novell Application Notes. In this article, it detailed the necessary steps for a NDS-based server DRP. Although the article was targeted at NetWare 4.11, but the procedure and theory is the same for NetWare 5. You can find it on the Web at `http://developer.novell.com/research/appnotes.htm`.

PROJECT: DEVELOPING A DATA RECOVERY STRATEGY

Using the information presented in this chapter and the October 1996 issue of the Novell Application Notes, develop a data recovery strategy—more commonly referred to as Data Recovery Plan (DRP) or Business Resumption Plan (BRP)—suitable for your NetWare 5 network. Your plan should include, but not be limited to, the following procedures:

- Alternative site at which you can install your new servers
- Backup WAN link and other communication infrastructure
- Off-site storage of your backup media
- Established and tested procedure for building new servers
- Established and tested procedure for restoring NDS
- Documented steps for restoring a single NDS object
- Established and tested procedure for restoring data
- Documented steps for restoring a single data file
- Provision for running mission-critical applications without a network

Keep in mind that you must test your DRP procedures regularly. Many businesses run a yearly (if not bi-yearly) DRP "drill" just to ensure everyone in the company knows what's expected of them and that the procedures are accurate and up-to-date. You really don't want to find out you overlooked something when you need to put the plan into reality.

## CHAPTER 26

SERVER TUNING FOR PERFORMANCE

In this chapter

DYNAMIC CONFIGURATION

Server performance optimization and benchmarking is a delicate subject because it is almost impossible to consider all possible variables. And, to add disarray to confusion, it is even harder to reproduce benchmark traffic that truly represents a real-world situation. However, everyone has an insatiable desire to push operating systems to the utmost limits. Therefore, this chapter is dedicated to optimizing the performance of NetWare 5.

From the inception of early versions of NetWare, its engineers have been concerned with performance. The growth and success of NetWare is an indication of their successful accomplishment of this goal. A large contributing factor to this success has been Novell's philosophy of *self-optimization*. This phenomenon is often referred to as *automatic optimization*, *automatic tuning*, or *dynamic configuration* (this chapter uses the term *dynamic configuration*). This dynamic configuration has bolstered NetWare's success because it leaves network administrators free to oversee the network, rather than having to continually try to optimize the network for performance.

In fact, performance optimization has almost been forgotten; network parameters go unnoticed and are simply left at default settings. Forgotten is the fact that several of these parameters, if fine-tuned, can increase network performance and make a server more efficient.

I begin by introducing the concept of NetWare's dynamic configuration and explain the portions of NetWare that are dynamically tuned. I then discuss, in length, some of the dynamically adjusted parameters that can be fine-tuned. You will gain an understanding of NetWare's dynamic configuration that will help you squeeze out of it every possible drop of performance.

Tip #260 from	Each time you bring your server down, NetWare's dynamic configuration mechanism has to start over. So if nothing else, this section informs you of parameters that you should watch. After the server has been in operation for some time, you can manually set the dynamically configurable parameters. Manually setting these parameters means that your server "gets back on course" the minute it starts up, rather than waiting hours, days, or months for it to optimize itself.
Peter	

NetWare's dynamic configuration has the capability to allocate a server's resources according to need and availability. When NetWare 5 is first started, all the server's memory is used for file caching. Other portions of the operating system require more resources, and if resources are available they will be allocated. For example, if the need for directory cache buffers increases or if more NetWare Loadable Modules (NLMs) are loaded, memory resources will be transferred, reducing the amount of memory that was previously being used for file cache buffers. Reallocation of resources isn't done instantly, however. The operating system waits a specified amount of time for existing resources to become available. If they do not become available in the specified amount of time, resources are taken from the file cache buffer area and reallocated.

Note

> The waiting period ensures that the operating system doesn't permanently allocate resources to activities that are infrequent, or for uncommon peaks in server activity.

The following sections cover some of the parameters that are dynamically configured by NetWare 5. Although these parameters are dynamically allocated, SET commands can be used to manually determine the amount of resources available to each process (at least the minimum and maximum levels).

Using SET commands to allocate server resources can be an extremely powerful performance tool and, at the same time, provide a more efficient server. The following sections explain how to set these limits and provides hints and tips on some of the more adjustable dynamic configuration parameters:

- Server cache memory
- Directory cache buffers
- Disk elevator size
- Memory for NLMs
- Service processes

SERVER CACHE MEMORY

All free memory, after all other processes have enough, is used as cache. The way NetWare 5 manages its free cache is different than in previous products. In NetWare 5, the available system cache is separated into cache pools for Novell Storage Services (NSS), file system, virtual memory; it also has the ability for others that can be registered. In order to manage the different cache pools, NetWare 5 implemented a "judge" process that acts as the ultimate deciding factor to move memory (cache) from one cache pool to another. Therefore, you don't have to worry about it. What you need to be concerned about is the amount of cache memory available for file caching.

NetWare servers provide faster file access by holding a copy of a file (a *cache*) in its memory (it can then retrieve the file directly from memory, rather than having to retrieve it from the hard disk. The more memory you have the more files that can be stored in cache, thus the faster (on average) file accessing will be. However, memory is usually a limited commodity, meaning it needs to be used efficiently.

Therefore, the file cache buffers parameter needs to be viewed in an opposite manner from dynamically configurable options (other areas grow in available resources). Thus, you set the minimum amount of memory to use for file cache buffers. Then when other processes ask for memory, memory designated for file cache buffers will only be allowed to get so low.

PART
VI

CH
26

Caution

A common question is "Where should I set the minimum value for file cache buffers?"

If you set it too high, you can save memory for the file caching processes that are never needed; at the same time you might handicap other services. But, if it is set too low, file retrieval speeds are only a smidgen of what they should be. NetWare 5 has several features that make monitoring cache utilization simpler. To determine whether you need more RAM for cache memory, follow these steps.

Select Disk Cache Utilization from the Options menu in MONITOR.NLM (see Figure 26.1). If, over time (say, 48 hours), the Long Term Cache Hits parameter remains less than 90%, you have too little memory to efficiently cache files. Also note the LRU (Least Recently Used) sitting time. The LRU time reflects how long cache buffers in the LRU queue were last referenced—you want this time to be as large as possible. If the Long Term Cache Hits is below 90% *and* LRU Sitting Time is less than an hour, you should seriously consider adding more RAM to the server; there is also the possibility that the Minimum Cache Buffer parameter is set too low.

Figure 26.1
Sample
MONITOR.NLM screen
showing cache memory usage.

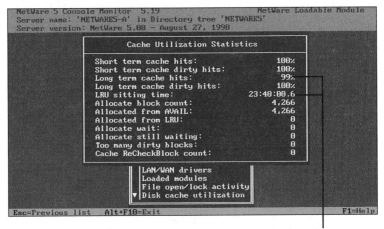

Note these stats

DIRECTORY CACHE BUFFER

Directory cache buffers is the portion of the overall memory pool that is set aside to cache (*file system*) directory requests. When a NetWare server is first brought up it will eventually receive a request for referencing a directory entry. When this first request to access a directory is processed, that directory table will be placed in the cache buffers (to speed up any subsequent access). By default, 20 cache buffers will be immediately created (the minimum default value). A directory entry requested will then stay in a cache buffer for as long as it is being accessed frequently. (The length of time the directory table stays in cache is determined by the NonReferenced Delay time; the default value is 5.5 seconds). When this time is elapsed, the buffer becomes available for another entry. Caching directory entries allows the most frequently used directories to be accessed more quickly, because they can be read from (fast) memory rather than the (slow) disk drive.

If more directory buffers are needed, NetWare waits a specified amount of time, which is called the Directory Cache Allocation Wait Time (default is 2.2 seconds), before it actually allocates any more memory to caching directory requests. During this wait time other resources might become available (NonReferenced Delay time might have elapsed on some entries). If no buffers become available, a new directory cache buffer is dynamically allocated. The memory for these directory cache buffers comes from memory previously allocated for file cache buffers (the amount of memory itself isn't dynamic). If enough directory requests are made, either directory cache buffers will reach the maximum value, or the entire directory structure will be cached.

Summarized here are settings related to directory cache buffers:

- The default minimum number of Directory Cache Buffers is 150. The range of supported minimum values is 10–2000.

- Default Maximum Directory Cache Buffers is 500. The range of supported maximum values is 20–4000.

- Default Directory Cache Allocation Wait Time is 5.5 seconds. The range of supported Allocation Wait Time is 0.5–2 minutes.

- Default Directory Cache Buffer NonReferenced Delay time is 5.5 seconds. The range of supported wait time values is 1 second to 5 minutes.

When memory is allocated to a directory cache buffer, it is not available to file cache processes and the only way to return the memory to the memory pool is to restart the server. If users are being warned that the server is getting low on memory, directory cache buffers is one of the first places that you will want to manually limit memory use.

Now, with NetWare 5, instead of typing the SET commands at the console prompt, you can use MONITOR.NLM to change directory cache buffer parameters (see Figure 26.2) and monitor the directory cache buffer usage (see Figure 26.3).

PART

VI

CH

26

Figure 26.2
Changing number of directory cache buffers using MONITOR.NLM.

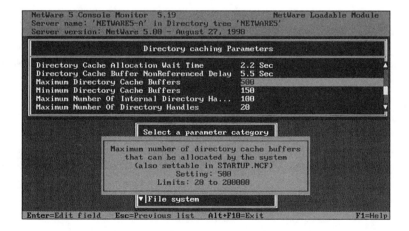

Figure 26.3
Checking the current number of directory cache buffers in use.

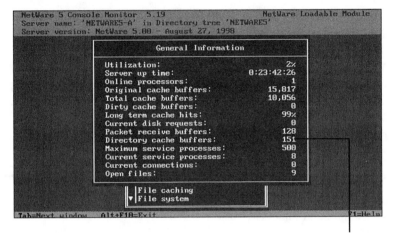

Currently in use

Tip #261 from
Peter

To change directory cache buffer parameters on NetWare 5 server, do the following:

1. Select Server parameters from the options box in MONITOR.NLM; it is the last entry.

2. Select the category Directory Caching.

3. Highlight the option you want to change.

4. Enter the new setting.

If you increase a setting, the change takes effective immediately. When a setting is lowered, it takes effect the next time the server is restarted.

DISK ELEVATOR SEEKING

Disk elevator seeking logically organizes disk access requests as they arrive at the server for processing. As disk requests are queued, they are positioned in the order that the disk heads retrieve the data (rather than simply in the order that they were requested). This allows the drive head operation to be a smooth sweeping fashion, rather than a completely random one.

Note

The term *disk elevator seeking* comes from its analogy to an elevator. Regardless of the order of the floors the passengers press the buttons (the order in which the disk seek is received), the elevator services the floors in order (the disk head moves from one track to another in order, rather than in a back-and-forth order akin to the order of the requests).

Elevator seeking can be fine-tuned by setting the Maximum Concurrent Disk Cache Writes. This setting determines how many write requests (for data in a buffer that has been changed) can be put into the disk's elevator at the same time, before the disk begins its seek procedure. The Dirty Disk Cache Delay Time parameter indicates the length of time NetWare 5 keeps a write request (not located in a cache buffer) in the buffer before it writes it to disk.

The best way to determine whether the Maximum Concurrent Disk Cache Write parameter needs changing is to watch the MONITOR screen. If the dirty cache buffers are more than 70% of the total cache buffers, you might want to increase the speed of disk writes by increasing the setting of the Maximum Concurrent Disk Cache Write parameter.

Tip #262 from
Peter

Increasing the number of Maximum Concurrent Disk Cache Writes can create more efficiency in disk write requests, while decreasing the number can create more efficiency in disk read requests. Therefore, if you have a write-intensive environment, set this to a higher value.

To change the amount, use the following SET command (or MONITOR.NLM) (supported values are 10–4000, default is 750):

SET Maximum Concurrent Disk Cache Writes = X

You can also increase the speed of disk writes by turning off software Read-After-Write Verification, if your hardware supports it.

Determining the most efficient setting for the Dirty Disk Cache Delay Time is not quite as easy as determining what needs to be done with the Maximum Dirty Cache parameter. It is not as easy because the most efficient setting is determined by the type of network traffic you have. The only tip that can honestly be given is that if your network traffic consists of many small writes, increasing the delay time increases efficiency.

PACKET RECEIVE BUFFERS

One of the most important dynamically configurable parameters in NetWare is the number of packet receive buffers (PRBs). Packets that are passed from another network, or workstation, to the server are first received in a holding area (which is appropriately named because packets receive buffers before they are processed). The packet is held until it can be processed by a service process, which creates a steady flow of work for the server.

If the packet buffer area is full, the server waits for 0.1 second (New Packet Receive Buffer Wait Time) before allocating more resources (memory) to the packet buffer receive area. If the number of packet receive buffers have reached the maximum value, the server's LAN channel runs the risk of being overloaded and packets will be lost (data will not be lost because the station will simply re-send the packet). This causes the network response to become very sluggish, especially if the server is routing between two network segments (one slow and one fast). In extreme cases, client station response times can be impacted to the point of being unusable.

PART

VI

CH

26

Note

Each buffer is identical in size and is set to the Maximum Physical Packet Receive Size for the operating system. The physical size of the packet is determined by the network media. Under NetWare, for example, Ethernet has a physical packet size of 1514 bytes, where as Token Ring's maximum physical packet size is 4202; the default Maximum Physical Packet Receive Size is 4224 bytes.

Fine-tuning the number of packet receive buffers setting should only be attempted after verifying it in fact needs to be adjusted. Three situations require you to adjust the default settings:

- You are in a multiple LAN segment environment (included are installations where multiple segments reside in the same server).
- The number of packet receive buffers are constantly reaching the maximum number.
- You have over 100 workstations actively using a server.

In a multiple server environment, packets are constantly being passed from one network to another, but this alone does not justify increasing the default setting of the number of packet receive buffers; increase the setting only if the server is constantly reaching its maximum value. To determine whether the server is reaching the maximum setting, simply look at the packet receive buffer indication on the MONITOR.NLM screen (see Figure 26.4).

Figure 26.4
Note the number of packet receive buffers used.

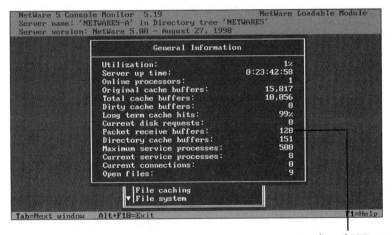

Number of PRBs used

Tip #263 from
Peter

Peak periods in usage can cause the packet receive buffers to inflate, so don't jump to conclusions the first time you see the buffers coming close to reaching the maximum limit. Change is only required if the limit is continuously being reached.

The default value of 500 usually proves to be sufficient; in large installations, however, it can be on the minimal side. In larger installations you should increase the packet receive buffers to include at least one buffer per workstation. Some EISA/PCI cards recommend you to increase the number of buffers. Check the documentation.

It is also wise to include 10 to 20 extra buffers for each bus mastering or EISA card in the server. If you see the Receive Discarded, No Available Buffers counter (in MONITOR, choose LAN/WAN Drivers, highlight the driver, press Tab, and look under Generic Counters), increase the PRBs in increments of 10 until the errors stop. Also you can watch the LAN Driver Statistics from the MONITOR.NLM screen to determine whether the LAN board is causing the errors (see Figure 26.5).

Figure 26.5
The Receive
Discarded, No
Available Buffers
counter in the
LAN/WAN drivers
menu was previously
known as No ECB
Available count.

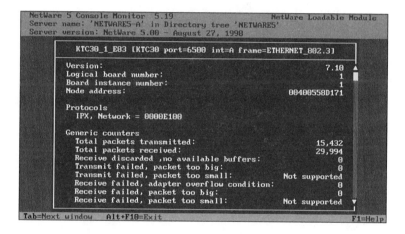

If the server continually reaches the maximum limit, it could point to a more serious problem. There are several situations where the number of packet receive buffers can climb to the maximum limit and actually hang the server, as in the following:

- Interrupt conflicts
- Faulty or poor network card drivers
- Bad cabling

In these situations, increasing the maximum value of the number of packet receive buffers will usually just prolong the time between server lock-ups—you're simply fixing the symptom and not the cause.

Watching the number of packet receive buffer limits becomes more of an issue if you are using fast workstations (whose CPU speeds are comparable to that of the server's) with NetWare 5 client software and have packet burst enabled. A single station employing packet burst (a discussion of packet burst can be found later in this chapter) can use several of the available packet receive buffers. Because it allows stations to stream packets and send as much as 64KB of packetized information in one stream. So if you have several fast stations using packet burst, carefully watch the packet receive buffer values.

> **Note**
>
> If you are upgrading from 3.1x, you will probably not need as many packet receive buffers. NetWare 5 has an increased the priority level of routing requests.

The default packet receive buffer settings are as follows:

- Maximum Packet Receive Buffers = 500
- Minimum Packet Receive Buffers = 128
- Maximum Physical Receive Packet Size = 4224 bytes
- New Packet Receive Buffer Wait Time = 0.1 second

It is possible to get larger packets, up to 24KB, with Token Ring; however, standard NetWare Token Ring driver implementation only support packet sizes up to 4202 bytes.

To change the number of packet receive buffer settings on NetWare 5, follow these steps:

1. Load MONITOR.NLM at the server console.
2. Select Server parameters.
3. Select Communications.
4. Select Maximum Packet Receive Buffers (see Figure 26.6).

Figure 26.6
Changing the maximum number of packet receive buffers using MONITOR.NLM.

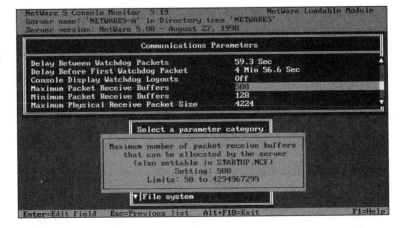

5. Change the value.

6. Press the Esc key twice to return to the main menu.

The change will then take effect immediately without having to take down and restart the server.

SERVICE PROCESSES

Resources available on a server can be divided into three classes: LAN, disk, and processor. LAN and disk resources are the number of buffers available, whereas processor resources are the number of service processes available. As a network packet arrives or a disk read or write is finished, there should be a buffer available for the data. If there is a buffer available, there should be a service process available to deal with it. Running out of any one of these for more than a brief period will cause high utilization on the server and delay for the users.

Service processes (also known as file server processes, or FSPs) are threads of execution that act as hosts to incoming service requests. NetWare 5 is capable of allocating up to 1000 service processes. To support 100 or fewer users per server, you can use the default service process settings.

Tip #264 from *Peter*	A good rule of thumb is set the maximum service processes to 2 or 3 per connection and set the minimum service processes to 1 per connection. Alternatively, you can simply set the maximum service processes to 1000 (the maximum number allowed). If the server does not require an additional service process, it will not allocate. You can also set new service process wait time to 0.3 seconds (default is 2.2).

Should you need to modify any of the service process parameters, it is easiest to set them using MONITOR. The change on the maximum setting will take effect immediately, whereas the change to the minimum setting will take effect at the next server boot—which is the only time they come into play anyway.

PART

VI

CH

26

MEMORY FOR NLMs

In previous versions of NetWare, specifically NetWare 3.x, memory was allocated into five different memory pools with each pool serving a different purpose. When an application (NLM) finished using the memory (unloaded), the memory often remained unused (wasn't returned to the "available" memory pool). This lead to memory fragmentation and even meant it was possible for an application to run out of memory. NetWare 5, on the other hand, has only one memory allocation pool, and when an application finishes using a section of memory that memory is instantly returned to the available memory pool. This allows the server to operate more efficiently (the server has to perform fewer memory management operations, memory isn't as fragmented, and the same segment of memory can be reused).

Tip #265 from
Peter

NLMs don't generally use as much memory when idle, as they do when performing tasks. However, if loaded, all NLMs use some memory. Simply put, unloading unnecessary NLMs provides more memory, thereby directly increasing performance (more memory to cache files, directories, and so on).

Memory fragmentation can lead to "insufficient memory" or "out of memory" errors when you try to run an NLM, even when you have lots of available cache buffers from which you can "borrow." This is because when a program allocates memory, the memory is allocated in contiguous blocks. And if you don't have a large enough contiguous block of memory, the NLM will fail to load or run. Consider this example: An NLM tries to allocate 1MB of memory; if the system has available this 1MB of memory but it is in 256 *separate* 4K chunks, memory allocation will fail. To reduce memory fragmentation, the operating system has to perform what's known as *garbage collection* on a regular basis to consolidate the fragmented memory blocks. The garbage collection process is like a disk defragmenter for the operating system's memory pool that is always running. This internal routine can be set or interrupted and runs in the background.

Note

NetWare 5 can use virtual memory by swapping to disk. When the overall supply of memory is low, however, swapping will happen more often. If the system is extremely low on memory, it might spend a majority of its time swapping in and out of disk and have no time to accomplish work. This is called *disk thrashing*. When disk thrashing occurs, you should add more RAM.

Note

The term *garbage collection* is used in computer science to describe the process of reorganizing the fragmented memory blocks into larger, contiguous blocks.

One SET parameter that affects how often garbage collection happens is the Garbage Collection Interval (default is every 5 minutes). Unless you're in a NLM development environment where NLMs are constantly loaded and unloaded or in a database server (running as an NLM) environment where large amounts of memory are constantly allocated and deallocated for tables, you should leave this SET parameter at this default five-minute interval.

Tip #266 from
Peter

If you need to increase or decrease the garbage collection time interval, keep in mind that a short interval can cause high CPU utilization because the OS will be busy doing garbage collection; too long an interval can result in inefficient memory usage, perhaps leading to reduced file cache buffers.

Be aware that the Garbage Collection Interval SET parameter is global; that is, it affects all NLM garbage collection. For this reason, great care should be given in changing the default parameters. An adjustment for one NLM to improve its performance can adversely affect another NLM. Novell recommends leaving these parameters at their default unless a NLM requires a specific change.

Note

Garbage collection can be triggered by demand on virtual memory. If the virtual memory is used heavily, garbage collection happens immediately.

Tip #267 from
Peter

Garbage collection can be forced to happen by a user through MONITOR. In NetWare 5, under the Load modules option, any of the system modules loaded can be selected. After it is selected you can press F4 to collect garbage on that specific module. Alternatively, under Virtual Memory, Address Spaces, you can free address space memory with F4.

VOLUME BLOCK SIZE

NetWare 5 can suballocate blocks. (For an in-depth explanation of suballocation see Chapter 1, "Features of NetWare 5.") From a performance standpoint, suballocation enhances the performance of write operations within the OS by allowing the ends of multiple files to be consolidated within a single write operation. Of course, this minor improvement will often be counterbalanced by the increased overhead of managing the suballocation process. However, as imaging, multimedia, and other workloads involving streaming data become more prevalent, large volume block size will become invaluable.

Based on performance testing, Novell recommends a 64KB block size be used for all volumes whenever possible (especially for large volumes whose size is 2GB or larger). The larger 64KB allocation unit allows NetWare 5 to use the disk channel more efficiently by reading and writing more data at once. This results in faster access to mass storage devices and improved response times for network users.

PART

VI

CH

26

Tip #268 from
Peter

If you are using RAID-5 disks, set the block size equal to the stripe depth of the RAID-5 disks.

If you are doing an in-place upgrade to a server, the server volume block sizes can't be changed. If you have a small block size, such as 4KB, you will definitely want to make sure that Read Ahead Enabled parameter is left ON (ON is default), otherwise performance will be drastically impacted. In order to change the volume block size, you need to re-create the volume.

Tip #269 from
Peter

You can consider using the Volume Block Resizer NLM from Novell Consulting Services to first increase the block size of your NetWare 4.x volumes before upgrading the server. The NLM can be found at http://consulting.novell.com/toolkit/tools/ resize.exe. Note that this utility is not supported by Novell and does not run on NetWare 5.

Large Internet Packet (LIP)

Increasing the size of the packet that the server can receive is just one more way to increase the performance of your NetWare 5 network. It logically makes sense if a packet's size is larger, more information can be sent at one time, thereby increasing performance. However, this will only help in certain situations. The most common being a network that contain routers (internal or external).

This is true because routers have no way to determine the packet size capabilities of the servers on the other side of the segment. So, in the past, these devices were forced to use the "least common denominator" 576 bytes (512 bytes of data, 30 bytes in the IPX header, and 34 bytes for the NCP/SPX header). By choosing a small packet size, the router is assured that the servers on the other side will be able to "handle" the packet.

With NetWare 5, you can set the server's packet sizing capabilities. Because of this, when a connection is made, the packet size negotiation routine will know what packets sizes are acceptable. If the server detects a router during the packet size negotiation, the server will no longer simply default to the lowest common denominator of 576 bytes. Instead, when the client workstation software negotiates with the server, it also tests to see the packet size that the router can handle.

By default, LIP is enabled in NetWare 5. However, if for some reason you need to disable LIP, use the following SET command:

SET ALLOW LIP = OFF

This will disable the *server*'s support for LIP, and not just for a given client connection.

Understanding and Tuning Packet Burst

Starting with the VLM (16-bit) workstation client software that shipped with NetWare 4, Novell implemented a technology known as *packet burst*. Packet burst takes advantage of wire's idle time by allowing clients to submit multiple read and write request for data blocks of up to 64KB. Each block of data is considered a *packet burst* and several packet bursts combined create a multipacket burst. The client and server are continually negotiating the amount of data that should be sent as the amount of network traffic is constantly changing. This helps optimize data delivery.

This burst mode NetWare Core Protocol (NCP) technology was created to increase data transfer rates for wide area network (WAN) links. WAN links using packet burst experienced speed increases of up to 400%! These tremendous speed increases on the WAN made NetWare LAN users wonder whether this technology would also increase speeds on local area networks. Now packet bursting technology is implemented in all the client software.

Traditionally, IPX/NCP "ping-pongs," whereas burst mode packets don't have to wait for a response packet. Responses are simply queued until the complete burst has been received. After the burst has been received, a single response packet acknowledges the transfer (see Figure 26.7). If errors occur during a transfer, the complete burst does not have to be retransmitted. Instead of sending a transfer complete response to the client, the server sends a lost fragment list. This list informs the client of the portions of the burst that didn't make it. Thus, it is only necessary for the client to re-send the fragments identified by the lost fragment response.

Figure 26.7
Packet burst protocol allows a group of packets to be sent for a single request packet.

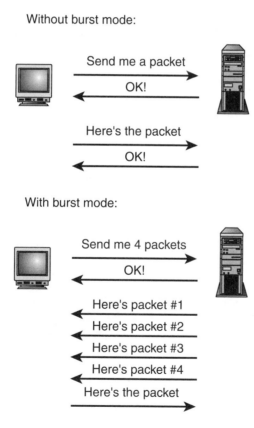

PART

VI

CH

26

A burst mode connection is only established if both the server *and* the workstation support burst mode. This doesn't imply that if you won't have a connection to your file server if packet burst is loaded on one side and not the other. It simply means that packet burst is disabled and that the standard request/response transfer mechanism is used. Also, not every workstation has to use burst mode. This interoperability lets you decide which workstations (or file servers) need packet burst.

Tip #270 from *Peter*	There is no SET parameter on the server to globally disable packet burst on the server. Therefore, to disable burst mode you need to turn it off at the client. To turn off the client's burst mode operation, include the following line in the NET.CFG file of the workstation if you're using DOS: PB BUFFERS = 0 For Windows 9x and Windows NT client, in the Advanced settings of the Client32 properties tab, set Burst Mode to Off.

Note	For the DOS client, changing the number of PB BUFFERS has no effect on the performance. Instead, a zero value disables burst mode and a non-zero value enables it.

Caution	A slow machine or NIC cannot transfer information fast enough to keep up with packet burst and the file server can completely overload the slow workstation (and possibly traffic-jamming the entire network). The workstation simply digests as much of the burst as it can—losing a majority of the multipacket burst—and then it has to send a lost fragment list to the server. The process starts all over again, with the server bombarding the slow station.

Tip #271 from *Peter*	Unless you have a specific reason for not using packet burst, such as occurrence of data corruption, and that there is no other solution, you should not turn off the burst mode support as you'll see much lower performance.

Increasing speeds through packet burst is simple, however, to truly optimize packet burst, the speed of file servers, workstations, network cards, and the amount of network traffic need to be taken into consideration, not to mention the wire type, topology, the number of users, and so on.

MONITORING AVAILABLE DISK SPACE

The amount of available free disk space has an impact on the performance of disk suballocation and file decompression routines of the NetWare 5 operating system. The symptoms of these two problems are high CPU utilization and sluggish server response. Their causes are discussed in the following sections.

SUBALLOCATION AND FREE BLOCKS

Suballocation uses free blocks to perform its function. When free blocks are low, suballocation could go into aggressive mode, locking the volume and driving the server utilization high.

It is important to keep more than 1000 "free blocks" and at least 10–20% free disk space on each volume with suballocation enabled. Suballocation uses these free blocks (as a scratch area) to free up additional disk space. To be warned on the number of free blocks available, you can set the Volume Low Warning Threshold and the Volume Low Warning Reset Threshold to 1024 (or higher) so that a broadcast message is sent when the thresholds are crossed.

High CPU utilization issues can be caused by the lack of disk space because suballocation is a low-priority thread. This means that under normal conditions, the suballocation thread runs only when the processor has nothing else to do and is idle. This condition of suballocation is a nonaggressive mode. When disk space is low, less than 10% available, suballocation can go into aggressive mode.

In its aggressive mode, suballocation is bumped up to a regular priority thread and can take control of the volume until is has cleaned up and freed up as much space as possible. This volume locking causes other processes, which are trying to use the volume, to wait until the lock is released. In large installations, this results in an increase of PRBs and FSPs. When the PRBs max out, the server drops connections and users are unable to log in. When suballocation completes its cleanup, the lock is released and the processes on the queue are serviced. This results in a utilization drop and the server returns to normal operation.

The lack of *free* blocks is different from a lack of disk space. When files are deleted, they are kept in a deleted state. This means the file actually exists but is not viewable to the user and does not show up in volume statistics as used space. The number of free blocks is determined by the following formula:

```
Free blocks = Total blocks - (Blocks in use by files +
Blocks in use by deleted files)
```

PART

VI

CH

26

Tip #272 from
Peter

To check how many free blocks you have, go into MONITOR.NLM. Choose Volumes and highlight the desired volume. Press Tab and then look at the statistic "free blocks" (see Figure 26.8).

Figure 26.8
Checking the number of free blocks using
MONITOR.NLM.

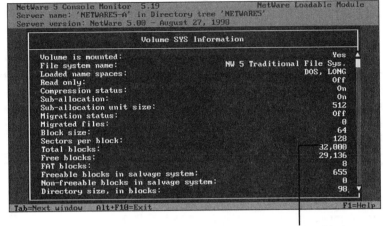

```
NetWare 5 Console Monitor  5.19                    NetWare Loadable Module
Server name: 'NETWARE5-A' in Directory tree 'NETWARE5'
Server version: NetWare 5.00 - August 27, 1998

                          Volume SYS Information

   Volume is mounted:                                              Yes ▲
   File system name:                         NW 5 Traditional File Sys.
   Loaded name spaces:                                      DOS, LONG
   Read only:                                                     Off
   Compression status:                                             On
   Sub-allocation:                                                 On
   Sub-allocation unit size:                                      512
   Migration status:                                             Off
   Migrated files:                                                  0
   Block size:                                                     64
   Sectors per block:                                             128
   Total blocks:                                               32,000
   Free blocks:                                                29,136
   FAT blocks:                                                      8
   Freeable blocks in salvage system:                            655
   Non-freeable blocks in salvage system:                          0
   Directory size, in blocks:                                    98. ▼

Tab=Next window   Alt+F10=Exit                              F1=Help
```

Number of free blocks

Hence, you can have 50% of the disk available, but there are no free blocks. These blocks are used by deleted files. If free blocks are low, run a PURGE /ALL from the root of the volume to free the "freeable limbo blocks" and move them to the "free blocks" pool. To avoid doing this often, you can set the P (Purge) attribute on directories that create a large amount of temporary files. The P attribute does not flow down the file system. This needs to be taken into consideration when setting the P attribute when you have subdirectories. Also, setting Immediate Purge of Deleted Files = ON at the server console will avoid the purgeable files taking all the "free blocks"—but you'll lose the ability to salvage deleted files.

Tip #273 from
Peter

> Suballocation does not have any SET parameters to adjust. Everything is done automatically. It is very important to monitor the disk space to avoid suballocation problems. Novell Engineering *strongly* recommends keeping 10–20% of the volume space free (or maintaining more than 1000 *free* blocks) to avoid suballocation problems.

FILE DECOMPRESSION AND FREE SPACE

Like file compression, decompression takes up CPU cycles as well. If you run a volume nearly full and compression is enabled, files are compressed and never committed as decompressed due to failure of allocating enough space on the disk to hold the decompressed version.

This can be caused by Minimum File Delete Wait Time being set to a large value, and thus not allowing any deleted files to be reclaimed for space to commit a compressed file. The full volume situation is usually indicated by the "Compressed files are not being committed" alert on the server console. This message can be addressed by setting Decompress Percent Disk Space Free To Allow Commit to a number lower than the current one. However, you must still remember that there must be enough space on the volume to allow for the decompressed version of the file to be committed in order for that file to be committed decompressed.

Note

Unlike the situation with suballocation where free disk space is required, decompression makes use of available disk space, which includes space occupied by deleted files.

As a file is decompressed, it does consume CPU cycles but it will relinquish control to allow other threads and PRBs to be serviced. A Pentium processor (133MHz) can decompress, on average, 2MB a second, which means that the decompression of a very large file, for example 100MB, could take close to a minute (50 seconds) on such a machine. If NetWare is decompressing a large file, utilization will be high for the duration of the decompression. This is normal.

Tip #274 from
Peter

You can determine whether a file is compressed using the NDIR command-line utility. When the file is compressed, a lowercase *o* is shown as part of the filename in the output, as shown in the following example:

```
F:\>flag 1.1

Files         = The name of the files found
Directories   = The name of the directories found
DOS Attr      = The DOS attributes for the specified file
NetWare Attr  = The NetWare attributes for the specified file or
➥directory
Status        = The current status of migration and compression for a
➥file
                or directory
Owner         = The current owner of the file or directory
Mode          = The search mode set for the current file

Files                         DOS Attr NetWare Attr        Status Owner
➥Mode
-----------------------------------------------------------------------
1.1                           [Rw---A] [---------------] Co
➥.sdk.DreamLAN   N/A
```

To get a list of all compressed files on a volume, you can use the following command syntax:

```
NDIR SYS: /COMP /S
```

PART

VI

CH

26

PROJECT: EVALUATING STATISTICS

To help you better understand the statistics reported by MONITOR, consider the following set of sample data. Before reading further, evaluate what these statistics are trying to tell you about the potential impact on system performance and consider some possible actions to take:

Utilization:	100%
Server up time:	30:01:10:34
Online processors:	1
Original cache buffers:	15,833
Total cache buffers:	4,926
Dirty cache buffers:	1,579
Long term cache hits:	87%
Current disk requests:	17
Packet receive buffers:	500
Directory cache buffers:	28
Maximum service processes:	50
Current service processes:	48
Current connections:	15
Open files:	1068

Among these statistics, the following six sets of counters should draw your immediate attention and, perhaps, concerns:

- **Utilization**—It is showing 100%. It might or might not be a cause of concern: Momentary spikes of CPU utilization to 100% are normal; sustained utilization, however, is not. You need to check this over a time period to see whether the high utilization persists before taking action.

- **Original cache buffers / Total cache buffers**—The total cache buffers reflect the current amount of RAM available for caching, while original cache buffers show how much memory was available at server start time (after the OS is loaded). The current total cache buffers is less than 50% of its original value. You should investigate where the memory is being used up. Try forcing a garbage collection on the loaded modules and see whether it helps. There might be an NLM that has a memory leak (not releasing memory) and should be updated. Or you simply need to add more RAM for the various NLMs that you're loading.

- **Dirty cache buffers / Current disk requests**—The current large value of dirty cache buffers suggest that a number of write requests have recently been submitted to the server. However, the low current disk requests suggest that the disk channel is processing the writes slowly. You should keep an eye on these two values for a few minutes to see whether they are changing much. If the number of dirty cache buffers remain high, you should consider raising the Maximum Concurrent Disk Writes parameter.

- **Long term cache hits**—This shows less than 90% suggesting possible RAM shortage. You should use the Disk Cache Utilization option to examine the LRU sitting time and other related statistics to see whether more RAM should be added.

- **Packet receive buffers**—The value as it stands is of no immediate concern. However, recall that the default PRBs is 500. Therefore, if you haven't upped the setting from the default, you need to investigate whether you should; check the Receive discarded, no available buffers counter in the LAN/WAN drivers menu. If the Received discarded counter is steadily increasing, you need to increase the PRBs.

- **Maximum service processes / Current service processes**—These two values are very close to each other. Recall from earlier in this chapter that service processes handle user requests. If the current number of service processes is close to the maximum setting, you should consider increasing the maximum so that PRBs are serviced quickly without having to wait too long.

To do a proper server performance evaluation, you need to monitor the statistics for a long period of time to establish a baseline. Then you'd be able to easily tell which component of the server (LAN, disk, or OS) is causing the slowdown.

## CHAPTER 27

TROUBLESHOOTING COMMON PROBLEMS

In this chapter

DIRECTORY SERVICES MONITORING AND UTILITIES

The Directory Services database is what Novell calls "loosely coupled." The entire database does not reside in one location, but is broken up into logical divisions, or partitions. Each partition has a master replica and should have at least two read/write replicas, or "copies." When a change is made to the database, it can take time to ripple through the tree, but sooner or later all servers holding replicas of a partition will show the same information.

Caution

> Before performing any replica or partition operations, always check the health of your tree first! If you have problems before you start, the operation you attempt will not finish, and you will have even more problems than you did before you began. And in addition to making sure that the directory replication status is OK, don't forget to check the time synchronization status also.

So you need the capability not only of monitoring the status of the NDS database, but also to add replicas, remove replicas, change replica types, and more. Partition operations such as adding and removing replicas are covered in Chapter 16, "Managing NDS Rights, Partitions, and Replicas." In this section, we look at the most common DS error, the –625, along with the DSTrace NLM, the DSTrace screen, and a utility called MakeSU, which will recreate a deleted admin user.

–625 ERRORS

Probably the most common error reported when checking synchronization is the –625 error, shown in Figure 27.1. The –625 indicates a failure to communicate. This isn't a problem with Directory Services itself, but is a fundamental communications problem; the servers simply cannot see each other. If they can't see each other, they cannot send and receive updates; therefore, getting the –625 errors cleared up is always the first thing you need to do. After the servers are talking, other errors might disappear because all the changes would have been on hold.

To clear up the –625, look at the basics. Is the NIC loaded, and the correct protocol bound? Are you using the correct frame type? Are the servers in question speaking the same language? Are the cabling and the connectors the correct type and properly installed? Are any routers or WAN links in the picture? If so, is any filtering being done? Is the server you are failing to communicate with even up at the time? If the server in question is down for maintenance or any other reason, the –625 error is perfectly normal; don't start in with elaborate partition operations until all the servers are up and in sync.

In Chapter 28, we covered the ping and tping NLMs, which you can use from the server console to ping a host, be it a workstation or another server. If you are using the IPX protocol, Novell also has an IPX ping utility, as shown in Figure 27.2.

Figure 27.1
Here, an outbound sync to Wizard2 has failed with a –625 error, a transport failure. The end result? `All processed = No`, which is not good!

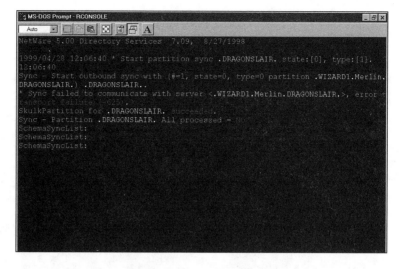

Figure 27.2
The IPX ping utility lets you ping another server or workstation using the IPX protocol.

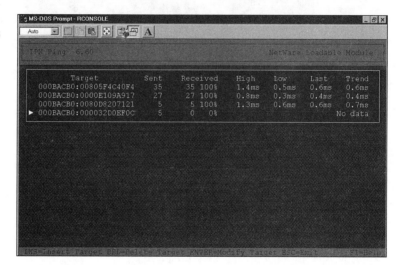

To run IPX ping, simply enter the command IPXPING at the console prompt. Enter the IPX network number and the node address of the target. The node address is the MAC address of the target NIC. You can also specify the seconds to pause between pings and the IPX packet size to send.

THE DSTrace.nlm

Prior to NetWare 5, to monitor NDS activity, you turned on the DSTrace screen. The DSTrace screen and all its arcane set parameters still work, and we will look at them later in this chapter. But a new utility, the DSTrace NLM, lets you monitor directory-services related traffic. When dstrace.nlm is loaded, you have the option of watching the traffic on a DSTrace console screen, logging the traffic to a file, or both.

The syntax to load the DSTtrace NLM is DSTRACE <options>. The screen shown in Figure 27.3 is the dstrace help screen; you can get here by loading the DSTtrace NLM and then entering the command HELP DSTRACE.

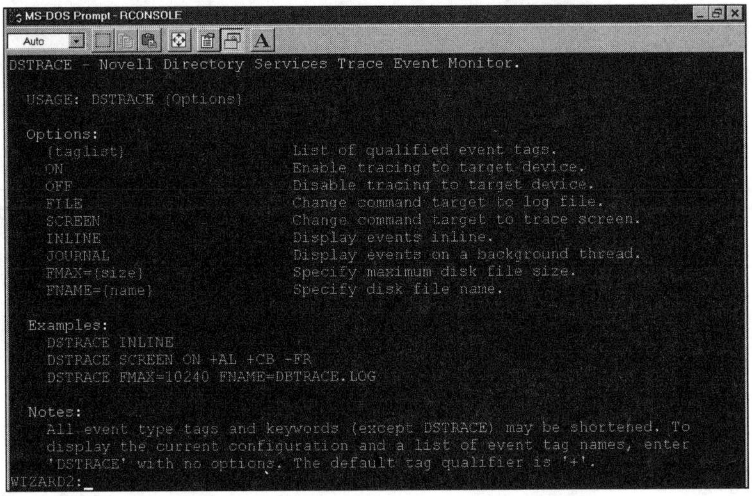

Figure 27.3
The DSTrace NLM has several command-line options; you can use these when you load DSTrace, or they can be changed on-the-fly after the NLM is loaded.

The DSTRACE options are listed here:

- {taglist}—The taglist is shown in Figure 27.5 later in this chapter. Basically, the tags are filters. You use the various tags to turn on and off events, so that you either see them or you don't.

- On/Off—These options turn tracking on or off.

- File/Screen—These options let you select the log file or the DSTrace console screen. For example, DSTRACE SCREEN OFF turns off the DSTrace console screen. DSTRACE FILE ON turns on logging to the dstrace.log file.

- Inline/Journal—This enables you to set foreground vs. background processing. Journal displays events on a background thread.

- Fmax/Fname—These options enable you to set a maximum file size when logging to a file, and also to name the file. The default file name is dstrace.log, located in sys:system.

Tip #275 from
John

You should definitely consider using the FMAX parameter to limit the size of the trace file. The default is unlimited. If you started the NLM logging to a file and then forgot it, you could easily fill up the sys volume!

The DSTrace console is shown in Figure 27.4. This screen is not to be confused with the Directory Services screen that you obtain by the set parameter SET DSTRACE = ON; the DSTrace console is independent of the Directory Services screen.

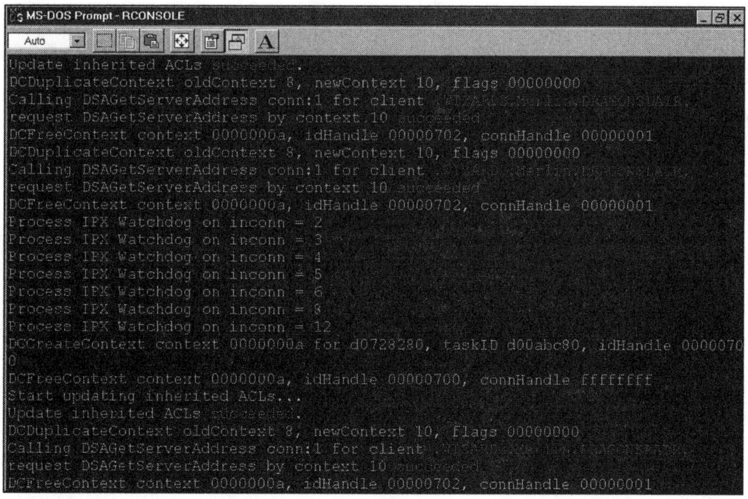

Figure 27.4
This is a view of the DSTrace console screen; this is not the same screen as the Directory Services screen that you can turn on by SET DSTRACE=ON.

A variety of information will be displayed on the DSTrace console, and you control what you wish to see by the use of the tags we mentioned earlier. You can obtain a list of the available tags by using the command DSTRACE TAGS or by entering the command DSTRACE with no parameters, after the NLM has been loaded.

In addition to obtaining the tag list, at the top of the screen shown in Figure 27.5 is the current DSTrace configuration and the status of the tags. For example, you can see that the trace mode is journal, the trace screen is on, the trace file is on with no size limit, and the file name is dstrace.log. You can tell if a tag is enabled by its color. If a tag is enabled, it is a nice bright cyan. If a tag is disabled, it is a dim gray.

Figure 27.5
The command DSTRACE TAGS not only displays the available tags, but also the current status of your tracking and which tags are enabled/disabled.

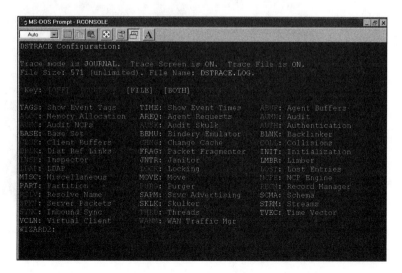

PART

VI

CH

27

Tags are enabled and disabled by using the + and –, followed by the name of the tag. Suppose that you were not interested in the times that events occur; you would enter the command DSTRACE -TIME. This stop the event times from showing, and the TIME tag toggles from bright cyan to dim gray.

Tip #276 from	The tags are not case sensitive, and you can save a bit of typing by using only the first two
John	letters of a tag; in other words, DSTRACE -BE is equivalent to dstrace -bemu.

The tag settings are persistent; if you disable a tag, then the next time you load the DSTrace NLM, that tag will *still* be disabled. This information is stored in a file sys:system\dstrace.cfg. If you have enabled and disabled a lot of things and want a fresh start, just delete this .cfg file, and you will be back to the defaults.

THE DIRECTORY SERVICES SCREEN (DSTRACE SCREEN)

If you enter the set parameter SET DSTRACE=ON, then a new screen appears at the console, the Directory Services screen, or what is commonly called the DSTrace screen. This screen is not to be confused with the DSTrace console screen covered in the previous section. The Directory Services displays the same information, except instead of enabling and disabling tags, you have to use a variety of arcane set parameters. There are also set parameters to force actions to occur. A very common use of the DSTrace screen, shown in Figure 27.6, is to check for All Processed = YES before beginning any partition operation.

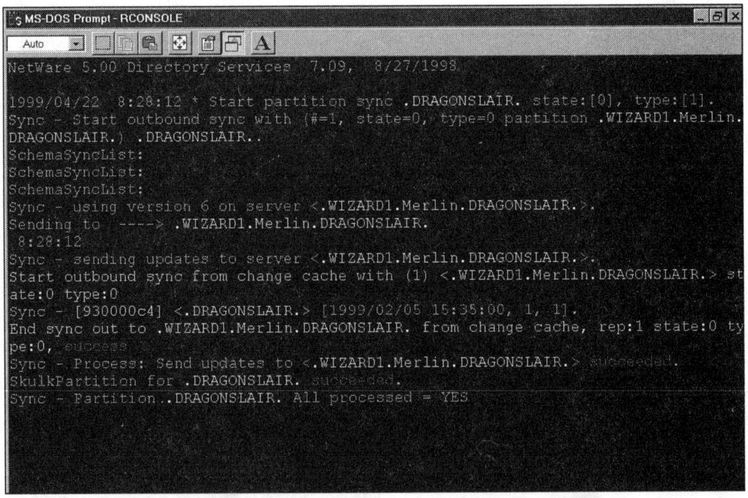

Figure 27.6
You can force an update to occur via SET DSTRACE=*H; you can then toggle to the DSTrace screen to see the results.

What are the various DSTrace-related set commands? Good question; it's a long list. Rather than list them all here, an excellent source both for the DSTrace parameters and an understanding of them is the February 1997 AppNote, "Using the Directory Services Trace (DSTrace) Screen." You can get this AppNote off the Web at `http://developer.novell.com/research/appnotes.htm`, from the support connection CD, or by calling Novell.

The syntax is always `SET DSTRACE=<some command or setting>`. For an example, try the following:

- `SET DSTRACE=ON` — This will turn on DSTrace, and you should now be able to toggle to the DSTrace screen; odds are it will be blank, with nothing at the top but the version of the DS NLM.

- `SET DSTRACE=*H` — The *h forces a synchronization to occur. Now toggle to the DSTrace screen, and you should see the same information as that in Figure 27.6: your server attempting to synchronize with the other servers in the replica ring.

- `SET DSTRACE=OFF` — This turns off DSTrace, and the DSTrace screen disappears. A few of the DSTrace settings are given in Table 27.1, but there are many, many more!

TABLE 27.1   ONLY A FEW OF THE DSTRACE SETTINGS

Set Statement	Function
Set dstrace=on	Enables the DSTrace screen.
Set dstrace=off	Disables the DSTtrace screen.
Set ttf=on	Start logging to the `dstrace.dbg` file.
Set ttf=off	Stop logging to the `dstrace.dbg` file.
Set dstrace=*r	Reset the trace file (start overwriting it).
Set dstrace=*h	Force an immediate synchronization.
Set dstrace=*.	Unload and reload the `ds.nlm`.
Set dstrace=*p	Displays the current settings of the tunable DS parameters.

DELETED OR IRF'D ADMIN—MAKESU

In the 2.x and 3.x versions of NetWare, user supervisor was installed by default. Supervisor had all rights to the system, and the user supervisor could not be deleted. To make another account have the same powers as user supervisor, security equivalence was used; you took the user account and made it security equivalent to user supervisor.

All this changed in the 4.x version of NetWare. No user supervisor exists; instead, there is the Admin user. And absolutely nothing is different about user admin from any other user; but user admin has all rights to the root, granted at the time you first create the tree.

NetWare 3.x administrators have been making themselves security equivalent to user supervisor for years. So quite naturally, when they move to NetWare 4 and NetWare 5, the first thing they do is make themselves security equivalent to user admin. And this works, but one problem occurs.

There is nothing special about user admin beyond the rights to the root of the tree; this means that the admin user can be deleted. And after the admin account is deleted, the security equivalence to admin goes right out the window. This leaves you with a tree that you cannot administer! Another thing that can happen is inadvertently putting an IRF (Inherited Rights Filter) on a container that locks out user admin.

Although experienced administrators might laugh at this, it is actually an extremely common problem. When the admin account is deleted, you have the following three options to resolve the situation:

- **Remove directory services**—This means that you will have to completely rebuild your tree from scratch. You get a new admin user all right, but only the smallest of shops would be able to completely start over and recreate all users, login scripts, printers, and so on.

- **Open a call with Novell**—Novell can dial into your network via something such as PC Anywhere and then recreate user admin. Be prepared to pay Novell for the call. You also need the PC setup for them to connect to, and paperwork is necessary to prove that it is your network and that you need Novell to fix it.

- **MakeSU**—A Novell-certified NLM written by Dr. Peter Kuo, one of the authors of this book. MakeSU will create a user in any context, including the root, with all rights to that context.

MakeSU has several security features; the first is that it runs only off a floppy at the server console. This means that you need to have physical access to the file server; without physical security, there is *no* security. The second security feature is that MakeSU is keyed to the name of your tree; it works only on the one network for which it was generated. If you order a copy of MakeSU, it will work only on one network; if you try to carry it elsewhere, it will not run because the treename would be different.

> **Note**
>
> MakeSU can be ordered online from MagicNet Network Consulting at http://www.jpence.com, a secure online service, or at DreamLAN Network Consulting at http://www.dreamlan.com.

But the main lesson you get for free because you're reading this book is *don't make yourself the security equivalent to user admin!* Instead, give your "backup" admin account all rights to the root of the tree. This way, if something happens to the admin user, you are OK. You can log in as your "backup" and create a new admin.

ABENDS

An *abend*, or *abnormal ending*, will generally ruin your day, especially if hundreds of people are accessing the server. Various types and causes of abends exist, caused both by hardware and software. Many abends, which I call "soft" abends, Novell can recover from, and the server will stay up; from others, it cannot, and the server will need to be restarted.

The first thing to do in preventing abends is to be proactive. Keep the server patched up to the latest patches, available at `http://support.novell.com`. Follow the link to the minimum patch list. Make sure that you are using the newest NIC and disk controller NLMs from the vendors, and the most current versions of third party NLMs.

The server hardware also needs to be up to the task; a server without enough memory will be problematic all the time. All cards and cabling need to be well-seated, and the server needs to be cooled enough to prevent overheating. The server should be on a UPS (uninterruptible power supply), which should also filter the power to prevent brownouts and spikes.

If the abend happens at the same time each day, look for what is going on at that time; for example, compression starts at midnight by default, and tape backup jobs are usually scheduled to kick off automatically at a certain time. Also, look for change; if the server has been running fine and suddenly begins abending, something has changed. Other NLMs have been loaded, or hardware is getting flaky.

CONTROLLING AUTOMATIC ABEND RECOVERY

The server can be set to automatically recover from an abend. As strange as it might seem, it is possible for you to have an abend and not know it, if you have the server configured for automatic abend recovery. This is especially true now that the clients will auto reconnect to the server when it comes back up. You could have an abend in the middle of the night, the server could restart, all clients reconnect, and when you get to work, all is fine. So keep an eye on the logs.

If you have a "soft" abend, one that the server can recover from, you will see the server name at the console followed by <some number>, as shown in Figure 27.7.

As you can see from Figure 27.7, server Wizard2 has encountered three abends. You can tell this by the number in the brackets (<>) following the server name. The server has been able to recover each time, but as you can see from the warning, "services hosted by this server may have been affected." The best thing you can do at this time is to restart the server as soon as possible.

PART

VI

CH

27

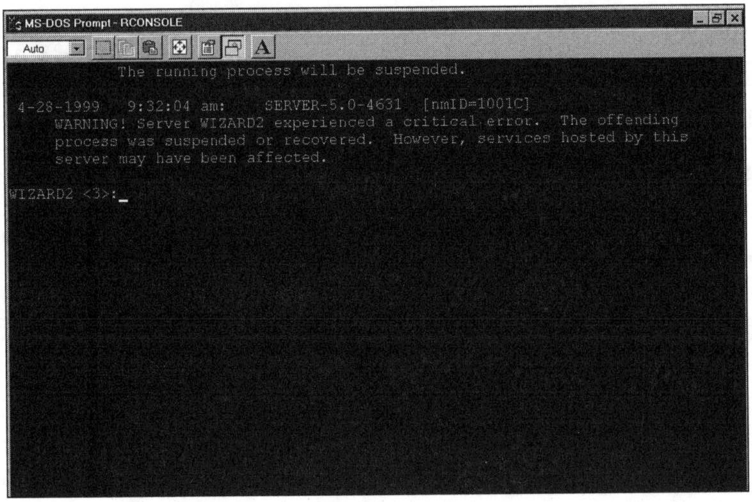

Figure 27.7
Server Wizard2 has
experienced three
abends; the server has
been able to suspend
the errant process and
is still up. This is a
"soft" abend.

```
MS-DOS Prompt - RCONSOLE

 Auto

                The running process will be suspended.

 4-28-1999   9:32:04 am:      SERVER-5.0-4631  [nmID=1001C]
     WARNING! Server WIZARD2 experienced a critical error.  The offending
     process was suspended or recovered.  However, services hosted by this
     server may have been affected.

 WIZARD2 <3>:_
```

Tip #277 from
John

If the server has downed and restarted itself, you will *not* see the server name followed by
<#>; all will look normal. The <#> happens only when the server recovers from the abend
and keeps itself up.

Automatic abend recovery is controlled by two set parameters (actually three, but the third
parameter, the Developer Option, would not be turned on in a production environment).
See Chapter 23, "Server Console Utilities," for information on setting the server's environ-
mental parameters. What are the two parameters that control automatic abend recovery?

■ **Auto Restart After Abend Delay Time**—This is the time in minutes that that server
will wait before automatically shutting down and restarting. The default is 2 minutes,
and it can be set from 2 minutes up to 60 minutes.

■ **Auto Restart After Abend**— Four values are possible:

   ■ 0—Do not try to recover from the abend. As the administrator, you will have to
   respond to the abend manually.

   ■ 1—This is the default setting. For software abends, NMIs, and Machine Check
   exceptions, the OS will attempt to recover, then down itself after the time configured in the Auto Restart After Abend Delay Time and restart. For other exception abends, the OS will suspend the faulty process and leave the server up. This
   is when you see the *servername <number>* indicating an abend from which the
   server has recovered. In Figure 27.7, we had the Auto Restart After Abend parameter set to 1, the default, and generated an abend. Next, we will set the Auto
   Restart After Abend parameter to 2, and you will see the difference in Figure 27.8
   when we generate the same abend.

- 2—For *all* hardware and software abends, the OS will down the server in the configured amount of time, then restart. The difference between setting the Auto Restart After Abend to 2 is that the server will restart for all abends, as shown in Figure 27.8.

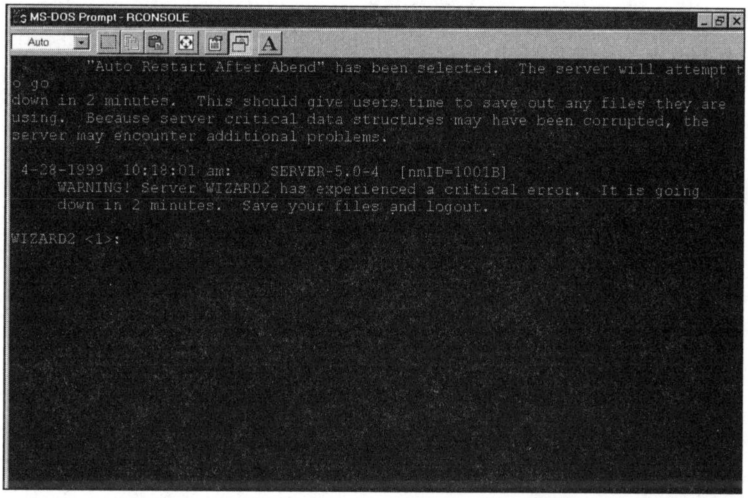

Figure 27.8
Even though we have generated the same abend as that shown in Figure 27.7, this time the server is going to restart.

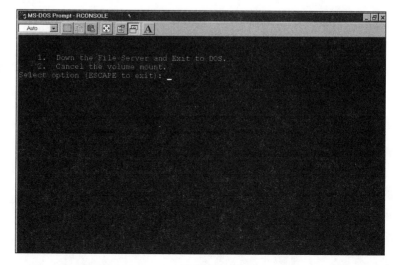

- 3—Setting the Auto Restart After Abend to 3 has the same effect as setting it to a value of 2. The only difference is that the server restarts immediately; the Auto Restart After Abend Delay Time setting is ignored.

If you have the Auto Restart After Abend set to 0, then you will have to manually handle the abend. Depending on the state of the server, you might have a prompt at the console to respond to. Other options are to enter the debugger and exit to DOS, or press Ctrl+Alt+Esc and choose to down the server and exit to DOS, as shown in Figure 27.9.

Figure 27.9
It might be possible to down the server by pressing Ctrl+Alt+Esc and choosing option 1.

THE Abend.log

Whenever you experience an abend, always check the abend.log in sys:system. The information in the log will probably point you to the culprit, and it is a lot easier than using the debugger to arrive at the same information. The abend log gets appended to, so you might want to either delete it or rename it after you have examined the log.

The abend log for server Wizard2 is given below; it is complete with the exception of the modules listing. The modules listing will list every module running on the server, and you can use it to check whether you have the most recent versions:

| Tip #278 from | When posting the abend log to the support forums, you don't need to post the entire log; |
| *John* | post the top portion minus the modules listing. |

```
Server WIZARD2 halted Wednesday, April 28, 1999  10:23:51 amAbend 1 on P00:
Server-5.00a: Invalid Opcode Processor ExceptionRegisters:
    CS = 0008 DS = 0010 ES = 0010 FS = 0010 GS = 0010 SS = 0010
    EAX = 00000004 EBX = D1FB0238 ECX = 02E9BEF0 EDX = 00000005
    ESI = D2046040 EDI = 00000000 EBP = 02E9BED0 ESP = 02E9BEC0
    EIP = D1FB0443 FLAGS = 00014297
    ABENDEMO.NLM¦DoInvalidOpcode:
D1FB0443 0FFF            ??FF
    EIP in ABENDEMO.NLM at code start +00000443h

Running process: Abend Demo Process
Created by: NetWare Application
Thread Owned by NLM: ABENDEMO.NLM
Stack pointer: 2E9BCE0
OS Stack limit: 2E98000
Scheduling priority: 67371008
Wait state: 5050170  (Blocked on keyboard)
Stack: D1FB02A1   (ABENDEMO.NLM¦MenuAction+69)
       D1FCD602   (NWSNUT.NLM¦NWSShowPortalLine+3602)
       --00000004  ?
       --00000000  ?
       --02E9BF20  ?
       --D0240060  ?
       --00000001  ?
       D1FCD949   (NWSNUT.NLM¦NWSShowPortalLine+3949)
       --00000010  ?
       --02E9BEF0  ?
       --02E9BEF4  ?
       --02E9BFAC  ?
       --D20440A0  (ABENDEMO.NLM¦programMesgTable+DD78)
       --00000006  ?
       --00000008  ?
       --00000012  ?
       --00000000  ?
       --00000019  ?
       --00000050  ?
       --000000FF  ?
       --00000001  ?
       --00000010  ?
```

```
--00000001  ?
--00000000  ?
--00000011  ?
--02E9BFDC  ?
--0000000B  ?
--00000000  ?
D1FCDBD9  (NWSNUT.NLM¦NWSShowPortalLine+3BD9)
--0000000B  ?
--00000000  ?
--00000000  ?
```

```
Additional Information:
    The CPU encountered an invalid instruction.  This was
    probably caused by corruption to the ABENDEMO.NLM code segment.
    It may have also been caused by a corruption to a process owned
    by ABENDEMO.NLM.
```

```
Loaded Modules:
SERVER.NLM        NetWare Server Operating System
   Version 5.00      August 27, 1998
   Code Address: FC000000h  Length: 000A5000h
   Data Address: FC5A5000h  Length: 000C9000h
LOADER.EXE        NetWare OS Loader
   Code Address: 000133D0h  Length: 0001D000h
   Data Address: 000303D0h  Length: 00020C30h
   <and more modules not shown>
```

At the top of the log is the server name, the date, and the time of the abend. This information is useful if you find that the server abends at the same time every day; the question then is what occurs at that time, such as compression starting or a tape backup kicking off. On the next line, the exact abend message is given—in this case, "invalid opcode processor exception."

The register values aren't going to be of any value to most of us. One thing you can do is look for a consistent pattern in the registers, which would indicate that the operating system was following the same code path each time. You can see that the instruction pointer (EIP) was in the abendemo.nlm, and the running process is "abend demo process." In fact, all indications seem to indicate that the abendemo.nlm is the culprit! But the NLM given is not necessarily always the culprit; it could have received a bad function of some sort from another NLM.

Often, the abend.log itself, or in conjunction with a search of the support connection CD or the support connection Web site, is enough to point you toward a solution.

CREATING A CORE DUMP WITH THE NETWARE DEBUGGER

Be careful with the debugger; you couldn't think of an easier way to abend your server than playing in this area. We mostly just want to make you aware of its existence; although a very experienced administrator might be able to recover from a file server abend via the debugger, about the only time most people would use it is if Novell asked them for a core dump. For more information on the debugger, I refer you to the various AppNotes available from Novell's Web sites.

PART

VI

CH

27

A core dump is a copy of the server's memory written to a file, which can then be sent to Novell for analyzing. Two types of core dumps are possible:

- Full, which copies the entire contents of the server's memory to a file.
- Full minus Disk Cache, which copies the server's memory but does not copy the file cache. This core dump will naturally be smaller, but for troubleshooting purposes, it has as much information needed as the full core dump.

You enter the debugger by a very arcane series of keystrokes—Shift+Shift+Alt+Esc. Obviously, Novell didn't want that series hit by accident! I find it easiest to use my right hand to hit the Shift and Alt keys, and my left hand to hit the other Shift and Esc.

Tip #279 from
John

Inside the debugger, you will have nothing but a # prompt. For help, enter *h* for the debugger command help screen. You can also enter .*h* for the debugger dot command help, and other help screens are available. For more information, search the AppNotes; several AppNotes cover the debugger in some depth. You might also try `http://www.avanti-tech.com` and follow the link to Network Management Tips.

To create a core dump, enter .`c` at the # debugger command prompt. You are then asked for the core dump type (one of the choices we have already covered—full or full without cache). You then enter a path for the core dump file; the default is `c:\coredump.img`. When you hit enter, the system begins writing the core dump out to the file.

After the core dump has been written, the command *q* will quit the debugger and exit to DOS. You could use this to shut down a hung server if you can still get to the debugger; it's the same as pressing Ctrl+Alt+Esc and choosing the option to down the file server and exit to DOS.

Depending on the state of the server, you can also enter *g* at the debugger command prompt. The g command will begin execution at the current EIP, which is the CPU's instruction pointer. For example, you can test this by entering the debugger, looking at the help, then entering *g*. You will exit the debugger and be back at the server console.

TIME SYNCHRONIZATION

The key to troubleshooting time synchronization problems is knowing how time synchronization works. Know the four types of time servers, which were covered in Chapter 7, "Time Synchronization," and how they interrelate. For example, if all the servers on a network are secondary time servers, then no time provider is available for them to contact, and time will not be in sync until that is straightened out.

The next key is knowing how your network is set up for time sync. You need to know which servers are the providers, which are just consumers, whether you are using configured time sources, and so on. More small networks exist than large ones, so most setups will have one single reference time server, and the rest will be secondary time servers.

GATHERING TIME INFORMATION

The timesync NLM is going to read the following information from the server's autoexec.ncf file:

```
set Time Zone = CST6CDTset Daylight Savings Time Offset = 1:00:00set Start
    Of Daylight Savings Time  = (APRIL SUNDAY FIRST 2:00:00 AM)
set End Of Daylight Savings Time = (OCTOBER SUNDAY LAST 2:00:00 AM)
set Default Time Server Type = SECONDARY
# Note: The Time zone information mentioned above
# should always precede the SERVER name.
```

Not only is the time zone and daylight saving time information given here, but also the time server type, secondary in the case of this server. Also, when you're editing, take note of the lines that the installation has added to the autoexec.ncf file; the time-zone information should precede the server's name. To see a servercentric view of the time status, enter the command TIME at the server's console:

```
Wizard2:time  Time zone string: "CST6CDT"  DST status:  ON  DST start:
Sunday, April 2, 2000   2:00:00 am CST  DST end:     Sunday, October 31, 1999
   2:00:00 am CDT  Time synchronization is active.
Time is synchronized to the network.Wednesday, April 28, 1999   7:40:43 pm UTC
Wednesday, April 28, 1999   2:40:43 pm CDT
```

By servercentric, we mean that the results of this command are only what the one server, Wizard2 in this case, thinks about its time synchronization status. What are you looking for when you issue the command time? You want to see that "time is synchronized to the network," as shown in boldface above.

```
WIZARD2:time  Time zone string: "CST6CDT"  DST status:  ON  DST start:
Sunday, April 2, 2000   2:00:00 am CST  DST end:     Sunday, October 31, 1999
   2:00:00 am CDT
  Time synchronization is active.
  Time is NOT synchronized to the network.
Wednesday, April 28, 1999   7:59:40 pm UTC
Wednesday, April 28, 1999   2:59:40 pm CDT
```

This time, when the TIME command was issued, you can see that time is not synchronized to the network. This indicates a problem, but again, this is a servercentric view; other servers might be synchronized. To quickly find out how a server is configured, enter the set command SET TIMESYNC TYPE with no parameters, as follows:

```
Wizard2:set timesync typeTIMESYNC Type:  SECONDARYMaximum length:  22
Description: The type of time source.  Choose from SINGLE reference,
          REFERENCE, PRIMARY, or SECONDARY.
```

The response will display the current setting for the timesync type—in this case, secondary. To get the big picture, load the DSRepair NLM by entering the command DSREPAIR at the server console. From the Available Options menu, select Time Synchronization and press Enter. The server then contacts every server known to the local NDS database and asks them for their time synchronization status, as shown in Figure 27.10.

Figure 27.10

Checking the time synchronization via DSRepair gives you information on the version of *DS.NLM*, the replica depth, the time server type, and the synchronization status of all servers.

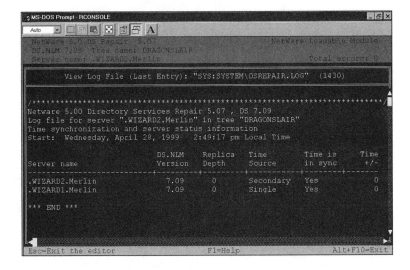

The Time Source field shown in Figure 27.10 is a bit misleading; DSRepair doesn't report the time source for each server, but rather the time server type. This is where you get the big picture, and you can see whether time synchronization is configured properly. As we pointed out earlier, if you saw both Wizard1 and Wizard2 as secondary time servers, for example, you immediately know that a configuration problem exists.

For the Time Is in Sync field, you want to see Yes. If it says No, find out who that server is trying to contact as its time source; the server showing No probably cannot contact its time source.

The time delta field (time +/–) shows how far out of sync the server is. In Figure 27.11, server Wizard2 is not in sync. The delta is given in the form of minutes:seconds. All your servers should be within one second of each other, or you will have problems. The time delta field will go up to 999:59, which is about 16 1/2 hours. If the delta is off by more than this, the value is given as –999:59. As you can see from Figure 27.11, Wizard1 is way out of line!

If you want to see what is going on in terms of a server's time traffic, enter the command SET TIMESYNC DEBUG=7. This will throw up a new timesync debug screen to which you can toggle like any other console screen. On the timesync debug screen, you can see the time-sync traffic. In Figure 27.12, the server is polling Wizard1, a Single reference time server.

Figure 27.11
Server Wizard1 is in sync, but a problem obviously exists with time synchronization; Wizard2 is not in sync, and the time delta on Wizard1 is –7:15.

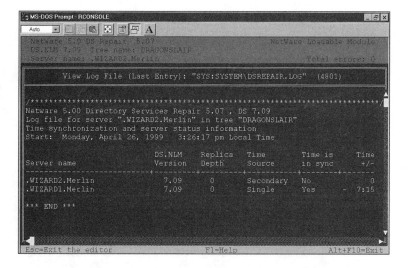

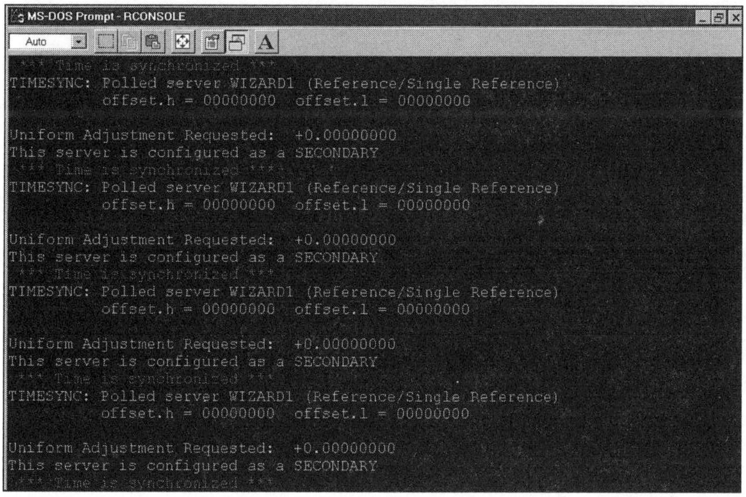

Figure 27.12
The timesync debug screen is a bit on the cryptic side. To turn it off, set the timesync debug to 0.

PART
VI

CH
27

SYNTHETIC TIME

When you modify an NDS object, (create, delete, and so on) the object is time stamped. If you set the time ahead on your network, that doesn't cause any problems at all, as long as you leave it that way. It's when you set the time back to the current time that you see problems, and that will be synthetic time being issued on partition *<some name>*, as shown in Figure 27.13.

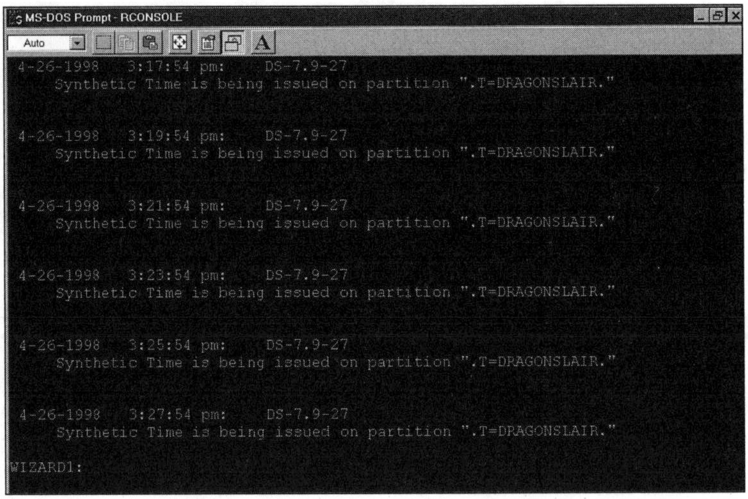

Figure 27.13
You will see synthetic time being issued if you set the time ahead and then later return the server to the actual time.

You will see this message every two minutes while the time sync process tries to close the gap, as it were. A small difference in time isn't going to affect things, and you can do nothing. The times will ultimately converge and the synthetic time messages will go away. But if you have set the time ahead by months, or even years, and then you return to the actual time, the time sync process isn't going to converge any time soon, and you need to take action to cure the situation. This is done via DSRepair using the -a switch.

Caution

What we are about to discuss—repairing time stamps and declaring a new epoch— will possibly generate a huge amount of network traffic.

The DSRepair NLM has many switches that Novell does not document. This lets them change the switches from version to version and keeps administrators from destroying their networks. The one that is both documented and consistent is the -a switch.

Load DSREPAIR -A, and select the Advanced Options menu. From the Advanced Options menu, select Replica and Partition Operations. Highlight the replica that is issuing synthetic time and press Enter. You will be at the Replica Options menu (see Figure 27.14).

Figure 27.14
The option to repair time stamps and declare a new epoch only shows up if you load DSRepair using the -a switch.

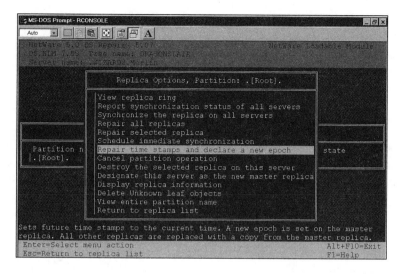

You want to choose Repair Time Stamps and Declare a New Epoch, which will only show up if you have loaded DSRepair using the -a switch. Select the option to repair time stamps and declare a new epoch; you will then be prompted to log in as the admin. After you log in, you will see the message "Repair time stamps has been scheduled, press enter to continue," and that's it.

What does this do, and why the caution given earlier? This sets the time stamps of all objects in the partition you have chosen to the current time, and it sets all replicas of that partition to a state of NEW, except for the master. This means that all the read/write replicas will receive a copy of all objects. Depending on the number of objects you are talking about and the number of replicas, this can add up to some serious network traffic and high server utilization.

Tip #280 from
John

Keeping the traffic and server utilization in mind, this procedure is best done during an "off" period on your network. Also, you want to make sure that all servers and replicas are up and available.

PART

VI

Cн

27

SUPPORT SOURCES

In this section, we take a look at some of the options you have for support. Often, when troubleshooting, you wind up in the middle of a finger-pointing contest. The vendor of a disk, NIC, or NLM will claim the problem lies with Novell, whereas Novell might claim that the vendor's software or hardware is the problem. The best way to resolve this type of conflict is by posting a message in the online forums, which we will cover later in this section.

Why the forums? Problems are going to follow a graph shaped like a bell curve; in the center of the curve, and the vast majority, are the common problems and the curve gradually diminishes to the truly exotic problems at the edge of the curve. These off the wall problems crop up only in certain setups. So the odds are extremely good that if the problem is with the OS itself, someone else has already seen the same thing you are seeing. Think about the millions of people running NetWare; the forums are the ideal way to ask them, "Hey, has anyone seen this before? Here is what is happening."

If the problem lies with the OS, you will almost certainly get an answer. If the problem lies with your setup, such as some odd brand of controller, probably no one else—or at least very few people—would have seen the same thing, so you might then look toward your own configuration.

ONLINE DOCUMENTATION

The days when you could line the shelves in your office with a long line of Novell red manuals have come to an end; now the documentation is all on one CD-ROM. The Online Documentation is an excellent resource; it installs and adds a bookmark to your Web browser, and it has a search engine and a print engine. I would recommend a hefty machine in terms of memory and processor power; otherwise, you won't be happy, especially with the Java-based search and print engines!

To install the online documentation, insert the CD and from the first menu, select Install Documentation. The next screen is a welcome screen; press Next, and then either accept the default file location of `c:\novdoc` or change it. On the next screen you select the language; this screen also has a button labeled Services. The Services button takes you to the Select Services screen, shown in Figure 27.15.

Figure 27.15
Why these are called services are beyond me; they are actually like chapters in a book.

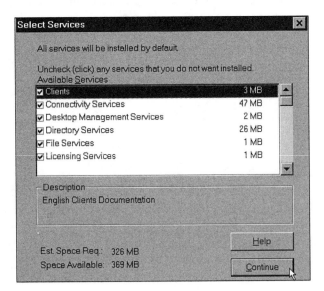

From the Select Services screen, you can uncheck any documentation you do not wish to have installed; by default, all the "services," or chapters, are checked. When you continue, the next screen merely shows you the options you have chosen. Press Next to continue, and then the file copy begins.

After installation, you will have a bookmark added to your Web browser pointing to the documentation files. Simply click the bookmark as you would when going to any site, and voilà, the home page of the online documentation appears. In Figure 27.16, we have selected the Contents link from the home page.

Figure 27.16
The online documentation is pretty good–definitely worth installing and using.

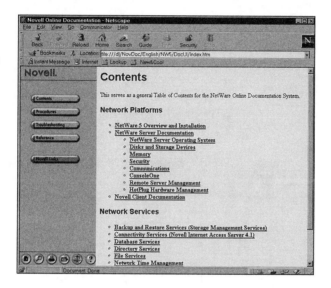

Most of the sections use frames, with the table of contents of each section in a frame to the left and the actual documentation in the pane to the right. The downside to online docs is that you can't take them with you, discounting laptops, of course. The upside to online documentation is that it is searchable; the search engine is Java based and is shown in Figure 27.17.

To run the search engine, click the icon that looks like a magnifying glass in the lower-left corner at any screen of the documentation. In Figure 27.17, we have searched for "nlsp"; the hits are returned in the lower panel. The Options tab lets you refine your search with options such as Match All Words (a Boolean AND) or "Match Any Words" (a Boolean OR). It's all fairly intuitive, like navigating any Web site, so play around with it.

The print engine is another neat feature; you can always choose File, Print Frame from the toolbar of the browser, but suppose you wanted to print out the entire chapter on Novell Public Key Infrastructure Services. Using the Print Frame choice from the toolbar would force you to navigate to each frame you wanted printed, and then print the frame every time. This is awkward, and it would be easy to miss something because it's all linked together. The print engine, shown in Figure 27.18, is much simpler.

PART

VI

Cн

27

Figure 27.17
The search engine and the print engine are Java based, so a machine with lots of memory and horsepower helps!

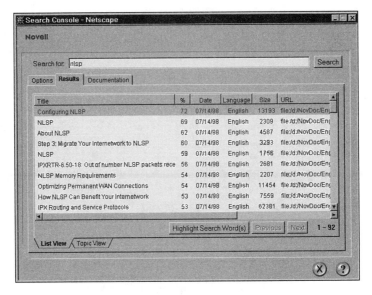

Figure 27.18
The print engine will let you drill down, make your selections, and then print.

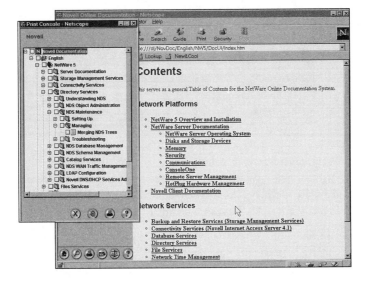

The print engine is launched the same as the search engine, except that the icon, looks like a printer. You can drill down and print only what you are interested in—an entire chapter or only a subsection of one.

SUPPORT CONNECTION NEWSGROUPS AND WEB FORUMS

Novell currently has the Web-based interface in beta; it's up and working, but a bit rusty as of this writing. You can get to the Web forum interface by starting at `http://support.novell.com` and clicking the Forums link. You need to provide a name and email address, and you are then presented with a list of the available forums. Choose the one you are interested in, and you can then view the messages as shown in Figure 27.19.

Figure 27.19
The Web interface to the Novell support forums is currently in beta; this interface would be useful to those who want to post and read only occasionally.

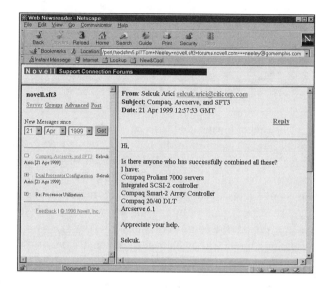

If you are interested in posting and reading messages only when you have a problem, the Web interface would be OK for you to use. But for any serious monitoring of the forums, you need a newsreader. Several newsreaders are available, and all are conceptually the same. A newsreader allows you to mark the messages you are interested in and then download them. This gives you the opportunity to read them offline at your leisure and to compose answers. When you have your replies ready, you can then reconnect to the server and post your responses.

A newsreader uses the Network News Transport Protocol (NNTP), and the news server for the support forums is at `forums.novell.com`. First, you configure the newsreader, which is a matter of putting in your name, email address, and mail server information. Then, point it to the news server and it will retrieve a listing of available groups for you to subscribe to (see Figure 27.20).

PART

VI

CH

27

Figure 27.20
This newsreader is Anawave Gravity. It has retrieved a list of 161 newsgroups, and you select the ones you wish to monitor from the list in the top pane.

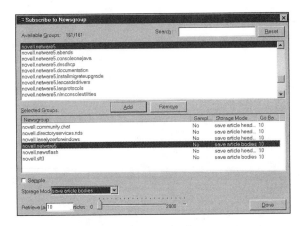

After the messages have been downloaded, you can read and reply to them offline. In Figure 27.21, the newsreader has three panes. In the top pane are the newsgroups subscribed to. In the middle pane are the message threads. A thread is an initial posting, followed by its replies and the replies to the replies, ad infinitum. A new thread is started whenever a message is posted that is not a reply to another message. It's helpful, and good etiquette, to use Reply to a Message when replying, not by starting a new thread with your reply. When you reply by starting a new thread, the continuity is broken, your reply is out of context, and no one knows what is going on unless they happen to remember the thread where your message actually belongs.

In the lower pane of Gravity is the actual body of the message along with the header information, such as the subject and who posted the message.

Figure 27.21
A newsreader will let you download and read messages offline. You'll have to make up your own mind about putting a slice of cheese on top of your NIC, but not all the forums have to be serious! This one is the Chat forum.

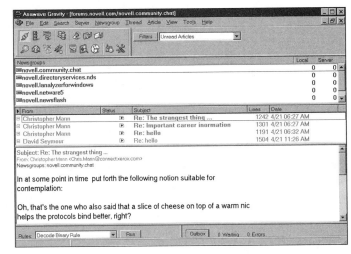

Tip #281 from *John*	Both Netscape and Internet Explorer have newsreaders built in. They will not be as full-featured as an actual newsreader program, however.

THE SUPPORT CONNECTION CD

I believe that any NetWare administrator should have two things: a copy of LANalyzer to see what is happening on the wire and a subscription to the support connection. There are those who might argue against the former, but everyone needs the subscription to the support-connection CDs!

The support-connection CD is a set of CD-ROMs that you receive once a month. The subscription cost is currently $495 for a single-user license (this price is for the U.S. and Canada), and CNEs get $200 off this price, so the cost to a CNE in the U.S. or Canada is $295. The support connection isn't only the Technical Information Documents (TIDs), but it also has software updates, patches, drivers, product documentation, the entire collection of AppNotes, and more.

You can obtain all this via Novell's Web site. However, you might not always have Internet access available, or you might be onsite at a customers location and not have Internet access. Also, downloading can be painfully slow, depending on the state of the Internet and your connection speed.

To install the support connection, insert the CD and run setup. Accept the license agreement, and then choose whether you want only the infobase viewer installed, or both the infobase viewer and the infobases. A full install of both the viewer and infobases will take 320,245K or 320MB, so that might be a consideration. After the file copy, select the Web browser to use with folio if both Netscape and Internet Explorer are installed on your system.

After installation, simply click the Novell Support icon, and you will be at the home page of the support-connection CD, as shown in Figure 27.22.

Before you even think about calling Novell, the first thing you should do is run a query of your own. If it's a known issue, you'll have your answer or some points to start looking from, instantaneously. To run a query, click the Query button and then enter the text you wish to search for, such as `sft3 & ip`. The results are displayed in a window like that shown in Figure 27.23. Double-click the result that most interests you, and the actual document appears.

PART

VI

CH

27

Figure 27.22
From here, you can run a query or use the existing links, such as the ones under product support.

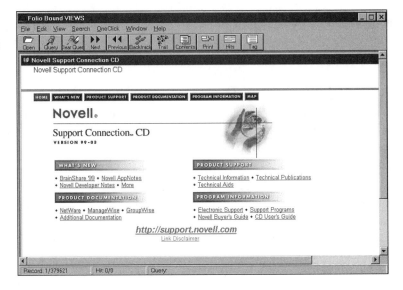

Figure 27.23
A search on `sft3 & ip` returns 31 hits. You double-click the document you wish to see.

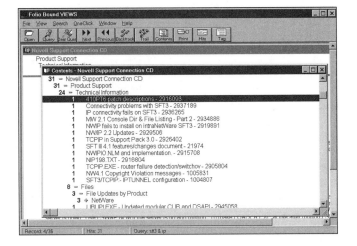

Tip #282 from
John

You might try running your query in more than one fashion. For example, a query on `sft3 & ip` returns 31 hits, but a query on `sftiii & ip` returns only 25. A search on `nlsp` returns 1,542 hits, whereas a search on `netware link services protocol` (nlsp) returns only 570.

support.novell.com

For support via the Web, you will want to start at `http://support.novell.com`, as shown in Figure 27.24.

Figure 27.24
From the Support Connection home page at http://support.novell.com, you can search and more.

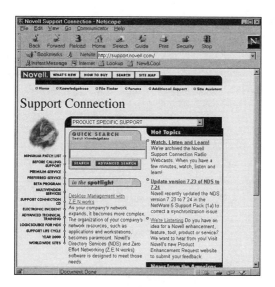

From the Support Connection page, you can access the file finder, the forums, the minimum patch list, and more. For example, we selected the link to the knowledge base from the Support Connection page, and then entered the words dead and server for the search criteria. The results are shown in Figure 27.25.

Figure 27.25
The results from a search on the words *dead* and *server*; the kind of search you would make when a server has been incorrectly removed from the tree.

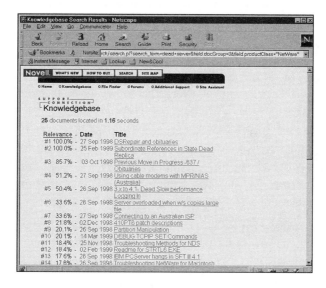

Why the words dead and server? When a server has been incorrectly removed from the tree, you are going to have serious NDS problems because the other servers all think the dead one is still alive. As a consequence, they continue to try to contact the missing server until eternity, unless the situation is corrected. If the results are too many and broad, simply go back and refine the search further or make a new one.

NOVELL

To open an incident with Novell, call them. Calling 1-800-NETWARE will point you in the right direction, and it is easy to remember. You can also get the correct telephone numbers at http://support.novell.com. The current phone number for America is 1-800-858-4000.

Be prepared to pay for the call on the front end with a credit card. If the problem turns out to be a bug in the NetWare OS, the charge will be reversed and the call is free.

LogicSource for NDS

If you really want to learn and study NDS, you should look into purchasing the LogicSource for NDS. This is a CD-ROM with extremely detailed NDS information. For more information, follow the LogicSource link at http://support.novell.com.

MORE TROUBLESHOOTING

The number of things that can go wrong is legion, and if you are a believer in Murphy's law, something will go wrong. Move slowly, and if possible, change only one thing at a time. If you jump in and put on a service pack, update some NLMs, and change the NIC card, you might fix the problem, but what exactly fixed it?

Document your changes and keep a log for each server. What you do now might seem so obvious at the time that you will never forget, but I assure you that in a year, you will be asking, "Didn't we see that once on server so and so? How did we get that fixed?"

Keep the server patched and use the newest NIC and disk drivers from the vendors. Simplify when troubleshooting; for example, the server with the tape backup is abending every night. Don't run the tape backup software and see what happens. If the server stays up, it's a pretty safe bet that you have found your culprit. Unload all third-party NLMs and get the server stable. Then, load them back one at a time until you find the guilty party.

Use the support sources that we have covered here to search for a solution to the abend method. As we pointed out, if the problem is in the operating system, someone else has almost certainly already seen what you are seeing.

Keep an eye on the synchronization status of both NDS and Time, and when working with NDS, move slowly; give the changes time to ripple through the network. Don't start any major NDS operations unless time and directory services are in sync and all servers are available.

PART VII

IMPLEMENTING INTERNET SERVICES

## CHAPTER 28

INTRODUCTION TO TCP/IP

In this chapter

NETWARE AND IP

In the dark ages, which were not too long ago, most networks were isolated, very few were interconnected, and even fewer were connected to the Internet. Internetwork packet exchange (IPX) has always been used by NetWare for communications between servers and workstations. In today's world, connecting networks to each other and the Internet is the norm rather than the exception. The Internet Protocol (IP) is the language of the Internet, so with NetWare 5, it is now possible to use to use IP instead of IPX.

NetWare 5 is the first version of NetWare that is capable of using pure IP. It has been possible to use IP in prior versions of NetWare, but this was done with encapsulation. Encapsulation takes the IPX data, and puts it into an IP envelope to be moved to its destination. At the other end, the IPX data is then removed from the IP envelope. With pure IP, there is no encapsulation; the servers and workstations communicate using only the IP protocol.

Most networks today have both the IPX and IP protocols running, which increases the complexity of the workstations and servers. Using only one protocol simplifies the configuration of the system, and possibly reduces traffic on the wire.

When you use the IPX protocol, assigning network addresses for the servers and workstations pretty much takes care of itself. As an administrator, you only have to set up two addresses: the internal IPX address for the server, which has to be unique, and the external IPX address that shows up on the wire. The external IPX address is common to all servers using the same frame type on the same segment.

In other words, if you have two servers on the same network segment running the same frame type, each server would have its own unique internal IPX address, but both would use the same external IPX address. Otherwise, server Y would begin complaining that server X says the IPX address is BACB0, and server X would argue that server Y says the IPX address is BA5EBA11. These router configuration messages would continue popping up on the server console until the situation was corrected.

In the IPX environment, the workstation's address becomes a combination of the external IPX address and the workstation's MAC (Media Access Control) address. The MAC address is "burned" into the network interface card (NIC) by the manufacturer. So the entire process was automatic, when the server addresses were assigned. As the burned in NIC address is unique, there was no need to worry about assigning addresses to the workstations.

You will find that addressing in the IP environment is much more complex than the automatic process used with IPX. Each workstation and server need to have a unique IP address, along with other addressing information to allow communication. Assigning these addresses can be simplified by using the Dynamic Host Configuration Protocol (DHCP), but a thorough understanding of IP and TCP is still required. This chapter is aimed at administrators moving to NetWare 5 and pure IP, who have previously dealt only with IPX and need a quick course in IP addressing and IP fundamentals.

IP ADDRESSING

An IP address is 32 bits, or 4 octets, in length and must be unique for every host on the network. The term *host* is used to describe a node on the network, such as a server or workstation. For example, you might give the server an address of 11001100 01001110 00101011 00000100. This is a perfectly valid address, and machines will not have any trouble understanding it at all. But for humans, the dotted decimal notation is generally preferred. Using dotted decimal notation, you take each octet and write it in decimal, and each octet is separated by a period. So the preceding address becomes 204.78.43.4, which is much easier for us to deal with.

Tip #283 from	In order to be able to deal with IP addressing, you need to have a good handle on converting from binary to decimal, and vice versa. The calculator that comes with Windows can be helpful here; switch the view to scientific, and merely by clicking the bin (binary) or dec (decimal) radio buttons, you can switch back and forth easily.
John	

In the address of 204.78.43.4, as you will see later in this chapter, some portion of this number represents the network address, and what remains represents the host address. Because each network address must be unique, there needs to be one central authority handing out the numbers. This authority is the InterNIC. The InterNIC assigns network numbers, and it is up to you as the administrator to assign the host IDs. http://rs.internic.net is a good starting point for the InterNIC.

If you plan on using IP, but do not plan on connecting your network to the Internet, you can use whatever IP addresses you want. However, if you later decide to change this, you will be faced with the possibly formidable task of renumbering your network. If you do plan on interconnecting your network, you need to obtain a block of valid addresses from your Internet service provider (ISP). Or, if you are in a wide area network (WAN) environment, it is possible that your corporate office has obtained a block of addresses for the entire corporation and you will use a portion of these.

SUBNET MASKS

Earlier, when discussing the InterNIC, it was mentioned that some portion of the complete address represented the network address, and the rest represented the host address. Saying "some portion" isn't being very specific, but until you know the subnet mask associated with the address, you simply cannot tell. The subnet mask blocks, or masks, a portion of the address, and says, "this part is the network number", and the rest is the host address.

For example, 11001100 01001110 00101011 00000100 is your network address, and 11111111 11111111 11111111 00000000 is the subnet mask. Or, in dotted decimal notation, which I will use from now on, the IP address is 204.78.43.4, and the subnet mask is 255.255.255.0. This tells you that you are dealing with host number 4 on IP network 204.78.43.0.

Why is the subnet mask important? A host can only communicate with other hosts on the *same* network segment. In order to communicate with a host on a different network segment, it is necessary to send the packet to a router. Routers have more than one interface, and are used to connect networks together, as shown in Figure 28.1.

Figure 28.1
A simple router, connecting two networks together. Using the subnet mask, the sending host determines whether the target IP address is on the same network. If the target is on the same network, the packet is sent directly. If the target lives on a remote network, the packet is sent to the default router.

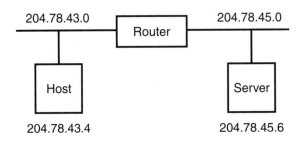

Figure 28.1 has a simple router with 2 interfaces. On one side is network 204.78.43.0 and, on the other side, is network 204.78.45.0. The workstation, or host, is 204.78.43.4. You want to send a packet to a server with an IP address of 204.78.45.6. The very first thing you have to decide is whether 204.78.45.6 is on the same network as you are. If it is, you can send the packet directly. If it is not, you have to send the packet to the router, and it is up to the router to forward the packet to the correct network. This decision is made using the subnet mask.

The simplest way to think about the subnet mask is this: a 0 in the IP address falls through as a 0, and a 1 falls through as a 1. For example,

```
11001100 01001110 00101101 00000110 = 204.78.45.6 = target
11111111 11111111 11111111 00000000 = our subnet mask
11001100 01001110 00101101 00000000 = result = 204.78.45.0
```

Note

The combination of the subnet mask and the IP address is actually Boolean addition, or what an electronics technician would recognize as an AND gate. The truth table looks like this:

Bit 1	Bit 2	Result
0	0	0
0	1	0
1	0	0
1	1	1

> You can see that this is what happens; the only time a 1 "falls through" to the result is when they are both 1s.

Notice that the result is 204.78.45.0, and from the subnet mask you know that the network is 204.78.43.0. So in this case, you send the packet to the router in order for it to reach its intended destination.

So the subnet mask is *very* important! From it, you determine which part of the address is the network portion, and you also use it to determine whether the host you are attempting to communicate with is on the same network segment as ourselves. An incorrect subnet mask renders communication virtually impossible and, when you're troubleshooting IP communication problems, the details of the workstations addressing setup should be one of the first things you check.

IP ADDRESS CLASSES

Now that you understand subnet masks, this leads nicely into a discussion of IP address classes. There are actually five classes of IP addresses, but I am going to touch on only three of them—class A, class B, and class C. Take a look at Table 28.1, and then you will go through the class B line of the table and see where these numbers come from.

TABLE 28.1 IP ADDRESS CLASSES

Address Class	High Order Bit(s)	First Octet Range	Number of Networks	Number of Hosts/Network	Default Subnet Mask
Class A	0	1–226	126	16,777,214	255.0.0.0
Class B	10	128–191	16,384	65,534	255.255.0.0
Class C	11	192–223	2,097,152	254	255.255.255.0

RANGE OF THE FIRST OCTET

The first octet of a class B address is always between 128 and 191. For example, you can look at address 145.97.32.41, and immediately tell that it is a class B address, because 145 falls in between 128 and 191.

NUMBER OF NETWORKS

You know that an IP address is 32 bits long. If the default subnet mask for a class B address is 255.255.0.0, you know that 16 bits will be used to specify the network portion of the address, and 16 bits will be left for the host ID. How high can you count in binary with 16 bits? 2 raised to the 16th power should do the trick, and $2^{16} = 65,536$. So why does the table show only 16,384 available networks?

The answer lies in the high order bits, which are 10 for a class B address. You cannot manipulate these 2 bits, because doing so would change the range or put you into another address class. So you do not have 16 bits available for the network portion, but only 14. And $2^{14} = 16,384$, which is the number of networks that can be assigned.

NUMBER OF HOSTS PER NETWORK

Again, the default class B subnet mask leaves 16 bits for the host IDs. $2^{16} = 65,536$. But the table shows only 65,534 host IDs available. The answer now isn't in the high order bits, but in the fact that you cannot have a host ID of all 0s or all 1s.

A host ID of all 0s (00000000 00000000) is invalid, because it is used to specify a network without specifying a host. If you remember from the discussion of subnet masks, it was said that 204.78.43.4 with a subnet mask of 255.255.255.0 indicated a host ID of 4 on network 204.78.43.0.

A host ID of all 1s (11111111 11111111) is invalid, because all 1s is used to indicate a broadcast address. If I send to 204.78.43.255, I am broadcasting, or sending a packet to *every* host on network 204.78.43.0.

So if you cannot use all 0s, or all 1s, you lose two numbers out of the available range, and the answer becomes 65,536–2, or 65,534 as the table shows. Remember that when assigning host IDs, you cannot use the first (all 0s), or last (all 1s) numbers in the range.

DEFAULT GATEWAY

Earlier, when discussing subnet masks, you learned that one of the things you use the subnet mask for is to determine whether a host you are trying to communicate with lives on the network, or whether it is on a remote network. A workstation, or host, can only send packets to hosts on the *same* network as itself. If, by applying the subnet mask to the target address, you determine that the target host lives on a remote network, the packet needs to be sent to the default gateway, or default router.

It is then up to the router to send the packet along on the next leg of the journey. If the default gateway is not specified, or is specified incorrectly, you will be able to send and receive packets only to hosts on your own network, pretty much rendering the concept of interconnectivity useless!

Tip #284 from
John

The default gateway is one of those subtle settings that can go unnoticed for a long time. Suppose you only have one network segment, and the network has been functioning fine for months. Then another network segment is added, and users on the new segment cannot connect to the server on the old segment. Your first thought will be "well, there is nothing wrong with my server, its been working fine". But the problem could be at the server in the form of a missing or incorrect default gateway, but the default gateway setting was never needed until now!

WINIPCFG AND IPCONFIG

You specify the IP addressing information, such as the IP address, subnet mask, and default gateway when configuring the client. But for troubleshooting purposes, it would be very convenient to obtain all this information without clicking through a bunch of tabs. There are two utilities you need to know about. The first, as shown in Figure 28.2, is Winipcfg for Windows 95/98 workstations.

Figure 28.2
The Winipcfg utility, for Windows 95/98, is a quick and easy way to obtain information about a workstation's IP configuration.

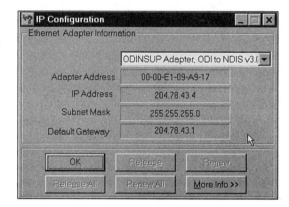

To run Winipcfg, simply go to Start, Run, and type `winipcfg`. The default view, in Figure 28.2, shows the adapter address, the IP address, the Subnet mask, and the default gateway. The More Info button takes you to the screen shown in Figure 28.3.

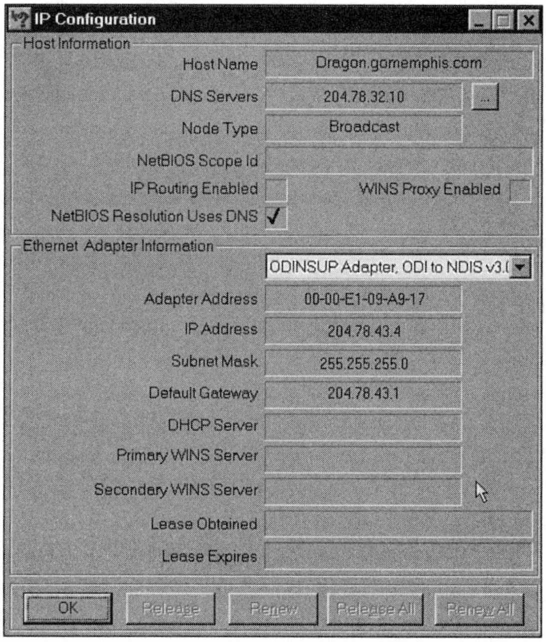

Figure 28.3
Additional information can be obtained by using the More Info button from the default Winipcfg screen.

PART
VII

CH
28

As you can see in Figure 28.3, you have the same information you had earlier, only with more information added to it. You can see whether the workstation is configured to use DHCP, obtain an address automatically, and see some Windows networking specific information, such as a WINS server address.

> **Note**
>
> WINS is a Microsoft networking thing; it stands for *Windows Internet Naming Service*. Windows networking uses NetBIOS names, and a WINS server is a NetBIOS name server. Workstations register their NetBIOS names with the WINS server, and then can query the server to resolve NetBIOS names to IP addresses.
>
> It is far more common to have a mix of operating systems on a network than to have only one, so a machine with both the Microsoft Client for Microsoft networks and the Novell Client for Novell networks is something you will see frequently.

It is extremely helpful to be able to walk up to a workstation and immediately obtain information about its IP configuration by using Winipcfg, but this utility is only for Windows 95/98. If you use Windows NT Workstation, you can obtain the same information, only without the nice GUI, as shown in Figure 28.4.

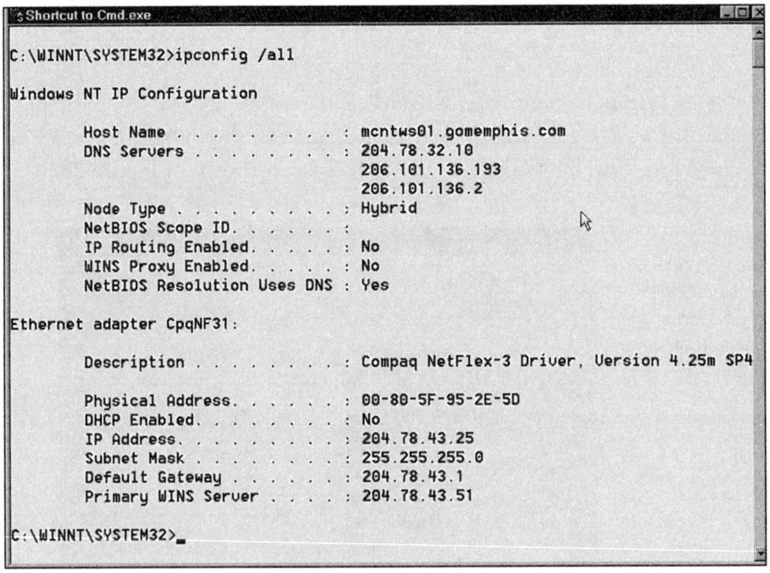

Figure 28.4

The `ipconfig /all` command is used on NT workstations to quickly obtain information about the workstations IP addressing.

```
 Shortcut to Cmd.exe                                               _ □ ×

C:\WINNT\SYSTEM32>ipconfig /all

Windows NT IP Configuration

        Host Name . . . . . . . . . : mcntws01.gomemphis.com
        DNS Servers . . . . . . . . : 204.78.32.10
                                      206.101.136.193
                                      206.101.136.2
        Node Type . . . . . . . . : Hybrid
        NetBIOS Scope ID. . . . . . :
        IP Routing Enabled. . . . . : No
        WINS Proxy Enabled. . . . . : No
        NetBIOS Resolution Uses DNS : Yes

Ethernet adapter CpqNF31:

        Description . . . . . . . . : Compaq NetFlex-3 Driver, Version 4.25m SP4

        Physical Address. . . . . . : 00-80-5F-95-2E-5D
        DHCP Enabled. . . . . . . . : No
        IP Address. . . . . . . . . : 204.78.43.25
        Subnet Mask . . . . . . . . : 255.255.255.0
        Default Gateway . . . . . . : 204.78.43.1
        Primary WINS Server . . . . : 204.78.43.51

C:\WINNT\SYSTEM32>_
```

You can *always* count on being able to go to a command line and running `ipconfig` or `ipconfig /all` to obtain information. However, if the workstation has had the NT resource kit installed on it, you can have the same GUI interface by running `WNTIPCFG.EXE`, which will be located by default in `c:\ntreskit`.

SUBNETTING

Suppose you have one network segment, several file servers, workstations, and a router connecting you to the Internet. Another system comes rolling in the door, this one to manipulate and work with large graphics files. You know that moving the files from server to workstation, and printing the images, is going to generate some pretty substantial network traffic, so you decide to put in another network segment. However, you only have one class C address to work with.

Because each network card in the server is going to define another physical network segment, how do you handle the IP addressing? It would be nice to simply keep on numbering with some of your unused addresses, but this isn't possible, because each network segment requires its own unique network ID. Both NICs in the server can't be 204.78.43.0, but this range is all that is available to you. The answer is subnetting. When you subnet, you steal some of the bits from the host ID portion of the address and add them to the network portion of the address. Remember, the subnet mask is something that you as the administrator define, so you do not have to take the defaults.

Hold on to your math hats, because subnetting is something that most people have a hard time getting a handle on—not because it is so complicated, but because most of us seldom think in binary. And to really understand subnetting, you need to be able to flip from binary to decimal and vice versa.

For example, using the default subnet mask of 255.255.255.0 for a class C address, take two bits away from the host portion and add them to the network portion of the address. Instead of 11111111 11111111 11111111 00000000, you wind up with 11111111 11111111 11111111 11000000, or 255.255.255.192. With these 2 bits, you have four possible ranges to work with, as shown in Table 28.2.

TABLE 28.2   SUBNETTING WITH TWO BITS

Binary Value	Decimal Value	Subnet Range
00xx xxxx	0	0–63
01xx xxxx	64	64–127
10xx xxxx	128	128–191
11xx xxxx	192	192–255

Now analyze two addresses that you might assign to the two NICs in the server, 204.78.43.65, and 204.78.43.129, each with a subnet mask of 204.78.43.192, by applying the subnet mask to each address. Remember, where there is a 1 in the address, and a 1 in the subnet mask, the 1 falls through into the result. And also, don't forget that if you are taking two bits away from the host portion of the class C address, you have only six bits available for host IDs, versus the default of eight bits that would normally be available to you:

```
11001100 01001110 00101011 01000001 = 204.78.43.65 (address for NIC number one
Âin the server)
11111111 11111111 11111111 11000000 = 255.255.255.192 (subnet mask)
11001100 01001110 00101011 01xxxxxx = the result, a network ID of 204.78.43.64.
```

So, in this case, the first NIC in the server has a host ID of 1 on network 204.78.43.64. Now, for the other NIC:

```
11001100 01001110 00101011 10000001 = 204.78.43.129 (address for NIC number two
Âin the server)
11111111 11111111 11111111 11000000 = 255.255.255.192 (subnet mask)
11001100 01001110 00101011 10xxxxxx = the result, a network ID of 204.78.43.128.
```

So, from one class C address, you have managed to come up with two separate network IDs, as shown in Figure 28.5.

Figure 28.5
Subnetting lets you spread your address range over multiple network segments. NIC 1 in the server is 204.78.43.65, subnet 64; and NIC 2 in the server is 204.78.43.129, subnet 128. The server acts as an IP router between the two networks.

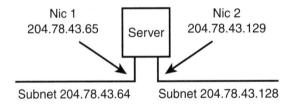

Now, the numbers in Table 28.2 should make a bit more sense, but be aware that when subnetting, you need to pay a bit more attention to host addresses. Any host address in the range of 64–127 winds up on subnet 64, and any host address in the range of 128–191 winds up on subnet 128. And, as I pointed out earlier, you cannot have a host address of all 0s, or all 1s, so valid addresses would range from 65 to 126. 64, or 01000000, which defines the subnet, would have the host portion as all 0s. 127, or 01111111, would have the host portion as all 1s.

At this point, you should know that historically all-1s subnets and all-0s subnets are not supported. However, the IP stack in NetWare 5 supports an all-1s or all-0s subnet, but make sure that other equipment on the network also supports these if you decide to implement them. By dropping the all-0s subnet and the all-1s subnet, you have valid host IDs of 65–126, and 129–190, cutting the class C address in half! Yes, subnetting costs you addresses.

> **Note**
>
> One point to consider is the switching technology available today. If you subnet in order to reduce traffic on an ethernet segment or to interconnect disparate network technologies such as token ring and ethernet, you might consider using switches. A modular switch lets you break your network up into many collision domains, interconnects differing technologies, and still leaves you a flat network with your entire range of addresses available.

In this example, you subnetted a class C with only two bits. What if you had taken three bits, or even four from the host portion? Using two bits, (11xxxxxx) or a mask of x.x.x.192 gave you two working networks, if you discarded the all-0s and all-1s subnets. Using three bits, (111xxxxx), or a mask of x.x.x.224, gives you how many useable subnets? The answer is going to be $2^{(\text{number of bits in the mask})}-2$, as shown in Table 28.3.

TABLE 28.3   SUBNETTING GUIDE

Binary	2^x	Decimal	Mask	# of Subnets	# of Hosts/ Subnet
01000000	2^6	64	x.x.x.192	2	62
00100000	2^5	32	x.x.x.224	6	30
00010000	2^4	16	x.x.x.240	14	14
00001000	2^3	8	x.x.x.248	30	6
00000100	2^2	4	x.x.x.252	62	2

Tip #285 from
John

$2^{(\text{number of bits in the mask})}-2$ gives you the number of networks available. $2^{(\text{number of bits in host portion})}-2$ gives you the number of hosts supported.

When considering subnetting, keep the following points in mind:

- The total number of network IDs required.
- The number of host you need to support on each subnet.

Then, define a subnet mask that meets your requirements. Consider the network shown in Figure 28.6.

Your task is to implement IP on these four network segments. Each segment has no more than 20 workstations. You have been given a class C address to work with, 204.78.43.0, and you must decide on an appropriate mask to use for subnetting. And preferably, you would leave room for future growth of the network.

Figure 28.6
Here, you have a network with four segments: the ethernet, the token ring, the WAN link, and the fiber. The Internet edge of the final router will be given an address by your ISP, so you do not have to worry about it.

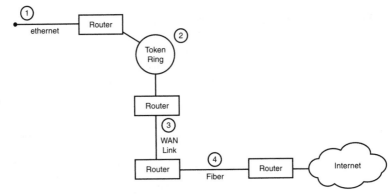

From Table 28.3, you can see that the absolute minimum would be a mask of x.x.x.224, (x.x.x.11100000) which would give you six networks available, each capable of supporting 30 hosts per network. This would leave you two network IDs for later growth, and room on each network to add up to 10 hosts. The six available network IDs are the following:

204.78.43.0	000xxxxx	This subnet mask is all 0s, and is discarded.
204.78.43.32	001xxxxx	Subnet 32
204.78.43.64	010xxxxx	Subnet 64
204.78.43.96	011xxxxx	Subnet 96
204.78.43.128	100xxxxx	Subnet 128
204.78.43.160	101xxxxx	Subnet 160
204.78.43.192	110xxxxx	Subnet 192
204.78.43.224	111xxxxx	This subnet mask is all 1s, and is discarded.

Notice that you have used steps, or increments, of 32. This is because with a mask of 224, you will be manipulating the three high order bits of the last octet. The smallest of these has a value of 32. As this bit toggles on and off, it defines the increments between the subnet ranges.

Now, which host IDs are available for each network ID? You will analyze only the first one, subnet 204.78.43.32, because they all work the same. The key is that you cannot change the first three bits of the last octet. The first three bits of the last octet are the ones we are stealing from the host portion to obtain our mask of 224. These three bits are shown in bold in the table below.

Since the value of these three bits is 001, that defines the 204.78.43.32 subnet. Changing these bits would put us into the range of another subnet, for example, if you changed them to 010, you would be in the .64 subnet range. So, leaving these three bits alone, you merely begin counting, as we have done ion the following table. You can count from 33 up to 63 before the value of your three bits toggles, and moves you into the next subnet range.

Tip #286 from John	Don't forget that host IDs are not allowed to be either all 1s or all 0s.

204.78.43.33	x.x.x.**001** 00001 = 33	(1)
204.78.43.34	x.x.x.**001** 00010 = 34	(2)
204.78.43.35	x.x.x.**001** 00011 = 35	(3)
204.78.43.36	x.x.x.**001** 00100 = 36	(4)
204.78.43.37	x.x.x.**001** 00101 = 37	(5)
204.78.43.38	x.x.x.**001** 00110 = 38	(6)
204.78.43.39	x.x.x.**001** 00111 = 39	(7)
204.78.43.40	x.x.x.**001** 01000 = 40	(8)
204.78.43.41	x.x.x.**001** 01001 = 41	(9)
204.78.43.42	x.x.x.**001** 01010 = 42	(10)
204.78.43.43	x.x.x.**001** 01011 = 43	(11)
204.78.43.44	x.x.x.**001** 01100 = 44	(12)
204.78.43.45	x.x.x.**001** 01101 = 45	(13)
204.78.43.46	x.x.x.**001** 01110 = 46	(14)
204.78.43.47	x.x.x.**001** 01111 = 47	(15)
204.78.43.48	x.x.x.**001** 10000 = 48	(16)
204.78.43.49	x.x.x.**001** 10001 = 49	(17)
204.78.43.50	x.x.x.**001** 10010 = 50	(18)
204.78.43.51	x.x.x.**001** 10011 = 51	(19)
204.78.43.52	x.x.x.**001** 10100 = 52	(20)
204.78.43.53	x.x.x.**001** 10101 = 53	(21)
204.78.43.54	x.x.x.**001** 10110 = 54	(22)
204.78.43.55	x.x.x.**001** 10111 = 55	(23)
204.78.43.56	x.x.x.**001** 11000 = 56	(24)
204.78.43.57	x.x.x.**001** 11001 = 57	(25)
204.78.43.58	x.x.x.**001** 11010 = 58	(26)
204.78.43.59	x.x.x.**001** 11011 = 59	(27)
204.78.43.60	x.x.x.**001** 11100 = 60	(28)
204.78.43.61	x.x.x.**001** 11101 = 61	(29)
204.78.43.62	x.x.x.**001** 11110 = 62	(30)
204.78.43.63	x.x.x.**001** 11111 = 63	This host ID is all 1s, and must be discarded.

So valid addresses in this subnet range would run from 204.78.43.31 to 204.78.43.62. Now that you have your valid network IDs and an understanding of subnetting, you can implement IP on the sample network as shown in Figure 28.7.

PART

VII

CH

28

Figure 28.7
Using a subnet mask of x.x.x.224 to implement IP on a network of four segments.

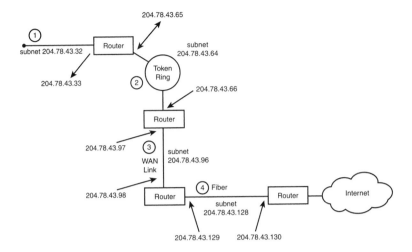

INTERNET PROTOCOL (IP)

IP, or Internet Protocol, is the backbone of the Internet protocol suite. All the data for Transmission Control Protocol (TCP), User Datagram Protocol (UDP), and Internet Control Message Protocol (ICMP) and others is moved via IP.

IP is a network-level protocol, which corresponds to layer three of the OSI model. IP is connectionless and unsequenced; it is simply best-effort delivery. There is no flow control or error control. In fact, in the event of an error, IP has a simple method of handling it; throw away the datagram and try to send an ICMP message back to the sender!

> **Note**
>
> By *datagram*, I mean a package of data transmitted over a connectionless network. Connectionless means that a session isn't set up between the sender and receiver, so that each party is aware of what he or she is sending and receiving, and can correct for lost or missing packets.

If you are coming from a background of IPX, you realize it's pretty much the same thing. In order to get sequenced and acknowledged transmission over IPX, you need to use sequenced packet exchange (SPX). To get sequencing and acknowledgements in the IP world, it takes TCP, which is discussed later. IP corresponds to IPX, and TCP corresponds to SPX.

TCP and SPX are transport-level protocols, and are concerned with reliable transmission of data. They do not have any network information contained in them; the network information is in the protocol they are riding on, which, in the case of TCP, rides on IP.

The NIC puts a frame onto the wire, and beyond the source address and destination address, all the rest is data as far as the NIC is concerned. IP datagrams also have a header that contains various fields, such as the time-to-live (TTL), which I discuss when using tracert later in this chapter, the source IP address, the destination IP address, and others. Beyond this IP header, and to IP, all the rest is data; it might be TCP segments, but IP neither knows nor cares.

Now take a look at part of an ethernet frame and see what kind of data is in the IP header:

```
DLC: ----- DLC Header -----
DLC:
DLC: Frame 225776 arrived at  13:31:27.7591; frame size is 60 (003C hex) bytes.
DLC: Destination = Station 3Com  D83F72
DLC: Source      = Station 000092A838FF
DLC: Ethertype   = 0800 (IP)
DLC:
IP: ----- IP Header -----
IP:
IP: Version = 4, header length = 20 bytes
IP: Type of service = 00
IP:       000. .... = routine
IP:       ...0 .... = normal delay
IP:       .... 0... = normal throughput
IP:       .... .0.. = normal reliability
IP: Total length    = 40 bytes
IP: Identification  = 32160
IP: Flags           = 0X
IP:       .0.. .... = may fragment
IP:       ..0. .... = last fragment
IP: Fragment offset = 0 bytes
IP: Time to live    = 255 seconds/hops
IP: Protocol        = 6 (TCP)
IP: Header checksum = 4F05 (correct)
IP: Source address      = [204.78.43.71]
IP: Destination address = [204.78.43.70], SNIFFMASTER
IP: No options
IP:
```

First, you see the ethernet information at the Data Link Control (DLC) level. Here you have the source address of the frame, the destination address of the frame, and the ethernet protocol type, in this case IP. You also have the frame size given of 60 bytes. Everything after this is nothing but data to the ethernet NIC; the ethernet card knows nothing of either IP or IPX. And you know that the source NIC and destination NIC have to be on the same physical segment in order to communicate.

Riding on this comes the IP header. The IP header is going to be a minimum of 20 bytes, and the header contains numerous fields. A complete analysis of the IP header isn't the objective here, but you can see several things immediately:

- The total length is the total length of the IP datagram, given in bytes, including the IP header itself.
- The time-to-live, or hop count, which you will see used later by the tracert program.

PART

VII

CH

28

- The source address is the IP address of the host sending the packet.
- The destination address is the IP address of the target host.

As I discuss UDP and TCP later in this chapter, you will develop a feel for the purpose of the other fields in the IP header.

There is also a fragmentation field. IP has to be able to handle fragmenting and reassembling datagrams. Why fragmentation? Different network topologies have different frame sizes. There is no reason that you could not have an IP router with one fiber interface, and one ethernet interface, and the fiber frame size can be much larger than the ethernet frame size.

As a network-level protocol, an IP header contains enough information to get a packet to the appropriate network. IP routers are responsible for routing packets from one network to another.

ROUTING

The sending host first examines the destination IP address, and, by using its subnet mask as I discussed earlier, decides whether the host can be reached directly. In other words, is the destination host on the same network as myself? If the answer is *yes*, the packet can be sent directly, and the sending host resolves the destination address into a MAC (burned into the NIC) address, and sends the packet.

Note The resolution of IP addresses to MAC addresses is done via ARP, or *Address Resolution Protocol*, as you will see in the following section. Remember, the network interface card knows nothing about IP, but only about ethernet, or token ring, or fiber, whichever the case may be.

If, after applying the subnet mask, the sending host determines that the target is on another network, the sending host checks to see whether the destination address is in the routing table. Any IP router has a routing table of either static routes that the administrator has entered or dynamic routes which have been discovered. The routing table grows when *networks*, not hosts are added. If the route is in the routing table, the packet is routed accordingly. If there is no entry in the routing table for the destination, the default gateway is used if specified.

Remember the default gateway discussed earlier? In this case, you have determined that the packet is destined for a remote network, but you do not have an entry in the routing table, so you use the default gateway. If no default gateway is defined, at this point you would receive an error. Table 28.4 shows the routing table for gateway Cheetah, which is also shown in Figure 28.8.

TABLE 28.4   THE ROUTING TABLE FOR GATEWAY CHEETAH

To Reach Hosts on Network	Route to This Address
202.78.78.0	Deliver Direct
204.43.59.0	Deliver Direct
192.200.201.0	202.78.78.2
212.1.1.0	204.43.59.2

Figure 28.8
Here you have three routers–Cheetah, Jane, and Tarzan– connecting four networks together. By examining the routing table for Cheetah, shown in Table 28.4, you can see that a router receives a packet on one interface, and it knows that its other interface is on the target network.

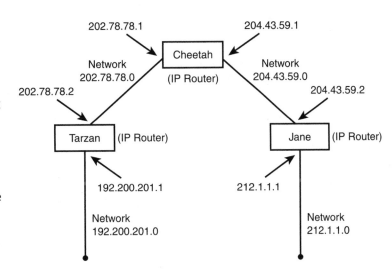

ADDRESS RESOLUTION PROTOCOL (ARP)

ARP, or Address Resolution Protocol, generally does its work behind the scenes, but you need to be aware of the whats and whys of ARP. You will also learn about the ARP cache and the ARP command.

Suppose you have two hosts on the same ethernet segment. The IP address of your target— say, 204.78.43.51—means something only to the IP stack. But when the packet ultimately needs to be sent, it comes down to one ethernet NIC sending to the other Ethernet NIC. And IP addresses don't mean anything down at the physical level where your NIC is.

So in some fashion, you need to obtain the hardware, or MAC address, of the target, and this is the purpose of ARP. When you ARP, you are essentially asking "Hey, 204.78.43.51, what is your hardware address?" 204.78.43.51 then answers with a packet containing the following information:

```
DLC:  ----- DLC Header -----
DLC:
DLC:  Frame 886 arrived at  11:47:09.0302; frame size is 60 (003C hex) bytes.
DLC:  Destination = BROADCAST FFFFFFFFFFFF, Broadcast
```

```
DLC:  Source     = Station Prteon8432BE
DLC:  Ethertype  = 0806 (ARP)
DLC:
ARP:  ----- ARP/RARP frame -----
ARP:
ARP: Hardware type = 1 (10Mb Ethernet)
ARP: Protocol type = 0800 (IP)
ARP: Length of hardware address = 6 bytes
ARP: Length of protocol address = 4 bytes
ARP: Opcode 1 (ARP request)
ARP: Sender's hardware address = Prteon8432BE
ARP: Sender's protocol address = [204.78.43.220], TARZAN
ARP: Target hardware address   = 000000000000
ARP: Target protocol address   = [204.78.43.68]
ARP:
```

The initial ARP request is a broadcast packet, which means its destination address is all 1s, as you can see from the FFFFFFFFFFFF in the destination address of the DLC layer. But even though the ARP request is a broadcast packet, it contains enough information about the node making the request that the response from the target workstation is a directed packet, as opposed the response being broadcast. In the preceding frame, the ARP request, you can see that Tarzan, with an IP address of 204.78.43.220, is ARPing for the hardware address of 204.78.43.68. Notice that in this frame, the target hardware address is all 0s, because Tarzan does not yet know it. But, in this request, Tarzan has filled in the hardware address, Prteon8432BE, so that 204.78.43.68 can respond directly:

```
DLC:  ----- DLC Header -----
DLC:
DLC:  Frame 887 arrived at  11:47:09.0445; frame size is 60 (003C hex) bytes.
DLC:  Destination = Station Prteon8432BE
DLC:  Source      = Station 00805F92C218
DLC:  Ethertype   = 0806 (ARP)
DLC:
ARP:  ----- ARP/RARP frame -----
ARP:
ARP: Hardware type = 1 (10Mb Ethernet)
ARP: Protocol type = 0800 (IP)
ARP: Length of hardware address = 6 bytes
ARP: Length of protocol address = 4 bytes
ARP: Opcode 2 (ARP reply)
ARP: Sender's hardware address = 00805F92C218
ARP: Sender's protocol address = [204.78.43.68]
ARP: Target hardware address   = Prteon8432BE
ARP: Target protocol address   = [204.78.43.220], TARZAN
```

In this frame, the ARP response, the sender (204.78.43.68) has filled in the requested information, and the sender's hardware address is 00805F92C218. Because the sender, in this case 204.78.43.68, already knows the MAC address of Tarzan, the ARP response is not a broadcast packet, but can be sent directly back to Tarzan, as you can see by once again examining the DLC layer, specifically the source and destination address.

The ARP cache is an extremely important part of this operation. A session between two hosts consists of hundreds, if not thousands, of packets. Imagine if you had to obtain the hardware address of the target each and every time you wanted to send a frame! In the ARP cache, you maintain a table of recently resolved IP addresses, and if the address is in the ARP cache, there is no need for traffic to be put on the wire; you already have the information that you need.

It is possible to view and manipulate entries in the ARP cache via the arp command. Figure 28.9 shows the syntax and available switches.

Figure 28.9

Using the arp command, you can view and manipulate the entries in the ARP cache of the workstation. Shown here are the available switches and the syntax.

```
 Shortcut to Cmd.exe                                          _ □ ×
C:\WINNT\SYSTEM32>arp

Displays and modifies the IP-to-Physical address translation tables used by
address resolution protocol (ARP).

ARP -s inet_addr eth_addr [if_addr]
ARP -d inet_addr [if_addr]
ARP -a [inet_addr] [-N if_addr]

   -a          Displays current ARP entries by interrogating the current
               protocol data.  If inet_addr is specified, the IP and Physical
               addresses for only the specified computer are displayed.  If
               more than one network interface uses ARP, entries for each ARP
               table are displayed.
   -g          Same as -a.
   inet_addr   Specifies an internet address.
   -N if_addr  Displays the ARP entries for the network interface specified
               by if_addr.
   -d          Deletes the host specified by inet_addr.
   -s          Adds the host and associates the Internet address inet_addr
               with the Physical address eth_addr.  The Physical address is
               given as 6 hexadecimal bytes separated by hyphens. The entry
               is permanent.
   eth_addr    Specifies a physical address.
   if_addr     If present, this specifies the Internet address of the
               interface whose address translation table should be modified.
               If not present, the first applicable interface will be used.

C:\WINNT\SYSTEM32>
```

Figure 28.10 shows the command arp -a being used to view the entries in the ARP cache. Notice the mapping of IP addresses to hardware addresses. Dynamic entries have been resolved in the normal course of things, and expire, as opposed to static entries that you would add via the command using the -s switch; those entries would be permanent.

PART

VII

CH

28

Figure 28.10
Using the command
arp -a to view the
entries in the ARP
cache.

```
Shortcut to Cmd.exe                                                    _ □ ✕

C:\WINNT\SYSTEM32>arp -a

Interface: 204.78.43.25 on Interface 2
  Internet Address      Physical Address      Type
  0.0.0.0               08-00-09-a0-2a-10     dynamic
  0.0.0.3               08-00-07-04-6a-2e     dynamic
  204.78.43.4           00-00-e1-09-a9-17     dynamic
  204.78.43.18          08-00-09-ad-0b-9d     dynamic
  204.78.43.19          00-60-b0-78-1a-25     dynamic
  204.78.43.20          00-60-08-2c-12-de     dynamic
  204.78.43.33          00-00-1d-6a-28-5f     dynamic
  204.78.43.40          00-00-1d-8c-45-b7     dynamic
  204.78.43.52          00-80-5f-19-b1-83     dynamic
  204.78.43.67          00-80-d8-20-71-21     dynamic
  204.78.43.68          00-80-5f-92-c2-18     dynamic
  204.78.43.100         02-07-01-14-11-f5     dynamic
  204.78.43.101         00-00-65-08-10-ca     dynamic
  204.78.43.104         00-00-65-08-33-57     dynamic
  204.78.43.105         00-00-65-08-33-b0     dynamic
  204.78.43.115         00-c0-7b-5d-84-de     dynamic
  204.78.43.116         00-c0-7b-5e-72-c9     dynamic
  204.78.43.120         08-00-09-d6-ab-ba     dynamic
  204.78.43.126         08-00-09-ad-cb-33     dynamic
  204.78.43.127         00-60-b0-40-95-95     dynamic
  204.78.43.128         08-00-09-af-15-e5     dynamic
  204.78.43.143         08-00-09-63-60-f7     dynamic
  204.78.43.150         00-60-b0-45-9c-c4     dynamic
  206.101.132.208       00-00-93-84-21-9e     dynamic
  206.101.132.247       00-00-93-84-20-e9     dynamic

C:\WINNT\SYSTEM32>
```

IP ADDRESSES

There are three types of IP addresses: broadcast, unicast, and multicast. Unicast packets are destined for only one target address, as the name implies. Broadcast and multicast packets are destined for multiple targets.

A broadcast packet has an address of all 1s in the host portion, such as 204.78.43.255. Normally, even though the NIC sees every packet that is placed on the wire, it ignores them unless it recognizes its own ethernet address. But because broadcasts are destined for every host, the NIC also dutifully passes these packets up to the next layers. Routers are generally configured not to route broadcast packets.

Are broadcast packets bad? Not really; they are very common. Services are advertised by broadcasting, and protocols such as ARP and DHCP use broadcasts. Broadcast packets are no different from a unicast packet in terms of traffic on the wire; it is still only one frame. The problem with broadcasts is that *every* workstation has to process them to some extent. The packet has to be handed up and either dealt with or discarded.

Now take another look at a broadcast packet you have already seen, the ARP request:

```
DLC:  ----- DLC Header -----
DLC:
DLC:  Frame 886 arrived at  11:47:09.0302; frame size is 60 (003C hex) bytes.
DLC:  Destination = BROADCAST FFFFFFFFFFFF, Broadcast
DLC:  Source      = Station Prteon8432BE
DLC:  Ethertype   = 0806 (ARP)
```

```
DLC:
ARP: ----- ARP/RARP frame -----
ARP:
ARP: Hardware type = 1 (10Mb Ethernet)
ARP: Protocol type = 0800 (IP)
ARP: Length of hardware address = 6 bytes
ARP: Length of protocol address = 4 bytes
ARP: Opcode 1 (ARP request)
ARP: Sender's hardware address = Prteon8432BE
ARP: Sender's protocol address = [204.78.43.220], TARZAN
ARP: Target hardware address   = 000000000000
ARP: Target protocol address   = [204.78.43.68]
ARP:
```

Notice the destination address of FFFFFFFFFFFF, or all 1s. Tarzan asks everyone on the wire "If you are IP address 204.78.43.68, send me your hardware address." Every workstation receives this packet and hands it up to the higher layers in order to decide whether they are indeed 204.78.43.68. Only one host answers the call, but every workstation had to process this packet to some extent.

Are excessive broadcasts bad? Most certainly. Excessive broadcasts generate more traffic on the wire, and from that you can derive that there will be more collisions. More collisions slow down access to the wire. And the workstations also slow down, because they have to pay attention to these frames.

Multicasting fits in between unicast and broadcast. Multicast frames are delivered to some *set* of users. Applications such as conferencing, or sending news to multiple recipients would be ideal for multicasting. You could send one copy of the data, whatever it may be, to multiple destinations. Otherwise, you might need to send the same copy 20 times.

USER DATAGRAM PROTOCOL (UDP)

UDP, or User Datagram Protocol, has no behavior; it is simply an unreliable, connectionless delivery service that uses IP as the transport. UDP rides on top of IP. When using a connection-oriented protocol, such as TCP or SPX, the applications do not have to worry about the integrity of the data they receive. Any dropped or corrupted packets are re-sent and acknowledged, before being passed to the application. Because UDP is connectionless, it is up to the application to make sure that everything is correct.

Examine a read request from host lzr2; lzr2 is making a read request from zen1. By examining this read request, which uses UDP, you will also gain a better understanding of IP, which you have already taken a look at.

In this first packet, take note of the IP identification number (15609), and the fact the one of the flags is set to indicate more fragments. Take note of the fragment offset field, and the fact that in the UDP header you can see that that not all the data is contained in this fragment. What is happening here is that the sender starts breaking up the required data into UDP datagrams and passes them to IP for transport:

```
DLC:  ----- DLC Header -----
DLC:
DLC:  Frame 128 arrived at  03:40:58.8718; frame size is 1514 (05EA hex)
DLC:  Destination = Station Sun    0650E4
DLC:  Source      = Station Sun    12BFB1
DLC:  Ethertype  = 0800 (IP)
DLC:
IP:   ----- IP Header -----
IP:
IP:   Version = 4, header length = 20 bytes
IP:   Type of service = 00
IP:        000. .... = routine
IP:        ...0 .... = normal delay
IP:        .... 0... = normal throughput
IP:        .... .0.. = normal reliability
IP:   Total length  = 1500 bytes
IP:   Identification = 15609
IP:   Flags        = 2X
IP:        .0.. .... = may fragment
IP:        ..1. .... = more fragments
IP:   Fragment offset = 0 bytes
IP:   Time to live  = 255 seconds/hops
IP:   Protocol     = 17 (UDP)
IP:   Header checksum = B25A (correct)
IP:   Source address     = [206.101.132.253], Zen1
IP:   Destination address = [206.101.132.244], lzr2
IP:   No options
IP:
UDP:  ----- UDP Header -----
UDP:
UDP:  Source port     = 2049
UDP:  Destination port = 1023 (Sun RPC)
UDP:  Length = 8300 (not all data contained in this fragment)
UDP:  No checksum
UDP:
```

In this next packet, the second in the sequence, you can see that the IP identification number is the same, 15609, and that you still have more fragments to come. Notice the fragment offset? In the first frame, the fragment offset was 0. In this frame, the fragment offset is 1480; that is because, of the data requested, 1480 bytes were sent in the first packet. Finally, you can see from the UDP header that there is also 1480 bytes of data sent in this packet, and that this packet is a continuation of the first one, IP ident=15609:

```
DLC:  ----- DLC Header -----
DLC:
DLC:  Frame 129 arrived at  03:40:58.8730; frame size is 1514 (05EA hex)
DLC:  Destination = Station Sun    0650E4
DLC:  Source      = Station Sun    12BFB1
DLC:  Ethertype  = 0800 (IP)
DLC:
IP:   ----- IP Header -----
IP:
IP:   Version = 4, header length = 20 bytes
IP:   Type of service = 00
IP:        000. .... = routine
IP:        ...0 .... = normal delay
```

```
IP:            .... 0... = normal throughput
IP:            .... .0.. = normal reliability
IP:    Total length    = 1500 bytes
IP:    Identification  = 15609
IP:    Flags           = 2X
IP:          .0.. .... = may fragment
IP:          ..1. .... = more fragments
IP:    Fragment offset = 1480 bytes
IP:    Time to live    = 255 seconds/hops
IP:    Protocol        = 17 (UDP)
IP:    Header checksum = B1A1 (correct)
IP:    Source address      = [206.101.132.253], Zen1
IP:    Destination address = [206.101.132.244], lzr2
IP:    No options
IP:
UDP:   [1480 byte(s) of data, continuation of IP ident=15609]
```

The next three packets are identical to the second; each time, UDP hands off 1480 bytes to IP for transport, and each of these packets is a continuation of the first, IP identification 15609:

```
UDP:   [1480 byte(s) of data, continuation of IP ident=15609]
UDP:   [1480 byte(s) of data, continuation of IP ident=15609]
UDP:   [1480 byte(s) of data, continuation of IP ident=15609]
```

In this last packet of the sequence, notice the flags pertaining to fragments. In other packets, you have seen that this is set to more fragments. Because this is the last of the series, it is now set to last fragment. Notice the fragment offset of 7400 bytes? So far, UDP has handed 1480 bytes to IP for transport, and has done this five times. $1480 \infty 5 = 7400$, so you can see how it all comes together. Another indication that this would be the last packet in the exchange is that this time UDP is sending only 900 bytes of data, fewer than the 1480 it had been sending:

```
DLC:   ----- DLC Header -----
DLC:
DLC:   Frame 133 arrived at  03:40:58.8778; frame size is 934 (03A6 hex)
DLC:   Destination = Station Sun   0650E4
DLC:   Source      = Station Sun   12BFB1
DLC:   Ethertype  = 0800 (IP)
DLC:
IP:    ----- IP Header -----
IP:
IP:    Version = 4, header length = 20 bytes
IP:    Type of service = 00
IP:          000. .... = routine
IP:          ...0 .... = normal delay
IP:          .... 0... = normal throughput
IP:          .... .0.. = normal reliability
IP:    Total length    = 920 bytes
IP:    Identification  = 15609
IP:    Flags           = 0X
IP:          .0.. .... = may fragment
IP:          ..0. .... = last fragment
IP:    Fragment offset = 7400 bytes
IP:    Time to live    = 255 seconds/hops
IP:    Protocol        = 17 (UDP)
```

```
IP:    Header checksum = D101 (correct)
IP:    Source address      = [206.101.132.253], Zen1
IP:    Destination address = [206.101.132.244], lzr2
IP:    No options
IP:
UDP:   [900 byte(s) of data, continuation of IP ident=15609]
```

To summarize, UDP has no behavior. It simply passes data to IP for transport, and it is up to the receiving application to check the integrity of what it has received.

TRANSMISSION CONTROL PROTOCOL (TCP)

TCP, or Transmission Control Protocol, is a layer 4, or transport-layer, protocol used for reliable delivery of data. The two hosts establish a session and data is acknowledged as it is transmitted. As you saw when discussing UDP, the application level had to take care of making sure that the data received was correct. TCP guarantees reliable delivery, so the upper application levels do not have to worry about data integrity. In essence, a virtual circuit is established between the TCP layers on each host. TCP does the same thing in the world of IP that SPX does in the world of IPX. Like UDP, TCP "rides" on top of IP.

CONNECTION SETUP AND TEARDOWN

In order for the sequencing and acknowledging of packets to work, both sides have to start off on the same wavelength. They first establish a connection, agreeing on which ports they want to use and the numbers they are going to use for sequencing. When the connection is established, the data can start flowing.

CONNECTION ESTABLISHMENT

The TCP connection is established by what is commonly called a "three-way handshake," because it take three packets to establish the connection. These three packets are shown here, where the source of 204.78,.43.220 is establishing a TCP session with the destination of 204.78.43.68:

SUMMARY	Delta T	Destination	Source	Summary
1	0.00051	[204.78.43.68]	[204.78.43.220]	TCP D=524 S=1027 SYN SEQ=13410 LEN=0 WIN=8192
2	0.00048	[204.78.43.220]	[204.78.43.68]	TCP D=1027 S=524 SYN ACK=13411 SEQ=171529568 LEN=0 WIN=23360
3	0.00056	[204.78.43.68]	[204.78.43.220]	TCP D=524 S=1027 ACK=171529569 WIN=8760

1—The requester, or source (204.78.43.220) sends a SYN segment specifying not only the port that the client wants to use, but also the client's initial sequence number. Here, the initial sequence number is SEQ=13410, and the source port used by the client is 1027, whereas the destination port the client wants to connect to is 524.

> **Note**
>
> Port? Either a wine or where you dock a ship? Not in this case. A *port* is a *portal*, such as a gateway or door. Numerous applications can use the TCP layer at the same time, so the port is used to differentiate between them. In your Windows directory (on 95/98), you have a file called `services` which lists the port numbers for well-known services as defined in RFC 1060. On an NT workstation, this file is in `c:\winnt\system32\drivers\etc`. And SYN? This is the S flag, abbreviated SYN, and its meaning is synchronize sequence numbers.

2—The server answers with a SYN segment of its own. This SYN segment contains the server's initial sequence number, and also an acknowledgement of the client's SYN by ACKing the client's initial sequence number plus one. The server's initial sequence number is 171529568, and notice that it has acknowledged receipt of the client's initial SYN segment by using the initial value of 13410 + 1 (ACK=13411).

> **Tip #287 from**
> *John*
>
> When discussing UDP, I spoke of *datagrams*. The unit of data the TCP sends to IP is called a *TCP segment*.

Now it is the client's turn to acknowledge, and in 3 the client returns a segment with the server's initial sequence number + 1, or 171529568 + 1 = 171529569.

Basically, the three-way handshake is SYN, SYN and ACK, and ACK. Then the session setup is complete.

CONNECTION TEARDOWN

The connection teardown follows pretty much along the lines of the setup. Like everything involved with TCP, both sides need to always know what is going on. So each side of the connection will tell the other that they are done, and each side will acknowledge this fact, as you can see in the following frames:

SUMMARY	Delta T	Destination	Source	Summary
25	0.03051	Server	Client	TCP D=524 S=1027 ACK=172508037 SEQ=18247 LEN=23 WIN=8104
26	0.00027	Client	Server	TCP D=1027 S=524 FIN ACK=18270 SEQ=172508037 LEN=16 WIN=22265

continues

continued

SUMMARY	Delta T	Destination	Source	Summary
27	0.00082	Server	Client	TCP D=524 S=1027 FIN ACK=172508054 SEQ=18270 LEN=0 WIN=8088
28	0.00019	Client	Server	TCP D=1027 S=524 ACK=18271 WIN=22264

In frame 25, you can see that the length (LEN) of the data the client is sending to the server equals 23.

In frame 26, the server has done several things; one is to acknowledge the data received. You can see this acknowledgement by the fact that the server has replied with an ACK=18270. The client's sequence number in frame 25 is 18247; the server has acknowledged the receipt of the data sent by the client by ACKing with 18270, which is 18247 (the sequence in frame 25) + 23 (the length of the data sent in frame 25). The other thing the server does in frame 26 is to set the FIN flag, indicating that the conversation is over. In addition, the length of the data the server sends in this packet is 16.

> **Note** FIN is the F flag; it is abbreviated FIN, and means that the send is finished sending data.

In frame 27, the client acknowledges the data (length of 16) and the FIN with an ACK=172508054. Then, in frame 28, the server ACKs merely by incrementing the client's sequence number by one.

To summarize the connection teardown, the server says "I ACK your data, and by the way, I'm finished" (the server sets the FIN flag). The client then responds with "I received your data, and I notice that you are finished. I'm done also" (the client sets the FIN flag). The server then replies with "Okay, I see that we are both finished" (ACKs the clients FIN flag).

In the section about UDP, I showed frames decoded with all three layers involved; the DLC layer, the IP layer, and UDP riding on top of it all. In this section on TCP, I have only showed the high level summary of the two TCP layers communicating. The following frame is to reinforce the fact that TCP rides on top of IP, as you can see:

```
DLC:  ----- DLC Header -----
DLC:
DLC:  Frame 67 arrived at  12:09:41.7714; frame size is 60 (003C hex) bytes.
DLC:  Destination = Station 00805F92C218
DLC:  Source      = Station Prteon8432BE
DLC:  Ethertype   = 0800 (IP)
DLC:
IP:  ----- IP Header -----
IP:
IP: Version = 4, header length = 20 bytes
IP: Type of service = 28
IP:        001. .... = priority
IP:        ...0 .... = normal delay
```

```
IP:        .... 1... = high throughput
IP:        .... .0.. = normal reliability
IP: Total length    = 40 bytes
IP: Identification  = 11264
IP: Flags           = 4X
IP:        .1.. .... = don't fragment
IP:        ..0. .... = last fragment
IP: Fragment offset = 0 bytes
IP: Time to live    = 128 seconds/hops
IP: Protocol        = 6 (TCP)
IP: Header checksum = DEEA (correct)
IP: Source address      = [204.78.43.220]
IP: Destination address = [204.78.43.68]
IP: No options
IP:
TCP: ----- TCP header -----
TCP:
TCP:  Source port           = 1027
TCP:  Destination port      = 524
TCP:  Sequence number       = 13301
TCP:  Acknowledgment number = 175449789
TCP:  Data offset           = 20 bytes
TCP:  Flags                 = 10
TCP:              ..0. .... = (No urgent pointer)
TCP:              ...1 .... = Acknowledgment
TCP:              .... 0... = (No push)
TCP:              .... .0.. = (No reset)
TCP:              .... ..0. = (No SYN)
TCP:              .... ...0 = (No FIN)
```

SLIDING WINDOW

TCP's method of flow control is called *sliding window*. I am going to spare you the protocol analyzer view of sliding windows (cheers from the gallery!), and touch on the concept. The idea behind the sliding window is to place a buffer between the application and the network.

Incoming data from the NIC is placed in the buffer, and the application can read from the buffer as it is able. As data is read by the application, space in the buffer is freed up for more packets from the NIC. The window is the size of the buffer, minus the data that is currently stored in it. If the application is slow at reading data, the buffer will be quickly filled up, and the window size will drop to zero. If the application can read data as quickly as it enters the buffer, the idea of sliding windows is still good; there can be multiple packets on the wire in transit, because the sender knows that there will be room for them when they arrive. This makes for more efficient use of the network than SEND/ACK, SEND/ACK, and so on.

The receiver will make window size announcements informing the sender of it current window size. Notice the WIN=(###) on each exchange in the following table? You can see that it changes from frame to frame; this is the window size announcement. Each side of the connection not only keeps up with the sequencing and acknowledging, but also informs the other party about its current window size:

SUMMARY	Delta T	Destination	Source	Summary
143	0.24429	Merlin1	client	TCP D=524 S=1027 ACK=223215073 SEQ=13715 LEN=30 WIN=7704
144	0.00042	client	Merlin1	TCP D=1027 S=524 ACK=13745 SEQ=223215073 LEN=29 WIN=22540
145	0.02104	Merlin1	client	TCP D=524 S=1027 ACK=223215102 SEQ=13745 LEN=108 WIN=7675
146	0.00100	client	Merlin1	TCP D=1027 S=524 ACK=13853 SEQ=223215102 LEN=54 WIN=22432
147	0.03087	Merlin1	client	TCP D=524 S=1027 ACK=223215156 SEQ=13853 LEN=120 WIN=7621
148	0.00084	client	Merlin1	TCP D=1027 S=524 ACK=13973 SEQ=223215156 LEN=54 WIN=22312
149	0.00200	Merlin1	client	TCP D=524 S=1027 ACK=223215210 SEQ=13973 LEN=124 WIN=7567

Each of the hosts is keeping the other side of the connection informed as to its current window size. When things are going perfectly, there is a balanced condition reached where packets are being sent in one direction, window announcements are coming back, and both are always in transit. As the application reads data, you announce a new window size, enabling the sender to adjust the amount of data it is about to send.

There are entire volumes devoted to nothing but TCP/IP, and what I have covered here barely scratches the surface. There are mechanisms for timeouts, resets, delayed acknowledgements, various flags, ways of dealing with congestion, keep alive timers, and more. It all happens underneath the hood, and just as you probably never deal with the bits and bytes of IPX, you will most likely never need to delve into the intricacies of IP. But hopefully, you have a bit better understanding of IP than you did before. As Novell says, "There's nothing like pure IP", or at least that's what it says on several of my T-shirts!

UTILITIES AND TROUBLESHOOTING

Troubleshooting IP communication problems will be no different than what you are used to when dealing with IPX, only in addition to the usual questions about the status of the cabling, connectors, and NICs, you have to verify that the IP addressing information is correct, whereas in the IPX world, the addressing was automatic.

When troubleshooting, it is best to gather as much information as you can before jumping in and changing things. If a host cannot communicate, ask the basic questions first. Is this a new installation, or has it been working and suddenly quit? Have any changes been made to the workstation's configuration? Can it communicate via IP with any other hosts, or is it having problems reaching only certain ones?

Run Winipcfg for 95/98 or Ipconfig /all for NT and make sure that the IP address, the subnet mask, and the default gateway are set correctly. And here is where a thorough understanding of what these parameters are will help. If you can communicate with hosts on your own network, but not remote hosts, the workstation's IP address and subnet mask are fine, and you would want to take a close look at the default gateway setting.

If you can communicate with remote hosts, but not one particular remote host, the problem almost certainly lies at the other end. Your IP address, subnet mask, and default gateway all are correct, but what would be the symptom if the remote host in question did not have its default gateway set correctly? Your packets would be reaching the remote host in question, but it would be unable to send them back.

And do not forget that a workstation can have a perfectly functioning IP stack, and still have name resolution problems. In this case, you will be able to ping by IP addresses, but not by names.

In any case, when troubleshooting IP, the first weapon in your arsenal is going to be ping, the IP troubleshooter's secret weapon.

PING

Ping, or *Packet Internet Groper*, is used to see whether another host is reachable. Ping is the duct tape of troubleshooting IP communication problems; you are always going to try to ping another host or even yourself. Ping works like the sonar you see in old World War II movies, or like shouting at the edge of a canyon. You send out a packet (shout), and if the other host is alive and capable of a response, you get a packet back (echo response).

Ping can be very helpful in troubleshooting, because it works at a very low level. Suppose a user is having problems with an application that uses TCP/IP, and she calls you. You try to ping her machine and get no response. It is then obvious that the problem has nothing to do with the application, but that there is a fundamental problem with the workstation's IP stack or configuration.

PART

VII

CH

28

Note

Technically, the Ping program sends out ICMP packets. ICMP, or *Internet Control Message Protocol*, communicates error messages and other situations that require attention. In the case of ping, you send out an echo request, and get back an echo response.

To use Ping, drop to a command prompt, and enter the command ping. Entering it with no parameters gives you numerous options, or switches for ping, as you can see in Figure 28.11. The most helpful of these I find to be the -t switch, which pings the other host continually until interrupted.

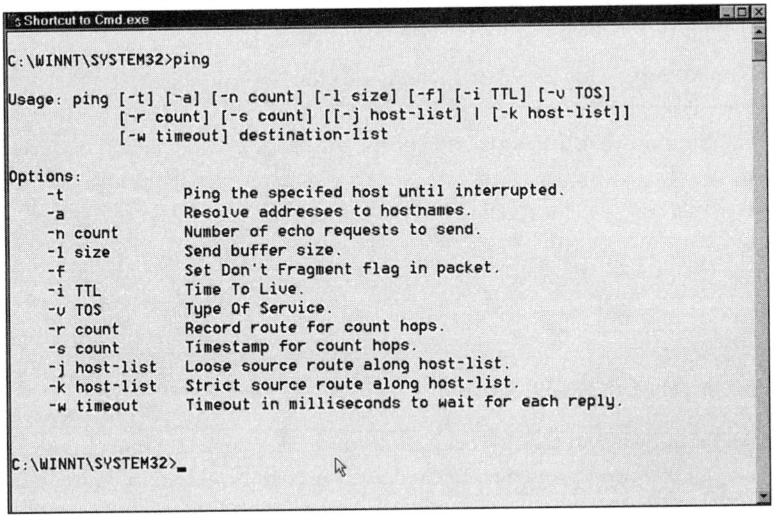

Figure 28.11
The various switches available when using the ping command.

```
C:\WINNT\SYSTEM32>ping

Usage: ping [-t] [-a] [-n count] [-l size] [-f] [-i TTL] [-v TOS]
            [-r count] [-s count] [[-j host-list] | [-k host-list]]
            [-w timeout] destination-list

Options:
    -t              Ping the specifed host until interrupted.
    -a              Resolve addresses to hostnames.
    -n count        Number of echo requests to send.
    -l size         Send buffer size.
    -f              Set Don't Fragment flag in packet.
    -i TTL          Time To Live.
    -v TOS          Type Of Service.
    -r count        Record route for count hops.
    -s count        Timestamp for count hops.
    -j host-list    Loose source route along host-list.
    -k host-list    Strict source route along host-list.
    -w timeout      Timeout in milliseconds to wait for each reply.

C:\WINNT\SYSTEM32>
```

You can ping another host in two different fashions: by name and by IP address. If you can ping by using the IP address of the target host, such as c:\windows> ping 204.78.43.4, but cannot ping the target by name, such as c:\windows\ping dragon, you have a name resolution issue, not an IP problem.

Note

Although names are easy for humans, they are meaningless to computers. If you enter the command ping elvis in some fashion, the name elvis needs to be *resolved* (name resolution) into an IP address that the ping command can work with. Host names are resolved either by using a hosts file, which is an ASCII text file that simply maps IP addresses to names, or via DNS, a domain name server, which responds with IP addresses to name queries. When using the IP address of the target host to ping, there is no need for name resolution; you have already supplied the address on the command line.

If you cannot ping a remote host by its IP address, you will not be able to ping it by name, and this indicates a problem on one of the two workstations in question. Figure 28.12 shows both methods of using the ping command. First, you enter the command ping 204.78.43.4, and you see that you get four replies, each taking less than 10 milliseconds to reach you. Secondly, you entered the command ping dragon, and you see that you again have received good response.

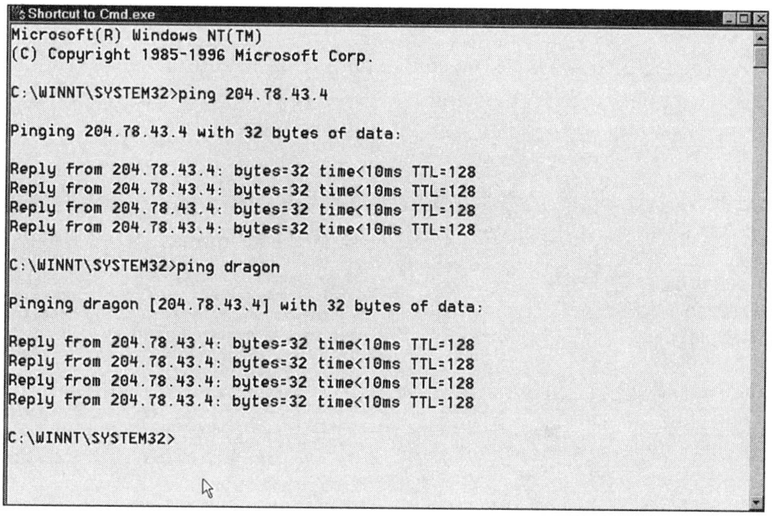

Figure 28.12
You can ping a remote host by either name or IP address. If you cannot get a response by using the IP address, you will not be able to ping by name.

```
Shortcut to Cmd.exe

Microsoft(R) Windows NT(TM)
(C) Copyright 1985-1996 Microsoft Corp.

C:\WINNT\SYSTEM32>ping 204.78.43.4

Pinging 204.78.43.4 with 32 bytes of data:

Reply from 204.78.43.4: bytes=32 time<10ms TTL=128
Reply from 204.78.43.4: bytes=32 time<10ms TTL=128
Reply from 204.78.43.4: bytes=32 time<10ms TTL=128
Reply from 204.78.43.4: bytes=32 time<10ms TTL=128

C:\WINNT\SYSTEM32>ping dragon

Pinging dragon [204.78.43.4] with 32 bytes of data:

Reply from 204.78.43.4: bytes=32 time<10ms TTL=128
Reply from 204.78.43.4: bytes=32 time<10ms TTL=128
Reply from 204.78.43.4: bytes=32 time<10ms TTL=128
Reply from 204.78.43.4: bytes=32 time<10ms TTL=128

C:\WINNT\SYSTEM32>
```

It might be that the problem lies in the setup of the machine you are working with; perhaps the IP stack was not installed correctly. Make sure that you try to ping your own IP address, and if that fails, try the local loopback address (127.0.0.1). If you do not get a response from the local loopback address, IP is not installed correctly on the machine and you need to address that issue before attempting to communicate with other hosts.

TRACERT

tracert is another command line utility that can be used to trace the route a packet is taking, and also to identify slow points along the route. The tracert utility works by manipulating the time-to-live (TTL) setting of the packets. Each IP packet has a TTL flag, and each time the packet crosses a router, or hop, the router decrements this setting by one. The TTL flag is essentially a hop counter.

When the TTL reaches zero, the packet is no good and is discarded. This keeps packets from looping endlessly around the Internet or your network. The router that throws away the packet then sends a message to the originating host that the time (hop count) was exceeded. The key to tracert is that this message contains the IP address of the router that tossed the packet.

PART

VII

CH

28

Suppose, as in Figure 28.13, you enter the command tracert www.jpence.com. The tracert program sends a packet to this destination, with a TTL of 1. The first router along the path receives this packet, discards it, and sends back the time (again, analogous to the hop count) exceeded message. Because this message contains the IP address of the router, you now know the first hop along the route, along with the time involved. Next, the tracert program sends another packet to the destination, this time with a TTL of 2. The second router along the path discards this packet, and sends us back information to that effect. And so on, each time, the TTL is incremented by 1 and then sent on its merry way.

Figure 28.13 shows both the command line options, which you can find by simply entering the command tracert and nothing else, and also the results from tracing the route to www.jpence.com.

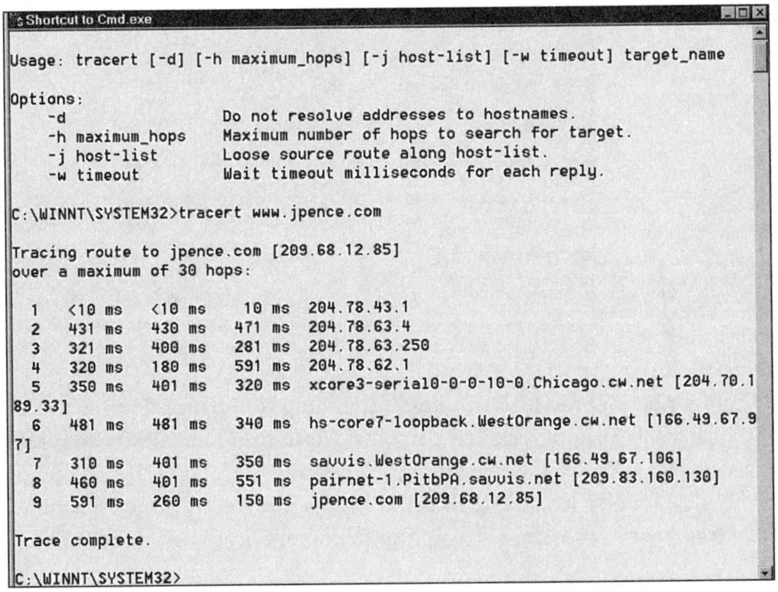

Figure 28.13
Here you can see the command-line switches available to the tracert program, along with the output when tracing the route to a destination, in this case www.jpence.com.

```
Shortcut to Cmd.exe                                              _|□|×

Usage: tracert [-d] [-h maximum_hops] [-j host-list] [-w timeout] target_name

Options:
    -d                     Do not resolve addresses to hostnames.
    -h maximum_hops        Maximum number of hops to search for target.
    -j host-list           Loose source route along host-list.
    -w timeout             Wait timeout milliseconds for each reply.

C:\WINNT\SYSTEM32>tracert www.jpence.com

Tracing route to jpence.com [209.68.12.85]
over a maximum of 30 hops:

  1    <10 ms    <10 ms     10 ms  204.78.43.1
  2    431 ms    430 ms    471 ms  204.78.63.4
  3    321 ms    400 ms    281 ms  204.78.63.250
  4    320 ms    180 ms    591 ms  204.78.62.1
  5    350 ms    401 ms    320 ms  xcore3-serial0-0-0-10-0.Chicago.cw.net [204.70.1
89.33]
  6    481 ms    481 ms    340 ms  hs-core7-loopback.WestOrange.cw.net [166.49.67.9
7]
  7    310 ms    401 ms    350 ms  sauvis.WestOrange.cw.net [166.49.67.106]
  8    460 ms    401 ms    551 ms  pairnet-1.PitbPA.sauvis.net [209.83.160.130]
  9    591 ms    260 ms    150 ms  jpence.com [209.68.12.85]

Trace complete.

C:\WINNT\SYSTEM32>
```

SERVER-BASED TOOLS

On the server side, there aren't that many tools to work with, but then, if you are having problems with the IP stack on the server, it will quickly manifest itself. The server will not be able to communicate with either the workstations or the other servers. I will take a look at the most useful ping tool, of which there are two flavors, and TCPCon, used to monitor TCP/IP statistics and activity.

TPING

tping is a command-line version of Ping and is used at the server console to see whether other nodes are reachable. The syntax is `tping host [packet size [retry count]]`. Each of these command line parameters is explained in the following list:

- Host can be either the host name, such as dragon, or the actual IP address of the target.

- Packet size is used to specify the size, in bytes, of the packet being sent.

- Retry count specifies the number of times you want tping to retry if there is no answer. The default is 5.

When tping receives an echo response from the target, it stops sending and displays a message that the target is alive (see Figure 28.14).

Tip #288 from *John*	It is worth noting that the loader has been changed in NetWare 5. It is no longer necessary to enter the command `load`, as in `load monitor` or `load tping`, but it still works. So `tping dragon` and `load tping dragon` are functionally the same.

Figure 28.14
tping is quick and dirty. Used from the server console, it is just like the Ping utility at the workstations. Here, you have entered the command `tping 204.78.43.4` and received from tping the message "204.78.43.4 is alive."

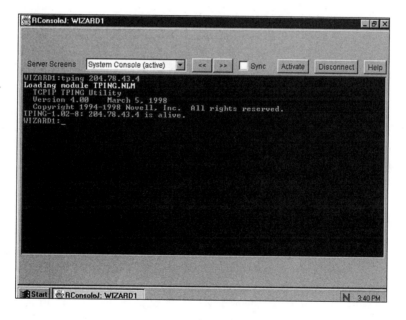

PING

Ping is also loaded at the server console, and functionally, is exactly like tping, only a bit fancier, as you can see in Figure 28.15. The syntax is `ping`, or `load ping`.

Figure 28.15
Ping gives you the same functionality as tping, only the interface is a bit prettier. Notice that here you are about to begin pinging a host named dragon.

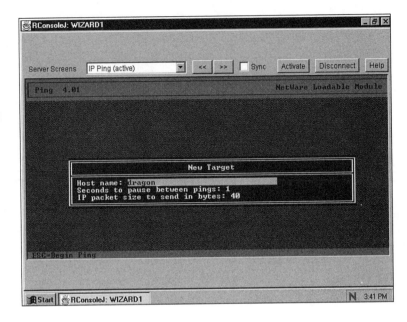

To select a target, enter either the host name or the IP address of the target. You can specify the number of seconds to pause between pings and also the packet size. To start sending packets, press Esc. The server continues to send echo requests until you press Esc again to stop pinging. One of the nicer features of Ping over tping is that you can press Insert and add additional hosts, so you can ping more than one host at a time.

Earlier, when discussing the ping command used at the workstation, I pointed out that you can ping either by host name or by IP address. When using the host name, some form of name resolution needs to occur, in order to map the host name to an IP address that the machine can use. If I try tping dragon, I get back a fairly cryptic message from tping that "host dragon is unknown." When attempting to use Ping from the server and reach host dragon, I still get an error message, only a bit more elaborate, along with some advice, as shown in Figure 28.16.

The advice is to make sure that netdb.nlm is loaded, and that sys:etc\resolv.cfg is configured correctly. What you are seeing in this case is a name resolution issue. Even though the host dragon (204.78.43.4) is up and alive on the network, the server cannot resolve the name, so the ping fails. When pinging by host name and failing, always remember to try to ping by IP address, to take name resolution out of the equation.

In Figure 28.17, you have backed up and entered the address of host dragon, 204.78.43.4, and you can see that this host is indeed reachable.

Figure 28.16
Ping cannot understand *dragon* as a host name or address.

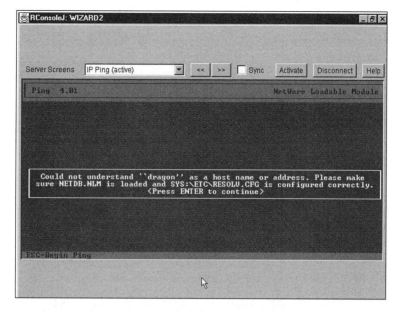

Figure 28.17
When pinging host dragon by IP address, you are successfully able to obtain replies. This indicates that there is a problem with name resolution.

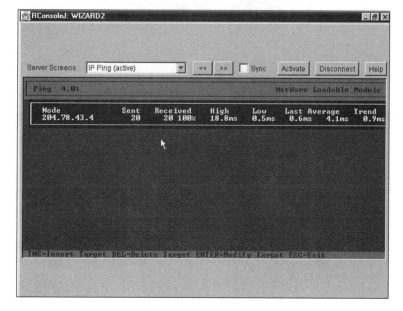

TCPCON

TCPCon is used at the server console to monitor TCP/IP activity. The syntax is `tcpcon`, or `load tcpcon`. TCPCon lets you do the following:

- View IP routes
- View network interfaces
- View configuration information and statistics about TCP/IP protocols
- Use Simple Network Management Protocol (SNMP) over TCP/IP or IPX to access remote nodes
- Access the trap log on the local system

The main TCPCon screen, as shown in Figure 28.18, has two main sections; the top has informational fields, and the bottom is the Options menu.

Figure 28.18
The main screen of
`tcpcon.nlm`.

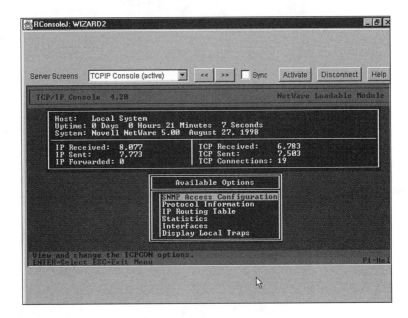

What information can you get from the main tcpcon screen?

- Host—The host name or IP address of the node being queried. (In this case, the local system).
- Uptime—How long since the host was last initialized (21 minutes, 7 seconds).
- System—Description of the selected host (Novell NetWare 5.00).
- IP Received—the number of IP datagrams received from all interfaces, including errors (8,077).

- IP Sent—The number of datagrams sent to IP for transmission (7,773).

- IP Forwarded—The number of packets forwarded, or routed (0).

- TCP Received—The number of TCP segments received, including errors (6,783).

- TCP Sent—The number of TCP segments sent. This field does not include retransmitted data (7,503).

- TCP Connections—the number of currently established connections (19).

From the Available Options menu, you can continue drilling down to access more information. In Figure 28.19, Statistics was chosen and then TCP.

Figure 28.19
Drilling down into the Available Options menu to obtain TCP statistical information.

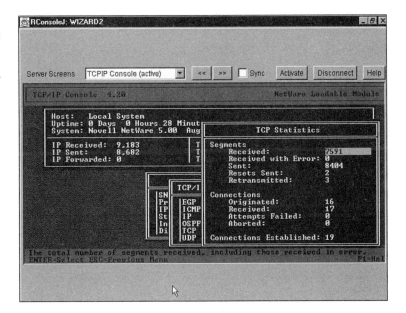

TROUBLESHOOTING

The ping command will always be the first weapon in your arsenal when troubleshooting IP connections. If you cannot ping another host by using the remote hosts IP address, you will never be able to ping it by name. Once you begin trying to ping using the name of the remote host, then name resolution comes into play.

It is important that you understand the process of name resolution used by your workstations. Do Windows 95/98, Windows NT Workstation, and a UNIX host all resolve names in the same fashion? What process is used for name resolution? For example, is it the hosts file and then DNS, or the DNS server then the hosts file? Understanding the process used by the workstations for name resolution will often help you to speed up establishing connections.

Also, although you do not need to know the low-level details of all the protocols, you do need to know that they exist, and what their function is. For example, ARP is used to resolve IP addresses into MAC addresses, because a NIC can only send to another MAC address. Knowing this will take you to the ARP command, where you can quickly learn that you can view and manipulate the ARP cache.

And remember to always break network communications down into its component parts; there is no magic here, it just seems that way. If you try and map a drive to a server and the drive mapping fails, then you have to systematically start in on the troubleshooting process, beginning with ping and moving on from there.

## CHAPTER 29

DOMAIN NAMING SYSTEMS (DNS)

In this chapter

INTRODUCTION TO DNS

When you point your Web browser to www.novell.com, this works for you quite well as a human, but to the computer, it is no good at all. The first thing the computer needs to do is find out the IP address of www.novell.com, and only then can it begin communicating. This name resolution process is handled by a domain naming systems (DNS) server, which has records of host names and their corresponding IP addresses. The first thing that your workstation does when browsing is ask the DNS server for the IP address of the URL you have just entered; then the browser is able to contact the site.

It is quite simple to test this: remove the DNS server entry from your IP configuration, and then try to Web browse. You'll get to see the hourglass for a bit, and then the browser will ultimately tell you that the site does not have a DNS entry and to check the name.

The DNS name space is like an inverted tree, very much like an NDS tree that you are already familiar with (see Figure 29.1). At the *root*, or top, of the tree are the root servers; all queries begin here. Below the root are the first level domains, such as .com, .net, .edu, and others.

Figure 29.1
The domain name space.

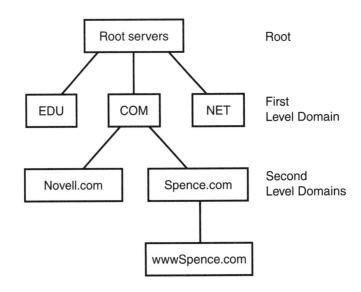

The complete name of a host is the path it takes to get back to the root, for example, the Web server www shown as a machine in the jpence domain (see Figure 29.1), has a fully qualified domain name of www.jpence.com. There should be a trailing period to specify the root, but you seldom ever see that.

A domain is a branch of the tree; like c:\windows\system is a branch of the directory tree on your c: drive. And like directories in DOS, domains can contain other domains. The .com domain contains Novell.com, Microsoft.com, Jpence.com, DreamLan.com, and many more!

These domains might be said to be child domains of their parent domain, or they could also be called subdomains. Table 29.1 lists some of the top level domains that you might be familiar with.

TABLE 29.1—TOP LEVEL DOMAINS

Domain	Used By
MIL	Military installations
EDU	Educational institutions
COM	Businesses
GOV	Government installations
NET	Networks
ORG	Miscellaneous organizations

In addition to the top-level domains, there are abbreviations that have been assigned to countries, as shown in Table 29.2

TABLE 29.2 COUNTRY CODES

Abbreviation	Country
AU	Australia
BR	Brazil
CA	Canada
DO	Dominican Republic
EG	Egypt
FR	France
DE	Germany
HK	Hong Kong
IN	India
JP	Japan
KW	Kuwait
MY	Malaysia
NZ	New Zealand
OM	Oman
PT	Portugal
UK	United Kingdom

If you have a private network, you can use any domain name you'd like, and any IP Addressing scheme. But if you want to connect your network to the Internet, your domain name needs to be registered, and you need valid IP Addresses. You can register a domain name at www.internic.net.

THE NAME RESOLUTION PROCESS

Think of how amazing it is; there are millions of names you can enter in an attempt to communicate. URLs for the World Wide Web, FTP servers; it would be one huge database. Imagine trying to host that on one machine? But the DNS name space is spread out over many DNS servers. Each DNS server knows the names it is responsible for because of the address records it holds. And the DNS server knows how to ask other DNS servers for names it is not responsible for. Each server has a small piece of the pie, and knows how to find the rest.

When you attempt to resolve the name www.jpence.com, the first thing you do is ask your DNS server. The odds are that your DNS server won't know anything about this address, but it can find out; first, your DNS server asks one of the root servers, "What is the address of www.jpence.com?" The root server won't know, but the root server does know the IP address of a machine responsible for the .com domain, so the root server gives you that, and suggests you ask the .com domain servers.

Your DNS server next asks the server responsible for the .com domain, "What is the address of www.jpence.com?" The .com server doesn't know that either, but it does know who is responsible for the .jpence.com domain, so it gives you this information, and suggests you ask the server responsible for .jpence.com.

Your DNS server next asks the server responsible for the .jpence.com domain, "What is the address of www.jpence.com?" This server, being responsible for the .jpence.com domain, will have an entry of the IP address of the machine that is www.jpence.com, so it will return this information to your DNS server.

All this time, your DNS server has been acting on your behalf; you have only sent it the one request, but it has had to query several DNS servers (make several requests) in order to find out the information that you are after. Finally, having received the desired address, your DNS server responds to your initial request.

No.	Source	Destination	Layer	Size	Summary
9	**JOHN**	**WIZARD2**	dns	0081	Std **Req** A www.gomemphis.com
10	WIZARD2	CISCO	dns	0082	Std Req A www.gomemphis.com
13	CISCO	WIZARD2	dns	0170	Std Req A www.gomemphis.com

No.	Source	Destination	Layer	Size	Summary
14	WIZARD2	CISCO	dns	0082	Std Req A www.gomemphis.com
15	CISCO	WIZARD2	dns	0186	Std Rply www.gomemphis.com A
16	**WIZARD2**	**JOHN**	dns	0186	Std **Rply** www.gomemphis.com A

This process is shown in the summary trace. John has made a DNS request for the IP address of www.gomemphis.com; he has made this request to Wizard2, as shown in frame number 9. Notice that Wizard2 then makes several queries, all directed out the Cisco router, because the DNS servers in question are out on the Internet, not local to the segment John and Wizard2 are on. Only in frame 16 does Wizard2, John's DNS server, respond to John with the IP address of www.gomemphis.com. The two local frames, 9 and 16, are shown in bold; in all the other frames, 10–15, Wizard2, not John, has been making the queries (Req = Request) necessary to obtain the requested information.

Consider the implications of the recursive requests that the DNS server needs to make when WAN (Wide Area Network) links are involved. Say the access point to the Internet is located at corporate headquarters, and the various properties are connected via WAN links. If you have a DNS server locally on each property, the client makes one local request to the DNS server; the DNS server then makes *several* requests over the WAN link to obtain the requested information, and, finally, gives the client a local reply. This scenario has generated more than two frames of traffic on the WAN link.

Now consider moving the DNS server to the corporate side of the WAN link; the client makes one request over the WAN link. The recursive queries done by the DNS server of other DNS servers stay off the WAN link, and finally, only the reply to the client travels back over the WAN link. This scenario puts less traffic on the WAN link; it might not seem significant, but if you have several hundred users browsing the Internet, it can and will make a difference!

DNS INSTALLATION

Several steps are involved in the installation of DNS services on your NetWare 5 server. The first is installing the DHCP/DNS console that you must use to manage DNS. There are snap-ins to make nwadmin32 aware of the objects, the schema must be extended, and more. Fortunately, setting it up is a lot easier than it sounds.

MANAGEMENT CONSOLE AND SNAP-IN INSTALLATION

To install the management console and the snap-ins necessary for NetWare administrator, follow these steps:

1. Run sys:public\dnsdhcp\setup.exe.

2. At the Welcome screen, click Next.

3. On the next screen, shown in Figure 29.2, make sure you have the Copy the Snap-in Files box checked.

Figure 29.2
When installing the DNS/DHCP Management Console, make sure you check the box to copy the necessary snap-ins for NWAdmin.

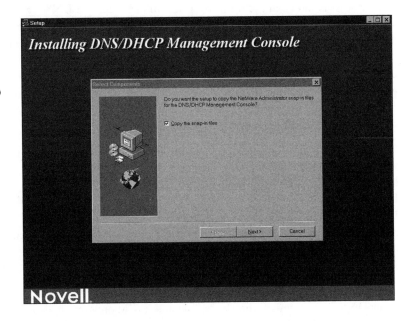

The default location to install the files for the management console is C:\ Program Files\Novell\DNSDHCP\.

4. Next, browse to the directory that contains the NetWare administration utilities, in this case, sys:public\win32.

5. After the snap-ins are copied, you have a chance to view the readme file; it's always a good idea to read this and print it when offered. The snap-ins are only going to let you see the new DNS objects that you will create later; you don't manage DNS from NWAdmin.

Setup is now complete, and you should have a shortcut on your desktop. Shortcut is to C:\Program files\Novell\DNSDHCP\dnsdhcp.exe. Note that at this point nothing has been done to the server other than to copy the snap-in files to public\win32; all you have done is to install the management console application on the workstation.

EXTEND THE SCHEMA

In order for you to be able to create DNS objects, the schema of your tree needs to be extended. You must have supervisor rights at the root of the tree in order to extend the schema. There are three ways to extend the schema:

- During installation, you can choose to install DNS. This isn't a very likely scenario, unless you are installing a new server with the intention of making it a DNS server. More likely, you will have a server already up, and then later desire to have it act as a DNS server.
- From the NetWare GUI, you can choose the Install.
- The simplest by far is the DNIPINST.NLM.

At the server console, enter the command LOAD DNIPINST, or simply DNIPINST. You are asked to log in, the schema is extended, and then you are asked where you want the following objects placed: the DNS/DHCP Locator object, the DNSDHCP-GROUP object, and the RootServerInfo zone object, as shown in Figure 29.3

Figure 29.3
In addition to extending the schema, DNIPINST creates the DNS-DHCP Locator object, the DNSDHCPGROUP object, and the RootServerInfo Zone object.

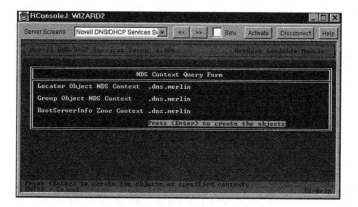

Before worrying about the context, what are these three?

- The DNSDHCP-GROUP object is a standard NDS group object. When a DNS object is created, the DNSDHCP-GROUP is automatically made a trustee. If you are a member of this group, you have access to the DNS objects; servers that you designate as DNS servers will be added to this group.
- The DNS-DHCP Locator object is unconfigurable; you will not see this when running the management console. The locator contains lists of DNS servers and zones. The management console can use the locator to find DNS objects without searching the tree. Later in this chapter, you will see how to speed up the launching of the management console by telling it the context of the locator object.
- The RootServerInfo Zone object is an important one. It contains the IP addresses of the root DNS servers, where all your DNS queries outside of your zone will begin.

You have placed these objects in .dns.merlin, a container that you will dedicate to DNS objects. Before doing any configuration at all, if you run nwadmin32, you can see the three objects that DNIPINST has created (see Figure 29.4).

Figure 29.4
In the specified context, running DNIP-INST has created the DNSDHCP-GROUP object, the DNS-DHCP locater object, and the RootServerInfo object.

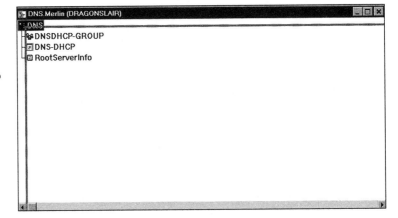

Even though you can see these three objects, thanks to the snap-in installation you did earlier, what happens if you try to manage them from within NWAdmin? If you double-click the DNS/DHCP Group, it is a normal NDS group object—nothing new there.

However, if you click the RootServerInfo object, you receive the following message: This is a zone record. You can launch the DNS/DHCP Management console configuration utility from Tool menu to configure it. In other words, as I have previously pointed out, you can see them in NWAdmin, but you manage them with the DNS/DHCP Management Console.

> **Note**
>
> If you double-click the DNS-DHCP object, you are told that this is a DNS-DHCP Locator record. You are also told to manage this via the DNS/DHCP Management Console, but, as I have already pointed out, this is not a configurable object, and you will not see it from the Management Console.

At this point, the schema has been extended, and the three NDS objects required for DNS/DHCP services have been created.

Tip #289 from
John

> DNIPINST extends the schema and creates the DNS-DHCP Locator object, the DNSDHCP-GROUP object, and the RootServerInfo zone object. To remove the schema extensions, you can load DNIPINST -R.

To start DNS running on the server, you run `named.nlm`. So far, you have extended the schema, which created three NDS objects, and you have installed the management console onto the workstation. But has anything been done to make the server functional as a DNS server yet?

At this point, if you run `named.nlm`, you will see the error `Unable to access DNS Server object, quitting` because you haven't done any configuration yet. The first thing you need to do is to create the DNS server object.

DNS CONFIGURATION AND MANAGEMENT

All configuration and management of DNS is done via the Java-based management console. As with any Java-based application, lots of memory and a fast machine cut down on your frustration!

LAUNCHING THE MANAGEMENT CONSOLE

There are two ways to launch the management console; the first is to use the shortcut on your desktop created by the setup program. The second is to choose the DNS/DHCP Management Console from Tools on the `nwadmn32` toolbar. The desktop shortcut points to `C:\Program Files\Novel\DNSDHCP\dnsdhcp.exe`, and the `readme` file gives you a tip to speed up the launching of the management console.

Tip #290 from
John

> To speed up launching the management console, edit the shortcut properties and add a `-C` option to specify the context of the locator object. This option eliminates the search for the locator object, and thus speeds up the launching of the management console. Remember, the locator is going to have a list of the DNS servers and zones. For example, in this case, the locator is located in `.dns.merlin`, so the shortcut or command line would be `C:\Program Files\Novell\DNSDHCP\dnsdhcp.exe -C dns.merlin`.

When you run the program, the first thing you are prompted for is the tree name to manage, as shown in Figure 29.5.

Figure 29.5
When running the management console, the first thing you do is choose the tree you want to manage.

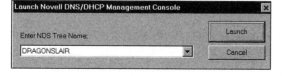

Enter your treename, click Launch, and you will see the console as shown in Figure 29.6.

Figure 29.6
This is how the
DNS/DHCP
Management Console
appears when it is
run for the first time.

There are two tables up at the top left of the console; one for DNS and one for DHCP. In this chapter, you are concerned only with the DNS tab. Notice that RootServerInfo zone that shows up? That's all; no servers, no other zones, and no locator objects.

CREATE THE DNS SERVER OBJECT

To create the NDS server object, follow these steps:

1. Start the DNS/DHCP management console.

2. Choose the DNS tab, and click the Create button.

> **Note**   The Create button is the cube at the left of the toolbar.

The Create New DNS Record menu appears, and DNS Server is highlighted by default.

3. Click OK and fill in the information in the Create DNS Server dialog box, as shown in Figure 29.7.

Figure 29.7
Here, you select the server you wish to act as the DNS server, along with assigning a host name and domain.

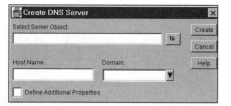

The Create DNS Server dialog box has the following text boxes:

- **Select Server Object**—This is the NetWare 5 server that actually acts as the DNS server and runs named.nlm. You can either enter the name or browse to the server; you have chosen Wizard2 to act as the DNS server.

- **Host name**—This is the host name for the DNS server. It does not have to be the same as the server name. You have entered Wizard2, the server name, as the host name.

- **Domain**—This is the name of the domain that the server will be responsible for. You are going to have this server in the domain dragonslair; more on DragonsLair later in the chapter, when you want your DNS server to resolve names for your own domain.

When the DNS server has been created, you will see a server icon down in the bottom left of the management console. Initially, this server has a red slash through it, because the DNS service hasn't been started yet. Later on, when you have had things working, then the red slash would be indicative of a communication problem between your workstation/console and the DNS server.

STARTING THE DNS SERVICE

At this point, you can test what you have done. Go to the server console you have created, and enter the command named to run the named.nlm. The red slash should disappear from the server icon, as shown in Figure 29.8, and you can now stop and start the service from the management console.

There are several command-line options for named, listed in Table 29.3. If you have already loaded named.nlm, you can still enter the command and options; the previously loaded module will be used re-entrantly. In other words, if named is running, and you want to turn on verbose mode, you would simply enter named -v at the console prompt. This would not load named again, but rather invoke the verbose mode.

Figure 29.8
You have done nothing yet but create a DNS server and start it running, yet it is already a fully functional caching DNS server. Notice the server icon in the bottom left of the console; the red slash has disappeared.

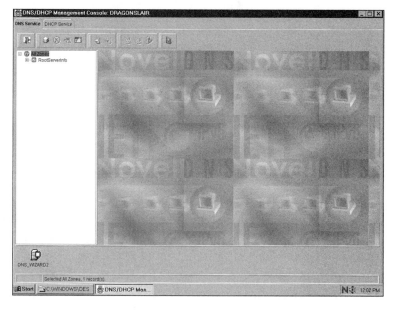

TABLE 29.3   NAMED COMMAND-LINE OPTIONS

Switch	Function
-a	Auto detect new zones. This is the default setting.
-b	Turns off auto detect of new zones.
-f <script.txt> <context>	Used to create zones with a text file in BIND bootfile format; context specifies the NDS context of the zone to be created.
-h	Shows help.
-l	Log in as Admin.
-m <zone.dat> <context>	Imports zone.dat to create a new primary zone; context specifies the NDS context of the zone to be created.
-q	Turns off verbose mode. This is a default setting.
-r <zone name>	Deletes <zone name>.
-rp	List of characters in the domain name to be replaced with -.
-s <zone name>	Print status information; the zone name is optional.
-u <file>	Imports file and updates an existing zone.
-v	Turns on verbose mode.
-zi <zone>	Forces zone in for the given zone.

When `named.nlm` is running, it creates its own screen that you can toggle to like any other server console screen. Depending on the `-v` and `-q` switch settings, you will see various status and operational messages; in any case, what you see will tend to be on the cryptic side.

Like any form of detailed logging, verbose mode takes more overhead, so you should accept the default setting of `-q` when loading `named.nlm`, and turn on verbose mode only when troubleshooting.

SETTING UP THE CLIENT FOR DNS AND TESTING

Before proceeding with more intricate DNS configuration details, you should test what you have already created. If all you need your DNS server for is to resolve names external to your network, you are finished. The server has access to the RootServerInfo zone record, which contains the IP addresses of the root servers. This means that you will be able to resolve any registered domain name.

As discussed earlier, you first ask the root servers, then the `.com` servers, and so on. If you want your DNS server to resolve names within your own domain, there is more work ahead, but first, set up the client to use your new DNS server and test what you have already done.

You will want to get to the Properties tab of the TCP/IP protocols, and choose the DNS tab (see Figure 29.9).

Figure 29.9
You must configure the client to use your new DNS server.

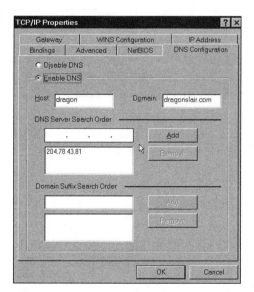

Enable DNS and enter the host name for your workstation, which by default is the same as the NetBIOS name, but it does not have to be. Enter the workstation's domain, and then enter the IP address of your new DNS server and click Add. As always with Windows, a reboot is required! When the workstation is back online, start your Web browser, point to a valid URL, and see what happens. If you have no luck at this point, skip ahead to the troubleshooting portion of this chapter. If all goes well, the name should be resolved by your new setup.

ZONES

By now, you should have a functional DNS server running on your NetWare 5 server; it should be able to resolve any registered domain name, because of the RootServerInfo zone record put there while extending the schema.

But suppose you have registered a domain name, and are going to be responsible for implementing your own domain name servers; you need to create a zone. A zone is a logical piece of the DNS name space, and it will consist of at least one domain. A DNS server has responsibility for a zone. For example, if you have responsibility for the zone dragonslair.com, you will maintain the resource records for that domain.

The .com servers at the second level domain don't need to know anything about dragonslair.com other than the fact that merlin2.dragonslair.com is responsible for the zone. When someone attempts to resolve the name www.dragonslair.com, the .com servers will refer him to merlin2.dragonslair.com, the DNS server responsible. Merlin2 will then be tasked with resolving the www portion of the name. So it wouldn't matter whether dragonslair.com had 10 machines or 10,000; the only thing the .com servers need to know is who is responsible for the dragonslair.com zone, or domain.

What I have been describing so far have been forward naming zones, those that resolve host names to IP addresses. But the reverse also exists, known as *IN-ADDR.ARPA* zones. An IN-ADDR-ARPA zone is used when you know the IP address, and you want to obtain the host name. An address record in the IN-ADDR-ARPA zone is written, as you might expect, backwards. For example, if the IP address of Dragon is 204.78.43.4, the IN-ADDR-ARPA record would be written as 4.43.78.204.in-addr.arpa. To create an IN-ADDR.ARPA zone, make sure that you fill in the Create IN-ADDR.ARPA button in the Create Zone dialog box (look ahead to Figure 29.10).

There are also IP6.INT zones; you can only have one IP6.INT zone in your tree. IP version 6 is the next generation of IP addressing. IPV6 will use 128 bytes for the IP address, versus the 32 bits used in IPV4, today's addressing scheme. The IP6.INT is used to resolve host names to IPV6 IP addresses. To create an IP6.INT zone, fill in the appropriate bullet at the Create Zone Dialog box shown in Figure 29.10.

PRIMARY (MASTER) AND SECONDARY (REPLICA) AND ZONE TRANSFERS

In any zone, there can be only one Master copy of the resource records; the DNS database. This copy exists on the Primary, or Master, Name Server. Changes to the DNS database are made at the Master, which is fine, but what happens if the primary server is the only one for a zone and it is not up? Name Resolution would fail.

In the event that the primary server is offline, you want a Secondary, or Replica server in place so that you can still resolve names. This is very much like the NDS Master replica and R/W replicas that you are already familiar with. A replica server can also take some of the load off of the primary.

Changes to the database are made at the master, and the Secondary, or Replica server, periodically downloads a copy of the database from the master; this is called a zone transfer.

ZONE TRANSFERS, PRIMARIES, SECONDARIES, AND NDS

In the traditional picture, you have your Master server and some replica servers; each replica server periodically does a zone transfer from the master. In essence, there are multiple copies of the DNS data floating around, and they are not necessarily always in sync.

Novell has done away with this by using NDS to hold the DNS information; you already have the NDS database, so why not use it? The zones and resource record information are stored in NDS, and are replicated like any other NDS data. So the concept of a primary and secondary server doesn't really exist, along with the idea of a zone transfer; there is only one copy of the data in NDS, and all servers have access to it.

CREATING A ZONE

In addition to resolving names out on the Internet, you also want your DNS server to resolve IP addresses for your fictional domain, DragonsLair.com, which you might find on the Internet, but it hasn't been registered by us! To create a zone, launch the configuration manager and select Create, Zone, Ok. The Create Zone dialog box appears as shown in Figure 29.10

The fields available in the Create Zone dialog box are as follows:

- **Create New Zone**—Select this to create a forward naming zone; one that resolves host names to IP addresses.

- **Create In-Addr Arpa**—Select this to create a reverse naming zone; one the resolves IP addresses to host names.

- **Create IP6.INT**—The next evolution of IP addressing is called IPV6; it vastly increases the available number of IP addresses by using 128 bits for the address, instead of only the 32 bits currently used by IPV4. There can be only one IP6.INT zone in a tree.

- **NDS Context**—Here, you specify the container where you want the zone record created; this is the normal NDS context that you are used to.

- **Zone Domain Name**—The fully qualified domain name, such as dragonslair.com or jpence.com.

- **Zone Type**—Zones are either going to be primary or secondary. A primary zone has the master copy of the records; a secondary gets a copy via zone transfer.
- **Assign Authoritative DNS Server**—This is the DNS server that will be servicing the zone; you created a DNS server object earlier in this chapter.
- **Host Name**—The host name for the server; it can be the same as the server name, but it does not have to be.
- **Domain**—The domain name of the server.

Figure 29.10
The Create Zone dialog has many options; it will default to Create New Zone.

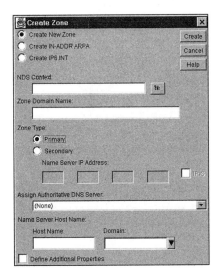

IMPORTING AND EXPORTING RECORDS

It is also possible to create zones by importing the data from a BIND master file. To import, launch the Management Console and choose the Import DNS Database button. Enter the name of the file, click next, and enter the NDS context in which the zone should be created. Assign a server, and then import. named.nlm also has switches to allow creation of zones by importing, via the command line.

You can also export the zone information contained in NDS to a file. Launch the Management console, and then highlight the zone you want to export. Choose the Export DNS Database button, enter a destination filename, and then choose export. You now have a BIND master file of your DNS zone. The following are the results of exporting the information for the fictional dragonslair.com:

```
$ORIGIN dragonslair.com.
@           IN    SOA     dragonslair.com. root.dragonslair.com. (
                  1999031401    ; Serial
                  10800    ; Refresh
                  3600     ; Retry
```

```
                    604800      ; Expire
                    86400 )     ; Minimum


$ORIGIN com.
dragonslair              IN    NS    wizard2.dragonslair.com.

$ORIGIN dragonslair.com.
wizard1                  IN    A     204.78.43.68
wizard2                  IN    A     204.78.43.81
dragon                   IN    A     204.78.43.4
```

Exporting the information has no effect on the information stored in the NDS directory, so you could use this method to back up your zone information. If you were to export the dragonslair.com zone, and then delete it, recovery would be as simple as importing the previously exported records.

RECORDS

A zone without resource records wouldn't be able to resolve many names! To create a record, highlight the zone in which you want it to be created, and hit the Create button. This will bring you to the Create Resource Record dialog box (see Figure 29.11).

Figure 29.11
The most common type of record you create will be an A, or Address record.

At the Create Resource Record Dialog box, enter the host name you are creating the record for and the IP address. The domain is automatically filled in. The radio button records are as follows:

- **A**—By default, this radio button is filled in. This is very much like your hosts file that you might be familiar with. The DNS server can only resolve names that it has a record for. You can see in Figure 29.11 that you have created records in dragonslair.com for dragon, wizard1, and wizard2; you can ping these stations by name. If you try to ping wizard3, the DNS server will not be able to provide you with name resolution; it knows nothing about wizard3.

- **CNAME**—This stands for *Canonical Name*, which is an alias. For example, suppose that the host name of your Web server is webserve.jpence.com. You would create an A record for webserve.jpence.com, but you could then create an alias of www, and point it to webserve.jpence.com, so that www.jpence.com would wind up pointing to webserve.jpence.com. If you are creating CNAME records, you don't supply the IP address of the host, like you did with the A record, instead, you supply the Domain name of the Aliased Host.

■ **Others**—There are many others, as you can see by selecting the other radio button and clicking on the drop-down list. To go over each is beyond the scope of this chapter, but you can research these by reading up on the numerous RFCs pertaining to DNS. The following are some of the more common ones:

- **SOA**—This stands for *Start of Authority*. The SOA record is the first record in a zone database file. It names the server that is responsible for the zone.

- **NS**—This is the Name Server record, identifying other name servers.

- **MX**—This is the Mail Exchange record, identifying email servers.

- **PTR**—This is the Pointer record, or IN-ADDR-ARPA record, used to resolve IP addresses to Host names, exactly the opposite of an A record.

TROUBLESHOOTING UTILITIES

When troubleshooting DNS, the first thing you need to do is verify basic IP functionality; in this section, I will look at some utilities that will help: Ping, Nslookup, and the logging you can enable at the DNS server itself.

PING

Assuming there are no network or configuration problems, you will always be able to ping by IP address. If you cannot ping by IP address, don't worry about DNS until you can. It is only when attempting to ping by name that name resolution needs to occur, and only for name resolution does the DNS server come into play. Suppose Wizard2 has an IP address of 204.78.43.81. You can ping this address by entering ping 204.78.43.81 and it works; but if you enter ping wizard2, you get no response.

Does the DNS server have an A record for wizard2, and is the information in the A record correct? If there is no record or if the information is wrong, the DNS server cannot resolve the name for you. The following is the output from entering the command ping wizard2:

```
Pinging wizard2.dragonslair.com [204.78.43.81] with 32 bytes of data:
Reply from 204.78.43.81: bytes=32 time=1ms TTL=128
Reply from 204.78.43.81:bytes=32 time<10ms TTL=128
Reply from 204.78.43.81: bytes=32 time=1ms
TTL=128Reply from 204.78.43.81: bytes=32 time<10ms TTL=128
Ping statistics for 204.78.43.81:
    Packets: Sent = 4, Received = 4, Lost = 0 (0% loss),
Approximate round trip times in milli-seconds:   Minimum = 0ms, Maximum =  1ms,
    Average =  0ms
```

Notice that even though you entered the command ping wizard2, the response comes back pinging wizard2.dragonslair.com, a sure sign that the DNS server is in the picture, because of the fully qualified domain name; you didn't enter it! Alternatively, to test, you could have used the command ping wizard2.dragonslair.com, using the fully qualified domain name of wizard2, which your DNS server would have to resolve.

NSLOOKUP

Nslookup is a diagnostic tool that comes with NT workstation. It queries and displays information from DNS servers. There are two modes to Nslookup: interactive and noninteractive. If you want only one piece of information, use the noninteractive mode. If you want more, or you want to query more than one server, you can go into interactive mode, where you actually have an Nslookup command prompt.

The command `nslookup www.jpence.com` returns the following information:

```
Server:  ns1.scripps.com
Address:  204.78.32.10

Name:    jpence.com
Address:  209.68.12.85
Aliases:  www.jpence.com
```

The first information, the server and its address, are the name and address of the DNS server you are using, set in the DNS tab of the TCP/IP properties. The second piece of information is the data returned on the query of `www.jpence.com`.

The available commands for Nslookup are quite extensive; a listing of the help output is given here in Table 29.4, but for more information, consult your online help.

TABLE 29.4 NSLOOKUP COMMANDS

Command	Function
Name	Print information about the host/domain name using default server.
Name1 Name2	Same as the previous entry, only use Name2 as the server.
Help or ?	Print information on common commands.
Set <Option>	Set an option.
Set all	Print options, current server, and host.
Set [no]debug	Print debugging information.
Set [no]d2	Print detailed debugging information.
Set [no]defname	Append domain name to each query.
Set [no]recurse	Ask for recursive answer to query.
Set [no]search	Use domain search list.
Set [no]vc	Always use a virtual circuit.
Set domain=<name>	Set default domain name to <name>.
Set srchlist=<nl>/<n2>/...	Set domain to N1 and search list to n1, n2, and so on.
Set root=<name>	Set root server to name.
Set retry=x	Set number of retries to x.

continues

TABLE 29.4   CONTINUED

Command	Function
Set timeout=x	Set initial time-out interval to x seconds.
Set type=x	Set query type (For example, A, any, cname, mx, ns, ptr, soa, srv)
Set querytype=x	Same as set type.
Set class=x	Set query class (Example: IN, ANY).
Set [no]msxfr	Use MS fast zone transfer.
Set ixfrver=x	Current version of user in IXFR transfer request.
Server <name>	Set default server to <name>, using current default server.
Lserver <name>	Set default server to <name>, using initial server.
Finger <user>	Finger the optional <name> at the current default host.
Root	Set the current default server to the root.
LS [opt] <domain> [> file]	List addresses in <domain>, optionally output to file.
LS -a	List canonical names and aliases.
LS -d	List all records.
LS -t Type	List records or the given type (for example, a, cname, mx, ns, and so on.)
View <file>	Sort an LS output file and view it with pg.
Exit	Exit Nslookup.

LOGS

Two logs are available to you, in addition to the information you might derive from the named.nlm console screen: the Audit Trail log and the Events log. By default, neither of these log files is activated; you have to turn them on.

From within the DNS/DHCP Management console, highlight the server you want to activate the logs on, and then choose the Options tab.

Under Event log, you can choose from one of three levels; None (the default), Major Events, or All. As always, remember that auditing and tracking has its own overhead, so you might turn on the logs only for troubleshooting purposes. If you want to enable auditing, you need to check the Enable Audit Trail box.

To view the logs, launch the console and select the server in question. Click the View Events/Alerts button and you will be presented with a range of dates; you can accept the range given or modify it to a particular time frame that interests you. After you okay the date range, you are viewing the Events/Alerts log as shown in Figure 29.12.

Figure 29.12
Remember, you have to turn on logging yourself. Once on, keep an eye on the logs!

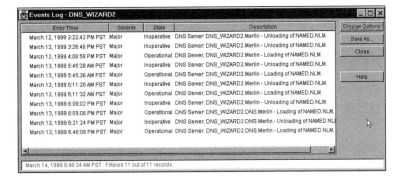

To view the Audit Trail log, simply click the View Audit Trail button instead of the Events/Alerts button.

TROUBLESHOOTING

When you have installed the management console, extended the schema, and created the DNS-DHCP locator, DNSDHCP-GROUP, and RootServerInfo objects, the only thing remaining in order to have a functional DNS server is to create the DNS server object, and start named.nlm running. At this point, you should be able to resolve any valid URL. But suppose it's not working?

As obvious as it might seem, is named.nlm running? named -s at the console command prompt gives you the status. And have you set your client up correctly to use your new DNS server in the TCP/IP properties?

The next thing to think about is the necessary connectivity. Does your server have a default gateway set? Without a default gateway, your DNS server receives the local request and begins trying to resolve it; however, it won't have any way to reach the root servers, which at this point is all it knows about!

If you can ping hosts on the Internet from the server, but DNS can't resolve names, something is possibly wrong with your RootServerInfo zone object.

Tip #291 from
John

You can ping the root servers and they will answer; you can get their addresses by expanding the RootServerInfo object inside the DNS/DHCP Management console.

CHAPTER **30**

Dynamic Host Configuration Protocol (DHCP)

In this chapter

WHY USE DHCP?

Why use Dynamic Host Configuration Protocol (DHCP) indeed? As you have seen, compared to IPX addressing, IP addressing is orders of magnitude more complex. With IPX, your workstation's address was a combination of the MAC address of the NIC and the external IPX address of the server. In essence, you as the administrator had to do nothing about addressing when using IPX, other than give the external address at the server when binding IPX.

IP, on the other hand, requires that each station have its own unique number. In addition to the IP address, each station needs at the extreme minimum a subnet mask. And for functionality, at least a default gateway. If you then add a DNS server to the mix, you are looking at entering at least four numbers at every workstation. The opportunities to make mistakes in this scenario are legion!

But assume that you have settled down to the task, and on a small network of 200 machines, have finally gotten it all correct. Now, what happens if the IP address of the router (default gateway) changes? Or the IP address of the DNS server? You are looking at making the round of all 200 machines and manually making the changes, again leaving plenty of room for human error.

And there is another place to make a mistake; you are going to have to keep a spreadsheet or some sort of database as to who has what address. And no matter how good your intentions are, it is only a matter of time until the spreadsheet is no longer accurate. In the heat of battle, you might assign or change an address, thinking you will update the spreadsheet later. Only later, you've forgotten!

It would be ideal if you could hand out the IP address assignments automatically. It would be even more ideal if you could hand out not only addresses, but also the other pertinent information, such as the subnet mask, the default router, the DNS server, and more. This is the purpose of DHCP. There are two pieces to DHCP: the server side and the client side. You configure the DHCP server with the information you want to hand out to the clients; then when the clients initialize, they ask the server for an address, and get it along with any other information you have configured.

This is the why; from one centrally managed server, you can automatically hand this information out to clients configured to use DHCP. It eliminates all error, and if you have to make a change, you have to make it only once, not 200 times! Using DHCP will vastly simplify the management of your IP addressing.

A client leases an address, in much the same way you would lease a house or apartment; the lease specifies how long the IP address is good for, and at the end of the lease, if the client has not renewed, it has to stop using the address. Later in this chapter you will see how to manually force a client to release or renew its lease.

DHCP THEORY OF OPERATION

There are four pieces to obtaining a lease from the server: discover, offer, select, and acknowledge. You will take a quick look at each of these packets, along with a look at the dhcpsrvr.log file which sums it all up nicely. The clients also attempt to renew their leases; after a client has successfully obtained a lease, it will later attempt to renew the lease.

DISCOVERY

I will show the entire DHCPDISCOVER packet, so that you can see that DHCP rides on top of UDP, which, as you already know, rides on top of IP. Notice at the DLC level that this is a broadcast packet; the destination address is all ones, or FFFFFFFFFFFF. Why a broadcast? The workstation is just coming online, and doesn't know the address of the DHCP server, so it must broadcast:

PART

VII

CH

30

```
DLC:  ----- DLC Header -----
DLC:
DLC:  Frame 116 arrived at  08:35:25.9751; frame size is 342 (0156 hex) bytes.
DLC:  Destination = BROADCAST FFFFFFFFFFFF, Broadcast
DLC:  Source      = Station Prteon8432BE
DLC:  Ethertype   = 0800 (IP)
DLC:
IP:  ----- IP Header -----
IP:
IP: Version = 4, header length = 20 bytes
IP: Type of service = 00
IP:       000. .... = routine
IP:       ...0 .... = normal delay
IP:       .... 0... = normal throughput
IP:       .... .0.. = normal reliability
IP: Total length    = 328 bytes
IP: Identification  = 0
IP: Flags           = 0X
IP:       .0.. .... = may fragment
IP:       ..0. .... = last fragment
IP: Fragment offset = 0 bytes
IP: Time to live    = 128 seconds/hops
IP: Protocol        = 17 (UDP)
IP: Header checksum = 39A6 (correct)
IP: Source address      = [0.0.0.0]
IP: Destination address = [255.255.255.255]
IP: No options
IP:
UDP:  ----- UDP Header -----
UDP:
UDP: Source port      = 68 (Bootpc/DHCP)
UDP: Destination port = 67 (Bootps/DHCP)
UDP: Length           = 308
UDP: Checksum         = 54E1 (correct)
UDP: [300 byte(s) of data]
UDP:
DHCP:  ----- DHCP Header -----
DHCP:
DHCP: Boot record type         = 1 (Request)
DHCP: Message type             = 1 DHCP Discover
```

```
DHCP: Hardware address type   = 1 (10Mb Ethernet)
DHCP: Hardware address length = 6 bytes
DHCP:
DHCP: Hops                    = 0
DHCP: Transaction id          = 20022002
DHCP: Elapsed boot time       = 0 seconds
DHCP: Flags                   = 0000
DHCP:    0... .... .... .... = No broadcast
DHCP: Client self-assigned IP address   = [0.0.0.0]
DHCP: Client IP address                 = [0.0.0.0]
DHCP: Next Server to use in bootstrap   = [0.0.0.0]
DHCP: Relay Agent                       = [0.0.0.0]
DHCP: Client hardware address           = Prteon8432BE
DHCP:
DHCP: Host name      = ""
DHCP: Boot file name = ""
DHCP:
DHCP: Vendor Information tag = 63825363
DHCP: Message Type              = 1 (DHCP Discover)
DHCP: Client identifier         = 010000938432BE
DHCP: Request specific IP address    = [204.78.43.50]
DHCP: HostName                       = "Tarzan"
DHCP: Parameter Request List: 8 entries
DHCP:    Request option code = 1
DHCP:    Request option code = 3
DHCP:    Request option code = 6
DHCP:    Request option code = 15
DHCP:    Request option code = 44
DHCP:    Request option code = 46
DHCP:    Request option code = 47
DHCP:    Request option code = 57
DHCP:
```

The most important thing to realize about the discovery packet is that is a broadcast packet, but there are other points of interest. Notice that at the IP level, the workstation is using an IP address of 0.0.0.0; this is because it has not yet initialized. You can also see that the DHCP message type is DHCP Discover and that the client is attempting to request a specific IP address of 204.78.43.50, the last one the client knew about.

OFFER

The server, having seen the client's broadcast asking for an IP address, responds with a lease offer:

```
DHCP: ----- DHCP Header -----
DHCP:
DHCP: Boot record type         = 2 (Reply)
DHCP: Message type             = 2 DHCP Offer
DHCP: Hardware address type    = 1 (10Mb Ethernet)
DHCP: Hardware address length  = 6 bytes
DHCP:
DHCP: Hops                     = 0
DHCP: Transaction id           = 20022002
DHCP: Elapsed boot time        = 0 seconds
DHCP: Flags                    = 0000
DHCP:    0... .... .... .... = No broadcast
```

```
DHCP: Client self-assigned IP address  = [0.0.0.0]
DHCP: Client IP address                 = [204.78.43.50]
DHCP: Next Server to use in bootstrap   = [0.0.0.0]
DHCP: Relay Agent                       = [0.0.0.0]
DHCP: Client hardware address           = Prteon8432BE
DHCP:
DHCP: Host name      = ""v
DHCP: Boot file name = ""
DHCP:
DHCP: Vendor Information tag = 63825363
DHCP: Message Type                = 2 (DHCP Offer)
DHCP: Server IP address       = [204.78.43.68]
DHCP: Request IP address lease time = 600 (seconds)
DHCP: Subnet mask = [255.255.255.0]
DHCP:
```

The server is offering the client an address of 204.78.43.50, and you can also see that the duration of the lease is 600 seconds, or only 10 minutes. You would not normally set the duration of your lease to 10 minutes, but you are trying to speed things up in order to get the traces! The problem with a 10-minute lease is that you would generate unnecessary traffic as the clients renewed their lease at the 50% mark, or every 5 minutes. Odds are that a workstation needing an IP address is going to need it for more than 10 minutes.

SELECTION

The workstation acknowledges the lease by sending a DHCP request packet to the server:

```
DHCP: Message type              = 3 DHCP Request
DHCP: Hardware address type     = 1 (10Mb Ethernet)
DHCP: Hardware address length   = 6 bytes
DHCP:
DHCP: Hops                      = 0
DHCP: Transaction id            = 20022002
DHCP: Elapsed boot time         = 0 seconds
DHCP: Flags                     = 0000
DHCP:      0... .... .... .... = No broadcast
DHCP: Client self-assigned IP address  = [0.0.0.0]
DHCP: Client IP address                = [0.0.0.0]
DHCP: Next Server to use in bootstrap  = [0.0.0.0]
DHCP: Relay Agent                      = [0.0.0.0]
DHCP: Client hardware address          = Prteon8432BE
DHCP:
DHCP: Host name      = ""
DHCP: Boot file name = ""
DHCP:
DHCP: Vendor Information tag = 63825363
DHCP: Message Type                = 3 (DHCP Request)
DHCP: Client identifier       = 010000938432BE
DHCP: Request specific IP address = [204.78.43.50]
DHCP: Server IP address       = [204.78.43.68]
DHCP: HostName                = "Tarzan"
DHCP: Parameter Request List: 8 entries
DHCP:    Request option code = 1
DHCP:    Request option code = 3
DHCP:    Request option code = 6
DHCP:    Request option code = 15
```

```
DHCP:     Request option code = 44
DHCP:     Request option code = 46
DHCP:     Request option code = 47
DHCP:     Request option code = 57
DHCP:
```

If you look at this packet, it looks very much like the DHCP discovery packet. But notice that this time, the client has the DHCP server address. The selection is also a broadcast packet.

ACKNOWLEDGEMENT

To complete the negotiation, the server responds with a DHCP ACK. Both sides now know that the IP address is taken; the client gets to use it for the duration of the lease, and the server knows not to hand that particular IP address out until it is released:

```
DHCP: ----- DHCP Header -----
DHCP:
DHCP: Boot record type          = 2 (Reply)
DHCP: Message type              = 5 DHCP Ack
DHCP: Hardware address type     = 1 (10Mb Ethernet)
DHCP: Hardware address length   = 6 bytes
DHCP:
DHCP: Hops                       = 0
DHCP: Transaction id             = 20022002
DHCP: Elapsed boot time          = 0 seconds
DHCP: Flags                      = 0000
DHCP:     0... .... .... .... = No broadcast
DHCP: Client self-assigned IP address   = [0.0.0.0]
DHCP: Client IP address                 = [204.78.43.50]
DHCP: Next Server to use in bootstrap    = [0.0.0.0]
DHCP: Relay Agent                        = [0.0.0.0]
DHCP: Client hardware address            = Prteon8432BE
DHCP:
DHCP: Host name      = " "
DHCP: Boot file name = " "
DHCP:
DHCP: Vendor Information tag = 63825363
DHCP: Message Type              = 5 (DHCP Ack)
DHCP: Server IP address         = [204.78.43.68]
DHCP: Request IP address lease time = 600 (seconds)
DHCP: Subnet mask = [255.255.255.0]
DHCP:
```

sys:etc\dhcp\dhcpsrvr.log

In the section on starting DHCP, you will see that there is a switch you can use when loading the DHCPSRVR.NLM which will enable logging. A portion of the log file is shown here, which clearly demonstrates the four steps of discovery, offer, selection, and acknowledgement. This is a view from the server side of the picture; you will see this same information on the dhcpsrvr console if you enable it:

```
1999/03/17 09:23:33  <DHCPDISCOVER> packet received from client <0:0:93:84:32:BE>.
 1999/03/17 09:23:33
Sending BOOTP/DHCP reply <DHCPOFFER> to <0:0:93:84:32:BE> as <204.78.43.51>.
```

```
        Get type:3, IPAddr: 204.78.43.51, LeaseTime:0
        DetermineLeaseTime: proposed=0, return=600, pSubnet->leaseTime=600
        SubmitJob called with addr=204.78.43.51,
            leaseExpiration=921684873, lease=600, operation=15
        AMAGet() exit type=3, err=0, addr=204.78.43.51
        1999/03/17 09:23:33
   <DHCPREQUEST> packet received from client <0:0:93:84:32:BE>,
 client requested IP address = <204.78.43.51>.
        1999/03/17 09:23:33  Sending BOOTP/DHCP reply <DHCPACK> to
                <0:0:93:84:32:BE> as <204.78.43.51>.
```

RENEWAL

The clients will attempt to renew their lease at the 50% mark; if the lease is set to three days, after 1 1/2 days has passed, the client will renew. This is nothing more than a request from the client and an ACK from the server.

```
1999/03/17 09:33:33  <DHCPREQUEST> packet received from client <0:0:93:84:32:BE>,
    client renewer IP address = <204.78.43.51>.
    1999/03/17 09:33:33  Sending BOOTP/DHCP reply <DHCPACK> to
            <0:0:93:84:32:BE> as <204.78.43.51>.
```

When the lease has been successfully renewed, both the server and the client reset their clocks; both sides know now that the lease is good for another three days. If the client cannot renew—for instance, if the server was down—it will continue to use the address and attempt to renew once again at the 87.5% mark.

If the client cannot successfully renew when the lease expires, the client must stop using the address. This will, of course, disable all communications over IP until the workstation can once again acquire a valid lease.

Tip #292 from	Both 95/98 and NT have the capability for you to manually release and renew a worksta-
John	tions lease. For 95/98 this is done with the winipcfg utility, and for NT, it is done with the
	command line ipconfig program using the release/renew switches.

DHCP RELAY

The lease requests made by the clients are broadcast packets. Generally, most routers are configured to not forward broadcast packets. This means that if you have a workstation that isn't on the same wire as the DHCP server, odds are the DHCP server will not see the client's request. To get around this issue, you need to use a relay agent.

A relay agent is software that receives the request and hands it on, just like the runners do in a relay race with the baton. The relay agent forwards the request, gets the answer, and gives the answer back to the workstation.

To use your NetWare server as a relay agent, you need to load the `bootpfwd` NLM. The bootpfwd NLM accepts the following parameters:

- `Server= <IP address/Name>`—This is the name of the target server to receive the forwarded requests.

- `Log= <yes/no>`—Logs forwarding activity to the screen of a log file.

- `File= <log filename>`—The filename of the log.

- `Info`—Displays the current operational status.

DHCP INSTALLATION

Several steps are involved in the installation of DHCP services. I am going to touch only briefly on them here, because they have been covered in detail in Chapter 29, "Domain Naming Services (DNS)." Chapter 29 covers DNS, and DNS/DHCP come together as a package; when you install one, you get both. They are even managed the same way, via the DNS/DHCP Management Console. So if you want more detail, refer to Chapter 29, and go back over the sections "Management Console and Snap-in Installation" and "Extend the Schema."

First, you need to extend the schema. This is done by running DPININST at the server console. DPININST will not only extend the schema, but will also create the three NDS objects required for DNS/DHCP; the DNSDHCP Group object, the DNS/DHCP Locator object, and the RootServerInfo Zone object.

Next, you need to install the Management Console at your workstation and copy the snap-ins necessary for NetWare Administrator to see the new objects; installing the console and snap-ins is done by running `sys:public\dhsdhcp\setup.exe`. The setup program will leave a shortcut on your desktop pointing to `c:\program files\novell\dnsdhcp\dnsdhcp.exe`, which you can run to launch the management console.

When the schema has been extended and the management console installed, you are ready to begin configuration and management of your DHCP server.

DHCP CONFIGURATION AND MANAGEMENT

The minimum requirements to get yourself going with DHCP are creating a DHCP server, a subnet, and a subnet address range. When you have created these three objects, you can start using your NetWare 5 server as a DHCP server. All managing and creating of objects is done via the DNS/DHCP Management Console.

LAUNCHING THE MANAGEMENT CONSOLE

The management console is a Java-based application, so you can save yourself some frustration by getting a machine with lots of memory and processor power to run it on! There are two ways to launch the management console: the first is to use the shortcut on your desktop created by the setup program; the shortcut points to C:\Program Files\Novel\DNSDHCP\ dnsdhcp.exe. The second method of launching the console is to choose the DNS-DHCP Management Console from Tools on the nwadmn32 toolbar.

PART

VII

CH

30

Tip #293 from *John*	To speed things up, edit the shortcut properties and add the -c switch to specify the context of the locator object, such as dnsdhcp.exe -c dns.merlin. This option eliminates the search for the locator object, and thus speeds up the launching of the management console.

The first thing you see is a small screen asking you which tree to manage, and then you see the console screen, which has two tabs in the upper left. One tab is for DHCP, and the other is for DNS.

CREATING A DHCP SERVER

The Create button is the small icon that looks like a cube. Click that, and then select DHCP server from the Create New DHCP Record dialog box. Select the server object, which is the NetWare 5 server that you are actually going to run the DHCPSRVR.NLM on. After you create the server object, it will appear as an icon in the lower pane of the management console. Initially, the server will have a red slash through it, because the DHCP services are not up and running yet.

There are a few server options that you can set, as shown in Figure 30.1. Click the server object you have just created, and then choose the Options tab.

Your choices for setting SNMP trap options are None, Major Events, and All; the same choices exist for the Audit trail and Alerts options. To view the events and alerts, click the View Events/Alerts icon; to view the audit trail log, use the View Audit Trail Log icon.

The mobile user option sets how the server will handle users that move from one subnet to another; when they move, they will attempt to renew their old address if they had not previously released it. The choices are self-explanatory.

Ping enable is an interesting feature; if you check this box, the server will ping the address it is preparing to let you have before it lets you have it. If there is no answer, the address isn't in use. The help warns that enabling ping increases network traffic, but it would be such a minimal amount of traffic that you can safely disregard it.

Figure 30.1
At the server's Options tab, you can set SNMP trap options, enable auditing and alerts, deal with mobile users, and enable ping.

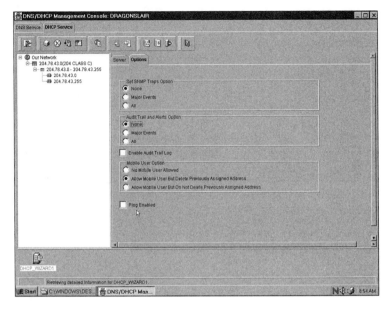

CREATING A SUBNET

The next thing you need to create is a subnet. The Create Subnet dialog box is shown in Figure 30.2. To get to the create subnet dialog, hit the Create Icon (the small cube), and in the Create New DHCP Record dialog box, choose subnet.

Figure 30.2
The Create Subnet dialog box.

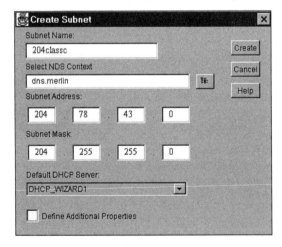

In the Create Subnet dialog box, you need to give the subnet object a name and an NDS context in which to create the object. Next, fill in the subnet address and the subnet mask, and then choose the server. After the subnet is created, if you expand it, you will see that two automatic exclusions have been created, x.x.x.0, and x.x.x.255. The .0 and .255 are illegal host addresses, hence the automatic creation of the exclusions. An *exclusion* means that this address will not be handed out (see Figure 30.3).

Figure 30.3
There are two automatic exclusions created, the x.x.x.0 and the x.x.x.255, which are illegal host addresses. An exclusion means the address will not be handed out.

Exclusions

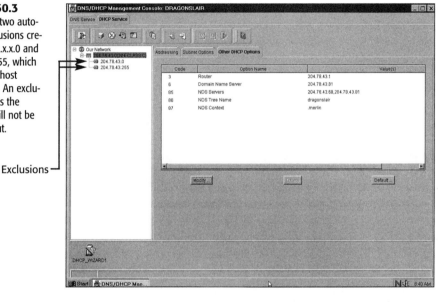

Earlier, when discussing why you should use DHCP, I talked about how a DHCP server could hand out more than just IP addresses. It can give the client other information that the workstation will need, such as a default router, DNS server, and more. Notice the Other DHCP Options tab in Figure 30.3. You can see that you are handing out the address of the router, domain name server, NDS server(s), the treename, and context to the workstation.

To modify the subnet options, go to the Other DHCP Options tab and hit Modify. This will pull up the Modify DHCP Options dialog box, as shown in Figure 30.4.

First, you need to select the option you want from the available options box on the left; then Click Add, and your choice will be added to the selected DHCP options box on the right. When it is there, highlight it and then choose Modify. In Figure 30.4, you are adding the IP address of the default gateway (router) to be used by the workstation.

Figure 30.4
To modify an option, first add it to the selected DHCP options, and then highlight it and choose Modify. Here, you are adding the address of the default router to be used by the workstation.

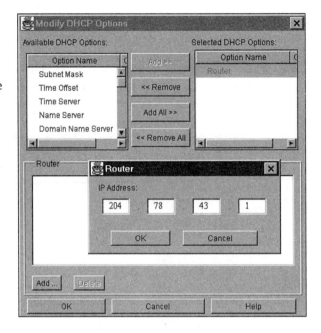

SUBNET ADDRESS RANGES

Having created the subnet, you now need to create a subnet address range. The subnet address range specifies the addresses within the subnet that the server can hand out. To create the subnet address range, highlight the subnet object you just created, and click the create icon (the cube). From the Create New DHCP Record dialog box, select Subnet Address Range. In Figure 30.5, you are creating a range of addresses from 204.78.43.50 to 204.78.43.125.

You don't need to put a lot of thought into creating the subnet address range; all it takes is a name, and the starting and ending addresses of the range.

Now that you have created the server object, subnet, and subnet address range, you are ready to load the DHCPSRVR.NLM on your server, and hand out addresses to the clients. In the next section, I go over starting the services, and then follow that with setting up the client to use DHCP.

Figure 30.5
To create a subnet range, you need specify only the name, and the starting and ending addresses of the range.

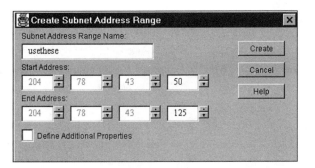

STARTING DHCP SERVICES

To start DHCP running, you load the DHCPSRVR.NLM at the console prompt. There are several command line options listed in Table 30.1.

TABLE 30.1   DHCPSRVR.NLM COMMAND LINE OPTIONS

Switch	Function
-d1	Enables background screen log of DHCP packets.
-d2	Enables background screen log of DHCP statements and packets.
-d3	Enables background screen of debug statements and packets, and logs to sys:etc\dhcp\dhcpsrvr.log.
-h	To obtain help - lists these options.
-py	Sets the global polling interval to *y* minutes.
-s	Forces read/write to the master replica.

An example of the log is given in the section titled "sys:etc\dhcp\dhcpsrvr.log" under "DHCP Theory of Operation," earlier in this chapter. As always, keep in mind that logging entails overhead, so you might want to use the -d3 switch only when troubleshooting.

If you are using any of the -d switches, you will have a dhcpsrvr debug screen, as shown in Figure 30.6. You can switch to the debug screen via Alt+Esc or Ctrl+Esc as you would any other console screen.

Figure 30.6
If you are using any of the -d switches when loading the DHCPSRVR.NLM, you will have a debug screen. You can switch to this screen like any other.

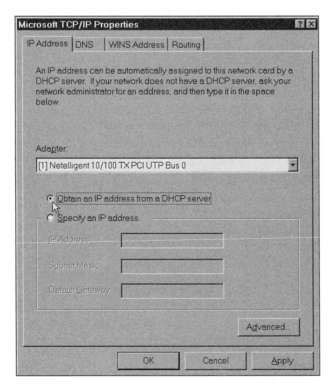

CONFIGURING THE CLIENT TO USE DHCP

Now that the server side is up and running, the clients need to be configured to use DHCP. Windows 95, Windows 98, and Windows NT are all configured the same way; get to the IP Address tab of the TCP/IP protocol, and select Obtain an IP Address from a DHCP Server, as shown in Figure 30.7.

Figure 30.7
The client must be set to use DHCP; this is done at the IP Address tab of the TCP/IP protocol.

On NT Workstation, any parameters that you have "hard-wired" into your IP configuration will override any corresponding values that the DHCP server hands out. For example, if you have hard-wired in a default gateway of 204.78.43.1, and the DHCP server is trying to hand out a default gateway of 204.78.43.57, the client would keep the 204.78.43.1 address that has been manually entered.

IP ADDRESS OBJECTS

You have already seen an example of an IP address object; when you created your subnet, there were two objects automatically created for you, excluding the x.x.x.0 and x.x.x.255 addresses. IP address objects can be created either to exclude an address, or to have it manually assigned.

Everyone has machines that need to be "hard-wired" in terms of their IP addresses, such as network printers or mail servers. When implementing your DHCP strategy, you might set your subnet address range to run from 75 to 254. This would give you the addresses below 75 and hard-wire the boxes whose addresses you want to stay consistent; all the rest could be handed out by the server. On the other hand, you could allocate the entire range from 1 to 254 to the server, and then create exclusions as needed for the addresses that you have hard-coded. Using exclusions would give you a chance to document things better than the spreadsheet; in the comment field of the IP Address Object, you could put "This address is being used by the WAN printer."

Alternatively, you can create manual IP address objects. Manual means static; it is a valid address in the pool, but only one device is allowed to have it. In Figure 30.8, you create an IP address of type Manual in the Create IP Address dialog box. To get to the Create IP Address dialog box, highlight your subnet object, and click the create icon (the small cube). From the Create New DHCP Record dialog, select IP Address.

Figure 30.8
An IP Address object of type Manual will only be handed out to a specific machine. You need to fill in the MAC address when creating the object, and only the workstation with that MAC address will get assigned this address.

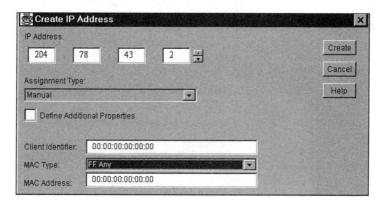

When creating an exclusion, there isn't a lot you get asked other than the number of the IP address to exclude. But when creating an address of type Manual, notice in Figure 30.8 that you need to fill in more information; in some fashion, you need to uniquely identify the client that you want to be assigned this address. The simplest and most common form is to use the MAC address of the workstation in question; because all NICs have a unique MAC address, it would be pretty hard to go wrong there! And, like exclusions, you would have a chance to document the network by filling in the comment field after the object is created.

SETTING OPTIONS

I looked at options when creating the subnet; the options are where you specify the information other than an address to hand out, such as the default router.

Options can be set at three levels: globally, at the subnet level (which you did earlier in this chapter), or at the IP address level, if it is an IP address of type Manual. The question naturally arises about priority; if at the IP address level, you have assigned a default router of 204.78.43.1, but at the subnet level, there is an option set for the default router of 204.78.43.254, what does the client wind up with?

The order of precedence works from the bottom up. Anything assigned at the IP address level takes priority over the subnet and global levels. And anything assigned at the subnet level takes priority over what is assigned at the global level.

To set global options, click the Global Preferences icon in the toolbar of the management console. You will see the Global Preferences dialog box, as shown in Figure 30.9.

Figure 30.9
To set global options, use the Global Preferences icon in the toolbar of the management console.

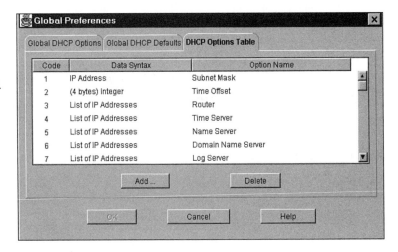

There are three tabs to the Global Preferences: Global DHCP Options, Global DHCP Defaults, and DHCP Options Table. Use the Global DHCP Options tab to set the information that you want to be global for all addresses, such as the treename, default router, and so on. The only thing you can do with the Global DHCP Defaults tab is set MAC addresses to be excluded. The machines with these addresses will not be able to use DHCP to lease an address. The DHCP Options Table tab lists the various parameters that can be handed out. For example, the router, DNS server, and so on are in this table. The only thing you would do here would be to remove an option, but why bother?

I have already covered how to set options at the subnet level, and setting options at the IP address level works exactly the same way.

IMPORTING

If you have a file of DHCP configuration information in either DHCP version 2 or version 3 file format, you can use the Import icon from the management console toolbar to import the database. This same import feature exists in the DNS side of things, and you can also export your existing setup, just like you could with DNS.

To export, use the Export icon, supply a filename, select the subnets you want to export, and then export.

Tip #294 from	You could use the export feature to back up your DHCP configurations.
John	

The file will have the following format; I have deleted quite a bit of the information about the individual IP addresses in the interests of brevity:

```
; DHCP3TAB - Please DO NOT delete this signature line.

[Globals]
    Subnet Attributes = \
        "204.78.43.0(204classc)"

[Subnet : "204.78.43.0(204classc)"]
    Subnet Address = 204.78.43.0
    Subnet Mask = 255.255.255.0
    Lease Time = 600
    Config Options = 00 00 00 00 03 04 CC 4E 2B 01 06 04 CC 4E 2B 44 55 08 \
        CC 4E 2B 44 CC 4E 2B 51 56 0B 64 72 61 67 6F 6E 73 6C 61 69 72 5\
        7 07 2E 6D 65 72 6C 69 6E
    Subnet Type = 1

[Subnet Address Range : "Subnet Server.204classc.DNS.Merlin"]
    Start Address = 204.78.43.0
    End Address = 204.78.43.0
    DHCP Server Reference = "DHCP_WIZARD1.Merlin"
    Range Type = 99
```

```
[Subnet Address Range : "usethese.204classc.DNS.Merlin"]
    Start Address = 204.78.43.50
    End Address = 204.78.43.125
    DHCP Server Reference = "DHCP_WIZARD1.Merlin"
    Range Type = 3

[IP Address Configuration : "204_78_43_0.204classc.DNS.Merlin"]
    IP Address Number = 204.78.43.0
    Assignment Type = 128

[IP Address Configuration : "204_78_43_255.204classc.DNS.Merlin"]
    IP Address Number = 204.78.43.255
    Assignment Type = 128

[DHCP Server : "DHCP_WIZARD1.Merlin"]
    DHCP Version = 3
    IP Assignment Policy = 2
    SNMP Trap Flag = 1
    Subnet Address Range Attribute = \
        "Subnet Server.204classc.DNS.Merlin" ,\
        "usethese.204classc.DNS.Merlin"
    Primary Server Reference = "WIZARD1.Merlin"
```

OBTAINING CLIENT TCP/IP CONFIGURATION INFORMATION

There is a much easier way to obtain information about your clients IP configuration than wading through the properties of network neighborhood; on the Win 95/98 platform, you can run the Winipcfg utility, as shown in Figure 30.10. To run winipcfg, select Start, Run, then enter the command winipcfg and click OK.

Figure 30.10
The Winipcfg utility is used to obtain information about the client's TCP/IP configuration.

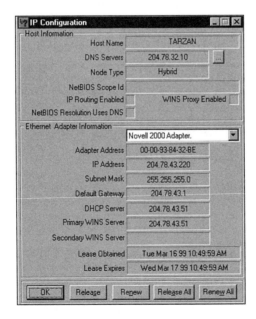

When you first run Winipcfg, you will only see part of what is shown in Figure 30.10; only the adapter address, the IP address, the subnet mask, and the default gateway are shown. However, you will see a More Info button; click that and the rest of the information shown in Figure 30.10 will appear. Note the Release and Renew buttons shown in Figure 30.10; you can manually force the client to renew or release the lease.

The NT platform doesn't have the nice GUI that the Windows 9x platforms do, but the information is still available. The equivalent in NT is the `ipconfig` command. To run `ipconfig`, drop to a command prompt and enter the command; entering `ipconfig` alone will give you the IP address, the subnet mask, and the default gateway. However, there are three switches available for the command; all, release, and renew. The command `ipconfig /all` will display the following information:

```
Windows NT IP Configuration

        Host Name . . . . . . . . . : mcntws01.gomemphis.com
        DNS Servers . . . . . . . . : 204.78.32.10
                                      206.101.136.193
                                      206.101.136.2
        Node Type . . . . . . . . . : Hybrid
        NetBIOS Scope ID. . . . . . :
        IP Routing Enabled. . . . . : No
        WINS Proxy Enabled. . . . . : No
        NetBIOS Resolution Uses DNS : No

Ethernet adapter CpqNF31:

        Description . . . . . . . . : Compaq NetFlex-3 Driver, Version 4.25m SP4
        Physical Address. . . . . . : 00-80-5F-95-2E-5D
        DHCP Enabled. . . . . . . . : No
        IP Address. . . . . . . . . : 204.78.43.25
        Subnet Mask . . . . . . . . : 255.255.255.0
        Default Gateway . . . . . . : 204.78.43.1
        Primary WINS Server . . . . : 204.78.43.51
```

Using the /all switch is the equivalent of hitting the more button on the Winipcfg GUI. The release and renew switches are used to release and renew the workstation's lease; the syntax is `ipconfig /release` or `ipconfig /renew`.

Tip #295 from
John

If you have the NT resource kit installed on your workstation, you have the GUI equivalent of the `ipconfig` command available to you; run `wntipcfg`, which is in `c:\ntreskit`, if you have installed the resource kit to the default location.

Dynamic DNS

In Chapter 29, you saw that the DNS server can resolve names only if it has a record for the host in question. And even though you are using NDS to store the data, you as the administrator still need to manually create each record; if there is no record for a particular host, the name resolution will fail.

Dynamic DNS is just like it sounds: When the DHCP server hands out a lease for an IP address, it lets the DNS server know about it and the DNS A and PTR records are automatically created for you! And the same process works in reverse; when the lease expires, the DHCP server lets the DNS server know, and the records are deleted.

There are a few prerequisites to using dynamic DNS:

- The DNS zone that you want to update must exist. In other words, you will need to create the zone at the DNS side of things before worrying about the DHCP side.

- The address range that you are going to have update DNS must be either dynamic DHCP or dynamic BOOTP and DHCP. The bootp protocol is the predecessor of DHCP, and works about the same. You don't have as many options available to hand out to the client with bootp as you do with DHCP.

- You must configure the address range to "always update".

In Figure 30.11, you have launched the management console and have selected a subnet from the DHCP tab. Notice (over the mouse pointer) that you have an option called DNS Zone for Dynamic Update. This is where you select the zone that you want to update. This is the zone that must already exist, as pointed out earlier. You have chosen your mythical domain, dragonslair.com.

Figure 30.11
The first thing you need to do is tell the subnet what DNS zone it is supposed to update. Here, you have chosen the mythical dragonslair.com.

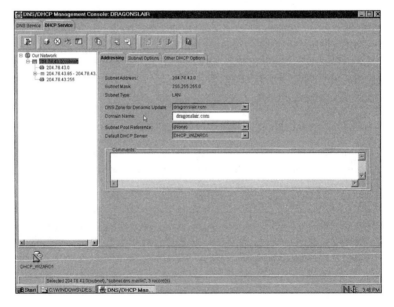

Next, you have chosen the subnet range you want to enable for dynamic DNS. This range runs from 204.78.43.85 to 204.78.43.95. Notice the DNS Update Option (over the mouse)? This is shown in Figure 30.12.

Figure 30.12
Having told the subnet what domain it is responsible for updating, now you need to tell the subnet range what to do; you have chosen Always Update; the other choice available is No Update.

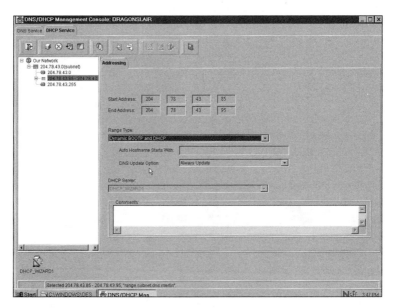

In order for the dynamic DNS updates to occur, you need to set the DNS Update Option to Always Update. If you choose No Update, that is exactly what you get!

If you restart the `DHCPSRVR.NLM` with the `-d3` option, and then look at the log in `sys:etc\dhcp\dhcpsrvr.log`, you will see something new when the DHCP server first initializes:

```
DHCP Server is ready at 3-17-1999 3:40:01 pm.
4    : connecting to server 204.78.43.81, port 53
       ReconstructConnection: TCPConnect successful, sending first packet
       Credential accepted by DNS server!!
```

Prior to enabling dynamic DNS, the DHCP server will have had no reason to contact a DNS server; the two processes, DHCP and DNS, are totally separate. Now, having enabled dynamic DNS, you can see that when the DHCP server comes up, it attempts to make a connection with the DNS server. In the portion of the log shown previously, the DHCP server attempts to connect to server 204.78.43.81 on port 53. 204.78.43.81 is the domain name server responsible for `dragonslair.com`, and port 53 is used by DNS.

When you have dynamic DNS configured, it is easily tested. You released the lease on workstation `tarzan`, and then rebooted the workstation. `tarzan` came up and got the first address available in the range, 204.78.43.85. If you then switch over to the DNS tab, you can see the entry for `tarzan` that was automatically created, as shown in Figure 30.13.

Figure 30.13
Notice the entry for
`tarzan`, 204.78.43.85?
This entry was created
automatically!

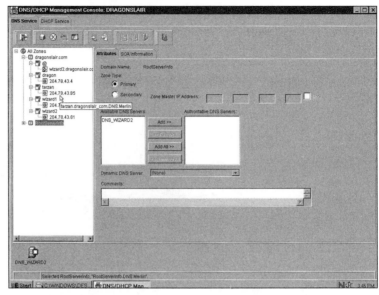

Tip #296 from	Think about whether you really need dynamic DNS; don't just implement it because you can. After all, do you really need the DNS server to resolve the workstation's addresses, or do you need the DNS server to resolve addresses for the boxes like the Web server and the email server?
John	

TROUBLESHOOTING

One problem you might encounter is that the workstation is unable to obtain a lease from the server. There might be several reasons for this—for example, does the DHCP server have any addresses left to assign, or are they all handed out? You can check this quite easily via the management console. Another possibility is the broadcast nature of the DHCP acquisition process; because most routers do not forward broadcast packets, is there a router between the workstation and the DHCP server? And as simple as it might seem, has the client been configured to use DHCP? Is the DHCPSRVR NLM loaded and running on the server?

The server's IP stack must also be functional; for example, if you can't ping the server by IP address from a workstation, and get a response, it certainly won't function correctly as a DHCP server! If the server is up and working, but it's handing out the wrong information to the clients, such as an incorrect address for the default gateway, you have simply configured the server wrong; the clients are fine.

And the problem might lie with the client itself; if a Windows 95 client responds with the message "Unable to obtain an IP network address," it could be a timeout issue. By default, the Windows 95 DHCP client has a two-second timeout between requests, or when it is expecting an ACK from the server. The Windows NT client has a four-second timeout, so you might see problems with the 95 client that do not show up with the NT clients. Microsoft has a patch available for 95 clients to extend the timeout to four seconds.

Don't forget that you can always enable logging and the three levels of debugging. This lets you see exactly what the server is doing, in terms of requests and responses. A portion of the log showing this activity is given earlier in this chapter under the section on the `sys:etc\dhcp\dhcpsrvr.log`.

## CHAPTER 31

NETWORK ADDRESS TRANSLATION (NAT)

In this chapter

WHAT IS NAT?

Each network that's directly connected to the Internet is required to have an officially assigned IP network address. Because you're connecting your network to a worldwide collection of systems, each of your workstations needs a unique IP address. Unless you have a registered IP *network* address from the InterNIC (Internet Network Information Center; the folks who handle IP network address assignments), you'll probably be stuck with only one or two IP *host* addresses assigned to you by your ISP. What's worse, you might have already set up your IP infrastructure (using arbitrary IP network addresses) before you need to connect to the Internet and now you have to change more than 500 addresses! Well, NAT can help you.

Short for *Network Address Translation* or *Network Address Translator*, depending on the context it is being used in, *NAT* is an Internet standard (RFC 1631) that enables a LAN to use one set of IP addresses for internal traffic and a second set of addresses for external traffic. A NAT box located where the LAN meets the Internet makes all necessary IP address translations (see Figure 31.1).

Figure 31.1
Using a NAT device to translate IP addresses between public and private networks.

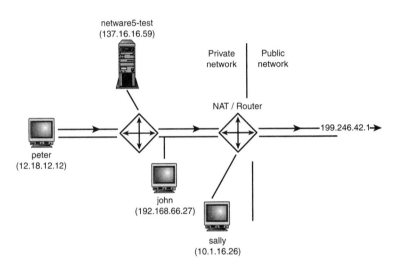

Tip #297 from
Peter

If you're interested in reading RFC 1631 to learn more about NAT, you can find it at one of the RFC sources mentioned in Chapter 28, "Introduction to TCP/IP."

The main feature of NAT is to enable an organization to use the reserved IP network addresses (such as the 10.0.0.0 Class A network) or *any* IP network addresses internally, while still permitting clients or servers on this (private) network to access, or be accessed by, the (public) Internet. NAT does this through a mechanism that substitutes a globally registered IP address into the source IP address part of a message leaving the private network, and restores the private IP address into the destination part of a reply message entering the private network. For example, consider the translate table shown in Table 31.1.

> **Note**
>
> The term private network is used here to designate the network that's "protected" by NAT. And the term *public network* generally refers to the Internet or the network that's unprotected by NAT.

TABLE 31.1   A SAMPLE NAT TRANSLATION TABLE

Host Name	Private IP Address	Public IP Address
peter	12.18.12.12	199.246.42.1
sally	10.1.16.26	199.246.42.2
john	192.168.66.27	199.246.42.3
netware5-test	137.16.16.59	199.246.42.4

A message originating from peter has 12.18.12.12 in the source IP address part of the message header. As it passes through the NAT to the Internet, the NAT substitutes 199.246.42.1 into that part of the header and recalculates the various message checksums. The message is then sent to the addressed host on the "outside" as though it originated from the public address. When a message arrives at the NAT from the Internet addressed to 199.246.42.1, the private IP address of peter is substituted into the destination part of the message header, the checksums are recalculated, and the message is delivered to peter.

Notice that even though the four internal hosts in this example are spread across different IP networks, their public IP addresses have been consolidated into the same external IP network (all are in network 199.246.42.0).

In summary, NAT serves a number of purposes. The following are some of them:

- **A workaround for shortage of registered IP addresses**—NAT allows clients using unregistered or private IP addresses to access the Internet with a registered, globally unique IP address that can be publicly routed. You *don't* need to reconfigure the clients.

  An unlimited number of users can access the Internet using just the one registered IP address. The result is that the packet destined for the Internet appears to have originated from the NAT router instead of from the client.

- **Hide private IP networks from Internet access**—When combined with an outgoing RIP filter at the router, NAT hides IP addresses used in your private networks. Only the public IP address assigned to the router is advertised outside your private networks. This offers some level of security against potential unauthorized access to your network.

  Because a hacker needs to know the actual IP address of a host in your private network to initiate an address spoofing session, NAT provides a basic firewall to protect against this type of attack.

■ **Secure areas of an intranet from unauthorized users**—Servers in a department's intranet that store confidential information can be secured by enabling NAT on all routers to the department's network. You can configure NAT routers to drop all packets addressed to those servers while letting packets addressed to the public servers in that department pass through. If packet filtering is enabled, NAT occurs before packets are filtered.

> **Note**
>
> Because NAT operates at the network layer, you can use *any* TCP/IP client on *any* platform, including Macintosh, UNIX, and OS/2, with NAT enabled on the router. No additional client software is required. However, NAT is for TCP/IP traffic only; it does not work for IPX networks.

IS NAT FOR EVERYONE?

Although NAT is a good solution for most environments, it doesn't work in all networks.

> **Note**
>
> From this point on, any discussion about NAT features and references to NAT are based on Novell's implementation.

The following are some NAT limitations that you should be aware of:

■ NAT only works with IP clients, not with IPX clients.

■ NAT does not support TCP/IP applications that use an IP address in the data portion of the packet. Some TCP/IP applications can embed and use IP addresses uniquely. Because NAT is not informed on how to handle these translations, it can't perform the translation of the IP address within the data portion of the packet.

> **Note**
>
> An exception to this limitation is FTP. Although the FTP PORT command uses the IP address in ASCII format, NAT uses a special table to handle these translations in the data portion of the packet.

■ NAT doesn't support unnumbered PPP connections. You must configure WAN interfaces that use NAT with numbered PPP or multiaccess connections. Unnumbered PPP establishes a type of virtual PPP connection without binding to a specific interface. Because a fixed IP address cannot be associated with unnumbered PPP, this type of connection cannot be used with NAT.

■ Multicast or broadcast packets are not translated.

■ NAT can't use NDS and access control to limit connections to the Internet.

■ NAT does not restrict access at the user level; it works at the network layer by looking at the IP addresses in the message headers.

■ Not all applications are supported by NAT.

- DNS queries are not supported. NAT does not translate private addresses embedded inside name lookups. For example, when an outside host makes a request to an internal DNS server, the DNS server responds with the private address. NAT cannot translate that private address embedded in the response to the public address.

MODES OF OPERATION

NAT can operate in one of the following three modes:

- Dynamic mode only
- Static mode only
- Static and dynamic mode

The mode you select depends on how you want to use NAT.

DYNAMIC MODE

NAT's *dynamic mode* can be considered the *automatic mode*, because you don't need to do any special configuration to make it work—simply enable NAT and select dynamic mode.

In dynamic mode, you bind *one* registered IP address to an interface on the NAT router that is used to connect to the Internet (the public side). All TCP, UDP, and ICMP packets from your network (the private side) have their source or destination addresses translated to the primary IP address on the NAT interface before they are sent out to the Internet.

> **Note**
>
> In the current Novell implementation of NAT, up to 15,000 users (up to 5,000 ports each for TCP, UDP, or ICMP connections) can access the Internet using a single registered public IP address at the router.

Here's how NAT's dynamic mode works. Each time a user connects to the Internet through the NAT router, the user's workstation IP address is dynamically translated in the packet to contain the public address (199.246.42.99 in this example) of the router before being forwarded (see Figure 31.2).

Multiple users share the *same* public IP address and NAT tracks, during each connection session initiated by a client, by dynamically assigning a unique port to that session at the router. When the NAT router receives a reply message addressed to its public address, it identifies the client that should receive the message based on the port number.

> **Note**
>
> NAT functions as a one-sided "mirror," because it will drop all packets originating from the public network that don't correspond to requests initiated from your private network.

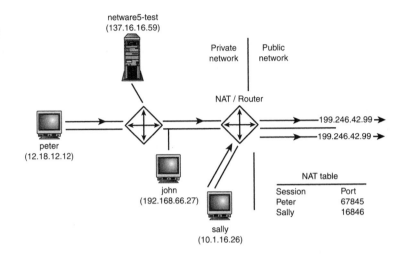

Figure 31.2
NAT's dynamic mode of operation.

Note that NAT translates the addresses in IP headers of inbound ICMP packets of type 0, 3, 4, 8, 11, 12, 17, and 18 before being delivered to the destination on your private network. Other types of ICMP packets are dropped. (ICMP packets contain a type field denoting the kind of message the ICMP packet contains.)

Following is a summary of the ICMP packet types, with those translated by NAT in bold:

Type 0 = Echo Reply

Type 1 = Unassigned

Type 2 = Unassigned

Type 3 = Destination Unreachable

Type 4 = Source Quench

Type 5 = Redirect

Type 6 = Alternative Host Address

Type 7 = Unassigned

Type 8 = Echo

Type 9 = Router Advertisement

Type 10 = Router Selection

Type 11 = Time Exceeded

Type 12 = Parameter Problem

Type 13 = Timestamp

Type 14 = Timestamp Reply

Type 15 = Information Request

Type 16 = Information Reply

Type 17 = Address Mask Request

Type 18 = Address Mask Reply

Type 19 = Reserved (for security)

Types 20–29 = Reserved (experimental)

Type 30 = Traceroute

Type 31 = Datagram Conversion Error

Type 32 = Mobile Host Redirect

Type 33 = IPv6 Where-Are-You

Type 34 = IPv6 I-Am-Here

Type 35 = Mobile Registration Request

Type 36 = Mobile Registration Reply

Types 37–255 = Reserved

Many ICMP packet types, such as Redirect (Type 5), are not supported by Novell's implementation of NAT due to potential security risks. With the right expertise, someone can use ICMP packets to gather information about your private networks that you don't want divulged.

Tip #298 from *Peter*	If you simply want to allow clients on your private network to access the Internet, use NAT's dynamic mode.

STATIC MODE

NAT's static mode can hide private IP networks from external access and allow access to specific services on your private network, such as FTP servers or Web servers. You can also use static mode to allow specific hosts access to the Internet.

> **Note**
>
> The primary difference between static and dynamic mode is that static mode requires a unique public address to be mapped to each private address for translation, whereas dynamic mode uses a *single* IP address for every private host.

To use static mode, you need to assign each private host its own public IP address on the NAT router. Add the public and private addresses for each host to a static NAT table on the NAT router. The corresponding public and private addresses is called an address pair.

> **Caution**
>
> If your router is configured so a remote router dynamically assigns its public address, you cannot use NAT in static mode because the public address is not a permanent assignment; you need to use dynamic mode instead.

Tip #299 from
Peter

NAT in static mode is particularly useful when some servers are designated for public use and others are only privately used.

Because external users access hosts using public addresses that have been mapped to private addresses, the private IP addresses of the hosts never become public information. By placing an address mapping in the NAT table for only public servers, private servers are protected from unauthorized access by someone outside your private network.

Note

Static mode can translate addresses for multiple systems in your private network, including UNIX, Windows NT, and NetWare servers and clients.

Whereas NAT in dynamic mode uses port numbers to identify hosts on the private side, NAT in static mode needs not, and does not, use port assignments because each host uses a different public IP address (as part of the address pair assignment). In essence, static mode uses a lookup table for the address translation.

Tip #300 from
Peter

Do not set the private and public addresses for each static NAT pair to the same address in the NAT table. Setting the private and public addresses in the static NAT table to the same address bypasses NAT's address translation feature.

Workstation john in Figure 31.3 can't access the Internet because the workstation's private IP address is 192.168.66.27 and doesn't have a public address mapped to it in the NAT table; any packets it tries to send through the NAT router are dropped. On the other hand, workstations peter and sally, whose private IP addresses are 12.18.12.12 and 10.1.16.26, respectively, have their packets forwarded by NAT, using their public addresses in the NAT table as the source addresses.

Figure 31.3
NAT's static mode of operation.

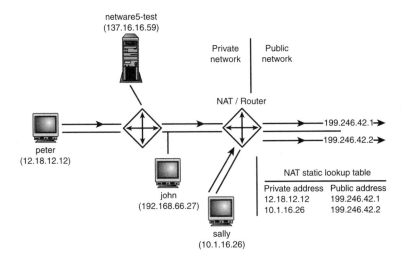

NAT static lookup table	
Private address	Public address
12.18.12.12	199.246.42.1
10.1.16.26	199.246.42.2

Similarly, packets coming through the NAT router in the reverse direction are either passed through or dropped based on the contents of the NAT lookup table.

Tip #301 from *Peter*	You will not be able to ping a public host (located on the private side) from the Internet (the public side) unless the IP address of that host is in the NAT table.

In summary, NAT's static mode performs the following actions:

- Forwards packets received from the public network only when the destination address corresponds to a public address in the NAT table
- Filters packets from the public network to a private host when the host does not have a public address assigned to it in the NAT table
- Filters packets from a private host addressed to the public network when the host does not have a public address assigned to it in the NAT table

MIXED STATIC AND DYNAMIC MODE

You can also configure NAT to support both static and dynamic mode of translation simultaneously. You use static and dynamic mode when you need to operate both modes simultaneously on the same NAT interface. You need to do this when, for example, your private network hosts need to access the public network and public hosts need to access some but not all private resources through the same router interface.

Dynamic and static mode requires more than one public IP address configured on the router. You must configure one public address for dynamic translation of outbound packets and the IP address of the public interface is used by default. You must also bind a second public address on the router for each private host that provides services to users on the public network and you must add a private-to-public address mapping to the NAT table.

In static and dynamic mode, NAT takes the following actions:

- Drops inbound packets from the public network that are not addressed to one of the public addresses mapped to a private host in the NAT table (when the actions for static mode apply)
- Drops inbound packets from the public network that are not responses to requests initiated by a private network client using the dynamic mode
- Translates outbound packets from any private host if they originate from a host with a configured entry in the NAT table (when the actions for static mode apply)
- Translates outbound packets if they originate from a host (located on the private network) that doesn't have an address mapping in the NAT table (when the actions for dynamic mode apply)

See the "Setting Up Secondary IP Addresses" section later in this chapter on how to bind multiple IP addresses to a single LAN interface.

Tip #302 from
Peter

TCP/IP's RIP Mode should be configured as Receive Only to prevent RIPing private addresses to the world. The RIP Mode is set using `INETCFG.NLM`, Bindings, TCP/IP, RIP Binding Options.

INSTALLING AND CONFIGURING NAT

The functionality of NAT was not included with the original shipping version of NetWare 5.0. It was added as part of Support Pack 1 and is configured using `INETCFG.NLM` Therefore, prior to your installing SP1 (or later), you'll see the option for Network Address Translation listed but you'll be unable to access it.

To install NAT, then, simply apply the latest available Support Pack for NetWare 5.0.

Note

Before you proceed to setting up NAT, you need to have two network interface cards installed in your NetWare 5 server, with TCP/IP loaded and bound to both NICs (thus creating a functional IP router).

Tip #303 from
Peter

It is possible to configure NAT using one single NIC. All NAT requires that a private and a public IP address be available on a TCP/IP host as it provides a routing function between addresses. In the case where the host only has one NIC, NAT works only if the following conditions are met:

- Two IP addresses (of different networks) are bound to the same interface card to create two logical IP networks.

- TCP/IP is loaded with the routing functionality enabled (`LOAD TCPIP FORWARD=YES`).

- The NAT-enabled IP address *must* be the first bound IP interface to the NIC.

Be aware that a NAT router configured in this manner have shown that other services (such as Web server) will experience sporadic performance hits under this configuration. Therefore, this option is recommended in testing environments only.

SETTING UP DYNAMIC NAT

The following procedure outlines, step-by-step, how to configure NAT for dynamic mode:

1. Load INETCFG at the server console. The first time you load INETCFG, you'll be prompted to transfer all LOAD and BIND commands from `AUTOEXEC.NCF` (see Figure 31.4). Select Yes.

Figure 31.4
Running INETCFG for
the first time.

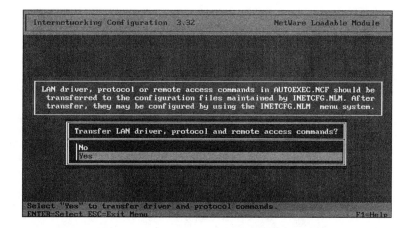

2. You're then prompted whether you want to restart the server for the updates to take effect. Select No. (You'll restart the server at the end of the configuration procedure.)

3. Select the standard setup method if prompted (see Figure 31.5).

PART

VII

CH

31

Figure 31.5
Use the standard
setup method to con-
figure NAT.

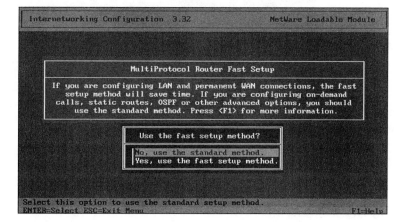

4. If necessary, configure the network board in your server using the Boards option in INETCFG.

5. If necessary, enable TCP/IP using the Protocols option in INETCFG.

6. If necessary, bind IP to the network board using the Bindings option in INETCFG. Specify the server's *public* address in the binding.

7. From the main menu, select Bindings. From the list of bindings, select the TCP/IP binding configured in the previous step.

8. Select Expert TCP/IP Bind Options, Network Address Translation, Status.

Tip #304 from
Peter

If you haven't applied SP1 or higher, you won't see Select to View or Modify in the Network Address Translation field.

9. Change the status from Disabled to Dynamic Only (see Figure 31.6).

Figure 31.6
Setting NAT to use dynamic mode.

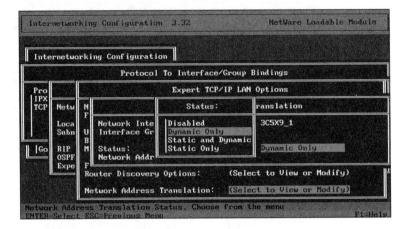

10. Press Esc three times. Select Yes to Update TCP/IP Configuration.

11. Exit INETCFG and reinitialize the system from the main INETCFG menu (second last option) or bring down and restart the server.

Tip #305 from
Peter

The reinitialize system command doesn't always work, depending on what changes you have made. If you find your changes didn't take place or you receive error messages, restart the server.

SETTING UP STATIC NAT

The steps on how to configure NAT for static mode is very similar to those for dynamic mode:

1. Load INETCFG at the server console. The first time you load INETCFG, you'll be prompted to transfer all LOAD and BIND commands from AUTOEXEC.NCF. Select Yes.

2. You're then prompted whether you want to restart the server for the updates to take effect. Select No. (You'll restart the server at the end of the configuration procedure.)

3. Select the standard setup method if prompted.

4. If necessary, configure the network board in your server using the Boards option in INETCFG.

5. If necessary, enable TCP/IP using the Protocols option in INETCFG.

6. If necessary, bind IP to the network board using the Bindings option in INETCFG. Specify the server's *public* address in the binding.

7. From the main menu, select Bindings. From the list of bindings, select the TCP/IP binding configured in the previous step.

8. Select Expert TCP/IP Bind Options, Network Address Translation, Status.

Tip #306 from *Peter*	If you haven't applied SP1 or higher, you won't see Select to View or Modify in the Network Address Translation field.

9. Change the status from Disabled to Static Only.

10. Select Network Address Translation Table.

11. For each host that requires a static NAT table entry, press Insert and enter the public and private addresses for the host (see Figure 31.7).

Figure 31.7
Creating static NAT lookup table entries.

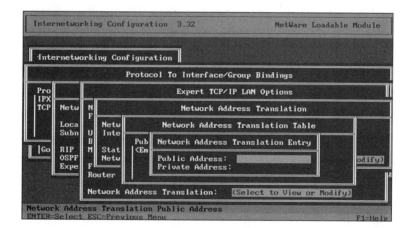

Tip #307 from *Peter*	You don't need to specify a subnet mask. The subnet mask for the primary IP address is used for all public addresses. Private addresses don't need a subnet mask configured because they are translated to the public addresses.

12. Press Esc four times. Select Yes to Update TCP/IP Configuration.

13. Exit INETCFG and reinitialize the system from the main INETCFG menu (second last option) or bring down and restart the server.

14. Bind the necessary secondary IP addresses to the public LAN interface (refer to "Setting Up Secondary IP Addresses" section later in this chapter).

Tip #308 from	The reinitialize system command doesn't always work, depending on what changes you have made. If you find your changes didn't take place or you any receive error messages, restart the server.
Peter	

SETTING UP STATIC AND DYNAMIC MODE NAT

The steps for setting up NAT to operate in the static and dynamic mode is very similar to those for dynamic mode:

1. Load INETCFG at the server console. The first time you load INETCFG, you'll be prompted to transfer all LOAD and BIND commands from AUTOEXEC.NCF. Select Yes.

2. You're then prompted whether you want to restart the server for the updates to take effect. Select No. (You'll restart the server at the end of the configuration procedure.)

3. Select the standard setup method if prompted.

4. If necessary, configure the network board in your server using the Boards option in INETCFG.

5. If necessary, enable TCP/IP using the Protocols option in INETCFG.

6. If necessary, bind IP to the network board using the Bindings option in INETCFG. Specify the server's *public* address in the binding. This address is used by dynamic NAT.

7. From the main menu, select Bindings. From the list of bindings, select the TCP/IP binding configured in the previous step.

8. Select Expert TCP/IP Bind Options, Network Address Translation, Status.

Tip #309 from	If you haven't applied SP1 or higher, you won't see Select to View or Modify in the Network Address Translation field.
Peter	

9. Change the status from Disabled to Static and Dynamic.

10. Select Network Address Translation Table.

11. For each host that requires a static NAT table entry, press Insert and enter the public and private addresses for the host.

Tip #310 from	You don't need to specify a subnet mask. The subnet mask for the primary IP address is used for all public addresses. Private addresses don't need a subnet mask configured because they are translated to the public addresses.
Peter	

12. Press Esc four times. Select Yes to Update TCP/IP Configuration.

13. Exit INETCFG and reinitialize the system from the main INETCFG menu (second-to-last option) or bring down and restart the server.

14. Bind the necessary secondary IP addresses to the public LAN interface (refer to "Setting Up Secondary IP Addresses" section next).

Tip #311 from
Peter

> The reinitialize system command doesn't always work, depending on what changes you have made. If you find your changes didn't take place or you receive any error messages, restart the server.

SETTING UP SECONDARY IP ADDRESSES

To allow a server to have more than one IP address (as is commonly done for Web servers so that one Web server can be accessed using different host/domain names), you can use *multihoming*. Each network interface on the server can have multiple IP addresses bound to it.

Note

> When a Web server is configured for multihoming, the additional, or secondary, Web servers are called *virtual servers*. (Netscape FastTrack and Enterprise Server for NetWare supports this feature.)

PART
VII
CH
31

Tip #312 from
Peter

> To create a virtual Web server using FastTrack, from the admin server's main menu, select Content Management, Hardware Virtual Servers.

In addition, binding multiple secondary addresses to the interface of a NetWare server that's acting as an IP router allows you to assign many public addresses to a single interface for static NAT use. The number of additional IP addresses (called *secondary IP addresses*) that can be added to a server depends on the amount of memory available.

To bind temporary secondary IP addresses to a network board, at the server console, enter the following:

```
ADD SECONDARY IPADDRESS IPaddress
```

Tip #313 from
Peter

> The keyword IPADDRESS is one word.

Note

> Secondary IP addresses added must be on the same network as the network interface. For example, if your NAT interface is bound to 10.16.1.1 with a subnet mask of 255.255.255.0, all secondary IP addresses for this interface must be on network 10.16.1.0. Secondary IP addresses 10.16.1.2 through 10.16.1.254 are allowed.

To delete secondary IP address bindings, at the server console, enter the following:

```
DELETE SECONDARY IPADDRESS IPaddress
```

You can display all secondary IP addresses bound by entering the following command at the server console:

```
DISPLAY SECONDARY IPADDRESS
```

Note that the secondary IP addresses are unbound when you do any of the following:

- Unbind TCP/IP from the network board
- Reinitialize the system
- Bring down and restart the server

Tip #314 from *Peter*	If you have many secondary IP addresses, create NCF files to add and delete them easily. In `AUTOEXEC.NCF`, you can also add a call to an NCF file to add the addresses each time the server is started.

Enabling Services in Static Mode

Because NAT in static mode hides the private addresses of servers behind the NAT router, services running on the NAT router *itself* might not work. These services can include Web servers, FTP servers, or DNS servers.

Because the service (IP) address is different from the public address, the services running on the router are not accessible because static NAT drops all packets that do not have an address mapping in the static NAT table. To enable these services to work properly with NAT, you need to configure the router's public and private address to be the same in the static NAT table.

For example, if your Netscape FastTrack Server is also running on the NAT router, its private address must be the same as its public address in the static NAT table for it to be accessible, as shown in Figure 31.8.

If you've enabled services (such as HTTP, FTP, or Telnet) on your static NAT router, you must also enable the following SET command from the server console:

```
SET NAT DYNAMIC MODE TO PASS THRU = ON
```

This setting is also called *implicit filtering*. The default setting is off. If implicit filtering is on, services can go through the router. If it is off, services are denied.

Tip #315 from *Peter*	You can add this SET command to `AUTOEXEC.NCF` so the command is set each time the server starts.

Caution	If your public connection is dynamic, implicit filtering might be turned off each time the connection is dropped and connected again. For example, when the connection is disabled, NAT is unloaded. When the connection comes back up, NAT is loaded, but the implicit filtering state stays off. It needs to be manually turned on again.

Figure 31.8
Services running on
the NAT router.

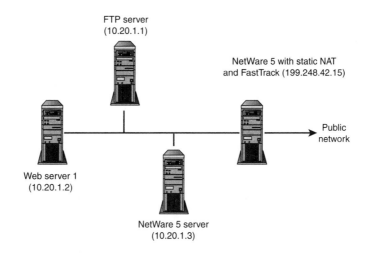

FTP server
(10.20.1.1)

NetWare 5 with static NAT
and FastTrack (199.248.42.15)

Public
network

Web server 1
(10.20.1.2)

NetWare 5 server
(10.20.1.3)

NAT static lookup table

Private address	Public address
10.20.1.1	199.248.42.31 — for FTP server
10.20.1.2	199.248.42.32 — for Web server 1
199.248.42.15	199.248.42.15 — for FastTrack

TESTING NAT

You can easily test your NAT configuration using your Netscape FastTrack Server. For example, to test your configuration of NAT for dynamic mode, complete the following steps (assuming you have FastTrack up and running on another server; see Figure 31.9):

Figure 31.9
Testing dynamic NAT
using the Netscape
FastTrack Server.

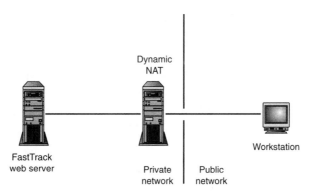

Dynamic
NAT

Workstation

FastTrack
web server

Private
network

Public
network

1. From your workstation, access the home page of your FastTrack server while NAT is not running.

Tip #316 from
Peter

> If NAT's already running, use INETCFG to disable NAT and reinitialize the system. Do not simply unload NAT.NLM from the server console.

2. Examine the Web server's access log by accessing FastTrack's admin server. Select Admin Preferences, View Access Log. A screen similar to that shown in Figure 31.10 is displayed.

Figure 31.10
Viewing FastTrack's access log.

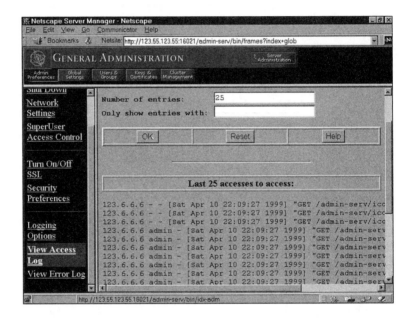

Tip #317 from
Peter

> You can also view the log file using any text editor; the file name is SYS:NOVONYX\ SUITESPOT\ADMIN-SERV\LOGS\ACCESS. The content of the Web server access log is similar to the following:
>
> ```
> 123.6.6.6 - - [Sat Apr 10 22:09:27 1999] "GET /admin-serv/icons/
>     ↪suite.gif"
> 123.6.6.6 - - [Sat Apr 10 22:09:27 1999] "GET /admin-serv/icons/
>     ↪title.gif"
> 123.6.6.6 - - [Sat Apr 10 22:09:27 1999] "GET /admin-serv/icons/
>     ↪back2.gif"
> 123.6.6.6 admin - [Sat Apr 10 22:09:27 1999] "GET /admin-serv/icons/
>     ↪suite.gif"
> 123.6.6.6 admin - [Sat Apr 10 22:09:27 1999] "GET /admin-serv/icons/
>     ↪title.gif"
> 123.6.6.6 admin - [Sat Apr 10 22:09:27 1999] "GET /admin-serv/icons/
>     ↪back2.gif"
> 123.6.6.6 admin - [Sat Apr 10 22:09:27 1999] "GET /admin-serv/icons/
> ```

```
            user_off.gif
   123.6.6.6 admin - [Sat Apr 10 22:09:27 1999] "GET /admin-serv/icons/
            clst_off.gif
   123.6.6.6 admin - [Sat Apr 10 22:09:27 1999] "GET /admin-serv/icons/
            pref_off.gif
   123.6.6.6 admin - [Sat Apr 10 22:09:27 1999] "GET /admin-serv/icons/
            keyscert_off
```

3. Enable dynamic NAT.

4. Access FastTrack's home page again from the same workstation.

5. Examine the Web server's access log again to locate your latest access entry.

If you see your server's DNS name (or IP address) in the access log, such as NETWARE5-TEST, you've configured dynamic NAT correctly. If you see your workstation's DNS name (or IP address) in the access log instead, you did not configure dynamic NAT correctly.

TROUBLESHOOTING

As you've no doubt realized by reading the configuration sections, NAT is rather straight-forward to set up. A number of little things, however, can be missed, resulting in everything seeming to be configured correctly, but not working. The following are two such examples:

- NAT is configured for dynamic mode. The workstation can ping the private IP address of the NAT server, and it can ping the public IP address of that NAT server, but it can't ping the router out to the Internet or anything on the Internet. When looking in TCP-CON.NLM, IP Forwarded shows packets being forwarded but nothing happening.

- NAT is configured for dynamic and static. The workstations can ping out to the Internet just fine, so dynamic is working, but the statically assigned IP addresses won't respond to pings or anything else. When looking at DISPLAY SECONDARY IPADDRESS, it shows both the primary public IP address and the secondary IP address that is statically mapped, but can't be pinged.

A couple of solutions can be applied. Sometimes for whatever reason, a duplicate entry for the configuration of NAT is added to the NAT configuration file, which is SYS:\ETC\TCPIP.CFG. Make a backup of the TCPIP.CFG file before editing it. Scroll through the file and look for all entries dealing with the IP address of the public interface that look similar to the following lines:

```
Interface {
    Address 199.246.42.4
    Port 3C5X9_PUBLIC
    Type lan
    RouterDiscovery no
    SolicitationAddress multicast
    NATStatus Dynamic
}
```

For the case of dynamic NAT, there should be one entry that has the public IP address showing *Disabled* and another exact duplicate entry of the same public IP address showing *Dynamic*. Delete the whole duplicate entry that shows *NATStatus Disabled*. You will need to delete everything from *Interface* to the ending *}*.

In the case of dynamic and static mode, there should be an entry that has the public IP address showing *Dynamic* and another exact duplicate entry about of the same public IP address showing *Both*. Delete the whole duplicate entry that shows *NATStatus Dynamic*. You will need to delete everything from *Interface* to the ending *}*.

Tip #318 from	There should be only *one* definition for the public IP address which contains configuration information for NAT. There will be other definitions in TCPIP.CFG for the public IP address, but they won't have NATStatus .... in the body of the definition, so be sure to delete *only* the duplicates that have NATStatus .... in the body.
Peter	

Second, the information areas towards the bottom that have the NATStatus should also be in a specific order. If not, NAT won't work properly. Review the information and make sure the public interface definition is listed first and the private interface information is listed second. If they are the opposite of this, do the following:

1. Use INETCFG to both the public and private TCP/IP bindings.
2. Reinitialize system.
3. Re-create both the public and private TCP/IP bindings, but create the public binding *first* and the private binding second.
4. If you're doing NAT static mode, ensure you enable the NAT mode of operation on the public interface only, and then add the static mappings.
5. Reinitialize system.

Another common oversight occurs with NAT. The default gateway (also known as default router or static route) of all workstations, clients, gateways, hosts, servers, and so on that go through NAT—through either static mode or dynamic mode—should point to the IP address of the NIC in the NAT router on their segment. If this fails to happen, NAT won't pick up the packet to translate.

Tip #319 from	If you have any services, such as Web or DNS server, running on the same NetWare server as NAT, ensure you have this command included in the AUTOEXEC.NCF file: SET NAT DYNAMIC MODE TO PASS THRU = ON.
Peter	

## CHAPTER 32

THE NETSCAPE FASTTRACK
WEB SERVER

In this chapter

SETTING UP YOUR OWN WEB SITE

Since the push for the Information Superhighway in the early 1990s, we have witnessed a rapid explosion of the Internet and intranets. The Internet and intranets provide you with an unprecedented opportunity to improve your productivity and, at the same time, to market your products and services inexpensively to millions of potential customers. Companies large and small, in almost every industry, are taking advantage of the Internet and intranet technologies to acquire, use, and provide information.

WHY HAVE A WEB SITE?

A company that has a Web server on the Internet has immediately established a global presence. This may be one of the goals of marketing for any company, regardless of size. On the other hand, *intranets* (private corporate networks that use Internet products and technologies) are sprouting up in many companies as a means to improving information distribution.

Companies can publish their important internal documents from a central Web server. The employees can look up the information at any time, electronically, using a Web browser. These documents typically include policy statements, manuals, product information, or even company newsletters. Using a Web server for central storage of such information can dramatically cut down on printing and distribution costs. What's more, the information will be up-to-date; as the saying goes, "as soon as something gets in print, it's out-of-date."

BENEFITS OF USING NETWARE AS YOUR PLATFORM

When choosing to build a Web server for either Internet or intranet use, you can choose from a wide range of software and hardware platforms. The following benefits are some of the reasons that NetWare servers make an excellent choice as your Web server platform:

- Performance
- Fault tolerance
- Ease of management
- Integrated security
- Ease of support

The performance of a Web server in an intranet environment is much more important than it is in the Internet environment. The reason is that if the Web server is on the Internet, the demand on it is limited by the connection you have. In general, small- to medium-sized companies will have a dedicated 56KB link to the Internet, whereas larger companies will have one or more T1 or T3 connections to the Internet. However, when compared with the intranet, where the connection speeds ranges from 10Mbps to 100Mpbs, accessing Web servers over the Internet is slow. NetWare servers are well-known for their high performance for file and print servers. That's what Web servers do—they serve Web pages and files to the servers. So, from the performance point of view, NetWare servers make an excellent Web server platform.

Furthermore, NetWare is also well-known for its fault-tolerance features, such as memory management and protection, disk mirroring and duplexing, dynamic bad disk block remapping (hot fix), to name but a few. Since 1992, Novell has offered customers a proven mirrored-server solution, SFT III (System Fault Tolerance), for NetWare. In addition to full server mirroring, SFT III provides automatic failover in the event of a server hardware failure. When the server is restarted, it automatically resynchronizes with the other one. The latest implementation of SFT III technology is the Novell StandbyServer for NetWare options and Novell High Availability Server for NetWare (NHAS; code name *Orion*) technology.

Note

StandbyServer greatly reduces server downtime by creating a complete copy (or *mirror*) of your server data and software components on a second server, which becomes the primary server in the event of a server failure. You can use any combination of Novell-certified server hardware for the mirrored pair, eliminating the need to deploy identical servers. You can locate the standby server anywhere–in the same room as the primary server, in another building, or in another city. StandbyServer is a much-improved SFT III implementation.

Note

The initial Orion implementation is a two-server solution, much like SFT III. However, Orion II, expected to be available sometime in 1999, will support multiple nodes.

As you have read in previous chapters, when you are using NDS, users and groups need to be defined only once, regardless of how many servers are on your network. You can easily manage all users and group objects and other network resources from a central location.

Many NetWare-based Web servers, such as Netscape FastTrack Server for NetWare and Netscape Enterprise Server for NetWare, take full advantage of the security features of NetWare, including NDS authentication, which enables you to secure access to your Web server and file system. In addition, access controls—based on IP addresses, username, host name, directory, document, users, or groups—let you limit access to specific Web documents. With these features, you can control who views which piece of information on your Web server.

If you are already using NDS to maintain security on your network, the same username and password list that is being administrated for the user's login process can now be used to secure the access to information on your NetWare Web server. All existing NDS users and groups can be used for this.

The NetWare operating system is designed so that most changes are dynamic. Therefore, when a new service, such as the HTTP service (Web server), is to be activated or deactivated, you either load or unload the corresponding NLMs. You do not need to reboot the server (thus increasing your server uptime), which is the case with many other operating systems.

PART

VII

CH

32

Tip #320 from
Peter

Should you encounter a genuine bug in any of the Novell software, you can open an incident call with Novell and obtain support at no cost.

BENEFITS OF USING THE NETSCAPE FASTTRACK SERVER FOR NETWARE

In June 1997, Novell and Netscape announced a partnership with the formation of a company called Novonyx. The goal was to deliver open, standards-based products to allow organizations to build full-service intranets without replacing their existing infrastructure. Novonyx ported the Netscape SuiteSpot servers to the NetWare platform, and as a result, a fully functional copy of Netscape FastTrack Server for NetWare is included with your NetWare 5 operating system—free!

Tip #321 from
Peter

The Netscape Enterprise Server for NetWare is now available for download from `http://www.novell.com/download`, free of charge.

Netscape FastTrack Server for NetWare is designed for small- to medium-sized businesses and therefore is easy to install and use. It enables organizations to create, publish, and distribute Web documents quickly and efficiently over the intranet or Internet.

The following list highlights some of the more salient key features of Netscape FastTrack Server for NetWare:

- **Remote desktop content management**—Files and directories can be created, deleted, renamed, and moved over the Internet from any desktop. This capability increases publishing productivity by eliminating intermediate conversion and manual data transfer steps.

- **Content access control**—Users control access to their documents using Access Control Lists (ACLs), in which they can specify who has read, write, search, execute, or delete permissions. This allows documents to be kept secure from public access while also being shared and managed across the intranet or Internet.

- **Web-based content view**—The directory and document structure visible to a Web browser do not have to be mapped to the actual file locations or directories on the server's file system.

- **Custom views**—Users can create dynamic pages that run queries against the server whenever they are accessed. For example, users can view all documents containing the word "contract" in the title, displaying the last modification date and author.

- **Cross-platform user and group management**—FastTrack Server for NetWare's management capabilities is tightly integrated with NDS. All users and groups in the Netscape server system can be managed through the NDS-based Directory interface to simplify and reduce the cost of managing an entire intranet.

- **NDS and LDAP integration**—NDS information is stored via LDAP calls, providing the same open standards to LDAP and NDS.

- **NetWare server configuration integration**—Web-based server configuration allows NetWare servers to be maintained through the browser on any browser-supported platform.

In addition, the following development environment is supported by the FastTrack Server:

- **Dynamic HTML pages**—Dynamic pages can be easily scripted on pages combining HTML with JavaScript. These are much richer and more powerful interfaces than are possible over HTTP.

- **Perl 5 support**—Supports Perl 5 language to protect your existing investment in Perl. Applications written in Perl with the previous Novell Web Server will run on FastTrack. A PERL5.NLM is included with NetWare 5.

- **NetBasic support**—Supports the NetBasic language to protect your existing investment in NetBasic. Applications written in NetBasic with the previous Novell Web Server will run on FastTrack. A NetBasic 6 NLM is included with NetWare 5.

Tip #322 from
Peter

You can use the scripting capabilities of Perl and NetBasic to manage your NetWare server and perform other tasks without installing FastTrack.

PART

VII

CH

32

- **JavaScript support**—Supports JavaScript language both on the client and the server. The use of Java, JavaScript, and plug-ins allows developers to extend the functionality of an application beyond the services provided by a standard Web server.

- **Oracle support**—Native support for Oracle's industrial databases for high performance database access.

- **Sybase support**—Native access to Sybase databases. ODBX support. Any ODBX-compliant database can be managed with FastTrack Server for NetWare.

- **JDBC support**—Any ODBC-compliant database can be managed with FastTrack Server for NetWare through the Java Environment.

Given the full spectrum of features available to Web masters, users, and developers, FastTrack Server for NetWare is an excellent Web server and will meet most, if not all, your Web server needs.

When you experience growth and need all the advanced features of a larger server, such as Netscape Enterprise Server, you can easily upgrade. Because FastTrack Server and Enterprise Server share the same architecture, core capabilities, and management interfaces, the transition is smooth and transparent to your users. The Netscape Enterprise Server includes these additional capabilities:

- **Document revision control**—Multiple users can share documents, which allows more effective collaboration. Documents are protected by check-in and check-out locking mechanisms while they are being modified. Users can check document versions or batch multiple documents for check-in or check-out.

- **Automated link management**—The Enterprise Server includes an advanced tool to manage document links and check for link consistency and validation. When changes are made, links are automatically updated in all documents on the same server. When a user moves a document from within Web Publisher by dragging it from one directory to another, all links referencing that document are automatically updated on that server.

- **Agent capabilities**—Users can be notified of content changes via email and custom views (Web pages).

- **Full-text searching and indexing**—Enables users to search the full text as well as the metadata of documents on their sites. Users can run searches on title, author, modification date, and other attributes. This allows powerful conditional searches, such as finding all documents modified by person X between date A and date B.

- **SNMP support**—Includes an agent allowing the product to be managed by several SNMP-compliant products, including ManageWise, Hewlett-Packard's OpenView, Tivoli/IBM's TME, BMC's Patrol, CA's UniCenter, and Sun Microsystem's Solstice.

- **Cluster management**—You can start or stop remote servers or update remote configuration files simultaneously. You can more easily manage multiple remote servers by treating them as a cluster, which can bring cost savings in administrative and maintenance overhead.

INSTALLATION REQUIREMENTS

Before you jump into the step-by-step installation procedure section, be sure that you have met the hardware and software requirements for installing your Netscape FastTrack Server for NetWare outlined in this section.

CLIENT REQUIREMENTS

The installation of the FastTrack Server is performed from a client workstation. On this workstation, you need to ensure the following:

- The operating system is Windows 95 or later.

- The workstation is running Client32 software and it can successfully log in to the NetWare server.

- You have installed and configured Netscape 3.x or later. A copy of Netscape Communicator is included on the NetWare 5 CD should you need it.

Tip #323 from
Peter

You can always download the latest version of Netscape Communicator from `http://www.netscape.com`.

- Have at least 100MB of free disk space to temporarily hold the installation files.

- If you're installing from the NetWare 5 CDs, your workstation must have a CD-ROM drive.

Tip #324 from
Peter

> If you don't have a CD-ROM drive on the workstation but one is on the NetWare server, you can mount the CD on the server as a NetWare volume.

SERVER REQUIREMENTS

On the NetWare 5 server that you're installing FastTrack to, ensure that the following requirements are met:

- The SYS volume, and any other volumes you plan to hold Web server content, needs to have long filename support installed. The NetWare 5 server installation would have the long name space already installed for you.

Caution

> Long name space support is automatically added to NetWare 5 volumes when the server is installed. However, it is not added to new volumes created after server installation or volumes other than SYS on a NetWare 5 server that has been upgraded from an earlier version of NetWare.

Tip #325 from
Peter

> To add long name support to a volume, type the following at the server console prompt:
>
> ```
> ADD NAME SPACE LONG TO volumename
> ```
>
> You need to do this only once.

PART
VII

CH
32

- If you want to integrate users and groups with other databases, the server must have LDAP installed. (Refer to Chapter 33, "Lightweight Directory Access Protocol," for instructions on installing the Novell LDAP.)
- Configure TCP/IP for the server. (See Chapter 28, "Introduction to TCP/IP," for information about addressing, subnet masks, and so on.)

Tip #326 from
Peter

> If the server does not have TCP/IP already configured when you do the installation, the installation program will prompt you.

- The server must have a minimum of 32MB of available RAM in addition to your current memory requirement; 64MB is recommended and is required if you are going to run Oracle8 on the same server.
- The server must have at least 100MB of free space on the SYS volume.
- Make sure DNS is up and running in the network and is accessible by the target NetWare server. (See Chapter 29, "Domain Naming Systems," on setting up DNS.)

Other Requirements

After you have your workstation and server ready, before you start the FastTrack installation process, check to see that you have the following:

- You're logged in as a user that has administrative rights to the SYS: volume of the target server.
- Know the IP address (or DNS hostname, if the server was previously set up) for the target NetWare 5 server.
- Know the netmask of the IP network to which the target server is attached.
- Know the IP gateway address (router) providing service to the target server.
- Know the DNS hostname for the target server and at least one DNS server that the target server will use for IP address resolution.
- Selected unique (and different) port numbers for the administration and the Web servers; Netscape FastTrack (and Enterprise) has an "administration server" (which you'll find out more about in the "Web Server Management" section later) that is separate from the Web server.

Tip #327 from	If you're unsure of the above, especially of the IP configuration data, contact your IP network administrator before you proceed with the installation. Without the correct IP information, you'll not be able to browse your FastTrack Server and you'll not know if there was a FastTrack issue or a workstation (browser) problem.
Peter	

Installing the Netscape FastTrack Server

Although the Netscape FastTrack Server for NetWare software is included with your NetWare 5, it is not copied to your server during installation. Unlike other NetWare products, you don't install it using NWCONFIG, but by using a workstation-based installation wizard (InstallShield Wizard). Do the following to install your copy of FastTrack (the steps assume you're installing it from the CD-ROM drive on your workstation):

1. From a workstation with the Novell client software installed, map a drive to the root of the SYS volume on your NetWare 5 server.
2. Insert the NetWare 5 Operating System CD into the workstation's CD-ROM drive.
3. On the Windows taskbar, Click Start, Run, and then type
   D:\PRODUCTS\WEBSERV\SETUP.EXE, where D: is the letter of your CD-ROM drive. Press Enter.
4. The Netscape FastTrack Server for NetWare Installation dialog box appears (see Figure 32.1).Click Finish to continue.

Figure 32.1
Netscape FastTrack Server's initial installation dialog box.

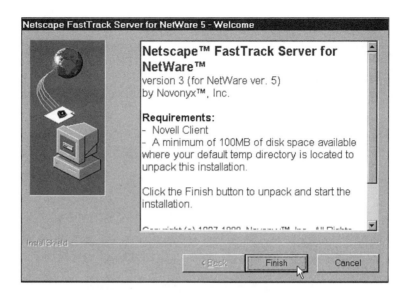

5. The files are extracted and the Welcome screen appears (see Figure 32.2). Click Next to continue.

Caution

The installation program uses the drive or directory pointed to by the TEMP environment. Therefore, ensure that you have sufficient space on that drive.

Figure 32.2
Netscape FastTrack Server's installation Welcome screen.

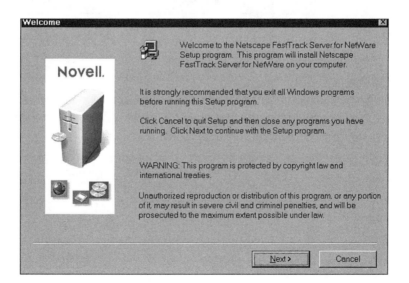

6. In the Software License Agreement screen that appears next, click Yes.

7. When asked for the Destination Folder, click Browse and specify the drive letter you mapped in step 1.

8. If your server has IP configured, its IP address will be shown on the Configure Server dialog box that appears next (see Figure 32.3). Otherwise, you'll be prompted to enter IP information to configure the server.

Figure 32.3
Configure the server's IP information.

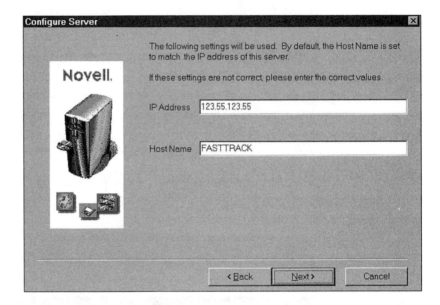

9. Enter a port number for HTTP access. The majority of the installations use 80, the default port number. Click Next to continue.

10. Specify a port number for the Admin Server (see Figure 32.4). The installation program generates a random port number for you (16021 in this case), but you can change it to any number, as long as it is not one of the well-known port numbers (generally less than 1024). Click Next to continue.

Tip #328 from
Peter

If you're going to use the randomly generated port number for the Admin Server, record it before going on to the next screen.

11. Enter a username and password for the Admin Server authentication and then click Next to continue (see Figure 32.5).

Figure 32.4
Specifying a port number for the FastTrack Admin Server.

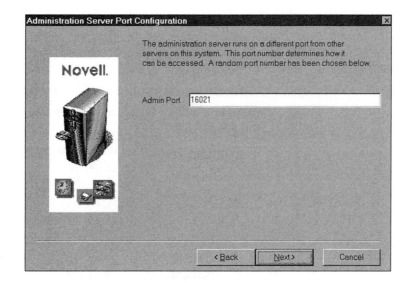

Note

This username/password combination is local to the Admin Server and is not tied to NDS.

Figure 32.5
Entering authentication information for the Admin Server.

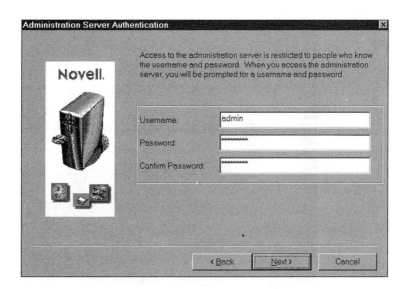

12. A screen about LDAP information is displayed next. Click Next to continue.

13. Select if you want the server's AUTOEXEC.NCF to be modified to include commands to automatically load the FastTrack Server when the NetWare server is restarted. Click Next to continue.

Note

If you have chosen to modify the AUTOEXEC.NCF file, the following lines are added to the end of the file:

```
# The following lines were added by Netscape Server for NetWare
NSWEB
# End of lines added by Netscape Server for NetWare
```

NSWEB.NCF loads the CRON.NLM to facilitate log file rotation and calls two other NCF files to load the Web and Admin Servers.

A NSWEBDN.NCF file is also created. This file contains all the commands needed to unload the FastTrack Server.

14. Review the information presented in the summary screen, record any information you need, and then click Next to begin copying files to the NetWare server.

Note

The setup program matches existing files that are currently on your server with files of the same name on the installation CD, and then determines whether they are newer or older. You will be prompted to overwrite files that are older than those on the installation CD. Any Web content you have developed should remain untouched.

15. A copy status bar informs you of the file copy progress (see Figure 32.6).

Figure 32.6
File copy in progress.

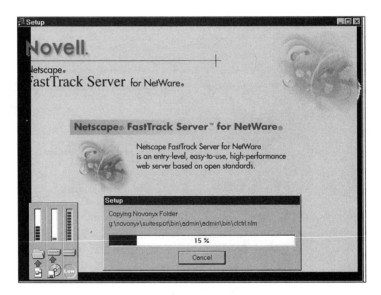

16. Select whether you want to view the readme file and launch the FastTrack Server immediately. Click Finish to complete the setup.

After the server is successfully installed, you can begin using the server by simply accepting all of its default settings. However, if you want to begin configuring your server, refer to the next section, which will give you the information you need to successfully modify and configure the server for your needs.

Tip #329 from *Peter*	You can test the installation by retrieving the FastTrack Server home page with a browser. If successful, the page shown in Figure 32.7 should be displayed.

Figure 32.7
FastTrack Server's home page.

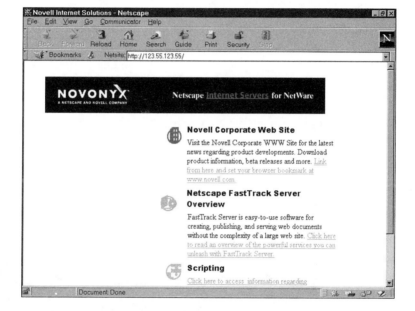

Directories used by Netscape FastTrack Server for NetWare

The installation process places all the files under the SYS:NOVONYX directory that you specified during installation. The following directories are created under the SYS:NOVONYX\SUITESPOT directory:

- admin-serv—Contains administration server directories.

- adminacl—Contains the files that store access control configuration information for the administration server.

- alias—Contains the key and certificate files for the Web server.

- bin—Contains the binary files for the server, such as the actual server, the administration forms, and so on.

- docs—The server's default primary document directory, where your server's content files are usually kept.

- extras—Contains a log analysis tool.

- httpacl—Contains the files that store access control configuration information.

- https-*webserverid* (for example, HTTPS-NETWARE5-B)—The directories for each Web server you have installed on the machine. Each server directory has the following subdirectories and files.

- include—Contains header files.
- js—Contains the Application Manager and the samples for server-side JavaScript.
- lcgi-bin—Contains support NLMs for local CGI calls.
- manual—Contains the online manuals for the product.
- ns-icons—Contains icons for FTP listings and Gopher menus used in "fancy" indexing lists.
- nsapi—Contains header files and example code for creating your own functions using NSAPI. For more information, see Netscape DevEdge Online at http://developer.netscape.com/library/documentation/index.html.
- plugins—Contains directories for plug-in options.
- userdb—Contains user databases and related information.

CONFIGURING SERVER PREFERENCES

The FastTrack Server is configured and managed using a browser, such as Netscape Communicator (included on the NetWare 5 CD). The Administration Server, which comprises a series of NLMs running on the NetWare 5 server, helps you manage the Netscape FastTrack Server from a single interface—the Administration Server home page (see Figure 32.8).

Figure 32.8
Admin Server's home page.

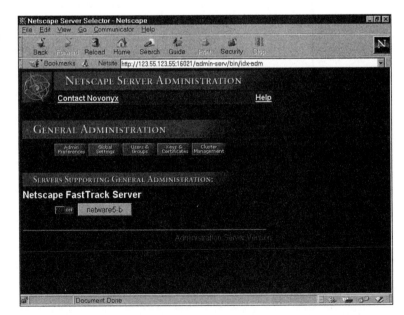

You can access Server Manager from Admin Server's home page. Server Manager is a collection of forms the Administration Server uses to configure and control your FastTrack Server.

ACCESSING THE ADMINISTRATION SERVER

Before you can access the Administration Server, the Administration Server NLMs must be running on the NetWare server. When the Admin Server is running, an NLM Novonyx Administration Server screen is present, and the first two lines on that screen are as follows:

```
Admin Server listening on port portnumber
Administration Server successfully started....
```

portnumber is 16021 in our example.

Tip #330 from
Peter

The commands to launch the Administration Server are added to the NetWare server's AUTOEXEC.NCF file during installation. If you need to manually launch the Administration Server, enter ADMSERV at the NetWare server console.

You can use any standard Web browser to access the Administration Server. Start your Web browser and enter the following URL in the Location field:

```
http:// server_hostname:admin_port_number/
```

Substitute *admin_port_number* with the number you entered or were assigned during the FastTrack Server installation. When you are prompted for a username and a password (see Figure 32.9), enter the username and password you chose during installation and click OK. When you have been authenticated, the Administration Server home page appears (refer to Figure 32.8).

PART
VII

CH

32

Figure 32.9
Admin Server's
authentication
dialog box.

THE SERVER MANAGER

The Server Manager is a collection of HTML forms you use to configure and control your FastTrack Server. Server Manager is accessed from the Administration Server home page. The Administration Server home page lists all the Netscape servers installed on your system. To access Server Manager, click the button displaying the name of your NetWare server (see Figure 32.10) and the Server Manager page appears (see Figure 32.11).

Figure 32.10
Accessing Server
Manager.

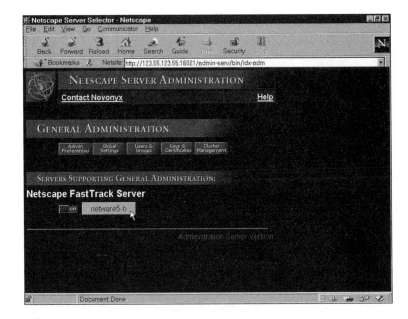

Figure 32.11
The Server Manager.

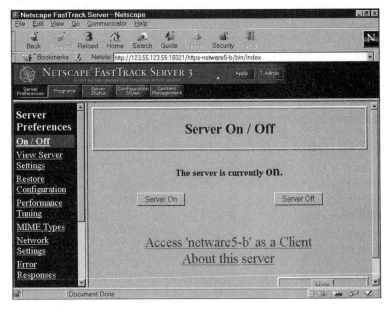

You can use the server configuration tabs in the top frame (just under the Netscape
FastTrack Server 3 banner) to configure the FastTrack Server. After clicking a tab, a list of
links appears in the left frame. When you click one of these links, the corresponding form
comes up in the main frame. If you need more information about a form, click Help for
context-sensitive help.

Most of the Server Manager forms make changes that apply to the entire FastTrack Server. However, you can use some forms to configure either the entire FastTrack Server or specific resources on the server, such as files or directories. You can use the drop-down list to specify the resource you want to configure. Many of the forms in Server Manager allow you to specify wildcard patterns to represent one or more items. Wildcard patterns use special characters.

After you submit a form, you are presented with a hypertext link that saves and applies your changes. When configuring your FastTrack Server, you must always save and apply your changes. When you have finished making changes with Server Manager, you can return to the Administration Server home page by clicking the Admin button in the upper-right corner.

You can use Server Manager to configure your FastTrack Server to provide an Internet or intranet Web server. Although many configuration options are available, this course covers the following topics:

- Modifying basic server parameters
- Modifying directories in the document tree
- Configuring document preferences
- Restricting access

MODIFYING BASIC SERVER PARAMETERS

Once installed, the FastTrack Server runs constantly, listening for and accepting requests. When FastTrack Server is running, you will see the On icon and its green light on the Administration Server home page, as shown previously in Figure 32.10. You can start and stop the FastTrack Server by clicking the Off and On buttons. You can also start and stop FastTrack using Server Manager:

1. Access the Server Manager page.
2. Select Server Preferences from the top frame.
3. Select the On/Off link from the left frame.
4. Click Server On or Server Off.

PART

VII

CH

32

Note

After you shut down FastTrack, the server might take a few seconds to complete its shutdown process and to change the status to Off.

Tip #331 from
Peter

You can also shut down and start up FastTrack from the NetWare server console using NSWEBDN.NCF and NSWEB.NCF, respectively.

You can also change the FastTrack Server's server port number using Server Manager. The server port number specifies the TCP port that the FastTrack Server listens to for HTTP requests. The standard insecure Web server port number is 80; the standard secure Web server port number is 443. The port number can be any port from 1 to 65535.

Keep in mind that changing the port number from its default will affect your users. If you use a nonstandard port, anyone accessing your FastTrack server with a Web browser must specify a server name and a port number in the URL. For example, if your server has a DNS hostname of consulting.dreamlan.com and you use port 8090, a user must specify the following URL to access your server:

```
http://consulting.dreamlan.com:8090
```

Figure 32.12 shows the Server Manager form you can use to change the server port number and other network information.

Figure 32.12
Changing network settings using Server Manager.

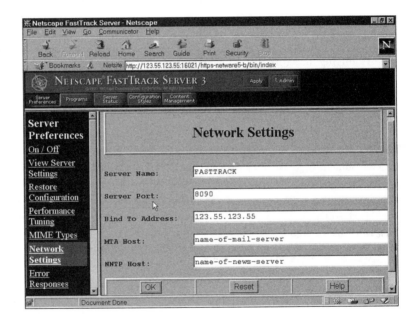

MODIFYING DIRECTORIES IN THE DOCUMENT TREE

FastTrack keeps its documents in a central location on the NetWare server. This location is known as the *document root*, or *primary document directory*. By default, the document root directory for the FastTrack Server is SYS:\NOVONYX\SUITESPOT\DOCS. The URL for your FastTrack Server maps to this directory.

For example, suppose your document root directory is SYS:\NOVONYX\SUITESPOT\DOCS and your FastTrack Server hostname is consulting.dreamlan.com. A user makes an HTTP request such as the following:

```
http://consulting.dreamlan.com/toolkit.html
```

The following file is retrieved:

```
SYS:\NOVONYX\SUITESPOT\DOCS\TOOLKIT.HTML
```

If you were to move all your Web content to a new directory on your NetWare server, you would have to change only the document root directory path that the FastTrack Server uses, instead of mapping all URLs to the new directory.

Note

The document root directory defaults to the SYS volume, but it can be changed.

To change your server's document root directory path, do the following:

1. In Server Manager, click Content Management.
2. Click Primary Document Directory.
3. In the Primary Directory field, type the full pathname of the directory that you want to make the new document root directory.
4. Click OK to save and apply the changes.

You can also serve documents from a directory outside your document root directory by configuring additional document directories. To add a document directory, you first need to choose a URL. Next, you need to create and specify the directory to be mapped to that URL. To add additional document directories, follow these steps:

PART

VII

CH

32

1. In Server Manager, click Content Management.
2. Click Additional Document Directories.
3. In the URL Prefix field, type the URL prefix you want to map (see Figure 32.13). For example, if you type marketing in the URL Prefix field and your DNS hostname is fasttrack, then users who access http://fasttrack/marketing/ with a Web browser will retrieve documents from the directory you specify next in step 4.
4. In the Map to Directory field, type the absolute path of the directory (including volume name) you want the URL prefix to map to.
5. Click OK to save and apply the changes.

Tip #332 from
Peter

Most of the time, you'll want to keep all your documents in the document root directory. Sometimes, though, you may want to serve documents from a directory outside of your document root. By serving from a document outside of your document root, you can let someone manage a group of documents without giving them access to your document root directory.

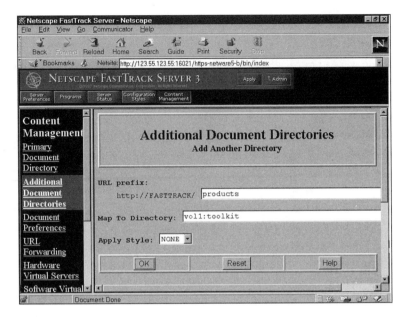

CONFIGURING DOCUMENT PREFERENCES

The FastTrack Server can respond differently to document requests from Web browsers, depending on your document preferences settings. You can configure the following preferences for FastTrack Server documents:

- **Index filenames**—FastTrack automatically displays the file you specify with this option when a filename is not explicitly requested in a URL (for example, `http://fasttrack/`). The defaults are `index.html` and `home.html`. If more than one name is specified, the FastTrack Server looks in the order in which the names appear in this field until one of the specified names is found.

- **Directory indexing**—If your document directory has subdirectories, you can allow clients to access an index of the contents of these directories.

Note

FastTrack automatically indexes directories using the following rules:

- The FastTrack Server first searches the directory for the file you configured as the index file.

- If the file is not found, the FastTrack Server generates an index file that lists all the files in the document root. The generated index has one of the following formats:

  - *Fancy* directory indexing, which includes a graphic that represents the type of file, the date the file was last modified, and the file size.

  - *Simple* directory indexing, which simply lists the files available. This format takes less time to generate.

  - No directory indexing. If the server does not find any index files, it will not create a directory listing to show the user and will return an error message.

- **Server home page**—By default, FastTrack finds the index file specified in the Index Filenames field and uses that for the home page. However, you can also specify the file you want to be used as the home page. Simply mark the option button next to Home page and enter the filename for the home page in the field next to the option button (see Figure 32.14).

Figure 32.14
Document
Preferences settings.

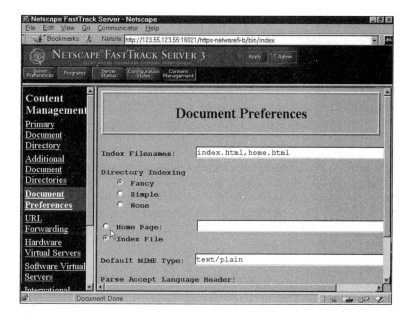

To configure document preferences, refer to Figure 32.14 and do the following:

1. In Server Manager, click Content Management.
2. Click Document Preferences.
3. Type a new index filename or add a file in the Index Filenames field.
4. Select the kind of directory indexing you want.
5. Specify whether you want users to see a particular home page or an index file when they access your FastTrack Server.
6. Click OK to save and apply the changes.

RESTRICTING ACCESS

One of the major selling features for using Netscape FastTrack (or Enterprise) Server for NetWare with your NetWare 5 server is its integration with NDS for security. Why set up users twice when you don't have to?

The default installation permits anyone to access your FastTrack Server with a Web browser and request documents in the SYS:\NOVONYX\SUITESPOT\DOCS directory or any of its subdirectories. This scenario is appropriate for public-access Web servers. If you need to restrict access to your FastTrack Server content, you need to complete the following tasks:

PART

VII

CH

32

- Bind the FastTrack Server to NDS.
- Create access restrictions.

BINDING THE FASTTRACK SERVER TO NDS

FastTrack comes with its own scaled-down directory service, which is automatically installed. The FastTrack Server uses this by default until you redirect it to another directory service. To provide a higher degree of security and centralized management, you can redirect the FastTrack Server to NDS. This allows FastTrack to leverage your existing directory information and to use the security features of NDS.

> **Note**
>
> Once you set FastTrack to use NDS, it does not allow public access to files. All users must be authenticated before receiving any content.

When the FastTrack Server is bound to NDS, it can determine access based on NDS and NetWare file system trustee assignments. To bind the FastTrack Server to NDS, complete the following steps:

1. Under General Administration, click Global Settings, Configure Directory Service.
2. Select Novell Directory Services (see Figure 32.15).

Figure 32.15
Configuring FastTrack to use NDS.

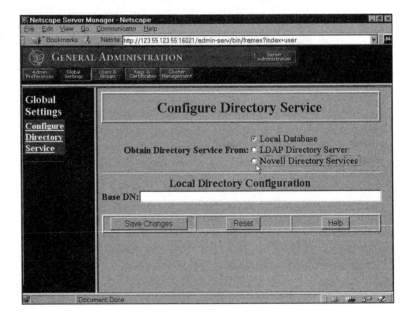

3. A dialog box appears to confirm that you want to use Novell Directory Services (see Figure 32.16). Click OK.

Figure 32.16
A JavaScript pop-up dialog box warning you of the consequences of switching to NDS as directory service for FastTrack.

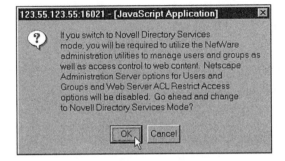

4. A Novell Directory Services treename will be displayed that represents the tree used by the NetWare 5 server on which the Admin Server is hosted (see Figure 32.17).

Figure 32.17
Configuring NDS context searching.

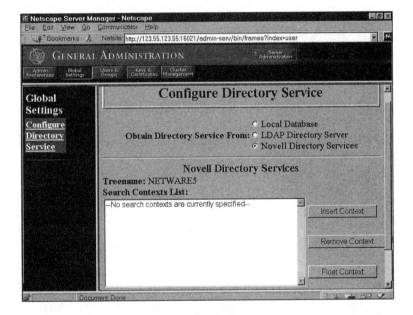

5. The Search Content List box allows an administrator to specify multiple NDS contexts in which to search for users during authentication. This allows users to specify a relative distinguished name, much like a UID for LDAP directories that provide a noncontextual-type login. The user search starts at the first context and continues until the relative name provided by the user is found.

Tip #333 from
Peter

> If the username is not found in any of the listed context, the user receives an `Authorization failed. Retry?` message on the browser.

6. Click Insert Context to add a new search context.

7. Click Remove Context to remove one or more search contexts.

8. Click Float Context to move the selected context to a higher-priority context.

9. Click Save Changes when done.

10. Shut down and restart the FastTrack Server. The administration server does not need to be restarted because its configuration is dynamically updated to refer to the Novell Directory Services operation mode.

CREATING ACCESS RESTRICTIONS

After you've bound FastTrack to NDS, you can restrict access to your Web server content by making trustee assignments for the desired NDS user, group, or container object to the file or directory you want to restrict. When users attempt to access a restricted file or directory, the Web browser displays a dialog box asking the user to enter a username and password.

To restrict access using NDS authentication, do the following:

1. Determine which users will be given access to the resource (file or directory).

2. Run NetWare Administrator.

3. Create a group and assign the users (identified in step 1) to it.

4. Make the group a trustee of the resource. You will need to give a minimum of Read and File Scan rights.

Tip #334 from
Peter

> If all the users in a given container are to have access to the resource, you can make the trustee assignment for the container itself instead of creating a group.

PROJECT: UNDERSTANDING ACCESS RESTRICTIONS

Here's a case study to help you better understand how FastTrack Server's NDS access restriction works. The following procedure outlines step-by-step how you configure FastTrack and NDS to allow only one of the users in a container to have access to one of the directories (thus its contents) in the document root area.

First, you need to configure FastTrack to use NDS for its directory service. Follow the steps given in the "Restricting Access" section. Make sure you include at least one NDS container (we'll call this `Consulting.Dallas.Company`) in the Search Content List. Then use the following steps to set up the restriction:

1. Make a directory named NOACCESS under the document root (SYS:NOVONYX\SUITESPOT\DOCS).

2. Using a text editor (such as Notepad), open a new file called INDEX.HTML and enter the following line:
   ```
   <html><body><h1>You're now in a restricted area!</h1></body></html>
   ```

3. Save the file in the SYS:NOVONYX\SUITESPOT\DOCS\NOACCESS directory.

4. Access this directory with a Web browser, such as http://ip_address/noacccess. You'll see a You're now in a restricted area! message, similar to the one shown in Figure 32.18.

Figure 32.18
Content of
index.html.

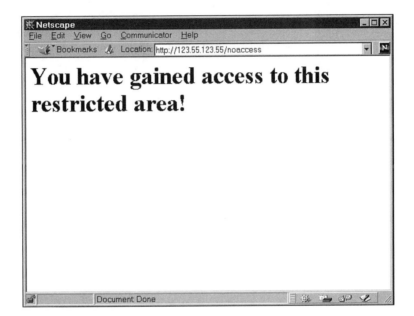

5. Use NWAdmin and give one of the users (for example, Sally.Consulting.Dallas.Company) Read and File Scan rights to SYS:NOVONYX\SUITESPOT\DOCS\NOACCESS.

6. Block access for all other users to the directory by making an explicit rights assignment for Consulting.Dallas.Company and removing the check marks in the Read and File Scan boxes.

7. Try to access the directory with a Web browser. You'll now be prompted with an authentication dialog box. Enter a username other than Sally. What do you see?

Tip #335 from
Peter

If you get an Authorization failed. Retry? message, the username you entered is not in any of the containers you specified in the Search Content List.

8. Try to authenticate as Sally. What do you see?

If you have correctly set up the NDS file system rights as outlined, at step 7 you'll receive a Not Found error message (see Figure 32.19). And in step 8, a screen similar to Figure 32.18 will be displayed.

Figure 32.19
Specified user does not have access to the URL.

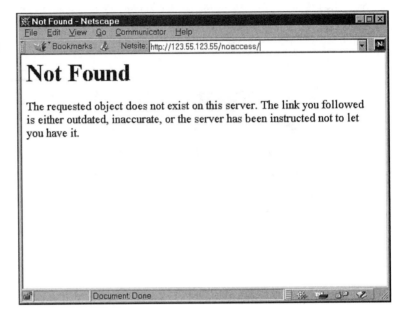

## CHAPTER 33

LIGHTWEIGHT DIRECTORY ACCESS PROTOCOL (LDAP)

In this chapter

WHAT'S LDAP?

The widespread acceptance and implementation of Internet and intranet technologies have made networks much larger and more complex than in the past. These larger networks, in turn, have created a greater need for a comprehensive directory service and a standard method for accessing information located in the directory.

As a result, *Lightweight Directory Access Protocol*, more commonly referred to as *LDAP*, was developed as an Internet communications protocol that allows client applications for accessing information directories stored on servers. LDAP is based on the standards contained within the X.500 standard, but is significantly simpler. And unlike X.500, LDAP supports TCP/IP, which is necessary for any type of Internet access. Because it's a simpler version of X.500, LDAP is sometimes called X.500-lite.

Tip #336 from *Peter*	If you're interested in finding out more about LDAP, two authoritative LDAP sources are the University of Michigan (`http://www.umich.edu/~dirsvcs/ldap/ldap.html`) and Critical Angle, Inc. (`http://www.critical-angle.com/ldapworld/index.html`). The following are some LDAP-related RFCs:

- RFC 1777—Lightweight Directory Access Protocol
- RFC 1558—A String Representation of LDAP Search Filters
- RFC 1778—The String Representation of Standard Attribute Syntaxes
- RFC 1779—A String Representation of Distinguished Names
- RFC 1798—Connectionless LDAP
- RFC 1823—The LDAP Application Program Interface
- RFC 1959—An LDAP URL Format
- RFC 2251—LDAP v3 Protocol.

Although not yet widely implemented (when compared with other directory services, such as NDS), LDAP has the potential to eventually make it possible for almost any application running on virtually any computer platform to obtain directory information, such as email addresses and public keys. Because LDAP is an open protocol, applications need not know about the type of server hosting the directory.

LDAP SERVICES FOR NDS

LDAP Services for NDS is Novell's implementation of LDAP. It is a server-based interface between NDS and LDAP-enabled applications. With LDAP Services for NDS, your LDAP client can communicate with various master servers that perform updates between servers. That means your LDAP clients can access information quicker, and changes are replicated throughout the network so users can have local access.

Unlike traditional LDAP implementations that use a master-slave data replication model, NDS uses a multimaster replication model instead. Consequently, if a server on your network goes down, another server becomes the new master and handles directory requests dynamically—and seamlessly to users. This (multimaster) replication model increases your network's reliability and enables you to construct a system where server failure, server maintenance, or a temporary loss of a communications link will not affect your users. And because NDS has a powerful replication engine, you get a network with unlimited scalability.

Tip #337 from
Peter

With the introduction of NDS 8 (discussed in Chapter 1, "Features of NetWare 5"), you can easily create a single NDS tree to support millions of objects.

At the time of this writing, LDAP is at v3 and LDAP Services for NDS (generally referred to as LDAP Services or LDAP for NDS, included with NetWare 5) is compliant with LDAP v3. This means LDAP for NDS supports the following features:

- Addition of auxiliary classes support required by Netscape and Entrust.

- Modified distinguished name (ModifyDN) requests that enable users to rename an object or move it to another place in the NDS tree. (LDAP v2 supported a ModifyRDN operation, which could only rename an object within its existing container.)

- Support for a RootDSE request from a v3 client. The RootDSE request allows the client to discover what features are available from the LDAP server (such as authentication mechanisms, controls, schema, and so on). Also supported through RootDSE are LDAP v3 extended requests (currently, none are defined in the v3 specification); any unsupported extended requests will result in a failure (which is currently done in NetWare 5).

Part VII
Ch 33

Note

In NetWare 5, the RootDSE object is Read-only. If the RootDSE were writeable, it would be possible to extend the NDS schema through a write operation on the RootDSE object.

- UTF-8 support for internationalization; UTF-8 is basically an ASCII-safe transformation of Unicode.

- Supports client bind request that includes v3 in the version field. Also supported is implied bind, if a request from a client is received without a prior bind request; an *explicit bind* (also known as *anonymous bind*) happens when a LDAP server receives a search request from a client that has not previously issued a bind request. A bind for this client as an anonymous user (a guest user) is first made and then proceed with the search request.

> **Note**
>
> An explicit bind authenticates the client to NDS as [Public]. Therefore, the search works only on those objects and attributes that [Public] has Browse rights to. However, you can also set up a proxy user to be used for explicit binds; see the "Configuring LDAP" section later in this chapter for more information.

- In LDAP v3, referrals were returned to clients by forcing them into an error field in the protocol. LDAP v3 provides for a new, more explicit method of returning referrals. The new mechanism is supported in NetWare 5.

> **Note**
>
> The referral that is returned is not a true NDS referral to an NDS server that contains the information requested. Instead, the user can enter, via the NWAdmin's LDAP snap-in, a single-server URL that will be returned in all referrals from this server.

In addition to the previous, the following features are enhancements offered by LDAP for NDS:

- **Access NDS data with an LDAP-compliant application**—With LDAP Services for NDS, you can specify the exact information you would like to expose to an LDAP client. In addition, you can identify the NDS information you want to make accessible using class and attribute mappings, which define the relationship between objects in LDAP and NDS.

- **Central administration**—LDAP Services v3 stores its configuration data in NDS rather than in a separate config file, as was the case with previous versions. Configuration can be updated using NWAdmin.

- **Improved security**—Instead of requiring clear-text passwords to be transmitted across the wire, Secure Sockets Layer (SSL), an Internet protocol, can be used to establish and maintain secure communication between SSL-enabled servers and clients.

  LDAP Services for NDS also supports *all* NDS security features and adds an LDAP access control layer that provides additional security features. Therefore, through NDS security, you can make certain types of directory information independently accessible to the public, to your organization, and to those groups or individuals that need to see some, part, or all of your directory information.

> **Note**
>
> The LDAP access control layer is an optional layer that operates on the LDAP client side of LDAP Services for NDS. Access Control Lists (ACLs) are part of the LDAP access control layer. These ACLs specify the rights an LDAP client has to specific LDAP information. The following rights are maintained by the LDAP Server Object ACLs:
>
> - **Search**—Enables clients to search for LDAP object attributes that are defined in the Access To List.
> - **Compare**—Enables clients to specify LDAP object attribute values that are compared to the corresponding (mapped) NDS values.

> - **Read**—Enables users to read the values of the object attributes defined in the Access To List. Read access also provides Search and Compare rights. You also receive Search access with the Read-access rights.
> - **Write**—Enables users to change the values of the object attributes defined in the Access To List. Write access also provides Read, Search, and Compare rights.

■ **Improve search request times**—By integrating with NDS Catalog Services, performance for search requests is dramatically improved compared to previous implementations.

Tip #338 from
Peter

> Because of the Catalog Services integration, implementing LDAP Services for NDS in a NetWare 4.1x environment means you'll need to install a NetWare 5 server and use that server as the LDAP server to access NDS. This also requires you to update the version of NDS (DS.NLM) on all the NetWare 4 servers in your directory tree to the version that supports NetWare 5.

Be aware that the following LDAP v3 features are not supported by LDAP for NetWare v3:

■ **SASL authentication**—LDAP for NDS supports only the simple authentication mechanism. It does not support the Secure and Security Layer (SASL) protocol used by LDAP v3 when an authentication mechanism other than simple is used.

■ **LDAP controls**—LDAP v3 specifies that a client can request or demand controls on a search request (sorted, paged, and so on). Supported controls are returned in a RootDSE response. If a client *requests* a control, it can be ignored by the server (which is done in NetWare 5). If a client *demands* a control (termed "critical control") and the server cannot handle it, it must return a failure (which is done in NetWare 5). LDAP for NDS v3 does not support any controls in NetWare 5.

The directory features available to LDAP clients depend on the features built in to the LDAP server and the LDAP client. LDAP Services for NDS allow LDAP clients to read and write data in the NDS database if the client has the necessary permissions. Some clients have the capability to read and write data; others can only read directory data. The following are some examples of the types of information that a client can request from a Novell LDAP server:

■ Look up information about a specific person, such as an email address or a phone number

■ Look up information for all people with a given last name or a last name that begins with a certain letter

■ Look up information about any NDS object or entry

PART

VII

CH

33

- Retrieve a name, an email address, a business phone number, and a home phone number
- Retrieve company name and city name
- Retrieve information stored in the NDS database

LDAP TERMINOLOGIES

To make full use of the LDAP Services, you need to have an understanding of the following topics:

- LDAP catalogs
- Class and attribute mappings between LDAP and NDS
- NDS and LDAP auxiliary class support
- Syntax differences between LDAP and NDS

LDAP CATALOGS

A catalog is generally a flatfile database that contains selected database information. A *LDAP Services catalog* (or simply referred to as a *LDAP catalog*) is a flatfile containing selected NDS data. It's stored as a stream attribute on an NDS object and provides rapid access to the selected directory data. Searching a catalog instead of an entire directory especially speeds searches in networks where some NDS objects are only accessible across a WAN link because searching across those links takes time and network bandwidth. A catalog also speeds searches because it contains only an indexed subset of data.

> **Note**
>
> When you install LDAP Services, you'll be asked if you want to enable LDAP catalogs. The default is Yes.

You can create different LDAP catalogs. For example, you could create an LDAP catalog for administrators to use and a different catalog for the users to use. The administrator's catalog might contain all the attributes for all user objects, whereas the users' catalog might contain only the username, telephone number, and email attributes. Each of these catalogs would have to be used by a different LDAP server.

LDAP catalogs are unique to the NDS tree, not the server. This means that all LDAP catalogs for a given set of information generated for any LDAP servers in the tree are identical. The LDAP catalog can be very large and can be replicated either by NDS or by a slave catalog. Therefore, other LDAP catalogs that contain the same objects and attributes and are generated for this tree merely waste disk space.

Tip #339 from
Peter

As a general rule, if you want to search a local copy of the LDAP catalog, install either an NDS or a slave catalog replica onto your server rather than generate a new catalog.

A *slave catalog* is a copy of a master catalog. Unlike NDS replication, LDAP requires each catalog to have a master catalog; slave catalogs are optional. The master catalog updates its information to the slave catalog. This means that the dredging of the catalog information occurs only once. The master catalog then copies the information to the slave catalog. This method saves the network bandwidth required by the dredging process.

Note

Dredging refers to the process of searching for the information to be put in the catalog.

CLASS AND ATTRIBUTE MAPPINGS BETWEEN LDAP AND NDS

As you recall from earlier chapters, an NDS class is a type of object in NDS, such as a user, a server, or a group, whereas an attribute is an NDS element that defines additional information about a specific object. For example, a User object attribute might be a user's surname or phone number.

Note

In NWAdmin and many NetWare-related documentation, you'll find classes are sometimes called object types or object classes, and attributes are called properties.

A *schema* is a set of rules that defines the classes and attributes allowed in NDS and the structure of an NDS tree (where the classes can be in relationship to one another). Because the schemas of the LDAP directory and the NDS database are different, mapping of LDAP classes and attributes to the appropriate NDS objects and attributes is necessary. These mappings define the name conversion from the LDAP schema to the NDS schema.

LDAP Services for NDS provides default mappings (see Figures 33.1 and 33.2). In many cases, the correspondence between the LDAP classes and attributes and the NDS object types and properties is logical and intuitive. However, depending on your implementation needs, you might want to reconfigure the class and attribute mapping.

In most instances, the LDAP class to NDS object type mapping is a one-to-one relationship. However, the LDAP schema supports a feature called auxiliary class support that allows an object to be associated with more than one class.

PART

VII

CH

33

Figure 33.1
An example of LDAP to NDS class mappings.

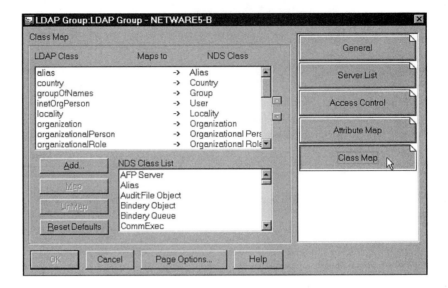

Figure 33.2
An example of LDAP to NDS attribute mappings.

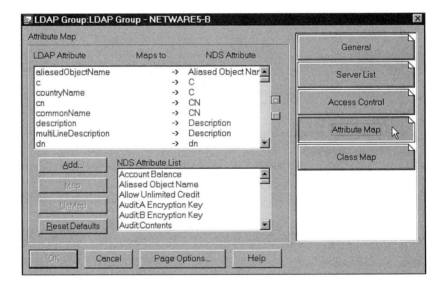

NDS AND LDAP AUXILIARY CLASS SUPPORT

In NDS, each object has a base class. The base class is part of a class hierarchy. The base class is a subclass of other classes and inherits the characteristics of the classes for which it is subclassed. For example, a User object (the base class) is a subclass of the Organizational Person, Person, and Top classes (see Figure 33.3).

Figure 33.3
User class inheritance
hierarchy.

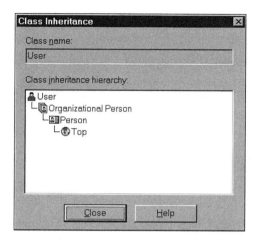

Only a single base class can be associated with an object.

To add more functionality (attributes) to an NDS object, you must extend the class by adding more attributes to the class definition. On the other hand, LDAP standard classes are static and cannot be extended as in NDS. However, the LDAP schema allows an object to belong to more than one class and to inherit attributes from more than one class. This association of multiple classes is called *auxiliary class support*.

Although the NDS schema does not allow multiple class associations, LDAP Services for NDS emulates auxiliary class support for the following selected subset of LDAP classes:

- strongAuthenticationUser
- certificationAuthority

LDAP Services for NDS extends the NetWare 5 NDS schema to allow User objects to have an auxiliary class of strongAuthenticationUser, and Organization or Organizational Unit objects to have an auxiliary class of certificationAuthority.

Tip #340 from
Peter

To emulate auxiliary class support for other NDS object classes, you can use Schema Manager (which is accessed through NDS Manager) to extend the schema for the NDS object class with the appropriate LDAP class. For example, an optional attribute called LDAP UserCertificate could be added, using Schema Manager, to a group object that would map to the LDAP User Certificate.

The strongAuthenticationUser and certificationAuthority auxiliary classes provide security features. They can be used to support a Public Key Infrastructure to maintain and store the digital keys necessary for secure applications such as secure email and electronic commerce. For example, the strongAuthenticationUser class contains a User Certificate

PART
VII

CH

33

attribute. This attribute holds the user's public key. This public key can be accessed and used to encrypt data and initiate a secure session with the user.

> **Note**
>
> Although the mappings for these object classes (User, Organization, and Organizational Unit) don't appear in the NWAdmin LDAP Group object Class Map page, you can't remap these object classes.

LDAP AND NDS SYNTAX DIFFERENCES

Because LDAP and NDS are different directory services, their naming conventions and naming syntaxes are different. Some important differences are in the following areas:

- LDAP uses commas as delimiters.
- LDAP uses typeful names only.
- LDAP has multiple naming attributes.

LDAP uses commas as delimiters between object levels, whereas NDS uses periods. For example, a *distinguished*, or complete, name in NDS looks like this:

`CN=SALLY.OU=DALLAS.O=CONSULTING`

Using LDAP syntax, however, the same distinguished name would be as follows:

`CN=SALLY,OU=DALLAS,O=CONSULTING`

NDS uses both *typeless* (`.JOHN.GEMINI.MARKETING`) and *typeful* (`CN=JOHN.OU=GEMINI.O=MARKET-ING`) names when referencing an object. LDAP uses only typeful names with commas as the delimiters (`CN=JOHN,OU=GEMINI,O=MARKETING`).

In both LDAP and NDS, objects can be defined with multiple naming attributes in the schema. For example, the User object has two naming attributes: CN and OU (see Figure 33.4).

LDAP uses the plus symbol (+) to separate the naming attributes in the distinguished name. If the attributes are not explicitly labeled, the schema determines which string goes with which attribute—the first would be CN, the second is OU. You may reorder them in a distinguished name if you manually label each portion.

INSTALLING LDAP SERVICES

This section covers the installation requirements and procedure for installing LDAP Services for NDS on your NetWare 5 server. Be certain that you're configuring LDAP services for NDS on a NetWare 5 server and not on a NetWare 4.x server. The NetWare 5 NWAdmn32 uses LDAP plug-ins that are installed when you install NetWare 5. Also, be certain that you're using the NWAdmn32 that came with your NetWare 5 software. Other NWAdmin and NWAdmn32 versions don't and can't use the LDAP snap-in (`LDAPSNAP.DLL`) supplied with the NetWare 5 CD.

Figure 33.4
Schema Manager
showing User
attribute definitions.

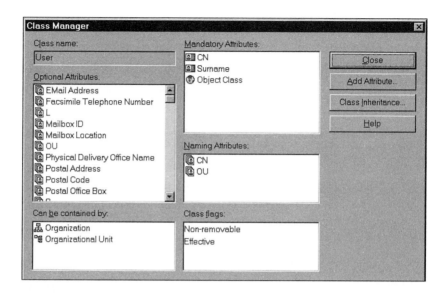

Tip #341 from
Peter

NWADMN32.EXE is located in SYS:PUBLIC\WIN32 and all its snap-ins modules are located in SYS:PUBLIC\WIN32\SNAPINs.

SYSTEM REQUIREMENTS

Before installing LDAP for NDS, ensure that you've met the following hardware requirements:

- NetWare 5 server
- 8MB disk space for LDAP Services
- 1MB of additional RAM for Novell LDAP Services, and 80KB of additional RAM for each LDAP connection

If you have previously installed a NetWare 5 Support Pack, don't forget to reapply it after LDAP Services is installed because some LDAP updates are available.

INSTALLING THE SOFTWARE

Like many other add-on products included with NetWare 5, LDAP Services is installed through NWCONFIG.NLM. Use the following steps:

1. Mount your NetWare 5 Operating System CD as a NetWare volume.
2. Load NWCONFIG.NLM at the server console.
3. Select Product Options.

4. Move the highlight bar to Install Other Novell Products and then press Enter.

5. Select LDAP Services from the Additional Products and Services page. Click Next to install.

The only issues you must immediately resolve when you install LDAP Services are the following:

- Whether to enable the use of the LDAP catalog on the server
- How to search the LDAP catalog

Choosing to enable the use of the LDAP catalog on the server means that an LDAP catalog will be loaded on the server you are creating. You don't always want to choose this option because multiple LDAP servers can share the same catalog. The following section covers this topic in more detail.

Note

When you install LDAP Services, you automatically install Catalog Services, regardless of whether you chose to enable the use of LDAP catalog on the server.

Tip #342 from
Peter

If you reinstall LDAP Services, you must first delete these objects using NWAdmin:

- LDAP Server object
- LDAP Catalog object associated with that server

The reinstall process does not write over these objects. Also, keep in mind that if you delete or reinstall NDS, you must also reinstall LDAP Services.

If you uninstall LDAP Services with the intention of reinstalling it again later, you should wait a significant period of time before attempting the reinstall. Since the schema needs to resyncronize across the tree, the time period you wait should be commensurate with the size of the NDS tree.

After the installation is complete, you'll find a LOAD NLDAP.NLM added to your AUTOEXEC.NCF; if you selected Yes to using LDAP catalog, a LOAD DSCAT.NLM line is also added.

Because an LDAP server can browse the entire NDS tree, you need to install only *one* LDAP server per tree. However, if you have WAN links, you should install one LDAP server per geographic location. If you require multiple LDAP catalogs, you must then install multiple LDAP servers because each LDAP server uses, at most, one catalog.

Note

Keep in mind that LDAP catalogs can consume large amounts of disk space on your SYS volume.

DETERMINING WHETHER TO ENABLE USING THE LDAP CATALOG

The first LDAP issue you must resolve happens during the LDAP Services software installation process and involves the use of the LDAP catalog. After you choose to install LDAP Services on the Additional Products and Services page and click Next, the LDAP Services for NDS Installation page displays the following message:

`Do you want to enable the use of the LDAP catalog on this server?`

As mentioned earlier, you generally should enable the use of only one LDAP catalog per geographic location. LDAP catalogs are stored as NDS objects and thus, can be replicated. If a replica of an LDAP catalog on another server is available locally, you should configure LDAP to use the replicated catalog using NWAdmin after the installation is complete.

If you decide to enable the use of the LDAP Catalog, a unique LDAP Catalog object will be created. This enables LDAP users to access NDS data from a catalog rather than from the entire NDS database. The use of the LDAP Catalog object provides significantly faster access, especially in an NDS tree that is widely distributed geographically or in a tree that is structurally flat with a large number of objects per container.

Selecting Yes to `Do you want to enable the use of the LDAP catalog on this server?` causes an LDAP catalog to be generated and installed on your LDAP server. This catalog contains a default set of information that you can change when you configure the LDAP Catalog object using NWAdmin. Selecting No means that no LDAP catalog will be stored on that LDAP server.

Tip #343 from
Peter

As a general rule, select No if you have already installed an LDAP catalog that is identical to the one you want this server to use. When you configure LDAP servers, you can assign the catalog to the server. However, if you want to create a different LDAP catalog, select Yes.

PART

VII

CH

33

CONFIGURING LDAP

Unlike previous versions of LDAP Services, LDAP Services v3 included with NetWare 5 stores its configuration information in NDS. That means you can manage all your LDAP servers from a central location using NWAdmin.

ADDING SNAP-INS TO NWADMN32

Administration of LDAP objects in NDS are facilitated by NWAdmin snap-in modules. You must use the 32-bit NWAdmin (NWAdmin32; `NWADMN32.EXE`) shipped with NetWare 5— not previous versions. If you have installed LDAP Services successfully, the necessary snap-in files are already in the correct directories.

If you need to manually add snap-ins to NWAdmin32, complete the following steps:

1. Put your snap-ins in the SYS:PUBLIC/WIN32/SNAPINS directory.

2. Resource DLLs and help files go into the SYS:PUBLIC\WIN32\NLS\<*LANG*> directory. For example, if you're using the English version, <*LANG*> would be ENGLISH.

3. NWAdmin32 automatically loads the snap-in DLLs, help, and resource files from its default directories.

Tip #344 from
Peter

If you're interested in a "quick start" guide, you can use the online help in NWAdmin to guide you through configuring LDAP Services.

THE LDAP SERVER OBJECT

The LDAP Server object stores configuration data for *one* LDAP Services for NDS server. During installation, an LDAP Server object named LDAP Server-*servername* (where *servername* is the name of the server on which LDAP Services for NDS is installed) is created; for example, if you installed LDAP Services on a NetWare 5 server called NET-WARE5-B, the LDAP Server object is called LDAP Server-NETWARE5-B (see Figure 33.5). The object is created in the same container as the NetWare Server object on which the product is installed.

Figure 33.5
The LDAP Server object.

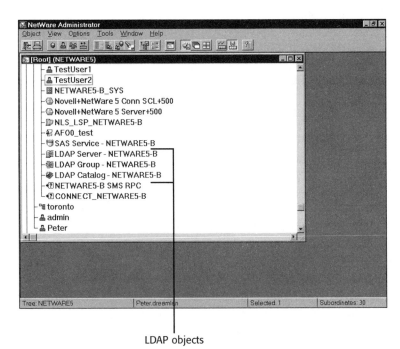

LDAP objects

Caution

> Each LDAP Server object configures one and only one LDAP Services for NDS server. Don't assign the same LDAP Server object to multiple LDAP Services for NDS servers. When you assign the LDAP Server object to another server, it is no longer assigned to the previous server.

The LDAP Server object contains five property pages (see Figure 33.6) from which you set configuration options:

Figure 33.6
LDAP Server property pages.

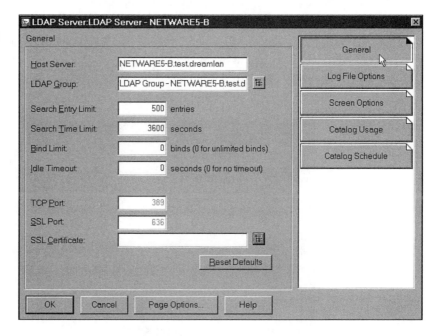

- **General page**—Use this page to configure server-specific properties, such as search limits.

- **Log File Options page**—Use this page to choose the types of events that are recorded in the LDAP Services log file and to configure log file parameters, such as name of log file and log file size limit.

- **Screen Options page**—Use this page to choose the types of events that are displayed on the console of an LDAP Services server. To enable a log event (such as displaying LDAP errors on the screen), select the corresponding check box.

- **Catalog Usage page**—Use this page to define how LDAP clients will be able to search catalogs—use catalog only, search NDS only, or search catalog first and if not found, search NDS.

- **Catalog Schedule page**—Use this page to determine when you want to update or refresh the Catalog object. All this information will be stored in the Catalog object. From this page, you can force a manual update.

PART
VII
CH
33

THE LDAP GROUP OBJECT

The LDAP Group object is used to store configuration data that can be applied to a single LDAP server or a group of LDAP servers. If you plan to implement the same configuration on multiple servers, the best way is to configure one LDAP Group object and assign it to each of the LDAP Services servers using the LDAP Server General property page in NWAdmin.

The LDAP Group configures the class and attribute mappings as well as security policies on the server. The use of this group object greatly simplifies configuration changes because one configuration change can be applied instantly to multiple LDAP servers.

Similar to the LDAP Server object, during installation a LDAP Group object named LDAP Group-*servername* is created in the same container as the NetWare server on which the product is installed. The LDAP Group object has five property pages (see Figure 33.7) with which you set various configuration options:

Figure 33.7
LDAP Group property pages.

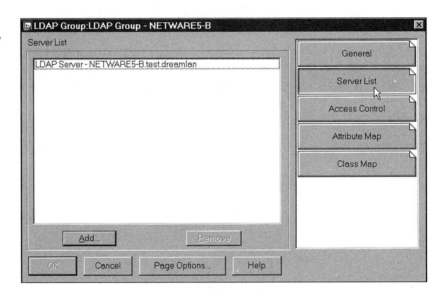

- **General page**—This page is used to configure the following settings: Suffix (the starting NDS context for LDAP requests; by leaving this blank, [Root] is assumed), referral (URL, of the form ldap://*hostname*, of an alternative LDAP server to handle the LDAP request if it's invalid for the current server's suffix setting), allow cleartext passwords (if set to Yes, it allows clients to send bind requests that include passwords over unencrypted connections), and proxy username (where you can specify a User object, instead of [Public], to be used for explicit bind requests).

- **Server List page**—This page allows you to view, add, and remove the servers that use the configuration data stored in this object. LDAP access to the servers in this list is logically equivalent with the same security restrictions and class and attribute mappings.

- **Access Control page**—Use this page to define and configure the ACL restrictions you want to use with LDAP Services.

- **Attribute Map page**—Use this page to define a relationship between any LDAP attribute and any supported NDS attribute. When an LDAP client requests an LDAP attribute from the LDAP server, the server returns the corresponding NDS attribute as specified by the mappings listed on this page.

- **Class Map page**—Use this page to define a relationship between any LDAP class and an NDS class. When an LDAP client requests an LDAP class from the LDAP server, the server returns the corresponding NDS class as specified by the mappings listed on this page.

To establish a mapping between an LDAP attribute and an NDS attribute, perform the following steps:

1. Access the Attribute Map property page (see Figure 33.8).

Figure 33.8
Establishing LDAP to NDS attribute mapping.

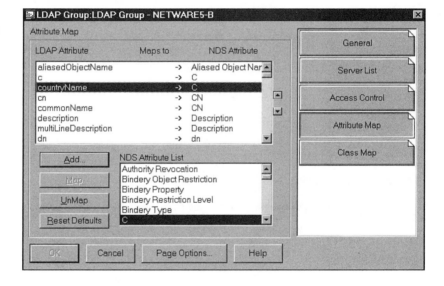

PART

VII

CH

33

2. Click the LDAP attribute in the upper window.
3. Click the NDS attribute in the lower window.
4. Click Map.

Note

If multiple LDAP attributes are mapped to the same NDS attribute, the order of the LDAP attributes listed in the upper window determines precedence; the first in the list takes precedence.

Tip #345 from
Peter

Use the arrow buttons to the right of the Attribute Map list to position the order of the attributes.

If the LDAP attribute you wanted to map is not in the displayed list, click the Add button to add it.

These steps can also be used to map LDAP classes to NDS classes.

USER OBJECTS

During the installation of LDAP Services, the NDS schema is extended. Specifically, User objects are updated to include a new E-mail Address attribute. NWAdmin will show a new property page called E-Mail Addresses where you can specify an Internet email address for the user.

Note

The Internet email address is not required for LDAP server operation. However, if an address is specified, that address will be delivered to the LDAP client when a user's email address is requested.

NDS RIGHTS FOR LDAP CLIENTS

To retrieve information from NDS, an LDAP client must authenticate to the NDS tree. The type of data searchable by the client then, depends on the NDS rights of the username used by the LDAP client.

Use the following steps to assign NDS rights for LDAP clients:

1. Determine which type of username the LDAP clients will use to access NDS:
   * Anonymous bind using [Public]
   * Anonymous bind via a proxy user
   * User bind using an NDS username

2. If users will use one proxy user or multiple NDS usernames to access LDAP, create these usernames in NDS.

3. Assign the appropriate NDS rights (such as Browse) to the usernames that LDAP clients will use.

The default NDS rights that most users receive provide limited rights to the user's own object. To provide access to other objects and their attributes, you must change the rights assigned in NDS. If the NDS rights assignment options do not provide the exact access level you want, you can implement additional controls using the optional LDAP Access Control List (ACL) feature (see the "Access Control Lists" section).

When an LDAP client requests NDS information, NDS accepts or rejects the request based on the LDAP client's NDS identity—the identity is set at bind time. The following tables serve as a reference to determine the NDS rights an LDAP client needs to complete the various types of LDAP client requests:

LDAP Object Access Type	NDS Object Rights Required
Search	Browse
Add	Create
Delete	Delete

LDAP Attribute Access Type	NDS Attribute Rights Required
Compare	Compare
Search	Compare
Read	Read
Write	Write

Note

Operations that require NDS Supervisor rights are currently not available through LDAP.

LDAP ACCESS CONTROL LISTS

When NDS security alone doesn't offer you the flexibility you need for your particular environment, you can use an Access Control List (ACL), an optional feature of LDAP Services that allows you to create an additional layer of security between LDAP clients and NDS. You can use ACLs to implement LDAP client access restrictions for all LDAP servers in an LDAP Group object.

You can accomplish the following objectives using ACLs:

- Create Container object attribute-level access controls that are inherited by the objects the container contains.

- Control client access based on criteria that NDS doesn't use (such as IP addresses).

- Implement more restrictive rights to NDS when accessed via LDAP (such as Read-only or publishing only names and email addresses).

Each ACL contains the following components:

- **Access To list**—This list determines which container or leaf object the ACL applies to, what rights are to be applied, and which LDAP attributes the ACL applies to (see Figure 33.9).

- **Access By list**—This list specifies who can access the objects and attributes defined in the Access To field and the level of access for those users (see Figure 33.10).

Figure 33.9
This ACL allows access to the telephone number attribute.

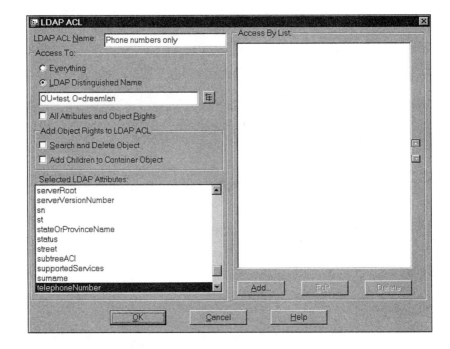

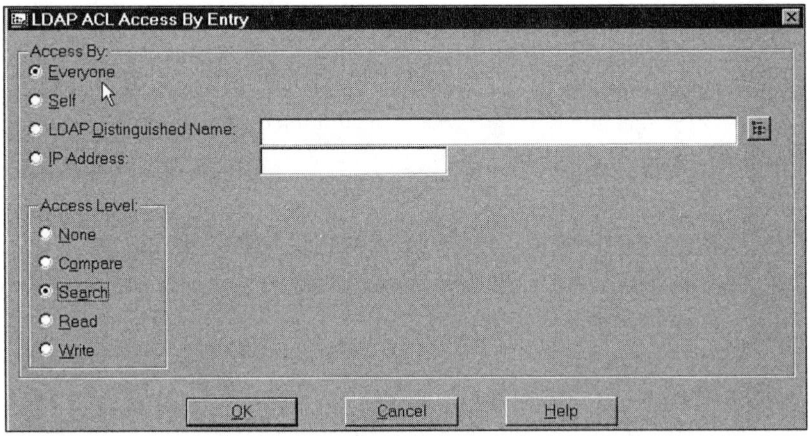

Figure 33.10
This ACL allows everyone to search the attribute.

Note

In the Access By list, the Compare right allows clients to verify known data for known objects—it does not allow clients to search for object attributes with which to compare values; the Search right allows clients to search for object attributes—it also implies Compare right. The Read right allows clients to read the values of the object attributes defined in the Access To list—it implies the Search and Compare right. The Write right allows clients to modify the values of the object attributes defined in the Access To list—it implies Read, Search and Compare rights.

LDAP ACLs are configured via the Access Control property page of the LDAP Group object using NWAdmin.

ORDERING OF ACLs

As discussed earlier, when multiple LDAP attributes or classes are mapped to a single NDS attribute or class, the order of the LDAP attribute or class listed determines precedence. The same is true with ACLs. When LDAP Services receives a client request, it searches the ACL list and uses the first ACL that specifies the requested attributes in the Access To list. LDAP Services then searches Access By list and uses the first entry that includes the LDAP client user. If no ACL is found, full NDS rights are given.

For example, suppose that you specified two ACLs: one for OU=Dallas and one for User object Sally within Dallas. Now suppose that the ACLs are in the following order:

```
ou=Dallas, O=Company
cn=Sally, ou=Dallas, O=Company
```

In this example, the ACL for Sally would never be processed because Sally is part of the Dallas organizational unit. Every request for Sally would be processed using the ACL for Dallas because Sally is part of Dallas. To provide separate controls for User object Sally, you need to move Sally's ACL to above Organizational Unit object Dallas in the ACL list:

```
cn=Sally, ou=Dallas, O=Company
ou=Dallas, O=Company
```

The same is true for the order of entries in the Access By list within each ACL.

PROJECT: SETTING UP A TEST CONTAINER

This section shows you how to set up a test organization within the NDS tree and give LDAP clients unlimited Read access to this organization. The procedures are to help you learn how to configure and use LDAP Services.

After installation and startup, LDAP Services is ready to process client requests for NDS information. However, your NDS tree might not yet be set up to support LDAP requests. For example, your LDAP clients can't access phone numbers if you have not populated the users phone number attribute in NDS. Also, LDAP clients can't read the phone numbers if they don't have the appropriate NDS rights.

Follow these steps to set up the test container:

1. Install LDAP Services.
2. Use NWAdmin to create a test container somewhere in the tree.
3. Create several users in the test container and assign values to the following properties: last name, given name, middle initial, title, location, email address, and telephone.
4. Create a user named LDAP_Proxy in the test container. This user will be used for anonymous user bind and will be given permission to read all the data in the test container.

5. Configure the `LDAP_Proxy` user to not Allow User to Change Password; don't assign a password to this user.

6. Make `LDAP_Proxy` a trustee of the test container and grant it NDS Browse object rights and Read and Compare rights to all properties.

Tip #346 from
Peter

If you allow NDS user binds, these users will typically not have sufficient rights to read and compare most attributes, even though all attributes and classes in the container that are mapped are readable by LDAP. Therefore, it is generally easier to set up a proxy user and use anonymous user bind instead.

---

7. Make the following changes to the LDAP Group object:

   • Enter LDAP_Proxy as the Proxy Username (in the General property page). This maps all anonymous LDAP requests to the proxy username for NDS authentication.

   • Enter the test container for the Suffix (in the General property page). This limits access by the LDAP proxy user to the test container. (Note the complete name of this container. LDAP clients need this name to configure their connections.)

   • Verify that your LDAP Services server appears in the server list (in the Server List property page). If it isn't there, click Add and use the Browse button to locate the LDAP Server object and add it to the list.

8. Click OK to save the changes when you're done with the modifications listed in step 7. LDAP Services will automatically load in the new configuration.

9. Make a note of the following information because you'll need it to configure the LDAP clients:

   • Your NetWare 5 server's IP address or DNS name

   • Distinguished name of the test container (refer to step 7)

Note

The LDAP distinguished name has no preceding period and uses commas to separate the components. For example, the NDS distinguished name `ou=test.o=dreamlan` must be entered at an LDAP client as `ou=test, o=dreamlan`.

---

10. If `NLDAP.NLM` and `DSCAT.NLM` are not yet running, load them on your NetWare 5 server. (You'll see a message after loading NLDAP that LDAP hasn't been configured with a valid SSL certificate, and all SSL connections will fail. This is expected because our procedure above didn't configure SSL.)

Netscape Navigator v4 and higher can function as an LDAP client. (A copy of Netscape Navigator is included with your NetWare 5 CDs.) You can use Navigator to access your LDAP server without having to first configure it; the first time you access your LDAP server, Navigator will prompt you with

```
Would you like to add xxxx to your LDAP preferences?
```

where *xxxx* is the name (or IP address) of your LDAP server.

Note
To configure Navigator's LDAP preferences, click Edit, Preferences, Mail & Groups, Directory. Click New to add a new entry. Depending on the version of Navigator, the menu selections may differ (see Figure 33.11).

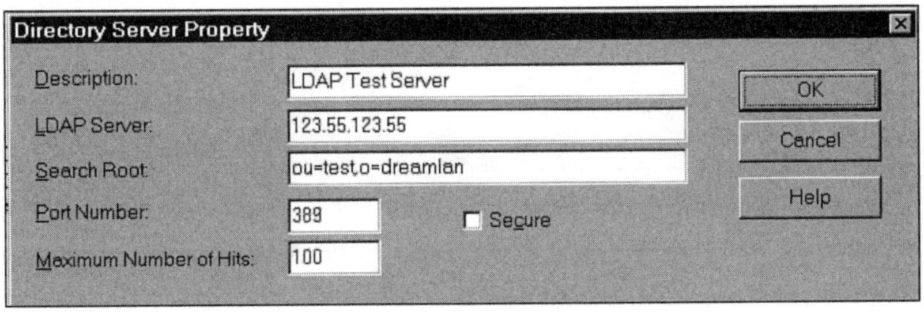

Figure 33.11
Adding a new LDAP server configuration to Navigator.

Here are some typical URLs you can use to access your LDAP server (the examples assume the server's IP address is 123.55.123.55 and the suffix is ou=test,o=dreamlan):

- To obtain a list of all objects in NDS starting at the suffix (see Figure 33.12), use the following:
  ```
  ldap://123.55.123.55/ou=test,o=dreamlan??sub
  ```

- To obtain a list of all objects in a given context (ou=test.o=dreamlan is used here), use the following:
  ```
  ldap://123.55.123.55/ou=test,o=dreamlan??one
  ```

- To show the specified NDS container only (ou=test.o=dreamlan is used here), use either of the following:
  ```
  ldap://123.55.123.55/ou=test,o=dreamlan
  ldap://123.55.123.55/ou=test,o=dreamlan??base
  ```

- To search for all NDS objects starting with "test" (see Figure 33.13), use the following:
  ```
  ldap://123.55.123.55/ou=test,o=dreamlan??sub?(cn=test*)
  ```

Figure 33.12
A list of all objects under
ou=test.o=dream-lan.

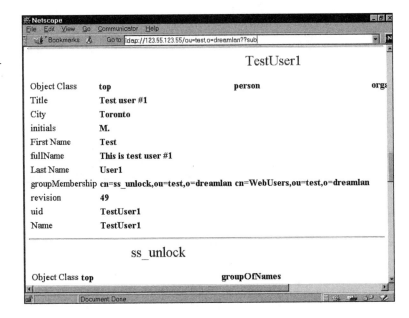

Figure 33.13
A list of all objects with names starting with test, under
ou=test.o=dream-lan.

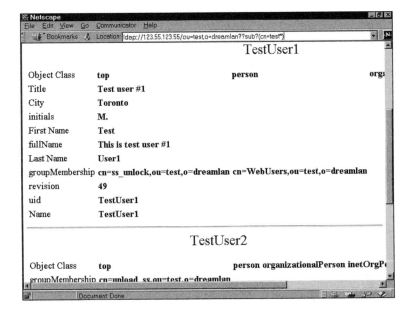

Tip #347 from
Peter

To search in NDS for names that have spaces in them (such as software engineering), use a %20 instead of the space. For example:

```
ldap://123.55.123.55/ou=software%20engineering,ou=test,
o=dreamlan??one
```

NOVELL INTERNET ACCESS SERVER (NIAS)

In this chapter

OVERVIEW OF REMOTE ACCESS

As companies expand, they increasingly rely on telecommunications technology to help run their businesses. Traveling employees, workers at branch offices, telecommuters, customers, and suppliers all find it necessary to contact growing companies electronically—for both voice and data communications.

Not surprisingly, these increased demands also radically alter the complexion of a company's computer networking resources. These demands force IS personnel to extend the reach of networking services beyond the traditional boundaries of the local area network—toward the "outer limit." Now, those in IS are grappling with the thorny issues of granting remote access to networked resources to a rapidly growing profusion of computers, telecommunications devices, and users.

It is "out there" that some of the networking industry's most exciting developments are occurring. Faster modems, improved data compression techniques, and new high-speed digital transmission services are making remote access more and more cost-effective and transparent to end users. But what's "out there," in the remote-access fringe, is also where many network managers fear to tread. There, they're concerned about security, management, and costs: major security problems without easy answers.

With the traditional LAN environment, you can selectively control user access to the network while also ensuring the security of the LAN-based resources. In addition, IS personnel are accustomed to dealing with standardized hardware interfaces such as hubs, bridges, and routers and their associated protocols.

Remote users, however, make strikingly different demands on a network than their local counterparts do. Their connectivity needs are intermittent—a dial-up session to pick up email a few times a day, for example. And they require different services, such as dial-up telephone lines rather than leased-lines. They also need a variety of new resources—in particular, modems, special software, and perhaps even specially configured user accounts on network servers.

The key requirements of a remote-access solution thus differ considerably from those of the local LAN. Moreover, these requirements introduce a new level of complexity into today's already-complex networks. How, for example, do organizations install, manage, maintain, equip, and support users at dozens of remote sites? And with an entirely new class of users now accessing networks remotely, how do organizations handle security?

This chapter looks at Novell Internet Access Server (NIAS), which is included with your NetWare 5. NIAS 4.1 remote access is a server-based software solution for remote computing. The remote access software runs on a NetWare server and provides a common platform for remote node and remote control technologies. With remote access, multiple remote users can access IPX- and IP-based networks, and network workstations can access host computers through telephone lines (including ISDN), leased lines, X.25 packet-switched networks, or direct connections.

It lets a wide range of different clients dynamically share common ports, thereby eliminating the need for dedicated ports or separate communications servers for each client type.

Whatever the end user's remote-access need, a network administrator's first critical decision about providing remote LAN access is to decide the best method for giving dial-up users entry to the network. Here, you have two choices: via remote control software or as a remote node on the network.

REMOTE NODE

With *remote node* (sometimes known as *remote client*) connections, the remote PC functions as if it were a workstation directly connected to the LAN: The modem functions like a network card and the phone lines become the data path to and from the server. All data required for a session (file data and application packets) is transferred over the communications link; data processing occurs on the remote PC (see Figure 34.1).

Figure 34.1
Remote node applications.

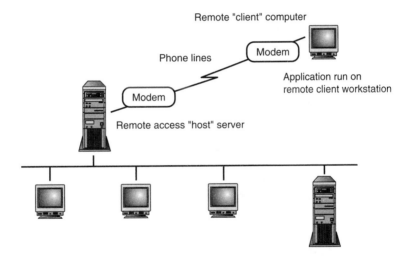

Remote "client" computer

Phone lines   Modem

Application run on remote client workstation

Modem

Remote access "host" server

Remote node solutions require powerful remote PCs and high-speed modems operating for optimum performance. Because applications run on the remote PC, remote node solutions do not, however, support real-time database applications efficiently (because the data has to transverse a slow communication link).

PART
VII

CH
34

REMOTE CONTROL

With remote control connections, the remote PC controls a dedicated workstation that's on the LAN (referred to as the *host*). The host software acts as sort of server, handling all data requests from the remote client. After receiving a request from the client, the host then transfers screen images and keystrokes over the telephone lines to the client, which displays the images on the user's monitor. Therefore, only keystrokes and screen updates are transferred between the two PCs over the communications link; data processing occurs on the dedicated workstation on the LAN (see Figure 34.2).

Figure 34.2
Remote control
applications.

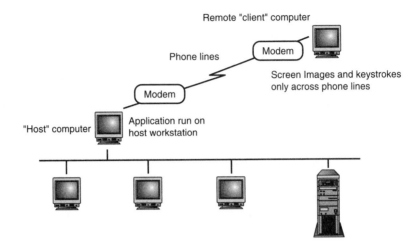

REMOTE NODE VERSUS REMOTE CONTROL

Choosing between the remote node and remote control when considering remote access needs can be a difficult task for several reasons. First, each offers end users features and benefits that the other lacks. Second, most remote node and remote control products are limited to 56Kbps data transmissions. Although remote node often provides what appears to be a transparent link between the PC and remote LAN, both it and remote control are considerably slower than the 10Mbps or 16Mbps rate offered by Ethernet and Token Ring LANs, respectively, and *much* slower than 100Mbps Fast Ethernet networks readily available today.

This means, among other things, that users' performance expectations must be clarified. It also means that companies must factor monthly long distance phone expenses into the costs of any remote LAN access solution.

A third reason they're also difficult to choose from is that both approaches generally require adding some form of communications controller, or server, to the network.

NIAS 4.1 is a consolidated communications platform that supports inbound *and* outbound services. It supports both remote control and remote node applications, over IPX, IP, and AppleTalk.

Macintosh remote node connections are made through Apple Remote Client and the AppleTalk Remote Access Service (ARAS) server. Because Mac client software support is not included with NetWare 5.0, the discussion of remote access will be limited to PC clients.

REMOTE ACCESS CONFIGURATION

To set up NIAS, you must complete several remote access design and configuration tasks. Although you don't have to perform these tasks in a specific order, the following is a recommended order:

1. Evaluate your current network and user environment in preparation for building a remote access solution.

2. Select an appropriate data transmission medium for use between the server and remote workstations.

3. Ensure that unauthorized remote users are prevented from accessing the network.

4. Tune remote client and server configurations for maximum performance.

5. Install and configure appropriate software to enable remote access on a network.

This section covers the last two tasks; task #3 is covered in the "Setting Up Security" section later in this chapter.

MAXIMIZING CLIENT AND SERVER PERFORMANCE

Each of the situations mentioned in the "Remote Node Versus Remote Control" section earlier can be improved by careful planning. The following performance-enhancing suggestions can be applied on the client side:

- Create minimal login scripts for each remote access user. If the remote user is also a LAN user, check the network address from which a user logs in from and if it's from a remote network, minimize the tasks executed by the login script.

- Install frequently used applications locally on the remote workstation.

- Set and use compression settings for the communication software on the remote workstation.

- Reduce the need to transfer files to and from remote workstations by rearranging work patterns, or proactively copying files to the remote workstation when connected to the LAN (such as a notebook PC).

- Create Windows shortcuts for commonly used remote files or servers on the remote workstation desktop. This eliminates the long wait for large lists of files or servers to be displayed when browsing.

- Upgrade slower modems to faster models.

- Evaluate alternative telecom services so you can get faster link speeds.

- Optimize workstation resources available to Windows.

- Train users to expect slow performance and plan their remote network use accordingly.

PART

VII

CH

34

Tip #348 from
Peter

Training users to efficiently use a remote access link and telling them to expect slow service are often a important step to increasing satisfaction.

At the same time, you should take steps on the server side to ensure maximum remote access throughput. The following are some suggestions that can be applied on the server side:

- The recommended amount of memory for the number of users expected to use it. NIAS 4.1 requires 5MB of additional memory which is sufficient for "normal use"; you might want to add more depending on your load.

- Available CPU resources to log in remote users and route their data to other locations on the network. Many sites use dedicated servers for remote access as a means to improve performance.

- Adequate LAN or WAN bandwidth to provide efficient connections to other locations on the network.

- The most recent remote access device drivers installed.

Installing NIAS

Before you install NIAS, make sure you complete the necessary hardware installation (such as modems and any necessary cables and telephone connections) and have available the following information:

- An IPX address that does not conflict with existing network addresses. If you set up remote nodes, the remote workstations are on their own IPX "network."

- IP addresses that do not conflict with existing IP devices. If you're to use DHCP services, have the address of the DHCP server handy.

- IP netmask information, if you're subnetting.

- If you're configuring IP remote node operations, the server needs to have IP configured.

NIAS can support connections over both WAN boards and modem (COM) ports. In this chapter, only modem configuration topics are covered. For detailed information about configuring NIAS, refer to your NetWare 5 documentation (which is on one of your NetWare 5 CDs, entitled "Online Documentation").

Tip #349 from
Peter

As you complete the product installation, Novell Internet Access Server 4.1 remote access runs an automated setup procedure that lets you quickly and easily set up and configure your remote access server for basic operation. The automated procedure runs the first time you select Remote Access Configuration from the NIASCFG menu. If you bypass or quit the automated setup, you can configure the remote access software manually.

The following steps show how you install and configure NIAS for IPX remote node operation (all operations are performed at the server console):

1. If you didn't select to install NIAS software during the server install, you need to install it from the OS CD. Use NWCONFIG, Product Options, Install Other NetWare Products, and then select Novell Internet Access Server from the list of products; 7.8MB of disk space on SYS: is required.

2. At the server console, type LOAD NIASCFG.NLM.

3. A dialog box informs you that in order for NIAS to run properly, driver commands need to be transferred to the NETINFO.CFG file (see Figure 34.3). Press Enter.

Figure 34.3
Transferring driver load and bind commands from AUTOEXEC.NCF to NETINFO.CFG.

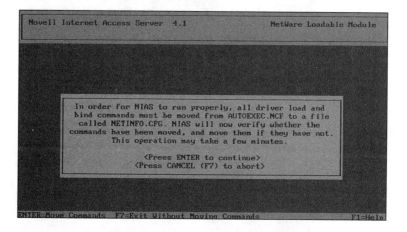

4. Press Enter to exit NIASCFG. The server is automatically shut down. Restart the server by running SERVER.EXE.

5. Load NIASCFG.NLM. Press Enter at the dialog box on moving driver load and bind commands to NETINFO.CFG. Press Enter again.

> **Note**
> You will not see the dialog box again the next time you start NIASCFG.

6. Select Configure NIAS from the NIAS Options menu (see Figure 34.4).

Figure 34.4
The NIAS main
configuration menu.

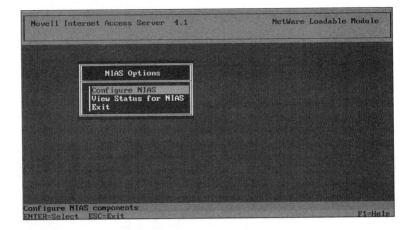

7. Select Remote Access. The very first time you access this option, a schema extension needs to be made to the tree (see Figure 34.5).

Figure 34.5
To use NIAS, a
schema extension
needs to be made.

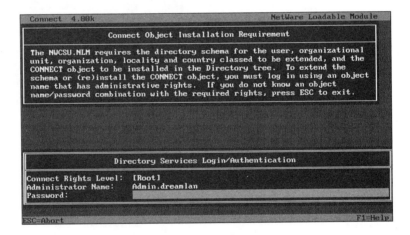

Note

The Connect Rights Level specifies the container below which the Remote Access object is granted administrative rights (Browse object rights and Read and Write rights to all properties), and users in this container *and* below can access this Remote Access Server. The default is [Root].

Tip #350 from
Peter

If you have difficulty displaying or selecting remote services, issue the following command at the server console prompt:

```
LOAD SVCDEF.NLM SYS:SYSTEM\CONNECT\SVCS.DEF
```

Then restart the server and try again.

8. Select Yes to Do You Want Instructions? to get an overview of the configuration process. Press Esc when complete.

9. Press Enter to begin the setup process.

10. Select No to Do You Have Any Synchronous Adapters? You will configure an asynchronous modem (using a COM port) for remote client access.

11. Select Yes to load and define an AIO port.

12. Scroll down to the Serial Port (COMx) entry and press Enter.

13. Press Enter when the console reports that the driver was loaded successfully.

14. Select No to Do You Need to Load More AIO Drivers? (If you had additional modems on other ports, you might say Yes and repeat steps 12 and 13.)

15. Ensure that your modem is connected to the server's COM port and that the modem is turned on.

16. Press Enter when you are ready for NIAS to look for your modem (see Figure 34.6).

Figure 34.6
NIAS will detect which ports have attached modems.

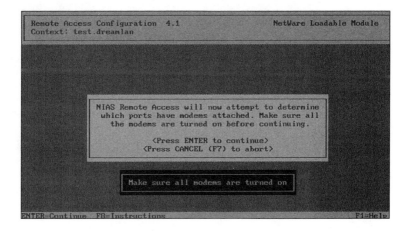

17. Ensure that NIAS found a modem on a licensed port (see Figure 34.7). If not, select Try Modem Discovery Again to repeat this process.

18. Select Continue With Automated Setup.

19. If prompted, select Yes to Auto-Detect Modem Types. (Due to the vast number of modem models and types, auto-detection does not always succeed.) If NIAS did succeed, proceed to the next step. Otherwise, complete the following:

   • Press Enter to continue if NIAS reports that it can't determine the modem type.

   • Press Enter again to display a list of modem types.

   • Scroll and select your modem.

20. Select PPPRNS from the Remote Access Services menu (see Figure 34.8).

PART

VII

CH

34

Figure 34.7
NIAS found one port with a modem attached.

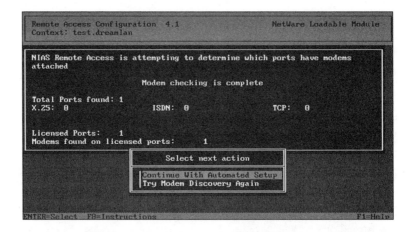

Figure 34.8
List of supported remote access services.

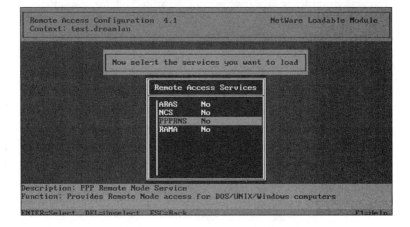

21. Select IPX.

22. Enter a unique IPX address.

23. Press Esc and select Yes to save and activate the change.

24. Press Esc and select Yes to save current settings to a file.

25. A dialog box appears indicating that the current configuration will be activated. Any active connections will be lost.

26. Press Enter to continue. Wait for reinitialization to complete.

27. Select Yes to Do You Want to Start This Service Now? (this will start PPPRNS).

28. Press Esc to complete the basic NIAS Remote Access configuration. Pay attention to the security note that states that all users can access all ports and services at all times.

Similar steps can be taken to set up remote control services and other services. To configure a new server, choose Set Up, Select Remote Access Services from the Remote Access Options menu.

SETTING UP SECURITY

Security is critical to any remote access design. To create an effective remote security solution, carefully consider security early in the design process. A remote access security solution imposed later on an existing remote access setup might be more difficult to achieve.

By default, NIAS Remote Access services are installed to offer *unrestricted* access to any user, and unlimited access to any service via any port. I strongly recommend that you adjust this default level of security before permitting users to dial-in.

When you've finished configured PPPRNS, you're automatically taken to the Remote Access Options menu (see Figure 34.9). Using this menu, you can configure basic NIAS Remote Access password security.

Figure 34.9
The Remote Access
Options menu.

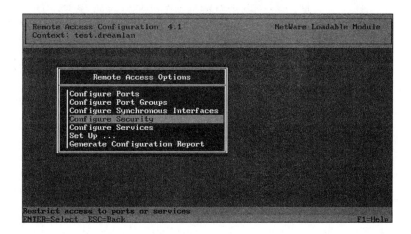

Continue with the following steps to begin this process:

1. Select Configure Security from the menu.

2. Select Set Remote Client Password Restrictions. Use this option to set parameters to ensure secure access to your organization (see Figure 34.10).

3. Select Enable Long Password. This setting allows passwords of up to 16 bytes instead of 8 bytes.

PART

VII

CH

34

Figure 34.10
Remote Client
Password Restrictions.

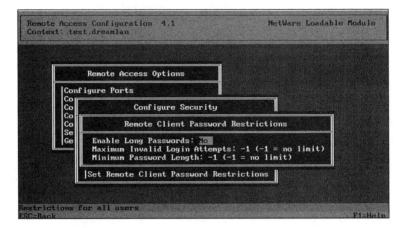

Legacy NetWare Connect servers do not support long passwords. Therefore, if you enable long passwords, users with passwords longer than 8 bytes will not be able to log in to any NetWare Connect 2.0 servers you have on your network. If you have any NetWare Connect 2.0 servers, you should upgrade them before you enable this feature.

You *cannot* disable long passwords after you have enabled them.

4. Set Maximum Invalid Login Attempts to no more than 3. A value of -1 allows unlimited attempts.

5. Press Esc and select Yes to save changes.

6. Select Set User Remote Client Password. A list of users and groups in the server's bindery context is shown. You can walk up and down the tree using the ".." (move up one level) and "+*containername*" (move down into the container) entries.

7. Select a user or group from the tree.

8. Enter the desired password and press Enter. Confirm the password. If you do not set up a password, users must use their password set up in NDS.

Note

The Remote Client Password is used by Remote Control users logging in to the Service Selector, ARAS users, and PPPRNS users when using the PAP or CHAP (but *not* NWCAP) authentication protocols. This password *is* case sensitive and is not as secure as the NetWare password.

Tip #351 from
Peter

To maintain the highest level of system security, it should not be set to the same value as the user's NetWare password.

9. Press Esc and repeat steps 7 and 8 as needed.

10. Inspect all other choices available. Set parameters to support any special security needs of your organization.

11. Press Esc to return to the main menu.

Your NIAS server is now ready to accept modem calls from remote clients.

CONFIGURING THE CLIENTS

Both Windows 9x and Windows NT provide a native remote access client (Dial-Up Networking, or DUN). To access your NIAS server over a dial-up link, you need to set up and configure the Windows native remote access client before you can connect to the NIAS server.

Hardware such as modems and cables might already be attached to your Windows client. If not, you need to install the necessary hardware before you can set up the client for remote access to the NIAS server.

CLIENT32 AND REMOTE ACCESS

The Novell Client32 software works with Windows to ensure a remote access user can properly connect to a NIAS remote access server and use all NetWare services.

Some versions of Client32 might feature a Dial-Up tab after you click the Advanced button displayed on the login window. The Dial-Up tab allows you to optionally set Client32 to always connect to the network using DUN.

CONFIGURING A REMOTE ACCESS WINDOWS CLIENT

You need to complete the following tasks prior to configuring a Windows workstation for remote access to NIAS:

- Make sure the latest Novell Client is installed in Windows.
- Install remote access hardware such as a modem.
- Install and configure Windows Remote Access Service or Dial-Up Networking (DUN) service.
- Configure network parameters to enable a connection to a server.
- Modify login scripts and security access to ensure adequate security and performance.

PART

VII

CH

34

The following steps outline the procedure you take to set up Windows to remotely access, via modem, your NIAS remote access server via IPX. Slight variations exist between Windows 9x and Windows NT; the following steps are for Windows NT and assume you already have DUN installed and properly configured:

1. Double-click the My Computer icon.

2. Double-click the Dial Up Networking icon.

3. Click New to add a new entry in the Windows NT phone book.

4. Enter a name for your new phone book entry (such as NIAS Server #2; see Figure 34.11).

Figure 34.11
Adding a new phone book entry.

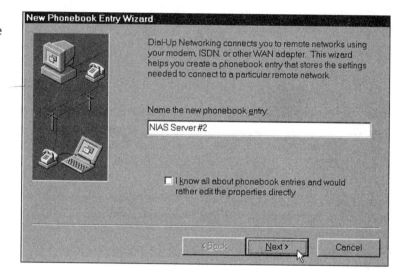

5. Click Next to confirm the name of the phone book.

6. Uncheck the I Am Calling the Internet box (if your dial up connection needs to support IP, check this box). If you are connecting via IPX, place a check in The Non-Windows NT Server I Am Calling Expects Me to Type Login Information After Connecting, or to Know TCP/IP Addresses Before Dialing box. Click Next.

7. Enter the phone number needed (including area code and other dialing codes) to access your NIAS server, and then click Next.

8. Click Point-to-Point (PPP) at the Serial Line Protocol window; click Next.

9. Ensure None is selected at the Login Script dialog box; click Next.

10. Ensure that 0.0.0.0 is entered in the My IP Address field; click Next. If you have configured NIAS to support IP, it can automatically lease the remote workstation an IP address. If, however, you want to manually configure an address, enter the workstation's permanent IP address instead of 0.0.0.0.

11. Ensure that 0.0.0.0 appears in both the DNS and WINS fields. An IP-enabled NIAS server can automatically provide the workstation with a DNS server address. If your want to manually configure DNS information, enter that information instead of 0.0.0.0.

12. Click Next.

13. Click Finish.

14. Click More and select Edit Entry and Modem Properties.

15. Click the Server tab at the top.

16. Uncheck the TCP/IP box and click OK to save the change.

> **Caution**
>
> If you didn't perform steps 14–16, NIAS will display a message on the server console when the workstation connects indicating that IP is not bound to the port.

17. Click Close.

Your Windows NT workstation is now ready to connect to a NIAS remote access server using an IPX connection.

CONNECTING TO NIAS

After you have configured both the server and client, you can test their connectivity. Connecting a remote client to a server is generally similar to the process of connecting and logging in to the network using a LAN connection:

- Launching a login utility
- Entering a user ID and password

Except that when creating a remote connection the login utility is a remote access login utility. In general, the only difference is that the remote access login utility might request the phone number of the remote server. When this information has been provided, the client's modem becomes the remote equivalent of a LAN card.

To dial in to your NIAS server from a Windows NT workstation running Client32, use the following steps (the procedure for Windows 9x workstations is similar to that for Windows NT). These steps assume you're running Client32 for Windows NT version 4.6 (which has a Dial-Up tab in its Advanced options):

1. Launch the NetWare GUI login utility.

2. Enter your username, password, and NDS context (just like you would when logging in via a LAN connection).

3. Click the Advanced button.

4. Select the Dial-Up tab (see Figure 34.12).

Figure 34.12
The Dial-Up tab in
Client32 for
Windows NT.

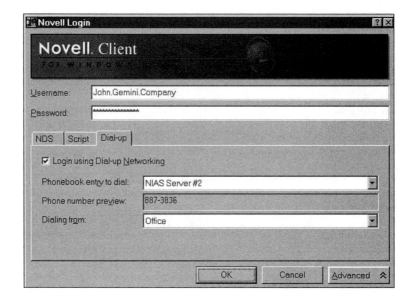

5. Check the Login Using Dial-Up Networking box.

6. Select the appropriate phone book entry.

7. Select the appropriate Dialing From location.

8. Click OK to log in.

9. A status dialog box similar to Figure 34.13 is displayed while the dial-up connection is being made.

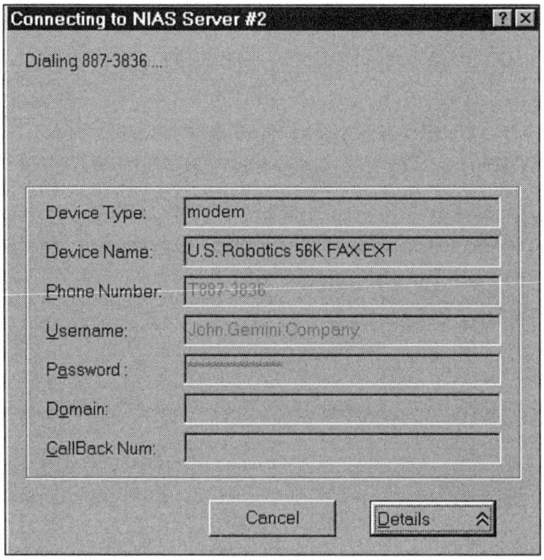

Figure 34.13
Client32 dial-up con-
nection status dialog
box.

10. After the connection is successfully made, the status dialog box and the GUI login screen are closed.

Tip #352 from
Peter

You can terminate the connection by either logging out (Shut Down in Windows) or using the Hang Up option in the Dial-Up Networking Monitor. Or double-click the DUN icon in My Computer and select Hang Up.

To confirm that your workstation has a live remote access connection, double-click Network Neighborhood and display the available servers and network resources. You should see a list of NDS trees and NetWare servers. Note the addition of a dial-up status icon in the task bar, normally next to the clock at the bottom right of your screen. The icons in Network Neighborhood and the Dial-Up Networking Monitor icon confirm that your workstation has a live remote access connection.

Tip #353 from
Peter

If you're not running Client32 or your version of Client32 does not have a Dial-Up tab, you can log in to your NIAS server using DUN directly. The steps are as follows:

1. Double-click the DUN icon in My Computer.

2. Use the pull-down list in the Phonebook entry to dial to select your NIAS entry.

3. Click Dial.

4. Enter the username, including context, and password in the connect dialog box (see Figure 34.14).

5. Click OK and wait for the modem to dial and connect to your NIAS server.

6. Click OK when you see the Connection Complete dialog box.

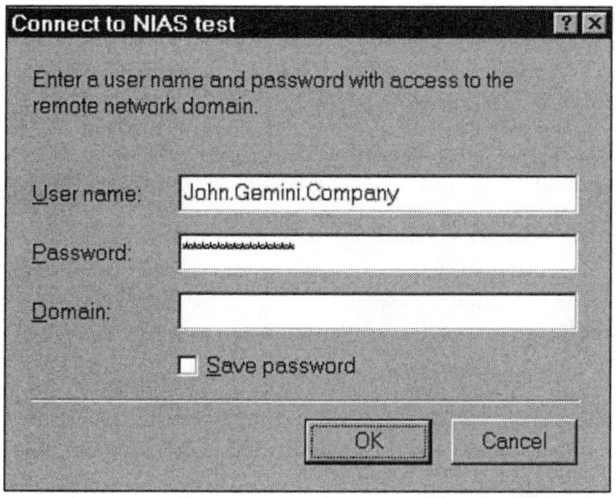

Figure 34.14
Make sure you enter the username with the full context.

Connect to NIAS test

Enter a user name and password with access to the remote network domain.

User name: John.Gemini.Company

Password: ****************

Domain:

☐ Save password

OK   Cancel

PART
VII

CH
34

TROUBLESHOOTING

One of the most common problems associated with remote access is that a user dials into a NIAS server for a remote node connection and the server answers but the two systems fail to negotiate communication parameters. This section discusses in general several potential causes of this problem.

This problem presents itself in several variations of symptoms:

- The phone line drops before the modems complete their handshake.
- The modems complete their handshake but the caller is erroneously presented with the Service Selection screen (which is for the selection of remote control sessions, such as via pcAnywhere, ReachOut, and so on).
- The modems complete their handshake but fail to negotiate PPP parameters.

Here is a list of some common errors displayed at the NetWare server console prompt. They can include, but are not limited to, the following (note that in some cases, IPXCP can replace LCP—Link Control Protocol—in these messages):

- `LCP is down: **Maximum reached for Config-Request retries - remote rejected the call**`
- `LCP is down: **Peer rejected Authentication negotiation**`
- `LCP is down: **Dial-up connection failure**`
- `LCP is down: **PPP did not receive a response from peer for the several Echo-Requests sent**`
- `LCP is down: **PPP did not receive an Authenticate Ack from its peer**`
- `LCP is down: **PPP has rejected peer's negotiation option value too many times**`
- `LCP is down: **Illegal peer ID/password in the Authenticate Request packet**`
- `LCP is down: **Peer rejected Authentication negotiation**`

Often this behavior is caused by a faulty modem script or improperly selected modem type. This can be true of the modem scripts on the server, the client, or both. You might be able to narrow down the problem as either the client modem or server modem by using another client machine/modem combination or dialing to a different NIAS server.

Tip #354 from
Peter

Anytime the error involved complains of authentication, username, or password, the user should verify his or her username, context, and password (which might be wrong or might have expired) before assuming another cause is responsible. Also note that different passwords can apply, depending on the method of dial-in. The NWCAP authentication uses the NetWare password. PAP and CHAP use the Remote Client Password, which is set in NWCCON).

You can also turn off NIAS security temporarily while you troubleshoot the problem. For example, to disable PPPRNS's security, load `NIASCFG.NLM` and from the NIAS Options menu, select Configure NIAS, Remote Access, Configure Services, PPPRNS, Configure Security, and then set Enable Security to disable.

Modem manufacturers often update the BIOS in their modems without changing the name or model, which changes how a modem responds to the same set of modem commands. As a result, Novell frequently updates existing modem scripts and creates new ones. The presence of a modem name in the selection list that seems to match the type of modem you have does not always guarantee that you have the appropriate script.

Tip #355 from Peter	Novell publishes its latest modem scripts in a downloadable file called `NWCMOD.EXE` (which you can obtain from the File Finder area on `http://support.novell.com`).

Many connection and negotiation problems can be resolved by applying the new updates to the server and client. However, take care to follow the instructions in `NWCMOD.TXT` closely. Also, note that sometimes there are many similar modem types listed in the updated list. The exact name to select can depend on the BIOS revision or the modem. After updating your modem scripts (which are a set of `.MDC` files in `SYS:SYSTEM`), you might want to reselect your modem type from the list in order to see what new options might apply to your modem. If it is unclear which of several similar modem names is best for your modem, you might want to try several of them.

Sometimes the symptoms described earlier are due to hardware issues. Even with updated modem scripts, the following might be responsible:

- Faulty modem or cabling
- Faulty or miswired 25-to-9 pin adapters or D-port-to-RJ adapters
- Different makes of modems that don't communicate well together
- A modem type or BIOS revision for which a script does not exist

If none of the updated modem scripts corrects your problem, you might want to contact the modem manufacturer to obtain appropriate modem scripts, or contact Novell technical support to verify that your problem is related to the modem script or to explore other possible causes for the failure.

Tip #356 from Peter	If you have a modem that the modem manufacturer doesn't have a script for (which is rare) and Novell doesn't include it on their list of supported modems, you can consider creating your own script using Novell's NWCWRT (a Windows-based modem script writer). You can find this software in the File Finder area at `http://support.novell.com` under the name `NWCWRT.EXE`.

## CHAPTER 35

FTP SERVICE AND LPR/LPD

In this chapter

INSTALLING FTP

FTP is a commonly used application and the standard for file transfer via the Internet. The FTP specification is defined in RFC 959. In order to use FTP, you must have an account on the remote computer; otherwise, the administrator needs to allow anonymous FTP.

FTP services are automatically installed, however, as part of the Unix Print Services (UXPS) installation. The prerequisites for installing FTP are the following:

- NetWare version 4.1 or higher.
- UXPS uses 12MB of RAM in addition to what NetWare itself requires. If RAM is tight, you might consider adding more before the installation.
- 8MB of free disk space on the sys: volume.
- TCP/IP loaded and configured.

Mount your installation CD as either a local volume or a volume on a remote server. Load NWCONFIG, choose Product Options, and select Install Unix Print Services, as shown in Figure 35.1.

Figure 35.1
To obtain FTP services, you need to install Unix Print Services via Product Options from NWCONFIG.

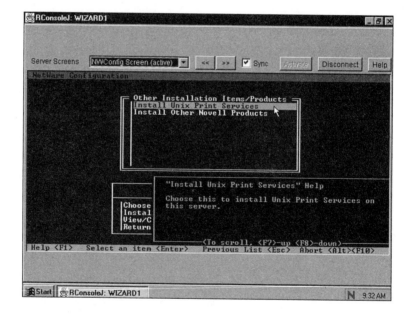

If you mounted your installation CD on a remote server, enter the path to the installation files when prompted. At the beginning of the installation, you have an option to view the README file; always a good thing to do. You are then prompted to enter the drive/path for booting NetWare, normally c:.

After the file copying is finished, UNICON starts and prompts you to login. UNICON, which you'll see more of later in this chapter, is how you manage and configure the FTP services. When you're successfully logged in, you are presented with the Available Name Service Options screen, as shown in Figure 35.2, where you must make a choice between Local NIS or Remote NIS. Unix Print Services, and thus FTP service, require the network information service (NIS).

Figure 35.2
You need to choose between Local NIS and Remote NIS.

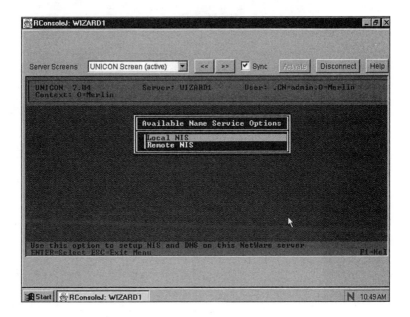

A discussion of NIS is beyond the scope of this chapter, but a search of the online documentation will provide you with quite a bit of reading. In brief, NIS is a distributed database that the print services use to obtain information about users and groups. There is one master server for the NIS domain, and other replica servers are possible. The choices presented to you in Figure 35.2 are either Local or Remote.

■ Local NIS sets up the NetWare server to act as a master NIS name server. You're able to manage the NIS database using UNICON, and the server is able to provide information to other client name servers (see Figure 35.3).

■ Remote NIS sets up the server as a client of an existing name server. You can't manage the database with UNICON but can only view it; hosts, users, and groups need to be configured on the remote master.

PART

VII

CH

35

Figure 35.3
Here, you have chosen Local NIS from the previous screen. These are all defaults; the only thing you can change on this screen is the NIS Domain and the DNS Domain.

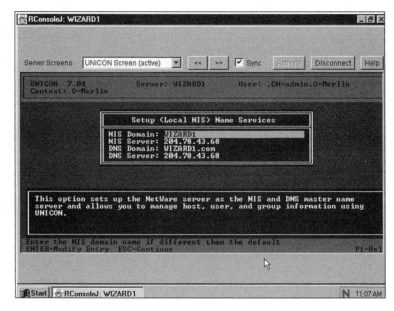

When you have chosen the name service option, the installation continues. The installation then displays the running services menu; you start FTP here by pressing Insert and then choosing FTP.

You might be prompted to reboot the server; if so, bring it down nicely and then back up.

CONFIGURING AND MANAGING FTP

FTP is configured using the UNICON.NLM; the main UNICON screen is shown in Figure 35.4.

There are many options on the main screen; what is pertinent to FTP is that you start and stop the FTP service from this screen. Highlight Start/Stop Services and, on the next screen, use the Delete key to stop a service and the Insert key to start it. To manage FTP, highlight and choose Manage Services, FTP Server, and you will be at the FTP Administration menu (see Figure 35.5).

Figure 35.4
FTP services are stopped, started, and configured via the UNICON utility.

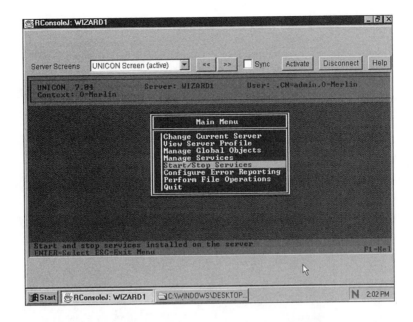

Figure 35.5
All management of FTP services is done via the FTP Administration menu.

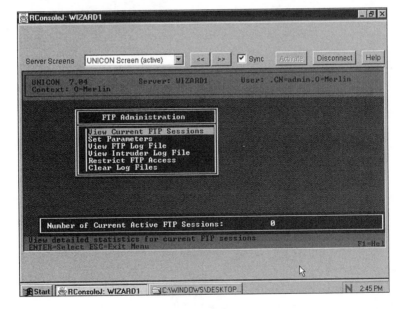

From the FTP Administration menu, you can view and clear log files, view current sessions, restrict FTP access, and also set the FTP parameters. To configure FTP, highlight set parameters and press Enter; the FTP server parameters are displayed as shown in Figure 35.6.

Figure 35.6
The configurable FTP Server Parameters. Pay attention to the Maximum number of sessions, which defaults to 9, a setting you will most likely need to increase.

The following are the configurable FTP server parameters:

- **Maximum Number of Sessions**—Set this to the number of concurrent FTP sessions that you want to have running.

- **Maximum Session Length**—This is how long a session can remain open, in minutes.

- **Idle Time Before FTP Server Unloads**—This is a very interesting parameter. The FTP server doesn't remain resident in memory; it unloads itself after the idle time that you configure here. This allows the NetWare server to put the memory that the FTP services were using to better use. After the server receives an FTP client login, the FTP service starts automatically.

- **Anonymous User Access**—defines whether an anonymous user can access the server; you will see an example of this in the next section, "Using FTP."

- **Default User's Home Directory**—This is the home directory of users who do not have home directories on the server. If the directory does not exist, you can create it here also. This property also applies if the user does not have his home directory entered into NDS. For example, remove the home directory value for user pence; FTP to the server, and do a pwd to obtain the present working directory. It will be the value set here for the default user's home directory—in this case, /sys/default.usr. Now set the home directory value for user pence, and again connect. A pwd now shows /sys/users/pence as the current directory.

- **Anonymous User's Home Directory**—The home directory used by anonymous users. You can create the directory from here if it does not exist. Make sure you change this to something other than the root of the sys: volume!

- **Default Name Space**—Either DOS or NFS.

- **Intruder Detection**—This is a Yes or No setting. If intruder detection is enabled, there are two other parameters that become active: Number of Unsuccessful Attempts and Detection Reset Interval.

  - **Number of Unsuccessful Attempts**—This parameter is active only if Intruder Detection is enabled. It is tied to the following parameter, Detection Reset Interval.

  - **Detection Reset Interval**—This parameter is active only if Intruder Detection is enabled, and works in conjunction with the number of unsuccessful login attempts.

  So how do these last three parameters work together? Assume that you have set Intruder Detection to Yes, Number of Unsuccessful Attempts to 2, and Detection Reset Interval to 5 minutes, which is the shortest time that you can enter. When there is an unsuccessful login attempt, the clock starts running; if there is another unsuccessful attempt within 5 minutes, the information is logged.

- **Log Level**—There are four choices for the logging level: None, Logins, Statistics, and File. None records no information. Logins records only logins; Statistics records files copied and includes logins. File is the highest level of logging: It records all FTP transactions and includes that which is recorded by Statistics and Login.

Depending on what you change when modifying parameters, you might need to stop and start the FTP service.

SECURITY CONCERNS

Don't just install Unix Print Services, start the FTP service, and walk away; there are a few things that you simply must do in terms of security. Make sure you thoroughly test your FTP access, so that clients can only access the files you intend for them to! At the very least, make sure that you enable intruder detection, and that you monitor the log files.

THE PASSWORD

The following is a summary trace of the packets being sent and received during an FTP session. In this brief session, user pence connects to the Wizard1 FTP server, which as you can see is NetWare version 5.00. The command get hello.jtp was issued at the FTP command prompt; you can see that it has translated into a RETR (retrieve).

Destination	Source	Summary
Tarzan	Wizard1	FTP R PORT=1054 220 wizard1 FTP server (NetWare version 5.00) ready
Wizard1	Tarzan	FTP C PORT=21 USER pence
Tarzan	Wizard1	FTP R PORT=1054 **331 Password required for pence**
Wizard1	Tarzan	FTP C PORT=21 **PASS gonovell**
Tarzan	Wizard1	FTP R PORT=1054 230 Successful Login
Wizard1	Tarzan	FTP C PORT=21 PORT 04,78,43,220,4,31
Tarzan	Wizard1	FTP R PORT=1054 200 PORT command okay
Wizard1	Tarzan	FTP C PORT=21 RETR hello.jtp
Tarzan	Wizard1	FTP R PORT=1054 150 Opening data connection for hello.jtp (Tarzan,1055)
Tarzan	Wizard1	FTP R PORT=1055 Text Data
Tarzan	Wizard1	FTP R PORT=1054 226 Transfer complete
Wizard1	Tarzan	FTP C PORT=21 QUIT
Tarzan	Wizard1	FTP R PORT=1054 221 Goodbye

The most important thing to gain from this summary trace comes right after the username pence is entered when prompted by the server; the 331 means that the username is okay, but that a password is required. In the next frame, the response from the user (the workstation's name is Tarzan), you can see PASS gonovell. Why is this important? The password is sent in the clear; definitely something to keep in mind! This isn't NetWare specific, the point is that your administrator password is being sent in the clear across the wire when you use the FTP client. And for those of you who might be thinking bad thoughts, gonovell isn't Pence's password!

Tip #357 from
John

> Don't log in as the administrator except to perform a specific task. Everyone, including administrators, should have her own account. But, human nature being what it is, most administrators don't like to log out and log back in to get something done; they stay as superusers all the time. Although this is convenient, it can also be disastrous if you inadvertently delete or move files, which is very easy to do with Explorer. Also, in a larger environment, you will have more than one admin, and just seeing in a log that something was done by user admin might not necessarily tell you who did it!

THE ANONYMOUS USER'S DEFAULT DIRECTORY

By default, the directory for anonymous users is /sys, or the root of the sys: volume. I discussed the Anonymous User's Home Directory parameter in the section "Configuring and Managing FTP," earlier in this chapter; make sure that you change this to an isolated subdirectory, and a volume other than sys: might not be a bad idea either. If you can get to a directory, you can get to its subdirectories, so dumping an anonymous FTP user into the root of your sys: volume isn't a good idea, and that is what will happen by default.

THE ANONYMOUS USER'S DEFAULT FILE ACCESS RIGHTS

It's bad enough that anonymous users are given the root of the sys: volume as a default home directory. But to add insult to injury, they have all rights there (see Figure 35.7).

Figure 35.7
The anonymous user has all rights to the sys: volume by default! Make sure that you take care of this one ASAP!

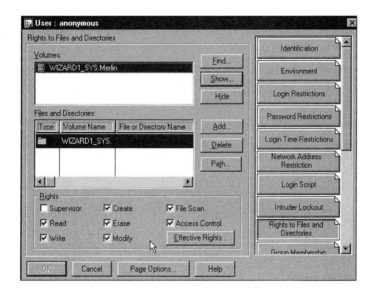

In Figure 35.7, you are looking at user anonymous's rights to files and directories. Notice that at the root of the sys: volume, this user has Read, Write, Create, Erase, Modify, File Scan, and Access Control. Make certain that you change these rights first thing; one can only wonder what Novell was thinking.

Tip #358 from
John

Move the default home directory to a directory on a volume other than sys. Give only the rights the users need for your purposes; you can always add rights, but after damage has been done, it might be too late to take them away!

PART

VII

CH

35

THE `restrict.ftp` FILE

The FTP access, sys:etc/restrict.ftp, defines who can access your FTP server. You can edit this file from the FTP Administration Screen, shown in Figure 35.5, by choosing Restrict FTP Access, or you can edit it in sys:etc. The default restrict.ftp file is given here, and the file is self documenting:

```
#                    FTP Server Access Control File
#
# This file determines who can access files through the ftp
# server. The user name must be specified to gain access.
# The default configuration allows all users access.
#
#    Syntax:
#
#    <username> [ACCESS=DENY,GUEST,NOREMOTE,READONLY]
#               [ADDRESS=<hostname>,<hostgroup>]
#
#    <username> All users.
#                    e.g. "*"
#               All users from a NDS context.
#                    e.g. "*.OU=sales.O=acme"
#               NDS user relative to the default context.
#                    e.g. "bill"
#               Complete Canonicalized NDS name.
#                    e.g. ".CN=Admin.O=acme"
#
#    <username> is required and must be the first field in
#               the line.
#
#    ACCESS=    This option limits user access to the server.
#               This option is case sensitive and is not
#               required.
#
#    DENY       Denies access to the server. This parameter
#               overrides a previously declared global access.
#
#    GUEST      Restricts the user to the home directory on
#               the server running the FTP server.
#
#    NOREMOTE   Restricts the user to the local server. User
#               cannot access any remote servers.
#
#    READONLY   Restricts the user from storing any files on
#               the server.
#
#    ADDRESS=   This option restricts access for users from a
#               specific host or set of hosts (hostgroup). This
#               option is case sensitive and is not required.
#
#    Examples:
#
#    1. The following example specifies that all users have
#       access to the local server but cannot access remote
#       NetWare servers.
#
#    * ACCESS=NOREMOTE
```

```
#
#    2. The following example specifies that all users from
#       the OU called SALES have full access, but must
#       connect from the host <hostname>.
#
#    *.OU=SALES.O=ACME ADDRESS=hostname
#
#    3. The following example specifies the user ADMIN cannot
#       access the FTP server.
#
#    .ADMIN.O=ACME ACCESS=DENY
#
#    The following default entry of "*" allows all users
#    access to ftp server.

*
```

THE LOG FILES

If you turned on Intruder Detection (which you should have) and set a logging level, there are two log files available, the FTP log file, located in sys:etc/ftpserv.log, and the intruder log file, located in `sys:system/intruder.ftp`. These log files can be viewed via the FTP Administration menu (refer to Figure 35.5).

THE FTP LOG FILE

Earlier, in the section on "Configuring and Managing FTP," you learned that setting the log level to File was the most inclusive. With the log level set to file, you will see the level of information shown here about an FTP session, and you can see that the login and statistical information is included:

```
----------------------------------------------------------------
Tue Mar  9 13:45:17 1999 FTP Session Starts from 204.78.43.220.
Tue Mar  9 13:45:26 1999 .CN=pence.O=Merlin login from 204.78.43.220.
----------------------------------------------------------------
Tue Mar  9 13:45:40 1999 Retrieved file /SYS/login/login.exe.
Tue Mar  9 13:45:44 1999 1 files copied from server.
0 files copied to server.
Tue Mar  9 13:45:44 1999 FTP Session Ends from 204.78.43.220.
----------------------------------------------------------------
```

THE INTRUDER LOG FILE

From the intruder log file, you can see a key piece of information: the IP address of the machine the intruder is using. You also have the time the intrusion was attempted, the name that was used, along with the password:

```
Intruder Alert. Address 204.78.43.220 has exceeded the limit
Time 3-9-1999 10:50:09 am  User .CN=ray.O=Merlin used password jjjjj .
Time 3-9-1999 10:50:00 am  User .CN=gates.O=Merlin used password hhhhh .
Time 3-9-1999 10:49:49 am  User .CN=Bill.O=Merlin used password jjjj .

4 unsuccessful logins from address 204.78.43.220
Time 3-9-1999 10:52:13 am  User .CN=noorda.O=Merlin used password llll .
```

```
5 unsuccessful logins from address 204.78.43.220
Time 3-9-1999 10:52:51 am  User .CN=norda.O=Merlin used password llll .
```

USING FTP

Now that the FTP server is up and running, how do you use it? In this section, I will look at the browser as a client, the FTP program that comes with Windows, and a few special NetWare-related commands.

THE BROWSER AS A CLIENT

You can use either the command line ftp.exe or your Web browser to access FTP services on your NetWare server. In order for you to use your Web browser as an FTP client, anonymous access needs to be enabled. Otherwise, you receive the message shown in Figure 35.8: The anonymous user account is not active and user anonymous has been denied access.

Figure 35.8
In order to use your Web browser as an FTP client, you must enable anonymous access when configuring FTP.

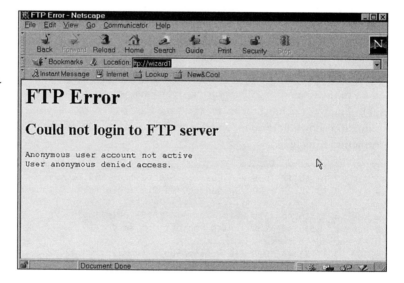

When anonymous access has been enabled, your browser can access the NetWare 5 FTP server by using the address ftp://<servername>, where <servername> is the host name or IP address of the server. The browser has a much simpler interface than the command-line FTP program, as shown in Figure 35.9.

Tip #359 from
John

If you enable anonymous access, you must start and stop the FTP service in order for it to take effect. The change will not take "on-the-fly".

Figure 35.9
When anonymous access has been enabled, the browser interface is much easier to use than the command line FTP program.

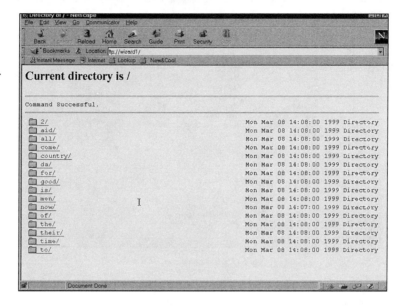

It is possible to use your browser as the FTP client and still not enable anonymous access. If you use Netscape, instead of just `ftp://<servername>`, use the command `ftp://username@<servername>`. This opens the FTP session with your username, and you are prompted for a password, which won't show up as you type. This syntax doesn't work with Internet Explorer; it does not pop up the box asking you for a password, so as a result, the login fails.

Tip #360 from
John

With both Internet Explorer and Netscape, you can use the syntax `ftp://username:password@<servername>`. The downside to this is that your password isn't hidden as you type it.

THE WINDOWS FTP PROGRAM

To establish a session using the command line FTP program, enter the command `FTP <servername>` at a command prompt, such as `FTP Wizard2`. You are then prompted for a username and password and will have an FTP command prompt. At the FTP command prompt, you issue the appropriate command, for example, `FTP> get hello.txt` would transfer the file `hello.txt` from the server to the local machine.

PART
VII

CH

35

To get a listing of the available FTP commands, enter ? at the FTP command prompt (see Figure 35.10).

Figure 35.10
To obtain a listing of the available FTP commands, enter ? or help at the FTP command prompt.

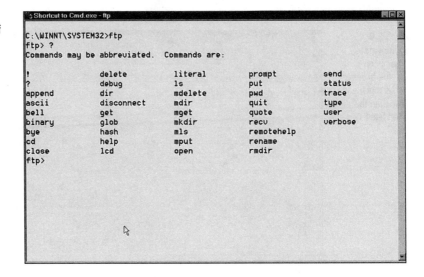

```
Shortcut to Cmd.exe - ftp
C:\WINNT\SYSTEM32>ftp
ftp> ?
Commands may be abbreviated.  Commands are:

!               delete          literal         prompt          send
?               debug           ls              put             status
append          dir             mdelete         pwd             trace
ascii           disconnect      mdir            quit            type
bell            get             mget            quote           user
binary          glob            mkdir           recv            verbose
bye             hash            mls             remotehelp
cd              help            mput            rename
close           lcd             open            rmdir
ftp>
```

To obtain help on a particular FTP command, enter help <command> at the FTP command prompt, such as help put. You then receive some rather cryptic help for the command; they certainly didn't waste any words on the help! The commands and the description that help returns are listed in Table 35.1.

TABLE 35.1 FTP COMMANDS IN WINDOWS 95/NT

Command	Help Description
!	Escape to the shell
?	Print local help information
append	Append to a file
ascii	Set ASCII transfer type
bell	Beep when command completed
binary	Set binary transfer type
bye	Terminate FTP session and exit
cd	Change remote working directory
close	Terminate FTP session
delete	Delete remote file
debug	Toggle debugging mode
dir	List contents of remote directory

Command	Help Description
disconnect	Terminate the FTP session
get	Receive file
glob	Toggle metacharacter expansion of local file name
hash	Toggle printing '#' for each buffer transferred
help	Print local help information
lcd	Change local working directory
literal	Send arbitrary FTP command
ls	list contents of remote directory
mdelete	Delete multiple files
mdir	List contents of multiple remote directories
mget	Get multiple files
mkdir	Make directory on remote machine
mls	list contents of multiple remote directories
mput	Send multiple files
open	Connect to remote FTP
prompt	Force interactive prompting on multiple commands
put	Send one file
pwd	Print working directory on remote machine
quit	Terminate FTP session and exit
quote	Send arbitrary FTP command
recv	Receive file
remotehelp	Get help from remote server
rename	Rename file
rmdir	Remove directory on remote machine
send	Send one file
status	Show current status
trace	Toggle packet tracing
type	Set file transfer type
user	Send new user information
verbose	Toggle verbose mode

NETWARE SPECIFIC FTP USAGE

There are two nonstandard commands that the NetWare FTP server supports, the stat and site commands. Each of these commands are preceded with the normal FTP quote command, which says "send everything after this just like it's typed", for example, FTP> quote stat.

The command quote stat returns the information shown in Figure 35.11.

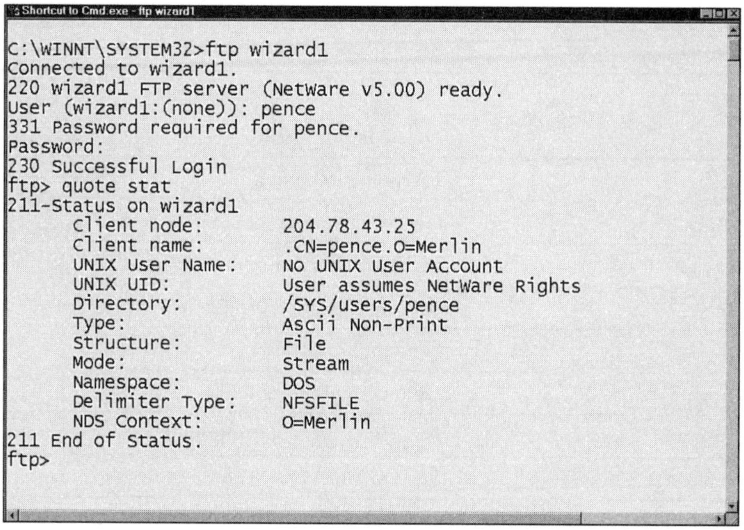

Figure 35.11

The quote stat command displays information about your current status and, as you can see, is NDS aware.

```
C:\WINNT\SYSTEM32>ftp wizard1
Connected to wizard1.
220 wizard1 FTP server (NetWare v5.00) ready.
User (wizard1:(none)): pence
331 Password required for pence.
Password:
230 Successful Login
ftp> quote stat
211-Status on wizard1
        Client node:       204.78.43.25
        Client name:       .CN=pence.O=Merlin
        UNIX User Name:    No UNIX User Account
        UNIX UID:          User assumes NetWare Rights
        Directory:         /SYS/users/pence
        Type:              Ascii Non-Print
        Structure:         File
        Mode:              Stream
        Namespace:         DOS
        Delimiter Type:    NFSFILE
        NDS Context:       O=Merlin
211 End of Status.
ftp>
```

The syntax of the quote site command is as follows:

quote site <help> <cx> <dos> <nfs> <ou> <path> <server> <slist>

For example, the command quote site ou gives the result Client's context is O=MERLIN.

The parameters of the site command are as follows:

- help—Lists the site parameters and their meaning.
- cx—Used to set the current NDS context.
- dos—Display files in DOS format.
- nfs—Display file in Unix format. This is supported only on NFS volumes.
- path—Displays available directory maps you can use as an alias for a pathname.
- ou—Displays suborganizations relative to your current context.
- server—Displays the local servers.
- slist—Lists all known file servers.

One very cool feature is that you can go through your NetWare FTP server and access files on other NetWare servers, even if they are not running FTP; the remote NetWare server doesn't even have to be running IP!

To access non–FTP-enabled NetWare servers, connect to your FTP server as usual. Then simply access remote resources by using the following syntax:

```
//remote server/volume/directory_pathname
```

There are a few caveats with this, such as it will not work with anonymous users, will support only the DOS namespace, and more. Search the online documentation for information on accessing remote servers via FTP.

TROUBLESHOOTING

FTP is very robust and is used daily on the Internet by thousands, so you shouldn't have any problems. The FTP program at the workstation uses the IP protocol stack, so the first thing to do is verify that you can see the FTP server. To do this, use the `ping` command. If you can ping by number but not by name, you have a name resolution issue. If you cannot ping the FTP server, you will not be able to establish an FTP session.

If you can successfully ping the FTP server, can you establish a session? If not, are the FTP services running on the server? If you can establish a session, but have other issues—for example, no files can be seen—check the rights of the user for the directory in question. The same would apply if the user were unable to upload to a directory. And find out if any problems affect all users, or if only one user is having problems. If it is only the one, leave the server side alone, the problem is with the workstation.

INDEX

K-L

P

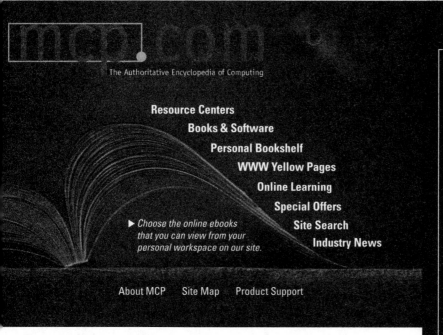

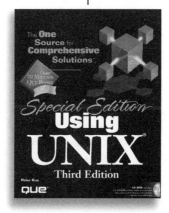

Other Related Titles

562
671
IPXPING   687
ARP   733
TPING   747
TCPCON   750